MONEY

—Ye shall have honest weights and measures

James E. Ewart

Principia Publishing, Inc.

Seattle, Washington

First Printing, August 1998

Copyright © 1998 by Principia Publishing, Inc., Seattle, Washington.

All rights reserved. Except for the Order Form and Reader Registration Form, no portion of this book may be reproduced without written permission from the publisher, except by a reviewer who may quote brief passages in connection with a review. The Order Form and the Reader Registration Form may be photocopied by anyone provided the copies are used only for their intended purposes.

Principia Publishing books are available at special quantity discounts as classroom course materials, as premiums, in sales promotions, or in employee training programs. For more information, please contact Principia Publishing at P.O. Box 98950, Seattle, WA 98198; 253-815-7821, fax 253-815-0265.

The bills shown on our dust jacket photo-composite are special. The $1 silver certificate, series of 1891, is one of only two series' – the other is 1886 — which bore the portrait of a woman, Martha Washington, on its face. The $10,000 bill, a Federal Reserve Note, is the largest denomination of the Federal Reserve Notes. The $100,000 bill is a gold certificate, and it is the largest denomination of the gold certificates. The bills shown on our dust jacket are also shown on their own pages in Chapter 9. When you look at those pages, please note also that the serial number for the $100,000 gold certificate and the $10,000 Federal Reserve Note is 1.

MANUFACTURED IN THE UNITED STATES OF AMERICA

Principia Publishing and PPI are trademarks of Principia Publishing, Inc. Zenger News Service and ZNS are registered trademarks and Zenger's Words and Phrases, *Principia*, Z-Gram, International Association of Independent Journalists, IAIJ, and ZYNDEX are trademarks of Zenger News Service.

10 9 8 7 6 5 4 3 2 1

Publisher's Cataloging-in-Publication
(Provided by Quality Books, Inc.)

Ewart, James E., 1936-
    Money : ye shall have honest weights and measures— / James E. Ewart. — 1st ed.
    p. cm.
    Includes bibliographical references and index.
    Preassigned LCCN: 98-091362
    ISBN: 0-9663570-0-0

    1. Money. 2. Money—Terminology. 3. Counterfeits and counterfeiting. 4. Legal tender. I. Title.

HG221.E93 1998   332,4
                                QBI98-285

Dedication

I owe special thanks to my father, James Edward Ewart of Glasgow, Scotland, and my mother, Amy Felton of Jamestown, North Dakota.

Dad, I thank you for teaching me about the horrors of war, as you experienced them at age seventeen as a World War I British soldier in France, and for your prescient warnings about government corruption.

Mom, thank you for taking us kids to the library so often and for teaching us to respect books, learning, and culture. Thanks also for teaching me the marvelous things you learned in the Catholic school you attended: etymologies, grammar, spelling, pronunciation, proper manners, and the other critically important aspects of civilized communication and living.

Dad, I'm sorry we couldn't ease the pain of the shrapnel wounds in your back.

Mom, I'm sorry I didn't appreciate how difficult it was for you to raise us kids after you lost your right arm and shoulder to cancer.

I thank you both for teaching me how to play the violin and piano, and helping me develop sensitivity to the spiritual elements of classical music.

Above all, I thank you both for teaching me about God and His principles of civics and citizenship.

For these and a thousand other reasons, I love you and dedicate this book to you.

I am also deeply grateful to these courageous souls, and to at least a hundred others who must remain anonymous. Their life experiences, research, writing or teaching — often under difficult circumstances — contributed materially to the form, substance and spirit of this work.

Gary Allen
George Bancroft
Frederic Bastiat
Taylor Caldwell
Alexander Del Mar
U.S. Representative Martin Dies, Texas
Victor Herman
Vivian Kellems
Sergei Kourdakov
John Locke
U.S. Representative Louis T. McFadden, Pennsylvania
Hulda Schneider Nagle
U.S. Representative Wright Patman, Texas
Franz Pick
Ayn Rand
Roger Sherman
Reverend Walter W. Skeat
Lysander Spooner
Booker T. Washington
Henry Grady Weaver
Robert H. W. Welch
and
John Peter and Catherine Ann Zenger

Epigraph

"Behind every great fortune there is a crime."
Honoré de Balzac (1799 - 1855)

"Federal reserve notes ... shall be redeemed in lawful money on demand at the Treasury Department of the United States, in the city of Washington, District of Columbia, or at any Federal Reserve bank."
12 U.S.C. § 411 (January 16, 1996).

IT is a word we use daily, yet almost no one remembers — or maybe ever knew — its precise meaning. It is misused by intelligent *and* stupid, informed *and* ignorant people; by the pillars and predators of every society. It is one of the most important words in any language. It is a term critical to every society's health and well-being, and a material factor in every major facet of civilization: commerce, science, religion, education and sometimes even romance.

The word?

Money.

You can survive without the information in this book, maybe even prosper, but you would do so without the peace of mind it offers, more peace of mind you may ever have experienced, newfound peace that will last a lifetime and enrich your heirs.

To understand money completely is to be able to protect your life and your freedom, and the lives and freedom of your loved ones. That's because, in today's society, some reject the Bible's moral lesson of Deuteronomy 25:15, which I've paraphrased to create this book's subtitle: Ye shall have honest weights and measures.

You will soon know who uses honest weights and measures, and you will also know who does not. You should move closer to all those who do, and you should stand apart from all those who do not.

For those who do not use honest weights and measures have formed alliances with one another, and they wield almost unimaginable power. They conduct what could be the largest criminal enterprise — perpetrating the largest crime — in history.

Jim Ewart
Seattle, Washington
June 4, 1998

Contents

Dedication iii
Epigraph v
Foreward by Alan Stang xi
Preface — "Verbicide" xiii
Acknowledgments xvii
Notice and Disclaimer xxi

Chapters

1	Berlin	1
2	Money	7
3	Currency	13
4	Dollar	17
5	Pay	23
6	Note	27
7	Tender	31
8	Bill	45
9	"Will Pay To (The) Bearer"	51
10	Usury	101
11	Inflation. Fundamentals	109
12	Inflation. Advanced Concepts	115
13	Inflation. Modern Mechanisms and Looking Ahead	135
14	Fraud	145
15	Your Security and Today's Money Substitutes	165
16	Your Future	185
17	Questions and Answers	195
18	Glossary	209
19	Postscript	225

Appendices

A	Bibliography, recommended resources, etc.
B	Reader Registration Form
C	Quotations on money
D	Act of April 2, 1792
E	Balance Sheets Federal Reserve System, 1996 United States Treasury, 1996
F	U.S. Secret Service letter, May 30, 1997
G	Biography of John Peter Zenger
H	*Oxford English Dictionary*: *money*
I	*Encyclopædia Britannica*: 1768 (First) Edition: *Money*
J	*Encyclopædia Britannica*: 1911 Edition: *Money*
K	*Encyclopædia Britannica*: 15th (current) Edition, 1997 printing: *Money*
L	Stock Ownership, Federal Reserve Bank of New York
M	Dow Jones Industrial Average graphs
N	Cases and Dictionary Definitions
O	United States Code, Constitution
P	Libertarian Party press release, *Pieces of Eight*.

Index 315
Colophon 325
Order Form 326

Figures

Page	Figure		Page	Figure	
xxii	1-1	Berlin, Germany: August 13, 1961.	62	9-11	1864, Confederate States of America, $10 bill.
11	2-1	*Money* defined.	63	9-12	1865, Treasury Note, $50, Interest Bearing, Gold Option, with five coupons.
12	2-2	Bank deposit ticket, *circa* October 1996.	64	9-13	1870, First National Gold Bank, San Francisco, $20 Gold Coin Certificate.
16	3-1	Cases, 1904 *Words and Phrases*.	65	9-14	1880, Silver Certificate, $1,000, from San Francisco Federal Reserve Bank.
22	4-1	1963, Federal Reserve Token (FRT), $1.	66	9-15	1882, Gold Coin Certificate, $100.
30	6-1	1950, Federal Reserve Note, $10.	67	9-16	1891, Silver Certificate, $1, Martha Washington.
36	7-1	1917, United States Note ("Greenback"), Face, $2.	68	9-17	1891, Treasury Note, $1,000.
37	7-2	1917, United States Note ("Greenback"), Back, $2.	69	9-18	1899, Silver Certificate, $5, Chief Ongepapa, "FIVE SILVER DOLLARS. . . ."
44	7-3	*Dollar* not defined.	70	9-19	1902, National Currency, $5, face and part of back (to show obligatory phrases), "WILL PAY TO THE BEARER," and, "IS RECEIVABLE AT PAR IN ALL PARTS OF THE UNITED STATES."
52	9-1	Counterfeiting, U.S.C.			
53	9-2	1690, Massachusetts Bay Colony Note, 20 Shillings; and 1776, New Jersey Colony Notes, Twelve Shillings.	71	9-20	1907, United States Note, $5, "WILL PAY THE BEARER," and, "IS A LEGAL TENDER." Face and part of back.
54	9-3	1776, Continental Currency Note, One Third of A Dollar; and 1780, Continental Currency Note, One Dollar.	72	9-21	1907, Gold Certificate, $10 "IN GOLD COIN," face and part of back (to show color).
55	9-4	1819, Farmers & Mechanics Bank of Ohio Banknote, $3.	73	9-22	1914, Federal Reserve Note, $10, face and part of back bottom to show obligatory phrases, "IS RECEIVABLE BY ALL NATIONAL" and "IN GOLD OR LAWFUL MONEY."
56	9-5	1840 (?), Republic of Texas Note, $50.			
57	9-6	1840, Bank of the United States Banknote, $3,000.	74	9-23	1918, National Currency (Federal Reserve Bank Note), $1. "SECURED BY . . . GOLD NOTES," etc. Face only. Back is shown on opposite page.
58	9-7	1850, Citizens' Bank of Louisiana "Dixie" Note, $10. Face and back.			
59	9-8	1861, "DEMAND" Note, $5. The first "Greenback," no reference to "legal tender."	75	9-24	1918, National Currency (Federal Reserve Bank Note), $1. Back only.
60	9-9	1862, Cherokee Note, $1; and 1862, Choctaw Note, Fifty Cents.	76	9-25	1917, United States Note, $2, "IS A LEGAL TENDER." Curved stuff on back, interesting.
61	9-10	1863, Fractional Currency Note, Fifty Cents, "IS EXCHANGEABLE FOR UNITED STATES NOTES;" and 1863, Fractional Currency Note, Fifty Cents, "RECEIVABLE FOR ALL UNITED STATES STAMPS;" and 1863, Fractional Currency Note, Ten Cents, face and back.			

Page	Figure		Page	Figure	
77	9-26	1922, Gold Coin Certificate, $50, "IS A LEGAL TENDER," face and part of back to show color.	91	9-40	1963, United States Note, $2, "IS LEGAL TENDER. . . ."
78	9-27	1923, Silver Certificate, $1, "IS RECEIVABLE FOR ALL PUBLIC DUES."	92	9-41	1963, Federal Reserve Note, $1. "IS LEGAL TENDER. . . ."
79	9-28	1928, United States Note, $2, "IS A LEGAL TENDER AT ITS FACE VALUE."	93	9-42	1976, Federal Reserve Note: $2.
80	9-29	1928, Silver Certificate, $1, "IS RECEIVABLE" and "ONE SILVER DOLLAR PAYABLE. . . ."	94	9-43	1923, German *Reichsbanknote*, 10 Million Marks.
81	9-30	1928, Gold Certificate, $10, "CERTIFICATE IS A LEGAL TENDER."	95	9-44	U.S. Gold coins.
82	9-31	1928, Federal Reserve Note, $10, "REDEEMABLE IN GOLD ON DEMAND . . . OR IN GOLD OR LAWFUL MONEY. . . ."	96	9-45	U.S. Silver coins.
			97	9-46	U.S. minor coins; U.S. Colonial coins.
83	9-32	1928, Federal Reserve Note, $10,000.	98	9-47	U.S. Privately minted coins, *circa* 1850 - 1855, "Mormon" gold, California gold.
84	9-33	1934, Gold Certificate, $100,000, "IS LEGAL TENDER."	99	9-48	Map of the Czech Republic and Germany, showing Jochymov (Joachimsthal).
85	9-34	1934, United States Note, $10,000 (replica).	100	9-49	1896 Silver Certificate, $1: "History Instructing Youth."
86	9-35	1934, Federal Reserve Note, $5, "IS LEGAL TENDER."	126	12-1	"Instalment [*sic*] Credit Note, 10/77"
			177	15-1	Gold and Silver Reserve, Inc.
87	9-36	1935, Silver Certificate, $1, "IS LEGAL TENDER."	184	15-2	Chart: National debt.
			267	G-1	The trial of John Peter Zenger, sketch.
88	9-37	1950, Federal Reserve Note, $100, "IS LEGAL TENDER" in small print.	268	G-2	*THE New-York Weekly JOURNAL*, Monday, November 12, 1733.
89	9-38	1953, United States Note, $2, "IS A LEGAL TENDER. . . ."	295	M-1	DJIA in terms of gold, log scale.
			296	M-2	DJIA in terms of gold, linear scale.
90	9-39.	1957, Silver Certificate, $1, "IS LEGAL TENDER. . . ."			

TABLES

Page		
223	17-1	Gold "price."
224	17-2	Cross-references.

Foreword

THIS book could provoke a revolution. Most people don't know how their bank works. I didn't. They may have heard of fractional reserve banking, yes, but don't know for sure what it is. They don't know what happens when they prepay a mortgage loan. They don't know what it means when the loan officer leans across the desk and unctuously asks, "Do you have an account with us?"

Jim Ewart is uniquely equipped to flay the hide off this beast. He is both an electronics expert and a wire service journalist, which means that he knows what he is talking about and that *MONEY* is written in a clear, often amusing style, despite the intricacy and deliberate obscurity of the subject. I believe that long before this book arrives at "critical mass," readers will overflow radio talk shows, will give their Congressmen permanent headaches the Congressmen deserve, and will picket the banks, because of it.

Years ago, when depositors found out that the money that was supposed to be in the bank wasn't there, bank presidents often wound up hanging from trees. It will be intensely interesting to see whether that happens again, after those depositors read *MONEY*. In the beginning, bankers lent money. Jim Ewart proves, from the mouths of the bankers themselves, that when they make you a loan today, they don't really lend you anything; certainly not money — nothing more than a computer entry. *But they expect you to pay them back with something real.* He shows you the language in the mortgage loan agreement the bankers use to steal your property. Did you know that they deliberately cause depressions and put you out of work? That they daily commit Insider trading that would land anyone else in jail? That they have stolen your gold? That they have as much conscience as Ted Bundy?

Jim Ewart calls the criminals who are doing this *Insiders,* and surgically exposes their crimes. I've never read this information anywhere else. Consider that none of it appears in the media, not a whisper; not so strange when you realize that the Insiders have used the literal trillions they have stolen to buy the media, and that millions of dollars of advertising are at stake. After you have read this book, ask yourself why its revelations are not on the front page every day. Then, take those revelations to Rush Limbaugh and prepare yourself for a shock.

Most of the problems in our country today originate largely in the fact that our "money" is phony. Inflation, recession, depression, unemployment, even crime and broken homes; you name it and that is the case. Long ago, Thomas Jefferson warned that if the bankers had their way, we could wind up strangers in our own land. Later, Andy Jackson promised to rout them out, and "by the eternal God" he did so! Andy did such a good job, they were out of power until 1913, when only a few Congressmen in on the scam passed the Federal Reserve Act in late December, 1913, while their colleagues left Washington for Christmas.

The job must be done again, and this incandescent book can do it.

Alan Stang
Los Angeles, California
February 1998

Preface

"Verbicide"

IN about 1890, Oliver Wendell Holmes, M.D.,[1] penned *The Autocrat of the Breakfast Table*, a humorous sketch of his perceptions of life and people. Dr. Holmes wrote:

> "What are the great faults of conversation? Want of ideas, want of words, want of manners, are the principal ones, I suppose you think.
>
> I don't doubt it, but I will tell you what I have found spoil more good talks than anything else; long arguments on special points between people who differ on the fundamental principles on which these points depend. No men can have satisfactory relations with each other until they have agreed on certain *ultima* of belief not to be disturbed in ordinary conversation, and unless they have sense enough to trace the secondary questions depending upon these ultimate beliefs to their source. In short, just as a written constitution is essential to the best social order, so a code of finalities is a necessary condition of profitable talk between two persons."

Speaking specifically to the point of this book, Dr. Holmes wrote:

> "Let me lay down the law upon the subject. Life and language are alike sacred. Homicide and *verbicide* — that is, violent treatment of a word with fatal results to its legitimate meaning, which is its life — are alike forbidden."

Finally, he wrote,

> "The great moralist says: 'To trifle with the vocabulary which is the vehicle of intercourse is to tamper with the currency of human intelligence . . . .' The infection spread to the national conscience. ***Political double-dealings naturally grew out of verbal double-meanings.***" [Emphasis supplied.]

Holmes coined the term *verbicide* to describe a serious danger to our nation. By succumbing to inaccurate terminology, we might became prey to those who would use our confusion as a weapon against us. The death (*cide*) of the nation could be wrought by an

---

[1] Dr. Holmes' son (1841 - 1935), appointed to the U.S. Supreme Court in 1902 by President Theodore ("Teddy") Roosevelt, retired from the court in 1932.

enemy whose most lethal weapons were terms whose meanings were twisted, perverted or vulgarized. We, as a people, would never commit political suicide but we might become victims of verbicide, which could be just as fatal to our freedoms.

Judicial Verbicide:
An Affront to the Constitution

Almost a century passed before Holmes' term would be widely used again. On October 22, 1980, Senator Sam J. Ervin, Jr., Watergate Special Prosecutor, spoke at Louisiana State University. Laying a foundation for his case against judicial verbicide, his speech, "Judicial Verbicide: An Affront to the Constitution,"[2] quoted Daniel Webster regarding:

> "these eternal truths: First, that 'whatever government is not a government of laws is a despotism, let it be called what it may. . . .'"

Next Senator Ervin quoted George Washington in his *Farewell Address*:

> "and second, that occupants of public offices love power and are prone to abuse it. . . ."

and this, quoting *Ex parte Milligan*, 4 Wallace 2, 120-121:

> "third, that what autocratic rulers of the people had done in the past might be attempted by their new rulers in the future unless they were restrained by laws which they alone could neither alter nor nullify."

Senator Ervin's phrase *judicial verbicide* describes the actions of Supreme Court Justices who "attempt to revise the Constitution while professing to interpret it."[3]

Senator Ervin also cited Chief Justice John Marshall's declarations:[4]

1. That the principles of the Constitution are designed to be permanent.
2. That the words of the Constitution must be understood to mean what they say.
3. That the Constitution constitutes an absolute rule for the government of the Supreme Court Justices in their official action.

Elaborating on paragraph 2, Justice Marshall said,

> "As men whose intentions require no concealment generally employ the words which most directly and aptly express the ideas they intend to convey, the enlightened patriots who framed our Constitution, and the people who adopted it, must be understood to have employed words in their natural sense, and to have intended what they have said."

Supplementing Marshall's view, Senator Ervin continues:

> "Judges who perpetrate *verbicide* on the Constitution are judicial activists. A judicial activist is a judge who interprets the Constitution to mean what it would have said if he instead of the Founding Fathers had written it."

Senator Ervin then returned to Daniel Webster:

> "Good intentions will always be pleaded for every assumption of authority. It is hardly too strong to say that the Constitution was made to guard the people against

---

[2] This speech, the second address in a series of Hubert H. Humphrey Lectures in Public Affairs, is reprinted in *A Blueprint for Judicial Reform* (Washington, D.C.: Free Congress Foundation, 1981). Senator Ervin represented North Carolina in the U.S. Congress for twenty years, also served as chairman of the Government Operations Committee, and was ranking Democrat on the Judiciary Committee and Chairman of its subcommittees on Constitutional Rights, Revision, and Codification of Laws, and of Separation of Powers.

[3] Paraphrasing Chief Justice Benjamin N. Cardoza in *Sun Printing and Publishing Association v. Remington Paper and Power Company*, 235 N.Y. 338, 139 N.E. 470 (1923).

[4] From *Marbury v. Madison*, 1 Cranch 137 (1803), and *Gibbons v. Ogden*, 9 Wheaton 1 (1824).

the dangers of good intentions. There are men in all ages who mean to govern well, but they mean to govern. They promise to be good masters, but they mean to be masters."

Senator Ervin continues:

"By committing verbicide on the Constitution, the judicial activists concentrate in the federal government powers the Constitution reserves to the states; diminish the capacity of federal executive officers and the states to bring criminals to justice; rob individuals of personal and property rights; and expand their own powers and those of Congress far beyond their constitutional limits. . . ."

"In charging in Chief Justice John Marshall's unhappy phrase that some Supreme Court Justices are making a solemn mockery of their oaths to support the Constitution, I am not a lone voice crying in the constitutional wilderness. I am, in truth, simply one member of a constantly expanding chorus.

"Judge Learned Hand, Alexander Bickel, Philip B. Kurland, and other profoundly enlightened constitutional scholars have made similar accusations. . . .

"One of the most lucid comments on the judicial verbicide of activist Supreme Court Justices is that of Justice Jackson in his concurring opinion in *Brown v. Allen* (1953). . . ."

Quoting Justice (Robert H.) Jackson:

"Whatever has been intended, this Court also has generated an impression in much of the judiciary that regard for precedents and authorities is obsolete, that words no longer mean what they have always meant to the profession, that the law knows no fixed principles. . . .

"I know of no way we can have equal justice under law except we have some law."

In his concluding remarks, Senator Ervin spoke bluntly:

"All history proclaims this everlasting truth: No nation can enjoy the right to self-rule and the right to freedom from tyranny under a government of men. The Founding Fathers framed and ratified the Constitution to secure these precious rights to Americans for all time. Judicial verbicide substitutes the personal notions of judges for the precepts of the Constitution. Hence, judicial verbicide is calculated to convert the Constitution into a worthless scrap of paper and to replace our government of laws with a judicial oligarchy. . . .

"A Justice who twists the words of the Constitution awry under the guise of interpreting it to substitute his personal notion for a constitutional precept is contemptuous of intellectual integrity."

The growing body of jurists gravely concerned about judicial verbicide is paralleled in a growing body of men and women who are equally concerned about verbicidal activity related to *money*.

Monetary Verbicide: Economic Warfare on Individual Liberty

This book may help you combat another form of verbicide, *monetary* verbicide.

Here you will learn the etymological histories of important words related to money, you will learn specific examples of correct and incorrect usage of important words and phrases related to money, and you will learn how corrupt individuals take advantage of public confusion about money-related words and phrases.

However, even though our topic is serious, the

information is presented to you in the most readable style; here you'll see that we avoided a stiff and scholarly approach in favor of a more comfortable and congenial one.

You may also note that we present some information in anecdotal form, so it reads much like a short story; we present other information satirically. Still other data is presented in such a way that you participate in the action described.

We adopted these reader-friendly methods in lieu of formal ones to help speed your understanding of important concepts.

Lengthy footnotes and legal citations are rare, to help make it still easier for you to read this book.

Finally, you should continue your study of money by examining the more-heavily documented materials listed in Appendix A. Your *preferred* next step may be to read *The Creature From Jekyll Island*, by G. Edward Griffin (Westlake Village, California: American Media, 1994). See also Appendix A.

Wisdom Begins
Wisdom begins by calling things by their right names. This ancient Chinese proverb explains why Zenger News Service emphasizes correct terminology. As we become more familiar with the correct names for things, our wisdom should grow.

People who don't call things by their right names, who object to "labeling," don't want you to know what they are doing.

By acquiring greater wisdom, our thoughts and actions should become more appropriate to our needs, and solutions may be found more quickly to our nation's problems.

As those problems are solved, the future for all Americans should become measurably brighter.

Indeed, as we in the United States begin to take remedial action against those who have sought to destroy *our* freedoms, we are likely to trigger the same action by freedom-loving people in other lands.

It is our hope that this small volume — and companion pieces under development — will help inspire valiant men and women everywhere to a higher standard of civic awareness, responsibility, and constructive action.

The Lord willing, history will record that this generation of Americans gave its full measure of devotion to the ideals of individual sovereignty and helped to implement a better understanding of those ideals in the hearts, minds and souls of all mankind.

Begin at the Beginning
The author encourages you to begin with Chapter 1, Berlin, and take sufficient time to analyze each major thought as it is presented.

Material in later chapters is presented in a form and style which assume you already understand the concepts, principles and terminology presented in earlier chapters.

As you progress from chapter to chapter, we suggest you resist any urge to skip over any material which, during a first reading, is unclear to you. We recommend you establish contact with the leader of a civic or patriotic group in your area. He or she may be able to help you get a better understanding of a principle which is puzzling to you. Or, in the alternative, you might visit a nearby university library or law library to look up pertinent words in older dictionaries.

Keep in mind that sometimes our ability to understand a concept is blocked by our misunderstanding of the meaning(s) of just one word used in the explanation of that concept. For this reason, we heartily recommend that while you read this book, a good dictionary should be at your side.

After reading this informal study, if you agree with the principles we discuss, we cordially invite you to complete and mail a copy of the Reader Registration Form provided in Appendix B. We will keep you informed about new products and services related to money and other vital subjects.

Principia Publishing, Inc.
Seattle, Washington
June 14, 1998

•

Acknowledgments

WHILE we owe our heartfelt thanks to the following organizations and individuals, our listing them here is for identification only and does not imply their endorsement.

Special thanks to Mr. Douglas Mudd, photographer, National Numismatic Collection, Smithsonian Institution, Washington, D.C., for many of the color photographs in this book, and the paper currency specimens shown on the dust jacket of the first printing.

Excerpts from *Pieces of Eight: The Monetary Powers and Disabilities of the United States Constitution* are used with the kind permission of the National Alliance for Constitutional Money, Inc., Manassas, Virginia, Edwin Vieira, Jr., Ph.D., J.D., president and author.

Excerpts from *A Blueprint for Judicial Reform* are used with the kind permission of the Free Congress Foundation, Washington, D.C.

Photocopies of parts of the articles on *money* from *Encyclopædia Britannica* are used with the kind permission of Encyclopædia Britannica, Inc., Chicago, Illinois.

Photocopies of definitions of monetary and legal terms from *Black's Law Dictionary*, First (1891), Fourth (1951) and Sixth (1991) Editions, are used with the kind permission of West Publishing Company, Saint Paul, Minnesota.

The map of the Czech Republic on page 99 is supplied by and used with the kind permission of the Czech Republic Consulate General in New York, New York.

Photocopies of definitions from the *American Dictionary of the English Language* (1828), by Daniel Webster, are used with the kind permission of the Foundation for American Christian Education, Washington, D.C.

The definition of *money* from the *Oxford English Dictionary*, in Appendix H, is used with the kind permission of Oxford University Press, Oxford, England.

Special thanks to Bowers and Merena Galleries, Inc., Wolfeboro, New Hampshire, and Mr. Douglas Plasencia, photographer, for the photographs of U.S. gold, silver, minor, and colonial coins in Chapter 9.

Special thanks to Ms. Robin Edgerly, Wolfeboro, New Hampshire, for the graphic design and layout of our coin montages.

We are also grateful for the assistance of Numismatic Guaranty Corporation, Parsippany, New Jersey, in locating photographs of the coins shown in our montages.

Quotations from *Golden Insights* are used with the kind permission of Mr. James U. Blanchard, III, President, Jefferson Financial, Inc., Jefferson, Louisiana.

ZNS extends special thanks to the Cornell University School of Law for hosting a marvelous web site: http://www.law.cornell.edu/uscode/, from which we obtained many of the United States Code sections quoted in Appendix O and elsewhere in this book.

Thanks to Mr. Robert Hoge, Curator, Museum of the American Numismatic Association, Colorado Springs, Colorado, for valuable assistance in finding photographs of U.S. paper currency and for historical information on U.S. and ancient coinage and important monetary terms.

Thanks to the American Numismatic Society, New York, New York, for historical information on U.S. coinage and assistance in finding photographs of U.S. paper currency.

Thanks to Mr. Stewart Westdal, researcher and numismatist, at Ponterio and Associates, Inc., San Diego, California, for data regarding nicknames of Spanish coins of the 1600s and later.

Thanks to Mr. Martin Gengerke, R. M. Smythe & Company, New York, New York, for helping us find several cleaner specimens of older U.S. currency. Mr. Gengerke authored the revisions to Title 18, United States Code, which now permits full-color reproductions of U.S. currency.

Thanks to internationally recognized expert on Japanese currency, Mr. Joseph E. Boling, Federal Way, Washington, for guidance regarding several obscure Civil War era paper currency issues.

Thanks also to J. E. Fosberg Design, Seattle, Washington, for last-minute technical help in producing the composite image of the $10,000 United States Note ("Legal Tender" Note replica) shown in Chapter 9.

Thanks to Mr. Fred Schwan at BNR Press, Port Clinton, Ohio, for helping us find the replica of the $10,000 United States Note.

Thanks to Mr. Arthur L. Friedberg, The Coin & Currency Institute, Inc., Clifton, New Jersey, for special assistance in our search for a color photo of a $10,000 United States Note.

Thanks to Mr. Ken Barr, U.S. and foreign paper currency dealer, San Jose, California, for the perfect replica of a $10,000 United States Note, which we used in Chapter 9.

Special thanks to Mr. Eustace Mullins for permission to photographically reproduce several pages from his book, *The Secrets Of The Federal Reserve* (Staunton, Virginia: Bankers Research Institute, 1984). These materials are shown in Appendix L.

Thanks to Brown Brothers, Sterling, Pennsylvania, for copyrighted archival material (drawing of the trial of John Peter Zenger, and a photo of the front page of Zenger's newspaper, *THE New-York Weekly JOURNAL*, for Monday, November 12, 1733), as shown in Appendix G.

Thanks to Mr. Dan Poynter, Para Publishing, Santa Barbara, California, for professional guidance on getting this book organized and to market.

Thanks to WinePress Publishing, Mukilteo, Washington, for help in solving technical and administrative problems on this project.

Thanks to Mr. Spencer Kope, Willow Creek Press of Washington, Silverdale, Washington, for advice and encouragement on how to overcome several technical and production problems encountered in producing this book.

Thanks to the George Edward Durell Foundation, Berryville, Virginia, for information on the Fort Knox Bullion Depository, Fort Knox, Kentucky, and the inventory of gold there and in other U.S. depositories.

Thanks to Mr. John Mueller, partner, Lehrman Bell Mueller Cannon, Inc., Arlington, Virginia, for details on the "World Dollar Base" method of analyzing commodity and other prices.

Thanks to Gordon Leitch, Jr., M.D. (ret.), Portland, Oregon, for providing us with rare archival information on the definition of *dollar* in colonial America.

Thanks to Mr. John Carter, Topline Investment Graphics, Inc., Boulder, Colorado, for assistance in developing the special Dow Jones Industrial Average graphs in Appendix M.

Thanks to Lawrence Parks, Ph.D., Executive Director, Foundation for the Advancement of Monetary Education, Inc., New York, New York, for special insight into a current monetary question.

We thank De La Rue Currency and Security Print, London, England (formerly Thomas De La Rue Limited) for current technical and operational information on producing and destroying paper currencies.

Thanks also to the World Gold Council, Geneva, Switzerland, for current information on gold production and use.

Thanks to former U.S. Representative William E. Dannemeyer for historical information related to the Federal Reserve Act of 1913 and amendments and laws relating to banking.

Special thanks to the United States Secret Service, Seattle, Washington, for valuable technical assistance related to publishing color photographs of U.S. currency.

Special thanks to Mr. Kaye Lawrence Jensen (founder, editor, and publisher of *Jurisdiction Journal*) for his outstanding support of the author during this project's earliest years. Mr. Jensen, a World War II combat veteran — United States Marine Corps in campaigns at Saipan, Tinian, and elsewhere in the Pacific — has performed "above and beyond the call of duty" his entire life. For his more than half a century of resolute service to the Republic and its God-given Constitution, ZNS salutes Mr. Kaye L. Jensen, without whose support this book would not have been possible. *Semper Fi*, Kaye.

ZNS also thanks Mr. Robert E. Pletka, American Awareness, Portland, Oregon, for our photos of Jochymov, Czech Republic, taken by Mr. Pletka on a photo assignment for ZNS in 1998. We plan to use Mr. Pletka's photos in a forthcoming work. Mr. Pletka has devoted most of his life to helping others better understand and appreciate two miracles: individual liberty and the United States of America.

The author also extends special, personal thanks to Mr. and Mrs. Drew Roddy, Grapeview, Washington, for use of their 1870 edition of *Bouvier's Law Dictionary*, and for the other support and counsel they have so kindly provided the author through the several years of this project.

Special thanks are also due these other Roddys — the staff and management of Rocky Creek Farm of Gig Harbor, Washington — for their support and counsel over the past decade. Thank you Kurt, Lisa, Taira, Morgan, and Noah. Thanks also to Simone, Fritz, Fritz's mom, George, Martha, and others of the Rocky Creek Farm menagerie. I thank you all very much, both for your support and for having me as your frequent guest – in *Eden*.

Thanks also to the following:

- U.S. Mint, Washington, D.C. and Fort Knox, Kentucky.
- U.S. Treasury Department, Washington, D.C.
- U.S. Bureau of Engraving and Printing, Washington, D.C.

U.S. Senator Slade Gorton (Washington).

U.S. Representative Ron Paul (Texas).

U.S. Representative Jack Metcalf (Washington).

British Royal Mint, London, England.

Bank of England, London, England.

Federal Reserve System, Washington, D.C.

Federal Reserve Bank, New York.

Federal Reserve Bank, Chicago.

Federal Reserve Bank, San Francisco.

Chase Manhattan Bank, New York, New York.

Consulate General of the Federal Republic of Germany, Seattle, Washington.

Embassy of Australia, Washington, D.C.

Embassy of Finland, Washington, D.C.

Embassy of New Zealand, Washington, D.C.

Embassy of Denmark, Washington, D.C.

Consulate of Denmark, Seattle, Washington.

New Zealand Consulate, Seattle, Washington.

Consulate of Norway, Seattle, Washington.

Austrian Consulate, Seattle, Washington.

Danish Mint, Copenhagen, Denmark.

Danish Trade Office, Seattle, Washington.

Embassy of Singapore, Washington, D.C.

Embassy of Estonia, Washington, D.C.

•

xx

Notice and Disclaimer

REPRODUCTION of United States currencies is legal only if the copy is more than fifty percent larger than, or smaller than three fourths, the size of the original; and the copy is black and white; and the copy is used in news or educational material related to money, finance, or monetary affairs, etc. Each reproduction must be referred to in adjacent or accompanying text. See 18 U.S.C. § 474, § 475, § 481 and § 504. Purchaser's failure to abide by applicable law is solely the responsibility of the purchaser. See also Appendix F for our authorization to reproduce color photographs of U.S. currency.

Brand names, product names, registered trademarks and trademarks used herein are the property of their owners.

This book is based on information from sources believed to be reliable, and every effort has been made to make it as complete and accurate as possible based on information available as of the printing date. Nevertheless, its accuracy and completeness, both typographical and in content, cannot be guaranteed. Despite the best efforts of the author and publisher, the book may contain mistakes. Thus, the reader should use the book only as a general guide and not as the final or ultimate source of information about money or the other subjects of the book. This book is not intended to reprint all of the information available to the author or publisher on the subject, but rather to simplify, complement and supplement other available sources. The reader is encouraged to read all available material and to learn as much as possible about the subject. Some of these materials are listed in Appendix A and elsewhere in this book. This book is intended to be an educational service to citizens of the United States of America and of each of the several states.

The material in this book is presented as general information only and is not intended to be specific, legal or other professional advice.

Readers should personally investigate federal, state and local laws regarding the matters discussed herein and, where appropriate, obtain further information from knowledgeable, professional sources. Readers should bear in mind that monetary and other laws change constantly as new cases are decided, as new laws and regulations are enacted, and as new technologies and products find their way to the marketplace. Thus, readers must make certain, through the assistance of professional counsel, that they rely on the most current and applicable law.

Occasional discussion of legal principles is greatly simplified and summarized, both to help non-lawyers understand the material and to keep the book's size reasonable. That is why you will see certain cautionary terms or phrases like "For example," "in general," "often," "usually," "sometimes," etc. These terms and phrases are intended to remind readers that the subject being discussed is much more complex than our discussion might imply. For this reason, please make sure you do not forget that there may be exceptions to a legal principle or a rule of law.

The purpose of this book is to educate, inform and entertain. The author and Principia Publishing, Inc., shall have neither liability nor responsibility to any person or entity with respect to any loss or damage caused, or alleged to be caused, directly or indirectly, by the information contained in this book.

Persons acting on information provided in this document do so at their own risk and responsibility.

IF YOU DO NOT WISH TO BE BOUND BY THE FOREGOING CAUTIONS AND CONDITIONS, YOU MAY RETURN THIS BOOK AND PROOF OF PURCHASE TO THE PUBLISHER WITHIN 30 DAYS OF THE PURCHASE DATE FOR A FULL REFUND OF THE PURCHASE PRICE.

•

Figure 1-1. *1961, Berlin, Germany, Sunday, August 13. This afternoon the Communists close the border between East and West Berlin and prepare to build the infamous Berlin Wall. The day's sharply increased military presence and nervousness of border police and troops reflect the heightened diplomatic tension. East German tanks line up at the Warschauer Bridge crossing point as the author enjoys his sightseeing tour of the Soviet sector. He is scheduled to return to the American sector at about 4:00 p.m. Copyright © 1998 by AP/Wide World Photos. Reproduced with permission. All rights reserved.*

1

Berlin

THE big guy had his submachine gun pointed right in our faces. The little guy had his submachine gun pointing down, but still at the ready. Standing next to our tour bus driver's seat and blocking the aisle, each soldier had a pistol in his holster and a surly expression on his face. Neither man looked very bright. Their cheeks were excessively red, not ruddy from being outdoors but *bloody* from ruptured capillaries. I suspected a long-standing relationship with vodka. Or maybe brake fluid. But for sure, long-standing.

The big guy, about 6' 2" and 225 pounds, effectively blocked anyone's attempted exit. He could spray the interior of the bus with .30 caliber submachine gun fire whenever he felt like it. His expression told me that he wouldn't be bothered much whether he hosed us down deliberately, under orders from his superiors, or accidentally, or even if he did it on a whim. (*"I thought I saw someone raise what looked like a gun."*)

The little guy, although "little" only in the sense that he was short, probably weighed as much as the big guy, had no neck, and he reminded me of a ball of gristle. His beet-red face was typically Russian-peasant round, his teeth were in conspicuously sorry shape, and his eyes were flat, dead, robot-like. Away from his face, his skin was almost gray, the color of recycled but unbleached newsprint, waxy and ashen, sickly looking.

I suspected neither soldier spoke English. I would soon also suspect neither spoke German.

The little guy, however, became my first "friend" in the People's Revolutionary Army of the Union of Soviet Socialist Republics. The USSR. He and his pal were Russian soldiers, part of a contingent of Red Army troops newly assigned to Berlin in the tense days of early August, 1961.

Our tour bus, based in West Berlin, had entered the Soviet sector about three hours earlier, about 1:00 p.m. this warm summer day. I'd been excited to go on this tour of the Soviet-controlled quadrant of Berlin (called *Der Ost,* the East, or the Eastern sector, the part controlled by the communists, the Russians). This afternoon I'd shot about six rolls of black-and-white film, thirty-six shots per roll, and had put the camera and exposed film in its carrying case and put the case under my seat. I thought it'd be safer there than *on* the seat where it could tumble off if the bus stopped suddenly.

The little guy turned to the first passenger on the right front of the bus and barked out just one word, loud enough so everyone in the front half of the bus could hear him: "PAHSS!" Meekly, the elderly German man held up two small green booklets, his passport and his wife's, to the Russian guard. After a moment of scrutinizing the pages, the guard handed the booklets back and then stepped to the second pair of seats on the right side of the bus. In a few moments I'd be invited to participate in the ritual of passport examination.

I thought: *Hmmm. Small problem, GI. You don't have a passport. Or a visa.*

Soon the guard looked down at me, expectantly holding his right hand out toward me. I gave him my Department of Defense ID card and my three-day leave papers, and began my explanation.

Very softly, so I wouldn't disturb others on the bus, I said, *Nyet penyamaiya Parushki,* just about the only thing I could say in Russian.

Then, raising my voice to almost a normal loudness, I continued, now in German: *"Ich bin eine Amerikanische fliegerman auf Flugplatz Spangdahlem in West Deutschsland statzioniert, und Ich mache hier heute nachmittags nur eine drei-stunde reise durch den Sovietische sektor. Wir gehen heute abend zuruck nach meine Flugplatz bie eisenbahn rund halb-seben uhr."*

Silence. Not even a flicker of understanding in the eyes. No change in expression. Nothing.

The Russian soldier then looked back at my "papers." They didn't look very impressive.

My three-day leave papers were 8 1/2 inch by 14 inch mimeograph sheets which I'd folded four times so I could carry them in my hip pocket. Because it was August and the weather was warm, those papers were noticeably soggy from my perspiration. Plus, they were almost impossible to read even when dry because *my* copies were the eleventh, twelfth and thirteenth carbons.

My United States Air Force ID card must have appeared equally suspicious. It was cracked diagonally across the center, and dust and perspiration had soiled a quarter-inch wide area on both sides of the crack. My ID card looked *very* "home made."

But it seems the gods were in a good mood that day because soon, with a little wink and the barest hint of a smile, the Russian soldier handed me my ID card and Leave papers and shuffled off. Now he'd inspect the documentation of the Italian couple sitting a few rows behind me.

It took only about fifteen minutes for the guard to go through the bus. Because of the tension at the border, about which I was blissfully unaware, the bus was only about one quarter full. I was the only English-speaking passenger and, although I thought the heavy Russian military presence was all very interesting, I was oblivious to the danger I was in. However I would soon learn I was the *only* person on that bus who was unaware of the danger I was in.

The guards finally got off, had our driver open the luggage compartment so they could check it for stowaways, and then they let the driver get back on board. In a few moments they gave him the okay to start the engine, and then to close the door, and eventually, to begin driving through the barriers. We crossed a bridge over the Spree River and entered West Berlin, turned left, and drove parallel to the river for about two blocks. Then, when we had a full city block of buildings between us and the Soviet sector, the driver slowed the bus, pulled to the curb, stopped, set the hand brake, and put the bus in neutral gear.

Boom! Suddenly, with an explosion of excited voices and shouts of laughter, all the other passengers sprang out of their seats and swarmed around me. Their voices were a raucous cacophony of Spanish, Swedish, German, Italian, and possibly a couple of other languages. I was amazed at the sight and sounds but I didn't have a clue as to what was going on.

Soon the guide pushed her way through the crowd and, laughing, and in perfect American English, she asked me, "Do you have any idea why these people are so shook up?" I was surprised that she spoke such fluent English, hearing her use the phrase, "shook up," so I answered in English. "No, I have no idea."

Her expression switched to serious and she asked, "Well, what do you think you said to that Russian soldier?"

I replied, "Oh, I just told him I was an American airman stationed at Spangdahlem Air Base in West Germany and. . . ."

She interrupted me, saying, "No, no, that was your German and it was fine. I mean, what do you think you said to him in Russian?"

I replied, "Oh, I just told him I didn't speak Russian."

"Oh, no, no, no! That isn't what you said!" She continued, "You didn't say the right words and you didn't say the words right. What you told him was to *not speak* Russian, I mean, *you told him to not speak Russian!*"

Oooooops!

Well, I never did feel like I had a handle on Russian. A few years earlier, when I was boot camp, a barracks pal from Russia had tried to teach me some Russian. It wasn't enough training for my contact with the Red Army that day.

Our tour guide, a petite German girl in her late teens or early 20s, went on. She said, "These people are shook up because they saw the whole thing. They are cheering for you and for the CIA."

CIA? I thought, *What the hell's the CIA?*

She went on, "We saw you taking all those pictures and we knew you were pointing your camera at the typical tourist sights, but we also saw you aiming in such a way that your pictures would also show the Russian artillery emplacements, machine gun positions, guard stations, and armored equipment.

"We are all very proud of you, tricking that Russian soldier into thinking you were a KGB[1] agent, making him think that you were penetrating to the West on the last day possible, hinting that confusion at the border might have prevented him from getting the word to watch out for you and make sure you got through okay."

Silently, I asked myself, *What the hell's the KGB? What is this girl talking about?*

Like a typical GI, I played along with her, smiling knowingly. I patted my camera case and gave the crowd a wink and a smile. But I really didn't have any idea what the deal was. CIA? KGB? Angrily, I asked myself, *What the hell's going on here anyway?*

About half an hour later I found out what the hell was going on here anyway. It was Sunday, August 13, 1961. In a move that caught the world by surprise, early that afternoon the communist government of East Berlin closed the border between East Berlin and West Berlin. It was the top story on all the television and radio news programs and in all the newspapers all over the world. I may have been the last American tourist out of the Soviet sector that day. It had been a close call. In a few days they'd begin sealing the border between East Berlin and the West. In a week they would begin construction of the infamous Berlin Wall.

If that soldier had spotted my camera case, and if he'd decided to try for a hero medal by dragging me off the bus for interrogation, I'd have been in a world of hurt. His superiors would surely have become curious about what was on my film. If they'd developed it, and if they didn't shoot me on the spot, I'd likely have been shipped to a *gulag* for at least ten years. That's because I'd been having a little fun with the camera, although it wasn't really *my* camera. I'd borrowed it from my buddy and roommate, Gordon Hobza, my best friend and fellow A1c (E-4) electronics tech at Spangdahlem Air Base, in the 49th Tactical Fighter Wing's Armament and Electronics shop. Thanks again, Gordy.

Three hours earlier, when I'd boarded the bus, the tour guide, upon seeing my camera, had told me that while we were in the Soviet sector it was okay to take pictures of anything I wanted *except military equipment.* Well, always the clever lad, I had thought, *Who's going to know? Who's going to pay any attention to me?*

I decided I might get a citation or something if I took a few sneaky shots of some of the Red hardware that was all over the place. I mean, you couldn't take a picture of anything, almost, without having some military stuff in the shot.

Here's the deal: If you took a photograph of an

---

[1] The KGB, the Russian equivalent of the CIA, is also referred to in Western nations as the Soviet Secret Police. KGB is the acronym for Komitet Gosudarstvennoi Bezopasnosti, meaning the (Russian) Committee for State Security. Those who are most informed about these matters say the KGB is *worse* than Hitler's Gestapo.

apartment building, you'd find that your photo also showed the Russian soldiers and their sand-bagged machine-gun emplacement on the roof. Or if you shot a picture of the Russian war memorial statue, if you were standing where I was, you couldn't help but include in that picture the Russian artillery unit in the park on the other side of the fence. So I said to myself, *To heck with it. I'm interested in military stuff and nobody'll pay any attention to me so I'll just take pictures of whatever I please. In fact, I think I'll take pictures of* everything *military that interests me.*

So I did.

I took pictures of apartments, including the troops walking patrol on their roofs. I took pictures of neighborhoods, making sure I focused on the Soviet armor parked in the adjacent vacant lots or at nearby intersections. I took pictures of troop formations at entrances to what appeared to be government buildings, and I took pictures of non-commercial aircraft overhead.

Once our tour bus stopped for a traffic light. Lo and behold, right there, outside of my window was a Russian Army communications truck loaded with radio gear. I snapped a few quick pictures of the front panels of a couple of the radio units, which I thought might tell the good guys something about the wavelengths the Russians used and what modulation flexibility they had, etc.

Click, click, click. Lotsa Soviet military stuff. Click, click, click, just like that. *Piece of cake. Noooooo sweat, GI.*

In a way I thought I was being pretty clever but in another way I thought that what I was photographing wasn't all that secret because, I thought to myself, *For crying out loud, it's all right out in the open and everything. I mean they aren't even trying to cover it up.*

Know what ah mean, Vern?

Anyway, after a tense train (and then bus) ride back to my base, Spangdahlem Air Base, I found we were on a full-scale war alert. I got a German friend to develop the film in Trier — about twenty miles south of our base, about 150 miles southwest of Frankfurt — a couple of days after I got back to the base. I had him make two sets of prints. I turned one set of prints over to our wing intelligence unit and they forwarded the prints to an intelligence unit in Berlin. About a month later, my Commanding Officer, First Lt. Nicholas Gionis (Gianis?), told me that while everyone appreciated my forwarding the pictures, there was nothing in them of interest to the military.

No medal for me, it turned out, and a while later I lost my set of the prints. Bummer.

But the experience was tremendously valuable for me. It gave me the emotional *and* intellectual motivation to find out more about international affairs. I soon found out about the KGB and the CIA, and I began a program of self-study that would continue for the rest of my life.

While in college I'd taken a speed reading course which increased my reading speed to about 2,000 words per minute and my comprehension to almost 100%. Since I'd never really enjoyed fiction, I focused on biographies. I'd soon read more than a hundred books by people who'd escaped from prison camps, or from Communist countries, or from Nazi Germany just before or during World War II. I read about people who'd been interned by the Japanese during World War II, and biographies of military and civilian captives during the Korean and Vietnam wars. I read biographies of KGB operatives, books about the CIA, and books about World War I, and World War II, and the Korean War, and the war in Vietnam. I read biographies of soldiers, sailors, marines, airmen, doctors, pilots, journalists, diplomats, business leaders, and even average citizens of various countries who found themselves caught up in world-shaking events.

Thus I learned about many of America's and the world's problems, from those trying to solve the problems and from those who suffered because of those problems.

I also met some interesting people.

- An American, imprisoned by the Russians right after World War II. This man spent ten years in a Soviet slave labor camp in Siberia.

- A former German soldier, now a U.S. citizen, who was captured and imprisoned by the Russians for several years right after World War II ended.
- A former KGB agent, a specialist in disinformation. He defected in India, became an American citizen, and now lives with his wife in California.
- A man-and-wife team who'd been in the U.S. diplomatic service corps for about thirty years. They'd worked in the American Embassy in Moscow for about ten years. They shared my concern, and many of my conclusions, about the state of the nation and where we were headed.

I've since met others who've helped reinforce my understanding of things. I met one man who was a pilot with the Flying Tigers of World War II, another pilot who is an expert on the shootdown of Korean Air Lines flight 007, another man who was the commander of a U.S. Navy ship which saw duty off the coast of Korea during the Korean war, and I've met many combat veterans: One from World War I (my dad); many others from World War II, Korea, and the Vietnam war. Virtually all of these people confirmed the truth of much of what I'd read. They encouraged me to continue my independent investigations and analyses.

My reading gave me a background which made me different from the average American. Because I've read biographies of people who were imprisoned by the Castro regime in Cuba, when I'd meet someone who had escaped from Cuba, for example, or a family member of someone who was still in Cuba, they could quickly tell I had an above-average understanding of the realities of life in the "worker's paradise" just ninety miles south of Florida. These and other immigrants also confirmed the truth of much of what I'd read.

Because I've read so many books by people who escaped from Russia, when I meet an immigrant from Russia, or the Ukraine, or Kazakhstan, for example, they can usually tell in a matter of minutes that I *know* something of what they've suffered and what they've seen. The bond of friendship with these people is often immediate, deep, and permanent.

Over the years, as I became more knowledgeable about world affairs, I began to look more closely at the political intrigues of the United States and at our nation's recent history. It didn't take long until I began to realize that there were serious problems in the United States and that the general public was, for the most part, grievously uninformed about the forces operating behind the scenes.

People in this country are generally unaware of the *real* movers and shakers, those who build their power by taking advantage of conflict. In fact, the record indicates that these people may sometimes *initiate* conflict when it will give them an opportunity to increase their power.

When you think of "movers and shakers," do you think of politicians, our nation's elected leaders, and the faces you see on the evening news, the TV news commentators, the Senators, the Representatives, the Supreme Court Justices, and the President? I used to think those folks were the nation's main movers and shakers too, but no longer.

Yes, I recognize that those people have power, a lot of power, but I've discovered that there are other movers and shakers in this country, and in other countries, and *these* folks have the ultimate power.

For the purposes of this book, let's just call these other movers and shakers by a single word, Insiders. Let's remember Insiders as movers and shakers who are rarely or never seen on TV, we rarely or never see reference to them in print, and their names and positions are not well known to the average American. In fact, although well-educated people may recognize a name or two now and then, only professionals in certain industries are usually well informed about who these Insiders are and what they do.

Coincidentally, on a crime program on TV a year or so ago, a former con artist told the reporter that the easiest people to con were the people who were the most educated. This reformed crook explained that the educated person tends to assume that *this stupid street-person* could not possibly pull anything over on him or her, they are too clever and knowledgeable to be tricked. The con artist said that taking an educated person to the cleaners is easy because their ego blocks them from seeing reality. He described his method as something like verbal *karate*, a fighting technique which takes advantage of an aggressor's off-balance condition when attacking, to make it easy to throw him to the ground.

The reformed con artist said scams work best on people who think they know a lot. College graduates, yuppies, wealthy teenagers, people who've never been in the military, all are prime candidates for scams because they are in the habit of dealing with honest people. In their heart of hearts they tend to think everybody is basically honest. They don't even *begin* to understand dishonesty, especially in their analysis of community leadership. Moreover, their inflated ego tends to make them think that they know all the important stuff, and that, logically, anything they don't already know is unimportant.

My reading gave me an insight into dishonesty. I think I've found that *some* of the most dishonest people in the world are the people we'd be least likely to think of as dishonest. We often see them on TV and we often see their names in print but we rarely or never hear about their dishonesty.

My investigations, however, revealed to me that the reason a prominent figure's dishonesty may not be widely discussed in the media is because the average news media representative, reporter, or investigator has a seriously impaired view of reality. News media personalities, in my view, tend to be fat, dumb, and happy.

My KGB friend, the disinformation specialist, said reporters from U.S. newspapers and magazines were easiest to fool. Their monumental egos made them like putty, easy to mold into supporting or attacking any philosophical or political position. KGB-generated slants on topics of interest (to the KGB) could be placed in U.S. newspapers and news magazines with ease, usually within a few months of the start of a disinformation campaign.

Since the disinformation campaigns were usually aimed at strengthening one group's power and weakening another group's power, it didn't take long to see the common theme in almost all of the disinformation campaigns, and their common result.

The common theme was that a conflict, real or artificial, was discussed widely. Then several solutions would be offered, but there would be only two or three "rational" solutions. The KGB didn't really care which one of the "rational" solutions was finally agreed upon. Any one of the "rational" solutions would achieve a target goal while also setting the stage for another conflict, so the KGB could manipulate our options once again.

The most common result of these "conflict followed by resolution" steps was an increased role of government — and commensurate erosion of the power of the individual — in the target country. Government (civil-service employee organizations) grew in size and power and the non-civil-service-employee citizen's authority weakened. The push was toward total control of an area by civil-service employees. But there was another facet to the KGB's operations. What I discovered was not so much an observation of what occurred as an observation of what didn't occur. You'll read about it in Chapter 12.

What I experienced in Berlin was *nothing* compared to what I experienced in my study of this country's most powerful institutions, and *money*.

You may soon see how you may have been a victim of what some call the largest criminal enterprise in history.

In any event, please turn the page now and let's get started, with *Money*.

•

2

Money

WHAT is *money*? Can you give a precise definition of *money*[1] without help from a dictionary? What is the difference between *money* and *currency*, between *dollars* and *legal tender*, or between *cash* and *coin*? Although this book discusses each of these terms, we begin by focusing on perhaps the most important one, *money*.

Roman Mythology and *Money*
Various objects have been used *as* money since man's earliest existence, but the first form of the *word* money did not appear until about 500 B.C.

Some sources say Roman mythology attributes the goddess Juno[2] — *in about 500 B.C.* — with giving the Roman legions a warning on the battlefield. Because her sage and timely advice saved the Roman army from sure defeat, she was given the epithet[3] *Moneta*, a variation of the Latin *monere*, which means *a warning*.

In about 344 B.C., sacred geese are said to have sounded the alarm of the Gallist invasion. A few years after the invasion, on the site of the home of the first person to hear the geese's warning, the Roman ruler Lucius Furius erected a temple to honor Juno (now Juno *Mone'ta*, the *Monitress*). Since Juno was considered the guardian of the Roman treasury, this temple was soon converted into a mint and used to manufacture silver coins, ases and denarii.

Rome's citizens soon began calling this temple *The Moneta*. Thereafter it was their custom to call *every* building in which coins were made, a *moneta*, and call ases, denarii and *all* other coins *monetas*, meaning "things which come from a *moneta*."

Etymology Of *Money* and *Mint*
Over the next thousand years or so, the spelling and pronunciation of *moneta* changed. As it related to exchange media (coinage), *moneta* began to be spelled either without the "ta," that is, *mone* (spoken to rhyme with moh-knee), or without the "a," as *monet* (moh-nay). By the time the Mayflower landed

---

[1] As a convention in this book, we italicize English words when their definition is our focus. Definitions may also be wholly or partly italicized for clarity or emphasis. We also italicize Latin and other foreign-language terms.

[2] Juno, wife and sister of Jupiter, queen of heaven, and chief protector of women, is also believed (by some scholars) to be the origin of our name for the sixth month of the year, June. The tradition of June being the best month for marriage stems from Juno's mythological protective covenant with women, which is also the root of today's European custom of women managing the household's money.

[3] An *epithet* is a tacked-on name which helps describe a person. In the names Richard the Lion-Hearted and Peter the Great, "the Lion-Hearted" and "the Great" are *epithets* of Richard and Peter, respectively.

on America's east coast, the English spelling had changed to *monie*, and several years before the Founders penned the United States Constitution, the spelling finally changed to *money*.

Another branch of this etymological tree takes us through a different sequence of spelling changes. The earlier *moneta*, the place (temple) in which Roman media of exchange were manufactured, became known by about 500 A.D. as the *mynyta*.[4] By about 1,000 A.D., the "a" was dropped, leaving *mynyt*, with the second "y" becoming a near-silent letter.[5] When the Pilgrims landed at Plymouth Rock, money was manufactured in a place called a *mynt*. Shortly after the American revolution, the spelling of *mynt* changed to *mint*.

Juno Moneta in America Today

Indeed, Juno Moneta's epithetical name endures to the present, unchanged by time or distance from her earlier domain, in our word *monetary*[6] and its variations.

One variation of monetary is *monetize*, a verb. When we convert metal into coins, we *monetize* the metal. Miners of gold and silver sometimes have their metal *monetized*, that is, made into money at a mint, often a United States Mint. *Demonetize* is also a verb. We *demonetize* money when we melt coins or grind them to dust.[7]

Contrary to what some might claim, one cannot demonetize *debts* (or accounts receivable, helium, love, rocks, 349, fish, or an old shirt). Simple logic tells us that we can *de*-monetize only that which is already monetized — *metal which is in coin form*.

---

[4] Pronounced my(th) + knit + uh.

[5] Often noted in Gaelic, Scottish, and early-English words.

[6] Moneta + ry (ry = Latin, *re*), meaning *money* + *regarding*.

[7] New Zealand recently withdrew two coins from circulation. The coins were sold as scrap with the provision that the buyer would melt the coins immediately. Once melted, the coins are demonetized, although the coins are considered to have been effectively demonetized when the New Zealand government issued the order to withdraw the coins from circulation.

The First Coins

Near the eastern end of the Mediterranean Sea, in what is now western Turkey, remains are found of the ancient kingdom of Lydia, sometimes called the Lydian Empire. Sardis, the Lydian capital, was founded in about 800 B.C.

In Sardis, as in most commercial centers of the day, trade was hampered by the lack of a trustworthy medium of exchange. Transactions were accomplished — with difficulty — through the most rudimentary methods of barter, although a crude coinage facilitated some trading. Believed to have been made as early as 750 B.C., this initial coinage, called *staters*, meaning *standards*, was irregularly-sized and -shaped lumps of *electrum*, a naturally occurring mixture of gold and silver.

Although rudely marked to show their weight and fineness, staters were gradually replaced by more-carefully made coins beginning around 500 B.C.[8] Since the newer coins were relative uniform in size, weight, and precious-metal content, prices could be expressed in multiples or fractions of the units of *weight* of the purchasing media, and transactions could occur without a need to weigh each object tendered. The invention of *uniform media of exchange* improved the efficiency of the marketplace and enhanced our ability to keep account of our actions.

Money: A Precise Definition

From this etymological review we see that a *mint* is the place where *money* is manufactured. We also see the most precise definition of *money*:

> **Money**: Coins or other mechanical devices manufactured in a mint — from gold, silver or other precious or semiprecious metals — to be media of exchange.

The "Why" of Money

If you ever wondered why money was invented, reflect on how difficult life would be without it. Money is an invention, much like the wheel, which helps us be less wasteful. Because of money, our transactions

---

[8] Historians believe the exact year was 463 B.C. or 465 B.C.

now are far more efficient than they were prior to our use of money to facilitate trade.

In fact, money's success is due in great part to sound logic. The best material from which to make money is a substance which is easily divisible, it has utilitarian value independent of any edict by government, it is durable, and is a relatively scarce yet ductile or mallable material. Silver and gold are the two substances which best meet that criteria.[9] The precious metal in U.S. gold coins, for example, could be fashioned into *objets d'art*, dental fillings, mirrors, electronic circuits, plating for specimens to be examined under an electron microscope, or as a heat reflector on components of spacecraft. The precious metal in U.S. silver coins could be fashioned into jewelry, cooking and eating utensils, mirrors, electrical conductors such as fine wires and solder, into germicidal[10] ointments and balms, and as heat-reflecting coatings on spacecraft components. Both metals resist oxidation and, when properly alloyed, are durable enough to be used as media of exchange. They may be easily fashioned into coins of small enough denomination to handle the transactions of children; a pre-1965 U.S. dime, for example, because of its silver content, may be exchanged today for a snack or small meal in any country in the world.

The industrial uses of silver and gold, combined with their relative scarcity, and their beauty, make them the ideal materials from which money might be made.

Universal recognition of the industrial uses and relative scarcity of silver and gold have made these two metals the preferred coinage material the world over. No governmental authority is needed to make gold or silver desirable. People want those two metals because their utilitarian value is known internationally.

Except in highly unusual circumstances such as war, no private or government mint would ever try to sell brass or lead or steel coinage because none of those metals are scarce enough to make that coinage a successful medium of exchange. Reasonable sized coins of steel would last a long time, especially if they were alloyed to resist rusting, but too many coins would be needed for even minor transactions, due to the relative low scarcity of steel. The same weakness is shared by almost all other materials: they lack scarcity, or they lack durability, or they lack international utilitarian or aesthetic value.

Logic also dictates the round shape of modern coins. Round devices do not tend to wear holes in our pockets, purses, or other containers. Round devices do not have corners to wear off, and round devices can be stacked and counted easily because they do not need to be first oriented a special way.

The relatively large flat surfaces of round coins are perfect areas for engraving or embossing special identification marks. Also, the relatively small edges of round coins are easily shaped with mill marks to protect against clipping.

What Is *Lawful* Money?
When gold bullion, for example, is converted into coins at a United States Mint in accordance with the Act of April 2, 1792,[11] as amended, those coins are *lawful* money, meaning money manufactured pursuant to Public *Law*.

Lawful money in France would be coins manufactured per French law. German lawful money would be coins manufactured according to German law. In fact, lawful money of one country might be manufactured in another country but according to the requirements of the first country's law. The lawful money of Jamaica is manufactured according to Jamaican law — *but in England, at the British Royal Mint*. The lawful money of Latvia is made according to Latvian law, but at a mint in Finland.

How To *Make* Money
You might say the best way to make money is to invent a product or service everyone needs, and then

---

[9] Platinum, due to its high melting temperature and softness, is rarely used to make circulating coinage.

[10] Some wagon-train pioneers settling the West in the 1800s hid their silver coins in their water containers. Families who adopted this practice avoided water-borne illnesses which befell other settlers.

[11] 1 Stat. 246. Please see Appendix D.

sell it at a reasonable price. However, that is only an informal use of the term *make*.

In strictly formal terms, *make* means create or manufacture, and the creation or manufacture of *money* is called *minting*. *Making money* is the function of a *mint*, and a mint is a specialized manufacturing facility.

Some folks attribute a mystical character to money, almost as if it is something to be worshipped. You should be on guard against becoming overly enthusiastic about money because it is really just a tool, an instrument like a pencil, wrench or other mechanical device which can perform services for humans. Money, like other useful tools, helps us but shouldn't control us. A silver coin or an ingot of gold holds no ethereal powers, and no government can attribute such powers to these mechanical devices, anymore than President Clinton, for example, can confer holy powers on wrenches. For money to serve mankind, there is no need for civil-service workers to comment on it. Money works, and it retains its intrinsic value, independently of all governments.

You should not make the mistake of deifying money, or falling into the trap that some governmental agency needs to be involved in the manufacture of money. Civil service workers are no more vital to the existence of money than they are vital to the existence of 3/4 inch box-end wrenches. Money will exist, as will box-end wrenches, even if there are no civil-service workers.

Watch Out For Poor Terminology
Some often-heard expressions about money are humorously incorrect.

Since "paper" and "money" are mutually-exclusive terms, the phrase "paper money" is without meaning.

Some economists talk about "monetizing" the public debt, but how can a debt be converted into coins?

People who are anxious to stop inflation sometimes call for a return to "honest money," but money, because it is inanimate, can be neither honest nor dishonest.

The phrase "interest-free money" is irrational. Money is a thing, and although a borrower of any thing may be charged for the *use* of that thing, the charge is not levied on the thing. Interest is often charged for credit, but credit is *not* money.

Another irrational phrase is "debt money." If one has a debt, one owes money to another. If one has money and has paid one's debts, that's the end of that story too. There is no such thing as "debt-money." If you hear someone discussing "debt money," you may wish to be on guard — that person may also use other irrational phrases. That's because "debt money" is just one of a dozen or so equally irrational terms or phrases used by people who have a poor grasp of the fundamentals of money and monetary matters.

While we recognize and appreciate the noble and sincere motives of those who utter these irrational phrases, we cannot help but also reflect on Voltaire's observation that, "Error flies from mouth to mouth, from pen to pen, and to destroy it takes ages."[12]

Watch Out For the Word *As*
Please notice that we did *not* define money as something to be used *as* a medium of exchange. Money *is* a medium of exchange. Money is manufactured solely to be a medium of exchange, although money may be used for other purposes. As an example of another purpose, pennies have (unwisely) been used as a temporary replacement for blown household fuses. Gold coins have become the centerpiece of necklaces, bracelets, watchbands, and earrings.

Wampum, stones, dead rats and wooden sticks have been used *as* money, but only when they were a medium of exchange; none of these things were, are, or *can be* money.

There are four forms or uses of the word *as*: adverb, conjunction, relative pronoun, and preposition. Since the specific usage of *as* cannot always be accurately determined by examining the context in which it is used, if you see *as* in a legal or financial document, determine *for sure* which form is being

---
[12] "Assassin," *Philosophical Dictionary* (1764)

used before you sign or otherwise act upon that document.

The adverbial form of *as* may be illustrated by the following analogy.

If I see a small nail which has worked its way out of my kitchen floor, I'd be expected to use a *hammer* to drive the nail back into place. But if I didn't have a hammer, I could use my wristwatch instead. (I have a really *big* wristwatch!) If I pound the nail down with my wristwatch, I am using my wristwatch *as* (meaning *in the manner of*) a hammer but your common sense tells you that my wristwatch has not *turned into* or *become* a hammer.

Criminals who specialize in *theft by fraud* take advantage of multiple meanings of words, knowing there's a world of difference between something which can be use *as* money, and real money itself.

Remember this point when you hear anyone — especially a politician, banker, lawyer, judge, or IRS employee — talk about you or anyone else using something *as* money.

Today, politicians talk about how much *money* is involved in a piece of legislation, or business executives tell us how much *money* their firm made or lost last year, or newscasters tell us how much *money* somebody won in a contest.

However, our etymological review tells you that these reports are inaccurate. Why are they inaccurate?

They are inaccurate because *there is no **money** in general circulation today—anywhere in the world. Fact.*

•

MONEY, *n.* plu. *moneys.* [Sax. *mynet*; D. *munt*, mint; G. *münze*; Sw. *mynt*; Dan. *myndt*, money or mint; Fr. *monnoie*; Ir. *monadh*; W. *mwnai*; Sp. *moneda*; Port. *moeda*, contracted; L. It. *moneta*. *Money* and *mint* are the same word varied.]

1. Coin; stamped metal; any piece of metal, usually gold, silver or copper, stamped by public authority, and used as the medium of commerce. We sometimes give the name of money to other coined metals, and to any other material which rude nations use as a medium of trade. But among modern commercial nations, gold, silver and copper are the only metals used for this purpose. Gold and silver, containing great value in a small compass, and being therefore of easy conveyance, and being also durable and little liable to diminution by use, are the most convenient metals for coin or money, which is the representative of commodities of all kinds, of lands, and of every thing that is capable of being transferred in commerce.
2. Bank notes or bills of credit issued by authority, and exchangeable for coin or redeemable, are also called *money*; as such notes in modern times represent coin, and are used as a substitute for it. If a man pays in hand for goods in bank notes which are current, he is said to pay in ready *money*.
3. Wealth; affluence.

Money can neither open new avenues to pleasure, nor block up the passages of anguish.
Rambler.

Vol. II.

MONEY. Gold and silver coins. The common medium of exchange in a civilized nation.

There is some difference of opinion as to the etymology of the word money; and writers do not agree as to its precise meaning. Some writers define it to be the common medium of exchange among civilized nations; but in the United States constitution there is a provision which has been supposed to make it synonymous with coins: "The congress shall have power to coin money." Art. 1, sect. 8. Again: "No state shall coin money, or make any thing but gold and silver a legal tender in payment of debt." Art. 1, sect. 10. Hence the money of the United States consists of gold and silver coins. And so well has the congress of the United States maintained this point, that the copper coins heretofore struck, and the nickel cent of recent issues, although authorized to "pass current," are not money in an exact sense, because they are not made a legal tender in the payment of debts. The question has been made whether a paper currency can be constitutionally authorized by congress and constituted a legal tender in the payment of private debts. Such a power has been exercised and adjudged valid by the highest tribunal of several of the states, but has not been passed upon by the supreme court of the United States.

For many purposes, bank-notes, 1 Younge & J. Exch. 380; 3 Mass. 405; 14 *id.* 122; 17 *id.* 560; 4 Pick. Mass. 74; 2 N. H. 333; 7 Cow. N. Y. 662; Brayt. Vt. 24; a check, 4 Bingh. 179, and negotiable notes, 3 Mass. 405, will be considered as money. To support a count for money had and received, the receipt by the defendant of bank-notes, promissory notes, 3 Mass. 405; 9 Pick. Mass. 93; 14 Me. 285; 7 Johns. 132, credit in account in the books of a third person, 3 Campb. 199, or any chattel, is sufficient, 4 Pick. Mass. 71; 17 Mass. 560, and will be treated as money. See 7 Wend. N. Y. 311; 8 *id.* 641; 7 Serg. & R. Penn. 246; 8 Term. 687; 3 Bos. & P. 559; 1 Younge & J. Exch. 380.

Money. In usual and ordinary acceptation it means coins and paper currency used as circulating medium of exchange, and does not embrace notes, bonds, evidences of debt, or other personal or real estate.

A medium of exchange authorized or adopted by a domestic or foreign government as a part of its currency. U.C.C. § 1-201(24).

See also Currency; Current money; Fiat money; Legal tender; Near money; Scrip.

Public money. Revenue received from federal, state, and local governments from taxes, fees, fines, etc. *See* Revenue.

Figure 2-1. Money defined. Left to right: Webster (1828); Bouvier (1870), and Black (1991). The etymology of money is evident in Webster and Bouvier but Black implies that the informal definition ("In usual and ordinary acceptation") is the only definition. However, Black also states that "notes" are not money, which is part of the formal, technical definition. Material from Black, © 1991 by West Publishing Company, is reproduced with permission. All rights reserved.

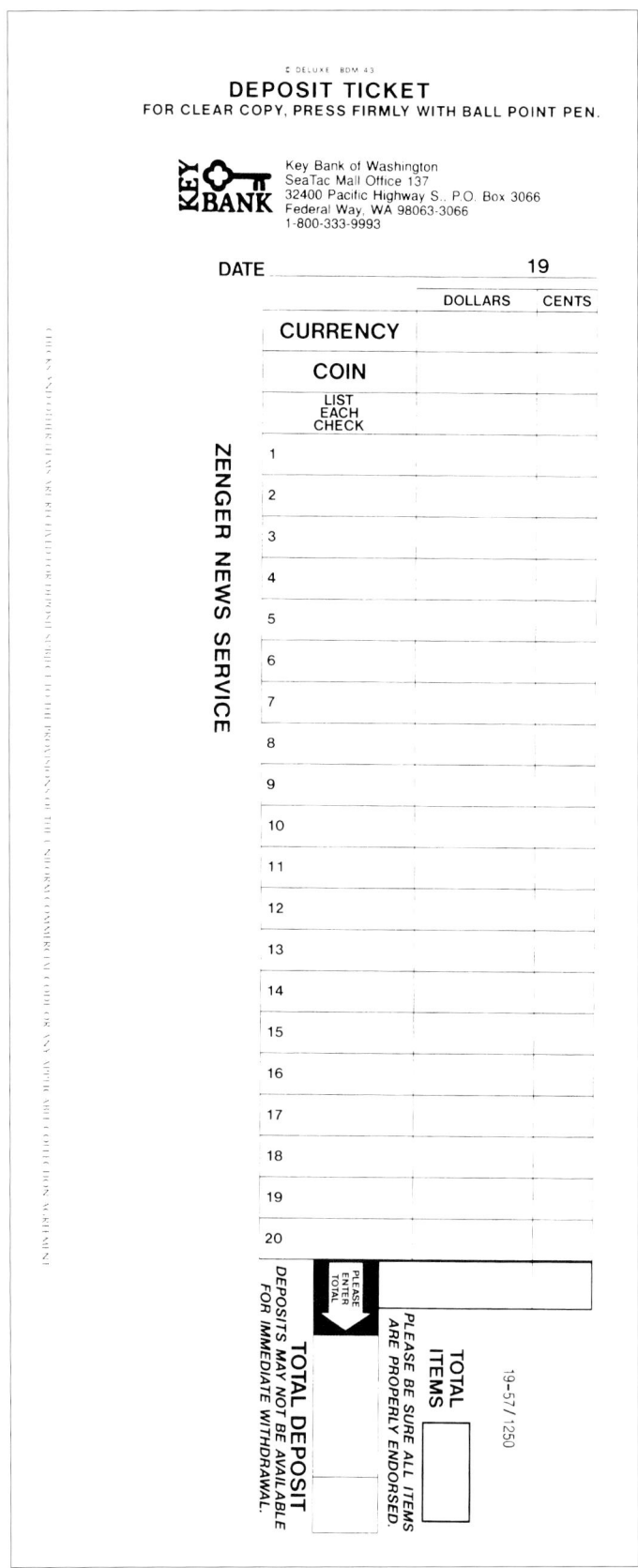

Figure 2-2. Deposit Ticket

3
Currency

THE word currency has two meanings, one already known to perhaps a majority of Americans, the other known to professionals in the financial community. Once you understand *both* meanings you should be well on your way toward a better understanding of the forces which shape world events today.

The First Definition
One meaning of currency may be illustrated by an analogy. Imagine yourself standing on the bank of a stream. You have two sticks in one hand, and you toss them together into the stream. A few minutes later you observe that one of the sticks has moved ahead of the other, because of the stream's swirling currents.

In our national economy, products and services flow in a complex and continuous swirl of currents which make up a stream of wealth. Various *media of exchange* (coins, wampum, cows, candles, and even cigarettes, etc.), when they are part of this stream, are called *currency*. Thus, our first definition is:

> **Currency**: media of exchange.

Classical economists rightly assert that a nation's media of exchange are often the most important products circulating in that nation's economy.

The Second Definition
The second definition of currency is known to, but not often publicly discussed by, top figures in the banking industry. These people may prefer that you never become aware of this definition, even though it has ties to other widely known accounting and bookkeeping terms. However, the banking industry itself can help us get a better understanding of the second meaning of currency.

Note that banking deposit slips have three separate areas for entering information related to the components of a deposit. These areas are *Checks*, *Coin* and *Currency*. (See Fig. 2-2, page 12.)

Since *Checks* means bank drafts, neither Federal Reserve Notes nor Silver Certificates, for example, would be entered in the area labeled Checks. And since *Coin* means metal objects, neither Federal Reserve Notes nor Silver Certificates would be listed in this area.

By a process of elimination, you can see that, to banks, *Currency* means only Dollar-bills, that is, Federal Reserve Notes or Silver Certificates, etc. If you hear someone refer to Silver Certificates as "*paper currency*," you should understand that he is using the first definition of currency, *not* the second definition, the one we are developing in this and the following paragraphs.

Textbooks on accounting practice tell us that a debt we don't need to pay for several years is called a long-term debt. A debt we must pay within the next twelve months is called a short-term, or *current*, debt.

When we discuss assets, liabilities, debts, receivable, payables, or other financial topics, *current* in front of one of those words indicates that we expect that the event or transaction will happen within the next twelve months. *Current* is therefore synonymous with either short-term, immediate-term, or "within twelve months," and the opposite of long-term or "beyond twelve months."

Next, please recall that until about 1968, Dollar-bills (20s, for example) made in the United States Bureau of Engraving and Printing, that is, Federal Reserve Notes, Silver Certificates, etc., were redeemable in lawful money at the United States Treasury, or at any Federal Reserve Bank, or at most other banks. More importantly, they were redeemable *on demand*.

Dollar-bills were *currency* then, *not* because they circulated in the economy but because they were to be paid *on demand*, which means instantaneously, and instantaneously is well within twelve months. Dollar-bills were *current assets* to their holder.

Therefore our next definition is:

> **Currency**: financial instruments convertible into money within twelve months.

Federal Reserve Tokens

In our transactions in the U.S. today, most of the pieces of paper we use are labeled "Federal Reserve Note." Researchers into what has become known as "the money issue" are quick and correct to point out that these pieces of paper are not *bona fide* Notes in financial and legal contemplation, although they obviously resemble the real Notes which were issued and used years ago.

The curious pieces of paper we now list on deposit slips, for example, might best be called *tokens*.

Our dictionary says a token is a piece of metal, somewhat like a coin, stamped for a higher value than the metal is worth and used for a special purpose, such as for subway or bus fare, or for entry into a game or other amusement.

While this definition of token may have been adequate in the early part of this century, today's monetary circumstances require us to use the following definition:

> **Token:** a thing labeled as having an extrinsic worth markedly greater than its intrinsic worth, used for a special purpose.

In this more comprehensive definition, if we substitute "piece of paper" for "thing" we may begin to see certain government-issued pieces of paper in sharper focus.

In regard to the Federal Reserve Tokens, abbreviated FRTs,[1] we now use *as* money, it is true that we list them on deposit slips under Currency, where we formerly listed *genuine* Federal Reserve Notes. But we can refer to today's tokens (FRTs) as currency only in the sense of our first definition, media of exchange.

We cannot rationally refer to FRTs as currency in the sense of the second definition because, in financial and legal contemplation, FRTs are not *current* assets to their bearer or holder. This is because FRTs are not convertible, at least not in the manner of *genuine* Notes or Certificates, into money at any time, much less within twelve months. They aren't convertible, that is, *redeemable* in *lawful money*, at either the United States Treasury or at any Federal Reserve Bank or at any other bank.

More Than One Special Purpose

Now let's consider what "special purpose" might be served by the issuance of Federal Reserve Tokens. For one thing, people who deposited real *money*, that is, coins of gold or silver, in banks long ago can no longer turn the tokens in and get their *money* back. That's a fact.

It also appears that banks, through complicity of the court system and other civil-service organizations, were allowed to keep the money while everyone else was compelled to keep the tokens.

But is this true? Did the banks really get real

---

[1] Abbreviated FRTs, pronounced "eff are tease" or just "furts."

wealth from our grandparents and then, with the complicity of the nation's federal civil-service workers, arrange for us, the voters, to get just the slips of paper? That question is the big controversy, that is "the money issue," and that is possibly one of the most intriguing questions of today. And because you are reading this book, you will soon have an answer to this question, once and for all.

It seems that starting in 1862, under the presidency of Abraham Lincoln, the federal government began printing tokens and trading those tokens for real wealth in the marketplace. This way President Lincoln financed the Union's participation in the Civil War. He and his administration were able to exchange real wealth for paper tokens only because of the unquestioned acceptance of the tokens by a patriotic but unsuspecting public.

Today, now that a seriously uninformed public is thoroughly conditioned to accepting bogus Notes, the vast majority of our financial transactions are accomplished by an exchange of imaginary credit-entries in the bank accounts of almost all individuals and organizations.

If this analysis is correct, today the forces which *legally* control the creation of tokens and credit-entries are steadily and *legally* acquiring effective ownership or control of all of the wealth of the nation.

Indeed, because almost all nations today are being victimized by *legal* alliances of banking institutions and civil-service employees, and because members of these alliances cooperate internationally, ownership or control of virtually all of the world's material wealth is being acquired by probably fewer than 1,000 individuals, perhaps far fewer than 1,000 individuals, *legally*.

Creating credit-entry purchasing power is even easier than creating pieces of paper. Today, creation of billions of "dollars" of purchasing power may be accomplished in seconds with a few keystrokes on a bank's computer terminal. Of course, to do it *legally*, a bank has to stay within the bounds set by civil-service workers. However, with the passage of recent laws, the limits on bank credit creation have been effectively eliminated.

The bottom line is that there are no real statutory limits today on how much purchasing power the banks are allowed to create. (See also Postscript.)

Absolute Power

We discussed some mechanics of a special purpose for which Federal Reserve Tokens and credit entries are created, but there is a wrinkle here we may soon have to face. Lord Acton warned: "Power tends to corrupt and absolute power corrupts absolutely."

If the money issue is as serious as some analysts would have us believe, we need to be alert to any attempt to trick us into supporting anyone seeking absolute power over us.

We might do well to study and learn the nature of the enemies of freedom, to understand their methods, and learn the steps we and our loved ones can take to establish a sound defense against their scheming.

If you find yourself intrigued by these issues and questions, you may wish to send us your name and address. We'll keep you informed on our progress as we continue our investigations into these fascinating subjects. Our Reader Registration Form is available for you in Appendix B.

Remembering Both Definitions

You've seen that *currency* has two meanings, each helpful to know. Imagine the stream and the two sticks to help you remember the first definition; visualize the stream of products — including coins and bills — and services in our economy.

Just think of "twelve months" to help you recall the second and possibly most interesting definition.

•

"Money," in its strict, technical sense, is coined metal, usually gold or silver, upon which the government stamp has been impressed to indicate its value; in its more popular sense, any currency token, bank notes, or other circulating medium in general use as the representative of value; a generic term, covering everything which by consent is made to represent property, and passes as such currently from hand to hand. The word designates the whole volume of the medium of exchange, regardless of its character or denomination. State v. Downs, 47 N. E. 670, 671, 148 Ind. 324; Hopson v. Fountain, 24 Tenn. (5 Humph.) 140; Miller v. McKinney, 73 Tenn. (5 Lea) 93, 96; Graham v. State, 24 Tenn. (5 Humph.) 40, 41; State v. Hill, 66 N. W. 541, 559, 47 Neb. 456; United States v. Lucius Beebe & Sons (U. S.) 122 Fed. 762, 767, 58 C. C. A. 562.

"The term 'money,' though it may have a popular import which in ordinary parlance means, or at least includes, bank notes, in its true technical import means lawful money of the United States, or, in other words, gold or silver coin, and, when used in judicial proceedings, is always to be taken in its technical sense; and thus an indictment for keeping a gaming table, at which a game of chance was charged to have been played for money, is not supported by proof that bank notes were played for. Pryor v. Commonwealth, 32 Ky. (2 Dana) 298.

"Money" does not include treasury notes. Foquet v. Hoadley, 3 Conn. 534, 536.

In legal acceptation, "money" means current metallic coins; therefore an indictment for embezzling "money" is not sustained by proof of embezzling greenbacks or national currency notes. Block v. State, 44 Tex. 620, 622.

The term "money" does not include bank notes. They pass as cash, and constitute a part of the circulating medium, and for many purposes are to be considered as money; but, in the strict sense of the term, they are not included therein. Dowdle v. Corpening, 32 N. C. 58, 60.

In Rev. St. § 152, declaring that the State Treasurer shall have charge of all moneys paid into the state, the term does not include promissory notes. State v. McFetridge, 54 N. W. 1, 16, 84 Wis. 473, 20 L. R. A. 223.

Promissory notes are not the kind of notes which pass as money, for they are not public tokens. Bank notes are public tokens—as much so as weights and measures or the alnager's seal. In practice, they represent the coin of our country, and pass currently as money. State v. Patillo, 11 N. C. 348, 349.

"Money," as used in Crimes Act, § 18, providing that any person stealing any money, the property of another, shall be guilty of larceny, cannot be construed to include bank bills, for strictly bank bills are not money, though for many purposes they are treated as such. Johnson v. State, 11 Ohio St. 324, 325.

The term "money" does not include bank notes. Hence an indictment under a statute making it an offense to play at games, etc., for money—the indictment charging that the defendant played at a game of faro for money—cannot be sustained by proof that bank notes were bet, nor would such an indictment be sustained by proof that property was bet. Hale v. State, 8 Tex. 171, 172.

"Money" as used in an indictment charging the betting of money, does not include United States treasury notes, such notes not being money in the legal acceptation. Williams v. State, 20 Miss. (12 Smedes & M.) 58, 63.

The term "money," in the statute defining robbery as taking from the person of another any money or personal property of any value whatsoever, with force and by violence, and with intent to steal or rob, does not include bank notes. Turner v. State, 1 Ohio St. 422, 426.

The term "money" does not include a bank note. Such a note does not differ in its nature from any other promissory note payable to bearer. Filgo v. Penny, 6 N. C. 182, 183.

It is not accurate to call currency in the shape of bills or notes money, for in the true sense they are not money. State v. Hoke, 84 Ind. 137, 139 (citing Boyd v. Olvey, 82 Ind. 294; Hamilton v. State, 60 Ind. 193, 28 Am. Rep. 653).

The term "money" or "moneys," wherever used in the chapter relating to the revenue, shall be held to mean gold, silver, or other coin, and paper or other currency, used in barter and trade as money. Rev. St. Mo. 1899, § 9123.

The word "money" may be extended to bank notes, when they are known and approved of, and used in the market as cash. Judah v. Harris (N. Y.) 19 Johns. 144, 145.

Webster defines money: "(1) Coin; stamped metal; pieces of metal, usually gold, silver, or copper, stamped by public authority, and used as the medium of commerce. (2) Hence any currency usually and lawfully employed in buying and selling as the equivalent of money, as bank notes and the like." Carter v. Cox, 44 Miss. 155.

Figure 3-1. *These quotations are from court cases cited in the 1904 edition of* Words & Phrases. *Notice that the last three quotations in the right column contradict the clear meaning expressed in the other thirteen quotations.*

4

Dollar

ALTHOUGH most of us use the word *dollar* daily, few Americans know what it really means. No one knows the meanings of all the some half million words in the English language, the world's richest, and that universal ignorance does no harm. However, failure to understand some *important* words can be disastrous.

This chapter makes the point that not only is *dollar* a *very* important word, but also that our failure, as a people, to understand clearly the concept behind it has caused us to make some potentially disastrous decisions.

Joachimsthalers
In about 1519 A.D., a fabulously wealthy Count named Stephen von Schlick[1] lived in Joachim's Thal, a valley in Bohemia[2] (formerly part of central Germany). Thal, pronounced *tall*, is the German word for valley. Because an ancient silver mine was on his property, von Schlick built a mint and, for about nine years, manufactured silver coins.

Count von Schlick's coins' original name was *gulden groshen* or *Guldengroshen,* which meant "golden ten-pfennig coin." A ten-pfennig coin was a *groshen* much like our ten-cent coin is a dime. *Gulden* meant golden, but in using *gulden* as part of the name of his silver coin, von Schlick intended for his coin to be recognized as equaling the purchasing power of the standard gold coin of the day, the *ducat*.

However, within a few years of their first issue, von Schlick's *gulden groshens* became most widely known as *Joachimsthalers*, meaning (the) *coins which came from Joachim's Thal*. After several more years, the *Joachim's* syllables were discarded as superfluous and von Schlick's coins were thereafter called *Thalers*, pronounced *tall´-ers*.[3]

Regulating Value
Thalers circulated widely because people had faith in von Schlick's high ethical standards. He had insisted from the start that his coins would be ninety percent silver and ten percent alloy, but, more importantly, he insisted that any coins which deviated more

---

[1] Occasionally spelled "Shlik" or "Slick."

[2] See map on page 99. In Bohemia, in the western end of the Czech Republic (part of the former Czechoslovakia), find the capital, Prague. About 110 km further west is a small city, Karlovy Vary (also called Carlsbad). About 15 km north of Karlovy Vary, Jachymov, a small town nestled at the base of the Erz Mountains (*Erzgebirge*). Count von Schlick built his mint and manufactured silver coins in Jachymov.

[3] In today's Germany, the Mark (or Deutschmark), the main currency unit, is divided into 100 pfennigs ("pennies"). Prior to 1871, before it became the German monetary unit, *mark* was a unit of weight, and the main circulating coins were the silver *thaler* and the gold *gulden* and *ducat*.

than five percent in weight from that standard were to be tossed into a scrap bin and melted to make new coins.

Establishing tolerances on precious-metal content and overall weight of a coin is called "regulating the value" of the coin. We can understand this concept clearly if we remember that *val* is Latin for *worth*. In *regulating the value* of a coin we assure close conformity between what weight is stated on the face of the coin and what the coin actually weighs.

By establishing strict tolerances on silver content and overall weight, von Schlick regulated the value or worth of each of his coins, and therefore regulated the truthfulness of what was said on their faces.

New Designs and New Names
As Thalers spread across Europe they acquired new names. For example, the Dutch called them *dallers* or *daalders*. When the Dutch later began making their own silver coins of identical weight, they gave them the same name, *dallers*.

Spanish officials, while having great respect for Thalers, recognized one shortcoming: their smooth sides. From time to time, unscrupulous people would clip, grind or file a thin layer off the sides of coins, a practice called "clipping." The clipped coins would be spent at the market as if they were of full weight, and the clippings were accumulated so they could be formed into new coins, or into jewelry. Coin clippers perpetrated *theft by fraud*. Since Thalers were manufactured with smooth sides, evidence of clipping was almost undetectable.

Spain decided to produce a better coin, one almost identical to the Thaler in silver content and overall weight but with a Spanish design — and with mill marks on the sides to discourage clipping.

The new Spanish coins were officially called *Colonatas*, but when they began to circulate where the Thaler also circulated, *they* shortly became known as *dallers* or *doleras* (or *dolaros*). The *Colonatas'* mill-marks gave rise to still another nickname: the *Spanish Milled Dollar*.

Pilgrims who settled in North America in the middle 1600s carried these Spanish coins with them, calling them either Spanish Milled Dollars or Pieces of Eight. The latter phrase came into use because the *Colonata* was divided into eight parts called *reales*, pronounced *ray-all´-ehz*, much like our current Dollar is divided into 100 cents.

Yankee settlers were disinclined to use the word *reales*. Instead of four *reales* for half a Dollar they often used the term four bits; two bits was often used, instead of two *reales*, for a quarter Dollar, expressions which have endured to this day.

Lawful Money of the United States
On April 2, 1792, about five years after the United States Constitution was signed, Congress passed our first coinage Act (hereinafter, the Act). The Act created the United States Mint, wherein our official money, coins of silver and coins of gold, were to be manufactured. Money manufactured according to law is called *lawful* money, and the phrase "Lawful money of the United States" means coins of silver or of gold which have been manufactured according to United States law in a United States Mint. Let's first look at what this law said about our silver coins. A little later we'll see what it said about our gold coins.

United States Silver Coins
The Act specified that our major silver coin would contain 371.25 grains of pure silver and would have an overall weight of 416 grains. The additional 44.75 grains would consist of alloy — about ninety percent tin and ten percent copper — to give the coins durability.

These weights were chosen to make the new American silver coins directly interchangeable with the then-circulating Spanish Milled Dollars. Thus there was no need for merchants to establish separate price schedules for the new money, and accounting problems were avoided.

In *regulating the value* of our money, Congress specified that coins deviating more than one-half of one percent (0.5%) from the standard weight would not be issued, and any coins later discovered to have deviated beyond this limit by wear and tear, etc., would be withdrawn from circulation. (Please see

Dollar: A Unit of Measure of Weight

The Act further provided that half-dollar, quarter-dollar and tenth-dollar silver coins were to be minted proportionate to the silver Dollar-coin as to both silver content and overall weight. In fact, if you examine a silver Dollar-coin closely you will see the words ONE DOLLAR in bold relief. The phrase ONE DOLLAR is not an indication of what the coin is worth; *it is the formal guarantee of how much the coin weighs.*[4]

Reflect for a moment on the specific and exclusive weight-measuring units used by jewelers. You could buy a diamond which weighs about one hundredth of an ounce but a jeweler would probably describe that stone as weighing 1.4 *carats*. *Carat* is the unit of measure specifically and exclusively for the weight of precious stones, and *dollar* is specifically and exclusively the unit of measure of the *weight of money* officially manufactured and issued by the United States of America. But there is more to know about *dollar*.

United States Gold Coins

The Act, in addition to authorizing the minting of silver coins, also authorized the manufacture of gold coins. Since equal weights of gold and silver were not of equal worth in the marketplace, a different dollar-unit was needed for gold. Congress established the overall weight of each gold Dollar-coin to be 27.0 grains, with the silver Dollar-coin (416 grains) about fifteen times heavier, closely approximating the relative worth of each of the metals in the marketplace of the time.

In fact, the Congress, via the Act of April 2, 1792, established that a Dollar of pure silver, meaning 371.25 grains of pure silver, would be *exactly* fifteen times the weight of one Dollar of gold. One fifteenth of 371.25 is exactly 24.75. The ratio of 15 to 1 was met by comparing the amount of pure metal in the coins, not by comparing the weights of the finished coins, because the finished coins contained different amounts of alloys, and the alloys, while adding to the coins' overall weight, did not add equally to their value in the marketplace. It was therefore imperative, in the interest of honesty and fairness, for the Act to base the 15 to 1 ratio on only the weight of the pure metal in each coin, and to ignore the weight of the alloys in each coin.

By establishing the worth (*regulating the value*) of a Dollar-coin of gold to be the same as the worth of a Dollar-coin of silver, prices set in terms of silver money could be paid with the same dollar-amount of gold money. This meant that a house costing $10,000 could be bought with 10,000 silver Dollar-coins or with 1,000 "Eagle" ($10) gold Dollar-coins, or with any combination of gold and silver coins totaling $10,000.

Some citizens of the Republic mistakenly believe that the U.S. Constitution's reference to *regulating the value* means that Congress is supposed to regulate the purchasing power of the nation's money. That is false. If you sell eggs, and if I buy some of your eggs, paying you one Dollar of silver for fifty eggs, our transaction is beyond the legitimate purview of the United States Congress and any other person.

Beware any "expert" who states that Congress is empowered, by *regulating the value* of our money, to "keep prices steady." Such confusion is stark testimony to the deplorable decline of public education in the United States in recent years.

Dollars of What?

The United States Mint in Philadelphia began manufacturing official silver coinage in 1794 and official gold coinage in 1795. In other words, in the latter part of 1794, if you had said you had "five Dollars" in your pocket, you would have *automatically* meant that you had about 1,856.25 grains of pure silver in your pocket. In late 1795, however, the same com-

---

[4] *Dollar* can not indicate the *worth* of the coin because its worth will vary. One Dollar of silver might be worth 100 pounds of potatoes after a bountiful potato harvest but another year, perhaps the next year, if the crop is poor, one Dollar of silver might buy only twenty pounds of potatoes. Thus the worth of 371.25 grains of pure silver may vary in terms of potatoes or any other commodity or service, but in *every* year, one Dollar of silver will always equal 371.25 grains of pure silver.

ment would have meant you had about 1,856.25 grains of pure silver *or* you had about 123.75 grains of pure gold — *or* a combination of the two substances — in your pocket or purse.

Unfortunately, however, by getting into the habit of hearing and saying just "I have five Dollars," we, as a people, began to lose sight of the precise meaning of our words.

Federal Reserve Tokens
When the United States of America was in its infancy, our currency was mostly foreign coin.

After 1795 we still had foreign coin, but we also had gold coins or silver coins from the United States Mint, plus some paper currency issued by the former Colonies and by banks.

In 1862, President Abraham Lincoln introduced the "Greenback" paper currency, the first United States Notes.

In 1914, the first Federal Reserve Notes were issued.

Through 1933, a common feature of almost every issue of our paper currency was its immediate and direct redeemability in lawful money: officially minted United States coins of gold or silver. It was generally understood that the paper was not the money. The paper was a claim on the money, in the same way that your dry cleaning ticket is a claim on your suit, and your pawn ticket is a claim on your stereo. Just as you get the real things only by turning in the tickets, so anyone who held a ten-dollar bill could turn it in and *demand* the money — the gold coin — because the words on the currency said that the money, the gold, would be paid "on demand," and it was. Because it was, American paper currency for a time had considerable prestige; it was thought to be "as good as gold," with the result that people stopped demanding it, preferring to carry light, foldable paper, rather than bulky, heavy coins. People started to forget what the words meant, which led to a gradual but insidious change in what we accepted *as money*.

In 1934, gold coins and gold certificates were removed from circulation.

Beginning in 1963, the redemption promise was no longer printed on our paper currency.

In 1968, the United States Treasury halted redemption in silver coin or bullion of the remaining money-substitutes — Silver Certificates, Federal Reserve Notes, and United States Notes.

Today, 1998, the only paper currency in general circulation in the United States is the "Federal Reserve Note."

Since today's "Federal Reserve Note" is not redeemable in lawful money or bullion, it is not a note. A note, in law, is a promise to pay at a certain time, like the note on your house or your car. When paper currency was legitimate, it did promise to pay a specific *weight* of gold or silver *on demand*. Today's "Federal Reserve Note" is also not a money-substitute in the traditional sense; it is not a financial instrument as contemplated by law.

In reality it is a kind of *token*, a *Federal Reserve Token*.

What Federal Reserve Tokens Are Not
Today, out of innocent habit, most Americans incorrectly use the word "Dollar."

The Federal Reserve Tokens — abbreviated FRTs — we use in daily trade are *not Dollars*. To say FRTs *are Dollars* is to say they, the FRTs, are units of weight, which would be an irrational assertion. Pieces of paper can not be units of weight.

FRTs are *not* "Dollar-bills." A bill is a writing at law. In the United States, a Dollar-bill, in financial contemplation, is a writing at law which describes a payer who must pay gold or silver to a payee, and the gold or silver must be counted by weight in *Dollar* units, whether the metal is in the form of coin, bullion, dust, nuggets, or plate. Officially issued Dollar-bills — Silver Certificates, Gold Certificates, some series of United States Notes, and series of Federal Reserve Notes prior to 1963 — have been withdrawn from circulation. Many people are surprised to discover that today, no actual Dollar-bills are in general circulation anywhere in the world.

FRTs are *not* money. Money is mechanical devices manufactured in a mint, from precious metals, to be media of exchange. Granted, FRTs *are* media of exchange but they are *not* manufactured in a mint and they are *not* made of metal, precious or otherwise. Moreover, in spite of their acceptance *as* money by a confused public, they have zero intrinsic value or worth. People accept them for the same reason the grocer takes your check when there is no cash in your account. He doesn't know.

So for an absolute fact, you know that FRTs are *not* "the same" as money, or "the same" as Dollars, or "the same" as gold or silver. *Fact*.

"The Same" Old Argument!
You might someday find yourself discussing these interesting matters with a middle-management civil-service worker, or a political office-holder or candidate, or a supposed expert from the banking field or from your local university.

In conversations with such people you might remind them that genuine money substitutes such as Dollar-bills are a lot like valid coupons because both are redeemable for things having intrinsic worth: shortening, paint, a quart of oil, silver coin, and so forth. Since FRTs are not redeemable, they are very much like *expired* coupons — *worthless*.

Should an "expert" argue that FRTs are actually "the same" as Dollars or money or gold or silver, ask him to consider a *coupon* for a hundred gallons of gasoline. Ask him to think carefully about that coupon for a moment, and then gently ask him these questions:

1. Is the coupon "the same" as the gasoline?
2. If the coupon has expired, is it still "the same" as the hundred gallons of gasoline?
3. If he tears the coupon into pieces and stuffs the pieces into his gas tank, will his car run?
4. If a coupon for one Dollar of silver is expired, isn't it just as worthless as an expired coupon for one hundred gallons of gasoline?
5. Would he be willing to accept *expired* coupons for gasoline or anything else in lieu of his paycheck?
6. Does he realize that today, when he "cashes" his paycheck, he *is* accepting "*expired coupons*?"

Confusion or Criminality?
To argue seriously that FRTs are the same as *money* or *Dollars* or *gold* or *silver* may not always be a sign of confusion or gullibility. It may be evidence of *criminality*. Here is why.

If you tricked someone into accepting an *expired* gasoline coupon in exchange for twenty pounds of sirloin steak, convincing the steak seller that your coupon was "the same" as the gasoline, you would have perpetrated *theft by fraud*. Similarly, those who *willfully* assert that FRTs *are* Dollars (or are "the same" as gold or silver, or are "the same" as money), and thereby trick us into giving up our property, may also be perpetrating *theft by fraud*.

Definitions of Dollar
Here are *some* better definitions of our subject.

> **Dollar**: 1) Unit of measure of weight of *lawful money* manufactured in a United States Mint;
>
> **Dollar**: 2) Unit of measure of weight of gold or silver coin, dust, nuggets, bullion, or plate, especially in the United States of America;
>
> **Dollar**: 3) Official unit of accounting for money transactions in the United States of America and several other countries;
>
> **Dollar**: 4) Nickname of coinage officially minted in the United States of America from 1794 through 1964;
>
> **Dollar**: 5) Variable of name of Spanish or Dutch coin *ca.* 1520 A.D., *et seq.*; and,
>
> **Dollar**: 6) Variable of nickname of German coin *ca.* 1517 A.D., *et seq.*

•

Figure 4-1. 1963. Federal Reserve Token (FRT). $1.

5

Pay

ONE of the most interesting English words is *pay*. When we receive pay we are usually pleased, less so when we must pay someone else. Yet payment between obligor and obligee is necessary if the peace of a community is to be maintained. Interestingly, *pay* is etymologically rooted in the Latin word *pax*, which means *peace*.

Since *pay* is a word which most adults believe they understand, readers may wonder why we would devote an entire chapter to it. We do so because we believe that *pay* contains some crucial surprises.

What Constitutes Payment?
When you hand your grocer a "Federal Reserve Note" in exchange for your groceries, have you paid him? The surprising answer is: No! People are confused about what *payment* means. In the United States, where our law specifies that the money of account shall be coins of silver or gold manufactured in a United States Mint, payment of most debts or obligations occurs only when lawful money is received. Since no lawful money or legitimate money-substitutes are in general circulation today, legal payment rarely occurs.

Contracts and agreements always specify or imply an agreed-upon medium of payment. Use of the Dollar sign ($) in contracts or agreements indicates that only lawful money of the United States shall be the accepted and legal medium of payment.

But, American courts generally held that receipt of genuine money-substitutes was tantamount to receipt of lawful money; for a time, *bona fide* Federal Reserve Notes, United States Notes, Silver Certificates and Gold Certificates were held to be effectively the same as lawful money, and when they were received, legal payment was held to have been made.

Presently, since neither lawful money nor *bona fide* money substitutes are in general circulation, legal payment does not often occur. Receipt of Federal Reserve tokens (FRTs) does not constitute receipt of either lawful money or genuine money-substitutes.

If you receive "in kind" compensation for services rendered, you are *said* to have been paid, although *pay* actually refers exclusively to the use of money. Some migrant agricultural workers receive partial "payment" (more properly, *compensation*) for services rendered in the form of housing. Some hospital workers are allowed to eat at reduced prices in the hospital cafeteria, as part of an employee *compensation* plan.

Generally, however, in the United States, because the medium of payment in contracts and agreements is most often stipulated by the Dollar sign, legal payment can occur only when the obligee or creditor receives either genuine money-substitutes or lawful money of the United States, that is, coins of silver or gold which were manufactured in a United States Mint.

Is Payment Possible by Check?

Many people believe receipt of a check is payment. They are wrong.

Suppose you work for me in my factory, and on payday I write your name on a check. Have you been paid? Of course not. Writing your name on a piece of paper, the check, would not constitute payment by me for your services.

If I wrote your name on the check in the space for the payee, and then signed the check as an authorized signer, would you then have been paid? Of course not. Writing words on a piece of paper does not constitute payment.

If I wrote your name on a check, signed the check, and then gave you the check, would you then have been paid? Of course not. Maybe there is no such bank; maybe there is no such account. If the bank is real and the account is valid, there still may be Not Sufficient Funds to pay the check.

Suppose I wrote you a properly signed check — in the amount of $1,000, for example — and you took it to my bank for payment, finding that there was a valid account for my company and there were sufficient funds credited to that account to pay the check. But suppose also that the bank happened to be short of cash that day. If the bank were unable to cash your check, would you have been paid? Of course not.

A check, also called a bank draft, is a financial instrument which orders the bank (where my money is supposed to be stored) to give you a certain amount of money from my account, on your order. Checks are called drafts because they enable us to "draw out" money from an account. Also notice on a check, in front of the payee's name, the words "Pay to the order of."

Now suppose, in keeping with the theme of the preceding paragraph, the teller said, "Gee, Mr. Smith, I'd like to cash your paycheck but we are short of currency today. How would it be if I gave you ten cashier's checks, each in the amount of $100? Would that be okay with you?"

If you answered Yes, and if the teller gave you the ten cashier's checks, would you then have been paid? Of course not. You might hold those cashier's checks until the following day, only to find out that, overnight, the bank had failed and was unable to make good on its liabilities (ten of which you hold in the form of those cashier's checks).

Suppose, however, instead of offering you cashier's checks, the teller offered you some promissory[1] Notes already printed in hundred-dollar amounts, ready for issue by the bank in case of a shortage of currency. If you accepted the Notes, would you have been paid? Of course not. You might accept Notes temporarily until the bank replenished its supply of currency. Eventually you would present the Notes for payment (in money). Only when you receive lawful money or genuine money-substitutes, in this example, would you be legally paid.

Now suppose, again using the "we're short of cash" scenario, the teller offered you ten already-printed promissory Notes, each having a face amount of $100, issued by a different bank? If you accepted these Notes would you have been paid? Of course not. And if these Notes were never paid in lawful money of the United States, you would never receive legal payment for your work for me in my factory.

Legal Considerations

In the event that you never receive payment of the Notes, you might be inclined to file a civil suit against me for non-payment of my debt to you. However, if I show a jury that you "cashed" my check, that you endorsed it before it "cleared" the bank, the jurors would probably agree with me that you must have been paid.

More appropriately, you might file a lawsuit against the issuer of the Notes. Under normal circumstances, you would probably win, but if the is-

---

[1] *Promissory* means "involving a promise." A Note (in financial contemplation) is a promise by a payor (or payer) to pay a payee a certain amount of money on or before a stated date. If no promise is stated, the instrument is not a financial instrument legally defined as a Note.

suer of the "Note" were the Federal Reserve banking system, you would probably be disappointed.

The Federal Reserve System and the Federal Reserve Banks, with the approval of the United States Congress, can legally dishonor the promissory Notes they've issued. This highly controversial action by Congress is the basis for all banks' refusal to redeem (pay) *bona fide* money substitutes issued by the Federal Reserve System, that is, Federal Reserve Notes from the series of 1914, 1928, 1934, and 1950.

While Congress' action in these matters may be deplorable, it has no bearing on the present impossibility of receiving payment — in lawful money of the United States — of Federal Reserve Tokens, the pieces of paper we use *as* money today. This is because, in legal and financial contemplation, FRTs are not Notes. Thus, there is no legitimate, legal requirement that they be paid.

Notes About Notes
To be a Note, at law, a written instrument must have four elements or features: maker, payee, Dollar amount, and due date.

Older paper currency, such as $10 Federal Reserve Notes from the series of 1950 (See Figure 6-1, page 30) said: THE UNITED STATES OF AMERICA WILL PAY TO THE BEARER ON DEMAND TEN DOLLARS   In this example the Maker is THE UNITED STATES OF AMERICA, the Payee is the BEARER (you, perhaps), the Dollar amount is TEN (for example), and the due date is ON DEMAND.

FRTs omit reference to THE BEARER and ON DEMAND. Since two mandatory elements (payee and due date) of a *bona fide* Note are missing, FRTs are not Notes. Because they are not Notes, their issuer, the Federal Reserve banking system, is under no obligation to pay you or anyone else who holds them, the FRTs, any lawful money of the United States.

If you accept FRTs in lieu of lawful money of the United States when you "cash" your paycheck, you are even worse off than our hypothetical Mr. Smith. By accepting tokens, you have no standing at law to sue the Federal Reserve System or anyone else for non-payment.

An Income Tax Question
Some Americans have refused to file federal personal income tax returns, basing their action on certain legal questions. Examples of these questions are:
- Who exactly is required to file;
- How can one be compelled to fill out government forms; and,
- How can one be compelled to give potentially incriminating information on the forms, since all information is potentially incriminating, especially when it is in the hands of the IRS?

While we cannot address these questions here, we will address one aspect of income taxes which relates directly to the word *pay*.

Since most Americans innocently accept FRTs *as* payment, and since they also unquestioningly accept the notion that their wages are "income," or are at least a "source" of "income," they file personal federal income tax returns. While we do not encourage anyone not to file his personal federal income tax return — if one is required to do so by law — we do encourage every reader to consider what we know about FRTs.

By now you know that if you have received a paycheck, you have not necessarily been paid.

Even if you "cash" your paycheck, if you accept FRTs in lieu of lawful money of the United States, you know you still have not been paid.

And because they are never paid — and need not be paid —by the banks, FRTs cannot possibly constitute anything except *evidence of a debt*, that is, evidence of an *account receivable*.

Doesn't the IRS always tell us that no income tax liability exists for accounts receivable? Isn't it IRS policy that only after accounts receivable are *paid* does any income tax liability accrue?

If you always receive FRTs *as* pay, doesn't it seem logical that you may not have any personal income tax liability and also that you may not even be required to file a return? We don't even pretend to know the answer to that question but you may want to consider it when your CPA calls in early April.

Ethics of Payment

One aspect of contemporary life is that we tend to specialize in one or two productive activities, and we trade our talents, time and energy — our personal products and services — for media of exchange, which we later use to buy products or services from others. Economists call this specialization the division of labor.

Sometimes we give our services to others without charge, as charity. Since charitable acts are almost universally applauded, you might think that giving everything away and living on savings would be totally good. Alas, things are not always as they seem.

If you were very kindhearted you might be tempted always to work for others free of charge. Some people believe such an approach to life is highly principled and spiritual. Is it?

Suppose you had many talents and abilities. If you always offered to work without pay at any task, you would probably be inundated with requests for your help. If you accepted them all, you would never be able to rest, spend time with your loved ones or take a vacation. Even if you had little talent, if you never charged for your services you would always be working.

Eventually, to avoid complete physical collapse, divorce and psychiatry, you would need to reduce the demand for your services. How? Well, you could offer your services for a fee of $1,000,000 (one million Dollars) per second, a fee-schedule which would likely discourage even the wealthiest potential employer. You would no longer be disturbed by many offers of employment but your earnings would drop to zero, your savings would run out, and, eventually, *you* would be living on charity.

However, by adjusting the amount you charge, you can control the demands on your time and energy. By asking $10 per hour, for example, you would probably still receive some employment offers from those who really want your services but you would also receive fewer requests from those who have no real need of them, or money to pay.

Since we in the "Free World" enjoy some freedom in the marketplace, and since we are still somewhat free to fine-tune the rates we charge for our services, many of us have time to enjoy the fruits of our labors.

We earn enough to buy many of the things we want or need, but we also have time to enjoy relatively peaceful lives. Thus we see that freedom and payment are keys to societal peace.

Lessons of History

Doesn't all this mean that if we remember the precise meaning of the word *pay*, and then if we get rid of FRTs and truly *pay* one another, perhaps our society would be more peaceful?

If we, as a nation, would return to the United States Constitution, and restore traditional American values, it is quite possible that greater personal, and social, peace would return to our lives and our country.

Conversely, if we don't do that, we could end up as slaves. If *we* end up as slaves, what would our grandchildren be? Who wants to be born into slavery?

War and Peace

War, the antonym of peace, is the word we use to describe the activity of one group of people who cooperate to steal as much as possible from another group of people as quickly as possible.

War is maximized theft.

If the opposite of war is peace, and if the free market helps ensure that peace, doesn't it follow that attacks against the free market tend to be destructive of peace and conducive of war?

If we truly desire world peace, that is, personal and social peace for everyone, we must comply with natural law. This means we must:

a) support the free market;

b) oppose intervention in the peaceful affairs of others;

c) oppose involuntary transfers of property; and,

d) ***pay*** our debts and obligations.

•

6

Note

WHAT is a *note*? One *note* is a musical tone; another is a written communication; still another is the verb (to) see or observe.

In this chapter we discuss the written communication meaning of *note*, and, in so doing, help demolish one of the grandest myths of this century.

The origin of the written communication meaning of *note* is found in Latin. Today we regularly use *notice* (observe, detect), *notary* (a witness), *notion* (mental picture), *notation* (written thought), and *connote* (indicate).

General and Specific Meanings

Actually, there are two written-communication meanings of *note*, one general, the other specific. An example of the general meaning would be a short note you wrote to a co-worker to let her know you would be out of the office for the remainder of the day. For an example of a specific meaning of note we must delve into the subjects of law and money.

Suppose you go to a bank to seek a loan, and complete a loan-application form. If a loan were approved, you would be asked to sign a document in which you agree to pay off the loan in a certain way: monthly payments of a certain amount, for a certain number of months, and including a certain interest payment, with payments to be sent to a certain address, etc.

This kind of document is sometimes called a Retail Credit Installment Note, or just a Note. For the remainder of this book, Note (with a capital N) refers to a *pay-back* agreement, at law. "At law" simply means, "in the eyes of the law."

At law, a pay-back agreement is called a Note only when it has four essential parts or elements. If a written instrument does not have all four of these elements, it is not a Note. What, then, are the four elements needed in a written instrument for it to be a Note at law?

The first element needed is the identity of the document's *maker*, or who originated it. In the case of your Note to the bank, you would be the maker.

The second element needed is the name of the party which is to receive payment. Again, using your loan-arrangement as an example, the bank is the party which is to receive payment, and is therefore the *payee*.

The third element needed is the *due-date*, a specific date when each periodic payment is due and payable, or the date the Note is to be paid by a single payment (as in a ninety-day Note).

The fourth and last element needed is the *Dollar-amount* of the loan or pay-back. For simplicity sake, if you borrowed $100 from a neighbor, and if there were to be no interest charged by him or paid by you, you might give your neighbor a Note explaining that you would pay him the $100 on or before such-and-such a date.

Let's list these mandatory elements again, for review:

1. Maker (you, for example)
2. Payee (the bank, or your neighbor)
3. Due-date (when the loan is to be paid off)
4. Dollar-amount ($100, for example)

Now you have a better idea of what the law requires in a Note.

Next, let's remind ourselves that a Note is a special form of *contract*.

Notes, Agreements and Contracts

A contract, at law, is generally defined as an agreement by one party to provide a service or a thing to another party for a "good and valuable consideration."

In your agreement with the bank, you (the maker of the Note) agree (promise) to give a consideration (pay interest) to the bank (the payee) for a service (the loan of money) for a designated period (which ends with the due-date). Remember that the phrase Promissory Note is used to distinguish payback agreements from routine memoranda.

Since no due-date is needed for an agreement to be a contract, we can correctly state that all Notes are contracts but not all contracts are Notes.

We introduce the subject of contracts because the law says something about them that, although simple, is often overlooked, even by professionals. That is, for a writing at law to be a contract, that writing *must* clearly express the intent of the parties.

For the intent of a contract to be clear, the contract must be written clearly. If you were to sit at a typewriter and type a few thousand fours and sevens on a sheet of paper, there would be no contract, even if you and your neighbor signed the paper. This is obvious because the fours and sevens do not express any intent.

If you wrote the following on a sheet of paper you would still not have a contract:

"I, Joe Blow — Sam Neighbor, $100 tomorrow."

This gobbledygook example would not be a contract, even if you and your neighbor signed it, because it does not make sense. The letters, punctuation marks and numbers may be clearly imprinted on the paper but the parties' intent is not clearly expressed because you used only isolated words and sentence-fragments. In contracts and agreements, clarity of intent is expressed through the use of complete sentences.

If a writing does not include at least one complete sentence — with subject and predicate, including a verb or verb-phrase — there is *no way* that writing can be a contract. If it cannot be a contract, it follows that it most assuredly cannot be a Note. Even if a writing involves many complete sentences, it still is not a Note unless those sentences contain the four elements which are legally required in Notes.

Of course, some people might call our gobbledygook example a Note, but the law would not, and what is decisive is what the law says, not what a neighbor or co-worker might say. Right? Right.

Even if you see a formal-looking, written instrument which has the word NOTE on it, don't jump to the conclusion that the instrument is a Note. You could spray-paint the word Note on your basement wall but that wouldn't make your basement wall a Note. Your father-in-law could neatly cut the word Note in the left front fender of your car with an acetylene torch but that wouldn't make your fender a Note.

Genuine Notes

If you wish to see an example of a genuine Note at law, look at the repayment agreement you signed when you took out that loan.

If you wish to see more examples of a genuine Note at law, jump to Chapter 9 and examine several photographs of U.S. paper currency, or visit a coin dealer who carries an inventory of old U.S. paper currency. Examine a specimen of any United States Gold Certificate, or any United States Silver Certificate, or a Federal Reserve Note from any of the following Series: 1914, 1928, 1934, and 1950.

You will observe on each of these instruments at

least one complete sentence which contains all four of the elements required for the instrument to be a Note. An example of the critical sentence on a *bona fide* Ten-Dollar Federal Reserve Note, Series of 1950 (see Figure 6-1, page 30), is:

>THE UNITED STATES OF AMERICA WILL PAY TO THE BEARER ON DEMAND TEN DOLLARS

In this sentence the subject is THE UNITED STATES OF AMERERICA; the predicate is WILL PAY TO THE BEARER ON DEMAND TEN DOLLARS, and the verb (verb-phrase, actually) is WILL PAY.

Also in this sentence are the four elements necessary for the law to call the instrument a Note:

>The maker is THE UNITED STATES OF AMERICA;

>The payee is THE BEARER;

>The Dollar-amount is TEN DOLLARS (or just TEN); and,

>The due-date is ON DEMAND.

Conversely, if you wish to see a piece of paper which many people think is a Note, but which most certainly is *not* a Note (at law, in financial contemplation), examine the contents of your purse or wallet.

Today's paper currency, those so-called Dollar-bills (ones, fives, tens, and twenties, etc.) bear the word NOTE in two places. Yet in legal contemplation, as financial instruments, that currency is no more Notes than the paper these words are printed on.

In reality, there are no Federal Reserve *Notes* in general circulation today anywhere in the world. The so-called Dollar-bills in general circulation today are most appropriately called Federal Reserve Tokens, abbreviated FRTs. (See example, Figure 4-1, Page 22.)

Be Prepared

Here are the main points you need to remember about Notes:

1. Four elements are required before the law will consider a monetary (financial) writing a Note.

2. Since a Note is a form of contract, the elements of a Note must be expressed in one or more complete sentences.

3. A complete sentence (with few exceptions, unrelated to this discussion) is comprised of subject and predicate, including a verb or verb-phrase.

4. If a financial writing lacks complete sentences, or lacks any one or more of the elements of a Note, that instrument is not a Note.

If you've found this chapter interesting, we respectfully suggest you take a few moments and review the previous four chapters. Then, re-read this one, and visit the nearest law (or other good) library.

Look at the *Oxford English Dictionary*, or *Bouvier's Law Dictionary* (two volumes), or *Black's Law Dictionary* (early editions preferred; later editions may not clearly distinguish between formal and informal constructions).

Also, locate the criminal code of your state, as well as the United States criminal code, called Title 18, United States Code, abbreviated 18 U.S.C.

You will likely benefit by carefully examining the definitions of each of these words: Note, fraud, counterfeit, crime, conspiracy, and *treason*.

•

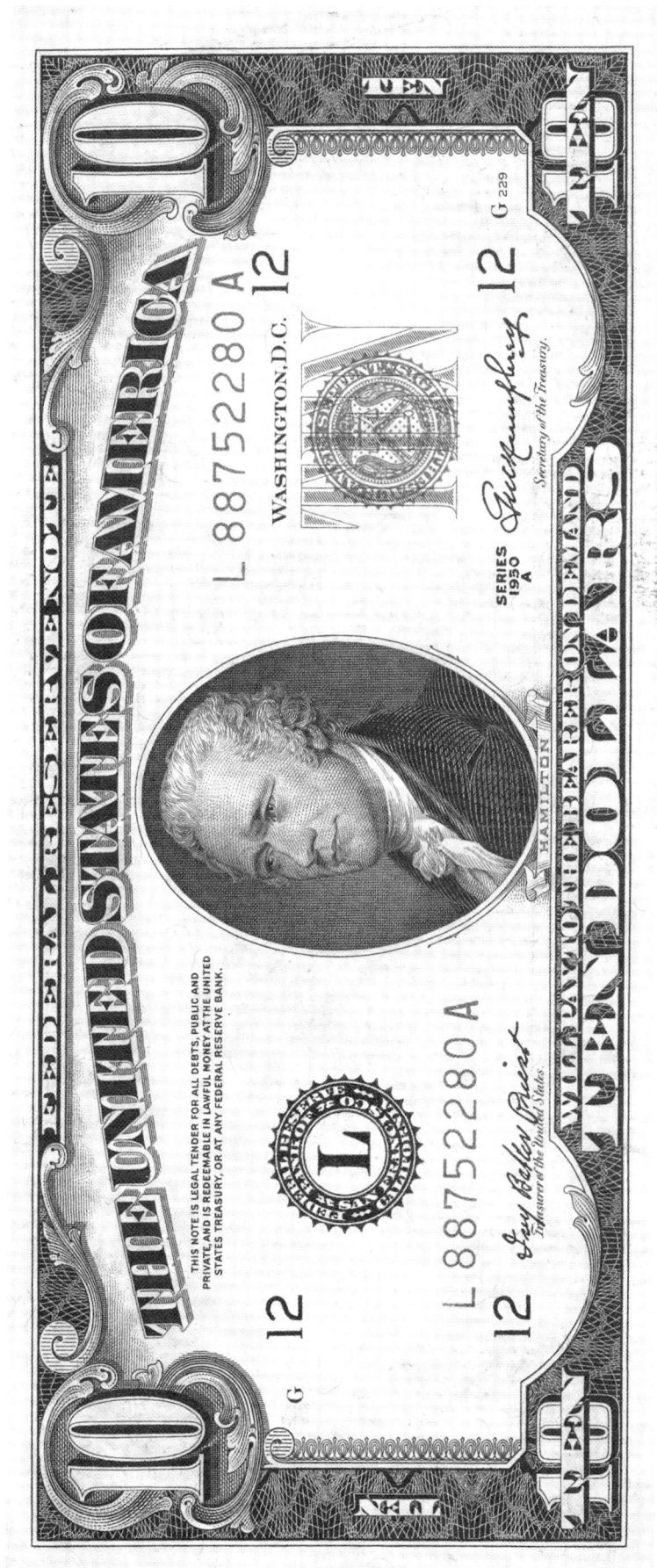

Figure 6-1. 1950, Federal Reserve Note, $10.

7

Tender

IN this chapter we examine *tender*, a word most people use correctly in adjective and noun forms but use incorrectly as a verb-transitive. Let's look at examples of each form.

> *Tender* (*adjective*): easily malleable or movable, opposite of unyielding or resisting. Ex.: "This meat is *tender*."
>
> *Tender* (*noun*): a thing which helps restore to, or sustain in, another thing its original capacity to operate. Ex.: (Naval officer says) "Our *tender* [a resupply vessel] should arrive soon."
>
> *Tender* (*verb transitive*): a motion or inclining toward, initiating movement. Ex.: "Please *tender* your rent payment directly to the manager."

The root of *tender* is tend, meaning action or motion just beginning. If you tend toward obesity, you are beginning to get fat.

Our focus in this chapter is tender's verb-transitive form. This form of *tender*, used almost exclusively in law and finance, has a narrow but important meaning.

Transactions and Tenders

A transaction begins when one party offers a product or service for sale, and another party says he or she wants to buy it. Let's explore the ways a prospective purchaser indicates his willingness to buy something.

If you went to a marketplace and saw a product you wanted, you might ask the seller what he was asking for it. Let's say he answered, "Five Dollars." Now let's further assume you had enough money to pay his price. You removed the exact amount from your pocket, held it out in your hand in plain view, with your arm and hand extended (ex-"tend"-ed) toward him. You *tendered* five Dollars toward consummation of the deal. You *tendered* the payment by *placing the money in motion* toward the seller.

Now suppose in response to your question about how much money the seller was asking for his product, he answered, "What'll you give me?" You might say, "I'll give you five Dollars." In other words, you made an *offer* but you did not make a tender because no thing — other than spoken words — moved from you toward the seller.

So a tender is made when money, or some other valuable thing, is placed in motion toward a seller. An offer is made when a prospective buyer offers a price, but no thing other than spoken or written words is placed in motion from buyer to seller.

In fact, the next time you hear someone claim he has made a "tender offer," don't think he's talking about an offer which could easily be chewed. If you tender 500 shares of XYZ, Inc. stock to a friend, and he offers you $5,000 for that stock, he is said to have made a "tender offer," that is, an *offer* (of $5,000) in response to your *tender* of 500 shares to him.

Now let's look at some other subtle aspects of tenders and offers.

Legitimate Tenders

Suppose you tell me one day that you have bought a car-washing facility. I say my car needs washing and ask how much you charge. You say, "$10," and I reply, "I'm broke today but I'll give you this portable stereo instead," and I pull a stereo from my briefcase and *extend* it toward you in the palm of my hand. By doing so, I have *tendered* one specific portable stereo to you in exchange for a car washing. You would probably examine the stereo closely, to see how it worked.

But suppose I had left the stereo at home. My phraseology might go like this: "Gee, I have no cash with me today but I have a nifty, portable stereo at home. I'll give you the stereo in trade for a wash job."

This time, I *offered* something, but I didn't *tender* anything. I didn't tender the stereo because I didn't place it in front of you, you couldn't examine it, or determine if it worked.

Legal and Illegal Tenders

Now let's take another look at the preceding scenario. Suppose I owned a small calculator, rather than a stereo, and I had it with me. I could have tendered the calculator instead. Or, suppose I had only $8 with me, presented it to you and said, "This is all I have today. Would you take it for a wash job?" Now I would be tendering $8 to you. The portable stereo, the calculator, and the $8 are equally usable in *legal* tenders.

Most tenders are called *legal* tenders because they are made to pay for something which is legal. Conversely, an *illegal* tender is one made to pay for something that is *not* legal, something that is a crime or misdemeanor.

Suppose someone approaches you and whispers, "I'll give you this digital watch," as he holds one out to you, "if you'll slash the tires on that car over there," gesturing toward a blue sedan parked nearby. Since slashing tires is a crime, the stranger's tender is illegal. The digital watch isn't illegal but the stranger's action, *tendering* something in payment for a crime, is illegal.

Tenders and the Law

Here's another aspect of tenders. Suppose you washed my car after I had tendered the stereo, but after the car was cleaned I changed my mind about giving you the stereo and, instead, tried to get you to accept my calculator. If you insisted on getting the stereo but I insisted on substituting the calculator, you could take me to court for my breach of our verbal contract. The court would undoubtedly order me to give you the stereo, ruling that because I had made *a legal tender*, and because that tender was accepted, I must follow through on it or be held in contempt of court.

Now suppose in the scenario of the stranger with the digital watch you did go ahead and slash the tires of the blue car. Then suppose the stranger said, "Gee, you sure did a nice job on those tires, but I've decided to give you this calculator," as he pulls one from his pocket, "instead of the digital watch, okay?" You say, "Absolutely not, Mister! You tendered the watch and that's what you gotta give me, period!" Well, let's say the stranger responds by saying, "Look, the calculator is worth more than the watch, and besides, the watch is an old family heirloom, so here's the calculator — take it or leave it!" Away you go to court, and the same judge hears the case.

The judge may surprise you with his response to this complaint. First, he's going to have the bailiff handcuff and book both of you on criminal charges. And as you are being led out of the courtroom you might hear the judge say, "For your information, Mister, there is no such thing as *a legal tender* for the commission of a crime!"

In other words, in legal contemplation, any object used in a legal tender may also be used in an illegal tender, to pay for an act prohibited by law.

From this and our other examples we should easily understand that a tender is only secondarily a physical thing. A tender is first the action or the event of holding a thing out toward a prospective recipient. We should never confuse the verb-transitive form of *tender* with the noun form, that is, when referring to the *thing* tendered as the tender.

Small Words, Large Significance
To round out our coverage of *tender* we must look closely at three little words: ***a***, ***an***, and ***the***. These words are called *articles* and, almost always, one of them must be placed in front of these words or phrases: legal tender, illegal tender, legal offer, illegal offer, tender, and offer.

In our hypothetical courtroom scenes, the judge might have said:

1. (Tire-slashing case) "There is no way to make ***a*** legal tender for the commission of a crime."
2. (Tire-slashing case) "***The*** tenders in this case were not legal."
3. (Car-washing case) "The respondent made ***a*** legal tender to the plaintiff."
4. (Car-washing case) "The attempted substitution of the calculator for the stereo does not mean that ***the*** initial tender of the stereo, once accepted by the seller, has been changed."
5. (Tire-slashing case) "***An*** illegal tender was made."

Notice that *legal* and *illegal* are the adjectives used to describe the types of offers or tenders. If no adjective is used, the assumption is that the offer or tender is *legal*. But please notice also how the judge used ***a***, ***an***, and ***the***.

Definite and Indefinite Articles
A and ***an*** are indefinite articles and ***the*** is a definite article. To illustrate their differences, please consider this: If I told you I saw ***a*** bird yesterday, you would correctly understand that I had seen one bird but you would have no idea which of Earth's billions of birds I had observed.

However, if I said I had seen ***the*** yellow bird that sings "Yellow Bird" for President Clinton every morning, and which was featured on the six-o'clock news on Channel 4 last night, you would have a definite idea of exactly which bird I had seen.

These examples show how a definite article is used to help give meaning to a sentence which would otherwise be vague.

Missing Articles
To illustrate further the necessity of articles (***a***, ***an***, and ***the***), consider this example of a meaningless sentence: *I saw bird yesterday.* Because no ***a*** or ***the*** is placed before *bird*, my utterance lacks specific meaning, especially at law.

Here's another example of a meaningless sentence: *John made legal tender to Charles.* Because no ***a*** or ***the*** was placed before *legal*, this sentence has no clear meaning at law or anywhere else. But the sentence *would* be perfectly clear if it read: *John made **a** legal tender to Charles*, or, *John made **the** legal tender to Charles.*

In other words, the phrase *legal tender* alone has no clear meaning, either in legal contemplation or in any other formal usage. There are, however, two colloquial (informal) uses of *legal tender* which are clear. Let's look at those uses and see how they came into existence.

Compelled Acceptances and Bad Habits
Well before the founding of the American Republic, courts all over the world had had to contend with disputes related to the substances of payment, that is, what constituted the correct or agreed-upon thing to be paid by debtor to creditor. Although the courts were generally successful in serving the ends of justice, the written descriptions of court opinions were somewhat complex. The public tended to describe those complex positions in purely colloquial ways, preferring the less cumbersome language and form of everyday speech over the precise, scholarly speech of those learned in the law. The colloquialisms were often legally imprecise or dangerously incomplete, despite which they were used in informal conversa-

tions. Indeed, precisely because they were used so often in informal conversation, they became "correct" and "the law" via repetition in the public mind.

Let's examine several colloquialisms now, in the context of how they came into existence. Once you see where they came from and how, you may also understand how dangerously incorrect they are and what trouble they have caused.

The Nation's First Coinage Act
The coinage Act of April 2, 1792 specifies that nickels and pennies, our minor coins, are to contain no precious metal. Because they contain no precious metal it would be an injustice to compel anyone to accept them in payment of large debts. The Act therefore specified, and the courts routinely sustained, that pennies and nickels could be used exclusively in tenders of amounts up to, but not more than, twenty-five cents. This meant that if someone owed you $150, and if he tendered 15,000 pennies to you, you could refuse 14,975 of them without waiving your claim to payment, at law.[1]

This special treatment given to subsidiary coinage by the courts gave rise to an informal but misleading use of the two-word phrase "legal tender." People began to say, "Pennies are *legal-tender* up to twenty-five cents; nickels are *legal-tender* up to twenty-five cents." This sentence was easier to say and understand than, "The courts will compel acceptance of pennies in tenders of amounts up to but not exceeding twenty-five cents," etc.

Although technically incorrect, this informal use of the two-word phrase *legal-tender* became deeply rooted in the national consciousness. From there it became the premise of yet another technically-incorrect colloquial use of *legal-tender*.

Payment of Debts
Assume that in 1800 a New York farmer sold a neighbor a cow on credit, and that the amount owed was agreed to be "ten Dollars." Now suppose that, after the agreement is made, the buyer tries to pay, with $10 in silver coin, but that the farmer refuses it because he wants gold. What would have happened if the farmer went to court? Well, the court might have ruled that by refusing a tender of ten officially minted silver Dollar-coins the farmer had waived his claim against the neighbor.[2] The court would have ruled that way, despite the farmer's preference for gold coin, because the agreement did not expressly state that the debt was to be paid that way, so it would have been an injustice to the neighbor to compel him to do it. This kind of decision led the public to say, "Gold coins and silver coins are *legal-tender* for any amount."

Also in the early 1800s, the courts had to contend with disputes about personal notes, Colony- or foreign-issued credit Notes, and foreign coin used by debtors to discharge obligations to creditors. Routinely, the courts would hold that a tender of foreign coin would not be upheld as *a legal tender* for the payment of a debt incurred in the United States. But the public then began to say foreign coins weren't *legal-tender*.

The courts would sometimes be asked to determine the worth of a Note, to determine if an obligation had been completely discharged and thereby make sure both parties received justice. If a Massachusetts Bay Colony Note, for example, had been used in a tender, and if the courts determined that the creditor must accept this Note (or waive his claim to payment of interest after the date of the tender), the public would colloquially describe Massachusetts Bay Colony Notes as *legal-tender* or *legal-tender Notes*.

As courts published their decisions about various media used in payments of debts or discharges of obligations, the public began to call each of those media *legal-tender*. The courts, of course, would normally use more formal and more precise language, but, in time, as colloquial uses of *legal-tender* became widespread, even legal professionals began to use them.

---

[1] Please see Chapter 18, Glossary: SUBSIDIARY COINAGE, and compelled acceptances of United States silver and gold coin today.

[2] Actually, if I owed you $10 and tendered ten One-Dollar silver coins to you, and if you rejected that payment, the court would simply deny you interest on the debt for the period after I made the tender.

But while legal professionals generally knew what the colloquialisms actually meant in the precise language of the courts, the public began to develop dangerously different understandings of them.

Money of Account
Another legitimate phrase, *money of account*, took on a colloquial form which, although acceptable for informal conversation, was even more dangerously inaccurate.

At the beginning of this nation's history as The United States of America, the phrase *money of account* was used to define what the word *dollar* meant *for accounting purposes*. In precise construction, it was proper to say, "The unit of the money of account of the United States is *Dollar*." This phrase meant that the accounts kept by the United States government, and by the governments of the several states, would be denominated in and organized on *Dollar* units of weight of money.[3]

However, the public and many professional people began to say, "The Dollar *is* the money of account" in the United States. Again, while this colloquial usage was imprecise, even dangerously so, there seemed to be little harm caused by using it. But as we've already seen, through repetition, the dangerously flawed colloquial expression became *formal* and *the law* in the public mind.

By the 1900s, the public began to describe Dollar-bills as just *Dollars*, and *paper currency* as *paper money* or *paper Dollars*. Indeed, as proof of how inaccurate one can become in the use of colloquial expressions, even educated people began using *Dollars* as a synonym for *money*.

In schools, a student might hear a business-law professor say, "The word *Dollar* is the unit of weight of the money of account of the United States of America." Several years later, a new professor might tell his students, "The Dollar is the money of account of the United States." Today we might hear a professor tell his students, "Dollars are what money is in the United States."

So it's no wonder that people now say, "Dollars are money." This is about as senseless as saying that units of weight are coins made of precious metal, or tons are sand, or quarts are milk, or miles are railroad tracks.

As the next several decades passed, we, as a People, began to lose sight of the concept behind the colloquial phrase *legal-tender*. Through repetition from generation to generation, its original meaning was forgotten and a new, incorrect and potentially lethal meaning was attached to it. This false concept, embraced even by legal professionals, was becoming ingrained in the public mind by the time of the Civil War, when President Abraham Lincoln issued the nation's first paper currency.

With public emotion riding high on war news, legitimate dissent to the proposed "paper emissions" was smothered. The nation got its first paper currency, colloquial expressions became "the law," and our Ship of State set a course toward monetary disaster.

Paper or Money?
In Figures 7-1 and 7-2, on pages 36 and 37, we see a reproduction (52% larger than actual size) of a "Greenback." These bills got their nickname because the imprint on the back side, shown in Figure 7-2, is *green*.

Looking at Figure 7-1, we see that this Two-Dollar bill is *labeled* a Note but since no due-date is given on it, we might describe it more properly as a quasi-Note. The courts of the time accepted this instrument as a genuine Note because, in the Act which created it, provisions were made for its ultimate redemption in United States silver or gold coins.

Now please look at the sentence printed across the top of the front side: THIS NOTE IS A LEGAL TENDER FOR TWO DOLLARS.

You can be sure that the structure of this sentence and the words in it were chosen with great care after much deliberation. After all, this bill was patterned after the first paper currencies issued by the United

---

[3] The unit of the money of account of your county or township may be *mill*, one thousandth of a dollar; your property tax bill may be quoted as "3.2 mills," meaning $3.20 for every thousand dollars of the assessed value of your property.

Figure 7-1. 1917 United States Note ("Legal Tender" Note), $2. Essentially the same as the U.S. Notes issued earlier, beginning in 1861 during the presidency of Abraham Lincoln, the first paper currency issued by the federal government. These bills were commonly referred to as "greenbacks" because the back side, as shown on the next page, was predominantly green. See also Chapter 9.

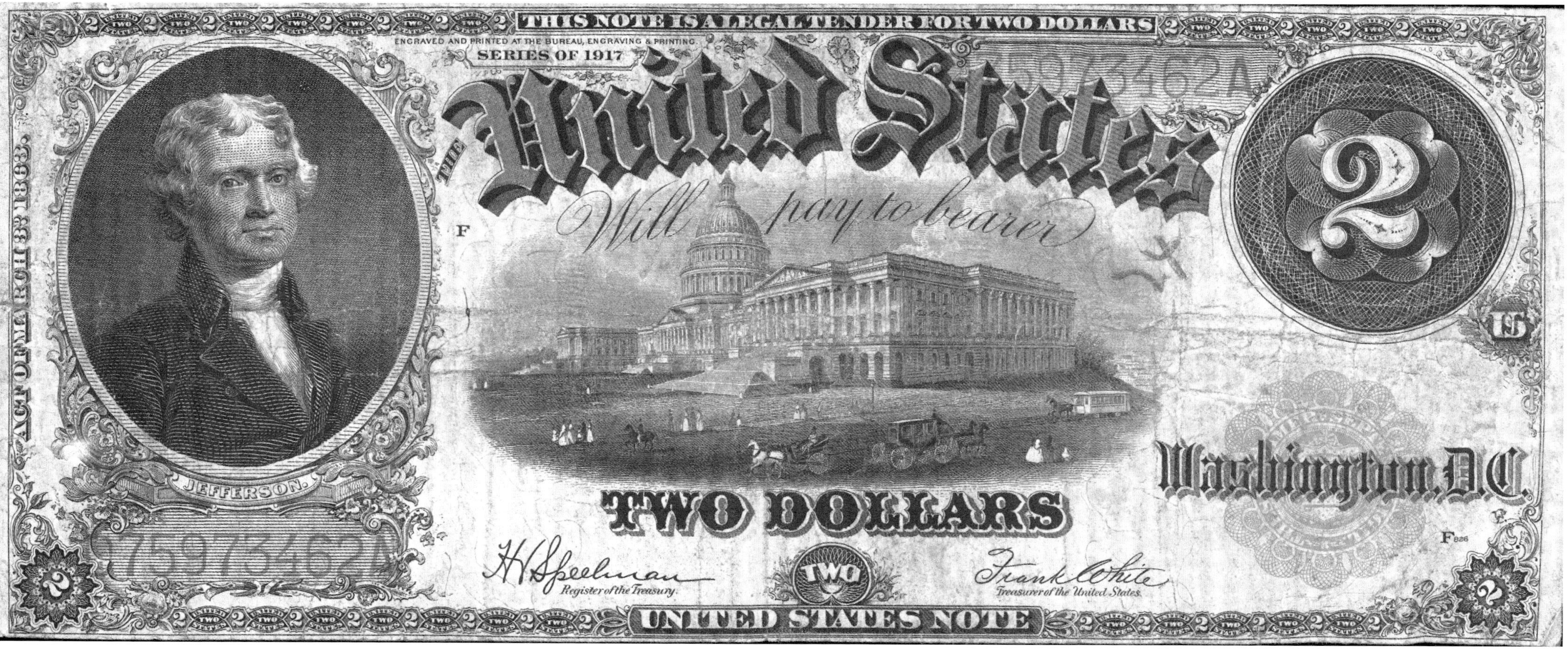

Figure 7-2. Back of "Greenback." The message on the back of this bill is interesting, particularly its anti-counterfeiting warning.

States, so let's look carefully at every word to see what we can learn.

THIS is used to distinguish *this* instrument from all the other Two-Dollar bills. We can distinguish *this* bill from all others by its serial number:

075973462A

We also see that this Two-Dollar bill was authorized by the ACT OF MARCH 3d 1863 and that it is one from the Series of 1917.

Further, we see that this instrument is self-declared to be A LEGAL TENDER FOR TWO DOLLARS (notice the indefinite article "A"). It is not legal tender (without the indefinite article), and it isn't legal tender "for all debts, public and private" (which today's paper currency says).

The phrase A LEGAL TENDER is most interesting. The indefinite article *A* indicates that THIS NOTE is just *one of many*. One of many *what*? Obviously, *one of many tenders*. Legal tenders? Legal tenders from whom to whom? Let's dwell on that a moment because it may be very important.

A Legal Tender

We must recall that a thing used in making a legal tender, such as tendering a digital watch to get a car washed, could also be used in an illegal tender, such as for slashing tires on an automobile. This piece of paper, this Two-Dollar bill, if used to get a car washed, would be used in a legal tender, *but it could also be used in a tender to pay for the commission of a crime*.

In other words, since the *use* of this piece of paper, this Two-Dollar bill, determines whether it is part of a *legal* tender or part of an *illegal* tender, what does the phrase "A Legal Tender" printed on it mean? History answers this truly *intriguing* question.

Warnings Ignored

The issuers of this bill faced a dilemma. Some members of the American public, remembering the nation's Founders' dire warnings about "paper emissions," were strongly opposed to any attempt to issue paper currency in the United States of America. Lincoln's critics feared they would end up holding a lot of worthless paper, which had happened to Americans who gave up real wealth in exchange for the Continental currency. Remember the phrase, "Not worth a Continental?" (See Figure 9-2, on page 53.)

The political figures of 1861 needed to pay for the Civil War but the federal Treasury was virtually empty. So rather than raise the money through taxes, they elected to borrow it from the citizens. The politicians used a "paper emission" to guarantee payment for the war-related goods and services they hoped to get from the public.

The Lincoln administration, aware of public aversion to even the *idea* of "paper emissions," may have used a psychological ploy in the form of the phrase A LEGAL TENDER. This phrase may have been placed in its prominent location to convey a message to the public:

> THINK OF THIS PIECE OF PAPER AS A GOVERNMENT AGENT STANDING BEFORE YOU WITH HIS HAND EXTENDED IN YOUR DIRECTION. IN HIS HAND YOU WILL NOTICE TWO DOLLARS OF EITHER GOLD OR SILVER MONEY. THIS MONEY IS YOURS IN EXCHANGE FOR THIS NOTE.

As many readers will recall, these bills were not redeemable when they were first issued. In fact, redemption did not begin until about 1879, some seventeen years later. Because the bills weren't redeemable, their purchasing power declined in the first several years following their introduction into circulation. But after they had depreciated to near zero worth, certain Insiders (wealthy speculators) began to buy them — at a huge discount from their face value. It was a "smart" move by these speculators. Had somebody tipped them off? A few years later, the government finally began to redeem those bills *at face value in precious-metal coin*.

The Insiders knew what they were doing, and made fortunes. Because they had great influence in the United States Congress, their "speculation" was as close to a sure thing as one could get. They knew what the future held because *they controlled many of the people who controlled the future*, the political figures of the time.

Greenback "Legal-Tender"

If a citizen refused to accept these "paper emissions" in a tender for payment of a debt, the courts held that he had waived his claim to interest after the date of the tender. Therefore, the public began to say,

> *United States Notes are* legal-tender, and
> *Paper money is* legal-tender, and
> *United States Notes are paper money*, and
> *United States Notes are money*, and
> *United States Notes are Dollars.*

Even the courts came up with some imprecise statements:

> *United States Notes are lawful money*, and
> *The lawful money of the United States includes the circulating coins and Notes of the United States.*

These colloquialisms, dangerously imprecise, just like others from earlier years, became more of "the law" in the public mind.

Except Interest On The Public Debt

In Figure 7-2, page 37, we see the back of a 1917 "Greenback." The critical writing reads:

> This Note is a LEGAL TENDER at its face value
> for all Debts, Public and Private, except Duties on Imports and
> INTEREST ON THE PUBLIC DEBT.
>
> Counterfeiting or Altering this Note or passing any coun
> terfeit or alteration of it, or having in possession any false
> or counterfeit plate or impression of it, or any
> paper made in imitation of the paper
> on which it is printed is Felony
> and is punishable by $5,000
> fine or 15 years Imprison
> ment at Hard Labor
> or both.

Placement of "all Debts, Public and Private" on the back of the bill is curious but understandable, particularly in light of the clever way the exception is phrased. INTEREST ON THE PUBLIC DEBT is in all capitals on a line by itself, indicating that the issuers did not want anybody to complain that he didn't know this Note couldn't be used to pay interest on the public debt.

Yet we must ask what prompted the exception. Why weren't the public creditors compelled to accept these Notes? If everybody else had to accept them, why make the exception for public creditors? Couldn't the public creditors, just like everyone else, exchange these Notes in the marketplace for goods and services?

The PUBLIC DEBT exception came about because certain Insiders of 1861, as we have seen, to whom a large part of the public debt would be owed, knew in advance that Lincoln's "Greenbacks" would depreciate to just a fraction of their face value. Because of the exception, the government could not force those Insider creditors to accept "Greenbacks," the only paper currency at that time, in payment of the debt.

However, when the "Greenbacks" depreciated sharply, the Insiders accumulated as many as they could. Only later, in 1789, when the government began redeeming the bills — at their face value in silver or gold coin — did those Insider creditors accept "Greenbacks" as payment for the debt they were owed. Then they had the government redeem all of their "Greenbacks" for gold or silver coin — to thereby double or triple their money.

Partial Justification for the Court's Actions

Sir Robert Burns (1759 - 1796), Scottish poet and philosopher, once said (in "To a Mouse"),

> "The best laid schemes o' mice an' men,
> Gang aft a-gley;"

Sometimes, our best intentions boomerang to our regret. This has happened to the nation's courts when they tried to do justice.

Since we rely upon the courts to provide justice for all, it is sometimes necessary that they consider informal speech and writing as expressing the intent of the parties to an agreement. For example, if a rancher used colloquial words and phrases to express the terms and conditions of a contract he and a neighbor entered, justice would not be served if the courts failed to consider the meaning or intent contemplated by the rancher and his neighbor, in spite of their use of colloquial expressions.

However, when courts published their opinions about such cases, lay and professional people alike would often adopt some of the colloquial expressions, even applying them beyond the focus of the court.

Idioms and vernacular phrases in one part of the country were thus lent national and formal acceptance and credibility because they were discussed in and by the courts.

In time, confusion about monetary terms spread everywhere in our society. Was this an accident? Maybe not, because it played into the hands of the tiny band of corrupt individuals, the Insiders we have already mentioned several times. We'll have more to say about these individuals later, but for now let's reflect on what we've just covered.

The cause of today's monetary problems is our use of imprecise colloquial expressions, especially in the courts and in the Congress. When one false premise led to a problem, other false premises were used to remedy it, thereby causing more problems. The cumulative effect of our use of false premises may be the root cause of *almost all* of America's current problems.

Redeemable Currency and the Courts
Following the introduction of government-issued paper currency in the United States (Act of February 25, 1862), until 1968, most of the time that currency was redeemable in specie — silver or gold coin — upon demand at government-chartered banks or at the United States Treasury.

In view of this easy and speedy redeemability, the courts held that if a seller refused a tender of any United States officially-issued paper currency, he waived his right thereafter to collect interest on the debt or obligation. This reasoning was essentially sound for in the view of the courts and the public, possession of such paper currency was tantamount to having actual money in hand.

The public began to paraphrase the courts in colloquialisms like, "You gotta accept paper money or you waive your claim to payment," or, "Federal Reserve Notes are legal-tender and legal-tender's what you gotta accept if you wanna get paid."

Again, although these errors in phraseology were unimportant in informal communications, through repetition they became both "formal" and "the law" in the public mind.

What About the "Legal Tender" Cases?
Following the first introduction of paper currency in the United States, by way of the Act of February 25, 1862 and the Act of March 3, 1863, two landmark decisions by the United States Supreme Court, called the "Legal Tender" cases, helped perpetuate several imprecise uses of terminology *and* several specious lines of reasoning. These two cases are *Knox v. Lee*, 79 U.S. 457 (1870), and *Juilliard v. Greenman*, 110 U.S. 421 (1884).

For the most clear and comprehensive discussion of these two cases, the reader is encouraged to read *Pieces of Eight: The Monetary Powers and Disabilities of the United States Constitution*, by Edwin Vieira, Jr., Ph.D., JD., Fort Lee, New Jersey: Sound Dollar Committee, 1983.

We don't have space to cover these cases here, but, after you read *this* book, we recommend you read Dr. Vieira's book. You should then be well-prepared to dispute the findings of these two courts because you would know exactly how the Justices came to their controversial conclusions.

Meanwhile, let's stress again that, through years and years of imprecise usage, the phrase "legal-tender" has come to be grossly misunderstood. Today, it is hard to find anyone who understands it correctly.

Can you see now why we say that only the phrases "*a* legal tender," "*a* tender," "*an* illegal tender," "*the* legal offer," "*an* offer," etc., express complete, proper and clear meaning *at law*?

However, to make absolutely certain we are not deceiving ourselves, let us turn back the clock. Let's see what the Founders said about tenders in the supreme Law of the land.

What the Constitution Says

The Constitution of the United States of America, in Article 1, Section 10, tells us what "a Tender" is.

> Section 10. No State shall enter into any Treaty, Alliance, or Confederation; grant Letters of Marque or Reprisal; coin Money; emit Bills of Credit; make any Thing but gold or silver Coin a Tender in Payment of Debts. . . .

If we eliminate the clauses between "No State shall" and "make any Thing" we will clarify the intent of the "Tender" clause.

> Section 10. No State shall . . . make any Thing but gold or silver Coin a Tender in Payment of Debts;

Further modifying the form of the clause, yet not disturbing the meaning of it, we could express it thus:

> States must make their tenders in payment of debts using only gold or silver coin.

Or,

> States may use only gold or silver coin in making tenders for payment of debts.

Thus, the nation's Founders understood that to pay debts, money must be tendered. Money is a device manufactured in a mint. The money contemplated by the Founders was coins of silver or gold. As proof of this assertion, please consider Article 1, Section 8, United States Constitution,[4] and the language of the Act of April 2, 1792,[5] the first coinage Act passed by the United States Congress.

The Founders, in the language of the time, said "make any Thing but . . . Coin a Tender." Today, of course, we would say "use anything but coins in making a tender." This minor difference in phraseologies — between making the coins a tender, and, making the tender using coins — has no material bearing on our understanding of *tender* or on how the word is to be used precisely today. In other words, even though the phraseologies between 1787 and 1998 differ slightly, the substance of the earlier construction is identical to what we advocate here.[6]

Please observe how the Founders show us their crystal-clear understanding of *tender* as the presentation of something of acknowledged worth to an intended recipient. Specifically, the Founders told us that States were required to use gold or silver coins, and nothing else, in making tenders for payment of debts.[7]

Now that you have completed this historical review, please pay especially close attention to what follows. Please remember that a Note is a promise to pay someone money, that a Note is an evidence of a debt. Now we want to expose you to something shocking.

Someone Is Myth-ing

Please remove your wallet or billfold from your pocket or purse. Next, remove a specimen of the paper currency you are carrying.

The odds are great that you are looking at a piece of paper which describes itself as a FEDERAL RESERVE NOTE. Observe that the piece of paper also pretends, via the words and symbols printed thereon, that it has something to do with money. Also recall that a Note, at law, in financial and legal contemplation, *must* identify a Maker, *and* a Payee, *and* a Dollar-amount *and* a Due-date.

Now notice that two of those four mandatory elements are missing from the collection of words and symbols printed on the thing in your view. Notice that the two missing elements are the Payee and the Due-date. Because these two mandatory elements are missing, you *know* that you are not looking at a

---

[4] "The Congress shall have Power . . . To coin Money, regulate the Value thereof, and of foreign Coin, and fix the Standard of Weights and Measures. . . ." — Art. 1, Sect. 8, U.S. Constitution.

[5] Please see also Appendix D.

[6] A third meaning of Art. 1, Sect. 10, bars the States from compelling citizens to accept tenders of anything but coins of gold or silver.

[7] If your state has a highway patrol, and if those officers aren't paid with *silver or gold coins*, isn't your state government violating the law?

genuine Note at law, insofar as financial or legal matters are concerned.

Next, please look at the eleven words in the upper-left corner of the front side:

> THIS NOTE IS LEGAL TENDER FOR ALL DEBTS, PUBLIC AND PRIVATE

These words mean absolutely nothing at law. Here is why:

1. First, the words THIS NOTE are irrational. You are not looking at a financial instrument recognized by law as a Note, an evidence of a debt, because two mandatory elements of a genuine Note are missing; Payee and Due-date are not identified. Even if the intent of the phrase THIS NOTE is to refer to a memorandum or other general written communication, the phrase is still irrational because no complete sentence is present, which will become unmistakably clear in a moment.

2. The phrase LEGAL TENDER is not preceded by an article, definite or indefinite (*the*, or *a*, respectively). Without a preceding article, LEGAL TENDER has exactly the same meaning as ABCDE FGHIJK, that is, no meaning at all.

3. FOR ALL DEBTS is irrational because a Note cannot be used to pay a debt. A Note or an IOU is *evidence* of a debt. If I owed you $100 and gave you an IOU as proof of the debt, would you have been paid? Of course not. Can you use your Note at the bank to pay off the mortgage on your house? Of course not.

4. ALL includes PUBLIC AND PRIVATE. Putting PUBLIC AND PRIVATE after ALL DEBTS is utterly redundant and useless. If ALL has any meaning whatsoever, there is no rational purpose to following ALL (DEBTS) with PUBLIC AND PRIVATE.

Proof of a Lie

Now let's do a Before-and-After comparison of the cluster of eleven words as they are printed on the "Note." Here's the Before:

> THIS NOTE IS LEGAL TENDER FOR ALL DEBTS, PUBLIC AND PRIVATE

A. Eliminate THIS NOTE. It's not a financial instrument.

B. Eliminate LEGAL TENDER. This two-word phrase has no meaning due to the absence of a preceding definite or indefinite article.

C. Eliminate FOR ALL DEBTS. The document, on its face, purports to be a Note. If it is a Note, DEBTS must be removed because Notes cannot be used to pay debts; OBLIGATION would have to be used instead of DEBTS. But because DEBTS *is* used, the phrase THIS NOTE cannot be used. Regardless of which error is accepted, the supposed meaning of the entire sentence is destroyed by removal of either NOTE or DEBTS. Also, since FOR ALL does not contain clarifying terminology — FOR *payment of* ALL or FOR *discharge of* ALL — the entire phrase FOR ALL DEBTS is barren of legal or financial meaning and therefore must be removed.

D. Eliminate PUBLIC AND PRIVATE. This phrase is superfluous. It has no substantive relationship to the preceding terms.

By eliminating meaningless and obfuscating words, here's what our "sentence" looks like, the After:

> IS

What does IS mean? Does it mean anything? Now please recall our observation about THIS NOTE in paragraph 1. Even if THIS NOTE were not eliminated we would still be left with an unintelligible cluster of words:

> THIS NOTE IS

What rational meaning can possibly be attached to either THIS NOTE IS or even THIS MEMORANDUM IS? Can you now see that what at first appeared to be a real sentence is only a collection of sentence-fragments, utterly devoid of meaning at law?

Please consider one other aspect of the curious wording on this and later "Notes" (bills). Placement of the wholly unnecessary terms PUBLIC AND PRIVATE after ALL DEBTS tends to imply that the only important question any "reasonable" citizen might raise about the paper currency might be: "Exactly which debts can I pay with this Note?" The "Note's" issuer then becomes the citizen's friend by answering the question in advance of it even being asked. The implied answer is that the Note can be used to pay *all* debts, meaning *all public and private debts*. However, the unnecessary terms and the odd construction tend to manipulate the citizen by planting or reinforcing the utterly false notion that a bill, a Note, can be used to *pay* a debt. This remarkably odd construction might tell us that its author was simply not skilled in writing, that he "accidentally" used an awkward construction which, purely by chance of course, helps perpetrate criminal fraud. Here are three questions you may wish to ponder: a) Who put this strange language on the nation's paper currency, poorly trained and unskilled clerk typists or highly skilled and well-trained lawyers? b) Is this odd construction accidental or was it put there deliberately? c) If deliberately, for what purpose?

Perhaps you can now better appreciate and understand why knowledgeable people refer to certain pieces of paper as Federal Reserve *Tokens*, abbreviated FRTs.

The Myth-ing Link

Ask your local banker to explain the meaning of the eleven-word mishmash given above. She will probably say, "Well, legal-tender is what you gotta take if it's offered to you, you know, in payment for something. If you want to buy groceries, the storekeeper's gotta take these Federal Reserve Notes. It's the law. Federal Reserve Notes are legal-tender and legal-tender's what's gotta be accepted or else you waive your right to get paid. That's why they're called legal-tender notes. Anybody that doesn't like paper money is a nut!"

Such limited understanding is epidemic in the United States today, as you may already be aware. This hypothetical banker, supposedly an expert in her industry, is blind to the fact that the pieces of paper to which she refers are *not* Notes. Some bankers and other professionals have been blind or silent about this and other critically important matters for years. Happily however, those who might persist in perpetuating such *myths*, after exposure to this book, could find themselves in serious legal jeopardy.

If you want to speed the restoration of sanity in this country, send copies of this book to public officials and political candidates, requesting comment. Responses might be amusing, or infuriating, or somewhere in between, but be sure to document your mailings or deliveries.

If you mail copies, it might be a good idea to use Registered or Certified mail, request a receipt, and keep the receipts when they are returned to you.

For greater impact, you might wish to do this: In the presence of two or more adult witnesses, enclose each copy in its own envelope. Write the intended recipient's name on the outside of the envelope. Have your witnesses document in writing what they saw you do. Then visit each intended recipient at his or her workplace during a normal workday. Take a witness with you, an adult not related to you by blood or marriage. When you and your witness have the opportunity to make your presentation, smile broadly and extend your little gift toward the intended recipient. Cheerfully say, "Here, this has your name on it."

After your recipient takes the package, quietly but cheerfully add, "You're served," and walk away. You and your witness are now experienced Process Servers! Complete and sign an Affidavit of Service of Process, and then store it in a safe place.

As with receipts from U.S. Postal Service delivery of your registered or certified mail, your Affidavits of Service of Process could become extremely important. Here is why.

Successful criminal prosecutions depend on proof of *mens rea*, Latin for *with bad intent* or *with bad purpose*. At trial, bad purpose (malicious intent, etc.) may be established by showing evidence of *willfulness*. Willfulness may be established by presenting evidence of *foreknowledge*. And foreknowledge may be established by presentation of your Registered or Certified Mail Receipts *and Affidavits of Service of Process*.

•

DOHSA. Death on High Seas Act.

Doing business. Within statutes on service of process on foreign corporations, means equivalent to carrying on, conducting or managing business. A foreign corporation is "doing business", making it amenable to process within state, if it does business therein in such a manner as to warrant the inference that it is present there. Or that it has subjected itself to the jurisdiction and laws in which the service is made. The doing of business is the exercise in the state of some of the ordinary functions for which the corporation was organized. What constitutes "doing business" depends on the facts in each particular case. The general rule is that the business need only have certain "minimum contacts" with the state to make it amenable to process in that state. International Shoe Co. v. State of Washington, 326 U.S. 310, 66 S.Ct. 154, 90 L.Ed. 95. And, such contacts may be as minimal as selling a single insurance contract. McGee v. International Life Insurance Co., 355 U.S. 220, 78 S.Ct. 199, 2 L.Ed.2d 223; Hanson v. Denckla, 357 U.S. 235, 78 S.Ct. 1228, 2 L.Ed.2d 1283. *See also* Long arm statutes; Minimal contacts; Transacting business.

The determination as to what constitutes "doing business" may differ as to whether the term is being used with reference to amenability to service of process or to taxation, and also may vary in definition from state to state.

Dollar averaging. Investment term for practice of purchasing a fixed dollar amount of a given security at regular intervals. *See also* Averaging up or down.

Dolus /dówləs/. In the civil law, guile; deceitfulness; malicious fraud. A fraudulent address or trick used to deceive some one; a fraud. Any subtle contrivance by words or acts with a design to circumvent.

Figure 7-3. *"Dollar" is not defined in* Black's Law Dictionary, *Sixth edition. This dictionary is a basic reference work for lawyers as well as for most other professionals and students. Did the editor decide there is no rational definition which will encompass all the ways "dollar" is used today? Copyright 1991 by West Publishing Company. Reproduced with permission. All rights reserved.*

8

Bill

THE word *bill* can mean either the beak of a bird, or an arrangement for the appearance of a performer, or a writing at law. The latter meaning is our subject in this chapter.

Early writing was done with either a feather (a quill), or with a bird's beak, or bill, fastened to the end of a stick. Because the point of a quill tends to wear quickly, quills were used primarily for general writing purposes. The bill kept its point relatively well, and was the preferred instrument when writing important, especially legal, documents.

One form of writing we use today derived its name from the instrument used centuries ago to create it: a bill. Today we hear of documents such as a Bill of Particulars, a Bill of Sale, and, of course, the Bill of Rights.

Today, if you have a telephone, you probably receive a bill from the telephone company each month. If you are a shipper you have undoubtedly seen bills of lading. If you are a building contractor you are probably familiar with bills of materials.

What a Bill is <u>Not</u>
Now that you know the names of some bills, consider also that there is one thing we know a bill certainly is not. We know it's not the thing or things described by the writing thereon. For example, a bill of lading which lists thirty grand pianos is most certainly not the grand pianos. A bill of materials is not the materials. The bill the waiter brings to your table is not the dinner you've just enjoyed. And the Bill of Rights is most certainly not the rights. A bill, then, is a writing about a thing or things, but it is NOT the thing or things.

However logical all of this may seem, you may be surprised to learn that there are people actually walking around loose on the streets these days who would argue the contrary. In this group of unusual individuals are a few IRS workers, lawyers and judges, politicians, bankers and even some of your neighbors. Maybe even your boss.

Now, this is not to say these folks are totally wacko, but you might be inclined to think so after you've finished reading this chapter. It contains some basic financial knowledge, so childishly simple you may wonder how it escaped so many people for so many years.

We reintroduce you now to the world-famous, almost universally misunderstood Dollar bill, or *Dollar*-bill. Let's first review what we've learned about the word *dollar*.

What is a Dollar Bill?
Dollar is defined in the Act of April 2, 1792, the

nation's first coinage act, as a unit of weight of silver or gold, in much the same way *carat* is a unit of weight of precious stones. A chunk of pure silver which weighs one dollar also weighs 371.25 grains or about 0.77 troy ounces. In the same way, a thing weighing one ton also weighs 2,000 pounds and also weighs 32,000 ounces. Ton and pound and ounce are units of weight, as are grains, carats, grams and *dollars*. One *dollar* of pure silver weighs 371.25 grains; one *ton* of anything weighs 2,000 pounds.

What, then, is a *Dollar*-bill? In law and finance, *Dollar*-bill generally means a writing which refers to Dollars, that is, a writing in which *Dollar* is the unit of measure. To be more precise, however, we should say that a *Dollar*-bill is a formal notice of indebtedness in which the indebtedness is measured in units called *Dollars*.

If you live in one of the United States, because your telephone bill is expressed in terms of *Dollars*, in a general sense, it is a *Dollar*-bill.

Federal Reserve Notes from the 1914, 1928, 1934, or 1950 series are all *Dollar*-bills. Let's look at the writing on one to see why. [See Figure 6-1, page 30.]

A Federal Reserve Note

On a Federal Reserve Note from the Series of 1950 we see what appear to be two complete sentences.

Here is Sentence A:

THE UNITED STATES OF AMERICA WILL PAY TO THE BEARER ON DEMAND TEN DOLLARS

And here is Sentence B:

THIS NOTE IS LEGAL TENDER FOR ALL DEBTS, PUBLIC AND PRIVATE, AND IS REDEEMABLE IN LAWFUL MONEY AT THE UNITED STATE TREASURY, OR AT ANY FEDERAL RESERVE BANK.

In Sentence A we see why the instrument is called a Note. It identifies the four elements required for the instrument to be a Note, at law: the Maker (the United States of America), the Payee (the Bearer), the *Dollar*-amount (in this example, Ten), and the Due-date (On Demand).

We run into trouble in Sentence B, because the words LEGAL TENDER FOR ALL DEBTS, PUBLIC AND PRIVATE, AND don't mean anything.

Remember that since the phrase LEGAL TENDER is not preceded by an article (A or THE), it has no meaning at law. The term FOR is ambiguous. Also, the term DEBTS is inapplicable to Notes, and the phrase PUBLIC AND PRIVATE is superfluous. However, if we eliminate the meaningless phrases and superfluous words, the following remains:

THIS NOTE IS REDEEMABLE IN LAWFUL MONEY AT THE UNITED STATES TREASURY, OR AT ANY FEDERAL RESERVE BANK.

Combining this sentence with Sentence A, we arrive at the following intent:

1. The United States of America (our federal government) owes somebody ten Dollars of money;
2. That somebody is the Bearer of the document (the Note);
3. The government will pay when the Bearer demands payment by presenting the document;
4. The Note may be presented for payment at either the Treasury of the United States or at any Federal Reserve bank;
5. Payment will be made in Lawful Money (of the United States of America); and,
6. There is no expiration date on this agreement.

Redeeming Features

If you presented this official document to either the United States Treasury or to a teller at any Federal Reserve bank, you would be presenting a *bill* for payment. You could also say you are presenting a Note for payment, or for redemption, or to get it redeemed. You are trying to get a *bill* redeemed. Since the bill in our example specified the amount of ten Dollars, it is referred to as a Ten-Dollar bill.

When this bill is redeemed, the bearer gets paid lawful money and the bill is taken out of circulation, thereby becoming, in accounting terminology, a *retired demand Note*. In the same way, you would take out of circulation — and probably destroy — an IOU, after the person who wrote it paid up.

In the phrase *lawful money*, *lawful* means created pursuant to public law, namely, the Act of April 2, 1792,[1] and *money* means coins made of silver or gold or other precious metal.

If you're still not sure how redemption works, remember how a supermarket redeems grocery coupons. First the coupon bearer presents the coupon for redemption. Second, the supermarket gives the coupon bearer the item or benefit described on the coupon (redeems it); third, the supermarket destroys the coupon so it can't be used in another claim.

By the way, please recall that these and other demand Notes are called currency for two reasons. In the public mind, *Dollar*-bills are considered currency because they flow in the economy like the current in a stream. But banks and other financial institutions call *Dollar*-bills currency for a different reason. They are payable (redeemable) on demand, and "on demand" means less than one year, the period during which transactions are "current." Thus, Federal Reserve Notes, Silver Certificates, Gold Certificates, and some other government-issued Notes are *current* assets to the person, bank or other financial institution holding them. This is also why, on the back of your bank deposit slips, counts of *Dollar*-bills (but not coins) are listed in an area labeled Currency.

Another Perspective on *Dollar* Bills

Question: How do you know how much to pay to the telephone company each month? Answer: "Why, the phone company sends me a bill." Okay, now let's assume you made a lot of long-distance calls recently and your bill this month is $1,245. When the bill arrives and you open the envelope and read the amount due, do you shout out to your family, "Hey gang, guess what? The phone company just sent us twelve hundred and forty-five dollars!"

Of course you don't. You know that the phone company sent that bill to you because they expect payment. Bills are a method of communicating to you how much you owe. Bills are things you pay, not spend. You cannot spend the phone bill you received in the mail — you must pay it. Exactly the same constraint applies to bills of $5.99, $208.50, $325.45, $50, or any other amount, regardless of who issued them.

When Uncle Sam prints a $20 bill, that bill — like any other — must be paid. And you can't spend Uncle Sam's bill any more than you can spend your telephone company's bill. Sam meant for that bill to be used as evidence of his debt to someone, maybe to you. Uncle Sam printed many bills, all to be paid by him at a later date. If you accepted one *as* money, you did so temporarily, but *not permanently*.

Let's say you are a postal carrier and, in payment for your work, Uncle Sam gives you some $20 bills. You accept money substitutes, temporarily, fully expecting to be paid at a later date, upon your demand. Whenever you feel like it, you can take the bills to "Uncle" in Washington, D.C., or to a teller in one of the Federal Reserve Banks, and present them for payment. That's when Uncle Sam must come up with the money. In other words, by accepting the $20 bills in lieu of money, you lent real money to Uncle Sam (to our civil service employees, actually), and you are to be paid (or paid back, if you prefer) upon your demand.

Since *on demand* is instantaneous, and since instantaneous is well within one year, your *Dollar*-bills are currency for two reasons: one, because they circulate in the economy (they are a medium of exchange); and two, because they are redeemable in money within twelve months.

At this point you might say, "Wait just a minute here, buddy. You might like to know that every time I go to the store, the storekeeper always accepts those bills in exchange for her products. She doesn't come after me for payment so I must have paid for those products with those bills you say I can't spend. It looks to me like they *can* be spent, and the storekeeper seems to agree. What do you have to say to that?"

The answer is another question: What do you

---

[1] The Act of April 2, 1792, still in force today, is conspicuously ignored by the Insiders who benefit from our confusion or ignorance.

mean by *pay*? Since you did not give the storekeeper actual money, you did not pay her. What you did was discharge your obligation to her, by giving her the government's promise to pay. She has your bills and will, or should, present those bills to the Treasurer of the United States for payment.

Remember our analogy about Uncle Sam and the postal carrier? Receipt of authentic government-issued money substitutes ($5 and $10 bills, etc.) is considered by the courts to be the same as receiving money, or tantamount to receiving money, because the bills could be redeemed for money upon (the storekeeper's) demand.

The storekeeper gets paid when Uncle Sam (or a bank, or another person) comes up with the money to pay the bills, but not before.

Legitimate paper currencies, that is, genuine money substitutes, the bills which we in the United States have used in the past **as** money, were called *Dollar*-bills because they were denominated in *dollar* units.

Bills can be denominated in Francs, Marks, Lira, or other monetary units. And remember, dollar is a unit of weight, like pound (i.e., British Pound), and the Biblical shekel and talent, weight-units for metallic media of exchange in ancient civilizations.

Using *Dollar* Bills
Unfortunately for most of us, there are no *Dollar*-bills in general circulation today (1998) in the United States, much less elsewhere in the world.

We say "unfortunately for most of us" because years ago, good people like yourself deposited a lot of silver and gold coin in banks in exchange for *Dollar*-bills. People preferred the convenience of paper currency and trusted the banks with their money, their silver and gold coins. At any time they wanted their money back, they took their *Dollar*-bills to a bank and presented them for payment. And payment was always promptly made, in lawful money of the United States of America.

Such trust wasn't misplaced, at least not at first. People all over the world would accept United States *Dollar*-bills in exchange for goods and services. Why would people in other countries that had their own money do that? They didn't have to but they knew that our paper currency, because it was redeemable in lawful money upon demand, was virtually "as good as gold" in their hands, pockets or purses, or bank accounts.

A Swiss hotel operator, for instance, who accepted United States *Dollar*-bills from American tourists, would deposit that currency in his bank. His bank would eventually present those *Dollar*-bills for payment in the United States, through international banking channels. And they would be paid.

Discharging Obligations
Actually, while *Dollar*-bills could never be used to *pay* anybody for anything, they could be used to discharge part or all of the obligation incurred when a person *without money* buys something. In other words, if a seller accepts *Dollar*-bills, the buyer's obligation to him is legally discharged. Actual payment would occur when the seller presented the bills for payment at his bank, or at any Federal Reserve bank, or at the United States Treasury.

Here's another way to look at discharging an obligation. Suppose I am a millionaire, that I am well known in the community as a responsible person, and that I give you a personal Note in the amount of $1,000 for something you've sold me. My Note is due and payable (by me) in one month. You, on the other hand, want to leave for vacation next week, but you don't have quite enough money to buy your airline tickets, which are going to cost $1,200.

If your travel agent will accept my Note, you need give her only $200 along with it to obtain your tickets; the remaining $1,000 owed on your ticket purchase will come from me when my Note comes due and payable. You are said to have discharged $1,000 of your obligation to her with my Note. The travel agent's acceptance of my Note is not mandatory, of course, but because she knows I am a responsible person, and because she believes I will pay the Note as promised, she accepts it rather than lose your business.

Bills and Payments

Now you certainly understand why bills can't be used to pay anyone. You certainly can't use your phone bill to pay your electric bill, and you can't use a Note from someone to pay your telephone bill. However, if your phone company accepted my Note (to you) in the amount of $1,000, your obligation to the telephone company would be discharged (reduced) by $1,000.

Here are the three most important points to remember about bills. Money is used to pay bills, and bills may be used to discharge obligations, but bills can *never* be used to pay anything.

Over the years, however, a few tricky changes have been made in the wording on our paper currency, rendering today's currency radically different from the versions used to get your elders to place their silver and gold coins in banks.

Tokens

Now that the wording printed on them is changed, we can no longer properly identify our paper currency as *Dollar*-bills, nor can we expect the banks to redeem our paper currency with either lawful money or any other kind of money. We are no longer empowered — by the writing on our paper currency — to get our silver and gold coins back from the banks. This is because the operative meaning expressed in the writing on authentic Notes and Certificates is no longer present on our paper currency. The present paper currency is not Notes, is not *Dollar*-bills, is not redeemable, is not directly related to *Dollars* in any way, and most assuredly is not money. So, since there is no direct relationship today between our paper currency and coins made of precious metal, it is suggested that the most appropriate name for these pieces of paper is Federal Reserve Tokens, abbreviated FRTs.

•

"All the perplexities, confusion and distress in America arise, not from defects in their Constitution or Confederation, not from want of honor or virtue, so much as from the downright ignorance of the nature of coin, credit and circulation."

President John Adams (1735 - 1826)

"Federal Reserve Tokens are like the 'green stamp' premiums of the 1950s, except that when you turn these green stamps in, all you get are more green stamps."

Mobley Milam, former assistant U.S. Attorney in San Diego, in a telephone conversation with the author in March 1998

9

Will Pay to (the) Bearer

"A man's word is his bond" means that his verbal promise is reliable. In previous generations, when there were fewer lawyers and fewer means to write agreements, one's reputation was extremely important. Verbal agreements, the basis for most trade at the time, played a critical role in neighborhoods as well as in the national economy.

Following the Pilgrims' landing on Plymouth Rock, native and newcomer alike soon discovered that a reputation for honesty was highly valuable. Credit at a local store, or with a farmer or blacksmith, could finance opportunity or even help save a life. Charity and forgiveness were traditions of America's earliest inhabitants but liars, sloths, deadbeats and perennial borrowers were quickly identified and shunned. Human parasites are not necessary to the well-being of a community, and such people don't keep their promises.

George Washington's honesty is exemplified by the quotation, "Father, I cannot tell a lie." The cherry-tree story has taught ten generations of young Americans the importance of telling the truth. In American law, deliberately false, verbal statements which harm a person are called slander. If the false statements are written, they are called libel. When someone knowingly writes a false document such as a bad check, the law calls that action, "uttering a fraudulent document." Utter, in a legal sense, often means *write*.

Starting in 1690, our paper currency, regardless of denomination, always bore the once-familiar phrase WILL PAY TO THE BEARER (or variations of that phrase). Our paper currency reflected our traditional values, namely, that we promised people we'd pay them whenever they demanded payment; they needed only to present our paper currency to an appropriate authority such as the United States Treasury or a bank, and payment would be immediate and without argument.

The immediacy of payment of America's bills — our Dollar-bills — gave rise to the global recognition that United States paper currency was "as good as gold." The government would pay a ten-Dollar bill, in gold coin or silver coin whenever you demanded it, so there was no need to do so. We Americans kept our promises, we were honorable people, and our word was our bond.

Now let's look at the nation's paper currency, from the first issue, the Massachusetts Bay Colony Note of 1690, to the $2 Federal Reserve Note (*sic*) of 1963. Pay attention to the two or three complete sentences on the bills. Watch for the elements of a Note: Maker, Payee, Dollar-amount and Due-date. Watch for complete sentences, but also for redundant, unnecessary, and obfuscatory words and phrases. Watch also for the indefinite article, A. You'll see a disturbing pattern which could be evidence of a major crime.

Order of Presentation

In the following pages, photographs of United States paper currency are presented chronologically, beginning with 1690. When specimens of more than one denomination are presented in the same year, larger-denomination bills are presented before the lower denominations. At the end of the series of United States paper currency, you will see one foreign bill.

In the following pages, most paper currency photographs are enlarged about 1.52 times the actual size of the bills. Title 18 U.S.C. requires that photos of U.S. obligations be more than one and one half times or less than three fourths actual size. We opted to enlarge most of our photographs an extra two percent to offset possible future shrinkage of the pages.

We reproduced some bills smaller than 1.52 times their actual size. Their reproduction size may be given in the caption, possibly as a percentage of the bill's actual size. Bills reproduced at their actual size are not subject to the size constraints of 18 U.S.C. § 474 *et seq* because they are not "obligations of the United States." Where no size information is given, conspicuously large reproductions are about 152% of the bill's actual size. Where a large reproduction is accompanied by a small reproduction, usually the opposite side of the bill in the larger image, the small image is about 73% of the bill's actual size.

Coins are reproduced actual size except as noted.

•

---

18 U.S.C. § 471.
Obligations or securities of United States. Whoever, with intent to defraud, falsely makes, forges, counterfeits, or alters any obligation or other security of the United States, shall be fined under this title or imprisoned not more than fifteen years, or both.

18 U.S.C. § 472.
Uttering counterfeit obligations or securities. Whoever, with intent to defraud, passes, utters, publishes, or sells, or attempts to pass, utter, publish, or sell, or with like intent brings into the United States or keeps in possession or conceals any falsely made, forged, counterfeited, or altered obligation or other security of the United States, shall be fined under this title or imprisoned not more than fifteen years, or both.

18 U.S.C. § 473.
Dealing in counterfeit obligations or securities. Whoever buys, sells, exchanges, transfers, receives, or delivers any false, forged, counterfeited, or altered obligation or other security of the United States, with the intent that the same be passed, published, or used as true and genuine, shall be fined under this title or imprisoned not more than ten years, or both.

Figure 9-1. *Counterfeiting, the crime and punishment per the United States Code, effective January 16, 1996.*

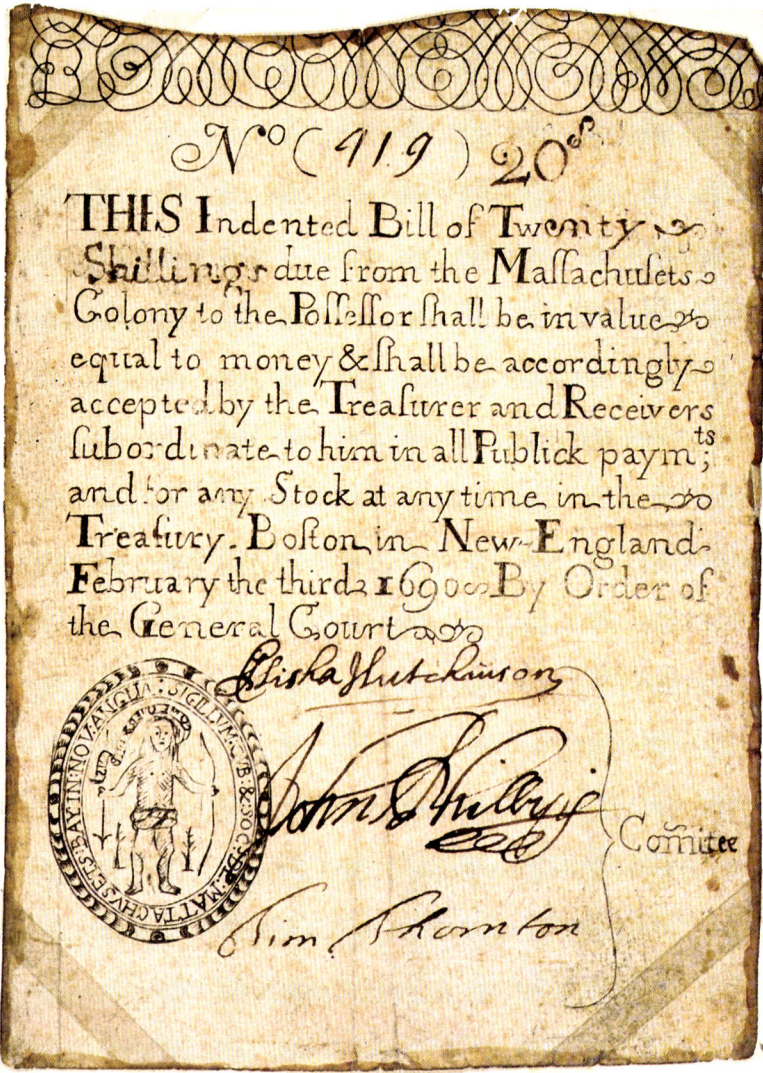
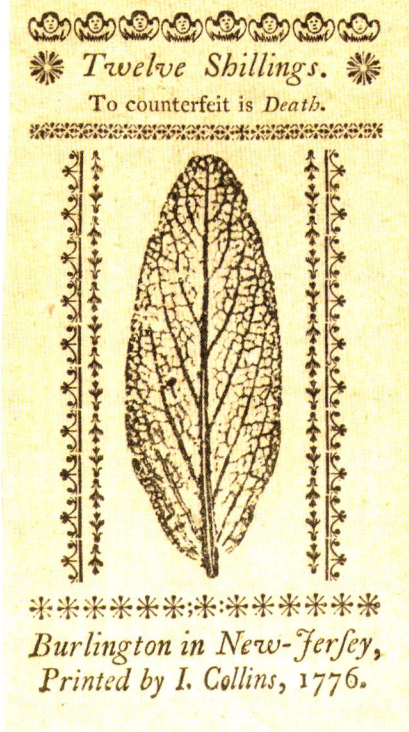
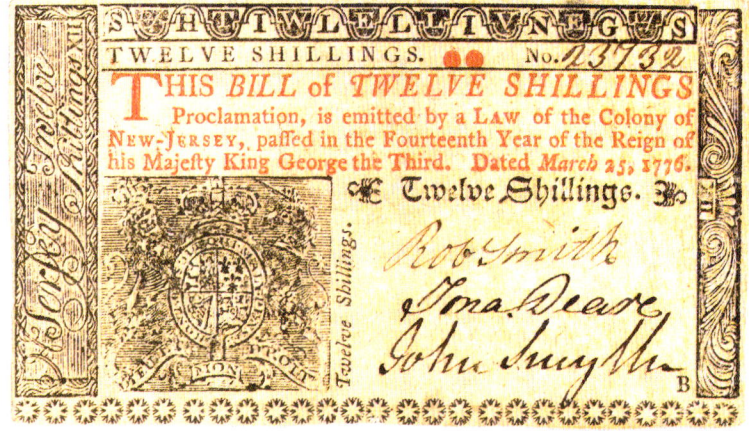

Figure 9-2. 1690, Massachusetts Bay Colony Note, 20 Shillings. This bill, the first paper currency in the Colonies, was issued about seventy years after the Pilgrims landed at Plymouth Rock. Photo courtesy of the Smithsonian Institution, Washington, D.C. Bottom, 1776 New Jersey Colony Notes, 12 Shillings. Photos courtesy of the Federal Reserve Bank of New York. Bills on this page are approximately actual size.

Figure 9-3. 1776, Continental Currency Notes. *One Third of a Dollar;* photo courtesy of the Smithsonian Institution, Washington, D.C. *One Dollar;* photo courtesy of the Federal Reserve Bank of New York. Continental Currency Notes depreciated to pennies on the dollar, giving rise to the saying, "Not worth a Continental." Both bills shown approximately actual size.

Figure 9-4. 1819, Farmers & Mechanics Bank of Cincinnati, Ohio banknote, $3. Photo courtesy of the Smithsonian Institution, Washington, D.C.

Figure 9-5. 1840 (?), Republic of Texas Note, $50. Hand signed and serial numbered. When this bill was issued, $50 would support a family of four for about a year.

Figure 9-6. *1840, Bank of the United States banknote, $3,000. Photo courtesy of the Smithsonian Institution, Washington, D.C.*

Figure 9-7. 1860, Citizen Bank of Louisiana "Dixie" Note, unissued, $10, face and back. French influence in Louisiana is clearly evident in its law, cuisine, and customs. The French word for ten is dix; and the prominent "DIX" on the back of this bill gave rise to the term by which the South would later be known: Dixie. Photos courtesy of the Smithsonian Institution, Washington, D.C.

Figure 9-8. *1861. "DEMAND" Note. $5. The first paper currency issued by the federal government of the United States, this bill has no reference to "legal tender." The back, printed with green ink, gave rise to the term "Greenback." Photos courtesy of R. M. Smythe & Company, New York, New York.*

Figure 9-9. 1862, Cherokee Note, $1. Redeemable in Confederate currency. 1862, Choctaw Note, $.50 (fifty cents), also redeemable in Confederate currency. Both bills shown actual size. Photos courtesy of the Smithsonian Institution, Washington, D.C.

61

Figure 9-10. 1875, Fractional Currency Note, Fifty Cents. 1874, Fractional Currency Note, Twenty-five Cents. 1863, Fractional Currency Note, Ten Cents. Bills shown about 1.52 times actual size. Denominations of U.S. Fractional Currency included seventy-five cents, fifty cents, twenty-five cents, fifteen cents, ten cents, five cents, and three cents. Photos courtesy of the Federal Reserve Bank of New York.

Figure 9-11. 1864, Confederate States of America, $10 bill.

Figure 9-12. 1865. U.S. Treasury Note, Interest Bearing, "Gold Option," $50, with five coupons, about 73% of actual size. Photo courtesy of the Smithsonian Institution, Washington, D.C.

64

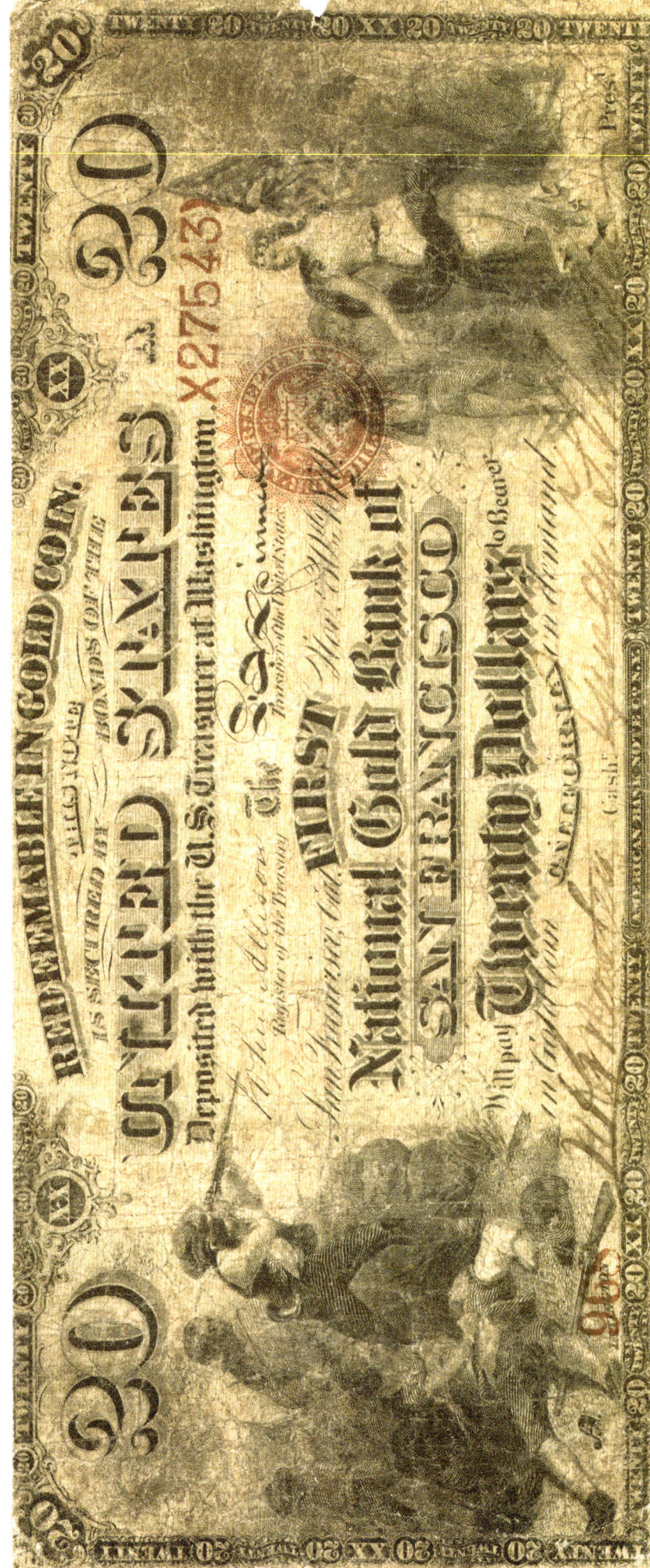

Figure 9-13. 1870, First National Gold Bank, San Francisco, Gold Coin Certificate, $20. Photo courtesy of the Federal Reserve Bank of New York.

Figure 9-14. 1880, Silver Certificate, $1,000, which is the highest denomination of U.S. silver certificates. Photo courtesy of the Federal Reserve Bank of San Francisco.

Figure 9-15. 1882. Gold Coin Certificate, $100. Photo courtesy of the Federal Reserve Bank of New York.

Figure 9-16. 1891, Silver Certificate, $1. The 1886 and 1891 series of $1 Silver Certificates were the only U.S. paper currency to bear a woman's portrait on the face. This bill is also shown on our dust jacket. Photo courtesy of the Smithsonian Institution, Washington, D.C.

Figure 9-17. 1891, Treasury Note, $1,000. Photo courtesy of the Smithsonian Institution, Washington, D.C.

Figure 9-18. 1899, Silver Certificate, $5, said to portray Chief "Running Antelope" of the Uncpapa tribe of the Lakota Sioux. This portrait, however, is actually a composite of the features of several Sioux chiefs. The tribe's name is also seen spelled as Hunkpapa, Oh-na-papa, Ongepapa, and Oncpapa. The latter variation gave rise to this bill's colloquial name, the "Chief Onepapa" (pronounced "one papa") bill. The Sioux (and Arapaho) treaty of 1868 includes both "Uncpapa" and "Hunkpapa" spellings. The Sioux nation ranged from Wisconsin and Iowa to the Rocky Mountains and north into Canada. The Lakota Sioux tribes lived near the Rocky Mountains. Photo courtesy of the Federal Reserve Bank of San Francisco.

Figure 9-19. 1902. National Currency, $5, face and part of the back. The language on the back of the bill is particularly interesting: "THIS NOTE IS RECEIVABLE AT PAR IN ALL PARTS OF THE UNITED STATES IN PAYMENT OF ALL TAXES AND EXCISES AND ALL OTHER DUES TO THE UNITED STATES EXCEPT DUTIES ON IMPORTS AND ALSO FOR ALL SALARIES AND OTHER DEBTS AND DEMANDS OWING BY THE UNITED STATES TO INDIVIDUALS CORPORATIONS AND ASSOCIATIONS WITHIN THE UNITED STATES EXCEPT INTEREST ON PUBLIC DEBT."

Figure 9-20. *1907, United States Note, $5, face, showing "Will Pay the Bearer," and back, showing "Is a Legal Tender."*

Figure 9-21. *1907, Gold Certificate, $10, face and back, payable in gold coin.*

Figure 9-22. 1914, Federal Reserve Note, $10, face and back, Act of Dec. 23, 1913. "THIS NOTE IS RECEIVABLE BY ALL NATIONAL AND MEMBER BANKS AND FEDERAL RESERVE BANKS AND FOR ALL TAXES, CUSTOMS AND OTHER PUBLIC DUES. IT IS REDEEMABLE IN GOLD ON DEMAND AT THE TREASURY DEPARTMENT OF THE UNITED STATES IN THE CITY OF WASHINGTON, DISTRICT OF COLUMBIA OR IN GOLD OR LAWFUL MONEY AT ANY FEDERAL RESERVE BANK." "GOLD" is explained in the caption of Figure 9-31.

Figure 9-23. *1918, National Currency (Federal Reserve Bank Note), $1, "secured by . . . gold notes," etc. Face only. Back is shown on opposite page.*

Figure 9-24. 1918, *National Currency (Federal Reserve Bank Note), $1*, back only. Face is shown on opposite page. The important language on the back is: "THIS NOTE IS RECEIVABLE AT PAR IN ALL PARTS OF THE UNITED STATES IN PAYMENT OF ALL TAXES AND EXCISES AND ALL OTHER DUES TO THE UNITED STATES EXCEPT DUTIES ON IMPORTS AND ALSO FOR ALL SALARIES AND OTHER DEBTS AND DEMANDS OWING BY THE UNITED STATES TO INDIVIDUALS CORPORATIONS AND ASSOCIATIONS WITHIN THE UNITED STATES EXCEPT INTEREST ON PUBLIC DEBT."

76

Figure 9-25. 1917, United States Note, $2. This bill is shown out of chronological sequence so the face and back sides of the 1918 National Currency Note could be shown on facing pages (to comply with 18 U.S.C., which says opposite sides of U.S. currency are not to be printed on opposite sides of the same page).

Figure 9-26. 1922. Gold Coin Certificate, $50, face and back, "... IS A LEGAL TENDER...." Photos courtesy of the Federal Reserve Bank of New York.

Figure 9-27. 1923, Silver Certificate, $1, "THIS CERTIFICATE IS RECEIVABLE FOR ALL PUBLIC DUES AND WHEN SO RECEIVED MAY BE REISSUED."

Figure 9-28. 1928, United States Note, $2. "... IS A LEGAL TENDER AT ITS FACE VALUE...."

80

Figure 9-29. 1928, Silver Certificate, $1, "... IS RECEIVABLE" and "... ONE SILVER DOLLAR PAYABLE...." This bill's obligation is to pay one Dollar of silver in the form of a One-Dollar silver coin, not with silver halves, quarters, dimes, or any combination thereof.

Figure **9-30**. *1928, Gold Certificate, $10, "... CERTIFICATE IS A LEGAL TENDER...."*

Figure 9-31. 1928, Federal Reserve Note, $10, "REDEEMABLE IN GOLD ON DEMAND . . . OR IN GOLD OR LAWFUL MONEY. . . ." Redemption in "GOLD" could be in the form of bars (ingots), plate, dust, or nuggets; redemption in "LAWFUL MONEY" could be in the form of U.S. gold coins or U.S. silver coins or a combination of U.S. gold coins and U.S. silver coins, but not in the form of gold bars (ingots), plate, dust, or nuggets.

Figure 9-32. 1928, Federal Reserve Note, $10,000, highest denomination of Federal Reserve Notes. Photo courtesy of the Smithsonian Institution, Washington, D.C. This bill bears serial number 1.

Figure 9-33. 1934, Gold Certificate, $100,000, highest denomination of gold certificates. This bill bears serial number 1. Photo courtesy of the Smithsonian Institution, Washington, D.C.

Figure 9-34. 1934, United States Note, $10,000, highest denomination of U.S. Note. This photo is a composite of an official souvenir – bearing no serial number or "Series" date – to which we added one missing element, the "serial number" of a replica, all zeroes, (taken from a black and white halftone photograph of an actual $10,000 U.S. Note replica). The souvenir and replicas were issued by the U.S. Bureau of Engraving and Printing, Washington, D.C.

Figure 9-35. 1934, Federal Reserve Note, $5, ". . . IS LEGAL TENDER. . . ."

Figure 9-36. 1935, Silver Certificate, $1, ". . . IS LEGAL TENDER. . . ."

Figure 9-37. 1950, Federal Reserve Note, $100, "... IS LEGAL TENDER...." Notice the small print used for the "REDEEMABLE" phrase.

Figure 9-38. 1953, United States Note, $2. "... IS A LEGAL TENDER...."

Figure 9-39. 1957, Silver Certificate, $1, ". . . IS LEGAL TENDER. . . ."

Figure 9-40. *1963, United States "Note," $2, "... IS LEGAL TENDER...." Observe that, as of 1963, the critical phrase, "WILL PAY TO THE BEARER ON DEMAND," is no longer used on U.S. paper currency.*

92

Figure 9-41. 1963, Federal Reserve "Note," $1. "... IS LEGAL TENDER...." Observe that, as of 1963, the critical phrase, "WILL PAY TO THE BEARER ON DEMAND," is no longer used on U.S. paper currency. Notice also that the critical terminology which belongs in the "REDEEMABLE" phrase is gone, and the font size of the remaining words has been increased so the new language (without the important terms) occupies the same area as the complete language on the 1950 series bills. Was that change in font size for artistic reasons or to take advantage of public confusion or apathy?

Figure 9-42. 1976, Federal Reserve "Note," $2.

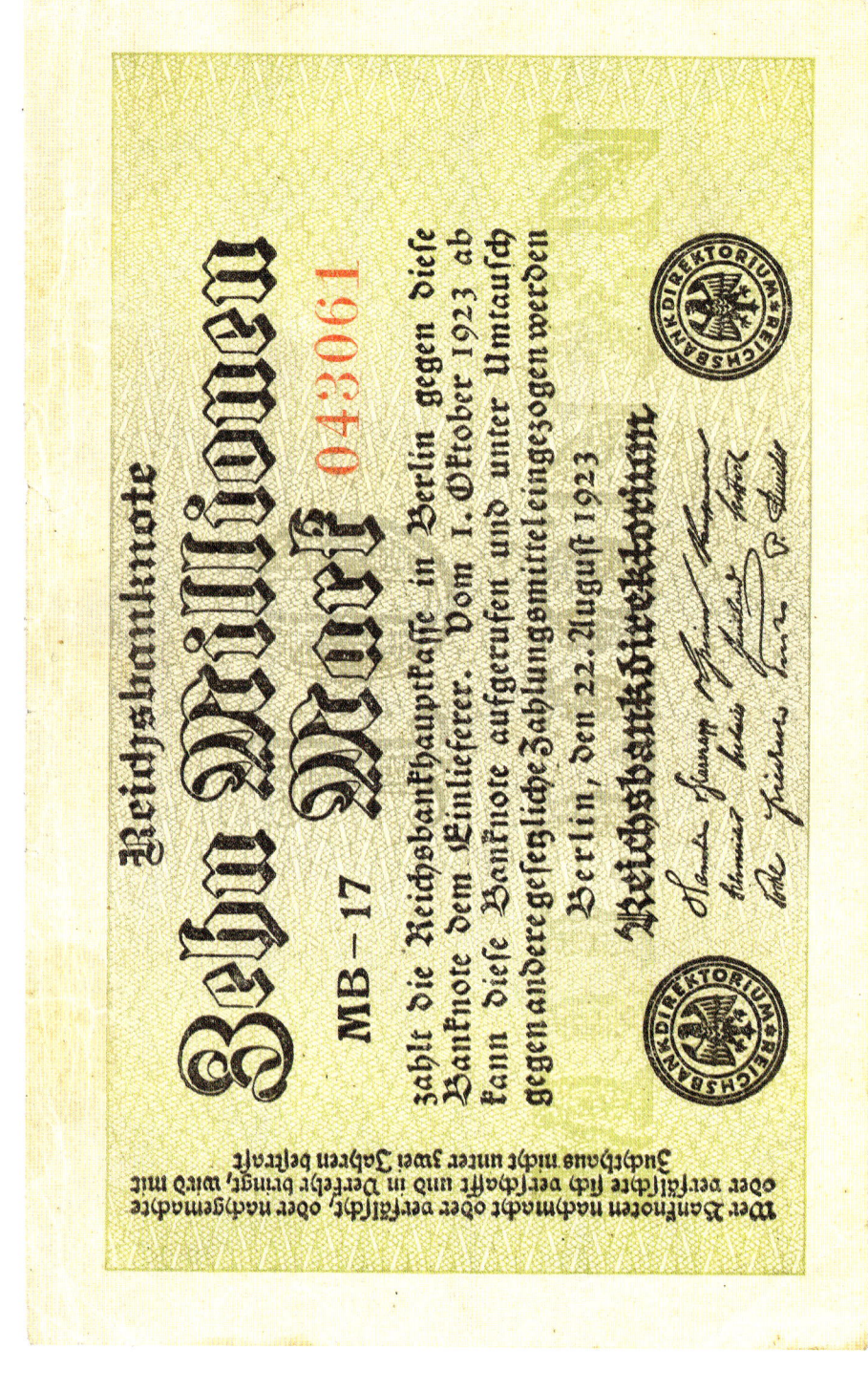

Figure 9-43. *1923, German "Reichsbanknote," 10 Million Marks, issued during Germany's runaway inflation of the 1920s. Printed on only one side because there was no time to let the ink dry; issued when workers were paid twice each day so they could try to buy at least something ahead of the next price rise. This "money" was "guaranteed" by the promises of the German government and the productivity of the German workers, citizens were told. U.S. paper currency today is supposedly backed by the same things that "backed" the Reichsbanknotes.*

U.S. Gold Coins

Obverse and Reverse of 1878 $1 Gold   Obverse and Reverse of 1849 $2.5 Gold   Obverse and Reverse of 1881 $3 Gold

Obverse and Reverse of 1879 $4 Gold Stella   Obverse and Reverse of 1909 $5 Gold

Obverse and Reverse of 1799 $10 Gold

Obverse and Reverse of MCMVII (1907) $20 Gold

Figure 9-44. U.S. Gold Coins. When a U.S. Dollar-bill was redeemed at a bank or at the U.S. Treasury, the person submitting the bill for payment was often given these kinds of coins, on demand. Coins are shown full size. Photos courtesy of Doug Plasencia, photographer, and Bowers & Merena Galleries, Inc., Wolfeboro, NH. Graphic art by Robin Edgerly, Wolfeboro, NH.

U.S. Silver Coins

1857 Silver
3¢ Piece

1839 Half Disme
(5¢ Piece)

1906 Barber Dime

1876 20¢ Piece

1926 Standing
Liberty Quarter

1834 Capped Bust
Half Dollar

1901 Morgan
Dollar

1883 Trade Dollar

Figure 9-45. U.S. Silver Coins. When a U.S. Dollar-bill was redeemed by a bank or the U.S. Treasury, the person submitting the bill for payment was often given these kinds of coins, on demand. Coins are shown full size. Blue discoloration indicates sulfate accumulation, not oxidation. Coins shown are rare collectibles, and remain discolored because cleaning or polishing would alter their surface sufficiently to lower their value. Photos courtesy of Doug Plasencia, photographer, and Bowers & Merena Galleries, Inc., Wolfeboro, NH. Graphic art by Robin Edgerly, Wolfeboro, NH.

U.S. Minor Coins

1883 Half Cent

1857 Large Cent

1909 Lincoln Cent

1943 Steel Cent

1864 2¢ Piece

1884 Nickel 3¢ Piece

1959 Jefferson Nickel

U.S. Colonial Coins

New England Shilling

Pine Tree Threepence

Pine Tree Sixpence

Pine Tree Shilling

Virginia Halfpenny

Fugio Cent

Continental Currency Dollar

Figure 9-46. U.S. Minor Coins. These coins contained no precious metal. Coins are shown full size. During World War II, a steel cent was issued and circulated, so more copper would be available for war production. A World War II Five-Cent coin (nickel) containing silver was issued and circulated (1943 to 1945), and twenty of these coins contained more silver than any other aggregate of $1 face value of U.S. coins. Several Colonial coins are also shown. Blue discoloration indicates sulfate accumulation, not oxidation. Coins shown are rare collectibles, and remain discolored because cleaning or polishing would alter their surface sufficiently to lower their value. Photos courtesy of Doug Plasencia, photographer, and Bowers & Merena Galleries, Inc., Wolfeboro, NH. Graphic art by Robin Edgerly, Wolfeboro, NH.

Private and Territorial Gold Coins

Obverse of 1850 $5 Mormon Gold   Reverse of 1849 $5 Mormon Gold   Reverse of 1849 $10 Mormon Gold   Reverse of 1849 $20 Mormon Gold

Territorial Gold Coins Shown Twice Actual Size

Reverse of 25¢ Octagonal Cal. Small Denomination Gold   Reverse of 25¢ Round Cal. Small Denomination Gold

Reverse of 50¢ Octagonal Cal. Small Denomination Gold   Reverse of 50¢ Round Cal. Small Denomination Gold

Obverse and Reverse of $50 Gold "Slug"

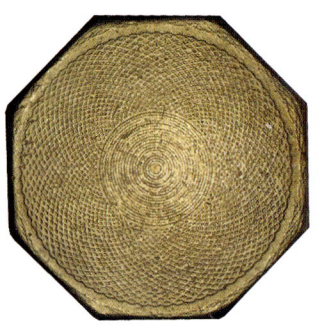

Reverse of $1 Octagonal Cal. Small Denomination Gold   Reverse of $1 Round Cal. Small Denomination Gold

Figure 9-47. *Privately minted U.S. gold coins. "Mormon" settlers in the Salt Lake area mined their own gold and minted their own coins, to facilitate commerce in the burgeoning West. California gold miners in the gold rush at Sutter's Mill also minted their own gold coins to facilitate trade. The $50 "slab" was minted privately but with U.S. government approval. The California miner coins are shown twice actual size; the "Mormon" coins and the "slab" are full size. Photos courtesy of the Smithsonian Institution, Washington, D.C. Graphic art by Robin Edgerly, Wolfeboro, NH.*

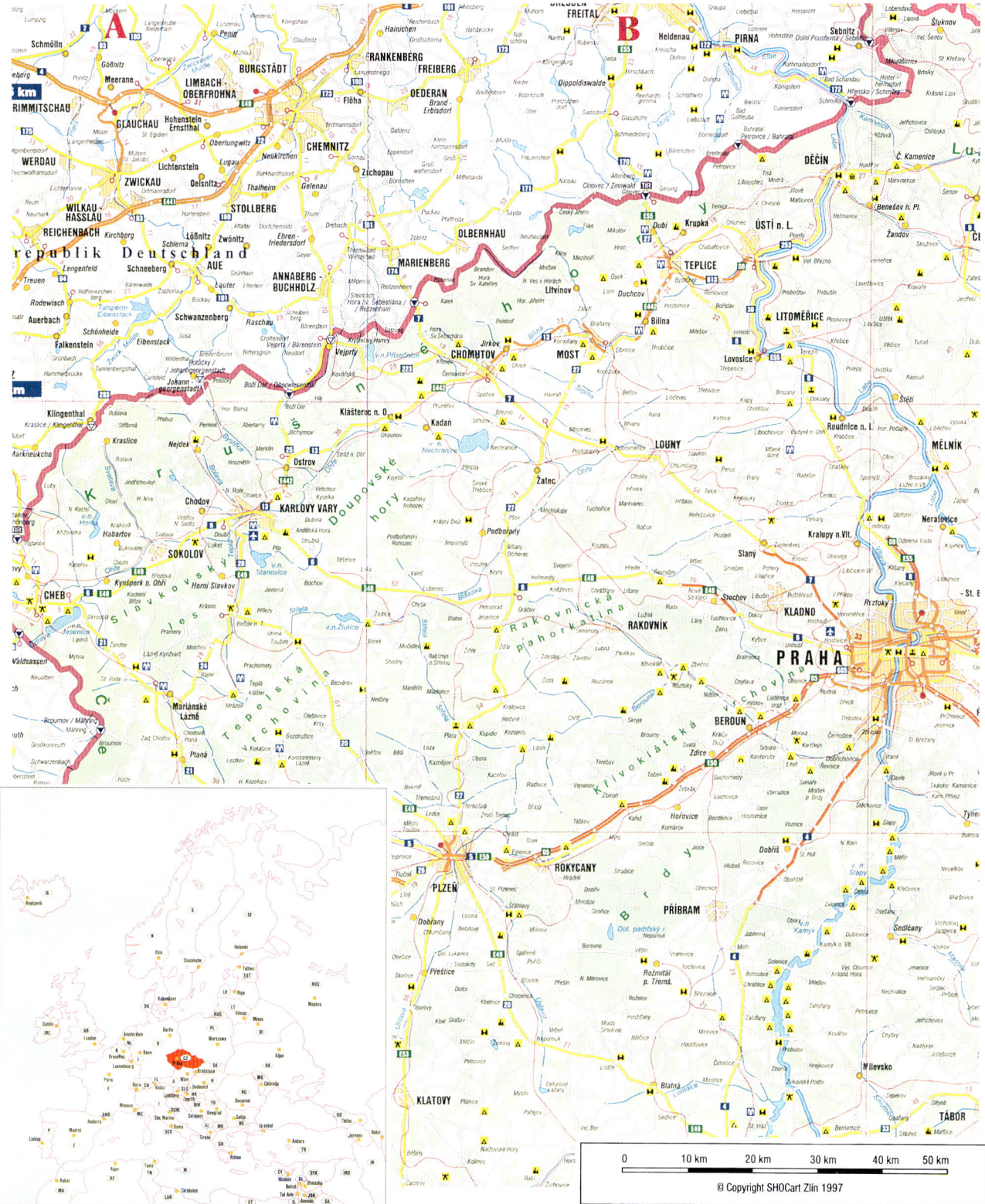

Figure 9-48. Map of the western end of the Czech Republic. Find Praha (Prague), go west about 110 km to Karlovy Vary (Carlsbad), and then north about 15 km to Jochymov (Joachimsthal). Jochymov is where Count Steven von Schlick mined silver and minted his gulden groshen coin in the early 1500s. A "Joachim's Thaler" coin dated 1592 is shown on our dust jacket. This area of the former Czechoslovakia is called Bohemia. Joachim is derived from the Biblical "Joseph," husband of Mary, the mother of Jesus Christ. Map courtesy of the Consulate General of the Czech Republic, New York, New York.

Figure 9-49. 1896, Silver Certificate, $1. This bill is considered by many to be the world's most beautiful. One of the "educational" series of bills produced in the late 1890s, this bill is referred to as "HISTORY INSTRUCTING YOUTH." Note the clear meaning of the bill's text.

10

Usury

WHEN you hear someone mention the word *usury*, what comes to mind?

Many Americans say, "The Holy Bible condemns usury," so it must be inherently evil. Don't most states have laws against it? Some of these good people say usury and "usurious interest rates" are destroying the nation.

Do you agree with these statements? What would you think if someone suggested that all of them were false? Regardless of what you may believe right now, there is much to be learned from a close examination of usury, interest, and usury law. When you finish reading this chapter, we think you will understand that not only are most Americans wrong in their beliefs about usury, but that they are *grievously* wrong.

What is Usury?
The average American today might define usury as "a rate of interest which is so high it is prohibited by law." This is the definition taught in most schools, it is also the definition given in most newer dictionaries, and it is the definition implied by the context in which *usury* is used in today's books, magazines and broadcasts.

But in spite of its widespread acceptance, this definition is incorrect. Spectacularly incorrect.

The noun, *usury*, is derived from the Latin word *usura*, an extension of two other Latin nouns, *usu* (or just *us*, rhyming with juice) and *uti*. In today's English we find stems from these Latin roots in utilize, utility, use, useful and usual. When a borrower of a thing pays the lender of that thing for "using up" the thing borrowed, the borrower is paying usury and the lender is receiving usury.

Usufrucht (today spelled *usufruct*), *usu* combined with *frucht*, meaning fruit, denotes "the fruit derived from a usage," meaning "the benefit enjoyed by the legal use of someone else's property." *Frucht*, in its modern spelling, is seen in expressions like "the fruits of crime must be returned to their rightful owners," and "we are entitled to keep the fruits of our labors."

In general, *usury* means using something up. In law or economics, *usury* is the name for the payment made in exchange for the benefit derived from "using up" a thing. The following hypothetical transactions are good illustrations of usury in practical settings.

A Rocky Start
A little boy loans his favorite rock to a schoolmate. At the end of the loan period, the schoolmate-borrower returns the rock to its owner, along with a fee in the amount and substance of one worm. The correct name for this fee, the compensation given by

the borrower to the lender for the borrower's possession or use of the rock, is usury. The amount and substance of the usury in this example, one worm, is also the profit derived from the transaction by the rock's owner.

Horse Sense
A man loans one of his horses to a neighbor for three years. At the end of the loan period, per agreement, the borrower gives the lender the following things:

    a) the borrowed horse;

    b) three more horses, each five years old; and,

    c) four pigs.

In a), the borrower is returning the main or principal thing, the capital item, less whatever of its original utility was used up during the loan period, to the lender.

In b), since a horse's productive life is about six years, and since the borrower used up about half the utility of the horse he borrowed, three additional horses, each with about one more year of utility left in him, are given to the lender, restoring the three horse-years of utility used up from the borrowed horse.

In c), the borrower "pays" a fee in the amount and substance of four pigs for the opportunity he had to derive fruit or benefit from his possession and use of the borrowed horse.

In this example, in legal and economic construction, a) and b) combined are a return of the capital, or repayment of the principal, of the loan. Four pigs, the profit derived from the transaction by the lender, is the usury.

Usury: A Moral and Private Matter
Notice that both these hypothetical neighbors — the owner of the horse and the borrower of the horse — are motivated by self-interest and act voluntarily.

The transaction is moral, ethical and correct in every sense. Both parties enter into it for the benefits they will enjoy. One neighbor wants the use of a horse; the other the fee the former will pay.

Although our hypothetical transactions described loans of a rock and a horse, and the usury that was charged and paid, the moral principles involved do not change if we were to describe loans of other objects, or if no usury was to be paid, or both.

When a thing owned by one person is loaned to another person, the morality of the relationship cannot rightfully be questioned by third parties as long as no force or fraud brought the lender and borrower to an agreement.

So if the thing lent is a rock, a horse, a cow, a bull, a lawnmower, or even the money to buy a lawnmower, the transaction — again, barring complaint of force or fraud — is moral, ethical, legal and beyond legitimate third-party intervention. This also means that the profit to the lender, which might seem "high" to some and "low" to others, is nobody else's business.

What About Interest?
Interest, in a strictly monetary sense, is related to the Latin word *terra*, meaning ground or earth. At death, one's remains may be *interred* at a cemetery. Interred means placed in the ground.

Interest, continuing in the monetary sense, describes a payment made for a particular kind of service rendered, a loan of money. This special association becomes crystal clear when we remember that money is a thing or things manufactured in a mint, *out of precious metal*, to be a medium of exchange. Payment for the use of money may be called interest because, in ancient times, *interessed* meant *among*. To be among those in a building, for example, meant you and your companions shared the blessings of safety and security provided by the building. This ancient term *interessed,* and its modern equivalent, *interest*, implies shared ownership or control of something. You could also think of lending money as much like placing the precious metal back *in the ground*. It becomes virtually inaccessible to the lender. If you *inter* your money in a bank, for example, the payment you receive is called <u>inter</u>-est. Or, you might think of it as "in terra est," meaning "In + the earth + it is."

Interest in a non-monetary sense denotes an involvement in an action, or, in a contract for the performance of an action. This form and usage of *interest* stems from the root *inter*, meaning "between."

For example, if you hold an interest in a corporation, you may own some or all of the corporation's stock. As a stockholder, you have a legal voice in the corporation's business. Before your corporate officers may act, they must obtain approval from you. You stand as a barrier *between* them and something they might want to do.

Therefore interest in its monetary sense is the same as usury. But interest in its non-monetary sense — for example, corporate ownership — is not even remotely related to usury.

Forms Of Payment

In regard to payment of usury or interest, the substance of payment could be coins of gold or silver, part of a crop, some cattle, or possibly a combination of these and other things of acknowledged worth.

Suppose the neighbors agree on a usury payment of two colts, but the colts die the day before the payment. The lender would be morally and legally obligated, under the laws of Moses — and of common sense — to accept payment in another substance or waive his claim to payment.

Today, courts often determine alternative forms of payment. Business disputes are often resolved in civil proceedings by juries which may award money, real property, or other things of acknowledged worth in lieu of whatever substance might have been agreed upon. Alternate forms of payment are appropriate because the law does not require or compel impossibilities.

Usury, Interest and the Free Market

As strange as it may first seem, loans are just a version of buying and selling. The thing sold in a loan is *time*. If it would take you six months to save enough money to take a vacation trip to Japan, and if you borrowed enough money to take the trip now, you might say you have borrowed or bought six months' time.

Like other traders, lenders vary their prices, their interest rates and collateral requirements, according to prevailing market conditions. In prosperous times, when their risk of loss is relatively low, lenders usually charge lower interest rates and require less collateral. In bad times, the reverse is true. Of course, in good and bad times, competition helps keep interest rates and collateral requirements at their lowest possible levels.

Lenders may suffer major losses if they make loans to individuals who fail to perform. Hence, lenders further adjust their interest rates and collateral requirements according to their perception of the unique risk characteristics of each loan. Nonetheless, in a free market a potential borrower may take his business elsewhere, if he is unhappy with the terms.

Crooks try to get loans so they can run off with the money. Sometimes they try to talk the lender out of his demand for collateral, or, failing that, they pledge collateral which isn't even their property. Lenders soon learn that to survive, they must stick to their lending criteria.

They must evaluate prospective borrowers without emotion, often suffering a reputation as cruel and insensitive. Without that self-control, however, they'd soon be broke, because it takes the interest from many good loans to recover the loss of principal of just one bad one.

Needless to say, the lenders we are defending here are in the business of lending something real — not the institutions that lend computer entry funny money.

So now let's look at a puzzling question. Since it is so reasonable to expect to pay someone for using up his property, and since decent behavior is highly esteemed among civilized people, why is usury now regarded as something bad, something sinful?

In Biblical Times

Scientific studies confirm that the region now generally embraced by Syria, Iraq, Israel, Lebanon and Jordan has always been hot and arid. Droughts spanning several years often devastated crops, cattle died and the people suffered.

The Holy Bible alludes to unscrupulous men of wealth visiting drought-stricken areas, not to aid their needy brothers, but to take their property. Perhaps feigning sympathy and understanding, a wealthy visitor might offer a *small, short-term* loan to a desperate farmer, explaining that maybe with this generosity the farmer and his family could survive until the drought ended and farm production returned to normal.

Scripture suggests that many farmers were compelled by circumstances to accept rapacious loans, even though the amount borrowed probably was barely enough to keep the farmer and his family alive for more than a few months, and even though he might have had to pledge his entire farm as collateral.

Of course, high collateral requirements for such loans would not be terribly unusual because high-risk borrowers have always had to meet high collateral requirements. But these were not ordinary lenders, nor were these ordinary loans, and certainly these were not ordinary times.

These lenders probably knew that if they kept the loan amount moderate and the loan period short, few borrowers would be able to pay back the loan per agreement. By implementing such a devious plan, a lender was almost certain to become the new owner of a farm for an amount which would normally be described as "a small down payment." And that is apparently what happened.

Form Versus Substance

Traditional American values hold that we should be good neighbors, good Samaritans, kind to our families and our neighbors near and far; that we should be fruitful and multiply, and exercise righteous dominion over everything we have. But our Judeo-Christian ideals also say we should be charitable, should "remember them that are in bonds" — not just in prison, but bound to other freedom-limiting devices too, such as drugs, perversions, poverty, etc. — and should be our brother's (and sister's) keeper.

In the Old Testament, the Bible condemns charging usury on loans to the poor. Scripture says nothing against usury *per se*, but trying to take advantage of the poor, those who should instead be given loving gifts.[1] Similarly, the Bible condemns charging usury on loans to family members, suggesting that family relationships should be based upon loving trust, not commerce.[2]

However, consider Proverbs 27:23: "Be thou diligent to know the state of thy flocks, and look well to thy herds." Also, the New Testament condemns the slothful servant who irresponsibly managed the master's money, and rewards the servants who used that money well.[3]

So, we can safely say that, except for the poor and family members, usury is not only permissible but encouraged. Moreover, by requiring collateral a lender manages his property well.

In those Biblical times of difficulty, the wealthy should have done everything within their power to ease the suffering of those in need. Instead, they prayed for a continuation of the drought so they could foreclose on the land and multiply their millions. Tragedy to a client meant profit to the lender.

In other words, the *form* of these loan arrangements was normal and ethical but their *substance* was malicious. Maliciousness is an attitude, a habit of thought, and Scripture condemns those with malicious attitudes: "for the Lord seeth not as a man seeth; for man looketh on the outward appearance, but the Lord looketh on the heart."[4] Also, "For as he thinketh in his heart, so is he: Eat and drink, saith he to thee; but his heart is not with thee."[5]

The point of all this is that what the Holy Bible condemns is not usury but *theft by fraud*.

What About Jubilee?

Today some people call for compulsory application of Jubilee principles to solve national monetary troubles. Often the same people call for "rigorous

---

[1] Exodus 22:25, Leviticus 25:35-38.

[2] Deuteronomy 23:19-21.

[3] Matthew 25:14-30 and Luke 19:12-27.

[4] 1 Samuel 16:7.

[5] Proverbs 23:7.

enforcement of the usury statutes" and a host of other inappropriate solutions to economic and monetary problems. Sadly, these people understand Jubilee no better than they understand usury.

Jubilee, a Biblical celebration which came every fifty years, was a time when debts were forgiven, lands were returned to their original (pre-Exodus) owners, and fields were left fallow for a growing season — in much the same way Sunday is the Christian day of worship, thanksgiving and rest.

However, confusion about Jubilee — and about our nation's economic problems — has caused a few well-meaning people to advocate inappropriate and unwholesome remedies for those problems.

The Ten Commandments are the bedrock of American law. Even atheists recognize that. However, compelled application of Jubilee would clash with the Ten Commandments.

Most often, people advocate compelled application of Jubilee principles to eliminate our huge national debt. But most of the present indebtedness of government and the private sector arose out of contracts that may be fraudulent. Our law says that contracts conceived in fraud are "stillborn" and are therefore dead. Performance under such contracts is not compelled by the law, so Jubilee principles, whether applied voluntarily or involuntarily, are not needed to solve "the problem of our national debt" or most private-sector debt.[6]

Next, the law can't justly penalize honest lenders or borrowers. If you loaned me $100 and I refused to pay you back, claiming Jubilee protection, I would be acting immorally. The Bible doesn't legalize theft, under Jubilee or anywhere else.

Also, if Jubilee principles were compelled under the law, lenders would raise interest rates sharply, just before the Jubilee year, to protect themselves from expected unpaid loans. Maybe they could buy insurance to prepare for that threat, but they would certainly pass the cost of it along to honest borrowers.

Lastly, some lenders and borrowers might enter loan agreements for periods ending just before the Jubilee year, and then enter new agreements for new loans (for the balance of the funds needed in the first place) *after* it. Of course, such arrangements would be inconvenient at the least. In short, to compel Jubilee principles by encasing them in laws, would be to make a travesty of the humane reason for them. Jubilee makes sense only when it is voluntary.

Christian Forgiveness — Moral and Legal
Suppose you lend something to a friend, and he becomes physically handicapped so he can't pay you back. It would be a gracious and Christian act for you to forgive the debt. If the law forced you to do so, despite the agreement with your friend, your "forgiveness" would be legalized theft, not Jubilee.

This common sense is the basis of our laws. If a man can't repay a loan because of an "act of God," the law would free him from repayment, because no one is accountable for acts of God. If an act of God takes my sight, for example, the courts would not compel me to keep repaying a loan. That is why, under the "reasonable man rule," the law expects lenders to carry insurance to protect themselves from acts of God.

What About Usury Statutes?
The name *usury statute* has misled people into thinking usury, per se, *must* be bad, because the obvious purpose of any law is to "prevent people from doing it." Well, maybe yes and maybe no.

Actually, usury statutes do not prevent usury at all. They simply forbid interest that is "too high," which falsely implies that interest payments which *are* "too high" *are* usury. And Americans have adopted this erroneous notion of usury. Remember that usury and interest are the same. To make usury illegal would be to make it illegal to charge interest for a loan.

Suppose I borrow a truck from you at a rental fee we both agree on, but the guy down the street thinks the fee is "too high." Is it any of his business? Of course not.

Suppose the guy down the street gets the neighbors together and they get a law passed that says any

---

[6] The mechanics of how contracts can be conceived in fraud is discussed in Chapter 11, *et seq.*

rental payment over a certain amount is illegal. If you and I go ahead with our agreement, you would be thrown into jail. That would not be Free Enterprise — it would be Fascism.

That is why usury statutes are immoral, unethical and noncommonsensical. In fact, that is true whenever the government intervenes to control how much I pay you for a service, be it a loan or a lawn mowing.

Usury laws, now on the books of all fifty states, are a stark testimony to moral decline in the American Republic.

The "Missing Dollar" Myth

Critics declare that interest on money is inherently bad because it's "impossible" to repay a loan if interest is charged. Their contorted reasoning goes something like this:

> Assume there is only one dollar in existence and I have it. You borrow that dollar from me for one year at 100% interest.
>
> One year later you give me the dollar back, but since the interest, also one dollar, is now due, and since there are no more dollars in existence, you can't pay. Now I have you at my mercy. I can legally foreclose on your property and take everything you have.

Our response:

First. The word *dollar* is a unit of measure, just like mile, ton, gallon, inch or ounce. There are never "only one" or "too few" or "too many" of them, and they are never "loaned out" or "lost" or "paid back." Fact.

Second. If there is one tractor in the world, and if I borrow it from you, agreeing to give you one more tractor as interest, rental, usury, or whatever you want to call it, I am an idiot. I have agreed to do the impossible. The law will not compel me to perform because I am certifiably insane. And, by the way, your agreement to this crazy arrangement means that you are also insane. Fact.

Third. If I borrow money or a tractor or a horse from you, and if I fail to pay you back either what I borrowed or the usury, or both, recourse and remedies are available to you at law. Let's say you sue me for $3,000 for breach of contract. I answer in court that I did my best to perform but things went bad and I don't have any money. The court awards you $4,000 *worth of apples* (which I grow in my orchard) as full settlement of your claim. The extra $1,000 in the award is to compensate you for the hassle of dealing with apples instead of cash. *Fact.*

Supporters of Usury Laws

Who supports usury laws? Totalitarian-minded people support them because they help "legalize" their interventions in the private, peaceful affairs of others. Adolf Hitler, Benito Mussolini *and most political figures in the United States today* fall into this category.

The mentally lazy support usury laws. So do the *ignorant*, which unfortunately means an embarrassingly large percentage of adults in the United States today. Also in this category are some patriotic citizens who, while striving to protect individual freedom, unwittingly endanger it by demanding "vigorous enforcement of the usury statutes."

Perhaps most conspicuously confused about these topics today are the so-called populists. Populism dates back to the late 1800s, when a political movement promoted public ownership of schools, railroads, utilities, and other socialistic controls on society. Fortunately for the United States, that movement died.

Italian dictator Benito Mussolini resurrected a version of populism in the 1920s. German dictator Adolf Hitler did the same in the 1930s. Americans who fought in World War II to stamp out Italy's Fascism[7] and Germany's National Socialism[8] did so because those systems were trying to enslave the world.

---

[7] See Glossary in Chapter 18 for definitions of *fascism* and other often-confused or misunderstood words.

[8] Hitler's *Nazi* Party might appeal to many uninformed Americans, just because of its name. In English it would be "The National Socialist Workers Party," and more than a few U.S. voters seem inclined toward a domestic "national socialist workers" party. See also Glossary.

In World War II we saw populism for what it really was and is, but a revival of populism is seen today in a fringe element of the movement to enforce the United States Constitution. Sadly, one so-called "conservative" leader says that "what America needs is a populist revival." Maybe he doesn't know he's actually calling for socialism. Among his top priorities is an end to what he calls "usurious" interest rates. There's no doubt that this man sincerely worries about the country, but the Socialist "solution" he proposes for a *symptom* of our nation's problems reveals a lack of knowledge of the fundamentals of freedom. Moreover, his attempt to cure a symptom instead of its underlying disease reveals a shallow perception of the nature of the nation's problems. Of course, it's not all bad for him — he has lots of company.

But bad leadership is not the only danger facing concerned Americans today.

A Trap For the Unwary
In some circles it is considered fashionable, even intellectual, to remark that "the meanings of words change with the times" or that "words which once had a bad connotation now have a good connotation, or vice versa." If you hear such a pronouncement, or if you see it in print, you may wish to consider it in light of the following.

A long time ago, *vulgar* is said to have meant routine, common, or everyday. Today, we are sometimes told, the word means crude, uncultured or uncivilized, which is only half correct. Long ago, when routine, common, everyday behavior *was* crude, uncultured and uncivilized, vulgar meant exactly the same thing it does today!

If someone tells you that freedom means to right to enjoy a 24-hour adult curfew, would you protest? What would you say if that person replied: "Well, freedom may have meant something else a long time ago, but, as you well know, the meanings of words change with usage, and today freedom means just what I say it does. Look at any dictionary if you don't believe me. Besides, that's what I learned in college, and I'm a lawyer."

If you want to hear someone actually say these things, just go into court, the higher the better. You will see smirking, arrogant brutes in expensive suits, who call themselves intellectuals and think their words mean whatever they want them to mean. They sincerely believe that their definitions are the definitions everyone else must use! Their pompous attitude is the hallmark of the real brutes of our generation, and we would be well advised to stand apart from them.

Verbicide
As we mentioned earlier, a growing body of law professionals and others have observed that the nation, its laws, and its traditional values are under attack. The attack is neither physical nor violent — yet — but it is just as life-threatening to our culture and our civilization. The attack involves a quiet but deliberate manipulation of the definitions of words, especially words which are used in law or in law-related fields. The sabotage often occurs when a legal fact is described colloquially, and then the colloquialism, through repetition (in the press and by the citizens), becomes the new legal fact. This meddling with definitions could ultimately destroy our nation. This dangerous activity is called verbicide. George Orwell wasn't the first to understand that if there are no words for certain things, then you can't think them.

Verbicide Through the Centuries
Propagandists throughout history have tried to conquer through manipulation. They know that "good" words can trick good people into doing bad things. Conversely, "bad" words can persuade good people not to do good things.

Today, all over the world, a verbicidal (semantic) war is being waged against individual liberty and sacred institutions.

Notice, especially in the United States, the gradual manipulation of our understanding of law, the subtle changes in the law textbooks, the definitions in law dictionaries, and even in the wording of the laws themselves.

Even the definitions of common words have been affected. In every case we know, the words that support freedom are the biggest victims.

Some of these changes pollute the definition by reversing the true meaning of the word. We have never observed a definition changed in a way which strengthened its use in a pro-liberty argument.

It should come as no surprise then, that there seem to be curious ties between some publishers and the "intellectuals" who revise and update these dictionaries, and the leadership of the schools which educated these "intellectuals."

Indeed, some American investigators have traced these ominous word games to the early years of the 19th century, and even back as far as the earliest days of the Republic.

A Warning to Truth Seekers

Americans should withdraw their support from individuals or organizations which rant about how "we are a Christian nation," but lust to use force or the threat of force or intimidation to intervene in the peaceful, private affairs of their neighbors, often through usury statutes.

Intelligent Americans should look again at those who profess to support our nation's Judeo-Christian ideals but whose political goals reveal an opposite philosophy, and who reveal themselves to be pawns of those who would destroy this country.

Those who support law and order should continuously review their actions to make sure they are not misled, through momentary confusion, to support a destructive program.

•

"Money, when considered as the fruit of many years' industry, as the reward of labor, sweat and toil, is not to be sported with, or trusted to the airy bubble of paper currency."

Thomas Paine (1737 - 1809)

"The official inflation statistics do not include the decline in quality of goods and services. Poorly built homes and new cars, poor education and other public services — and more — are not figured in official figures. If you include declining quality as an inflationary factor, a good rule of thumb is that the actual inflation rate is twice the official rate."

George Steve, associate of Franz Pick, June 27, 1980.
From Blanchard (see Appendix A, Gold Newsletter)

"We are in danger of being overwhelmed with irredeemable paper, mere paper, representing not gold nor silver; no sir, representing nothing but broken promises, bad faith, bankrupt corporations, cheated creditors and a ruined people."

Daniel Webster (1782 - 1852), speech in the U.S. Senate, 1833

11

Inflation
Part 1: Introduction

INFLATION isn't discussed as much as football and the movies — but it's close. Most people think inflation means this:

> A rise in the general price level, caused by a relative increase in the supply of money and credit.

While this definition might be correct as far as it goes, it doesn't go far enough. In fact, it falls very short. Possibly criminally short.

The roots of inflation are hidden from public view today by the dominant media's imprecise use of money-related words and phrases. In previous chapters, we looked at some of the most important English words and phrases related to money. Now, because you better understand the basic terminology, you are well prepared to examine inflation. Welcome to World War III.

Etymology of *inflation*
Inflate stems from a past-participle form of the Latin *inflare*, which means (to) blow into or puff up. A variation of this root is found in *flatulence*, wherein *flat* means windy. The root *flat* is also used in the Latin word *flatus* (with a long "a"), which means breath.

The Innocent Definition
A rise in the *general* price level is usually the result of an increase in the supply of money or credit. Consider a familiar example, a county fair at which an antique vehicle is auctioned. If the population of the county has enjoyed several prosperous years and saved some money, the successful bidder will probably pay a somewhat high price for the antique vehicle. Conversely, if the county has experienced a few bad years, and if people necessarily have had to rely on savings to make ends meet, the reduced funds available for bidding would probably reduce the purchase price. This is an example of how the supply of money and credit can influence prices paid in the marketplace.

Consider a corollary situation in which the supply of goods and services — not the money and credit — is reduced. People who really want those goods and services would bid against one another, which would raise the selling price. For instance, at a sports event, the sole in-stadium soft drink vendor charges perhaps twice as much as a nearby supermarket. Many fans are willing to pay the vendor's higher price rather than walk several blocks to a market for a lower price.

However clear the above examples may be, none of them relates to inflation because inflation causes a *permanent* rise in the *general* price level, not a *temporary* price rise in *narrow or isolated* markets.

What, then, is "a rise in the general price level?" The *general* price level of a community, county, state, or nation is determined by monitoring the prices voluntarily paid for a long list of products and services.

Remember, inflation is a *cause* of a rise in the general price level, much like rain is a *cause* of wet streets.

Always remember this common-sense rule:

> *Wet streets don't cause rain and price increases don't cause inflation.*

Three major influences

The three most important factors influencing the general price level of a society are the:

1. Supply of money and credit (purchasing media).
2. Supply of goods and services.
3. Availability of people to buy the goods and services.

Here are three circumstances, any one of which can cause an *increase* in the general price level:

A. The supply of purchasing media *increases*.

B. The supply of goods and services *decreases*.

C. The population (demand) *increases*.

Here are three circumstances which can cause a *decrease* in the general price level:

A. The supply of purchasing media *decreases*.

B. The supply of goods and services *increases*.

C. The population (demand) *decreases*.

Since the population and supplies of goods and services are continuously fluctuating, a certain amount of "jiggle" will usually be seen in a graph of any society's general price level. The jiggle isn't as important as the trend.

A Classical Study

Since productive people almost always find better (less wasteful) ways to do things, in a simple trading society, one which doesn't use money or other media of exchange, productivity almost always increases. As individual or social productivity increases, everyone's standard of living improves.

Each of us has his own "personal computer" called our brain. When we use our "computer" properly, our standard of living, from generation to generation, steadily improves because we continually find less-wasteful ways to do things.

As long as the availability of our purchasing media remains relatively stable, which it does when we use gold or silver coins, prices tend to decline from generation to generation, in spite of the increasing demand for products and services from an ever-larger population.

If you live in a society which adheres to traditional American values, as you grow older the prices you pay for almost everything would be relatively lower and your standard of living would be relatively higher.[1] When you reach old age, your standard of living would be highest because the prices of almost everything would be at or nearly the lowest you have ever seen.

Present world circumstances suggest we *Homo sapiens* have done something radically wrong.

History of Purchasing-Media

In past centuries, purchasing media were slaves, stones, prisoners of war, sticks of wood, cows, weapons and ammunition, sea shells, bones, tools, cigarettes, metal coins, skins of animals, nylon stockings, dead rats, women and a host of other interesting and inherently valuable things. Nevertheless, the most widely accepted purchasing media were paper receipts for precious-metal coins which had been stored in a safe place.

In this country's earliest years, coins of gold and silver quickly became the most popular purchasing

---

[1] Traditional American values, via their *laissez faire* economic climate, also foster investment (capital formation) rather than consumption, thereby protecting natural resources. If you want to see an environmental disaster of monumental proportions, visit the "former" Soviet Union, the world's preeminent "scientific socialist" country for at least seventy years.

media. Later, with improvements in printing technology, paper receipts for the coin replaced it as the preferred purchasing medium. Paper receipts (certificates and bills), used *as* money, are correctly called *money substitutes*. Still later, with the advent of the computer, electronic impulses began to replace the paper receipts. Therefore, electronic impulses are sometimes used *as* money.

We Became Apathetic
Over the years, with each improvement in technology and in our standard of living, we became apathetic. We failed to pay attention when certain government and industry leaders began to tout the virtues of a "flexible" currency, which some of us thought meant portable or convenient to use.

The men who smoothly used the word flexible also smoothly told us that "the dollar is as good as gold," which we thought meant that the paper receipts we carried were more or less "the same" as gold (or silver).

Then these men or their replacements, as political figures or lions of industry, told us that "credit" was even better than "paper money," that "credit" could be electronically transferred around the world in seconds, could never be lost at sea or burned up in a fire, could never (well, almost never) be stolen, and would therefore always be "safe." Electronic "funds" transfer, they said, was here to stay. Well, maybe yes and maybe no.

A One-Minute Course in
American Monetary History
The Founders of our wonderful Republic despised even the *idea* of "paper money." They built a mint in Philadelphia and manufactured our nation's first gold coins and silver coins. These and other official coins were the nation's primary purchasing media for about 100 years. Our burgeoning prosperity and high quality of life were the envy of the world. There were adjustments in our economy but they quickly corrected themselves.

In 1862, President Abraham Lincoln printed some paper currency which eventually was redeemed in coins. You could turn the paper currency in to a bank and you'd get an appropriate number of gold or silver coins. Our prosperity and high quality of life continued to amaze the world.

By the early 1900s, people had become accustomed to the compactness and light weight of paper currency. They began to leave almost all of their gold coins and silver coins in the care of their local banker. Our prosperity, while still great, began to be hampered by government controls and restraints.

On "Black Tuesday," October 29, 1929, bankers suddenly shut off the credit they'd extended to stock purchasers. The equity markets collapsed and the Great Depression began.

In 1933, the Franklin Roosevelt administration, using the Great Depression as an excuse, said private ownership of gold was "contrary to public policy" and issued a decree which made it illegal for most Americans to own gold or gold certificates. The gold certificates and coin were replaced by silver certificates, or by United States Notes, or by Federal Reserve Notes, or by silver coin. Although we were beginning to recover from the depression, the foundations of our economy began to show signs of severe weakness.

In 1963, the federal government changed the wording on some of the paper currency we were accustomed to seeing. The nation's paper currency, our receipts for the gold coin and silver coin we'd stored with bankers, was changed. The wording on new issues no longer said anything about being able to turn them in so we could get our coins back. Currency bearing the new wording was introduced into circulation as the currency bearing the old wording was withdrawn.

The banks, from 1963 onward, could legally keep our gold and silver coins. Where before there was stability, today our economy convulses from boom to bust, from growth to recession.

In 1968, the government stopped honoring the receipts they'd given to people who had stored silver bullion in the United States Treasury.

Today, people don't know they've been robbed. They've forgotten about the gold coins and silver coins their grandparents stored for them in the banks, and cycles of recession and boom now seem to be naturally-occurring phenomena.

In about eighty years, we, as a people, have experienced a revolution in what we use as purchasing media. We began our monetary history, as a nation, with the exclusive use of gold and silver coins. Then we began using a mixture of precious-metal coins and redeemable paper currency. Later we were shuffled into the use of only one kind of precious-metal coin and one less kind of redeemable paper currency. Still later, we were manipulated into using only base-metal coins and non-redeemable paper tokens.

Today, we use metal tokens, paper tokens, and imaginary "electronic funds." The economy appears healthy but "We, the People," are edgy, the fabric of our society is being torn asunder by a thousand plagues. We are up to our sideburns in all kinds of criminal behavior, and we are witnessing the steady deterioration of the family, our culture, the church, our educational system, and, to some extent, even our military organizations.

Indeed, the very foundation of the Republic, the United States Constitution, is largely unknown to the voters and a thorn in the side of most politicians and many leaders of industry.

Could there be a direct relationship between our present problems and what we use as purchasing media? The most-serious investigators think so, and we believe there is a parallel between the sickness in our society and a sickness that afflicts a human body: a disease called syphilis.

The Symptom is Not the Disease

Syphilis is a deadly, venereal disease. The syphilis spirochete, a bacterium or "bug," takes several years to multiply enough to be fatal to the victim. Death is preceded by a devastating decline in the victim's physical and mental health. Madness, compounded by excruciating physical pain, precedes death.

Most victims of syphilis, within a year of contracting the disease, develop a kind of "cold sore" or chancre on or near their upper or lower lip. In early times, victims would apply an ointment to the chancre, and then breathe a sigh of relief as it slowly disappeared. Later, however, they'd die — of syphilis.

In the 1930s, medical science discovered that with syphilis, the chancre was just a symptom of the disease; researchers were astonished to discover that the chancre would go away of its own accord, whether ointment was applied or not.

The symptom went away but the disease continued its deadly advance. Syphilis: fatal unless treated properly.

Inflation is a lot like syphilis. The main symptom of inflation is a permanent rise in the general price level. As with syphilis, the symptom of inflation can go away — prices may remain steady for a while, or even decline — but, without proper treatment, the inflation disease will eventually kill.

Inflation can surely cause the death of a nation, and a society, and a culture and its people. You, I, and our children.

Inflation — Debasement of the Purchasing Media

Earlier in this chapter we saw that one cause of a *permanent* rise in the *general* price level of a society might be a relative and permanent decrease in the supply of goods and services in that society.

Another cause might be a relative and permanent increase in demand for those goods and services by a larger population.

A third cause could be a relative and permanent increase in the supply of money and credit in a society.

Supplies of goods and services, however, never decrease permanently. Drought, flood, pestilence and other transitory events cause only *temporary* reductions in the availability of foodstuffs, for example. A fire might destroy a lumber mill, *temporarily* reducing the availability of lumber. Other transient phenomena may cause equally transient decreases in the availability of other goods and services. But never, in all recorded history, has the availability of goods and services *permanently* declined. Therefore we can safely say it is highly improbable that a decrease in the availability of goods and services is a major factor in the permanent rise in the general price level we've seen in the United States during the past century.

A larger population might increase demand for a relatively fixed supply of goods and services, but throughout recorded history, especially in this nation's first hundred years, no permanent increase in the general price level was observed.

Indeed, prices tended to decline, or quality rose notably, in spite of increased demand from an expanding population, because that population continuously improved its productivity. Healthy people learn from their mistakes, and since most people in any society are reasonably healthy, their productivity improves more rapidly than does their demand for goods and services.

Thus we can eliminate an expanding population as a primary cause of the permanent increase in the general price level we've noted in the United States in recent years.

By a process of elimination, we see that the permanent rise in the general price level of this country *must* have been caused by a permanent increase in the supply of our purchasing media.

Our Purchasing Media
Today we realize that the total purchasing power of our country is far greater than the amount of paper currency and coins in circulation; that credit is the largest component of our nation's overall purchasing power.

We also know that permanent increases in the amount of extended credit have the same impact on the general price level as might a permanent increase in the amount of money (coins of gold or silver) or money substitutes (clad coins and paper currency) in circulation.

In the United States today, since the most widely used purchasing media are credit and Federal Reserve Tokens (themselves a form of credit), in that order of importance, we should ask ourselves three critically important questions:

1. How is the supply of purchasing media increased?
2. Who is causing this increase?
3. Why are they causing the increase?

Now that we have some good questions, let's see whether we can come up with some equally good answers.

Debasement of Purchasing Media
In times past, counterfeiters manufactured fake coins and spent them into circulation, achieving a profit in their purchases of goods. Other crooks would hollow out a gold coin, replace the removed gold with lead, and pass the debased coin in trade at its face value. The removed gold would be accumulated, eventually to be exchanged for more gold coins, after which the cycle would begin anew. Counterfeiting and debasing are means of stealing. The law calls these crimes *theft by fraud*.

Bogus paper currency is produced by counterfeiters who are good at engraving. But while the mischief of a few home-grown domestic counterfeiters could hurt the standard of living of others, it is inconsequential compared to the counterfeiting by government.

In World War II, Adolf Hitler's agents produced plates for manufacturing counterfeit American currency. Hitler's plan was to use bogus American currency discreetly to buy much-needed war materials in the United States and elsewhere. If his counterfeiting operation were discovered, he planned to print tons of the illegitimate currency and inject it into the American economy — to cause a sudden and permanent rise in prices and an equally sudden and permanent misallocation of goods and services, both of which would have disrupted our nation's war effort.

Some readers may recall that a special branch of the United States government was created to counter this threat from the Nazis. This special branch was the Economic Warfare Division, a part of the nation's defense establishment, then called the War Department.[2]

---

[2] The German manufacture of bogus currency was conducted under the Nazi's "Operation Bernard" and involved U.S. $100 bills and U.K. Five-Pound notes.

In recent years a new form of counterfeiting has emerged. Criminals skilled at computer programming hack into bank computer records by telephone. By manipulating a bank's records and computer programs, crooks can cause the bank to disburse non-existent "funds" (credit) automatically and without much chance of early detection.

This credit, often in the form of deposits to an existing (albeit temporary) checking account, allows crooks to buy things in the marketplace. They write real checks backed by imaginary deposits.

This activity is *electronic theft by fraud*.

As we move to Chapter 12, which is Part Two of our discussion of inflation, please remember these conventional criminal tactics so you can compare them to what has been made "legal" by acts of your employees: members of the United States Congress.

•

"I sincerely believe . . . that banking establishments are more dangerous than standing armies, and that the principle of spending money to be paid by posterity under the name of funding is but swindling futurity on a large scale."

President Thomas Jefferson to John Taylor, 1816

"Specie is the most perfect medium because it will preserve its own level; because, having intrinsic and universal value, it can never die in our hands, and it is the surest resource of reliance in time of war."

President Thomas Jefferson to John Wayles Eppes, 1813

"A government that robs Peter to pay Paul can always depend upon the support of Paul."

George Bernard Shaw (1856 - 1950)

12

Inflation
Part 2: Modern Mechanisms

WHEN you ask people how they think the federal government raises its operating funds, often they answer, "Through taxes." Actually, however, only part of the federal government's operating funds is obtained through anyone's payment of taxes.

Most financial professionals will tell you that today's federal government raises a substantial percentage of its operating "funds" through the "sale" of "bonds." Notice that we enclosed "funds" and "sale" and "bonds" in quotation marks. We did that because none of those words is appropriate to describe what the government is actually doing.

Government workers, certain bankers, and other Insiders use *those* words because, if they used the right words to tell what they are doing, they would soon be serving long terms in federal penitentiaries.

We'll explain this later but for now let's pretend we're a fly on the wall of the Oval Office in the White House. Sssh! The President is sitting at his desk. Suppose you were the President and you "needed" operating funds. How would you raise them?

Tricks of the Trade
You have your secretary type the following sentence on a blank sheet of paper:

I, John Doe, as President of the United States of America, hereby and herewith pledge the wealth of the People of this nation as collateral for a loan to the federal government of the United States of America in the amount of ONE MILLION DOLLARS ($1,000,000).

After signing the document you give it to your Treasury Secretary who, in turn, notifies the banking community that you want to sell a bond. The bond is the collateral you are offering. You want the bankers to bid on how much interest they are going to charge you.

In a few days the bids are in. The lowest bidder is the Federal Reserve Bank of New York (which we'll abbreviate "FRB"), which has said it will charge you only 7% per year. What a great deal! You notify the FRB that they've won the bid and that you want the money in one week.

They say, "Okay, Mr. President." And you smile. You love your job.

Ordering the "Money"
You deliver your bond to the FRB and they hold it as an asset, collateral for their loan of one million dollars to you. The FRB then calls the United States government's Bureau of Engraving and Printing (which we'll call the BEP) and orders 50,000 Twenty-

Dollar bills. A week later — barely dry — the bills are delivered to you at the White House and you use them to pay for a federal highway project.

Each year, from now on, you will have to pay the FRB interest payments of $70,000, which is 7% of $1,000,000.

About thirty days after printing the 50,000 Twenty-Dollar bills, the BEP sends their statement of charges to the FRB. How much does the BEP charge to print 50,000 Twenty-Dollar bills? About $3,000.

In other words the FRB pays about $3,000 to buy something which, when it is loaned to the government, will bring them $70,000 per year in interest payments, *forever*. Not a bad return on their one-time investment of $3,000, wouldn't you say?

Of course, as President, you don't have to worry about making the interest payments. You use tax revenue, most of which you extract from the people who work and create the wealth.

The "one million dollars" you borrowed from the FRB is "one million dollars" of additional, extended credit in the nation's economy. Every time the government borrows this way, the amount borrowed is added to the national debt.

This is the primary way our national debt grew to its present size.

The total national debt today, our nation's accumulated net *deficits*, is reported to be about five trillion dollars. In the United States, a trillion is one million million, which means the national debt is about $5,000,000,000,000, or $5 trillion. However, that $5 trillion is only the debt which is due and payable within twelve months. Our total long-term debt is reliably estimated to be more than $19 trillion.

This debt of $19 trillion dollars is called "mostly unfunded" because Congress hasn't yet figured out where it's going to get all that money. The amount needed works out to about $71,000 for every man, woman and child in the United States, about 265 million people — every one of whom is born screaming about it!

If you are married, and if you and your spouse have two children, the four of you owe the Insiders about $287,000. The Insiders expect our children and our children's children to pay off the national debt. Put another way, the Insiders expect that *our* children will pay $19,000,000,000,000 to *their* children.

But that won't happen, because the law will protect us.

Fractional Reserves and Loans of Nothing

We all know that banks seek deposits they can lend to borrowers. This is the way banks have made their money since they first started doing business, but many people mistakenly believe this is *still* the way banks make most of their money. It isn't, not really. Let's learn now about the stupendous prestidigitation[1] of "fractional reserves."

Funds deposited in a checking account are referred to as demand deposits, meaning that the funds can be taken out of the account "on demand" of the account holder.

When funds are placed in a savings account, or when they are given to a bank in exchange for a certificate of deposit, they are called time- or long-term deposits.

Congress, through various banking Acts, has made it legal for banks to loan something they don't really have. Today, if a bank can show that it has funds in a *demand* deposit, for example, it is permitted to make loans of up six times that amount.

As we have seen, the banks don't have any *money* in any account — because there is no *money* in circulation — but they *pretend* that they have money on deposit, and they *pretend* to loan six times that amount to borrowers. This is the reality of operating a bank today under the constraints of a "sixteen percent reserve of demand deposits." On the other hand, borrowers are not permitted to *pretend* to pay the "money" back.

If a bank can show that it has funds in *long-term* deposits, Congress has enacted laws which allow the bank to *pretend* to loan up to *sixteen* times that amount. This is the reality of operating a bank today under the constraints of a "six percent reserve of time

---

[1] Trickery, sleight-of-hand.

deposits." Again, borrowers are not permitted to *pretend* to pay the "loans" back.

Since it is so important, we want to cover this "fractional reserve" magic in just a bit more detail. We want you to understand not only the *effect* of its operation, but we also want you to be aware of the day-to-day mechanics of it.

Mechanics of Fractional Reserves

When someone deposits one thousand dollars in a checking account, the bank may loan all but sixteen percent of that amount. This is an example of a bank keeping a sixteen percent reserve of its demand deposits.

When someone deposits one thousand dollars in a savings account or purchases a $1,000 certificate of deposit, the bank may loan all but six percent of that amount. This is an example of a bank keeping a six percent reserve of its time- or long-term deposits.

Many people who hear about these reserve requirements don't see anything wrong with them. On the contrary, they think that these reserve requirements are a protection to depositors; that by restricting the bank from loaning *all* the money its customers have deposited, the bank will almost always have enough money on hand to cover occasional withdrawals. This line of thinking is perfectly logical, and it is valid as far as it goes. Unfortunately, it doesn't go far enough.

Let's look at some numbers now, tracking one thousand dollars deposited in a savings account. Assume, for example, you are the owner of a new bank and you open your doors for business on January 1st. A friend of yours, Mr. Zulu, comes in to open a savings account. Once he's filled out your forms, he makes his initial deposit of $1,000. You pay 5% interest per year on savings deposits.

A few minutes later, Mrs. Able, also a friend of yours, comes in to see about a loan. You know you are allowed to loan up to $940 to her because you have $1,000 in a time deposit and the law says your reserve of time deposits needs to be only six percent, or $60. And as chance would have it, Mrs. Able wants to borrow exactly $940 for one year.

You give her some forms to fill out, which she does. Your review of the information on those forms tells you that she is a good risk, so you decide to make the loan. You give her $940 in cash. You charge fifteen percent simple interest per year on loans.

Now let's assume you did no more business through the year, and next January 1st Mrs. Able comes back in to pay off her loan. She gives you back the $940, the principal of the loan, and she also gives you an additional $141 in interest.

A little later that day, Mr. Zulu comes in to close out his savings account. You give him back his $1,000, and you give him $50 as his earned interest for the year. You got that $50 from Mrs. Able's $141.

You close your bank, observing that you have made a net profit of $91 ($141 - $50 = $91) from your banking operations that year.

But this example is a trick. It's a trick because it doesn't even *hint* at how banks operate today. If you believed it was a fairly accurate description of bank operations today, you are probably living in a fractional-reserve paradise.

A Real World Bank of Today

Let's say you open your own new bank on January 1st. Your first ten customers open checking accounts, each depositing $100. Ten deposits of $100 each total $1,000. Because "the law" requires you to keep a reserve of sixteen percent of demand deposits, you are allowed to loan up to $840 of the total of $1,000 deposited in these checking accounts.

Later that day, Mrs. Able, one of those who opened a checking account, comes back in to see about a loan of $840. She's willing to pay your interest charges, fifteen percent per year, and when you ask her if she has an account at your bank, she answers Yes. You explain that you asked that question because you like to know something about your loan customers, how they handle their money, etc., and that for this reason, you are not too interested in making loans to people who don't have accounts at your bank.

But, you go on to explain, since she does have an account, you'll go ahead and make the loan. Mrs. Able thanks you, explaining that she understands your policy, that she thinks it makes sense, and that if she were a banker she'd probably implement the same policy.

As you prepare the Note for Mrs. Able's signature, you casually ask if she has her checkbook handy. She says Yes, that she always carries it wherever she goes. You ask her for a deposit slip, saying "I'll take care of it this way." She innocently gives you a deposit slip, thinking you are such a nice man, that you'll save her even the need to endorse one of your bank's checks by simply making a deposit of the $840 directly into her checking account.

A few minutes later you return to your desk and give Mrs. Able her deposit slip, which is now imprinted with today's date and "$840." You've made a "deposit" directly to her account, and all she has to do is add $840 to the running balance she carries in her check register. Mrs. Able is pleased about the courteous and efficient service you've given her. You are, however, even more pleased.

Loaning Loans
You are more pleased than Mrs. Able might ever suspect. You know that when you made that deposit of $840 to her checking account, you simultaneously increased the total of your bank's demand deposits from $1,000 (which came in through the ten original depositors, including Mrs. Able) to $1,840.

Now you can make another loan to another borrower, this time "lending" most of Mrs. Able's $840 which you just "deposited" in her checking account. Since "the law" requires that you keep a reserve of sixteen percent of demand deposits, you are permitted to loan up to eighty-four percent of the $840 you just "added" to Mrs. Able's checking account. Eighty-four percent of $840 is about $700. (A requirement to keep a reserve of sixteen percent is the same as permission to loan eighty-four percent.)

About an hour after Mrs. Able leaves, another of your original checking-account holders, Mrs. Baker, comes in to see about a loan. Mrs. Baker wants to borrow $700, and because she has an account with your bank, and because she looks like a good credit risk, you make the loan. You use one of her deposit slips to "deposit" the $700 directly into her checking account.

Shortly after Mrs. Baker leaves your bank, another of your ten original checking-account holders, Mrs. Charles, comes in to see about a loan of $575. You can make this "loan" because $575 is slightly less than eighty-four percent of the $700 you just "deposited" in Mrs. Baker's account.

You do your cute deposit-slip routine with Mrs. Charles, making a "deposit" of $575 to her checking account.

A little later, Mrs. Davis, another of your original checking account depositors, comes in to see about a loan. How large can this loan be? "The law" says it can be eighty-four percent of the $575 you just "deposited" in Mrs. Charles' account, and eighty-four percent of $575 is about $480.

Let's say you "loan" $480 to Mrs. Davis, "depositing" the "money" to her checking account.

Now would be a good time to look back on the day's events.

You received $1,000 in demand deposits. Your first "loan" was in the amount of $840, the second was in the amount of $700, the third was in the amount of $575, and the fourth was in the amount of $480. $840 plus $700 plus $575 plus $480 equals $2,595, or almost $2,600. $2,600 is almost three times the $1,000 placed in those checking accounts by the original depositors.

If we continued our sequence beyond these four "loans," the size of each succeeding "loan" would be smaller than the one immediately preceding it. If we continued our sequence until the amount loanable (eighty-four percent of the amount of the immediately preceding "loan") reached $1, our total of "loans" made possible by the original deposits of $1,000 would be very close to $6,000, six times the amount of the original deposits.

One year's interest at fifteen percent APR (annual percentage rate) on $840 is about $126, but on $6,000 it is about $900.

Did you know about this multiple-loan capability? If you didn't, you might think a sixteen percent reserve requirement means that if $1,000 is deposited in a checking account, only $840 of it could be loaned, and that the interest paid by borrowers would come to about $126. *That's what the public and much of the business and professional community thinks.*

Sometimes when we try to explain this multiple-loan business, people get irritated with us. They think we're wasting their time telling them something which is just a minor aspect of the way one industry happens to work. They sometimes angrily ask us, "What's so important about all this, anyway? What's the big deal about fractional reserves? So the bank makes $900 in interest instead of $126; what's so significant about that?"

Can You Really Borrow a Loan?
If you try to explain these things to a neighbor, for example, you may become frustrated by his lack of interest in what you say. But you might do well to stop and consider his perspective. First, he sees only the difference between $900 and $126. He also sees that this difference isn't coming from just one borrower, and that none of the several borrowers is complaining. Your neighbor, however, by looking at just the interest paid, overlooks the most important aspects of fractional-reserve banking techniques.

First, your neighbor misses the fact that this multiple-loan activity of banks is not really loans of money but loans of *credit* ("pretend" money). This credit being pumped into the nation's economy is the *cause* of a permanent rise in the general price level, and remember that a permanent increase in the general price level of a society is the *symptom* of inflation.

Second, remember that only part of the increase of the general price level is due to banks' pretended loans to private-sector borrowers. Another part of the increase is caused by banks' pretended loans to government.

The combined effect of all those pretended bank loans is the root cause of inflation. "Loans" to private-sector entities plus "loans" to government entities combine to increase the supply of money and credit, thereby producing what we call inflation, a permanent rise in the general price level.

So, *the fundamental cause* of inflation is "fractional-reserve" banking, made "legal" by the United States Congress.

Indeed, let's look at some other things the banks do.

Dealing With a Loan Officer
Bank employees, particularly loan officers are, in the main, low paid and low ranking people on a bank's totem pole of authority. Loan officers are usually nice people but the bank treats them like real "nobodies." They are low paid, just like other bank employees, because low-paid employees have little wiggle room, and can be easily intimidated by their superiors. Loan officers soon learn to not question the bank's policies. Banks may even *prefer* insecure or immature loan officers because insecure or immature people are less likely to suspect they're being used. Even if they do, they probably won't have the courage to ask questions.

Most people think the senior officers of a bank are important, and that the tellers are people who count, because they are the ones people see. In fact, they are regular nine-to-five workers much like the rest of the work force in a community. The people who really do count in any bank are the stockholders, and the people who count most are often the stockholders who are also members of the bank's board of directors.

Loan officers, even if they are called Vice President, do as they are told or suddenly find themselves on the street. They are instructed to tell borrowers and potential borrowers certain things, and if they don't follow those instructions to the letter, they are terminated. Loan officers are the chief *patsies* for the bank's stockholders.

Often they don't tell the truth. They know that much of what they are told to say is false and makes no sense. But most important, some of the things they say help cover up a monstrous crime, the crime of *theft by fraud.*

Let's look at a typical day in the life of a typical banker and analyze some of his statements and actions.

Do You Have an Account Here?
Let's pretend *you* are a bank's loan officer and I tell you I want to borrow $50,000. You ask me whether I have an account at your bank, and I say, "Yes, a checking account."

If I ask you *why* you want to know whether I had an account at your bank, you would probably say what you've been told to say. "Well, we like to know who we're dealing with, you know. We can't go around making loans to just anybody. We want to know a person's track record, you know, like how he manages his money and like that. We prefer to loan to our present accounts because we know them and know how they handle their money. We don't like to make loans to people we don't know. You can understand that, I'm sure."

Sure.

This statement by a loan officer is a *smokescreen* but most borrowers, naïvely believing that today's banks are legitimate lending institutions, don't question the truth of it. (Admittedly, some loan officers also believe this statement is legitimate but we'll soon see why it's not only not legitimate, it doesn't even make sense.)

Think for a moment.

Do you recall ever being asked that question — "Do you have an account here?" — by any other institution where you tried to do business?

Has any gas station attendant ever required that you have an account there or be a previous customer, before he agrees to sell you gas?

Has a department store sales clerk ever told you that, if you've never bought anything at that store before, or if you don't have an account there, they don't want to do business with you?

We think it's likely your answers are No, No and No.

Isn't it also true that in most other businesses — we're tempted to write *all* — when they find out you don't have a charge account with them or have never done business with them before, they treat you royally in hopes you'll become a regular customer? Don't most businesses make a special effort to *attract* people who have never been to their store before or who don't (yet) have an account at their store?

Of course they do, because they are in business to do business, and that means expanding their customer base. The last thing a real business would do is discourage or deny business from new customers. What kind of business doesn't want to do business?

In fact, if any other business behaved like the banks, most of us would run for the exit. Nobody does it — *except the banks.*

Why?

Some readers might say, "Well, banks loan money, and they operate on a small spread between what they take in from interest on loans and what they pay out in interest to savers. They have to watch their money carefully because it takes the interest payments from a lot of good loans to cover the loss of the principal of just one bad one."

Well, there's truth in that response but keep in mind that a bank investigates a potential borrower's financial picture, evaluating his assets, liabilities, earnings and disposable income, as well as maturity and credit record; and possibly even checks for a criminal record. No bank would loan even a small sum to anyone who failed to meet all the bank's requirements for personal responsibility and ability to repay the loan. So the question, "Do you have an account here?" is not related to a potential borrower's creditworthiness. *The question obviously relates to something other than a potential customer's ability to repay a loan.*

Yes, banks used to operate on a small spread between loan income and payouts for deposits but that is no longer true. Let's take an even closer look at the internal operation of a bank.

Variations On a Theme
Remember how banks use fractional-reserve techniques to pyramid their ability to make loans? Remember how demand deposits can be lent some six times over and how time deposits can be loaned some sixteen times over?

Let's say you are a banker and your bank runs an advertisement in your local newspaper, soliciting new accounts, especially savings accounts. A stock broker responds to the advertisement and deposits $10,000 in a savings account. To show your appreciation for his business you give him an electric alarm clock — which you bought (in 100-unit lots) for about $2 apiece. Because of fractional-reserve banking laws, you are now able to make a series of loans of up to $160,000, but to simplify this example we'll have you make *one* loan of the entire amount to just one person.

A little while later a businessman, Mr. Factory Owner, comes into your bank to see about a twelve-month loan of $160,000.

You go through your little song-and-dance about "Do you have an account here?" Because he replies that he has a business checking account in your bank, you give him a loan application form to complete.

A few days later, after you've notified him that his loan has been approved, he returns to your bank.

Your secretary has drawn up the papers and you present the Note to your client for his signature. You assure him, "It's the standard form everybody uses nowadays," so he signs it without hesitation.

You gently ask him if he happens to have his checkbook with him, and he says, "Yes." You ask for one of his deposit slips, smoothly explaining that you'll use the deposit slip to "take care of it" so that he won't need to carry around a check or even endorse it. He innocently tears a deposit slip out of his checkbook and, after he hands it to you, you say, "I'll be back in just a moment. Would you like Ann," who just happens to be a real *fox*, "to get you a cup of coffee or a soft drink?"

Your client takes you up on your offer and walks with "Ann" over to the office coffee dispenser. Your client enjoys his conversation with "Ann," and you've done your little trick in less than one minute.

What was the trick?

When you walk away with that deposit slip you know you are about to make a killing. You walk up to a posting machine, insert the deposit slip, enter "1-6-0-0-0-0-.-0-0," and then press the "Enter" button. "BRRRrrinnng," goes the machine, and the imprinted deposit slip is kicked up for you to pull from its slot.

You walk back to your desk to rejoin Mr. Factory Owner and "Ann," ready for a little break. It's been a tough day for you, what with all that ham-acting and button-pushing.

One Year Later
One year later Mr. Factory Owner pays off his loan in a lump sum, having had a prosperous year of producing widgets. His payoff check is in the amount of $184,000, which is $160,000 as the principal of the loan plus $24,000 in interest, at fifteen percent APR.

A little later that day our stock broker comes in to close his savings account. With your generous interest payment of five percent APR automatically credited to his account, his current balance is $10,500.

When you give him a check in the amount of $10,500, you see that he's obviously pleased. But you have reason to be just as pleased, maybe even a little more pleased.

Your *pretended* loan to Mr. Factory Owner brought you a cool $24,000 in interest. When you deduct the $502 (interest, plus the cost of the electric alarm clock — don't forget the alarm clock) you had to pay the stock broker to get his $10,000, you've netted $23,498 on the deal. That's not a bad return for your thirty seconds of *work* pushing the buttons on your posting machine. Isn't that interesting?[2]

Here's something even more interesting. Remember how you, as a just-pretend banker, deposited the principal amount of that loan in your client's checking account? Remember how easy that was, just pushing a few buttons on a machine? Do you realize that without fractional-reserve banking techniques you would have needed the $160,000 in savings deposits in order to make that loan? That would have been a real bummer, wouldn't it? It was so much more fun, and it was so much more profitable, to concoct the $160,000 just by pushing those few buttons.

One way of looking at the "Do you have an ac-

---

[2] Although it's only a minor point, let us ask you a question: If a banker loans *nothing*, in reality, but receives, say, $24,000 in interest, isn't that evidence of an *infinite* rate of interest? Isn't an *infinite* interest rate at least a little greater than what your state's usury law permits? We think it is. Have you ever heard of a bank being prosecuted on a charge of violating a state's usury law? We haven't, at least not recently. Isn't that interesting?

count here?" question relates to the bank's ability to make multiple loans. Another way to look at the "Do you have an account here?" question is this: If your client didn't have an account at your bank, you would have had to write him a check for the $160,000.

He would of course deposit your check in another bank, which would weaken *your* bank's ability to make more loans and would simultaneously strengthen *his* bank's ability to make loans. You don't want to hurt your bank and you don't want to strengthen another bank. The "Do you have an account here?" question is the precursor to the "deposit slip" routine, which is the guarantee you need, as a banker, to make sure the "money" *stays* in your bank!

These are the main reasons banks won't loan to you if you don't have an account with them. It also explains why banks *will* agree to make a loan to you barely two minutes after you open your first checking account with them. So much for the "We like to see how a person handles his money" blather.

Fake Loans But Real Paybacks
We're still not finished. There's still another element in this transaction. Actually it's the largest element in the transaction but few people even suspect it exists. With all the hoopla in the media about the prime rate, the discount rate, and points — and with some "Christian Patriots" bellowing about "usurious interest rates" — it's no wonder that the general public hasn't picked up on it. But have *you* spotted it yet?

As a banker, you spent maybe thirty seconds in "productive labor" pushing the buttons on your posting machine. For this "work" your pay was a cool $23,498. It would have been an even $24,000, if you hadn't had to buy that darn $2 alarm clock. Thank God you can deduct it.

But what about the $160,000 you received as "repayment" of the "principal" of that "loan?" In reality, you *pretended* to make a loan of $160,000 but Mr. Factory Owner *didn't pretend* to pay you back, did he? He gave you a net $23,498 as his interest payment, *but didn't he also give you an additional $160,000 you didn't have before*?

He sure did.

Subtract the $10,000 you gave back to the stock broker and you are ahead not just the $23,498 in net interest but *also $150,000, the net payoff of the principal of the "loan!"*

This means that for thirty seconds of productive labor at the posting machine, *you actually took in a total of $173,498!* Now with this in mind, how important is the prime rate to you? Or the discount rate? Concern about interest rates in a fractional-reserve banking environment is about as rational as worrying whether the cat's been fed when your house is burning down.

What we're saying is this: Banks make their *biggest* killing by *pretending* to make the loan. When borrowers pay off the principal, the bank gets something *real* which, without the help of the borrower, it could only *pretend* it had. Once the banker has the *real* $160,000 (in FRTs), he uses a small part of that amount to cover checks written against it (taking full advantage of a perpetual float), and he pyramids the balance in new loans. Through pyramiding, really big bucks are created and controlled by the banks. (Caution: Please see also the Postscript.)

Now do you understand why bankers cringe at the mere thought of millions of Americans closing their bank-type checking, savings and other accounts?

Now do you see why bankers almost tremble at the thought of millions of Americans cutting up their credit cards?

Now do you understand why the bankers wince at the notion of private citizens making private loans to, or borrowing from, their neighbors or friends.

Now do you comprehend why bankers have nightmares worse than LSD flashbacks, about Americans who stop using bank-supplied electronic funds transfers and start using strictly cash (FRTs), or Internet-based and encrypted transactions, or even coins of gold or silver?

Now do you understand why there are such complicated laws prohibiting you and me from pooling our surplus funds and making them available commercially to our neighbors through loans? Now do you see why all commercial loan activity, to be "legal," must be arranged through chartered (licensed) lending institutions?

Now do you understand why we don't see FRTs in denominations larger than $100 anymore — circulating paper currencies used to be available in denominations up to $10,000 — and why the Insiders now push for elimination of even the $100s and $50s?

Now do you see why Insiders mumble about "drug money" and "counterfeiting" as the reason for pulling in the $100s and $50s, when the fact is that they, the bankers, want to make it ever more difficult for all us non-bankers — non-drug smugglers, non-counterfeiters — to use cash? The truth is that the banks want to prevent us from leaving *their* system.

Conversely, if we begin to use cash for more of our transactions, and if we begin to borrow from and loan to one another, bypassing banks and other chartered financial institutions, the Insiders would soon start to feel the pressure. But, until that happens, the Insiders, as bank stockholders, do very well, thank you, very well indeed.

Bank Employees: Please Take Note
Notice we said that "bank *stockholders* do very well." Please also notice that we *didn't* say bank executive officers, bank loan officers, bank tellers, bank cashiers, bank janitors, bank advertising department workers, bank computer programmers, bank guards, bank secretaries, or bank clerks.

No, the people who play the fool to the tune of the stockholders, and tell the lies, and trick the public and do the ham-acting: they don't benefit.

Oh, they may get to keep their jobs, or maybe they get a small raise from time to time, but aren't they also the ones who get *murdered* by disgruntled farmers, for example, whose farms are foreclosed upon?

Aren't they the ones who are physically assaulted and verbally abused by customers who are beginning to see through some of the fraud?

Aren't they the ones who are blown to bits by the terrorist bombs, and aren't they the ones who place themselves at risk every day, dealing with some of our incredibly stupid neighbors?

You bet they are.

So how much do the *stockholders* care about what happens to the president or other employee of their bank? Not much, usually. If one president gets killed, they just hire another, or maybe they promote a deserving, young loan officer, a promising vice president. (We think it is safe to say that the larger the bank, the more likely it is that the stockholders really don't give a *damn* about the bank's employees. If you are a bank employee, especially if you support a family, you might want to keep this in mind as you consider your career options.)

Are we a tad too harsh on bank stockholders? It's true that banks have to beat the bushes pretty hard with advertisements these days to get enough victims to come in for their "free gift" electric alarm clocks. Advertisements and alarm clocks don't come cheap nowadays. Remember that the alarm clock in our scenario cost a whole $2 before deduction. It's also true that bankers have some overhead in those palatial, downtown business facilities and that "Ann" must be paid at least something for her work, but when you get right down to it, fractional-reserve banking is the most profitable scam ever devised — for bank stockholders.

Collateral is Also Part of the Scam
When a loan officer recites his little question — "Do you have an account here?" — to someone desperate for a loan, the potential borrower tends to be intimidated; easily persuaded, because of his desperation, to pledge extra collateral so he can get his loan.

Banks prefer to have loans solidly collateralized, backed two, three or more times the principal of the loan by real property or other assets like long-term annuities from an insurance company.

Most people believe that banks are not wrong in demanding high collateral, that they are just protecting themselves from difficulty they may have selling property they may acquire by default of a borrower. Again, such is not really the case, at least not most of the time. Then why do banks demand extra collateral, you ask?

A grand jury may have found part of the answer.

A Grand-jury Investigation
In the Portland, Oregon area a few years ago, a grand jury was asked to issue criminal indictments against certain persons who were picking up distressed properties, mostly single-family residences, which had been foreclosed upon by local banks. It seems the average equity being purchased was about $30,000 but the average payment *to the banks* which had repossessed the properties was only about $10,000.

Investigators learned that the banks were taking huge write-offs on their taxes through those supposed losses, but what the grand jury was even more interested in was that, in a majority of the cases the grand jury examined, the persons buying the distressed properties were relatives, business associates or close friends of the officers of the banks which had initiated the foreclosure actions.

While this grand jury did not return any indictments (to the best of our knowledge), it's possible that the right kind of evidence wasn't presented to them. Sometimes the wrong kind of evidence is presented to a grand jury so certain persons can say, "Well, the grand jury investigated us on that question and they didn't indict anyone, so we couldn't be doing too much wrong, heh, heh." But rather than rely too much on what these certain persons might say, let's look at some common sense.

If you took out a loan, pledging as collateral your home equity of perhaps *five times the principal* of the loan, wouldn't your banker rejoice if you were late for a payment? He could then foreclose, sell the house at a low price to his brother-in-law, and write off any "loss" against the bank's taxes. After a few deals like this, the banker, his brother-in-law or a select list of stockholders could become very well off. Their naïve neighbors might say, "Well, those boys sure have a way of buying low and selling high," or, "Those fellows certainly have a knack for making money."

Yes they do. It's called successfully perpetrating *theft by fraud*.

Let's keep on pretending you are a bank's loan officer. You have me fill out an application for a $20,000 loan and I agree to pledge my house — fully paid for and worth about $100,000 — as collateral. You mumble something to the effect that, "The loan committee meets on Wednesday," and that you'll let me know if my loan is "approved."

First, let's analyze your comment about "the loan committee." In reality, most of the time there is no "loan committee" because there is no need for one. The bank's lending policies are well established and well known to every loan officer, and if you don't meet their loan criteria, you don't get a loan. That's the way it should be and that's the way it is. A loan officer can usually tell whether you meet the bank's lending criteria within a few minutes of first looking at your application.

But loan officers use this mostly non-existent "loan committee" to take the blame if your financial condition doesn't warrant a loan. Pleading and emotional outbursts in the lobby or public areas of a bank are avoided, thanks to the "loan committee" which met on "Wednesday."

If you continue to plead, the loan officer may cheerfully suggest you write a letter to the bank, outlining why you think the "loan committee" made a mistake in not granting your loan. Your letter is a waste of time. The bank will mail you a form letter which thanks you for the additional information, but also "regrets that the loan committee will be unable to approve your loan at this time," etc. Even the phrase "at this time" is meant to make you think you are possibly just a short way away from getting a loan, but conditions ("loan balances," etc.) just aren't favorable for your type of loan right now, etc. You would have been better off writing to Santa Claus.

But back to our story.

On Thursday morning you call me with the good news. My "loan" has been "approved" by the "loan committee" and I go down to your office to sign the Note. When you notice that I'm actually beginning to *read* the Note, you quickly say, "Uh, that's just a *standard* installment Note, uh, *everybody* uses much the same thing nowadays, uh. . . ."

You don't want me to read that Note. You don't care what my mother told me about reading something before I sign it. You want me to back off from reading it *right now*!

You are so afraid I might start asking "a bunch of stupid questions," you launch into another of your ham-acting routines, the one which implies that if I keep reading the Note, I'll offend you, or confirm the impression that I'm just a *hick* who doesn't know *anything*. Your little act is meant to tell me, through your body language and feigned impatience, that *everybody knows* "the wording on there is okay," and I shouldn't be a jerk and take up a lot of your time reading it. You might even mumble, with your impatience barely concealed, that you've "got a call to make" or, "*We* should wrap this up so *we* don't hold *you* up any longer than necessary."

As an experienced loan officer, you've become quite an actor or actress. Bravo! But readers of the next few paragraphs are going to see some things you don't want them to see.

Installment Credit Notes
You *definitely* don't want me to read that Note.

You are deathly afraid I'm going to start asking a lot of questions, and if you answer them in your usual fashion, I might see through your arm-waving, patronizing, little show.

Plainly stated, you're beginning to perspire.

Why are you getting so nervous?

Well, there are several reasons.

Please read this "Instalment [*sic*] Credit Note" on the next page.

On the front of this Note, observe that if I sign it, I am agreeing to repay the loan in *lawful money of the United States*. Just before those words is the blank where you or your secretary would type $20,000.

Lawful money of the United States is a phrase which is clearly defined in the law of this country. As we mentioned back in Chapter 2, this phrase means coins of gold or silver which have been manufactured in a United States Mint. In early 1998 it will cost me about $85,000 in FRTs to buy that much silver coin in order to pay your bank the face amount of this loan.

Do you think such terminology is just a mistake or oversight on the part of the bank's highly-paid legal department? If "push comes to shove" in the courts, I'd be required to perform as agreed. Yes, it is true that banks have used this form since about 1977 and to date they've never tried to compel anyone to come up with actual lawful money. But isn't it curious that such specialized wording came to be on the Note in the first place?

Do you suppose this phraseology might be the banking industry's way of protecting itself if we, as a People, come to our senses, get rid of FRTs, and start using precious-metal coinage again?

Didn't older versions of these kinds of documents refer to "legal tender of the United States?" Did bank legal departments begin to realize that that phrase has no meaning at law?[3] Some investigators say the answer to both questions is Yes.

Next, please notice the language of the last sentence of the first paragraph. It begins with, "If any of said instalments [*sic*] is not so paid. . . ." What this sentence says is, if I miss an installment, the principal and interest become due and payable immediately.

Of course, of course.

But look at the last sentence in the next paragraph of the Note: "Prepayments of principal will be applied to the most remote unpaid instalments [*sic*] of this note." Do you have any idea what that means? Here's a short story for you.

The Trip to Hawaii
One day in 1978, a friend overheard me talking about "the money issue." He asked me if I'd be willing to look over a mortgage Note he'd signed at his bank about two years earlier. I agreed, and asked him to bring the Note to work with him the following day, which he did.

He and his wife were taking a six-week trip to Hawaii, planning to pay five mortgage payments in advance just before leaving on the trip. They wanted to make sure their payment record wouldn't be interrupted if an airline strike, or something else, delayed their return.

---

[3] Do you have any old Notes you've signed? Zenger News Service would like to see and analyze the phraseology on any photocopies you'd be willing to send us. Your privacy will be protected and your response will be considered strictly confidential.

FRONT

INSTALMENT CREDIT NOTE   No. _____

$ _____   _____, Oregon,   _____ , 19_____

For value received, each of the undersigned, jointly and severally, promises to pay in lawful money of the United States of America to the order of FIRST NATIONAL BANK OF OREGON, at its _____ Branch, $ _____ , with interest thereon at the rate of _____ percent per annum from date until paid, in monthly instalments of not less than $ _____ in any one payment, including the full amount of interest due on this note at the time of payment of each instalment. The first payment shall be made on the _____ day of _____ , 19 ____ , and a like payment shall be made on the same day of each month thereafter until _____ , 19 ____ , when the whole sum of principal and interest then unpaid shall be paid. Interest shall be computed daily at the rate per annum set forth above on the declining principal balance. If any of said instalments is not so paid, the whole sum of both principal and interest shall become immediately due and payable at the option of the holder of this note and the principal shall continue to bear interest computed daily at the rate per annum set forth above.

The principal of this note may be prepaid in whole or in part at any time. In the event this note is prepaid in full and the loan evidenced by this note is not in renewal or extension of a prior loan, a $15.00 charge in lieu of interest will be paid by the undersigned unless interest to the date of prepayment exceeds that amount. Prepayments of principal will be applied to the most remote unpaid instalments of this note.

Payments will be applied as follows: First to credit insurance premiums, if any, accrued to the date of receipt of such payment; then to interest accrued to the date of receipt of such payment; and the remainder to principal.

If suit or action is instituted to collect this note, or any portion thereof, each of the undersigned, jointly and severally, promises to pay such additional sum as the trial court and any appellate court may adjudge reasonable as attorney's fees in said suit or action, including any appeal therein.

THE TERMS AND CONDITIONS PRINTED ON THE REVERSE HEREOF ARE INCORPORATED HEREIN.

NOTICE TO THE BORROWER

Do not sign this note before you read it. This note provides for the payment of a penalty if you wish to repay the loan prior to the date provided for repayment in this note.

Address _____   _____
                                                                                                                BORROWER'S SIGNATURE

Telephone _____   _____
                                                                                                                BORROWER'S SIGNATURE

TPL-4 10-77   Use for FirstLoan

BACK

TERMS AND CONDITIONS

The holder of this note may cause additional parties to be added hereto or release any party hereto either with or without notice to any of us, either as co-makers, endorsers or guarantors, or may once or often extend the time for making any instalment provided for herein for any term, or may accept said instalment in advance, all without affecting the liability of us or any of us hereon.

Each and all of the parties to this note do waive presentment, demand, protest and notice of protest, dishonor or nonpayment, and do agree that if they or any of them remove from the addresses indicated on the face hereof, fail in business, become insolvent or commit an act of bankruptcy, or if any attempt is made to attach or garnish any deposit or other property in the possession of the holder of this note which may be due, owing or payable to any of them or in which any of them may have an interest, the entire amount then owing on this note shall, at the option of the holder hereof, become immediately due and payable without demand or notice and the principal shall continue to bear interest computed daily at the rate per annum set forth on the face hereof.

Figure 12-1. "*Instalment* [sic] *Credit Note, 10/77.*"

Their payments, about $500 per month, were on an original loan of $55,000. Because they had made a down payment of $25,000, their current equity was about $30,000.

We analyzed the wording on his Note (identical to the one in Figure 12-1) and discovered that, even though his next payment check would be $2,500, and that about $500 would be applied toward his next payment, the remaining amount of $2,000 *would not* be applied to his next four payments. The remaining $2,000 would be applied "to the most remote unpaid instalments [*sic*]."

This meant that even though he'd given the bank enough to cover his payments for about five months, the bank would apply most of the amount of his check — the remaining $2,000 — to payment numbers 237, 238, 239, and 240, the most remote unpaid installments. *This also meant that about thirty days after he left for Hawaii, by falling in arrears on his payments, he would be in default on his loan.*

Because he would be in default, the bank could legally foreclose on his house, and, according to the language in other sections of this Note, the bank was not obligated to notify him either that he was in arrears, or that they were foreclosing on his home. He wouldn't have known about it until he returned from Hawaii and found that the locks had been changed.

Further, if they did foreclose on his home, they could sell it for a sum far less than the unpaid principal of the loan, and then charge off the "loss" against their taxes.

Still further, this bank's president could make sure that one of his buddies, possibly the president of another bank, got a chance to pick up the $30,000 equity in my friend's house for perhaps only $10,000.

Bank presidents may, from time to time, reciprocate on these kinds of "professional courtesies." (It was exactly this kind of "professional courtesy" that the Oregon grand jury was supposedly looking into.)

Now you know how banks deliberately word their Notes so as to benefit handsomely from someone else's misfortune or misunderstanding.

Now you may understand why borrowers are told, "That's the *standard* form that *everybody* uses these days."

The Bottom Line For the Insiders

We've seen how, for the cost of a few newspaper advertisements and a few electric alarm clocks, a bank can make a real killing in its loan business, thanks to "fractional-reserve techniques" made "legal" by the United States Congress.

We've also seen how it is the bank's stockholders who win big, thanks to fractional-reserve banking.

But while the stockholders of small banks may be a few of your neighbors, and while they are likely uninformed about the mechanics of fractional-reserve banking, other stockholders may not be innocent at all.

The real ownership of bank shares can not be determined by examining the list of stockholders. Notice that we said, CAN NOT.

Whoops! You may be thinking, this author is losing his grip! How could one NOT know the names of the owners if one is looking at the list of stockholders? That's a good question and here is its equally good answer.

First, honest people, average investors, may have no qualms about letting their names show up on a list of stockholders of a local or even regional bank. After all, one buys stock with a view of profiting by the investment, and, when it comes to investing, the paramount goal is preservation of capital. Bank stock, to some investors, provides that kind of solid protection because, as a rule, banks are very well managed and rarely lose money. Who's going to give you a bad time because you own 200 shares of such-and-such bank?

Second, other honest people don't buy a bank's shares directly but do own the shares indirectly through purchase of mutual funds, or by investing in shares of a credit union which keeps part of its capital in shares of bank stocks. Is anyone going to give you a bad time because you own $10,000 worth of stock in a mutual fund, one which carries the shares of a few banks in its portfolio?

Neither of these two scenarios offers a clue as to

what does or doesn't show on the list of shareholders of bank stock. Please pay careful attention to the following paragraphs. You may be surprised by what you read, but you'll sleep better knowing that this information is getting out to the general public, to the voters.

When wealthy people buy stock, they often do not want their names to show on shareholder lists. Such lists can be an invitation to robbers, extortionists, kidnappers, swindlers, high-pressure promotion firms, and to a host of other problems.

The really wealthy, and some privacy-sensitive modest investors, do not buy stock the way you might buy stock. There are two other ways they do it. Read now about "street name" and "nominee" purchases.

"Street name" is a phrase well-known to people close to the world of equity investments. Let's say your investment strategy includes some short-term purchases, and that you hope for a quick profit in stocks. You do not want the stock certificates to be issued and then mailed to you because you don't plan to keep the stock for a long time, maybe just a few days or weeks, and you don't want to have to sign off the certificates in front of a witness or notary, and then deliver the signed-off certificates to your broker. By keeping the certificates in the name of your broker, or at least in the name of the brokerage firm where you transact your investment business, you can execute a sale of that stock with a phone call to the broker. Once she gets your sell order, she executes that transaction and, a few minutes later, the shares are removed from the brokerage firm's vault and are signed off by their "back office" staff and mailed to the clearing house. Your name would never appear on any list of persons who owned shares of that company.

Another way to own shares without your name showing on a list of shareholders is to buy the stock through a nominee, usually a lawyer. Your relationship with your lawyer involves privileged communication, that is, not subject to scrutiny by others, even the government, except under highly unusual circumstances not related to our topic. The lawyer, acting on your instructions, receives $10,000 from you, deposits that money in a bank account set up in the lawyer's name or the law firm's name, and you sign a document in which you authorize that lawyer to invest that money according to your instructions. Your first instruction is for the lawyer to buy 200 shares of such-and-such bank. The lawyer's name, not yours, will appear on the shareholder list. Your privacy is assured.

Nominee purchases offer protection to the innocent as well as the not-so-innocent. A Mafia "Don" could use several nominees to buy a controlling interest in a casino, for example. A KGB-controlled immigrant could, through her lawyer-nominee, buy stock in several firms heavily involved in defense contracts with U.S. military organizations. Such a purchase could mask the real purpose of the spy's visit to the company's premises, and delay FBI detection of the KGB's interest in a particular company or industry.

However, the most likely method of masking strong, criminal involvement in a company or industry is simply an extension of street-name and nominee ownership, a method which also may be used by non-criminal investors.

Let's say you are a movie star and you have managed to save a few hundred million bucks from your last couple of films. You don't want to be bothered with the details of investing — it's such a total bore — but you have a friend, a one-time star who is nearly eighty years old, and the old-timer strongly recommends you talk to an accountant at one of the big accounting firms. You think that's a good idea so you, your lawyer, and your business manager, meet with a few folks at the offices of one of the world's largest accounting firms, in their office in Los Angeles.

The meeting goes well, you sign a few papers, and the rest of your afternoon is free for more stimulating activity.

Here's what the accounting firm will probably do for you. They'll buy shares in a host of different companies in a host of industries, and they'll also buy some shares in a few mutual funds, all for your account and with your money. They will deduct a small percentage of the transaction amounts as part of their fee, plus they'll also deduct an annual fee to cover their overall service of your account. You couldn't care less about the fees or anything else, so long as your bucks are well managed and your business manager and lawyer agree the accounting firm will do a respectable job.

In your case, your name doesn't show on any stock certificates. Your account at the accounting firm will grow, year by year, with some stocks held, some sold, and some new ones purchased, all as may be determined by the management of the accounting firm. Perfectly legal, ethical, clean as a hound's tooth. Everything on the up-and-up.

But let's now consider an Insider. We'll call her "Ms. Donchano." She wants her involvement in the equity markets completely hidden from public view, and she's no ditzy movie star. She knows banking, investments and international finance, she got her M.B.A. at Yale and has a couple of years' advanced training at a very private institution in Switzerland. She's been learning about these things since she was five years old, at the knee of her daddy, the late Pompous J. Bighead, founder, president and chairman of Megalopolis Enterprises of Brooklyn, New York. Megalopolis, by the way, is now known simply as ME, and ME now operates out of a small office in the back of a small bank in Schenectady, New York. ME is actually a mail-clearing office, staffed by a long-time trusted secretary, a junior attorney, and an elderly accountant. Mail is forwarded by courier to an address in the World Trade Center, which happens to be a prestigious law firm. The packages are addressed to the president of the law firm but he has his staff process courier packages according to the wishes of his client.

The law firm coordinates ME's investments through a network of law firm nominees in seventeen major U.S. cities and twelve accounting or law firm nominees in nine foreign countries. These nominees buy and sell shares for ME, of course, but ME's name never shows on the stock certificates because all of the nominees are instructed to keep all the stock purchased in street name.

When stockholder meeting notices are mailed, the brokerage firms dutifully forward the notices, and associated proxy forms, to the law firms in the field. The head law firm, the organization in the World Trade Center, knows which stockholder meetings are important, when they are scheduled, and which corporate officers need to be replaced (and by whom) and who should be reelected. Appropriate instructions are sent to the field nominees, who process and mail the proxy forms to the corporation for application to the voting at the stockholder meetings.

Thus Ms. Donchano exerts her influence in businesses globally.

But Ms. Donchano funnels some of her funds into a foundation, which she controls indirectly through two or three lawyers. The foundation is a tax-exempt entity, it funnels money to public-interest groups which support certain political positions, perspectives which, as chance would have it, tend to drive business to the companies whose stock she owns via the World Trade Center law firm and its network of lawyer-nominees.

Of course, Ms. Donchano's sister has a foundation too, and so does her husband, who happens to be the brother of a former Secretary of the Treasury. Wow, what a coincidence!

If you believe only in coincidences — if you thnk it's a coincidence that *every* Harrison Ford movie stars Harrison Ford — you may not see anything unusual in what we've discussed, using the hypothetical Ms. Donchano as our heavy-hitter Insider. On the other hand, if you recognize that sometimes crooks work together to accomplish their criminal ends, you may suspect that there is more to the relationship between Ms. Donchano and the Treasury Department and other "friendships" which seem to serve her and her family so very well.

Friendships can be valuable. Some friendships can be *especially* valuable in business, especially in international business. Families which have been involved in international business for several generations usually have a lot of friendships, some of which have served them very well because the friendships are with high officials of governments. Some of those friendships are not well known to persons of limited means because we — I put myself in that category — tend to be so preoccupied with our own survival and have little time to investigate our suspicions. In fact, even if you showed us proof something illegal was going on, we might not recognize it because we don't understand the words used to describe the crime. Cops say it takes a thief to catch a thief; we have to think like Insiders to understand what they might do to advance themselves in business and international affairs.

All the foregoing discussion of ways to hide one's financial interests may help you realize that some individuals can and do exercise immense influence in world affairs without the knowledge of the public, press or even many industry and political specialists.

Despite their carefully nurtured anonymity, we believe that the ultimate goal of the Insiders is complete control of all material wealth in the world. To achieve that goal they would first need to control the world's people, and to do that they would need to control the world's purchasing power. The Insiders in New York and London, through a myriad of interlocking international relationships, including central banks in other countries, have been taking charge of the grand design.[4]

And while having "ambitious goals" is often laudable, we might remember the wisdom of Lord Acton (1834 - 1902) — so wise it has become a cliché — when he said, "Power tends to corrupt and absolute power corrupts absolutely." Do you want to live under a world government controlled by persons who are corrupted absolutely?

Indeed, perhaps we can catch a glimpse of what the "American" Insiders have in store for us. Let's look at what their present — "legal" — banking practices do to the people of the United States.

An Open Letter to Banking-Industry Friends of the Insiders

Your *pretended* loan caused an injection of purchasing power of $160,000 into the economy of the nation. It became a *permanent* addition to the supply of "money and credit" of the United States. When this "loan" is repaid, the $160,000 becomes the *permanent* property of your bank.

Earlier in this chapter we learned how *permanent* increases in purchasing power cause *permanent* increases in the general price level. How does that relate to what you are doing?

First, the $160,000 Mr. Factory Owner paid you, as the banker who made the "loan," came from people who bought his widgets. To be able to pay for those widgets, those people had to work.

What you have done is stuck a siphon into the productive labor of everyone in the nation. Your siphon is in the arms of men, women, and even children, sucking the fruit of the labors of blacks, whites and every other race; no one can accuse you of racial discrimination. You take from teen and pre-teen girls who baby-sit or help with housework, and you take from young boys who mow lawns or deliver papers. No one can accuse you of age discrimination.

You sit in your bank, chatting once in a while with "Ann," while the rest of us, unaware of what Congress' law-making has done to us, have to get out and hump to make a living.

As a banking-industry friend of the Insiders, through your manipulation of the supply of credit in the economy, you manipulate the stock markets, the commodities markets, the real estate market, international and domestic trade, insurance premiums, wholesale and retail prices, and even the value of retirement benefits.

Through your deft control of available credit, you manipulate interest rates, because you know that changes in the interest rates effect virtually every facet of the American economy. You determine the price changes of almost everything. You know *for sure*, but no one else does, when the Dow Jones Industrial Average or the price of gold, in terms of FRTs, will begin a long climb or descent. Naïve and ignorant people exclaim that you have a talent for investing wisely. Yes, you most certainly do have a talent, but the name of it is *perpetrating theft by fraud*.

With your enormous, ill-gotten purchasing power,

---

[4] I've read more than a thousand non-fiction books on recent history and not one told of communist rioters anywhere attacking a bank (supposedly the epitome of capitalism, the communists' arch enemy).

you are able to influence elections so political prostitutes are elected to offices high and low. With your pernicious influence over government workers, you make sure investigations into your affairs don't get very far.

And you manipulate the dominant media to make sure you always appear honest and credible, but those who challenge you are made to appear ignorant or unstable.

But your impact on the standard of living of the rest of us is becoming better known now. We look at the overall impact you and your Insider associates have had on our nation, and we are horrified.

We have nothing more to say to you now. For most of you, discussion would be a waste of time. But you can be certain that we *will* continue this discussion — perhaps in an American court of law.

Have Any Not Been Harmed?
There are some people — other than Insiders and their supporters in the United States Congress — who have not been directly harmed by inflation.

That harm has been possible only because we have continued to use the purchasing media which the bankers have power to inflate: banking-system "credits," Federal Reserve Tokens, and clad coins.

Fiat currency, or fiat "money," is created by *fiat*, which means by the order of someone in authority. If Americans accept and use FRTs on the orders or "authority" of the Insiders, We, the People, have surrendered our independence. We have voluntarily placed ourselves in the status of serfs, or bondsmen, under the criminal dominion and control of Insiders and their political pals.

However, for those who may have continued to conduct their daily transactions with specie, meaning precious-metal coinage, inflation simply doesn't exist. Specie has not been inflated (debased) because counterfeiting or debasement of specie is difficult to do on a large scale; and if it *is* done it is relatively easy to detect.

If you were to buy a new tire for your car today using officially minted United States silver coin, for example, the Dollar-amount of your purchase *today* would not be much different from the Dollar-amount you might have paid forty years ago, except that because of the improved productivity of workers in the tire manufacturing industry, today's price might be a little lower.

Also, if you examine your new tire closely, you'd probably discover that its quality is markedly improved over what was available forty years ago.

So for those who did not switch from silver or gold coins to "credit" and Federal Reserve Tokens, their world has been relatively undamaged by inflation. However, the phrase "relatively undamaged" is important.

Even if you *had* refused to use "credit" and Federal Reserve Tokens, you still *would* have been damaged because the quality of your life depends greatly upon your safety. If the society you live in is being destroyed by inflation, as it seems to be, your safety is jeopardized.

Oh, you might be more comfortable than others, at least for a while, but when the ship of state sinks, you go down with it too.

A great part of your standard of living is dependent upon the performance of others. If their performance stops, meaning if they die, no amount of silver or gold coin is going to improve your standard of living much beyond that of a stone-age cave dweller.[5]

The only way we are going to survive this monetary holocaust is for those of us who know what's going on to pull together and bring fractional-reserve banking crimes to a halt. Period.

Bankers Still On the Gold Standard?
Did you know that the Insiders, at least those who own capital stock of the member banks of the Federal Reserve System, are still on the gold standard? That is correct. They were quite successful in getting the rest of us to switch to the exclusive use of banking-system credits, FRTs, and clad coins, but they didn't make the switch themselves, except as may have been necessary to advance their criminal ends.

---

[5] Attention militia members: No amount of "survival training" or knowledge of "escape routes" is going to protect you because it's not that kind of battle. Fact.

(We can almost hear older readers of these lines growling, "Whaddaya mean, *they* didn't switch?")

Few Americans pay much attention to annual reports of *private companies* like the Federal Reserve Bank of New York. But some do read those reports and a few years ago a copy of one page of a recent "Fed" annual report was widely circulated among groups of concerned citizens.

This report, an official publication of the Federal Reserve Bank of New York, listed a very interesting item in the asset section of their balance sheet.

That entry placed a value of about $4.56 billion on assets described as "Gold Certificates."

Now isn't that interesting?

The Federal Reserve's Gold Certificates
In checking our copy of *A Guide Book Of Modern United States Currency*, by Neil Shafer (Racine, Wisconsin: Western Publishing Company, 1973), we discover that, in 1934, two series of officially printed United States gold certificates were issued to the Federal Reserve System, for what Shafer describes as the "exclusive use" of the Federal Reserve.

The denominations involved are $10,000 and $100,000.

In other words, while Alan Greenspan and his friends continue to belittle the worth of gold and gold-backed currencies *for you and me*, he and his pals have a nice survival-stash of them in their vaults *right now*.

But what's even more interesting is that the United States government printed 36,000 of the $10,000 denomination and 42,000 of the $100,000 denomination; they all went to the "Fed."

What we're talking about is a face value of $360,000,000 ($360 million) in just the $10,000 bills (gold certificates). The face value of the $100,000 gold certificates is a tidy $4.2 billion.

What is the significance of "face value?" Well, it means that if the United States had never called in the gold coins, and if there were plenty of Eagles ($10 coins) in circulation, the "Fed" could "buy" about 456 million of them with their holdings of gold certificates. If no Eagles could be found, the "Fed" could present those certificates to the United States Treasury, demanding that the certificates be redeemed at once, in gold or gold coin.

How do you suppose the Treasury would round up enough gold to manufacture 456 million $10-denomination gold coins? Do you realize how much coinage that is?

Since one $10 gold coin contains about 232.2 grains of pure gold, and since one troy ounce is equal to 480 grains, 456 million of those coins would contain about 220.6 million troy ounces of pure gold.

This mass would weigh about 15,126,000 (fifteen million one hundred and twenty-six thousand) *pounds* (avoirdupois, the same units we Americans use to weigh ourselves on a bathroom scale), or 7,560 tons!

At today's gold price of about $300 (FRTs) per troy ounce, 222.6 million troy ounces would set you back about $66 billion — $66,780,000,000 to be more precise.

But there's more. If you were to examine a recent (say, 1996) report of the United States Treasury, you would discover that the total liabilities of the United States to the "Federal Reserve," as of September 30, 1996, were "$11,049,674,663.38" representing 261,702,958.6 fine troy ounces at $42.2222[6] per ounce.

That's about 41,000,000 (forty-one million) more troy ounces than we listed in the two paragraphs above.

Now we're talking about a mass weighing 8,975 tons!

Two hundred sixty-one million troy ounces of gold, at about $300 FRTs per troy ounce, would cost about $78,300,000,000 (seventy-eight billion three hundred million dollars in FRTs). Call it $78 billion in round numbers. Seventy-eight billion. That's not petty cash.

Do you see now what a return to the gold standard would mean? Knowledgeable citizens recog-

---

[6] This valuation, $42.2222, was a standard footnote on U.S. Government and "Fed" balance sheets but not so in recent years. Perhaps the U.S. Treasury and the "Fed" believe "everyone knows" this is the vaulation they use for the gold listed in their reports.

nize that one of the first things the "Fed" would do is raid the Treasury for all the gold bullion owned by the federal government.[7]

By the way, do you know how much gold bullion the United States government owns?

According to *The World Almanac and Book of Facts* for 1997, the United States owned, in 1995, "261.7 mln. oz t." We interpret this entry to mean 261.7 million troy ounces. If the "Fed" were to make its move on the Treasury, they'd take *all* the gold we have, and we'd still owe them roughly 12 million more troy ounces of it.

Think about it. The United States owes every ounce of gold it owns (plus about 12 million troy ounces) to a private banking entity. And nary a word on "the news" about it. Not a word in the *Wall Street Journal* either. Nor in *Fortune*. Nor in *Business Week*. Nor on TV's "Wall Street Week" or the "Nightly Business Report."

Interesting. Very interesting.

Some reflections on Part Two

Readers with investment or business experience should quickly recognize the validity of the following observations, other readers may be surprised by them, but every reader should carefully consider these thoughts before continuing into Part Three.

Leveraged investments pay off best if the investor has correctly forecast the overall market trend. Insiders and their close friends know about every major market trend *before* it begins because the Insiders *cause* those market trends to happen. The Insiders not only know the direction of the trend, but they also know about when it will begin, about when it will end, and therefore, about how long it can be expected to last.[8]

Because they always tend to win, and because they multiply their winnings through leveraged investments, the Insiders are more than able to offset decreases in the purchasing power of their cash and other current assets.

Our losses in various investment media provide the Insiders and their friends with *their winnings*. As the bad guys win, and as we lose, we have fewer resources with which to fight back. We are becoming weaker with each passing day.

The Insiders also know that *war* is the best stimulus for making markets move, and war makes markets move fastest. Whether you are leveraged or not, if you can manipulate governments, you can trigger wars whenever and wherever you wish.

If you *know* a war is about to begin or about to end, you also *know where* you should and shouldn't invest. You can make out great, whether you are leveraged or not. In fact, you can take your time getting into your position, and you can take your time getting out of it. After all, if you are an Insider, *you* control *all* the engines that move the markets, including war.

War is "good" to the Insiders and their fellow conspirators for another reason: War is good for "loan" business. In time of war, governments and industry borrow lots of "money" and those "loans" help make the Insiders even richer than they are.

Wars also *destroy* a lot of wealth. Most of the wealth destroyed in wars is really the wealth of the little people who live in the countries involved in the wars. Insider-bankers loan "money" for producing the weapons of war, and later they loan the "money" needed to rebuild the country damaged by those weapons. The labor is supplied by the little people in those countries; their work is controlled by the Insiders through their influence in that government.

By way of example, the loans which supported Adolf Hitler in his rise to power in Germany were supplied largely by agents of one of the best known families in the eastern U.S.; after the war, politicians closely linked to that family promoted the Marshall Plan. We call that family, and others like it, the *Insiders*. Other researchers in the U.S. and elsewhere

---

[7] While it is definitely a good idea for us, as a nation, to return (or advance again, if you prefer) to a precious metal standard, you may understand now why we respectfully suggest that we *first* put the Insider conspirators behind bars.

[8] The past several year's increase in the U.S. "money" supply hasn't changed the U.S. general price level much but it may have contributed to the spectacular rise in the Dow Jones Industrial Average. It may have also been, in substantial part, loaned to foreign entities, which will further delay its influence on the U.S. general price level.

do the same. A few of the best of their works are cited in Appendix A.

By the way, Insiders may occasionally see some of their *stocks* go down in price, prior to, during, or after a war, but these losses are usually more than offset by the profits they make in war-related investments.

War is the friend of the Insider for yet another reason. War, or the threat of war, especially when featured prominently in the dominant media every day, tends to work public emotion up to a frenzy. When our neighbors are emotionally concerned about a war or the threat of a war, they are not likely to evaluate objectively our warnings about what the Insiders are up to.

Parenthetically, some readers may believe that inflation benefits government because as the general price level moves up, individual workers and corporations move into higher-*percentage* tax brackets. But civil service employees do not benefit from this increased flow of wealth. On the contrary, they suffer much like the rest of us as their fixed salaries have to be stretched more and more to match the rise in the general price level. But *the Insiders* and their friends benefit when the rest of us move into higher-percentage tax brackets. When we pay higher taxes, we have less wealth to use in our battle against the Insiders.

So, as we move into Part Three of our look at inflation, let's remember that in this country today there are four kinds of people.

- Those who don't even suspect that something's wrong;
- Those who know about the nation's problems but, because they are immature, won't act;
- Those who are part of the scam, who know what's going on and are articulate, dedicated, conscious, active participants in it; and,
- Those who know what's going on and have joined the battle on the side of honest weights and measures, and freedom.

We hope you will investigate these questions and, if you agree they are legitimate and serious, that you will join with others already enlisted in this educational effort.

Now we'll move to Part Three of our discussion of inflation, where we'll give almost everybody good reason to enroll in the educational effort.

•

"Paper money eventually returns to its intrinsic value — zero."
Voltaire (1694 - 1778)

"Paper is poverty, . . . it is only the ghost of money, and not money itself."
President Thomas Jefferson to Edward Carrington, 1788

"Money is coined liberty."
Fedor Dostoevsky (1821 - 1881), House of the Dead (1862)

13

Inflation
Part 3: Looking Ahead

PRIOR to the advent of fractional-reserve banking a popular candy company sold their famous chocolate bars for a nickel apiece; bars weighed about two ounces and they were made with real cream. Today, one of their bars costs about fifty cents, ten times the original price, it weighs less than the original bar, and it is made with lower quality ingredients. In effect, the price of that delightful chocolate bar has increased more than ten times.

But because that company's employees are always becoming more productive, a price increase of more than ten times has been avoided. Their improved productivity has *masked* some of the effects of inflation, with the beneficial effect that the price increase has been limited to "only" ten times.

Federal Reserve Ointment?
This is a *critically important* observation. Confused people sometimes call for "increased productivity" as a *cure* for inflation. We know a prominent Ph.D. who offered this suggestion, not in *The Daily Worker* or other communist publication but in a monthly patriotic magazine whose subscription fee was $120 (FRTs) per year. People who subscribed to that magazine paid $10 a month to be confused. This doctor was suggesting an ointment for a syphilitic-type disease. Increased productivity is a fine cure for the *symptoms* of inflation but if we follow this doctor's prescription, our freedom and prosperity will die. Regrettably, he's not alone in his confusion.

The Cruelty of Inflation
Years ago, many elderly people looked forward to a peaceful and comfortable retirement on "a guaranteed $40 per month." At that time, not so long ago, $40 per month *was* a comfortable amount to retire on. However, fractional-reserve banking has destroyed the dreams of many retiree's, whose constant fear is that they will outlive their money and become a burden to their children.

Inflation has stolen the productive wealth they accumulated over a period of perhaps forty or fifty years. Like every other swindle, this one has been concealed by fraud, often including political manipulation and enormous cruelty.

Today the banks make loans of their credit, despite the fact that it is illegal to do that. But the bank Insiders aren't punished. Their flunkies in Congress have arranged for them to do whatever they like, while the rest of us have to obey the law.

Banks and the U.S. government make "loans" to our nation's declared enemies, which use those credits to augment and modernize their armies and their arsenals. Then, when war is imminent, the U.S. government borrows more money to buy weapons and equipment for *our* military organizations. Then there are the big "loans" to weapons manufacturers, to help them gear up for the production orders they are sure to get from the U.S. government.

Defense contractors know they are promoting inflation, but their enormous military profits will stop if they don't keep their mouths shut.

The Real Bottom Line
We've seen that fractional-reserve banking has *caused* a permanent rise in the general price level in this country. We've seen that because of fractional-reserve banking our national debt is astronomically high. And we know that the Insiders control Congress and our turbulent economy, for the obvious reason that if there is an effect, there must be a cause.

What do they want?

Many people are confused because the Insiders look like us. In fact, they look better. They are handsomer than we are, smarter than we are, healthier and better educated than we are, certainly much richer than we are, and considerably more charming than we are. When they enter a room, it lights up. They have "presence." When scandal or crisis erupts, they don't panic. We sometimes see their pictures in the papers.

Well, if they have all these qualities, what could be wrong? In the nineteenth century, doctors would have called them insane. Today's doctors would call them "psychopaths." Their insanity consists of having no conscience. Something upstairs isn't connected. They are incapable of feeling guilt or remorse. When the rest of us feel those things, the psychopath smiles. He smiles when he lies in your face, and when he sticks a knife in your back.

For instance, how could Ted Bundy kill all those women? We'll probably never know how many. No doubt he was immensely charming. He was also insane. Soviet spy Alger Hiss was said to be one of the most charming, urbane, witty men on this planet. He was all those things when he betrayed the nation to his Soviet clients. Hitler was so mesmerizing, he could reduce strong men to tears. Castro is a perfect example. So charming. That's why he's been dictator for almost forty years.

There are different types of psychopaths. Some, like Bundy, are free-lancers. All they want to do is kill women in peace. Others are the subject of this book. They are Insiders. They want *total* power over people and things. *They want world government*, and *plan to be the power behind the figureheads they install* in that government. George Orwell made that clear in *1984*, and Mr. Orwell, a thoroughly disenchanted British socialist, knew what he was talking about.

As the Insiders progress toward their goal, they keep the rest of us off balance, mentally, emotionally and spiritually, with an endless parade of wars and other emergencies. These mostly-manufactured crises give the political Insiders justification to increase the power and reach of civil-service workers and weaken our God-given individual sovereignty. This includes *every* war we have fought in the Twentieth Century.

If we let the Insiders consolidate their control over us, all we'll be allowed to do is procreate, work and die. (Of course, there would be a few six-packs between shifts.) If that is okay with you, do nothing.

Is This Insanity Satanic?
Some say it is. Others argue that it's a mania which, much like other manias, appears in cycles. Still others claim it's an example of mankind ignoring the economic lessons of history, and that people will eventually come to their senses and change their ways.

Whichever of these theories you buy, never forget that the Insiders who did all this have broken the law.

Crimes of the Insiders
To list all the laws the world's Insiders have broken would double the size of this book. But from a practical standpoint, to bring their criminal mischief to a halt, we need only successfully prosecute the American Insiders for their major violations of U.S. law. Fortunately, that is a fairly short list.

First on the list, and perhaps the easiest violation

for most readers to verify on their own, is the matter of lending credit. Federal banking laws, and most state banking acts, prohibit banks from doing certain things. These prohibitions fall on banks because they are chartered institutions, which means they are corporate entities. Because corporations are *artificial persons* in the eyes of the law, much of what they do and don't do is controlled by law. Banking laws prohibit banks from lending credit, yet today, ALL banks violate this law. NO banks today loan *money*. Why not discuss this the next time you take your state's attorney general to lunch.

Next, remember our discussion of "theft by deception," and "theft by fraud." Theft is a crime, and Insiders are perpetrators of this crime. Insiders steal from everyone else through fractional-reserve banking techniques. Insiders derive much of their wealth from theft by fraud. While theft is usually prosecuted on a state level, interstate racketeering — which is almost always what the Insiders do — may properly be prosecuted in federal courts as well.

Insiders also wage a form of economic *warfare* against most other American citizens, and ample legal precedent exists for also prosecuting them on this charge in state and federal courts.

Some members of the Congress are Insiders, and they are helping other nations wage economic warfare against the United States. Waging war against the United States, or aiding and abetting those who wage war against the United States, is defined in the law books and in the United States Constitution as *treason*. Treason is tried in the federal courts.

But treason is not just a federal offense. Insiders may be charged with treason against your state, by virtue of the economic warfare they wage against you and your neighbors, as citizens of your state.

The definition of treason in the California Constitution, for example, is the same as that given in the United States Constitution. Waging war against the state of California, or aiding and abetting those who wage war against the state of California, is *treason* against the state of California. The Constitutions of Washington, Utah, and Oregon contain similar language. Your state's constitution may say much the same thing.

There's another aspect to these charges which you should not overlook. The law is well settled on the point that when two or more persons cooperate to commit a crime, each of the parties to the plan is called a *conspirator*, and the plan itself is called a *conspiracy*. A *global conspiracy* involving bankers, political figures and key industrial leaders is behind almost all the havoc in the world today.

What is a conspiracy? The dictionary says it's two or more persons agreeing in secret to commit a crime. The Latin root of *conspire* means "to breathe together." A conspiracy doesn't need to incorporate or issue membership cards. The participants in a conspiracy *always* do everything they can to prevent others from discovering that the conspiracy exists. If one conspirator should be apprehended by the police, other conspirators will circulate rumors that he was a "loner," that he acted strictly on his own, and that it would be "witch-hunting" to suggest that others might be involved with him.

Apprehended conspirators cooperate in this policy because, as long as the conspiracy itself is safe, it will help them at trial and thereafter. Strange things happen. Trials can bog down, attorneys get sick and judges have heart attacks. Protection of an arrested member is in the best interest of a conspiracy, but sometimes, when things get touchy, the arrested individual is killed. The murder of one of their own is standard practice for conspirators because sometimes that is the only way to stop an investigation. The national media say Secretary of Commerce Ron Brown was about to be indicted and had threatened to sing. Then he turned up with that convenient hole in his head.

Second, the law provides much harsher punishment for conspiracy. For example, if someone acts *alone* under the "color of law" to deny you your rights, he commits a *misdemeanor*. Upon conviction, he faces up to one year in prison and a fine of up to $1,000. But if he operates *with another* person, he is now part of a conspiracy and he commits a *felony*. He now faces up to ten years in prison and a fine of up to $5,000.[1]

---

[1] See 18 U.S.C. § 241 and 242; also see 42 U.S.C. § 1981 *et seq.*

The *last* thing an Insider wants is for someone to begin investigating him as a suspect in a conspiracy. When someone attacks the Insiders, they pull all their strings to get the attacker off their collective back. For example, the John Birch Society was the first organization to raise the question of an international conspiracy for world government, and that organization was *vilified* by the dominant media. Years later, President George Bush, for instance, made speech after speech advocating world government, which he called the "new world order."

Fruits Of Crime
A basic doctrine of American law says: The fruits of crime must be restored to their rightful owner. This means is that stolen property must be returned to its rightful owner. For example, if a bank repossessed your farm and if the loan on which you defaulted was a loan of credit — not a loan of coins of gold or silver, that is, *money* — the loan was illegal. The bank stole your property and must return it.

Your spouse, your parents and your children are probably also victims of theft. Ditto with your neighbors, your relatives and almost all other Americans. When the courts begin to act on these matters in accordance with American law, the stock, bonds, real estate, airplanes, cars, and other property of the Insiders will be confiscated. *Their wealth is the fruit of their crimes.* They don't get to keep it; *they have to give it back to its rightful owners.*

All the Insiders' wealth will likely be placed on the public auction block, with the proceeds of the sale going to the same place as the proceeds from an auction of an extortionist's new Cadillac: to the Treasury of the United States of America.

Civil Process Against the Insiders
Another maxim of American law says that any contract (which was) conceived in *fraud* is *stillborn* (dead), and as such, has no life or operation whatsoever. It has no force or effect on any party, and it will not be sustained in any court of law. It is as if it had never been written.

Anyone who might try to compel performance under an inoperative contract would place himself in legal peril under the federal criminal code, Title 18, United States Code, abbreviated 18 U.S.C.

If the reality of a *debt* is contingent upon the operation of a contract which was conceived in fraud, there is no debt. So, since virtually the entire national debt of this country — supposedly owed directly or indirectly to the Insiders — came about through the operation of contracts which were conceived in fraud, there is no national debt.

Essentially, the national debt as we know it today has *never* existed, at least not legally. The only reality it can legitimately claim is in the minds of the Insiders' confused, manipulated and defrauded victims.

To be successful in civil actions against the Insiders, juries must first be made aware of the totally *fraudulent* nature of fractional-reserve banking. Litigants and their counsel, in preparing a case, should make jury awareness their number-one consideration. Does it seem strange to you that a subject as important as fractional-reserve banking is never taught in the schools and never explained by the dominant media, with the logical result that few Americans understand it, or have even heard of it? But once this understanding has been achieved, civil recovery may be realized on a stupendous scale.

To have standing to sue, a party must have suffered an injury. In civil actions against the Insiders, most borrowers probably *do* have standing because — as we have seen — they probably paid back, in FRTs, much more than the bank loaned. Those borrowers suffered financial injury.

If you borrowed $1,000 (FRTs) and paid that amount back, you probably paid far too much; the bank probably loaned you only about sixteen percent of this amount, about $160 (FRTs), thanks to fractional-reserve techniques. Your suit might seek to recover $840 (FRTs), plus the cost of prosecuting the suit, plus damages.

If you presently have a "loan" balance outstanding (that is, an unpaid balance outstanding), your suit might seek to have the "loan" declared invalid. You should not have to pay back a penny more than sixteen percent of the face amount of the loan.

Civil actions take several different forms.

A *group* of borrowers might initiate a class-action suit. A group may be better able to afford the costs of protracted litigation, and it may command more respect from local media — which could label a lone individual quixotic.

A third form of civil suit, initiated by individuals or groups (as class actions), could be directed against various agencies of government. These suits, also seeking recovery of damages, would argue that inaction on the part of a governmental agency contributed to the Insiders' ability to harm the community. Such a suit might charge culpable negligence, mal- or misfeasance of office, breach of a fiduciary trust, or even violation of oath of office, a form of perjury.

For example, consider a civil suit against your region's United States Attorney and the United States Department of Justice. You might charge either or both of these entities with failure to investigate the matter of banks making loans of their credit, and charge that the banks did this on an interstate basis, and that even though a formal complaint was filed with the United States Attorney, he or she failed to act on it. This kind of suit might be initiated under Title 42, Section 1983, of the United States Code.

But while recovery through civil action may become popular *in the United States* in the next few years, we should also keep in mind that there is an *international* aspect to this matter of fraud by the Insiders.

Since most indebtedness of the United States *and* foreign countries came into existence through machinations of the Insider crowd, as far as United States law is concerned, most foreign nations don't *legally* owe any of "our" banks even a penny. For this reason we safely predict that Brazil is effectively out of debt, and that Mexico is effectively out of debt, and that almost all other countries are effectively out of debt, at least as far as any debt to a U.S. lending institution.

But even that's not all. As we discuss these cheerful things, we may have a moment or two of concern as to how we're going to adapt to a monetary environment where loans of credit, fractional reserves, and FRTs no longer exist. The most obvious question is . . .

What Will We Use As Money?
Some readers may ask, "What will we use as money if we get rid of FRTs?" The most astute analysts of the money issue predict that, initially, silver or gold coin will be restored as our fundamental monetary instruments. But silver and gold coins won't be used **as** money; silver or gold coins *are* money!

The next most obvious question is, "Is there enough gold to go around?" What this question really asks is, "Is there enough gold *and silver* available to manufacture all the coins we'd need?" This is a perfectly logical question but its major premise is that, at today's prices in terms of FRTs, there may not be enough silver and gold bullion available for the manufacture of enough coins for trade use. After all, the argument goes, there are more people and more vending machines now, which means we'd need even more coins than we needed back in the 1930s, for example.

This premise *incorrectly* assumes that $10 in gold (258 grains, 900 fine) would be the price of something costing $10 in FRTs. Actually, prices today, in terms of dollars of gold, are about one twentieth (1/20, or five percent) of FRT-prices; prices in terms of dollars of silver are about one fourth of FRT-prices. Another way of saying this is that FRTs have depreciated 95% against gold, and 75% against silver.

But it is valid to ask, "With industrial uses of silver expanding, and with the world supply of silver decreasing, isn't it likely that the purchasing power of a given silver coin will continue to increase into the foreseeable future and beyond?" The answer to this question, at least with today's knowledge, is an emphatic Yes.

Another valid question is: "If silver keeps getting more scarce, and if gold maintains its current rarity, isn't it going to be difficult to regulate *legislatively* the ratio of value between dollars of gold and dollars of silver?" The answer is, No, it's not going to be difficult; it's going to be *impossible*.

This observation tells us that we may need to

adjust our thinking along lines slightly different from those of the Founders of the Republic. Because of the new industrial demand for silver, *legislative* control over the ratio of value between equal weights of gold and silver will remain a thing of the past.

This observation about industrial demand also tells us that we may eventually experience difficulty if we try to use silver coins as our nation's primary monetary instrument. Industrial demand and ever smaller supplies of silver are expected to cause listed prices — in terms of silver coin — of all products and services to decline steadily, probably faster than would be tolerable.

In the earliest years of this country's history, the free-market ratio of value between equal weights of pure gold and pure silver was about 15 to 1; an ounce of pure gold would buy about fifteen times as many pounds of potatoes, for example, as would an ounce of pure silver. The 15:1 ratio remained relatively stable for a few decades, but by the late 1800s, the free-market ratio was approaching 16:1. In 1900, in adherence to the Constitutional provision to "regulate the value thereof," Congress changed the ratio (of a dollar of gold to a dollar of silver) to 16:1. But today we see that a 16:1 ratio diverges greatly from the ratio established by free markets. In recent weeks (July 1998), an ounce of gold would buy about $300 FRTs; an ounce of silver would buy $6.00 FRTs. The ratio between 300 and 6.00 is about 50:1 (fifty to one).

Metals-industry analysts suggest that we'll eventually see a sharp and continuing increase in industrial consumption of silver. This would drive the FRT-price of silver up, thereby moving the gold-silver ratio back toward 16:1. In fact, increases in industrial consumption, and reductions in availability (as mines begin to peter out), may produce an event which has never occurred before: We may come close to running out of an element of matter — silver.

What this means, however difficult it may be to accept, is that silver may become more valuable than gold, perhaps very much so, and perhaps within the next fifty years. So in considering what kinds of coins we should use in daily trade, we must not forget what the not-too-distant future may hold for silver.

But for the immediate future, say for the next ten to twenty years, silver coin would probably work just fine.

How Many Coins Would We Need?
Next, we should realize that we probably would need *fewer* silver and gold coins today than the number we needed in the 1930s.

In spite of today's larger population, because we now use checks, credit cards, wire transfers, Internet transactions using electronic "money," and a host of other methods to transfer purchasing power, now we have a *reduced* need for precious-metal coins.

Even the present proliferation of vending machines may not require more precious-metal coinage. We must remember that, when we re-establish a Constitutional (non-FRT) monetary system, *prices will drop sharply*. For this reason, most machine-vended products will be purchased with *pennies and nickels* (and possibly, in some cases, with "intelligent" credit or debit cards). Since our minor coins contain only base metals, and since there is no shortage of base metals, the popularity of vending machines is not a factor in the question of whether there is enough gold and silver available for coinage.

Also, expected productivity improvements could well lower prices even more. A candy bar, now priced at about fifty cents in FRTs, might cost only *two* cents in a post-FRT vending machine.

For all these reasons, we can safely say that the number of *gold* coins needed today is perhaps ninety percent less than the number needed in the early 1900s. That's good news, to be sure, but it isn't the whole story, not by a long shot. Don't forget that many of the gold coins which once circulated in the United States *are still around*. They're alive and well, safely in the hands of people who traded FRTs for them. Once prices are again denominated in lawful money, we may see many of those gold coins return to circulation — *without legislative action*.

Although the same can be said for silver coins, it is possible that, for a few months, there might be a shortage of them. Again, some silver coin has been melted for use in industry. But since silver is epithermally deposited (found near the surface of the Earth), it is relatively easy to mine. Moreover, since most silver is obtained as a byproduct of mining copper and other industrial metals, an improving economy should spur rapid development of this kind of mining and smelting. Shortly after the Insiders' schemes are stopped, the free enterprise system should automatically produce and supply all the silver we'd need for our national coinage.

One last concern might be the need to accommodate the increased purchasing power of silver. One dollar of silver, about 0.77 troy ounces, will buy a nice meal in most neighborhood restaurants. A silver dime will buy an item selling for $.50 FRT. Thus, it *may* be necessary for us to investigate what problems, if any, might arise from the widely different intrinsic values of a nickel and a dime.

In conclusion, however, we have to say Yes, there *is* enough silver and gold to go around, more than enough.

What Kind of Paper Currency Will We Have?
Remember that the United States Constitution, the supreme law of our land, grants the federal government *no power whatsoever to issue paper currency*.

This conspicuous absence of power is not an oversight, for in *The Federalist Papers* and other documentation of the Founders' beliefs and principles, we see only the harshest condemnation regarding "paper emissions," meaning government issuance of paper currency. Had there been an attempt to allow it at the Constitutional Convention, there would have been a walkout, by delegates who remembered that, during the War for Independence, paper currency was "not worth a Continental."

Some have suggested that the *states* adopt a standard pattern for a national paper currency, and then issue that currency to banks and other institutions which store officially-issued gold and silver coins for depositors. This would merely produce another version of the corrupt FRT except, in lieu of the symbology identifying which Federal Reserve Bank was the issuer, special symbols and wording would indicate which state was the issuer. The idea goes on to suggest that the states use the same paper and inks now used for FRTs, and even have the Bureau of Engraving and Printing produce the currency. The trouble is the whole idea is illegal. The U.S. Constitution prohibits the states from issuing "Bills of Credit" (paper currency) in Article 1, Section 10.

Another suggestion is that banks and other private-sector institutions issue their own paper currency. Banks once issued their own banknotes as part of a "National Currency" concept established by the National Banking Act of 1862.[2] National Currency banknotes circulated along with Federal Reserve Notes, Silver Certificates, Gold Certificates, and United States Notes, and were secured by United States government bonds. The last National Currency banknotes were issued in about 1935 but have not been seen in circulation for many years.

The idea of banks and other financial institutions issuing their own paper currency may have merit but the National Currency experience was an administrative nightmare. More than 3,000 banks issued their own banknotes. Damaged or otherwise unserviceable Notes discovered by tellers, often in banks thousands of miles distant from banks that issued them, had to be returned to that bank for proper disposal. Otherwise the issuer's records would descend into chaos. So, this type of private-sector approach to the issuance of paper currency may have serious drawbacks.

Still another suggestion is that the Constitution be amended to grant the federal government power to issue a paper currency, provided that the currency would always be redeemable in lawful money (gold or silver coin) upon demand. This suggestion has great appeal from an administrative standpoint in that it would result in Gold Certificates and Silver Certificates, *but no other paper currency*, produced by the federal government. However, under today's circumstances, with so few statesmen in Congress or elsewhere in government, a Constitutional Convention would pose *extreme* danger to the Republic. Of

---

[2] This Act was superseded by the National Currency Act of June 3, 1864.

course, the change could be made by the Congress and the states, *without* a convention.

An Interim Paper Currency
From the foregoing we can see that the paper currency question is not a simple one. But, if only for reasons of personal privacy and convenience, we probably ought to have at least one paper currency.

Here's our suggestion for an interim answer to the question as to what paper currency we should use. We think Silver Certificates, in denominations up to $1,000, would be our best choice for the type of currency. We also think the federal government should be the issuer, acting in the interest of the states and the people, under Executive powers associated with national defense. We will be recovering from the effects of economic warfare.

As to implementing a paper-currency changeover, we suggest that the federal government exchange Silver Certificates for FRTs at prevailing market rates — so many FRTs per dollar of silver — for one year. After that redemption period, FRTs would no longer be accepted by the federal government.

Silver Certificates would be used for perhaps one more year until we, as a nation, ascertain whether a paper currency is really needed, and, if it is, what its character should be and who should be its issuer.

Government-held FRTs would be destroyed as property is seized from the perpetrators of the economic warfare. Once the stolen property is recovered, the last FRTs would be destroyed. Over a period of several years, this property would be auctioned to private-sector bidders, with the proceeds going to the federal treasury.

A Booming Economy
Some people fear that a radical change in the form of our purchasing media might trigger violent reactions in the stock market, the commodities markets, and all other major segments of our economy. These people may politely listen to much of what we say, but eventually they say something like, "Yeah, but if we did *that*, the economy would collapse."

Again, we understand the questioner's concern, but permit us to draw a couple of parallels, one imaginary and one real.

As to the imaginary one, consider a car with a hand brake which doesn't fully release — the driver is going to get poor gas mileage from having to overcome the effect of the partially-applied brake. Would his gasoline economy plummet if he gets that hand brake fixed so it would completely release? Of course not. Fixing the brake would enable the car to get the fuel economy it was designed to get. Fixing the brake may seem "dangerous" to someone who hasn't thought much about how brakes work, and doesn't know that cars with the least friction get the best mileage. The Insiders have been acting like a brake on our economy — no matter how finely we tune our carburetor, we're going to have a hard time getting any performance out of the old jalopy until the brake is fixed.

The *real* parallel can be seen in the experience of Germany right after World War II. There was a huge injection of capital into Germany, primarily from the United States and secondarily from other Allies, which produced an economic miracle, or *Wirtschaftswunder*, as it was called. In spite of Germany's near-total destruction at the end of the war, with a tremendous injection of capital (and an end to National Socialist intervention in the marketplace), the German economy bounced back to life.

If the bankers and their fractional reserve gimmicks are stopped in *this* nation, there would be the same effect. Our economy will surge back to vigorous life.

No More Taxes?
Those billions upon billions of dollars of wealth recovered from the Insiders should pay for the *legitimate* operation of the federal government for years.

Federal taxes might no longer be needed. Elimination of the federal tax load could boost everyone's prosperity. (We had no internal federal taxes at all, from 1817 until 1862.)

Further, because the Insiders won't be funneling purchasing power and other aid to tyrants, the threat of war will fade and appropriations for national defense, normally one of the largest federal budget items, will drop to its lowest level in perhaps a century.

There would be "No More Vietnams." Or Koreas. Or World War IIs, or World War Is, or Civil Wars, or any more wars at all. The most important thing someone who is truly opposed to war can do, is to help restore honest weights and measures to America.

The Communists Are In The Red
The Insiders, operating through entities such as the World Bank and the International Monetary Fund, have financed and otherwise aided the Soviet and Chinese communist regimes since the days of Lenin and Mao. But since these dictatorships haven't the slightest chance of maintaining their rule without continuous support from the Insiders, within about six months of the beginning of the *criminal trials* of the Insiders and their pals, *every* communist regime in the world will begin to collapse, and not one shot need be fired.[3]

The last of the 5,000 or so slave labor camps in the Soviet Union will be emptied of their prisoners, which would already have been done if *glasnost* and *perestroika* were what we have been told they are. This massive influx of productive workers into the Russian economy should help produce a substantial improvement in the standard of living of not just Russians but also the citizens of neighboring countries, the Central and Western European lands which are Russia's natural trading partners.

The newly-freed Russian and Chinese economies will begin to blossom, and the fictional threat of nuclear war will be recognized for exactly what it has been all along, a ploy of the Insiders to make more of their *artificial* loans to *societies made fearful of their neighbors*.

A Post-War Economic Miracle
With the Insider's game halted, and with the damage they've done repaired, our economy ought to take off like a rocket to the moon. Even the nation's drug-damaged youth and the infirm elderly should be able to find appropriate and satisfying employment.

The influx of illegal aliens will stop, because economic miracles would be happening where these people come from. Indeed, many foreigners already here who have not yet been assimilated may elect to return to their homelands for the same reason. It would be economically sensible for them to return because, at home, they know the language, they would be getting in on the ground floor of an economic revival, and they would be near friends and loved ones, who share their ethnic and cultural values.

Also, when the Insiders are routed, their venal influence in a host of industries will cease. All manner of capital investment avenues will open up to the entrepreneur, the venture capitalist, and the experimenter. Funds will be available for investment in dozens of private-sector industries which have heretofore, thanks to the Insiders, been the exclusive province of a veritable *army* of beleaguered, frustrated and demoralized civil-service workers.

Hundreds of thousands of civil-service workers will find satisfying employment in a vigorously growing private sector. Even low-level workers from the civil-service ranks will find new and more pleasant employment in the private sector (which means, for instance, that fewer workers would be shot in the post office).

Life in the United States will likely be emulated around the world. Our Constitution may be adopted by many other nations, giving the blessings of individual freedom and prosperity to almost all mankind — for the first time in history. We are on the threshold of a great new era of personal freedom, mental and physical and moral and spiritual and environmental health, and all of this, not just in the United States and her sister nations of the West — but globally.

Inflation: The Popular Definition
Remember the simple definition of inflation given at the beginning of this chapter? Doesn't it now seem laughably inadequate? Here it is again:

---

[3] Of course, we are talking about a *genuine* collapse, not about *glasnost* and *perestroika*, which promote "convergence" between the United States and the Soviet Union.

> Inflation is a rise in the general price level, caused by an increase in the supply of money and credit.

Almost everybody believes this definition is adequate. But it *isn't* adequate, any more than this is an adequate definition of *arson*:

> *Arson is heavy smoke and flames, caused by rapid oxidation of combustible materials.*

This definition fails to include reference to the most important element of arson, *the perpetrator*. Arson is a crime. Crimes are committed by people. People who commit crimes, who act with criminal intent, are criminals. Criminals are subject to criminal prosecution.

The definition of inflation quoted above is deficient for the same reason: its failure to include reference to a perpetrator, the most important element of inflation. Because this definition makes no reference to a perpetrator, the public is unaware that inflation is the *natural result* of one form of crime: *theft by deception*, or, *theft by fraud*. The public does not suspect that, ultimately, *people* cause inflation. Criminals cause inflation.

Because this *criminally* inadequate definition is widely published, it is widely accepted by an unsuspecting (gullible) public. Because so many people rely on this definition, they don't suspect that inflation is the result of the acts of *people*. The public has been deceived by the people who write and publish this inadequate definition.

Some Questions and Answers

Is inflation caused by the operation of fractional-reserve banking practices? Yes.

Are Insiders aware that fractional-reserve banking practices are beneficial to them and harmful to everyone else? Yes.

Do some members of Congress know that fractional-reserve banking practices benefit some people and harm the rest of us? Yes.

Do Insiders and their friends in Congress know that fractional-reserve banking practices are a form of theft by fraud? Yes.

Is theft by fraud a crime? Yes.

Is more than one person involved in perpetrating this particular crime? Yes, we think so.

Are these persons cooperating with one another in perpetrating this crime? Yes; we believe the evidence supports this argument.

If two or more people cooperate secretly to accomplish a crime, aren't they conspirators? Yes, that's what the law says.

Are the perpetrators of this "theft by deception" involved in a conspiracy? Yes.

Is this conspiracy international? Yes, it is.

Would we therefore be correct in saying that inflation is one of the primary symptoms of an international conspiracy whose principal crime is theft by fraud?

Yes.

Inflation: Better Definitions

Here are three definitions of inflation which we believe are more accurate and more comprehensive than the one which is so commonly and innocently accepted:

> **Inflation**: 1) A symptom of the fact that megalomaniacs have seized control of a society.

> **Inflation**: 2) A form of theft by deception, perpetrated by an international conspiracy and evidenced by a permanent rise in the general price level, and accompanied by a commensurate and permanent deterioration of everything good, clean, healthy, and worthwhile in a society.

> **Inflation**: 3) A form of treason wherein the warfare waged is primarily economic, but which may also be psychological, chemical, military or spiritual, depending upon the wish of its perpetrators.

•

14

Fraud

YOU may think you know what *fraud* is but, unless you are a lawyer or law-enforcement specialist, you may be in for a surprise. New ways of perpetrating fraud are almost unbelievably effective, deceiving even mature professionals. You and your family need to know what the world's crooks have planned for you.

Fraud, as a term of law, comes to us from the Old French term, *fraude*, which stems from the Latin *fraudem*. That Latin word, by the way, is the accusative of the Latin words for guile or deceit.

Fraud is intentional deceit which results in injury to another person. Fraud is a crime. Federal statutes on fraud are in Title 18 of the United States Code. There are state laws against it, too.

You would be a victim of fraud if you suffered an injury because you acted on information which was false or materially incomplete or inaccurate, and the person who provided that information to you knew it.

Fraud does not involve force or a threat of force. Fraud is a strictly non-violent crime. Fraud is a form of theft in which the perpetrator of the crime does not always receive the thing stolen, or does not receive a direct benefit.

In fact, you might also be a victim of fraud if you suffer an injury, even if the person who provided the information to you that caused it did not know it was false or materially incomplete or inaccurate.

If fraud is perpetrated knowingly, the crime is *actual* fraud. If the perpetrator is unknowing, the crime is *constructive* fraud.

Constructive fraud is easy to prove if the perpetrator is a lawyer or other well-educated professional who would reasonably be expected to know the falsity, inaccuracy or incompleteness of the material provided to the injured party.

So you could be the victim of fraud if you've suffered an injury which happened because you acted on information provided to you by another, if that information was false, incomplete, or materially incorrect.

The most important aspect of the crime of fraud is therefore not necessarily the intent of the perpetrator but the false, incomplete or inaccurate information.

However, if a store clerk innocently repeats a manufacturer's claim of a product's durability or superior performance, the law will focus not on the clerk but on the manufacturer who misled the clerk and possibly others who sell that product.

Constructive Fraud

An essential element in establishing *constructive* fraud

is that the perpetrator must have breached an equitable or legal duty, trust or confidence which results in damage to another. An example of this aspect of fraud might be the professional tax preparer who obtains your business by promising that you'll pay less federal personal income tax if you let her, a CPA, prepare your return. Fraud could be at work if later you are fined heavily by the IRS because your tax return did not reflect the $100,000 you made selling hot dogs at the stadium.

Here is a short and wholly fictional story that will test your susceptibility to fraud. It doesn't take long to read but it will serve a valuable purpose. People who cannot quickly, accurately and positively solve the problem posed by this story may be highly susceptible to fraud. If you have trouble answering the question at the end of the story, be on guard. You may not be able to recognize a fraud.

Where is the Missing Dollar?

Once upon a time, in the dead of winter, three men are traveling by car in the midwest. Late that day a sudden snowstorm makes driving hazardous so the three decide to spend the night in a local hotel. The desk clerk tells them that the hotel is full except for one room, which costs $30 for a night. The men agree to take that room, and each man gives the clerk $10. About half an hour later, the clerk discovers that he overcharged the men. The room was only $25 per night, so he gives the bell captain a $5 bill and asks him to take it back to the three men. On the way to that room, the bell captain tries to figure out how much to give each man. When he realizes it's going to be awkward finding small change and one-dollar bills to distribute the funds equally to the men, the bell captain comes up with a plan. He knocks on the door, and when the men answer, he tells them that the hotel accidentally overcharged them for the room. He gives each man $1 and bids them good night. The men thank the bell captain and retire for the night.

Here's the puzzle. The men initially paid $10 each for the room, for $30 total paid. Each man got $1 back, which meant that each man paid only $9 for the room. Three times nine is 27, plus the $2 in the bell captain's pocket, equals 29. Where did the other dollar go? [The answer is hidden elsewhere in this book.]

This story is an example of the kind of reasoning used by con men, who perpetrate fraud by first gaining the victim's confidence. The victim, confident that the perpetrator is truthful and honest, falls for a trap.

While studying hypothetical situations can help you safely prepare for potentially dangerous ones, you're now ready to examine several *real* situations, scams which have victimized several generations of Americans.

Ponzi

The name "Ponzi" is known to most adults over forty, and certainly most police officers, FBI agents, and investment advisors and economists. In fact, the name is so well known it has become an adjective. That's because Mr. Charles A. Ponzi, a Boston entrepreneur in the 1920s, and a consummately skilled con man, bilked a reported $15 million out of about 40,000 "investors" who bought into his scheme.

Ponzi advertised it in the Boston newspapers, claiming that he could make unheard-of investment profits, and that he was willing to share his good fortune with anyone who wished to invest.

Unsuspecting victims, lured by the promise of big returns, lined up to give Ponzi their money. To keep the suckers coming, he would occasionally send a big check to an early "investor." Of course, the check was big enough to be newsworthy, which attracted the attention of the press, and motivated more sheep to invest in his bonanza.

However, Ponzi had no magic formula for making money. He invested in nothing and made no profits. He simply held the money the first investors gave him, then gave one or two of them their money back with a profit large enough to stimulate another news story. Then, as more "investors" gave him their money, Ponzi would wait a while before giving some other lucky investor a huge profit on his investment.

Eventually, Ponzi could not continue the charade. Obviously, he could not give out more money than he received, and his high-on-the-hog lifestyle was exposed as part of the scam.

Ponzi went to jail, thousands of people lost their "investments," and the Boston area got a hard lesson in Latin, learning the meaning of *caveat emptor*[1] and one or two other choice phrases.

"Your Room is Guaranteed"
We travel now to New York City, it is the summer of 1995, and your airline and hotel reservations have been arranged by your employer's travel agency. Just in case your flight is delayed and you are unable to arrive at your hotel before 6:00 p.m., the travel agency gave the hotel your American Express card number so your room would be guaranteed; that is, your room will be waiting for you even if you arrive very late at night, long after the normal check-in deadline.

There's only one problem: your travel agency doesn't know that the hotel is *crooked*.

Your flight is delayed and you arrive in New York at La Guardia airport at about 8:15 p.m. Sure, you're exhausted, but why worry. "Your room is guaranteed." You can take a hot shower and be in bed by 11:00 p.m. You can sleep like a rock and be up in time for breakfast — before the convention, the reason for your business trip, begins.

Your cab drops you and your luggage off at the front door of the hotel but you notice that the concierge seems tired so you grab your own luggage and head inside, tossing the concierge a smile and a quick, "I've got 'em; I need the exercise." But as you struggle past him and enter the building, he rushes (no, not rushes, but he *does* move) to get a cart for your luggage. You suppose that means you will have to tip him after all.

You approach the registration desk, give the clerk your name, and say you believe you have a guaranteed reservation. The clerk, who should get an Oscar for his performance, dolefully reports that the hotel is inadvertently overbooked, due to an oversight between shifts (or due to a computer error, or whatever), but for you not to worry because you'll be placed in a "nicer" hotel just a couple of blocks away and the hotel will pay your cab fare to get you over to the other hotel, and the concierge will bring your luggage back here for you in the morning.

Oh, well, people make mistakes. You make a comment to this effect to the clerk, and he nods, not looking at you. Did he actually hear you? He seemed so distant, so absorbed in his study of the computer screen.

Soon you are back outside with your luggage, wondering how long it's going to take to get a cab. The ever-helpful concierge flags one in less than five minutes, and, you load your bags into the trunk. You tip him because he holds the trunk lid open while you do so. As soon as his hand closes on that tip, he heads back to the hotel lobby so you close the trunk lid yourself, then open the door of the cab and get in. It's a good thing the rain is letting up.

The ride to the alternate hotel took less than ten minutes because it was just three blocks away. Your cab fare was $3 but you let the driver keep the "five dollar bill," because you didn't want to seem cheap. Because the clerk at the registration desk was called by the clerk at your first hotel, all you have to do is sign a registration card. You have no idea that both hotels are owned by the same firm, and that the song and dance ("due to a computer error we accidentally rented your room") is a well-exercised routine.

The room wasn't all that great, but, as tired as you are, you have no trouble falling asleep, although you don't take time for a shower because you have to be up extra early in the morning. You have to re-pack your luggage so it can be delivered to the first hotel while you are at your convention.

This story is true. It happens every day. It is a sign of the times. Here's the scam, just in case you didn't pick up on it.

The first hotel management realizes that a cer-

---
[1] "Let the buyer beware." A principle of American law says that, absent *fraud*, buyers are solely responsible for their judgments in the marketplace.

tain number of people who reserve a room will not show up. That's fine, but when it guarantees a room, something else happens. Here's what it is. The hotel charged your American Express card, and did it right after your travel agent booked your travels, two weeks ago.

The hotel now has your money. If you don't show up, they have legitimately charged your card for the room they held for you all night. But the twist on the story is not immediately apparent. If you do show up late, as you did, the management is in a bind because they didn't really hold your room for you. At 6:00 p.m., when you didn't show up, they rented your "guaranteed" room to another guest, and they kept on doing that until their hotel was filled.

You are the *only* "guaranteed" guest who showed up after 6:00 p.m. After long experience, the hotel knows that if such a guest doesn't show by 6:00 p.m., chances are he won't show up at all. Every day about 75% of the rooms will have a turnover; one guest will leave and another will arrive. During the summer, this hotel is usually full every week night and most of the time is full every weekend night. In fact, during a typical week there are about fifty no-shows, people who simply don't show up and don't cancel their "guaranteed" rooms.

To the hotel management, these no-shows are a Ponzi bonanza. Instead of leaving a room empty all night, it deliberately overbooks the hotel by five percent. Suppose the hotel has 200 rooms, about 175 new guests are scheduled to arrive each day, and all of them will have guaranteed rooms. However, the management knows that about five percent of these 175 new guests will not show up at all. They will pay for their rooms but will not be there to occupy them. Five percent of 175 is about nine people, and, the odds are that only one of them may actually arrive later that night. So as the evening wears on, the hotel keeps renting more rooms, double-renting eight or nine rooms, knowing that eight or nine people with guaranteed reservations won't show up at all.

Double-booking rooms is profitable. In this hotel, rooms rent for about $125 and up per night, so double bookings alone may bring the hotel $1,000 in extra profit per day, which is $30,000 per month or $365,000 per year. That's not peanuts and that's why hotels do it.

The "accidental" overbooking is no accident. It proves the wisdom of the old Russian proverb: "When money speaks, the truth keeps silent."[2]

While the double-booking isn't illegal — perhaps — it's just one of dozens of scams. The hotel makes money from the confidence of their guests (via a con game), and the lowly night clerk suffers the occasional outburst at the registration desk. Maybe management pays him a commission on each double-booking. Since this is New York, he probably needs it — for his tuition at acting school.

Now let's look at a typical fraud, a crime.

The Pigeon Drop

The "pigeon drop" scam works like this: You walk down the street, and a stranger walking in your direction starts talking to you. After a block or so he suddenly stops and points to a pile of trash. A $20 bill is barely sticking out of a crumpled paper bag. The stranger asks you if you see what he sees, and of course you do. The two of you look in the bag. Whoopee! It contains about $5,000. The stranger says a lawyer should hold the money until it can be distributed legally. The lawyer, who is the stranger's partner, demands payment of, say, $1,000 in "earnest money" which you and the stranger gladly pay. The lawyer tells you his office will notify you in thirty days that the money is yours to pick up, and his fee will be half of the earnest money. While you savor the idea of paying $500 to get $2,500, the lawyer and his friend move to a different town — after pulling this scam on dozens of other unsuspecting citizens in your town. You never see either man or the $5,000 or your $500 "earnest money" payment again.

A "Need Money" Scam

You are a male welder, age about thirty-five, and you are walking down a busy city street. An attractive young woman, probably in her twenties, stands on the curb near the crosswalk. Her expression is one of

---

[2] We've also seen this proverb quoted: "When money speaks, the truth is silent."

grave concern, almost fear, and she's holding what appears to be a business envelope. Her lower lip is pursed and trembling. She appears to be on the verge of crying.

You remember your Boy Scout training, how it is good to be helpful to those in distress. You approach the young woman and, gently, you ask her whether anything is wrong.

With a halting voice she explains that her mother has died suddenly and she's been notified that the estate is in limbo because of a legal technicality, and that she has to come up with $500 in cash to pay a bank escrow fee by noon or she'll lose her claim to the funds in the account, $35,000. The problem is, she explains, she doesn't have the $500, and she's spent her last dollar on bus fare just to get downtown, her kids are home alone, and her paycheck won't arrive in the mail until next week. She's going to lose a $35,000 inheritance if she can't get $500 in the next fifteen minutes.

Being a good Scout, you offer to loan her the $500, which you can get from a nearby ATM. She suggests that you wait for her in front of the bank, and, of course, you agree. She'll pay the escrow officer, get her inheritance in cash, and will not only pay you back your $500 but she'll give you an extra $500 as an expression of her gratitude. Of course, you tell her that the extra $500 is not necessary, that the good feeling you're getting from helping her is reward enough, etc. You even thank her for giving you this opportunity to do a good deed.

You visit the nearby ATM, give her the $500, and you wait outside the bank as the two of you agreed. However, after an hour or so, you become concerned. You decide to enter the bank and locate the escrow department. The receptionist there informs you that no such woman has been to the escrow department all day, and that no $500 escrow fee need be paid in cash, and that you are the sixth or seventh man in the past two weeks who has come to that desk with the same story, and who described a similar or the same young woman. When you look around the main lobby to the bank, your stomach sinks as you notice that there is another doorway, one which allows exit to a side street.

You wait another fifteen minutes, just to be sure, and then you call the police. A detective tells you the young woman's name, describes her to you, tells you she's from Chicago, even tells you some of the phrases she used. The detective also tells you that this person is just one of a group of young female con artists who arrived in your city a few months ago, and that arrest warrants have already been issued for her and two of her associates.

The detective asks if you'll come to the station to fill out a report. You decline, since your time is valuable, and you've already wasted most of the afternoon. Although you don't say so to the detective, you don't want to be bothered with going to a trial and testifying; it just isn't worth it. After all, you lost only $500, and you make almost that much in a few days as a welder. You write the whole thing off as a learning experience.

However, the other victims also are writing *their* losses off as learning experiences. They, too, lost only $500 or $1,000 or $2,000. The perpetrator and her friends know that if the dollar amount they take from each victim is relatively small (in the eyes of the victim), few if any victims will take the time to make a formal report to the police, much less sit through a trial and testify and undergo cross examination.

Con artists work the odds. They know that if they hit a lot of people for just a little money, and if they move from town to town, they are unlikely to get caught. If they do get caught, they are not likely to be convicted, but if they are convicted, probably they won't serve time because they are considered just a minor nuisance, not a serious danger, to society.

Such treatment teaches these kinds of offenders that we, the law-abiding members of society, *deserve* what they do to us. Because we tolerate them, they logically believe that what they are doing is not all that bad, really, so they continue harming others by theft by fraud, and they make a career out of crime. We, the law-abiding members of society, tell such crooks that, in effect, what they're doing is "no big deal" to the rest of us.

Did you know that fraud now adds about twenty percent to the price of all consumer products in the United States? And Medicare overpayments currently cost us about $50 million *per day*!

"Your Roof Looks Like it Could Use an Overhaul"
On a nice summer afternoon, a roof-repair truck drives slowly up the street. The driver and his partner are experienced con artists and they are looking for a victim. Here's how their scam operates.

They drive to a nice neighborhood and watch for a house which does not have a new roof, and which has an elderly person on the porch or in the front yard. If they see a particularly nice house, they may knock on the door. If a young person answers, they may not go through with their scam but if an elderly person answers, they will likely go ahead with their practiced routine.

Let's say an elderly woman answers the door. They introduce themselves as brothers, "Frank and Leo," and they give a false last name. They explain that they've been assigned to fix the roof at "1105 S. 21st Street." They are on the porch of 1103 S. 21st Street and there is no house number 1105 on this street. They give a fictitious name for the supposed customer, and the elderly person replies that she has lived in this house for thirty-five years and there has never been anyone by that name in any nearby house on this street.

The con artists then offhandedly comment that they have all the materials to fix a roof, including hot tar, and it's a shame to see it wasted. They'll mention that they noticed a couple of places on the elderly lady's roof which need repair, and if she'll give them the okay and just $500, "in advance, of course," they can do the job right now, while they are supposed to be working for the party who "gave them the wrong address."

The elderly lady will also be told that today's prices for roof repair would ordinarily mean she'd have to pay more than $2,000 for the repairs they can do for just $500 today, if she acts now.

By a process of experimentation, these con artists know which appeal is most likely to get an older person to trust them with the roof repair.

One aspect of this scam involves getting the victim to pay cash. If the victim pays by check, there is a chance the perpetrators may have trouble cashing the check if it is made out to a company which does not exist, or if it is made payable to a person whose name is different from that of either crook. Asking for a check to be made payable to cash may raise suspicions.

Most of the time, these crooks will say the $500 price is good only if the customer comes up with cash (in advance), and they may wink at the customer when they say they have to have cash, to imply that the cash transaction can be kept off their books and therefore untaxed, or away from their boss or the owner of the roofing company.

To ensure that they get cash, one crook may feign dejection and return to the truck. The elderly person will ask why the other man is so dejected, and the lead con artist will tell a tearjerker that belongs on General Hospital, to appeal to the good nature of the elderly person.

A typical story would be that the other man's wife is seriously ill, he needs every cent he can earn to buy medicine, and their family includes seven kids and her mother, or that he's about to lose his home because an illness or death in the family took all of his ready cash, etc. There will also be a mention of his daughter's illness, or some other tragedy, etc., all of which are likely lies.

If the elderly person succumbs, the men slop some tar on the roof, make noises with hammers for five or ten minutes, then move around on the roof "inspecting and repairing small leaks."

After half an hour or so, the men come down from the roof, puffing and panting from all the "work" they've done. Counting on the elderly person's feeble faculties, they'll imply that they've been on the job a couple of hours already, and they've "got to get back to the shop to be dispatched on another job."

The elderly person may never suspect that he or she has been victimized. If there are no leaks in the roof, the victim may believe the men were honest and did a good job. However, if a leak develops, since the elderly victim is not likely to remember the men or their vehicle, detectives will have little evidence of the crime.

A recent television documentary program exposed a nationwide gang of roof-repair and driveway-repair con artists. These men and their families live in the same South Carolina community, in the same neighborhood, and they cooperate with one another, knowing the illegality of what they do. They agree ahead of time which city to hit each year, changing cities from year to year to reduce the chances that a victim will spot them again, and they change the paint schemes on their vans and other vehicles so previous victims will not be alerted to their return.

Victims may not wish to help prosecute these crooks because of the time-consuming nature of cooperating with detectives, writing affidavits as to what happened, and testifying in court. Also, although they may not mention it, elderly victims may be embarrassed to admit they were conned, or embarrassed because they remember so few details, or they may fear reprisal.

This scam operates continuously in most metropolitan areas of the country, it is rarely prosecuted, yet the "take" from these scams allows the perpetrators to live in very nice homes in a nice neighborhood. The average cost of these homes, in terms of FRTs in 1998, appears to be about $200,000 to $300,000.

Who says crime doesn't pay? In the U.S. today, crime *does* pay and it pays well. We Americans are *so* tolerant, *so* loving, and *so* understanding.

"You Have Already Won a Prize"
A California firm was in the news recently. It seems that this firm sends "You have already won a prize" mailings to addressees all over the U.S. While this operation is well known to the authorities, criminal charges have not been filed. Consider what this company does and then see if you think its officers should be charged criminally.

You may have already received a mailing similar to this company's, a promotional piece which announced that you had already won a prize but that the amount of the prize would be determined by what you send back to the company. Perhaps you had to peel a sticker from one place and stick it on a reply card, or you had to fill out a form with employment or education information about yourself. Indeed, addressees are presented with a bewildering assortment of choices for applying stickers, checking blocks, etc., or the person can call a 900 number and just give the company representative a code number which is printed on the mailed material.

A lot of people won't go though the time-consuming and arduous task of reading all the confusing "instructions" and "explanations." They will just call the 900 number and "get it over with."

Calls to 900 numbers, in case you weren't aware, are billed to your phone number and are expensive. For example, calls to this promotion company on their 900 number cost about $3 (FRTs) per minute. In the first minute of the call, a female voice rapidly tells the caller that the rate charged on this call is $2.99 per minute, but because the recorded voice speaks so fast, and the instructions are so confusing and complicated, the statement about the cost is indecipherable. A slow-thinking person, or someone hard of hearing, would not likely pick up on the fact that the call could last approximately seven or eight minutes and that the cost of the call is $2.99 per minute. The voice uses awkward phraseology and occasionally complex terms, and when combined with the rapid-fire delivery, makes the introductory message highly confusing. By the way, the promotion company pays for the first minute of the call; the charges to the victim's phone do not begin until after the first minute.

After the first minute, and now that the cost of the call is being billed to the calling party, the voice slows way down, sometimes unnecessarily repeating instructions or repeating congratulations that the caller has won a prize, etc. Ultimately, after seven or eight minutes of further recorded information, congratulations and instructions, the caller is asked to enter the authorization code number. A moment or two later, the caller is told that his prize is a new ball-point pen or other inexpensive item, and that the prize will be mailed in four to six weeks, or some such period. The recorded voice then thanks the caller for participating in the *game* and wishes him success in his future participation, expressing a wish that he will win the grand prize the next time he plays the *game*.

Actually, only a few callers "win" a prize of any substantial value. In fact, the vast majority of the callers receive a "prize" which is worth less than $5 (FRTs) but the phone call's average cost (which is automatically charged to the caller's phone) is $25 to $30. The promotion company makes a huge profit on the phone calls.

In effect, the talk of "prizes" and "winning" are inducements to naïve people to read the mailed promotional materials. Once they become frustrated reading the deliberately complex printed matter, they are likely to call the 900 number. Once they call the 900 number, it is likely they will stay on the line for the full seven or eight minutes until they get to enter their "secret" authorization code or whatever it might be called.

Not discussed in the TV documentary was the fact that this company need not reply to mail from any "contestant" or "prize winner." That's because mail sent First Class, even if delivered, is not considered by the courts as received unless the sender can prove the addressee received that specific piece of mail. Proof of mail receipt is usually established by a Registered or Certified Mail delivery Receipt. If you don't get a delivery receipt, you may not be able to prove easily that an addressee received your mail.

In the TV documentary, the company's chief executive said he did not think the company was doing anything unethical or illegal, and the California authorities agree, apparently. This promotion company is highly profitable because of the gullibility of its customers, the people who play the *game* and pay up to $35 or more for a "free prize" like a ball-point pen or other inexpensive item.

Is it a crime to take advantage of naïve people? Is it unethical to do what this company does? Or is it as some suggest, no more unethical than many of the other foolish offers naïve or gullible or unsuspecting people fall for all the time?

We mention this company's operation because it is "on the edge" of the law, so to speak. It may seem illegal and fraudulent to some yet to others it will seem only foolish, essentially harmless.

Regardless of what you may think about the promotion company, knowing how it operates may help you spot similar attempts to get your money.

"We're Liquidating Our Inventory"

Another scam involves the telephone. A stranger calls and offers you a special deal on a product you may need. Recent reports suggest you should be alert for a call from someone "liquidating" an inventory of computer equipment or computer supplies. The pitch may go something like:

"Hi, my name is Fred Buzzoff and I'm with Unnamed Liquidators here in" (insert the name of a city more than 1,000 miles from your city) "and we got your name from a list agency which compiles information on computer owners." Here the caller will pause a moment to see if you say, "But I don't own a computer." If you say nothing, the caller knows you have a computer. The caller will go on to say that because of an unusual circumstance, several million dollars of new computer equipment is available for "fifty cents on the dollar, and even more off" for some products.

The promoter will then ask if you need any computer equipment or if you have been looking at adding to your current system, or if you want to upgrade your system with something like a new laser printer or new monitor, etc.

If you stay on the line, the caller will "do a lookup" and "find" exactly what you want. He'll say he can hold this one for you only if you can get the funds to him, in the form of cash or a blank money order, by courier *but not the U.S. mail*, in not more than forty-eight hours.

The "lookup" is likely imaginary, as is the successful "find" of the price. The use of cash or a blank money order is required because the promoter wants to remain hidden from you. He says he's calling from a city more than a thousand miles from you because he doesn't want you or anyone else to find him, ever.

That's also why he insisted that you send your funds to him via a courier instead of the U.S. mail. If fraud is involved, the U.S. Postal Service and the FBI can get involved, and the penalty for mail fraud can be a long, all-expenses-paid vacation at "Club Fed."

The "company address" is usually a privately operated mail-service facility, one which rents boxes to people who need a street address from which they can pick up their mail after normal post-office hours. In years gone by, one could mail a letter to General Delivery, for example at Tanana, Alaska. Mail addressed to you "Care of General Delivery" would be held at the Tanana post office, and if not picked up by you within ninety days, would be returned to the sender.

Today, private-sector mail-box services augment the General Delivery services of the U.S. Postal Service but the private-sector firms have no investigative powers. The supposed seller of computer equipment may give you an address something like "Unnamed Liquidators, 9999 S. 99th Avenue, Suite 19" and then the city, state and ZIP.

This street address is probably legitimate except "Unnamed Liquidators" is just the name the crook gave on his application to the mail-box provider, and "Suite 19" means his mail is delivered to box number 19. Nobody at the mail-box provider service pays much attention to what is put on the application form. The information on that form would interest no one except official investigators, and then only after someone has complained formally to a law-enforcement or postal agency about a suspected scam operating from that address.

The computer equipment probably doesn't exist. The caller is probably calling from a motel, and probably not even a motel in the city to which he asks you to send the money. Courier deliveries to the mail-box service will be held for the scam artist for a few days, at which time he'll either pick them up all at once, or merely ask that they be boxed and shipped to him — via courier — in still another city.

If the crook orders the material forwarded on Friday afternoon and asks for Saturday delivery, he knows it is unlikely that law-enforcement personnel will be around on the weekend to either intercept his package or to arrest him when it arrives. In fact, by using Saturday delivery, the con artist can be sitting on the front steps at about 9:00 a.m., the appointed hour for delivery. The address can be that of a business which either hasn't opened yet, or the business can be open but small, and the con artist can jump up and approach the delivery person when she gets out of her vehicle. "Hi, if that's for Dave Buzzoff at Unnamed Liquidators, that's me."

The crook knows what's on the address label because he instructed the agent in the pick-up mail-box service as to what should show on the package arriving Saturday morning. That label will show whatever is most likely to assure uncomplicated delivery by the courier to the crook.

After getting the package, the crook will then return to his motel room, pull all the cash and money orders from the envelopes, toss the envelopes in the nearest dumpster, and drive to another city or another motel for his next week of "work." This "businessman's" overhead is his motel room and the cost of the calls. His calls could have been placed on a stolen telephone credit card, and he might have paid for his motel by charging the cost to a stolen VISA or MasterCard.

Because the victims have no written record of their transactions, there is no easy way to track the perpetrator; the victims will likely never see their money again. It is equally likely that they'll never receive any computer equipment.

Of course, legitimate liquidation sales do occur. Someone who requires a fast turnaround on an order isn't necessarily a crook. A requirement for cash can be perfectly honest. On the other hand, if you see all three of these elements in an offer from an individual and company you don't know, or whose offer you can not verify independently of the caller, you should be suspicious of what you are told.

One effective protection is to ask for the street address of the business and the name of the salesperson. You might say that the deal sounds great and that you would like to take advantage of it but your business partner lives in a suburb of whatever city the caller says he's in, and you want your partner to deliver the cash tomorrow, personally, and then pick up the merchandise. If you hear something like, "We don't have any way to take walk-in business," or "We aren't set up to deliver like that because our warehouse is in another state and we send everything by courier," you'll have further grounds for hanging up the phone.

One final test: Tell the sales person you are entertaining important guests right now but you are definitely interested and you want to get back to him as soon as your visitors leave. Ask for a phone number. If he gives you one, make sure you have it down right. Read it back to him and make him confirm it. Then call information in that city and see if there is a listing for that company, and whether the phone numbers match. If they do, the call may have been legitimate. If there is no listing for that company, you will know the caller probably wasn't.

If the caller says it's now after business hours and their switchboard is closed, tell him you will call back in the morning. Get a number or hang up. The next day, during normal business hours, you can try calling the company.

If you suspect you have been victimized by fraud, call your local police at once, along with your state's attorney general office. You could also notify the Better Business Bureau.

Another form of sales deception is pandemic today, but, surprisingly, many people don't know of it. It isn't a crime, it does not involve tragedy or payment of cash or near cash, or even a time constraint. It's called

Bait and Switch

Here's the scene. You are a field sales representative for your Seattle-based company, you are on a business trip in Los Angeles late Friday afternoon. Your older car begins to lose power and overheat. You pull off the freeway, stop at a convenience store, and as you shut your engine down, you notice it sounds very strange, almost "sick." Unknown to you, the drain plug in your crankcase became loose and your oil leaked out. Your engine has seized, it is ruined, and the cost of repair will probably exceed the price of a good used car. So you buy a copy of the local paper and look at used-car advertisements.

You see an ad for an almost-new, low miles sedan of the type you've had your eye on for some time. You hail a cab, rush down to the lot, and, as the cab pulls away, you start looking for the car you read about in the advertisement. A used car salesman you probably wouldn't vote for walks up to you and says, "Hi, I'm Cindy. Are you looking for something in particular or are you just window shopping, heh, heh."

When you tell "Cindy" what brought you to the lot, she apologetically tells you that "the car in the advertisement was sold yesterday" but, because she now knows what kind of vehicle you want, she leads you to their stock of that particular kind of vehicle.

In an hour or so you drive away with another vehicle, similar to the one in the advertisement but which cost you quite a bit more than you'd expected to spend. The car that caught your eye in the ad was probably a vehicle owned by an individual who drives to different car lots, takes a picture of his car on that dealer's property, and then sells that picture to the dealer for use in an advertisement. "Cindy" probably never owned the classy car. She just used it to draw customers to her lot, where she switches you to a different car.

Actually, because you arrived in a taxi, and because the taxi drove off, "Cindy" knows you probably won't quibble about a few bucks added to the cost of the wheels she's going to sell you. You need to be back on the road, selling life-size decorative flamingos, on Monday morning.

"Cindy" has an advantage over you, thanks to the "bait and switch" operation. She baited you with the imaginary car, then switched you into something she had in inventory.

An African Parallel

The Serengeti Plains encompass several thousand square miles of central Africa. Millions of large animals roam the Plains during seasonal migrations. All of these millions of animals die, and are eaten by predators or scavengers, but there is no trace of their corpses. Even their bones are gone.

The food chain in Africa does a nice job of keeping "litter" to a minimum. Every scrap of the dead animals returns to nature. It is nature's way.

Some crooks believe that naïve people should be shorn of their money, that such shearing is nature's way of keeping them from power. That is how many crooks justify their thievery to themselves.

Some people commit an occasional petty theft or burglary because of temporary need, but crime is the "day job" of those who believe they have a right to take money or property from anyone "stupid enough" to fall for their schemes.

Young offenders, perhaps during their first incarceration, learn this philosophy. Fellow inmates teach them new criminal techniques, which they use in new swindles when they are released. "Never give a sucker an even break," is their philosophy, and they sneer at all who don't share their belief.

A common belief among many criminals is that only suckers obey laws. Criminals obey only when the laws benefit *them*, the crooks. As Lenin put it: "Promises are like pie crusts, made to be broken."

An essential component of our limited constitutional Republic is obedience to the law. Early training in social graces and etiquette taught us self-control and respect for the person and property of others. As adults, our voluntary compliance with the law helps make this society function.

However, when a sizable minority of any society begins to *dis*obey the law selectively, that society is headed for the scrap heap of history. That's because the cost to catch, prosecute and jail the burgeoning criminal element will soon become more than that society's law-abiding majority can pay.

Society usually pays for crime *in*directly. The total cost of crime may be seen in the cost of law enforcement, courts, legal counsel for indigents, jails, probation, medical care for inmates, legislative attention, insurance, time lost from work and its impact on employers, permanent physical and emotional damage to victims, plus hospitalization and convalescence, and associated emotional trauma to relatives and friends of the victims. The total cost to society of just a small amount of crime is truly great.

Because of our crime problem today, American society is like a fish to which a lamprey eel has attached itself. A healthy fish can feed one or even two small lampreys but as theses parasites grow and multiply, the host fish becomes less and less able to survive. Ultimately it dies and the lampreys seek another host.

You are the "host" to all criminals, petty and otherwise. Every crook in the country is a kind of lamprey eel which has attached itself to your skin, to the skin of your spouse and your children, and to the skin of all of your friends and neighbors.

Crooks are society's lamprey eels, blood-suckers, because they suck the wealth of the law-abiding members of society. The next time you see a "telecaster" wink and smile when she discusses vandals who spray-painted their gang symbols on the side of a police car or city bus, keep in mind that the telecaster is winking and smiling about a lamprey eel which is fastened to your child's body, and to your body, and even to the telecaster's body.

To smile and wink at crime and criminal behavior suggests confusion so terrible as to border on madness. Similarly, to coddle criminals, or to indulge in a "dialog" with someone who exhibits gross anti-social behavior, is equally irrational.

Your Best Protection

The Scout's motto is "Be Prepared." That's good advice, even if you aren't a Scout. Here's what we mean.

To survive and prosper, you must preserve your capital, and to do that you need high quality information. You need to be forewarned about dangers to your capital.

To protect your capital from human predators, keep alert to the methods crooks use. The four most essential things to know are:

1. If it sounds too good to be true, it probably isn't true.

2. Crooks feed off the productive segment of society, and use lies and every other form of deceit.

3. Crooks like nothing better than to steal *your* wealth. They use every trick they can think of to do that. *You* are a target for them today, *right now*.

4. Crooks do not look like "crooks." Crooks, such as the roof-repair frauds, look like ordinary workers. "Pigeon drop" specialists look like ordinary citizens. White-collar crimes are committed by people who appear professional in every respect; they may be your biggest danger, especially if they are civil-service workers, especially if they were elected or appointed.

Your main concern should be to avoid falling for a fraudulent sales pitch. To avoid the "hook" you must remember the three hallmarks of a scam.[3]

a. The approach, which may seem normal, will often involve an alleged human tragedy.

b. A time-factor usually dictates that you must act at once; you do not have time to investigate the perpetrator's claim or offer, nor do you even have time to call a friend or other trusted advisor.

c. Cash or near-cash is almost always required.

Here are a few guidelines on how to respond to a pitch which you suspect is part of a criminal scheme.

First, ask questions about specific details like addresses, phone numbers, the names of supervisors, owners, coworkers, agents, legal counsel, accountants, and ask for the rank, title or positions of each person, along with specific phone extensions or phone numbers where possible. Evasiveness should be your cue to hang up.

Second, if you suspect you are dealing with a con artist, if you are face to face with the person, simply say, "Thank you for your time," and walk away. If you are in a city and want to help your neighbors, or if there is a question about your safety, go into a building where you can see anyone following you, and call the police. An officer may be dispatched to get your report. Possibly you'll provide the testimony the police need to arrest the perpetrator.

Third, if the pitch was by phone or mail, call the police and ask for their guidance. You may be asked to call a detective, or to mail a copy of the promotional materials you received, or to notify your telephone company that you received a call you suspect is from a criminal enterprise. It may also help for you to contact the nearest Better Business Bureau office, a lawyer or your clergy or accountant. Make your concerns known to competent professionals, and keep a written record of what happened and what steps you take to notify the authorities.

We need to discuss three other scams currently in vogue in the U.S. These are not all fraud, *per se*, but they are dangerous and you need to be aware of them.

Rear-end Collision
In Los Angeles, Miami and other cities, two or three punks drive around in junker cars, watching for possible victims. The scam begins with a rear-end collision. The punks pull in front of their intended victim, and, when traffic is moving slowly, they slam on the brakes so the victim hits the rear of their car. The punks get out of their car, look at the "damage," and complain of sore necks. They suggest they'll be willing to forget the whole thing if you'll give them $500 cash "to get x-rays," etc., and have their neighbor, who is a "mechanic," "repair" the "damages." These guys may use the same car in a dozen or more "accidents" and then, when necessary, go buy another junker to continue their "day job."

A cash payoff appeals to many victims to preserve their driving record, and their insurance company never finds out about the "accident." Also, the punks feign anger, which inspires the victim's fear that if he doesn't pay cash he'll be beaten or killed.

A variation on the rear-end accident is the one in which two drivers cooperate. One drives into the other, and the drivers and their passengers sue the insurance companies for bogus injuries, etc. Crooked lawyers file the suits, crooked medical doctors issue

---
[3] Scam: Underworld slang term meaning swindle, originated as a carnival term to mean a rigged game or concession.

bogus diagnoses of permanent disability, and all participants to the scheme win. The losers are you and other law-abiding citizens who pay the multi-million dollar claims, through higher insurance premiums.

Another variant of this kind of fraud has come to the attention of the metropolitan transit authorities in New York City and Philadelphia, where people claim lifetime disabilities from injuries suffered in a car-bus accident which is a simple fender-bender. In one accident like this, several people claimed permanent disability and sued for at least $25,000 — yet the bus driver, the driver and other witnesses all agreed that, at the time of the collision, the bus had no passengers. At other car-bus collisions, pedestrians have boarded the bus after the accident and waited to be taken by ambulance to a hospital, so they could make a claim against the bus service.

More recently, enterprising crooks in the rear-end collision scam have eliminated the need for vehicles. They report a non-injury accident which is completely bogus: they generate a fake police report, fake photos of an accident and damage to vehicles, fake repair estimates, and a fake repair bill.

Friendly Persuasion, Texas Style?
Here's another kind of fraud, from Texas.

You are driving to work one weekday morning in Dallas when suddenly you see a blur and then everything goes black. You regain consciousness in a local hospital about an hour later, where you are attended by a doctor and two nurses. As you slowly awaken, the doctor talks to you. She explains that your car was hit broadside by a tractor-trailer unit whose load had shifted and thrown the truck out of control. You have a broken back and broken legs and will be hospitalized for about thirty days. Then you'll likely need physical therapy for a year, and you'll be unable to work for probably a year after that. Since you have a family and mortgage to support, you'll need financial help, and soon, so your husband looks in the phone book for a lawyer who specializes in accident injury cases.

You soon contact "Louise," who explains that she's been representing accident injury cases for thirteen years. "Louise" will be happy to take your case on a contingency basis, collecting "only thirty-three percent of your award, plus expenses," only *after* she wins a settlement for you. In other words, "Louise" explains, she doesn't get a dime until she gets a settlement for you. You agree to have her represent you, and you sign an agreement to that effect. "Louise" tells you she has every confidence she'll have an award for you "soon," probably within six months.

Unknown to you, "Louise" is a crook. After a few weeks of keeping you on edge, she calls you to report that she's made tremendous progress on your case, and that there probably will not even be a need to go to trial, that she's been able to "straighten out" the claims department at the insurance company and that "they now see the light." "Louise's" enthusiasm is infectious and you are anxious to learn how much the award is going to be. A family friend has told you that in a similar case in the news last year, the injured party was awarded about $500,000. Your bills are piling up fast; you hope "Louise" can get a big award soon.

A week later, "Louise" calls with a "good-news, bad-news" report. It seems she's got the insurance company in a mood to settle out of court, and generously. The bad news is that there's a provision in the insurance code under which the federal regulation's don't apply because the trucking company was not involved in *interstate commerce* at the time of the accident. Because only Texas rules apply, the larger settlement is no longer possible. So, "Louise" explains, the maximum "we" can expect to receive if "we" go to trial is about $150,000. Moreover, "Louise" explains, in this kind of case, each party has to cover his own court costs, which "Louise" expects would be about $50,000 on "our" side. Then, after the court granted her percentage of the settlement, you would get about $80,000. However, she thinks she can put a little more pressure on the insurance company claims department and get them to settle for $125,000 right away, if they think they can avoid going to court. Of course, don't get your hopes up too high. "Louise" asks for your okay to accept an offer about that size, and of course, you give it.

Although you didn't major in math, you realize that sixty-six percent of $125,000 *right now* is much better than *maybe* $80,000 a couple of years from now, when you might even lose the case at trial. "Louise" compliments you on your clear thinking, saying you are a "lawyers' dream" (because you are so clear thinking and intelligent) and says she'll be back in touch in a few days.

On the following Monday, just after lunch, "Louise" calls and says she has a check made payable to you in the amount of $82,415, your part of the settlement, after she took her fee plus about $85 in expenses. You are ecstatic, overjoyed, and you agree to let her come by your home this afternoon so she can get your signature on the "settlement papers" that will release the insurer from further claims arising out of the accident. After you sign it, "Louise" also gets your endorsement on the back of the settlement check, and even fills out one of your deposit slips. On her way back to her office, "Louise" deposits your settlement check in your bank account, which she didn't have to do. You marvel at your good luck at finding "Louise" and having her represent you in your time of crisis.

As you give thanks for great lawyers like "Louise," you are blissfully unaware of a couple of facts. First, "Louise" is a practiced hand at settling cases out of court. Your case was just one of about 1,500 similar cases she's settled out of court in the past five years. Here's how she did it.

"Louise" knows the people in the claims departments of all the major accident insurance companies in the Dallas-Fort Worth area, and she's dined with many of their top executives. In your case and in most of the others, she told the claims manager that if he paid her a consulting fee of $25,000 (an estimate), she would "try" to get her client to accept an out-of-court settlement of *about fifteen percent of what would normally be awarded at trial*. Of course, the insurance company agreed. When you accept a "low ball" settlement offer of $82,415, it writes a "consulting fee" check to "Louise" for about $25,000, and nobody is the wiser.

If you had been represented by an ethical lawyer, whether or not your case had gone to trial, your award would likely have been closer to $500,000.

While the ethical lawyer's fee would have been about a third of the amount awarded to you, or about $165,000, "Louise" avoids trials because they are "iffy," preparing for them takes hundreds of hours, and they are very stressful. Her approach gets her smaller but more frequent and certain checks, she avoids the labor and stress of trials, and makes more money.

However, you are very thankful to get the $82,415, you pay your bills, and the agony of your convalescence keeps your mind occupied. You never suspect that "Louise's" representation was anything but professional.

Although such unethical conduct by any lawyer would disbar him forever, we suspect that unethical cooperation between plaintiff counsel and insurers is not limited to Texas and is not limited to the profession of law; a few medical professionals may also be tempted to compromise their ethics when big bucks are involved.

Two Fortune Tellers

You respond to a knock on your door one day and greet two women. The older woman announces that she is Madame such-and-such, her daughter is the other woman, and they are here to see "Mrs. Davis" (or other made-up name). You inform Madame that there's no "Mrs. Davis" at this address, etc. Madame says her answering service must have written the address down wrong, and she launches into a casual spiel intended to whet your appetite for a "psychic reading" or similar service.

Basically, these two women produce a series of contrived events designed to trick the unwary into believing that "good spirits" want to do good things for him. The victim merely has to prove his sincerity by destroying some money in a prescribed and witnessed way.

Madame and daughter suggest the victim meet at Madame's office at an appointed time in a few days and bring along, say, $1,000 in cash. Madame charges "only $25" for the visit and, under instructions from the "spirits," burns the $1,000 in the fireplace in plain view of the victim. Or so it seems. In fact, the room is very dimly lit, and Madame is able to replace the package containing the $1000 with an identical package which contains newspaper cut into the size of paper currency. The newspaper package is tossed into the fire and the $1,000 is hidden until the mark leaves.

By means of such "spirit" instructions, these women can bring in many thousands of dollars per month. It's a scam which takes advantage of a darkened room and people's fear of offending the gods, as it were, people who are insecure or guilty about something. Anyone's latent guilt or insecurity makes him susceptible to manipulators of every stripe — not the least of whom may be the day's political figures.

Three-Card Monte
"Monty." That's what the locals call it. You meet "Monty" for the first time as you walk down a quiet neighborhood street in Brooklyn, New York, enjoying a nice spring morning. In front of a deli you notice a man standing behind a small folding table, and he looks like he's demonstrating something to two or three other men.

As you approach, you see that the men are playing a card game. There is money on the table. The "dealer" puts three cards, two Aces and the Queen of Clubs, on the table. The trick, you soon see, is to guess which card is the Queen of Clubs. After a few games, and after one of the players wins $20, the dealer asks if you want to try your luck, adding that it costs you $1 minimum to play a game.

You decide to give it a try, partly because you sense that the dealer is a little dim, and because you've easily followed his manipulation of the three cards in the games you've watched. In your first game or two, the dealer moves his hands slowly and lets you win. Then he invites you to bet a little more because he has to go somewhere soon. You increase your bet to $5, and after a win and a loss, feel a little anxious to hit this guy for a good one; you up your bet to $50. This time the dealer wins, but he acts surprised that you didn't guess the right card. Then comes the clincher: the dealer offers you a chance to break even, to bet once more but for the total of what you've already lost, say about $75.00.

You agree, he deals the cards, and you lose. You're now out $150 and you've been playing Three-card Monte for only about ten minutes. The dealer says good-bye to everyone and heads down the street, and the two other men go their separate ways. You continue to your destination, $150 less affluent, and wonder how you could have been so accurate in the first few games yet fail so miserably in the last few.

The answer is simple. The dealer manipulated the cards in a way you didn't suspect. In the games he wanted you to win, he moved the cards slowly enough for you to follow his moves. When he wanted to win, he moved the cards just fast enough to confuse your eye but not so fast that you realized you were dealing with a real pro. The dealer never wants you to become aware of how fast he can manipulate those cards, but to be able to beat the really alert bettors, he has to be able to do it at truly blinding speed. You were suckered into the game, and he thought you deserved to get taken to the cleaners.

A variation on this game comes after you have lost a bundle. A stranger walks up and whispers that he also has lost a pile to this guy. He says he has an idea on how to get "our" money back, saying that if you want to place a bet on his money, he'll pull a little trick on the dealer. He'll play "one more time," but say he first wants to examine the cards. The dealer lets him do so, and the stranger bends a corner of the Queen, so he can easily spot that card. Your new friend bets $200 and you add $150 to the pot, hoping to win back what you've already lost. The dealer takes the cards back and deals, but you see that he has bent the corners of the other two cards, the two Aces, so your partner now has no way of knowing which card is the Queen. You lose again, yet you don't dare accuse the dealer of cheating because you and your partner have just attempted to cheat him.

Later you discover that your "partner" is a pal of the dealer's and that they have been pulling this trick on people for years.

In fact, the other players were also part of the

scam. It takes several "shills" to lure "marks" (victims) to the dealer. This is three-card Monte and it's been taking gullible tourists and locals to the cleaners for nearly a century.

What other dangers lurk in today's marketplace? The following paragraphs should help you avoid some financial dangers because we are about to examine how radically different are the attitudes, the habits of thought, of criminals and law-abiding people.

Beware the Automated Teller Machine
ATMs are a fact of life in America today and they will probably be for a long time. They already are like pay phones, something you can ignore that is there when you need it. We discuss ATMs more extensively in the next chapter but here we introduce the subject because most law enforcement and bank security officials categorize ATM crimes as *fraud* cases.

If you lose your ATM card or a typical credit card or debit card, no one else can use it for a cash withdrawal unless he also knows your access code, the four-digit or four-character code which permits access to your account or accounts. Writing your access code on your ATM card is a bad idea because if you lose it, the finder may use the access code to withdraw the maximum daily limit from your account, sometimes for several days in a row, before you discover you've lost your card. By the way, notifying your bank *after* a crook withdraws your money will usually not protect you from that loss.

If you are not careful when you punch in your access code, a stranger standing nearby may be able to see what buttons you push, and thereby learn your access code. If you leave your transaction receipt, that crook may also learn your ATM-card number, and possibly also the amount of your withdrawal and the balance in your account.

The crook who has your account number can create a new card with that account number. The number gives him the information on the bank which issued the card, and thereby enables the crook to code the new card's magnetic strip appropriately. By knowing the amount you withdrew, the crook will know whether your wallet or purse would be worth stealing for the cash. For example, by knowing your access code, the crook who is a pickpocket can lift your wallet, quickly remove your ATM card, and then place your wallet where it will be found right away and returned to you. If you lose your wallet and get it back right away, you will likely assume that nothing is missing, especially if all your cash is still there.

If the crook is watching you, he or she will watch how you behave when you search through your wallet. If you show no concern, you probably didn't notice that your ATM card is gone, and the thief will feel safe "hitting" your account later that day or early the next, for the maximum amount possible.

Crooks not only look for ATM, credit and debit card access codes, they also try to detect phone-card access codes. A stolen phone card with a valid access code can be sold to another crook for hundreds of dollars. Particularly susceptible to this kind of crime are persons using ATMs or phone cards in busy public places such as airports and train stations.

To help protect their customers, ATM providers now place the machines in well-lighted areas, and program them to print only a part of the account number, without the account balance.

Banks say that a four-digit number is the longest PIN most customers can remember. Perhaps the password recognition software can be modified to permit a longer PIN because a familiar word of eight or ten letters could be memorized just as easily. Also, ATMs may soon be programmed to take digital pictures of the person involved in every transaction, and to send that picture to the card-issuer's headquarters for processing prior to dispensing any cash.

Protect Your Assets
We respectfully suggest that every reader make a list of his credit cards, debit cards, and any other similar cards, and keep that list at home or at the home of a trusted friend or at a law office. If you should ever lose your wallet or purse, that person could call each card issuer to report the card stolen. You will not likely be held responsible for charges to those cards after the issuer has been notified. If you don't wish to ask this kind of help from a friend or lawyer, pri-

vate companies offer the same service for a small annual fee.

Federal legislation may be forthcoming to penalize those who steal another's identity. A college student recently (September 16, 1997) testified before the U.S. Senate Banking Subcommittee, reporting that when her purse was stolen, her identification was copied and then used to get new credit cards in her name. The crook charged $27,000 in purchases in about a year. The victim testified that she received virtually no help from any government agency or card issuer during her ordeal. She did say she was pleased that once the fraud exceeded $25,000 she could notify the United States Secret Service, but that agency never called her back. The credit-card companies and other businesses that had been defrauded did call her back. They continued to plague her.

During the Senate hearings, a security representative from a major credit-card company said that Internet transactions were, in some ways, more secure than store transactions because, on the Internet, there are no carbon copies or other written record of the transaction which might be found in a trash barrel or dumpster by a crook who specializes in "dumpster diving" for that purpose. In fact, testimony before this committee suggests that Internet transactions may now be the safest "place" to use a credit card.

Cell Phones; Radio Phones
If you insist on using a radio phone or cellular phone, fine, but you should realize that others may be monitoring your calls. Such eavesdropping is easy because electronic scanners, some available for less than $100, let anyone, including crooks, monitor cell and radio phone traffic. If you call a firm and order a product or service, charging the purchase to your credit or debit card, a crook might be listening and even recording everything you say. Your answers to all the questions the seller may ask are available to the world, via your cell or radio phone and an inexpensive scanner. Some crooks leave their scanners on all day, and record the intercepted traffic on a tape recorder. At the end of the day, the crook plays the tape back at twice normal speed, which allows him or her to find quickly the calls involving credit card transactions.

If you do not use a cell or radio phone, your calls are still subject to easy interception. Many mail-order firms offer telephone tap equipment and "bugs" at reasonable prices and no questions asked. That equipment can be carried in the trunk of a sedan, and may be used to eavesdrop on calls and other conversations in your home by detecting the feeble electrical signals generated when your voice vibrates the carbon granules in your home or office telephone microphone; your phone can act as a 'bug' even when the receiver is on the hook, that is, when your phone is hung up. Such a phone is said to be "hot." Also, invisible laser beams can be bounced off any wall or window in your home, apartment or office, and the vibrations of your voice will be detectable even to inexpensive eavesdropping equipment perhaps a block or two away. Today's eavesdroppers need not physically connect their equipment to your phone line. You must be discreet about what you say over the phone, especially if you are wealthy or even just comfortably well off. Professional thieves may already be monitoring your communications.

Criminal Process
We'll close this chapter with a few observations. One hallmark of a dying society is a worsening crime rate. Criminals tend to "progress" from minor rudeness, to serious anti-social behavior, to petty crimes and then to major crimes. Few criminals commit murder to launch their careers. Most serious crime is committed by experienced criminals.

To foretell accurately a society's future health we need look only at its current level of anti-social behavior and petty crime. When anti-social behavior and petty crime increase, ten to twenty years later we should expect an increase in *major* crime.

In the United States, we are living in an unstable society. Please reflect on the following issues and questions, and a few examples of anti-social behavior.

- **FAMILY:** Is an *in-your-face* attitude characteristic of a person likely to commit violence against law-abiding citizens and their family members? How often do we hear of battered women and children? How prevalent is cruelty to children, the elderly, and animals? How much of a problem is domestic violence? How about alcohol and drug abuse?

- **ADULT RESPONSIBILITY:** How much do we, as a People, seek pleasure and immediate gratification as opposed to saving for a rainy day? Are we, as a People, becoming less mature? How well do we as voters really understand our nation's history and the important principles upon which our government is based? How many eligible voters study the issues and vote in every election? How many of us look forward to jury duty? How many of us know and understand the important principles involved in the United States Constitution?

- **MANNERS:** How much public rudeness is there in movie theaters, restaurants, in apartment complexes, at your local public (civil-service-worker-operated) schools? How much emphasis is there on raising our nation's young people to be respectful, polite, patriotic, honest, law-abiding, and physically and morally clean and productive citizens? How many times have you seen obscenities displayed publicly, such as in a vehicle window decal or bumper sticker? How often have you heard obscenities and profanity in public places? How often on TV? How often in movies? How often in public by teenagers or pre-teens?

- **NEIGHBORS:** How many of your neighbors can you count on to own and responsibly handle firearms? How many of your neighbors or co-workers know first aid and CPR?

- **SCHOOLS AND YOUTH:** How much teenage and pre-teen insolence and vulgar behavior do you see at local shopping malls? How often do you hear about crime in the public schools? How serious is it? Are younger and younger children committing ever-more-serious crimes? What do you think of self-destructive tendencies such as "beauty wire" punched through noses, lips, ears, tongues, and even genitalia? What do you think of black clothing, lipstick, hats, black everything, as emulation of ghoulish "heroes" from the acid-rock and heavy-metal bands? How about drugs, tattoos, and rejection of all traditional American values? How soon will the nation's teens begin wearing bones in their noses, grossly stretching their lips and ears, or adopting still other *tribal* behaviors?

- **VEHICLES:** How many people drive below the speed limit, especially on freeways? Do you? How many people think it's okay to drive with their boom-boxes blasting everyone else, even at three o'clock in the morning? How many drivers deliberately adjust the headlights on their cars and motorcycles so *they* can see better, not caring that their headlights now blind oncoming traffic? How many drivers continue through intersections on left turns after their signal turns red?

- **SPORTS:** How much intentional and wholly unnecessary violence is there in sports? How about hockey? Do the fans relish the fights? How much of this willful violence is prosecuted *at law*? We'd say virtually none. Sports is sometimes touted as wholesome, yet *criminal assault* is a key entertainment factor in some of the most popular sports. Ever wonder where children get the idea that hitting is okay? Why wasn't Mike Tyson charged with criminal assault when he twice bit Evander Holyfield's ear, tearing a piece off, in their boxing match in June 1997? Tyson was prosecuted and fined by the boxing commission but why was there no *criminal* prosecution?

- **POLITICS:** Anti-social behavior may manifest itself as corruption in politics and government. Evidence of anti-social attitudes in political leaders may be seen in their avoidance of principle, avoiding the critical issues, much talk but little constructive action, pandering to the whims of the mob or the dominant media, and essentially zero interest in the historical or ethical foundations of law and legislation. Most national political figures in the United States today exhibit anti-social symptoms such as megalomania,[4] partly because voters may not recognize the symptoms or understand the danger of anti-social behavior in political affairs.

Our list of questions could continue, of course, but you probably see our concern. People in all parts of the United States say that the number and severity of anti-social incidents in their area, even if rural, seems to be rising.

Fraud: A Symptom of Megalomania?
The United States is in trouble, some of our most sacred institutions are crumbling, and an all-pervasive, anti-social subculture is perverting them. Fraud is a major component of today's anti-social and criminal activity, including violent and white-collar crime (which includes political crime). Fraud is a real "growth industry." A television news show reported, in November 1997, that fraud cost American consumers (U.S. citizens) $400 billion in 1996. Since the U.S. population is roughly 265 million, the per-capita cost of fraud in 1996 was about $1,500.

Our schools and other public institutions instill anti-social attitudes in young people. The entertainment industry — sports, TV, "popular" music, etc. — reinforces trashy values.

White-collar criminals, particularly Insiders who hold tremendous monetary power, instill *sophisticated* anti-social and criminal attitudes in their children.

Will the Insider's children compel *our* children to live in a truly horrific future? Will we, as a People, continue our blasé attitude about fraud?

Notice how so many civil-service agencies can no longer be reached by phone; how often do we get only a recorded message, or put on eternal Hold, or switched to a voice-mail box, guaranteeing anonymity — it's hard to pin blame on a nameless worker. Civil-service workers love to mumble about "budget cuts" and "low manning levels." Today, they never need take a call from any citizen. Are civil-service workers operating like the long-distance scam artist who is also most anxious to preserve *his* anonymity?

Please also consider your legislator's plea that "this bill must go through to solve the problem of," and here you finish the sentence with your favorite crisis-*du-jour*. Remember the scam artist who pleads for help because of the needs of a sick relative or family emergency? Is there also a parallel to the scam artist's insistence on cash or near-cash?

Haven't we been trained in the government schools to expect government to solve every problem from housing to psoriasis? Have some civil-service entities (government agencies) and other major American institutions themselves become scams? Are some of the civil-service workers who run the government perpetrating fraud?

Many scholars today believe there *are* legitimate grounds to charge not just several individuals but even several *groups* of individuals in the government with actual or constructive fraud, and in some cases, *conspiracy* to commit fraud.

As the new millennium approaches, the main question we Americans might ask ourselves is:

When will there be a formal investigation of these concerns, and, if not soon, why not?

•

---

[4] Megalomania, pronounced meg-uh-low-main´-ee-uh, is a psychological illness characterized by delusions of one's importance to the world, or by an obsession with doing things on a vast scale, globally, etc.

"I object to the claim that banks are a rip-off. They're part of the monetary system. Sure, there is hocus-pocus in the money game, but people know that. It's an acceptable fraud."

A middle rank Canadian banker, *as quoted in* Towers of Gold, Feet of Clay, by Walter Stewart *(Don Mills, Ontario, Canada: Collins Publishers, 1982), p. 1*

"The history of the great events of this world is scarcely more than the history of great crimes."

Voltaire *(1694 - 1778)*

"Whoever controls the volume of money in any country is absolute master of industry and commerce."

President James A. Garfield *(1831 - 1881), as quoted by Paul Hein, M.D.,* All Work & No Pay *(Sewanee, Tennessee: Spencer Judd, Publishers, 1986)*

" The transition from gold to fiat money will be greatly smoothed if the State has previously abandoned ounces, grams, grains, and other units of weight in naming its monetary units and substituted unique names, such as dollar, mark, franc, etc. It will then be far easier to eliminate the public's association of monetary units with weight and to teach the public to value the names themselves. Furthermore, if each national government sponsors its own unique name, it will be far easier for each State to control its own fiat issue absolutely."

Murray N. Rothbard *(1926 - 1995),* Man, Economy and [the] State, *Volume II.* From Blanchard *(see Appendix A,* Gold Newsletter*)*

15

Your Security and Today's Money Substitutes

IN recent years, many new things have been used as money. A blizzard of new financial products and services offers more convenience and efficiency. Just twenty years ago we would have considered most of today's offerings as strictly science fiction, not even remotely possible until well into the next millennium.

Today's banking services, for example, are marvelous, but, to some, bewildering. This chapter will help dispel that confusion.

BANK SERVICES TODAY
Automatic Teller Machines (ATMs)
ATMs now dot the globe. They are in every major city in the world, and in most smaller towns and even remote areas in the most highly developed countries such as the United States and Canada. They are also in the major cities of the advanced countries of Asia and the Middle and Far East. Africa and the Latin American countries lag but not by far. You can get cash, in the local currency, in almost every major airport and rail station, and major bank, in almost every country now, from ATMs. Currency conversions, where needed, are automatic.

There are two main dangers with ATMs. First, they produce a printed receipt of each transaction. As you learned in Chapter 14, Fraud, you should always take your receipt with you after you use an ATM because you do not want a crook to learn anything about you or your financial affairs. Second, if you don't shield your fingers from prying eyes, someone watching with a telescope or binoculars from across the street could easily read your hand or finger movement and learn your access code and the amount you withdraw.

Another danger with ATMs is that prying eyes may see how much cash you withdraw. A drug user who needs a fix may be ruthless in his or her attempts to get their drug of choice. Everyone, regardless of their physical size or strength or stamina, is a potential victim of a crazed drug user who is desperate for a fix.

In fact, you should know that if you are young, physically strong, alert, and well able to defend yourself, you are in the greatest danger. A drug user who is truly desperate for a fix won't threaten you. He will shoot you in the head, probably from behind, and then take your wallet or purse. You will have no chance to give him your money; the thief, recognizing your health and physical prowess, won't take a chance on getting into a fight with you. Because of your size and obvious mental alertness and physical strength, he will just blow you away. You may not feel a thing but your family and other loved ones will suffer the agony of your death for a long time.

Of course, the frail, elderly or obviously ill or physically disabled are also prime targets for ATM-location robberies. Sometimes the thief will brutally beat these people because they cannot defend themselves; some criminals derive great satisfaction from inflicting pain and suffering on others. A drug user, already weakened by his addiction, may physically attack a feeble victim, to rebuild his shattered ego. Cocaine users, in particular, are known to inflict horrible injuries on their victims, even when the victim has voluntary handed over his or her money to the thief.

Where addiction abounds, and when anti-social attitudes are "acceptable," the crime rate will be high. Addicts are finding that ATMs are great places to get money!

Wire Transfers
You can easily and safely send money to another state or country electronically, and one way to do it is to have your bank send a wire transfer to your choice of destination. A wire transfer is a transfer of funds on a phone or teletype wire. Of course, a "wire" is not necessarily used anymore because most electronic communications today travel on microwave radio links or fiber-optic cables.

To send funds to a relative in Scotland, for example, you would visit your bank's department which handles wire transfers. It can't be done by phone. You will fill out a form, indicating the account from which you want the money taken, and the number which identifies the destination bank and account. A fee of about $15 applies, and you must present adequate identification to prove you are authorized to access the account from which the funds will be transferred.

Wire transfers are usually done only from a bank's main office, so if you visit a branch to do the transfer, it may be delayed until the next business day. That's because the paperwork and other information must be transferred from the branch to the main office, which might be many miles from the branch you visited.

In many cases, the branch will fax your application form to the wire-transfer department, where it will be processed when time permits. That is because today, in all but the largest banks, wire transfers are not a popular service. The bank employee who handles wire transfers may work most of the time on another activity, doing the transfers only when needed.

Delays can occur, sometimes inexplicably. In 1993, on a Wednesday, I think, I tried to send a wire transfer to a company in New York. I drove to the nearest bank branch to do the paperwork, but since the clerk who processed my application was not familiar with the process — few wires were sent from that branch — she misrouted the paperwork. It ended up in the wrong department at my bank's main office and the error wasn't discovered for two days, until late Friday that week.

The main office didn't send the wire-transfer message until the following Monday. When I called the company to which I'd sent it, their bank had not yet notified them that the funds had arrived. On Tuesday I got the same response, but finally on Wednesday, late in the afternoon, an accounting department employee said their bank had called to say that my wire-transfer had crawled in. She also said the wire transfer had actually arrived on Monday but that because such transfers are so rarely received by that bank, the employees there didn't know what to do with it. It took them three days to figure out how to apply the funds and to notify the receiving company.

A week after I filled out the forms and paid the $15 fee, my money was delivered to the company in New York. For less than fifty cents I could have mailed them a check and it might have arrived sooner.

Wire transfers are particularly valuable for transferring large sums, especially to foreign recipients. Let's say you want to buy a ranch in Costa Rica. The price, in U.S. "dollars" is $247,875, probably too much to charge to a credit card. Also, there would be potential delays in processing a cashier's check. You would probably elect to "wire" the funds to the proper account, converted to Pesos by your bank, where you get the most favorable exchange rate. Your transaction could be handled in a few days, safely and securely.

For the latest information on wire transfers, contact your bank.

Debit Cards
A debit card is the opposite of a credit card. To get a debit card you must have funds in the bank which issues the card. The advantage of a debit card is that you don't have a balance to pay and no interest charges apply. A debit card lets you buy things over the phone, for example, or in stores, without the need to carry a lot of cash. Also, you receive a monthly statement from the issuer, showing all of your transactions through the month. That statement can help you spot spending habits which are bad for your financial health. You might even graph your expenditures for a year or so, to see how they may be changing.

A debit card should be protected, however, because if you lose it, and if you have written your access code on it, an unethical person or crook could empty your account.

Some debit card issuers offer insurance to protect you against such loss but it may cover losses only after you notify the issuer that the card is lost or stolen. Other insurance may not cover losses if the insurance company believes you have improperly secured the card.

Debit cards are sometimes touted as a great mechanism for a young person to build his or her credit rating. That's not really true because no credit is involved, no credit report is issued, and no interest payments are made because nothing is lent. However, using a debit card may help some people build confidence in their own ability to manage their money, and that is a valuable benefit.

Debit cards have another benefit. They eliminate the need to carry a lot of cash, which reduces spending for non-essential items. Few vending machines will accept a debit card. Snacks, trinkets, and other "small ticket" purchases will be less frequent if we carry only small change and a debit card.

Credit Cards
Credit cards are possibly one of the most valuable financial innovations of the century, although, like other powerful tools in the hands of the unwary, they can be dangerous.

Credit cards create instant credibility with strangers, even strangers far away, even without the need to meet them.

Because of that instant credibility you can buy a product or service from someone you don't know and who doesn't know you. The credit card issuer approves you to the seller and the seller to you. You and the seller identify each other as reliable and responsible, at once.

The "at once" is the key benefit of a credit card. "At once" means zero time, and "time is money." If you don't have a credit card, your must pay more "time" for your purchases, meaning you pay a higher price.

However, the extra power a credit card gives its holder can undo him. If we run up a huge debt, the interest on that debt may become an onerous burden. It is not uncommon these days for someone to owe so much on a card that he cannot pay even the interest, much less make payments on the principal.

A credit card user may succumb to the power and buy things he doesn't really need. Eventually, he could pay a heavy price. The card may not be worth it.

However, if a credit card is used properly, and if all of our expenditures are carefully considered, we will benefit handsomely because we will pay a little less for things and we will have a wonderful written record of our transactions. We will also have extra purchasing power available in event of an emergency.

Presently in the U.S., credit-card debt is about equal to the indebtedness of the federal government, but where credit-card debt could be paid off in less than two years, based on the average worker's disposable income, the federal debt is another story.

The federal government's *current* debt, that is, the debt which must be paid within twelve months, is about five trillion dollars, or $5 trillion. In the U.S., a trillion dollars is a million million dollars. However, this is only part of the story. The real national debt is closer to four times that amount because the "national debt" we hear about on TV and in the press is just the *current* debt, the amount due and payable within one year.

The nation's long-term debt, *also* called the national debt, is not discussed very often because it is huge. It is about $19 trillion today, in the spring of 1998, and the Congress hasn't a clue as to how "we" are going to pay it off. See Figure 15-2, page 184.

Most of the real national debt is unfunded. That means the Congress has obligated the country — you — but Congress has not determined how those funds will be raised. If taxes are raised, the economy falters, people are laid off, plants are closed and overall government revenues decline. A similar situation faces individuals who build up such great credit-card debt that their entire paychecks won't even cover the interest payments, much less allow any payment of the principal.

The United States Congress is composed of supposedly well-educated and responsible adults. Some are lawyers, a few have backgrounds in accounting or other professions. Yet, with the ready assistance of countless thousands of other professionals who work in government offices such as the Treasury and the Congressional Budget Office, they have put this country's financial health in serious peril. Their profligate spending patterns, often to win votes, have placed an almost impossible burden on today's children, a burden they will have to bear as adults, a burden which they had no hand in creating. We have saddled our children with a horrible future, and we ought to be ashamed of ourselves.

Credit cards are a wonderful invention, and can help us reduce waste and conserve our resources, but to do those good things, they must be used wisely.

Smart Cards
A "smart card" is a credit card or debit card which contains a tiny computer chip. The purpose of a smart card is to keep track of its use, and provide that information to the user.

For example, if you use a smart card for a transaction, the display device which processes that transaction may interact with the smart card to tell you that you've reached your budget limit for that kind of purchase this month. Your smart card may be programmed to alert you when you have less than $1,000 in credit, or it may alert you that today you also need to pay a certain amount on a particular account or at a particular store.

Smart cards are likely to play a larger role in our financial affairs in the future, so here are some of the things such a card might be used for in a few years.

A smart card may alert you when you need to gas up your car, or to get it greased or change the oil, or when your eldest child is due for a medical or dental checkup.

A smart card could also record your blood pressure and pulse, if you insert the card in a blood-pressure measuring machine at your supermarket or drugstore. Your cardiologist will likely have a machine to download those readings from your smart card and produce a graph of your heart condition. He can make copies of the graph, one for you and one for your patient file.

Smart cards could also help convert money when you are traveling in foreign countries. A gas station in Germany may sell a liter of unleaded gasoline for "M 10.20" ("*zehn mark zwanzig*") but your smart card will convert this unit price to "$4.27 per gallon," which you'll see in the pump's price window. The gas station will be paid in German Marks but your credit card, because it is smart, will record the sale as a gasoline purchase on that date in the amount of $51.93.

Another use of smart cards might be in keeping tax-deductible or business expenses separate from personal ones. If you program your smart card appropriately, your purchase of medicine and medical services will be coded as tax-deductible, as will be purchases of office supplies, etc., but dinner in a restaurant will be coded as personal entertainment or meals, unless it has a business purpose.

Smart cards could also contain medical information about you, if you wish. If you are injured or fall ill suddenly, your smart card could save your life. If you are unconscious and can't tell the emergency room doctors about your medical history, your smart card could provide vital information on your medical history, medicines you take now, and the names and phone numbers of your doctors and other medical advisors. If you are an American, and if you faint while visiting New Delhi, India, your smart card might tell the emergency room doctor that you take Cardizem (diltiazem hydrochloride), 100 mg daily, for hypertension, and that you have a family history of high blood pressure and cancer, and that your blood pressure was 190 over 110 with a pulse of 105 just yesterday, when you checked your blood pressure at the airport in Tokyo. That may be all the examining physician needs to see to rush you off to the cardiac care unit.

The future of smart cards is bright. Keep an eye out for developments in this area. They are bound to be interesting, and potentially valuable for you to know about. However, when we said, "Keep an eye out," we meant something special. Here it is.

New "Eye-D" (ID) For You?
Technology can and often does dazzle the eye with spectacular achievement. Such is the case with a new and unfolding technology which promises to end much criminal mischief with checks, credit cards, and identification generally.

Scientists have determined that, much like fingerprints and ear shapes, your retina and iris patterns are different from the retinal and iris patterns of everyone else in the world. The retina is the inside back surface of the eye; it is the surface on which light is focused by the lens. The iris is the area which determines the color of one's eyes; blue, brown, green, etc.

Computers can scan your retina or iris, store the pattern digitally, and then link information about you to that digital image.

The benefit of this technology is that you would no longer need to carry a credit card, driver license or other form of identification. You wouldn't even need to carry cash for commercial transactions. When you want to buy something, the store clerk, for example, would scan your iris, and the store's computer would then instantaneously transfer the amount of the sale from your bank account to the store's. You'd get a receipt and the transaction would be reflected on your bank statement.

This would greatly lower the risk that you'll be the victim of a robber or a thief. If no cash changes hands, there would be zero chance that the clerk might give you the wrong change.

If police units are equipped with scanners, fake driver licenses will become a thing of the past. Outstanding warrants could be tied to a crook's digitized iris or retinal image.

This technology could also help identify murder victims or the remains of persons who are otherwise unidentifiable. If a body is found shortly after death, the new identification systems can help locate family members as well as the victim's last known address, place of employment, and other vital information.

Also, a child who becomes separated from a parent or guardian at a baseball game, for example, could be identified immediately by a scanner in a police unit, or by a scanner in any nearby business. A lost child could be reunited with his or her parents quickly.

With ID based on one's iris or retina, some forms of crime will likely fade into obscurity, thereby improving everyone's standard of living. "Eye-D" is not far off but it is kind of *far out*! Unfortunately, this boon could be a bane in the wrong hands. Imagine Hitler or Castro using it. "Your papers, please!"

Auto-deposit, Withdrawal, Transfer
Banks and other financial institutions nowadays can automatically receive your paycheck, transfer funds to your savings account, and even pay your bills for you. Your pay is available to you on the day you expect it, and you don't need to drive to the bank or even endorse a check. The transfer is done electronically between your employer's computer system and the bank's.

Even if your employer subcontracts the payroll activity of the firm, the payroll service company can electronically deposit your pay into your checking account with ease, and at no cost to you.

One requirement for automatic payroll deposit might be that you have your checking account at your employer's bank. Your employer's accounting department personnel may be able to tell you your options and limitations in this area.

The main advantage of automatic payroll deposit to employees is that there is no check to lose, nothing to endorse, and no need to travel physically to the bank to make the deposit. The savings in gas and time may not be great for just one payday but over a period of years, the savings are substantial. To avoid the loss of just one paycheck would be a tremendous saving in itself.

To arrange for automatic payroll deposit takes only a minute or two. Typically, you sign a form authorizing your employer to deposit your pay automatically, and you provide your account number. Your employer will be happy because he no longer has to buy paychecks, print your pay information on them, and keep them after they've been returned to the company from the bank.

Automatic payroll deposit benefits banks too. They don't have a check to read and enter into their system, they don't have anything to guard while it is on their premises, and they don't have anything they need to mail back to your employer.

Automatic payroll deposit saves everyone time and money. It's a good deal.

Of course, we must enter the usual *caveat*. As we have seen, the Insiders will use every trick to keep us in their "funny money" system. Cash means freedom and anonymity. The "cashless society" we've heard so much about means records. In innocent hands, no problem. In a megalomaniac's, it means you'll hear, "Your papers, please!" Automatic payroll deposit means no cash. Notice also that, effective January 1, 1999, all Social Security recipients must open bank accounts for the direct deposit of their checks. Those deposits will vastly increase fractional-reserve banking.

Safe-deposit Boxes
Safe-deposit boxes, sometimes called "safety" deposit boxes, have been around for a long time. Basically, they are small metal boxes, hundreds of which a bank keeps in a vault made of metal and concrete, which has a huge, incredibly thick, steel door. The door, when locked, makes that room essentially impenetrable. It probably has both a combination lock and a timed lock. Once the door is closed at the end of the business day, even someone who knows the combination cannot open it until the time lock automatically opens. The time lock, usually set to unlock only at the beginning of the next business day, prevents an employee from reentering the vault at other times.

A safe-deposit box may be used to hold family valuables such as jewelry, birth and death certificates, small and precious heirlooms, wills, deeds, prenuptial agreements, and other valuable or important items. Many individuals and business owners store their computer backup disks or tapes in bank safe-deposit boxes.

Safe-deposit boxes are available in a wide range of sizes but their length is about eighteen inches. The smallest box is usually about three inches wide and two inches high. Documents can be folded to fit in this box, if necessary. Expect to pay about $15 per year to rent this size box.

The largest safe-deposit box is about the size of a drawer in a filing cabinet. This drawer would be about twelve inches wide, twelve inches high, and of course, the standard length of that bank's safe-deposit boxes, probably about eighteen inches. The rental fee for the largest box may be about $500 per year.

The least expensive safe-deposit boxes will be found in bank branches, particularly those in small towns or rural areas. The most expensive boxes will be in a bank's main office, usually downtown.

For personal use, the safety and convenience of a nearby branch office will likely be satisfactory for you. However, if you own or manage a business, and if your business records are extremely important to you, it may be worth the extra cost to use a downtown vault. However, it would be risky to drive to and from the downtown location to access your safe-deposit box.

For most of us, either as individuals or as business owners or managers, a bank's branch office safe-deposit vault will be safe enough while still offering us the convenience of being near our home or office.

All-hours Access
Today's wonderful banking environment includes 24-hour access, by phone, to many bank services. Perhaps the most valued benefit of after-hours service is the ability to find out whether a check or deposit has cleared your account. Since banks cooperate to provide these services, a bank customer-service specialist is as close as a phone call, 24 hours per day, seven days per week, even on holidays. You can call to see if your paycheck has been deposited in your account, or to see if a check you wrote to a relative has been processed by the bank, reducing your available funds by possibly a large amount.

If you maintain personal and business accounts, you may transfer funds from one to the other, simply by calling the special after-hours number for your bank. Some banks allow you to make transfers by using your phone keypad to enter the account numbers and then follow prompts given by a recording.

You may also be able to transfer funds to and from a savings account, at any hour of the day, without the need to talk to a customer service specialist.

Other after-hours services include applying for a loan, or for a credit card, or for a debit card, or for business advisory services.

Some bank customers are intimidated by the wide range of services offered by banks today, but we've found that the people who process your call after hours will be helpful, friendly, and competent to answer your questions. We use after-hours banking services often and we encourage you to become familiar with your bank's services. We think you'll find them very valuable to you and your family.

Bank Security
Banks today are faced with a nearly bewildering range of real and potential attacks against their security. We'll discuss this jeopardy briefly because you'll benefit by knowing about it when you consider the fees banks charge these days.

Computer fraud is a huge concern to banks today. A "hacker" is a computer programmer who uses his or her talents for destructive and other illegal purposes. A hacker may try to penetrate the bank's computer system, by modem, late at night or on a weekend, and transfer funds from customer accounts to the hacker's account, possibly in another country. Recently a Russian computer whiz transferred a few million dollars from several New York banks to a bank in Europe, where the Russian and a couple of his pals picked up the money. It was a classic example of "hacker" activity.

Another danger to banks is that a crook will learn the access codes used on credit and debit cards the bank has issued. As we have seen, once the crook has this information, he or she can use a credit-card imprinting machine to duplicate the credit card, and use it at ATMs for cash withdrawals or to purchase products in stores. Products purchased are taken to a pawn shop and exchanged for cash. Or, the crook will visit a "fence," which is a criminal-operated enterprise that pays cash for merchandise known to be stolen. Fences will often transport the stolen items to another city or state and attempt to sell them at "garage sales" or other low-profile untaxed and unlicensed events.

Banks must also be alert to bogus checks. If you lose your purse and your checkbook is in your purse, an unscrupulous person can keep your checkbook. Crooks will write several checks payable to "Cash" and then use the checks to buy things from unsuspecting merchants, or from unsuspecting clerks who may work for merchants. A stolen check written for the amount of $100 payable to Cash may be used to buy an item priced at $20. The crook hopes to get $80 in cash as change, plus he can sell the $20 item to a friend for possibly $10. Thus a crook can get $90 by using just one of your blank checks made payable to Cash.

Deposit slips can also pose a peril to a bank and its customer. If a crook finds a deposit slip, he or she can visit the bank which has that account, get a "counter check," and make it payable to Cash. A counter check is a blank check available in most bank lobbies, offered as a courtesy to a customer who may have forgotten to bring his or her checkbook on a visit to the bank.

The counter check made payable to Cash has a place for the user to enter the number of the account from which the funds are to be drawn. The crook simply copies the number from your deposit slip to the counter check, and he's ready to "rock and roll" — with your money.

Another form of fraud perpetrated against banks is the person who approaches a teller and tries to cash a check made payable to a third party. Suppose the teller suspects that the endorsement is bogus. For example, let's say you are a teller at XYZ Bank of Busted Hump, Arkansas. One day a young woman approaches your teller's cage and asks to cash a check. You look at the check and see that it is drawn on the account of a major aircraft manufacturer whose headquarters are in Los Angeles, California. The check is wrinkled and smudged, and dated a couple of months ago. The signature on the check is not a real signature but an impression made by a machine which stamps a signature of an officer of the aircraft manufacturing company.

However, what really gets your attention is that the check is made payable to "William Jefferson Blythe, Esq." You realize that the "Esq." after the payee's name indicates that this person is probably a lawyer, but the young woman presenting the check for payment doesn't appear to be even close to the age of a lawyer, who usually needs five or more years of college to get the degree, and she doesn't look anything like a William. Also, the endorsement appears to be the writing of a sociopath, horribly disorganized and virtually illegible. The girl appears disheveled, is nervous, and keeps looking at a beat-up older car sitting in the parking area, with the engine idling and a seedy looking young male sitting in the driver's seat.

So, you approach your boss, the branch manager, who consults a computer system for lost or stolen checks. Nothing comes up to indicate that this check is anything other than valid. You cash the check for the girl, give her the $3,709.24, the amount of the check, and she leaves the bank, gets into the beat-up car, and she and her seedy-looking boyfriend hit the road again. Come to find out though, Mr. Blythe is the girl's father, he is a lawyer, and he gave her that check for college tuition just before she hit the road with her boyfriend.

However, the next person in line was a matronly gal in her early sixties and well tanned from a recent trip to Miami. She has identification, driver license, Social Security card, etc., and wants to write a check for $1,000 for, as she put it, "to buy gifts for the grandchildren," while she and her husband are in town over the weekend on vacation. The check is drawn on a local bank, you cash the check, and the lady thanks you and heads out the door.

Suddenly, you hear sirens. The parking lot fills with police cars. With guns drawn, the police arrest the woman and her husband. A state trooper and two FBI agents enter the bank and interview you on what just happened in the bank. You explain that the woman cashed a check and you show it to the officers. The agent in charge explains that the woman and her husband have been the focus of a three-state search, and that the pair are wanted on a host of federal and state charges involving stolen checks, stolen credit cards, bogus checks and credit cards, and wire fraud.

The young girl and her seedy-looking boyfriend were innocent of wrongdoing — despite their appearance — but the matronly lady and her distinguished-looking husband were the crooks. Bank tellers are trained to watch for what's really wrong and not just symptoms of possible criminal behavior. If a bank pays a check to the wrong person, the bank may be liable for the loss, and, even if the loss is covered by the bank's insurance, repeated losses at the teller windows will drive the rates sky-high. Tellers have to be meticulous in their screening of payouts, otherwise they get fired. If you deal with a teller who seems unduly critical, you can always ask to speak to his supervisor, who may be more pleasant or reasonable, but in the final analysis, banks are the target of virtually every thief, and the banks know it. Conduct your affairs professionally and the banks will love you; act like a loose cannon and you'll be treated accordingly. Fact.

Bank fees are higher today because of overhead. Instead of one bank "downtown," major banks today have branches all over the place, as a convenience to customers. Few of us today would be willing to drive "all the way downtown" to cash a check or visit our safe-deposit box. The expense of branches is passed on to bank customers through higher fees for specific services. If you think banks are awash in a sea of cash, start your own bank and retire a millionaire in just two years, or however long you think it would take you to rake off a couple of million. Actually, local banks don't do badly but if they don't guard against fraud, they don't do very well.

If you operate a business that receives a lot of paper currency, you may wish to buy a small, handheld device which will help you spot counterfeit U.S. currency. The device is a battery-operated scanner which, when swiped across paper currency, will beep and blink if the currency is good. This device detects the metallic particles in modern paper currency. Counterfeit bills, which don't contain metallic particles, will not cause the device to beep or blink its light. One model of this device, available now at office supply stores, sells for about $30 and uses a 9v battery.

The Internet
Developed by the U.S. government, beginning in about 1959 with ARPAnet,[1] the Internet is a set of computer software and hardware instructions manufacturers and users have agreed to. In the beginning, the Internet allowed universities and other large organizations to communicate with one another via their computers and telephone lines.

Access was extended to non-government entities beginning in the late 1980s and the Internet soon became the world's most universally-accepted medium of electronic communications, surpassing even the telephone in rate of growth. At one time in the early 1990s, new Internet accounts were being established at the rate of more than 20 million per month.

If you aren't acquainted with the Internet, or just the "Net" according to some folks, listen up and we'll give you a quick and non-technical overview.

You have a computer. You install a software program on it, perhaps under Windows. You now see a little picture, an icon, labeled "Program Manager." Then you click on an icon labeled "Internet" and a new screen display pops up. On that display you click on an icon labeled "E-Mail" and soon your computer shows you another screen, and you see some blanks to fill in.

The blanks are for data about an "Internet Service Provider," or ISP, a company which connects people to the Internet. You phone a local ISP, give them your credit card number and expiration date, and they give you some information to enter into the blanks on your screen. Your cost for their services will be about $20 per month.

You enter the information into the blanks on the screen and then follow whatever remaining instructions you see. Now, you are ready to "log on" (connect) to the Internet.

Logging on is as easy as anything you've ever done with a computer. Typically, you double-click sequentially on three or four icons and then you hear your modem dialing. A minute or two later you hear a hissing sound and some strange chirps. Then all is quiet and your screen shows several icons representing choices of activity in which you may engage. The three most popular activities are:

1. Sending and receiving email, which is an abbreviation for "electronic mail."

2. Surfing or browsing the web, which is slang for "visiting various Internet web sites."

3. Newsgroups, which is a "place" (actually, a series of screens and supporting software programs) which displays public commentary about topics under discussion.

Email, or e-mail, is electronic mail one person sends another. Unwanted commercial email messages are called "spam" or "junk email." You can type a short email message, enter an email address in a field la-

---

[1] ARPA is the acronym for Advanced Research Projects Agency, a subdivision of the United States Department of Defense.

beled TO:, and then click on a button marked SEND. Your email message is on its way and it may show up at the recipient's ISP in just a few seconds, probably less than a minute, even if you are in New York and the addressee is in Kuala Lumpur, Malaysia. And email is free. Messages can be several pages long, you can ATTACH a small picture or other kind of file to your message, and you can request and receive a "receipt," an acknowledgment from the addressee's ISP that the message was received okay by that ISP. The receipt may even show the date and time the addressee's ISP received your message.

Email may be used to communicate with sellers of products and services. However, if you supply a seller with your credit card number and expiration date, etc., there is a chance that others will see that information. As a rule, it is not a good idea to consider email private because it is like sending a post card — any postal worker can read it while it's in postal-service custody.

Very few people report problems with email information coming back to haunt them. Millions of dollars of transactions take place every week on the Internet, usually in complete safety. Nonetheless, insurance that could protect you from criminal use of your credit card, is available.

If you exit your email program and then click on a button which activates a software package called a browser, meaning a program which allows you to browse around on Internet web sites, you will probably visit a *search engine*.

A search engine is a special Internet web site which helps you find other web sites. You might visit a search engine called Web Crawler. When Web Crawler is on your screen, you will see a blank field into which you can type a word or two. Let's say you type "gold." Then if you click on a button possibly labeled SEARCH, your computer will sit idle for a few moments and a list will begin to show on your screen. Some words in the list are one color, perhaps black, and other words are blue. The black words are probably part of a description of a web site somewhere which has something to do with gold, and the blue words are the Internet address or formal name of that site. If you see a description which looks interesting, click on the blue words and you'll soon be looking at the "Home Page" or main screen of that web site, perhaps a gold-mining company.

Browsing the Internet is also called "surfing the Net." Surfing often goes faster after the business day ends because fewer people use the web (the Internet) after working hours. "Surfing" can be fun but unless you have a new and very fast computer and modem, things can move slowly on the net.

You can visit web sites which offer things for sale. You can enter your credit card information into fields at that site, build a list of products you want to buy, click on a button to confirm the sale, and away your order goes. Moments later, that company's computer processes your order and sends you an invoice to confirm it, tell you which products are on back-order, how the merchandise will be shipped, and when it is expected to arrive.

For example, if you'd like to buy another copy of this book, you can do so by visiting this address:

    http://www.amazon.com

The company's formal name is "Amazon.com, Inc." and its address is spoken as "Amazon dot calm." Notice that "calm," as in what follows a storm, is how you pronounce "com." "Dot" is how you communicate that a period is between "Amazon" and "com."

Amazon.com warns its customers that it does not guarantee that your credit card information will not be intercepted by someone, but amazon.com is, as of July 1998, a very large bookseller — from whom you can order more than 2.5 million different titles. They would not have grown to that size if there had been a serious problem with credit card numbers intercepted by crooks.

Once you give Amazon.com your credit card number, etc., you need not enter it when you make subsequent purchases. As long as you remember your password, your transactions at Amazon.com will be charged to that credit card.

Buying items over the Internet is good in some ways but not so good in other ways. It is good because it is fast, it is available all day every day, you don't have to try to communicate with someone who may not understand your speech, and it avoids personality clashes over the phone. Also, it gives you a written record of the transaction, almost as soon as it is complete. The bad things are that you don't get to see and touch the product before you buy, it has to be shipped (you can't take it home with you), and you may have to wait a while before it arrives.

At least one web browser, Netscape, provides some security to credit-card transactions conducted on the Internet. Unfortunately, recent releases of Netscape have had weaknesses which could be exploited by persons familiar with transaction security programming. Netscape has eliminated those weaknesses but transaction security on the Internet, while good, still is not perfect.

Encryption

Encryption means changing a message so it can't be read or understood by anyone other than you and your intended recipients.

As a child, you may have used a "secret code" tool to write a note to a friend, but the note would appear incomprehensible to everyone else.

A very simple encoding (encryption) scheme might be just to shift all the letters of the alphabet one place to the right. To communicate the letter "a" you would write a "b." To communicate a letter "z" you'd send an "a." To send a letter "m" you'd send an "n." Using this encryption scheme, the word "love" would appear to be "mpwf." Who could make any sense of "mpwf?"

Simple codes like this can be broken easily because English and every other written language has patterns which can be analyzed by a computer. For example, in English, "e" is the most frequently used letter, "t" is the next most-often used letter, and so on through the alphabet. A test of any coded message may show which symbol is the letter "e," the "t," and many other letters, all determined by the frequency the symbols appear. Once a substantial percentage of the letters are known, it may be easy to see what the missing letters are.

A very good encryption program, PGP, which stands for "Pretty Good Privacy," was created by American computer whiz Phil Zimmerman. Zimmerman believes that civil-service employees, and others, are sometimes snoopy, and he wanted to do something to stop snoops. He invented PGP to "put an envelope" around your email messages.

His PGP program processes a plain message like "I love you!" so it may resemble this:

> Z3wCJ0meWBmYrT0wpjN4zb

Since this would take a long time to unravel, you could use this scrambling system with some degree of confidence that few would take time to try. But with a computer, decrypting this kind of message wouldn't take long. Using our example of replacing a letter of the alphabet with another letter or a symbol, unscrambling might take less than one second if you use a fast computer and a good analysis program.

PGP works better than simple letter replacement. It uses each letter as a multiplier against a number which is changing according to a mathematical formula. To unscramble an encrypted message takes another program at the recipient's end, and that program must use a special unscrambling program called a "public key." It is called a public key because you can give it to anyone. It can unscramble messages you send to one recipient, but not messages you send to anyone else.

PGP is effective. If you send a short message, say twenty-five words, and you encrypt your message with PGP, a typical computer could not break that message during the *normal lifetime* of the recipient. However, using your public key, he could decrypt the message in less than a second, and read it as easily as you are reading this paragraph.

PGP protects our privacy, an essential element of our freedom. However, civil-service employees want the ability to peek at our email messages, for "law enforcement and national security" purposes.[2] We believe these arguments are just a pretext for civil-service workers to intrude still further into our lives.

---

[2] "Necessity is the plea for every infringement of human freedom: it is the argument of tyrants; it is the creed of slaves." William Pitt, the Younger, in 1793.

PGP and other forms of encryption are ideal tools that help keep financial affairs and electronic communications private. Information on the commercial version of PGP, called "ViaCrypt," may be obtained by contacting:

> Network Associates
> 3965 Freedom Circle
> Santa Clara, CA 95054
> Phone: 408-988-3832
> Fax: 408-970-9727
> Sales: 800-338-8754, ext. 2752
> Web site: http://www.nai.com

One book we found very helpful is *Digital Money: The New Era Of Internet Commerce*, by Daniel C. Lynch and Leslie Lundquist (New York: John Wiley & Sons, 1996).

E-Banking
Electronic banking is now offered worldwide. It is a service which allows customers to access their account information after hours and by computer, to effect transfers of money between accounts, or to pay bills, or to transfer funds to businesses which are set up to do business on the Internet.

E-Cash
Readers wishing to investigate electronic banking should be sure to contact the Mark Twain Bank at 800-926-4922 or 314-418-0224. You can leave a message and someone will call you back. For faster service, send the bank an email message at:

> Ecash-info@marktwain.com

Or visit the bank's website:

> http://www.marktwain.com

The Mark Twain Bank is at P.O. Box 524, St. Louis, Missouri 63166. The first Mark Twain bank opened in 1963, and through acquisitions, now is part of a group of sixty-three banks, and is in the top 100 banks in the U.S., with assets in excess of $3 billion. "Ecash" and "ecash" are trademarks of Mark Twain Bancshares, Inc., the owner of Mark Twain Bank.

E-Gold
E-metal and E-gold (and e-metal and e-gold) are registered trademarks of Gold & Silver Reserve, Inc., 1013 Centre Road, Suite 350, Wilmington, DE 19805. Call G&SR at 800-909-6590. This address is the office of Mr. Barry Downey, attorney at law, and vice president of G&SR. President and founder of G&SR is retired Florida physician Douglas L. Jackson. G&SR is an Internet-based service whose customers conduct business in either a currency or in units of a precious metal, worldwide. For example, you could pay for a Swiss watch, perhaps sold by a store in Geneva, Switzerland, with perhaps a fraction of a troy ounce of gold or maybe 200 Swiss Francs, by executing the transaction through G&SR. For more information on e-metal accounts and other services, email G&SR at:

> admin@e-gold.com

Their web site is:

> http://www.e-gold.com

G&SR is a fascinating concept and it merits the attention of everyone interested in helping to resolve the world's monetary dilemma. G&SR is on the leading edge of the movement to restore honest weights and measures, and sanity, to the world's monetary systems. See also Appendix A.

DigiCash
A relatively old hand in the Internet realm, DigiCash has recently begun a national television advertising campaign to attract new clients to its electronic "money" product. DigiCash works with banks in a manner something like a travelers-check mode. You "buy" some "cash" which you then send, in an encrypted message, to a seller who also is a client of DigiCash. If your DigiCash funds are stolen or lost, you get an adjustment similar to a partial refund. If you buy anything, the seller never sees your credit-card numbers or anything else about you that you choose to keep private. Contact DigiCash at:

> http://www.digicash.com/

Figure 15-1. Gold & Silver Reserve, Inc., the world's leading source for gold-denominated transactions, as well as transactions denominated in silver, platinum, and currencies. Metal-denominated transactions can be in various units: Dollars, troy ounces, fractions of an ounce, etc. Offers privacy and security, locally and internationally. Visit http://www.e-gold.com.

CyberCash

CyberCash is the brainchild of the two geniuses who founded VeriFone, the company that achieved remarkable success by providing vendors with the machines which verify and process credit-card transactions. Their current service, CyberCash, is similar to others, provides automatic encryption and other privacy protection, but is priced differently than similar service providers. You can find out more about CyberCash at:

> http://www.cybercash.com/

Mondex

You'll surely hear a lot about Mondex in the near future. With Mondex, you use a smart card to access a host of services, not the least of which are financial. This system, now controlled by MasterCard International, will likely eventually also allow storage of things like one's medical history and authorized prescription drugs, allergies, eyeglass prescription, access code for your employer's computer network, your encryption "public key," and other important items.

Other

You may also benefit by investigating First Virtual Holdings, Inc., Open Market, Inc. (or just OMI), NetBill (a product of VISA International and Carnegie Mellon University), and Netscape Communications Corporation. Most of the current crop of on-line transaction services offer protection via encryption but their range of services and pricing varies widely. Investigation will reveal the best combination of services and prices for your needs.

Computer Viruses

A computer "virus" is a computer program which cannot be controlled by the computer operator. Some viruses are pranks — all they do is display a silly or puzzling message at unpredictable times. Other viruses are extremely damaging to the computer, erasing information from a hard-disk drive, or scrambling that data, or possibly polluting that data with random errors. People who produce and distribute computer viruses to unsuspecting computer users are malicious criminals who deserve harsh punishment under the law. They have done untold millions of dollars of damage to computer systems around the world. To protect your computer from viruses, you must do several things.

First, you must be cautious about what you put into your computer. Viruses can get into your computer from a floppy disk, or from something you download from a bulletin board system (BBS), or from the Internet. As long as you are downloading strictly ASCII (plain text) files, you probably won't receive a virus. However, if you download a "free" utility or other program, you may be falling for a trap — viruses are usually distributed by the appeal of something for nothing. You may see an offer for a free utility program which will keep your hard-disk free of viruses, only to find that *it* is a virus that destroys all the data on your hard-disk before you realize what it is doing.

If you download only text files, which is what you do when you receive email, you probably won't receive a virus. If you avoid bulletin boards, you will go a long way toward keeping your computer free of viruses. Being careful about the floppy disks you put into your computer is also helpful.

Second, to increase the likelihood that you will never be harmed by a computer virus, you should buy and use an anti-virus software program. These programs cost up to $200 per copy but they work well and can give you a lot of peace of mind.

Anti-virus software programs usually include a small program or routine[3] which stays alert while you operate your computer. This kind of program tells you about unusual activity on your hard-disk drive, and offers instructions on what you might do. If it prompts you that it has detected a virus, if you say OKAY, it will "kill" that virus, and then erase it from your hard disk so you'll never be endangered by it again.

Anti-virus software manufacturers keep abreast

---

[3] A program which loads into a computer's memory and stays active is often referred to as a "Terminate and Stay Resident" program, or "TSR."

of the newest viruses being spread around the world. When you buy an anti-virus software package, it usually comes with a comprehensive list of all the known viruses and, you can be sure, it knows how to detect and erase them all. Of course, new viruses are created regularly and your old anti-virus software may not know about them.

If you buy an anti-virus software package, you should be alert to communications from the manufacturer, who will likely notify you when an upgrade to its software is available. Upgrades often include an expanded list of viruses which can be detected and foiled by that software. Upgrades to anti-virus software are usually inexpensive, easy to install, and worth their cost.

Third, even if you have the latest and greatest anti-virus software, you could still suffer terrible damage from a new and devastating virus. For this reason, even if you have strong anti-virus protection on your computer, you should remain cautious about what you download from Internet web sites, or what you accept as ATTACHments to email, what you download from a BBS, and what you copy from a diskette.

For more information on anti-virus software, you may contact your local computer software store, or a local computer-user group, or the computer science department at a nearby college or university.

Computer Cookies
A "cookie" is a special program which monitors your activity on the Internet, stores that information, and sends it to another party. You may be unaware that a cookie has been downloaded to your computer, or you may have agreed to allow an Internet web site or browser to install one. However, some web browsers and web sites can install a cookie on your system without telling you they have done so.

A cookie is usually a simple program which tracks your activity on the Internet so as to develop a consumer profile of you. It may track things like the web sites you visit, purchases you make on the Internet, the dollar amount of those purchases, and, if you buy software, whether that software is for a PC or a Macintosh, etc.

The web site which inserted the cookie on your system will likely read the information collected by that cookie the next time you visit that web site. The creators of that web site will develop a database of visitors, and then use that information for marketing purposes, possibly selling it to others.

Cookies can benefit you, in a way. Let's say you are interested in investing in mining companies which focus on gold and silver. If you visit dozens of search engines and continuously search for "gold" and "silver," etc., that information may be recorded in a cookie and then transmitted to a search engine you use quite often. Your email address might then be added to a list of email addresses of persons who have an interest in gold, silver, coins, jewelry, or precious-metals investments. You could receive commercial messages on those topics from businesses which specialize in those products or services.

On the other hand, the promotional messages you receive may be unwanted, if, for example, you sought the information because it was part of a class on economics you were taking, for a post-graduate degree in business administration or political science.

PC users can search their hard-disk drive for files like cookie.txt and Macintosh users might look for MagicCookie. Look into those files and see what is there. You may wish to erase the file if you did not agree to install those cookies.

To keep current on the debate about cookies, visit any search engine and search for "Electronic Privacy Information Center" or just EPIC. That group, located in Washington, D.C., monitors the cookie debate and regularly posts new information about it, and related topics, on their web site. EPIC may be contacted by email at:

>   info@epic.org

EPIC's main web site is at:

>   http://www.cpsr.org/cpsr/privacy/epic/

In this address, the "cpsr" stands for Computer Professionals for Social Responsibility, which is one of the two organizations which fund EPIC. The other organization is the Fund for Constitutional Government. Contact EPIC at:

> Electronic Privacy Information Center
> 666 Pennsylvania Avenue SE, #310
> Washington, D.C. 20003
> Phone: 202-544-9240
> Fax: 202-547-5482

Transaction Security

The most fundamental guideline of transaction security is to keep what you do and don't do away from everyone but the person with whom you do business. Some discussion of your financial affairs will involve your spouse or business partners, or your accountant, etc., but you should avoid casual discussion of your affairs with everyone else.

Talking on the telephone is risky if you are known or thought to be well off. Crooks can monitor your phone calls with electronic equipment carried on their persons or mounted in a vehicle. Sound-detection systems can also be trained on your home or office to eavesdrop on business or family discussion.

Cellular and radio phones are much less secure than a regular phone, and a regular phone is not secure at all. Inexpensive electronic systems can be used to monitor cell phone and radio phone conversations, and other electronic devices may be used to monitor signals on a regular telephone line. Nonetheless, unless you are known to be wealthy, and unless you discuss financial affairs on a phone, you will likely not suffer a loss because of your telephone conversations.

Law-enforcement agencies are now said to use a monitoring system which can reproduce and record the activity on a computer system. If you use an encryption system, and you believe your electronic communications are safe from prying eyes, you might be only half correct. While PGP and other encryption schemes protect your message while it is enroute to a recipient, your computer monitor shows your message to you, as you compose it, in "plain text." If you can see that message in plain text, and if your recipient can also see it in plain text, then an electronic snoop *may* also be able to see it that way by monitoring your computer's electromagnetic radiation.

Last, carrying cash is a good way to reduce the chance of a credit card rip-off. But, if a crook sees you with a fair amount of cash, he may be desperate enough to kill you for it, especially at night, or in a bad part of town. Even daylight and a crowd of people will not deter an addict who is twelve hours past his or her need for a fix, and wants it *now*. The desperation of such addicts may be illustrated by the fourteen-year-old found in an Eastern U.S. city a few years ago. He bled to death from his fingertips, which he'd clawed to the bone while trying to scratch through a locked wooden door in a doctor's office. The youth was hooked on heroin or cocaine, and had broken into the doctor's office looking for any kind of drug. His body was found on Monday morning when the staff arrived for work. Addicts are driven by a desperation which is almost beyond the understanding of everyone else. Keep that in mind the next time you are tempted to use cash for a large purchase. It's a good idea to keep large transactions as private as possible. Your life may be at stake.

International Considerations

Almost every large bank has an international department, which may be helpful when you do business overseas. Also, almost every bank has a correspondent relationship with banks around the world, and correspondent banks cooperate with one another to provide special services to their customers.

Perhaps most valuable is a bank's ability to execute a wire-transfer to another country in the currency of that country. Buy a boat in Italy and wire the payment there in Lira.

Additional advice regarding international transactions may be obtained by contacting the Export-Import Bank, or the U.S. Department of Commerce, or the United States Department of State, or even the United Nations. The U.S. Postal Service may also help because it now offers International Priority Mail service.

Finally, in most non-U.S. lands there are social groups comprised of citizens of other countries. For example, in San Jose, Costa Rica, there is a small community of Koreans. If you are Korean or of Korean extraction and can speak Korean, and possibly Spanish, a few calls to San Jose to locate a Korean business might open a door to the Korean community in that city. Those people may be able to give you special insight into doing business in that country, and possibly also details about the Costa Rican company with which you plan to do business, etc.

Most large universities maintain lists of students from other countries, who may be helpful if you plan to call prospective clients or businesses in their homelands. Exchange students can advise you, help you make the phone call, or translate your questions into their language. For example, an initial fax to a Saudi business written in Arabic, will open a door much wider than one written in English.

Consider arranging a conference call. The student can remain on campus, you can stay in your office, and you two can be connected by phone before an operator places the call to the third person, your prospective client or supplier, etc., in Saudi Arabia, for example.

It wouldn't hurt to learn a few words of in Arabic before the call. It's not hard to learn a couple of phrases and one sincere *salaam a leckam* or *shukrahn* can make a big difference in how the next conversation goes, or even whether there will be a second conversation.

ECUs and SDRs

You'll not likely to need to know much about ECUs and SDRs but because they are acronyms which show up in financial material more and more often these days, here's what they stand for and what they mean.

ECU is the abbreviation of European Currency Unit, now called the "Euro," a proposed universal currency to be used in European countries. The Euro would mean prices for Swiss goods could be easily compared to prices of identical or similar goods manufactured in Belgium or any other European country. Not all European countries have agreed to adopt the Euro-based pricing idea, though, so we offer this information as advance notice to persons who plan to travel or trade in Europe.

SDR stands for Special Drawing Rights, a label applied to an attempted global currency-type device created in 1960 pursuant to goals of the Bretton Woods Conference (1944). The governments of many of the world's major powers agreed to support the concept of a purely fictitious "currency" based on bookkeeping entries in which one SDR was equal to one U.S. dollar, which at the time meant one thirty-fifth of a troy ounce of gold. Thus, the SDR was referred to euphemistically as "paper gold."

The thinking behind the creation of SDRs went something like this: We're Britain, see, and when our citizens buy a lot of stuff in the U.S., for example, the U.S. makes a claim on our gold. That's not cool because when gold flows out of Britain, that forces us to reduce our money supply — we're allowed to create only a limited amount of bogus currency in the form of credit. When we lower our supply of money and credit, our economy falters, people are laid off work, businesses fail, and the natives get restless.

Other countries remarked similarly, so the SDR bookkeeping system permitted participating countries to deposit a certain number of U.S. dollars' worth of their currency into a pool. When gold began to flow out of their countries, as in the example of Britain shipping gold to the U.S., the country losing gold could borrow SDRs, "paper gold," sufficient to offset the loss of (real) gold, and thereby not need to reduce its supply of money and credit. Brilliant, eh wot? One might ask why the country losing the gold even bothered to use SDRs to mask the loss. Why didn't it simply *not* reduce its supply of money and credit? The fact is, they couldn't help what happened because when the gold began to flow out, knowledgeable citizens began to exchange their Pounds or French Francs or whatever for anything of fixed value. They did so because the amount of gold their currency would convert to was declining. Who in his right mind would buy a stock which is collapsing?

In our example of Britain shipping gold to the U.S., the British currency, the Pound, was loosely tied to gold. Therefore, when the number of Pound notes in circulation remained constant but the number of ounces of gold backing that currency declined, the number of ounces, or fractions thereof, backing *each* Pound declined. It became smart to trade Pound notes for articles which were not going down in value. Later, when the articles may be going down in value but the Pound note is going up, you could sell the articles and hold the Pound notes you receive from the sale. That is just common sense but the bureaucrats dreaded that reaction to the shipment of gold out of their country. Actually, there is a flaw in their reasoning too. Have you spotted it yet?

The flaw is as follows: Yes, the gold left Britain and yes, the purchasing power of the Pound tended to sag a bit, but that is the natural consequence of normal market forces at work. There was no real need for SDRs because for each ounce of gold which left the country, an equal amount of goods and services entered the country, the result of the purchases made by Britain's citizens which caused the drain on the gold supply. The real net worth of the country hadn't changed because an equal value of merchandise came into the country. Thus, whenever the country wished to replenish its gold supply, all it needed to do was sell some of its products to another country. *Voilà!* The money flowing back into Britain could now be presented to its issuer, such as the United States, for gold.

When the world's financial markets were thrown into a turmoil due to growing Arab reluctance to accept FRTs in payment for oil, a quasi-currency was created to allow participants to exchange some FRTs for gold. A certain number of FRTs had to be converted to SDRs, and only the SDRs could be presented to the financial community for redemption in gold. The SDR concept, in essence, meant that the FRTs we gave to the Arab countries for oil were backed at least partially by gold. This *idiocy*, which filled the world's financial press for weeks, is akin to saying to the Arab nations:

> Okay, *sultan*, we will give you fake Dollars, you use them to buy SDRs, and then you give us the SDRs, and we will give you a little gold, and you can spend the remaining Dollars as you wish in the world economy.

The public isn't exposed to much discussion of SDRs in the financial press these days because in 1971, President Richard Nixon "closed the gold window" (and "the silver window") by refusing to redeem SDRs with gold or silver. Essentially, at that time, the U.S. withdrew from the Bretton Woods agreement. However, SDRs still interest those who follow the international commodities markets, particularly the markets for currencies and precious metals.

Money Laundering

In our older law dictionaries we do not find a definition of "money laundering." However, what is termed "money laundering" in the statute, 18 U.S.C. § 1956, is the practice of investing drug and racketeering money in legal activities so that the money's source cannot be identified.[4] There is considerable "money laundering" today, but the government often applies the term to perfectly legal transactions.

For example, in the Whitewater controversy which has swirled around President Clinton for several years, the independent counsel charged that one defendant had avoided reporting a transaction of "$10,000 or more" by having a bank issue him two cashier checks, one for $6,000 and the other for $5,000. The bank would have had to report a check for $11,000 to the U.S. Treasury Department. The banker and his customer were charged with "money laundering" even though there is no law which makes what the bank did illegal.

If the law covers two checks on the same day if they total more than $10,000, does it cover two checks in one week, or two checks in the same month, or even in the same year? Very quickly, we get into absurdity. The fact is that the law says *nothing* about

---

[4] While some may see this as humorous, others may view it with alarm: Our *Black's Law Dictionary*, Sixth Edition (© 1991), defines "money laundering" under the entry "Laundering." However, our Fourth Edition (© 1951), has no reference to "money laundering" in the section on "money" or in the section where "laundering" would be listed.

two checks that total more than $10,000, on the same day or any other interval.

Nevertheless, we encourage every reader to obey the existing law and avoid even the appearance of breaking it. If you stay away from the edge of the law, you are not likely to be disturbed in your financial affairs. Of course there is no guarantee of that, as we have seen, but we believe it will be true most of the time.

Money Orders
Postal money orders today are a good way for transients to mail funds safely. For example, a Latino migrant worker may buy a postal money order in the amount of $500 and mail that instrument to a family member in Mexico. The funds are relatively safe if the money order is made payable to a specific person, so it isn't advisable to leave the Payee line blank. A stolen blank money order from any financially-sound source is as good as cash. A money order made payable to your uncle, whose full name is printed clearly on the money order, is not so likely to be cashed by a thief.

Money orders are even more valuable in another way. A money order can protect you if you need to pay a person or company you think may be crooked. If you are at an auction, you can use three money orders, in the amount of $100 each, to buy a machine for which you bid $275. The auctioneer can stamp the money orders "FOR DEPOSIT ONLY" and then give you $25 cash as your change. That way the auctioneer never knows the name of your bank, or your bank account number, or your phone number or mailing address. Your transaction ends when you take delivery of the machine and they take the money orders. Use money orders to help protect your privacy and safety.

Travelers checks can be used in a similar way. When you buy a travelers check, you sign it *once* before you leave the seller's premises. You sign it again to make it valid. That way someone who finds your lost travelers checks can't cash them unless the finder (or thief) can accurately copy (forge) your signature. When you sign a travelers check a second time, you are said to be *countersigning* it.

Banks and other financial institutions are careful to check signatures on travelers checks, which lowers the chance yours would be used if they are lost or stolen. If your travelers checks are lost or stolen, you can easily get replacement checks. Your loss will be confined to the day or so of time lost until the replacement checks arrive. Travelers checks are a good idea, especially for persons traveling outside of the United States. Contact your bank's international department to ask if travelers checks are advisable in the countries you plan to visit.

Bank money orders and cashier checks (also called "teller checks") are similar to postal money orders in function and cost.

In the end, your safety using money substitutes is probably a lot higher than if you use money — coins of gold or silver — or paper currency. If you use credit or debit cards, you have greater freedom and financial clout.

In these days of economic uncertainty, it will serve you well if you investigate the Internet, encryption, and e-cash, e-metal (e-gold and e-silver), and other modern financial tools.

•

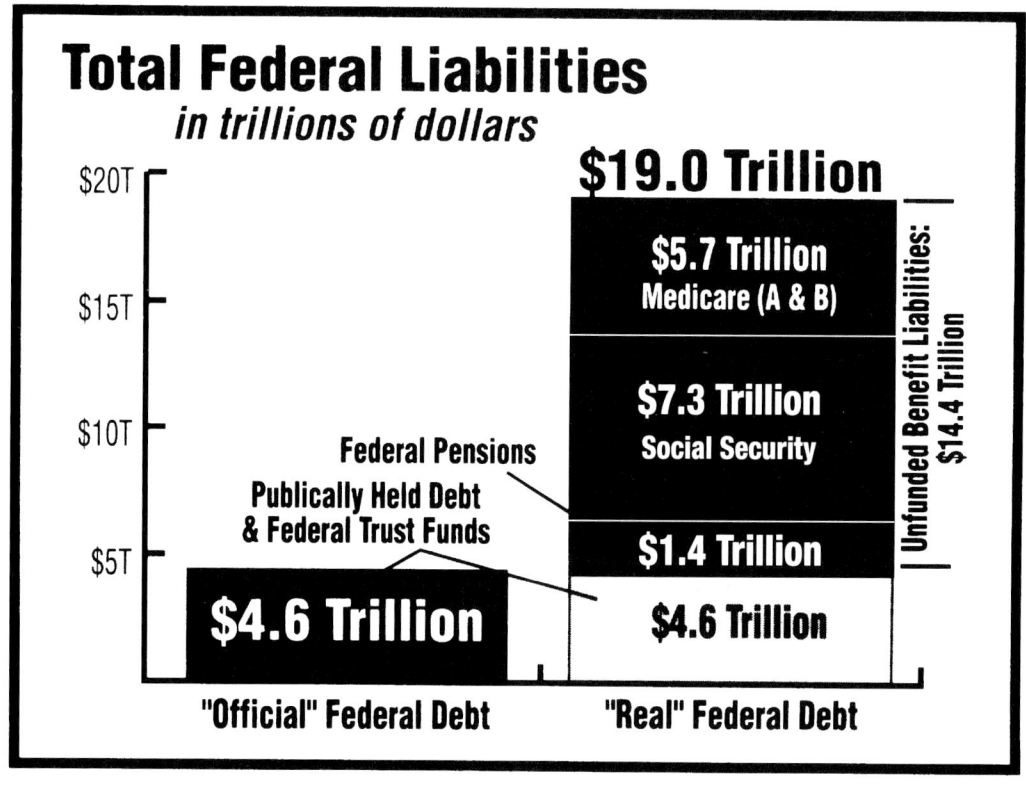

Figure 15-2. *The national debt. Chart courtesy of* The Fleet Street Letter. *See Appendix A.*

16

Your Future

THE question arises of what can be done with the knowledge in this book. Of course, you can drop the subject and continue your life as before, or you can learn more. Should you choose the latter course, you'll benefit by completing and then mailing the Reader Registration form in Appendix B, and we will do our part in keeping you informed on new developments.

You are doubtlessly aware that few if any of the facts and arguments presented in this book are even mentioned in the dominant media. No major magazine, newspaper or network television broadcast, in the U.S. or elsewhere, has shown much if any interest in these issues. To the dominant media, they are non-issues, nothing to be concerned about right now or in the future.

However, in contrast to the impertinent attitude of the dominant media, we are making a list of possible action programs related to the issues. Among the actions already suggested are a class-action lawsuit about fractional-reserve banking, and a project which would help a federal grand jury investigate.

We will keep you informed on our progress if you give us your mailing address, etc. You may also be invited to participate in one or more educational programs, some of which may be a lot of fun; you could donate time or money, or you could act as a contact for us in your city, county or state. We think you may find that your participation in one or more of our projects may be among the most rewarding things you've ever done.

Nevertheless, while there is a long list of things which *could* be done, some of those things are not prudent, many are likely to be inefficient, and quite a few have been tried but resulted in failure.

This chapter will introduce you to a host of ill-considered "solutions," activities you may benefit by avoiding. You will also learn about a few things which could be done, things which you could become involved in without risk to yourself, your family, or your financial well-being.

Much of what follows will either amuse, anger, or sadden you. Few action programs promoted in the past will likely interest you. However, once you are familiar with this range of options — including a few action programs which may work but command too high a price — you'll be better able to judge what may be the best program for you.

First let's talk about what's been tried and found wanting. You may wish to avoid these activities, or at least examine them carefully before you commit to supporting them.

"Illegal Tax Protest"
I've always enjoyed seeing the two ways this header is printed. Those who protest taxes, the activists, are described in newspapers as "illegal tax protesters." However, those who pay attention to details often wonder if a hyphen shouldn't be in that phrase, and where the hyphen should be placed.

If we talk about *illegal-tax* protesters we talk about people protesting against illegal taxes. On the other hand, if we talk about illegal *tax-protesters* we discuss people who protest against taxes in an illegal manner.

Placement of hyphens aside, let's look at the tax protest movement to see what we can learn. Here are the ten supremely important things for you to know about this once-huge movement.

1. Most people in it are sincere, they are motivated by high ideals, and they are, in the main, fine Americans. Some people are in the movement because they are angry with a particular aspect of the tax code or the IRS which has cost them significantly. A very small part of the movement is comprised of people motivated by their egos; in their search for power over others, they may lead a group to disaster.

Take a hard look at the leadership of any group that interests you. Avoid groups based on the leadership of a lone zealot. Lean toward a group which has an accounting system and CPA, a bank account, professional people who run it, and titular leaders guided and controlled by a board of directors or board of trustees. Otherwise, an organization probably lacks the stability to survive, much less serve a membership, or consistently serve the best interests of the community at large.

2. The idea of challenging the federal government or any part of it is not likely to bear fruit because your target has a virtually inexhaustible supply of resources to use against you. Practically every "David" who has dared to attack the federal "Goliath" has lost most if not all of his worldly assets, and, to a certain extent, his credibility. It is great to lead people to victory; it is anything but great if you lead people to defeat, especially easily predicted and total defeat.

Most tax-protest leaders have led their followers to defeat, big time. The most obvious indication of "amateur night" is the leader who says he's taking on the IRS personally because he won't ask anything of his membership which he isn't willing to do himself. That sounds great when you say it fast but on close examination it falls apart. Here's a short story to illustrate what you need to think about.

George Patton was a kick-butt U.S. Army general in World War II. He was not afraid to be near or at the front lines — in fact, he wanted to be there — but most of the time he remained at the rear, where it was safer. He stayed there because he knew that his primary duty was to win the war, not impress others. He knew that a dead general cannot lead his troops. Alive, and safely at the rear, he could organize the attack of his thousands of men, the ones who drove the tanks and fired the weapons. To do his job effectively, Patton had to avoid direct, personal contact with the enemy.

If you find a group leader who loves to get into the foxhole and exchange small-arms fire with the enemy, steer clear of this guy and his organization. He probably lacks the vision necessary to lead an organization, and an organization without good leadership is destined for ignominious defeat. Choose your leaders carefully — or you're toast.

3. Many of the issues which form the basis of the tax protest movement have merit. Students tell us that the Supreme Court says our tax system is "voluntary," and therefore that a return is "testimony," which the Fifth Amendment forbids if it is compelled. Most tax returns lie when they say the taxpayer received "income" because the word *income* does not mean what most people think it means, in the eyes of the law. The 16th Amendment, presumably the basis for today's personal federal income tax, was not properly (legally) ratified, so that portion of the IRS code is illegal. Since 1963, nobody has received lawful money so nobody since 1963 has been required to fill out a return, much less pay anything to the federal government. Most people are confused about what constitutes "income." The arguments go on and on but the main issue might really be: what works?

None of these arguments has borne fruit in court, although in a handful of cases, the protesting citizens won two or three partial or temporary victories.[1]

4. What is needed is a viable (rational) means of opposing what is wrong, but without jeopardy to one's financial, emotional or family security. We have a few ideas on the subject, and will explain them to those readers who fill out and send us their Reader Registration form.

5. "Sure-fire" court procedures, court arguments, and techniques for dealing with the IRS have been largely unsuccessful. Experts tell us they failed, not because of any legal or procedural flaw but primarily because either the court or the jury was unfamiliar with the principles upon which the arguments were based.

For example, if you were a juror in a trial involving the theft of Federal Reserve Tokens, and the law under which the accused had been charged referred specifically to "Federal Reserve Notes" and "lawful money," you might vote for an acquittal because you know that the accused person didn't take any *bona fide* Federal Reserve Notes or lawful money of the United States.

But a jury composed of persons who have not read this book, for example, would not likely follow your reasoning.

What we are saying is, *uninformed* jurors, no matter how moral, ethical and patriotic they might be, should *not* be expected to follow your arguments because they have never heard anything like them. Your arguments might sound perfectly valid to you when you present them in court as a defendant, but in the quiet privacy of jury deliberation, every juror falls back on what he or she "knows" to be true; the average juror's life experience simply does not support your arguments — so you are found guilty. That's what appears to have happened in most tax-protest and similar cases in court.

6. Practical considerations prevent you, the individual, from succeeding in court. Your opposition, the federal prosecutor and the IRS, for example, have a huge budget for not just nailing you in court but for doing it in a big way. They want pages of publicity to discourage others from trying what you are doing. That's why the court orders you to forfeit your home, real property, car, stocks, bonds, and other assets, and to pay a massive fine. While your argument may be based squarely on the law, the jurors probably don't know the law; it has been withheld from them. They will vote to convict you, even though they may sympathize with you and your family and friends. Often, the judge will tell them to do so, almost in as many words, and they will do it. To the jurors, you are a lawbreaker, although admittedly a "grievously misguided" lawbreaker.

Your loss in court will be featured on local television, in local newspapers, and will be the subject of discussion at every meeting of patriotic citizens for weeks to come. Yet, when it comes to helping you and your family with the expenses of the trial, such as fines and attorney fees, if any, your friends will become distant. They will not be there to help pay your bills because "you took your chance and you blew it," your loss "set the movement back ten years," or it was the fault of your own incompetence, and you should have used a different approach or argument. You'll be all alone, looking for the people who had encouraged you to take your case to court: "We're right behind you, Charlie." You're broke, probably out of a job, you have huge bills to pay, nowhere to live, no car, no phone, and perhaps not even a mailing address. Welcome to the world of tax protest, at least the old way of doing it.

7. Beat the IRS at its own game; that's the siren song of folks who produce their own equivalent of the FRT. Their creation, their "monetary instrument," is a "draft," a bogus piece of paper, often incompetently printed, which resembles a money order but which is drawn on a fictitious entity at a post office box somewhere, or perhaps a street address of a mail-forwarding service — in Guatemala, Borneo, or Rwanda. Clever. Really clever.

---

[1] A major exception is the Supreme Court ruling that you can't be convicted if you sincerely think you are right. That's because your sincerity means there is no *mens rea*, that is, no criminal intent.

The "draft" scheme has people mailing "drafts" to one bogus entity after another, in effect, exchanging IOUs. Suppose you sell me a car and I give you an IOU for $1,000. Then you use my IOU to "pay" for a computer. You might be able to pass my IOU on to the computer dealer if it looks official enough, but his bank certainly will not accept that "draft" as a deposit.

"Drafts" made to resemble money orders have been used by protesters to "buy" even large-ticket items. Your humble editor knows one fellow who used one "draft" to "buy" a new Cadillac and another to "pay off" his mortgage. Unfortunately for him, the bank and the car dealer became angry when his paper hit the fan. They cooperated with the U.S. attorney and our enterprising pal now sits in a federal can. The Cadillac went back to the dealer, his wife and children are trying to keep up the payments on their property, and everyone the protester involved in his "clever" scheme has lost thousands of dollars (of purchasing power). Also, a couple lost their homes, several of his pals are in federal prison, and one friend was murdered. Want to join this crew? Just help fight the "Fed" using "drafts." It's a plan which is almost guaranteed to wipe you out financially, destroy your credibility, and put you in the slammer.

8. *Pro se* and *pro per* court action is also virtually guaranteed to take you to the poor house. A *pro se* or *pro per* litigant is one who handles his or her own case. If you do battle with any person in court, and if you handle your own case, you are said to be acting *pro per* or *pro se*. (*se*, by the way, is pronounced *say*.) Here's how it works.

You do considerable "legal research," you devour a ton of newsletters filled with other protesters' opinions and then you tackle the IRS on the "16th Amendment was never ratified" issue.[2] You begin by not filing tax returns for several years. You respond to every computer-generated IRS mailing by sending back longer and longer "letters" explaining how the 16th Amendment was not properly ratified, so therefore the IRS code is not legal, etc. Great.

For the first four or five years you con yourself into thinking you have the IRS exactly where you want them. You believe in your heart of hearts that you can't lose because if the IRS takes you to court, you'll bring in all the letters you sent to them and you'll explain to the judge and jury how the 16th Amendment was not ratified. But that isn't what happens.

What actually happens is that you are charged with willful failure to file, and the judge warns you not to raise the subject of the ratification of the 16th Amendment or you'll be held in contempt of court. You are stunned. Your main argument is the 16th-Amendment ratification issue. The judge tells everyone that the matter of the ratification of the 16th Amendment is not a subject heard by this court, that it is reserved to the Supreme Court, or that it is "well settled" that the 16th Amendment *was* ratified. In any event, your main argument is disallowed because it is considered bogus from the onset. The trial judge may tell you that if you believe she is acting improperly, you may always raise the issue on appeal, etc. You are speechless.

So you are convicted of willful failure to file, you have no funds with which to initiate an appeal, and your case is so weak, at least in the eyes of local attorneys, that even the patriotic lawyers won't consider representing you *pro bono* (free of charge, as a contribution to the public interest, etc.) on your appeal. You're toast, pal, and the prosecutor, judge, IRS personnel, and some of your neighbors knew it all along. Your zeal to address a public wrong is commendable, of course, but you were blind to reality. But don't feel alone, friend: you have *lots* of company.

9. You decide to attack "the system" by dropping out of the system. You decide "the whole Social Security thing is pure socialism" and you decide you want no part of it. After all, if you are going to stand on principle, you have to take this kind of action, oth-

---

[2] Beware "legal research" materials offered in protester newsletters. A few years ago your humble editor received a list of about forty "legal citations" supporting a refusal to file a personal federal tax return. I visited a local law library, checked the citations, and found that *every one* contained one or more errors, or was inappropriate to cite as legal opinion, or both.

erwise people will think you're a hypocrite, right? Right.

So you not only drop out of the Social Security system, you close your bank accounts because part of the bank's records on you include your Social Security Number. You also destroy your driver license because that either has your Social Security Number on it or it has a link to your Social Security Number. Then you take your license plates off your car, you no longer use a ZIP code as part of your return address, and you respectfully decline to give your employer your Social Security Number.

For a few months, nothing happens. Then, you get pulled over for not having a license plate or tags, your car gets towed and impounded, and you get canned from your job because your employer has more important things to do than get involved in your "stupid battle with the IRS."

Now you can't get mail or phone calls because, without your job, you can't pay a phone bill or pay rent. You can't get a new job. You can't even look presentable at an interview. You are now a "street person," one of the nation's "homeless," your credibility is shot, and no prospective employer wants you on the premises because you're a troublemaker who would soon have the other employees in a turmoil. Of course, IRS agents will be frequent visitors to any potential employer's accounting department. You're toast, friend, even if you are a veteran, or a physician, or a truck driver, or whatever. T–O–A–S–T.

10. Here's another route to self-immolation, if you're interested. Be an entrepreneur, support free-enterprise, and start your own consulting service. Do all kinds of legal research, make photocopies of the pages of court cases and your briefs, memoranda, points and authorities, etc., and sell copies of your material to others. Tout your materials as "guaranteed to beat the IRS." Accept only cash or postal money orders, use a mail service as your mailing address,[3] and contract with an answering service to take phone calls for you. Pay everybody with cash only, so you leave no "paper trail." Return calls only to those who have paid you a handsome fee in advance. You call them back collect, from a pay phone or the phone of a friend or sympathizer.

Things go well until a few of your clients find themselves in really hot water with the IRS or other government agency. Your instructions to your clients are getting more and more radical and your clients are becoming more and more irrational, mostly because they see the handwriting on the wall. They should never have become involved "in this stupid business," and they should never have relied on "you and your stupid arguments." But by the time your clients wake up to the superficiality of your instructions, it's too late.

Soon, all of your clients have caved in to the U.S. attorney and IRS; they have decided to accept the U.S. attorney's generous offer of dismissal of the charges against them; all they have to do is file tax returns within ninety days, pay all the taxes due, pay IRS the $500 fines imposed on each of them, *and testify against you.* In other words, your clients walk (serve no time in jail) if they testify about *everything* you sent to them or told them.

Soon, good buddy, you're gonna get a chance to put all your legal skills to the test. You're going to get a chance to represent yourself in court, facing federal charges of wire fraud, mail fraud, and a few other tried and true means of getting self-ordained ministers of truth, justice, and constitutional law off the streets and into the gray-bar hotel.

"If You're Not Having Fun You Aren't Doing It Right"

"Illegal tax protesters" and other protesters would do well to reflect on this warning from George Gordon, a former Idaho businessman who produced several instructional video tapes on how to confront the authorities regarding issues which, according to Gordon, were illegal, unconstitutional, or both.

Mr. Gordon's arguments were impressive, at least to non-lawyers. Probably several hundred followers used Gordon's materials to launch their own offen-

---

[3] Call it a "mail drop," and use other spy terminology, to impress your friends. The conversation in which you first mention your "mail drop" will likely be the last conversation most of those friends will voluntarily have with you.

sive against the forces of darkness. But the results were predictable: almost everyone who used Gordon's materials had some early success but, ultimately, the power and resources of the state crushed the opposition.

The last I heard, Mr. Gordon had abandoned his wife and kids, run off with a younger woman, and was teaching gardening classes in Missouri. Some of his more ardent disciples have done time in the gray-bar hotel.

You may wish to reflect on the preceding realities the next time some sincere individual tries to get you to challenge "Big Brother" — unless you are suicidal. Going into battle against "Big Brother" is, in your humble editor's opinion, akin to juggling quart jars of nitroglycerin, and doing it when you are drunk. You are likely to destroy not just yourself but your loved ones too. Think hard, my friend. Think very hard.

Of course, these horror stories should not be taken as proof that nothing can be done. We have just given you the basics of what not to do, and what to avoid, and whom to avoid and why. Now let's look at what you might find worth your time, money and effort to do, in an offensive against perpetrators of fraud.

What Does Recent History Tell Us?
Since the 1950s, in the U.S., tax protest, private armies, separate states, separate countries, issuing "drafts," and other solutions to the nation's problems have been tried by others. Regrettably, with heavy losses to individual participants, virtually all of these approaches failed. A few hardy souls continue the fight in each of these areas but the credibility of their actions may have been damaged by the defeats of others who've already pursued that approach.[4]

Several on-point educational organizations have been solidly successful, however. The Cato Institute, Toward Tradition, the Foundation for Economic Education, and the Acton Institute are just a few organizations whose ideology suggests understanding of at least some of the most important principles discussed in this book. We also think *all* of these organizations are professionally managed and deserve your support.

We might ask ourselves what common characteristics distinguish successful organizations from those which fail. We offer the following as a guide to those who are thinking of starting one.

1. The leadership must be open-minded about factual matters but resolute in their adherence to principle.

2. The organization must be educational in nature, or more educational than anything else. By education, we mean the members must take pains to inform themselves on the issues, and then they must take steps to inform others. Education of the public is absolutely essential to long-term success.

3. The organization must eventually involve the services of professionals in leadership positions. No group has ever achieved real success without having an accountant and a checking account, a legal advisor, a marketing consultant, and an advisor regarding insurance matters. Remember: Marketing, Accounting, Insurance, Legal, or M-A-I-L. Remember M-A-I-L and you won't go wrong. We might add that a computer technology advisor would also be valuable to a new or existing group. Moreover, a professional writer, someone who can and will edit the printed matter which the group issues, would be worth a lot.

4. The organization operates like a successful business. It buys and sells things, keeps good records of its transactions, and it files all the reports and pays all the fees and taxes required by law.

5. The organization is a good neighbor, always seeking to sustain and support the good things in the community rather than just seeking to tear down and destroy the bad things in the community. A balanced approach to community activity is vital to maintaining a balanced perspective on life and the organization's direction in life.

6. The leadership of the organization must have a sense of humor. Without a sense of humor in the

---

[4] In about 1987, ZNS records indicated existence of about 1,000 "illegal tax protest" groups and key personalities in the United States. An informal survey in 1998 indicates that the number had declined to about ten.

leadership, few members will feel comfortable discussing their questions, fears, and ideas for improvement. Without constructive input from the membership, the leadership will be unable to "grow" the organization into an effective body. If the organization cannot grow, it will fail.

7. The cost of participation should be low but it should not be zero. For example, few people who've protested against the personal federal income tax, and who have lost their home and property in the battle, are much interested in doing that again. Also, if the organization is led by professionals, they will quickly see that a reasonable dues schedule will generate greater operating revenue. A lower membership cost means more of their neighbors can afford to join and support the group.

8. The aims of the organization should be spelled out clearly in a mission statement, and should be available on a single sheet of paper. This statement should be expressed in as few words as possible.[5]

9. Reports to the dues-paying members should be brief, brutally frank, and should discuss failures, setbacks, and losses. However, the group's reports should also include brief discussions of work-arounds, alternative plans and new opportunities. Members will support honest leadership, even in times of adversity, but those once-supportive members may want to sue or file criminal charges against leaders who lie or cover up problems.

10. The organization's leadership must maintain friendly relations with other leadership in the community. Alienating possible supporters is not a legitimate role of management. Diplomacy can reap huge rewards, often when support is desperately needed. Successful leaders already know this truth; would-be leaders should be reminded of it regularly.

11. Every entity should devote part of its resources toward pleasant activities, enjoyable events which will attract members who may be too timid to participate in the group's more serious activities. Also, every group should donate some of its resources toward community service, such as providing volunteers to place sandbags during a flood. Further, the serious business of the organization should be conducted in the most businesslike manner possible. No organizational activities should tolerate indulgence in alcoholic beverages or illicit drugs; the organization and its members should strictly adhere to the highest standards of personal behavior. Their behavior should be a beacon to all other upstanding members of the community. If a member wishes to consume alcoholic beverages, for example, encourage that member to restrict his or her drinking to places other than the group meetings or other group activities.

12. The organization's leaders may wish to consider how they will relate to the varying religious beliefs of the members and the community. Few successful business organizations begin their staff meetings with prayer, even though all who attend may be very religious. For some groups, a public prayer at the start of a meeting helps set the tone for the meeting. For other groups, a prayer may look like grandstanding, trying to piggyback on religion. While Congress begins its sessions with a prayer, so may your group, but you may also wish to consider the approach of local, and highly successful, businesses. Religious fervor, whether real or affected, is no substitute for sound business management.

"What Can I Do?"
When you discuss the revelations of this book with friends, they may ask, "What can *I* do about it?" We suggest the following:

1. Send in the Reader Registration Form. You'll find it in Appendix B. That is a critically important step because once ZNS has your address, we can keep you informed of developments, some of which could be very beneficial to you.

2. You may wish to buy extra copies of this book and loan, give, or sell them to friends. The education provided by reading this book could help that friend become your ally in possibly challenging times ahead.

---
[5] For an example of a clear and succinct mission statement, see the Libertarian Party's statement at their web site: http://www.lpusa.com.

The support of friends who share your understanding of national and world affairs would be helpful. Friendship with mature, kindred spirits is synergistic.

3. Adopt a friendly and gentle rather than belligerent approach to others. Ask questions, particularly ask for their opinions on the more familiar issues. Perhaps ask them if they've heard the latest estimate of the size of the national debt. See what kind of answer you get and pursue the subject if you think the person who answered your question is approachable. Possibly ask your friends if they'd be willing to volunteer to support a group which is trying to root out corruption in government. Another question might be to ask if they would donate money to a group trying to keep the country strong but do it in a way which would eliminate the need for a personal federal income tax. We suggest these questions, not because ZNS is involved in any of these activities but because we think we'll be able to refer readers and their friends to organizations which are professionally managed and which do have these and other worthwhile goals.

4. ZNS may soon have a few special projects which will interest almost every reader. These projects will involve essentially zero risk to your hide or your financial or emotional stability. However, they won't be boring, either. We think they might be best described as fun, possibly hilarious, and definitely *interesting*. To get the word on these events, you will need to do only one thing now: fill out and mail us the Reader Registration Form in Appendix B.

5. If you are already on-line on the Internet and have an email address, you are in great shape to have a lot of fun with us in the near future. We encourage those readers who are not Internet capable, but who have been thinking about it, to get on-line as soon as possible, provided however that they can afford to do so. The cost of an adequate computer system and software might be about $2,000, which would include an ink-jet or similar medium-quality printer. Access to the Internet may cost about $20 per month. Typically, you could be on-line with an email address within a couple of hours after you get your new computer system home from the store and set up and running. It might be a good idea to pay a little extra to have a technician set your system up properly to "surf the Net." ZNS' most helpful and valuable friends have computers, use Microsoft Word or other good word-processing software, have good printers, and have modems and Internet software (such as Netscape Navigator, Internet Explorer, etc.), and an email address. An extra $20 per month could be used for a separate phone line for your computer and modem; with a fax-modem, you can send and receive faxes with your computer and its printer.

6. If you send us the Reader Registration Form (Appendix B), and if you have a moment, please jot a short note telling us a little about your current employment, education, hobbies, or any other thing you think possibly valuable for us to know about you. Tell us if you are a lawyer, pilot, accountant, engineer, teacher, pastor, computer guru, programmer, etc. We also want you to tell us if you are a mom, a homemaker, a truck driver, a disk jockey, or you do anything else with your time. Even if you are retired and quite inactive, we'd like to know that too.

7. We have a special interest in supporting United States military personnel. If you are a veteran, or if you are currently on active duty or in the reserves or National Guard, anywhere, we would very much appreciate your letting us know that. We have an especially strong interest in identifying veterans with combat experience, including those who may have been wounded or disabled by combat injury. We have an equally strong interest in knowing if you are the spouse of a military person who was killed in action or is currently listed as missing in action.

8. ZNS would like to hear from you if you are a published writer, editor, wordsmith, advertising copy writer, grammarian, or English teacher at the high school or university level.

9. ZNS would also like to hear from persons currently or recently employed in the broadcast or newspaper or magazine publishing field. If you are

now or have recently been a newspaper, magazine, or newsletter editor or publisher, or you are now or have recently been a broadcaster (talk show, interview program, producer or director) on radio or television, we'd like to hear from you.

10. If you have a resumé or *curriculum vitae*, we invite you to include it with your Reader Registration Form. Also, if you are reasonably sure ZNS is on the right track, and if you would be willing to support us occasionally with a financial contribution, please put a dollar sign ("$") in the box in the upper left-hand corner of your Reader Registration Form. ZNS deeply appreciates those willing to give us the freedom we derive from financial support. If you should elect to provide us with financial support on any project, you will find out what we mean.

A New Journey
Your journey through this book may have been an eye-opening experience. I know it certainly was an eye-opening experience for me to gradually discover these things over thirty-five years. I can only imagine what it must be like to read this book and learn all of these things in a relatively short time. Nonetheless, I have one more thing to mention to you, and this may be the most shocking aspect of our topic.

In the Epigraph (page v) I said I think you and I may be the targets of possibly the greatest criminal enterprise in history. While many Americans already know at least a little about this enterprise and the danger it poses, only a few understand its *modus operandi* well enough to effectively oppose it. Unfortunately, if those of us who know about the Insiders don't soon get our act together, at least through an informal but professionally managed effort, our future will be grim.

Is there anything *you* can or should do about the Insiders?

Perhaps you are pondering that question right now. It's a legitimate question, one everyone should ask himself. To help you answer it, please carefully consider the following facts.

In about 1955, the editors of the highly respected Paris newspaper, *Le Monde*, investigated the Communist movement and the horrors it had inflicted on the world. In their lengthy report, the *Le Monde* researchers estimated that since its inception in 1917, the Communist movement had directly or indirectly caused the unnatural deaths of 149 million men, women and children — through war, starvation, torture, terrorism, hideous drug and chemical experiments, assassinations, slavery, and the most grotesque forms of imprisonment.

U.S. researchers such as journalist Gary Allen and scientist Antony Sutton confirmed what the *Le Monde* editors had uncovered, but they also found that U.S. Insiders supplied significant support to the global Communist movement since its inception.

Now a host of researchers have documented Insider support for Adolf Hitler and Emperor Hirohito prior to and even during World War II.

Moreover, research has also uncovered evidence of Insider financial and political support for freedom's enemies prior to and during the Korean War, prior to and during the Vietnam War, and even (for Iraq) prior to, during, and after the Gulf War.

I believe the number of unnatural deaths caused by Insider-supported criminal "governments" is now at least 20 million more than *Le Monde* estimated in the 1950s.

Consequently, as of 1998, the Insiders may have contributed to the unnatural and untimely deaths, often by the most horrible means, of 169 million innocent men, women, and children.

This unnatural loss of human life occurred during eighty-one years, from 1917 to 1998, and averaged about 2,000,000 deaths per year, or 170,000 deaths per month, or about 5,800 deaths per day. Think about it: 5,800 unnatural deaths, by the most horrible means imaginable, every day for eighty-one years.

Now please recall that in the United States our government is based on laws, not on men. Our Constitution is our supreme statutory law but we know it is based on a higher, spiritual law we honor in our minds and hearts. That higher law, which many consider the basis of all of our written laws, is: Thou shalt not kill.

Thus we say the highest purpose of the law in the United States and most other countries is the protection of innocent human life.

But the evidence suggests that the Insiders act against that law. If that is true, the Insiders have arrogated to themselves power to give and withhold life: they have *deified* themselves. If they believe they are gods, they may demand that we worship them. Is our use of their "money" a form of worship? Is our use of dishonest weights and measures a form of "sacred" obedience to the Insiders? Are FRTs and fractional-reserve banking the icons and sacraments of a Satanic church?

You and I have a simple choice. We can ignore the Insiders and the mounting evidence of their evil, or we can act responsibly, as mature men and women who discover a criminal scheme aimed at our selves and all that we love and cherish.

Obviously, the immature and the evil among us will ignore the Insiders and their criminality.

It is equally obvious, to me anyway, that those who send me their Reader Registration Form will be this generation's most mature and responsible people, those who stand on principle and refuse to ignore a criminal enterprise which uses dishonest weights and measures to harm the innocent.

I think the Insiders want those who know the score to remain out of touch with one another. They want us to remain strangers, or constantly feud and bicker among ourselves, even over petty issues. *The Insiders don't want us to become friends* because that would improve our communications and thereby hasten the day they have to face the music.

So, dear friend, I cordially invite *and urge* you to please send me your Reader Registration Form — today. Let's embark on a new journey together.

To the utmost of my ability and resources, I will keep you up to date on these exciting developments. Over time, I'll invite you to voluntarily participate in a series of exciting and enjoyable projects. Some projects, if you volunteer to participate in them, may involve a small cost. Other projects will not involve any expense at all on your part. Still other projects will be mostly for those who, due to their circumstances, prefer to just contribute financially. Still, all of the projects will be important, enjoyable, and effective, though none will put you or your family or your business in any jeopardy whatsoever. Essentially, these projects will just be pleasant ways to help speed public awareness of what's going on.

Everyone who sends me their Reader Registration Form will receive a benefit. However, *as a special bonus to early-birds, I promise that those whose Reader Registration Forms arrive first will get a surprise (but for now, secret) benefit.*

Your Reader Registration Form represents both a once-in-a-*lifetime* opportunity and a once-in-a-*millennium* opportunity. The sooner I receive your Form, the better. *You get only this one chance to be an early-bird reader of MONEY!*

So, here's looking forward to meeting you and shaking your hand sometime soon. Until then, I thank you for sending me your Reader Registration Form, and for your support of traditional American values, including honest weights and measures.

May God be with you until we meet again.

•

17

Questions and Answers

BY now, you probably have many questions about what you've read. Here are some of them, no doubt, along with our answers. We encourage you to discuss them with others who know what the terms in this book mean. Of course, it would be pointless to discuss them with almost everyone else.

1. All this talk about FRTs doesn't make sense. Our family has no money problems now and we don't expect any problems with the money you say isn't really money. Why should we pay any attention to you?

   A. You don't have to pay any more attention to me than you might pay to a neighbor who, after your community suffers a series of unexplained fires, warns you that an arsonist may be operating in your neighborhood. Ignore me if you wish but please continue to guard against danger to your financial well-being. As long as you stay alert to possible danger and consult with knowledgeable professionals, you should be just fine.

2. There's not very much gold in the world today, compared to an ever larger world population. How can so many people have gold and silver coins?

   A. If a candy bar costs fifty cents today, in terms of FRTs, that candy bar could also be purchased with a coin which contained about one hundredth of a troy ounce of gold. A silver coin of the same purchasing power would need to contain only about one tenth of a troy ounce of silver. Thus, the existing stocks of gold and silver would be adequate to manufacture the world's coin needs. Also, denominating a nation's currency in gold or silver would not require an inordinate amount of either metal because it is just that scarcity of the precious metal which gives the currency its purchasing power. A precious-metal backed paper currency, if denominated in Dollar units, would likely be very powerful — a new home costing $200,000 today in FRTs might cost only $20,000 or less in currency backed by precious metal.

3. If precious-metal coins are needed, which would be better, gold or silver?

   A. This question needs to be studied thoroughly before the country decides its course for the next ten or twenty years, but we guess that markets would accept coins made from either metal.

4. Is there any reason a private firm couldn't make gold and silver coins? Why wait for the government to get its act together? Why not start a company and mint our own coins?

   A. There does not appear to be any legal reason you could not start your own coin-manufacturing company, but you might have trouble getting your neighbors to accept the coins in trade unless your production standards were well known and respected. Getting the public to learn about you and trust you would take a serious marketing effort, the cost of which would likely be high because of the general public's lack of knowledge about these subjects.

5. If all we get are FRTs, and if FRTs are not money, we don't ever get paid. That means nobody has to pay taxes. Why doesn't the country fall apart?

   A. The nation's founders set the country up so that it could be supported by voluntary taxes. Today, the government is mostly doing things the founders would call blatantly unconstitutional, and voluntary taxes (customs, imposts, excises, etc.) can't pay for them. Thus, because we strayed from constitutional principles, we can no longer support our "government" with constitutional taxes. As a nation, we're making good "progress" on the road to social and economic destruction.

6. If your theories are correct, there's no way this country isn't going to collapse. What sense is there in even thinking about fighting your so-called Insiders?

   A. If the theory of an Insider cult manipulating the world's supply of "money and credit" is correct, then they would not permit a total collapse because it wouldn't be in their interests. They might, however, slowly increase their power, and slowly erode the power of others (you and me), until they could exercise their financial power and authority without raising the suspicions of any but the most diligent investigator. Suppose, for instance, that you tapped into the U.S. Treasury computer system and reprogrammed it so you received a check every month forever. You, alone, would control the amount of the check, and you alone would have the authority to stop the payment. Wouldn't you then also have an interest in seeing that the U.S. Treasury remained the government agency which received all federal taxes and other receipts, and paid most of the bills? Of course you would. The Insiders are like lamprey eels fastened to your body; if they suck too much blood they will kill you, and they would die too. The Insiders show no suicidal tendencies.

7. If you're so smart, how come the Insiders haven't killed you?

   A. The Insiders probably don't know about me, or, if they do, they don't consider me a threat.

8. If everybody used silver coins, prices would be too high. Your idea is nuts.

   A. If you bought a new Lincoln Continental car today using Dollars of silver, the price would be about one fourth its price in FRTs. If you were paid in Dollars of silver instead of FRTs, your paycheck likewise would be about one fourth what it is today. However, with only one-fourth the pay, your taxes would be much lower and you could apply the extra money to the car. That's the way it was when this country grew from a wilderness to the emigration goal of suffering people around the world. What's "nuts" about that?

9. During the past several years, the stock market has climbed to new records. Things can't be very bad in this country if the economy is healthy. Doesn't that undermine your argument?

   A. Inflation can be masked a couple of ways. First, the components of the Consumer Price Index are always subject to changes. Recently, meat was removed from the list because its price had supposedly risen too far too fast. The CPI is therefore not always a reliable indicator of inflation. Some analysts say the past year's increases in the supply of "money and credit" are influencing the markets but the most dramatic increase in prices has been in the "bull" market in stocks, and will only later show up in a rise in the general price level.

10. All your talk about money and FRTs is interesting but don't you think there are more serious problems in this country, like drugs, guns and crime?

   A. The other issues you mention are serious, of course, but while they have captured headlines, few people are aware of the seriousness of the issues raised in this book. Also, there is considerable evidence that the Insiders play a role in fomenting crime, illicit drug usage, and a host of other problems. Indeed, the fact that our money system has been perverted is one of the main causes of those problems.

11. Why don't I hear about FRTs and the money issue on TV?

   A. TV is not a good teacher when the subject is serious. "TV watchers" have become a subclass of modern society. While there may occasionally be TV programs which promote understanding of serious issues, their number may be declining because the really thoughtful people in this country now recognize TV for what it does best: amuse and entertain. If you are interested in light amusements, watch TV. If you want laughs or entertainment, watch TV. TV is also not good for children because it exaggerates almost everything it broadcasts, and the increasingly bad grammar and affected behavior of the announcers, along with the non-music and trashy subject matter, make TV especially corrupting for children and young adults. A local critic refers to TV as the "Trash Vendor."

12. Your arguments are persuasive but why don't I see confirmation of them *anywhere*?

   A. You aren't looking in the right places. Confirmation of the facts in this book may be found in selected investment newsletters, testimony of former Insiders and federal banking investigators, and in books whose narrow focus parallels this book's. Unfortunately, those books do not enjoy wide distribution because they are not carried by the nation's largest booksellers, or bought by many of the nation's libraries. However, small publishers have discovered ways to avoid the marketing problems which beset them in the past. Watch for wider distribution of better materials soon.

13. Your book stinks! My pastor says usury is a sin and I believe him more than I believe you.

   A. Your pastor undoubtedly has your best interests at heart and I would not fault him for that. On the other hand, when people are in the habit of believing something, change is sometimes difficult. Be patient with your pastor — he would no doubt admit readily that he doesn't know everything. Continue your own investigations into this issue and I'm confident you'll reach the right answer on this and other questions.

14. Why should anyone believe you? Lots of other people, lots better known than you, never say anything about the Fed or the other things you're upset with. Why is that?

   A. What do you think reality is? Recently scientists discovered that high-frequency sounds can produce tiny bubbles in water. When the bubbles collapse, they produce a faint blue light and generate highly localized temperatures approaching that of the sun, many thousands of degrees Fahrenheit. Did you know about that? Probably not, if you don't follow the literature of technology. Similarly, many magazines which appeal to more generalized audiences do not cover topics like the bubbles in water or fractional-reserve banking. Congratulations though, because your curiosity tells me you will take the trouble to investigate. Send in your

Reader Registration Form and we'll help keep you up to date on the issues.

15. I have about $100,000 in the stock market right now and I don't know whether to stay in or get out. What do you suggest I do?

A. Find a broker who caters to your age and your income. Otherwise, buy low; sell high. As financier Bernard Baruch put it, buy when the blood is running in the streets. Then wait.

16. My husband is a CPA and he told me your arguments about fractional-reserve banking are nothing new to him. But what we want to know is, what can anyone do about it?

A. Continue your investigations, be prudent in your financial affairs, and use sound judgment in your choice of counsel. Also, send us the form in Appendix B and we'll keep you informed about new developments.

17. I have a friend who raised the same arguments you raise but he did it in court and he lost. He lost his house, his car, his acreage, and his farm equipment. What do you have to say about that?

A. Using the money issue as a defense in court may not be wise, especially in a trial where you represent yourself, if neither the judge nor the jury knows the facts well enough — which is usually the case.

18. I heard of a lawyer, I think it was in California, and he raised the same arguments as you but he did it trying to get a $50 Silver Certificate paid. He didn't have any luck at all. Any comment?

A. You may be thinking of the former assistant U. S. Attorney in San Diego, Mobley Milam. In about 1970, while in private law practice, Milam attempted to get the Los Angeles branch of the Federal Reserve Bank to give him lawful money, which was promised to him on a $50 bill, a Federal Reserve Note from the series of 1950, we believe. The bank offered him $50 in various denominations of FRTs but refused to give him lawful money. Milam sued, lost at trial, and also lost his appeal.[1] He didn't get the lawful money which was due him but the story of his attempt to get it helped alert thousands of Americans to the issues raised in this book.

19. What do you think of President Clinton?

A. We agree with the analysis of Paul Fick, Ph.D. (psychology), in his book, *The Dysfunctional President* (New York: Citadel Press, 1996). Mr. Clinton's sometimes strange behavior and stranger priorities are typical of an adult who, as a child, suffered the adverse influence of an alcoholic parent. Mr. Clinton, while intelligent, may be driven by unhealthy forces.

20. A few years ago I bought a lot of silver one-ounce "rounds." Should I keep them? Will they ever be used as coins? Also, what do you think about investing in jewelry?

A. Any mechanical device which resembles a coin and which contains precious metal has value because of its precious-metal content. On the other hand, if the mint or minter of the device is not well known and well respected, the public may be reluctant to accept the device in trade. In general, one's investment portfolio is considered balanced only if it contains some holdings of precious-metals denominated assets, but your age, health, and financial circumstances may suggest another approach would be better for you. You should discuss your financial circumstances with a competent professional.

21. You explain your position very well but there seems to be a problem, not just in the problem itself but how to resolve it. If a criminal enterprise is involved here, and I think there may, this thing has been

---

[1] See 524 F.2d 629 (9th Cir. 1974) (Kilkenny, Trask, and Craig, JJ.).

going on for more than a hundred years. Wouldn't the statute of limitations bar any prosecution, plus bar any recovery via civil process?

    A. Our legal advisors are still out on this question but they are considering it in light of a couple of things. First, while it is true that if a crime is known to the community for a long time and nobody does anything about it, the courts or prosecution can legally consider that the misbehavior no longer constitutes an offense. On the other hand, a court holding I read a few years ago said something like, "The longevity of a crime confers no sanctity upon the act or affords any protection to its perpetrators." Either way, if the Insiders perpetrate a *continuing fraud*, the statute of limitations on just the most recent acts should allow plenty of time to investigate and prosecute the matter.

22. If there is or was a criminal conspiracy at work regarding our country's money, why haven't we heard anything about it before?

    A. A conspiracy is sometimes difficult to prove, and most publishers avoid discussing a topic which could get them sued for libel. Thus, general-circulation periodicals and broadcasts may skirt the question of conspiracy in favor of less dangerous issues. Also, sometimes serious damage is done by well-meaning but innocent people who cry "conspiracy" without valid cause. We should keep investigating these issues, and we should act appropriately on our discoveries, but we should be careful to not accuse as conspirators persons who may have just been ill-informed or confused about an issue.

23. I have a friend who says the Jews are behind all of the world's turmoil, especially the money problems. Could you comment on that outlook?

    A. Like the members of every other group, there are Jews on every side of this issue. Beware voices who accuse any race, creed, culture or religion of complicity in what may be the crime of the millennium. Always remember that crimes are not conducted by races, for instance, but by *criminals*.

24. I notice that you don't mention Montana's Freemen or the Texas sovereignty movement. They are saying some of the same things as you are so why don't you give them credit?

    A. Ill-advised, ill-considered, and illogical movements exist, and should be expected to exist, in a free country. Many voices have raised the issue of our country's unbacked paper currency but only a few of those entities, in our opinion, offer high-quality materials or leadership. Some entities we think you might find valuable to contact are listed in the appendices.

25. A big part of the tax protest movement of the 1970s and 1980s was based on what you're arguing but that movement has been wiped out. Why should anyone believe you, with that kind of track record behind you?

    A. The movement still exists but it has changed its focus. Instead of direct confrontation with the IRS, adherents now tend to support alternative activities such as a national flat tax or the balanced-budget idea. Some leaders have been replaced; the movement's new leaders seem to prefer a more practical approach to the issues. Always remember that, whether you agree with them or not, the "civil rights" demonstrators of the 1960s went to jail to get the legislators' attention. The tax protesters of the 1970s and 1980s have done the same thing. Without them, would Congress now be talking about abolishing the income tax?

26. My church believes in obedience to the government because of Romans 13. You seem to be going against that teaching. Are you?

    A. No. We should obey the government — but not when it violates the law, harms innocent people, and breaks the Eighth Commandment. Isn't Scripture full of kings — governments —

like Saul, brought down by disobedience? Also, remember that *we* are the real government, and we have a contract with our employees, the civil service workers, who are bound by the U.S. Constitution. If they violate our work rules, we need to give them more training, or find others who will do as they are told. Romans 13 does not mean blind obedience, which is a recipe for Hitler.

27. All your fancy talk about etymologies is hooey to me because you're ignoring the fact that Jesus threw the moneychangers out of the temple, which proves that your arguments are Satanic.

A. Jesus threw the moneychangers and a few other business people out of the temple because the temple was meant to be a place of quiet worship, not noisy mercantile activity. Jesus did not condemn the moneychangers but he did condemn others. Moneychangers offered a worthwhile service to the community and, in so doing, contributed to the well-being of all.

28. It seems to me that if you force everyone back on gold and silver coins, prices would skyrocket and millions of people would starve. How would you avoid that little problem?

A. If gold and silver coins begin circulating, and if Dollar-bills also circulate, prices will adjust to the availability of the purchasing media. How those prices change will not change the two critical things. First, the number of people on the earth will not change, and, second, the amount of food and other forms of wealth will not change. If prices change to reflect the availability of the purchasing media, the real cost of any good or service, in terms of the labor involved in earning the purchasing media, will not change. If it now takes you an hour to earn a nice meal in a restaurant, after the new media of exchange are used, it will still take about an hour of your work to earn enough purchasing media to buy a nice meal in a restaurant.

29. My wife and I are on Social Security. If the country goes back to gold and silver coins, what would that mean for us?

A. Please see the answer for question 28, above.

30. Gresham's law says bad money drives out good, so if the U.S. went back to gold and silver coins, why wouldn't Gresham's law cause all the other countries' low-quality currency to flood into this country and thereby cause our good money to flow out?

A. Today the world's weakest currencies do not flood this country because there is no benefit to a U.S. citizen to use that currency. Gresham's law applies to circumstances like the runaway inflation in Germany in the early 1920s. If you'd been there at that time, and if you had a gold coin, you would keep the gold coin and spend the junk money (aluminum coins, paper bills). You'd get rid of the junk money because its purchasing power was declining; you'd keep the gold coin because its purchasing power was at least holding steady. Gresham's law is just another way of saying that sane people will always act in ways which will help assure their survival. Insane people will often act in ways which assure their destruction. Be sane. It's more fun, it costs less, and it is much less filling.

31. Which of the two political parties is most likely to support your ideas?

A. Both major political parties (Republican and Democrat) have their strengths and weaknesses but generally, the Libertarian party seems to be most likely to offer the most reliable leadership because Libertarians advocate education as the best means of solving problems, not behavioral changes compelled by government. Libertarians advocate private-sector, free-market and voluntary means of solving problems, a refreshing approach when one considers the phenomenal sums of the national treasure which have been expended by or through representatives of the Democrat and Republican parties.

32. Why don't the schools teach what you say?

A. Most of the people who run them work for the government. Civil service workers, in general, may initially oppose reductions in the size of "government" because they mistakenly believe their personal security will be jeopardized. However, they need to realize that if the nation *doesn't* change course, and quickly, their jobs will evaporate and their civil-service organizations will likely be shut down by opportunistic politicians to appease growing public sentiment against "big government." That awakening is far from complete but it is happening, if only slowly.

33. If you could move to any other country, which would it be?

A. If *compelled* to move to another country, I'd probably choose Switzerland. I love the Alps, the snow, the lakes and the trains, and the climate would be ideal for me. The Swiss are generally polite, responsible and law-abiding people; they'd be good neighbors in time of crisis. Also, if I lived in Switzerland I could easily travel to many other European countries. But if I were not compelled to move to another country, I'd stay right here in the U.S.

34. I have a collection of old paper currency, including a few silver certificates. How much are they worth today?

A. If you live in the western half of the United States, you might contact the American Numismatic Association, Colorado Springs, Colorado, for information on ANA activities in your area. If you live in the eastern half of the United States, you may wish to contact the American Numismatic Society in New York City. A member of either group who lives in your area may be able to help you obtain a reliable appraisal of your collection.

35. Are you being funded by a big company or foundation? Where is your money coming from?

A. I pay my own way and always have. Long ago, personal friends helped me on some projects. If you'd like to stay in contact, please fill out and mail us the form in Appendix B. We'll notify you if we seek support on a specific project, etc.

36. What are your favorite sources of information on money and related subjects?

A. Please see the appendices.

37. We have kids reaching college age. Which school would you recommend?

A. Generally, the college or university may not be as important as the people who teach the courses. Look for a like-minded faculty member, preferably a professor of the discipline your children plan to pursue, and consider that person's advice. Also, complete and mail us a copy of the form in Appendix B.

38. My wife and I work for the post office and plan to retire in 1999. What will happen to our retirement?

A. Your retirement, whether paid in FRTs or silver coins, will probably be adequate to your needs, but if paid in silver coin or silver-backed paper currency, your standard of living, and everyone else's, might rise.

39. I've collected coins for years and have heard a lot of what you say, but I'm still wondering if I should sell my gold and silver coins or keep them. I'm sixty and won't be able to retire for a few more years. What should I do?

A. Contact the American Numismatic Association for help in getting an appraisal of your coins, and then contact a professional investment counselor for further guidance.

40. Are you going to come out with a video or paperback book?

A. We plan to offer a paperback edition of this book in the near future, and we are discussing a CD and a video. Let us know who you are by completing and mailing us the form in Appendix B.

41. What you say is fascinating but almost unbelievable. What can we (husband and wife) do to check you out?

A. Forget about me. Check out what I say. Start with the bibliography. Most of what I've reported here can be confirmed by multiple sources, some of which are listed in the appendices.

42. What do you think of home schooling?

A. If home schooling was good enough for Abraham Lincoln, it's also good enough for many Americans. Home-schooled children have two advantages over other children: they mature more rapidly because they are around adults more than they're around other children, and they are more emotionally stable than most children I know who attend "public" schools. To be successful, one must be intelligent *and* emotionally balanced. In the main, most home-schooled children have these characteristics, and most other children do not. Moreover, home schooled children have *internalized* Judeo-Christian values — they are well-behaved, considerate of other people and property — because those things they have been part of their lives, not just something learned from a lecture or story.

43. The newspapers recently told of Swiss banks holding on to money deposited by German Jews during the rise of Hitler and World War II. Those banks are reluctant to give the money back. Any comment?

A. The Swiss banks have a big problem. Some depositors, or the descendants of depositors now dead, have little documentation to establish that they are the rightful heirs to the deposited sums. Also, some Nazis spirited their funds to Switzerland at the same time, and some people demand that those funds be distributed to Holocaust victims. Third, because of a couple of fires in buildings in which these records were stored, it may be very difficult to learn who deposited some of the funds. Last, the banks have an interest in continuing to hold on to the funds. With each passing year, more potential claimants die, thereby leaving their deposits as property of the banks. It's a tough period for the Swiss banking community. Also keep in mind that the criminals we have exposed in this book have long hated Switzerland, which has been a refuge for assets they covet. The Insiders have tried to demonize Switzerland with the propaganda usually reserved for people who invest offshore. That propaganda could be at work in the present dispute.

44. Suppose I could get my boss to pay me in silver coin, which would mean, instead of about $50,000 per year, my salary would be about $12,000 per year. That would put me into a much lower tax bracket wouldn't it?

A. IRS probably would argue that you must report the coins on your 1040 form "at their fair market value," which the IRS would likely determine was about $50,000. You might also face a fine and other penalties for filing a "frivolous return."

45. In the past year or so, the supply of "money and credit" in the United States has increased sharply but the deficit is lower and there has been little change in the Consumer Price Index. Why haven't we had continued inflation if the supply of "money and credit" has increased?

A. The deficit is lower because of cost-cutting in administrations prior to President Clinton's arrival in the White House. Evidence of a rise in the general price level may be hidden because components of the CPI may be discarded if they experience a rapid price movement. Second, some of the extra "money and credit" is showing up in exploding public investment in mutual funds, which may be a large part of the reason the Dow Jones Industrial Average has been climbing so high so quickly. Third and finally, a lot of the increase of "money and credit" may have been distributed in loans to businesses and governments internationally. If so, it may be a while before this distribution of extra "money and credit" causes a noticeable rise in the general price level in the United States.

46. Why doesn't the Congress or the President do something about the Federal Reserve Banks?

A. You may not fully understand the mess we are in. The Federal Reserve Banking System is a private organization. Yes, it has tremendous power but it is not part of the U.S. government. It is just like AT&T or IBM. It provides services for other banks and for the United States government but it is not operated by civil-service employees, it is not a tax-exempt entity, and each Federal Reserve Bank is an incorporated entity with stockholders, just like the stockholders of AT&T and IBM. There is no dispute about this. The Federal Reserve says so itself. The "Fed" is owned mainly by other banks and other private corporations. Individuals who own large amounts of "Fed" stock have that stock in the name of nominees, which means the real owners' names don't show on stockholder lists. The nominees are often lawyers or law firms, or the ownership is hidden by additional layers of ownership. If the "Fed" ever decided to do so, it could close down its operations in just a month or two. Interest rates would then follow market forces and would not be subject to direct manipulation. The power of the "Fed" is often underestimated by the American public because the average citizen thinks the "Fed" is part of the government. On the contrary, the "Fed" may be the world's most powerful private-sector entity. Those who own the "Fed" are the most powerful people in the world, more powerful than political leaders in any country, including the United States. For example, the U.S. President does not act unless he first confers with his advisors, almost all of whom have been directly or indirectly linked to the "Fed" — for the past seventy years or so. The "Fed" may control the President of the United States in the nation's most important policy decisions. Since 1913, for eighty-five years, those decisions have been enhancing the power of the "Fed's" owners to the detriment of almost everyone else.

47. What is the answer to the puzzle you gave us at the beginning of Chapter 14, Fraud?

A. The answer is that the question itself is fraudulent and cannot be answered. It can't be answered because it is irrational. Here's why. Three men paid $27 for the room. $25 is in the hotel cash register and $2 is in the bell captain's pocket. There is no missing Dollar. But a devious manipulator might phrase the question the way we did in Chapter 13: "Three times 9 is 27 plus the $2 in the bell captain's pocket makes 29. Where is the other Dollar?" Focus on the word "plus" and you'll see that it's wrong. The only way to logically use "three times 9" and "$2 in the bell captain's pocket" would be like this: "Three times 9 is $27, which is the $25 in the cash register plus $2 in the bell captain's pocket." This puzzle is a good example of the kind of patter a con man uses. That's why professional advice in money matters is often helpful. Some people, perfectly intelligent, fall victim to their own sincerity, which scam artists are able to turn into a weapon.

48. I know about the problems of unbacked currency but I've had bad luck explaining them. What's the simplest way you know to get someone to understand how dangerous unbacked paper currency is?

A. There are no guarantees, of course, but you may want to try these five analogies.

1) Your grandparents put gold coins weighing about 200 troy ounces, in the bank. The bank gave your grandparents receipts. The receipts were called Dollar-bills. When your grandparents died, your parents inherited the Dollar-bills. When your parents died, you inherited the Dollar-bills. Now you want to take the bills back to the bank and get the 200 troy ounces of gold. The bank refuses to give you the gold, saying you have the Dollar-bills and they "spend" just like the gold coins did. You argue that the 200 troy ounces in gold coins will still buy a house but the "paper money" (Dollar-bills) won't pay more than a month's rent on a house. The banker accuses you of being unpatriotic because a law was passed which made it legal for her to keep the gold. That law also said you had to keep using the Dollar-bills. The banker closes the conversation with a warning that you'd better move along or she'll call the police. The difference in purchasing power between 1900 and today is the loss you suffer. It is also someone else's gain. Who got the purchasing power that you lost? How would you like to get it back?

2) The federal government alone is allowed to print "Dollars." Everybody else has to work for them. But the people who control interest rates — the "Fed" — subtly control how those "Dollars" are spent. Since the "Fed" knows ahead of time what the nation's interest rates will be, the "Fed" makes the prices in our economy trend up or down. By knowing that, the Insiders who own the "Fed" can buy and sell stock and make other investments with little chance of loss. You and I will lose, because we don't know what they know. Because the odds are stacked in their favor, the Insiders will win and win until they control virtually all the world's material wealth. You and I might own a few things — toothbrushes and underwear — but to interact with others, we'd probably be dependent on the wealth the Insiders own or control. Ownership of those few things would satisfy some citizens but, in reality, our freedom would be gone. That's the end-game of fractional-reserve banking. It's a slow process, a fraud scheme that is barely detectable to its victims, but the end is ordained — unless we stop it. We lose everything, the Insiders win everything, and our freedoms are gone.

3) Suppose the President announced that he had turned the nation's military over to Lemon Motor Company. From now on, the defense department will remain independent of the government because defense is so important that it should be "above" political influence. The President says that an "independent agency" will be a healthy sign of "democracy" at work, and that he pledges the "full faith and credit" of the country behind Lemon Motor Company. A few months later, Lemon Motor Company representatives establish offices in every major country worldwide, and work closely with the leaders of those countries. From now on, wars and other forms of violent conflict erupt at regular intervals around the world, as political and military leaders vie for control of one country after another. The world population declines, because people are being killed in wars faster than the nation's birth rate can replace them, and environmentalists tell us that is "good." None of this is an accident; the President wanted to reduce the rest of the world's population and that's how he and his Insider friends accomplished it. They did it because they knew that such a tactic would make most other countries less desirable to live in. The wealthy of those countries would tend to move to the United States, making the Insiders' real estate investments in the United States more valuable. They would use the profits later to buy real estate in war-torn countries at extremely low prices, and then manipulate those wars in one country after another, at the Insiders whim. Their real estate holdings in a peace-

ful country would grow to great value. They would sell that real estate just before they brought a war to that country and depressed real estate prices again. By controlling the war-making capability of governments, the Insiders control the value and price of real estate, which means they can leverage their current wealth into effective ownership of the world.

But assigning the nation's defense responsibility to Lemon Motor Company isn't the only way to accomplish the migrating-war scene described above. Another way would be to give any company, even Lemon Motor Company, the responsibility for the nation's "money" supply, and therefore interest rates. With knowledge of interest rates and the direction they are going, the Insiders can pyramid their wealth, possibly by fomenting wars and making large loans to arms manufacturers, and, after the wars, making large loans to the companies who are tasked with repairing the war damage. That's what the Insiders have done for almost a century. It works.

4. You and three friends decide to go to Dave's Burger Joint for lunch. Three of you have $5.00 apiece in cash but Linda has a coupon for one meal. She bought the Dave's Burger Joint coupon a year ago for $5.00. The meal is described as "One double cheeseburger, with lettuce, pickle, onion, ketchup, mayonnaise, mustard, and two slices of American cheese; biggie fries, and one full-size milkshake (any flavor)." The coupon says the meal will be provided to the bearer on demand. Your party arrives at the nearest Dave's Burger Joint, everyone places his order and then pays for his meal. Linda "pays" for her meal with her coupon but the clerk says that her coupon will buy only the pickles, and that she'll have to pay an additional $4.75 for the meal. The clerk explains that "inflation" caused the problem, and that while they used to honor the coupons for the full meal, they couldn't afford to do it any longer. Since Linda thought the coupon would be honored at face value, she didn't bring any cash with her, so while everyone else eats a nice meal, she eats the two small slices of pickle and wonders where the missing $4.75 of value went; she remembered being told by the Dave's Burger Joint employee, when she bought the coupon, that the coupons were "the same" as the meal, and that the coupon was "backed" by the "full faith and credit of Dave's Burger Joint" which had been in business for more than 100 years. While Linda savors the last taste of the two small slices of pickle, she notices Dave drive away in his new Mercedes convertible. She wonders how a guy who fries burgers for a living can afford such a classy set of wheels.

5. You realize that your family can't eat gold or silver so you take a major part of your savings and use it to buy certificates for a year's supply of food for each member of your family, which is composed of you and your spouse and your daughter and son. A few years later a fire destroys your business so you decide to feed yourself and your family by turning in the food-reserve coupons. However, when you enter the storehouse, a clerk there says "We haven't redeemed those things," referring to your coupons, "for many years. But we can give you some 6-month and 3-month coupons in exchange for your 1-year coupons. Would that be okay with you?" You are not interested in exchanging a one-year coupon for two six-month coupons because what you want is food for yourself and your family. Suppose the clerk tells you to take the coupons down to the local store, because "all commercial establishments will accept your coupons in trade." You decide to do just that, and you visit a local supermarket. The clerk looks at your one-year coupons and says you can pick out enough food for one person for two weeks, and that's all. The clerk sees your expression of dismay and explains, "That's all anybody gets for those coupons nowadays. It's the law. You're the only one who's ever complained."

49. Your book is interesting but the problem of inflation is over. The "Balanced Budget" and "Flat Tax" amendments are sure to pass and when that happens, the Insiders' game will be over.

   A. The "Balanced Budget" amendment and other proposed monetary reforms have been ballyhooed around this country for the past decade or so. Some of the people who promote such reform seem confused. Please consider the following.

   1. A proposed "Balanced Budget" Constitutional amendment would not prevent inflation. Inflation is an increase in the supply of money and credit relative to the supply of other goods and services. Today, inflation is caused by huge federal deficits, and by the pernicious effect of fractional-reserve banking. The "balanced budget" proposal does not prevent government from spending more every year. If a "balanced budget" is mandated, and if the government spends more every year, taxes would have to rise each year to keep the budget balanced. Our tax payments would have to be borrowed or otherwise taken out of the private sector. Thus, ever-increased spending by government will have the same effect on the general price level, both before and after a "balanced budget" amendment. Because of the amendment, taxes would rise, as government spends more. Right now we pay the extra tax in the form of inflation, which is caused by government deficits. If we eliminate those deficits but continue government's profligate spending patterns, our taxes would probably have to be paid with funds borrowed from the banks. Thus, the supply of money and credit would continue to increase, just as it did when caused by government deficits. When the Balanced Budget amendment is passed, inflation will continue but now it will be caused by taxpayer borrowing to pay additional taxes.

   Yet there are two more-serious aspects to this issue. First, there is extreme danger in convening a Constitutional Convention because the clearly confused or corrupt politicians and their pals could easily rewrite the entire Constitution and delete the Bill of Rights. Also, recall that there was a limit on the national debt enacted into law in the 1950s yet, almost every year, the Congress raises the limit on the national debt. If Congress violates the intent of the debt-limit law, why should we expect Congress to pay any heed to a balanced-budget law? Congress doesn't seem to understand or respect many other aspects of the U.S. Constitution, so why should we expect Members to understand and respect a Balanced-Budget amendment? The bottom line is that honest and ethical members of Congress need no balanced-budget amendment to help them solve the problem of inflation; what the nation needs is Members of Congress with honor, ethics and courage. Until we, the People, elect them, we'll never solve the problem of inflation. You now know a few of the reasons its more caustic critics say the Balanced Budget amendment is a fraud upon the American public.

   2. In some circles the Flat Tax movement is also considered a form of fraud upon the people. This movement says nothing about the amount of control civil-service workers have over We, the People, but it does permit them to take more tax money from us, and to take it more efficiently. Flat Tax legislation does not attempt to reduce government spending. If tax savings accrue they will accrue only to the civil-service workers, because in the United States today, it is too easy for the public to be misled about money-related matters. We would agree that a really simple federal tax system would benefit everyone but not if it hastens the demise of the country, and that is exactly what critics say the recently-proposed Flat Tax plan would do.

50. If you were President, what would you do?

   A. I'd impanel a committee of top accounting and economics experts and ask them to investigate the country's current problems. My guess is that this committee would recommend we re-establish a redeemable currency, phase out FRTs over a period of a year or two, and end all personal federal taxes, including the personal income tax. The committee would likely also recommend the safest and quickest steps to reduce and restrict the size and scope of the federal government so that once again it operated within Constitutional limits, and to return the savings immediately to the public. (I suspect the committee would suggest radical change in how the federal government is financed, but I'll save that for another time.) The committee's recommendations would become *my* top priorities, as President.

•

"Whenever the paper has not been convertible into specie, and its quantity has depended on the policy of the government, a depreciation has been produced by an undue increase, or an apprehension of it."

President James Madison (1751 - 1836)

"Warburg's revolutionary plan to get American Society to go to work for Wall Street was astonishingly simple. Even today, . . . academic theoreticians cover their blackboards with meaningless equations, and the general public struggles in bewildered confusion with inflation and the coming credit collapse, while the quite simple explanation of the problem goes undiscussed and almost entirely uncomprehended. The Federal Reserve System is a legal private monopoly of the money supply operated for the benefit of the few under the guise of protecting and promoting the public interest."

Anthony Sutton, Wall Street and FDR *(New Rochelle, New York: Arlington House, 1975), p. 94. As quoted by G. Edward Griffin,* The Creature From Jekyll Island *(Westlake Village, California: American Media, 1994), pp. 18-19*

"Throughout history, periods of high moral attainment have been periods of sound money, while periods of moral disintegration have followed the debasement of the monetary unit. Fiat money, printing press money, or money without intrinsic value is dishonest money, and the moral laws having been violated, moral degradation is inevitable."

> Howard E. Kershner (1891 - ?), Gold, God and Government, *as quoted in* Gold Newsletter, *March 1988. From* Blanchard *(see Appendix A,* Gold Newsletter*)*

"For the last five years, we have been in a new era in this country. We are making progress industrially and economically, not by leaps and bounds, but on a heroic scale."

> Forbes *magazine, in its issue for June 1929, just three months before the horrendous stock-market "crash" of 1929 and the start of the Great Depression. [Sent to me by Hal Lindsey's office. Mr. Lindsey wrote* The Late Great Planet Earth *and co-hosts the* International Intelligence Report *TV news commentary program on Trinity Broadcasting Network. je.]*

18

Glossary

INFORMAL DEFINITIONS OF MONEY-RELATED WORDS AND PHRASES

Definitions given here pertain only to law, finance, money and related subjects. Parts of speech (verb, noun, etc.), homonyms, and antonyms are usually not identified. This glossary is provided for general reference only. It is meant to be a guide, not a rigorous study of the meanings of these or any other words. Readers should refer to Appendix A for titles of suggested supplementary reading and scholarly reference works, and should refer to their own dictionaries (plural), the older the better, for assistance in seeing how meanings have been corrupted or otherwise varied over the years.

A

A — An indefinite article. Indicates *one of a group* or *one of a series*. Generally used when the next word starts with a consonant.

ACCOUNT — From the Old French *a*, meaning *to*, and *conter*, meaning *(to) count*.

ACTUARY — From Latin *actuarius*, meaning the person who records (writes down, reports about) the actions of others.

AMORTIZE — French *a*, meaning *to*, and *mort*, meaning *death*. To track until (its) death.

AMOUNT — French *a*, meaning *to*, and *mount*. To pile up.

AN — Indefinite article; *one of a group* or *one of a series*. Generally used when the next word starts with a vowel.

AS — Occurs in four forms: adverb, conjunction, relative pronoun, and preposition. Look *as* up in a regular dictionary. When you see *as* in print, especially in legal documents, make certain you know which form is being used. If you are even slightly uncertain, don't sign the documents.

ASSIGNAT — Fiat paper currency first issued in France April 1, 1790, originally backed by real property but, with later issues added to already-circulating issues, the amount of real property backing each piece of paper got smaller and smaller. When the public became fed up with them, they were burned. Use of *assignats* plunged France into an economic collapse from which some say it has not yet (1998) fully recovered. Pronounced ah´ + seen + yacht.

AUDIT — From Latin *auditus* (with a long *i*), which means *a hearing*. See audible, audio, auditory, etc.

AVOIRDUPOIS — Pronounced awe + vwah´ + due + pwah, with emphasis on the second syllable. From the French *Avoir*, meaning *goods* (originally *avoir* meant *to have*), plus *du*, which means *the*, plus *pois*, which means *weight*. Originally spelled *avoir de pois* (or Anglo-French, *de peis*), meaning *goods of weight* or *heavy articles*. A system of weighing in which sixteen ounces equal one pound. (Counterpoise means counterweight.)

B

BANK — Originally *banc*, for *bench*. In a monetary or financial sense, a bank is a structure specially built for the safe storage of *money*. As an operating entity, a bank stores money for some clients and rents that money to other clients, receiving a rental fee from the borrowers, which fee is shared with the persons who placed the money in storage with that banker. According to this classical definition, *there are no banks operating anywhere in the world today because there is no money in general circulation anywhere in the world today*.

BANKRUPT — Literally, a *bank* which is *broken*.

BAR (of gold) — See *INGOT*.

BARTER — From the Old French *barater*, which means *to deceive*. Earlier European versions of *barater* (tied to *barratry*) meant *haggle* or *exchange*.[1] Some etymologists also see a link to *bargain*. Many people think a *barter system* is a market system without money, where people trade things without benefit of a medium of exchange. That is a popular but etymologically incorrect notion. Barter takes place in every market, whether a medium of exchange is used or not. When we negotiate for a better price, in terms of money or anything else, we are bartering.

Libya to Trade Cash For Barter System

LONDON (UPI) — Libya plans to abolish money and replace it with a barter system, Libyan television said Friday.

The television, monitored by the BBC, quoted the state news agency JANA as saying "the new system of barter will be adopted" in accordance with Libyan leader Col. Moammar Gadhafi's political philosophy.

"This will end dealings in money, which will become a unit of measurement only," the television said.

It gave no further details.

Salt Lake Tribune, Sept. 27, 1986

BOND — Related to bind, band, shackle, restraint, and tie (attach). Also related to farmer, one who is tied to the land or soil. Also related to *bauer*, German for farmer, and to bondage, bondsman and serf.

BORROW — From Anglo Saxon *borgian*, meaning *pledge*. Also related to *borough*, which relates to *castle* and to *burgus*.

BULLION — Related to French *bouillon*, a boiled soup, and Latin *bulla*, meaning *bubble*. When silver or gold ore is processed by high heat, the precious metal melts first, and is thus easily separated from the dross or slag.

BUY — Anglo Saxon *bycgan*, meaning *to purchase*. *Purchase* relates to *pro chase*, or *as a result of a chase* or *what I caught*.

C

CARAT — Related to Greek *karation*, meaning a *little horn*, or *fruit of the carob tree* (whose fruit is shaped like a small trumpet), or a *small weight*; equal to exactly 200 milligrams or 3.086 grains. Carat is a unit of weight exclusively for precious stones.

CASH — From French *casse*, a box or case in which money was kept. Not related to the French word *cache*, pronounced cash + ay´, which is a place to *hide* things. *Cache* rhymes with the name of the French painter, Monet, in which the last syllable is accented.

CATTLE — From Latin *capitale*, meaning stock or capital; also tied to *chattel*, and to *capita*, or *head*. How many *head* are in your herd? (*Herd* is not related to *hoard*.)

CENT — One one-hundredth, also *one hundredth part*. Century: Cent + ur + y, or *hundred + year + period of*. See also DIME. Officially, one Dollar is equal to 100 *cents*, not 100 *pennies*.

---

[1] Barratry originally meant buying or selling jobs.

CHANGE — From Latin *cambiare*, meaning *exchange*.

CHARGE — From French *charger*, meaning *to load*.

CHATTEL — From Late Latin *capitale*, meaning *property*. Be sure to also look at *property* (*pro per + ty*), meaning *a tie* to what belongs to a person.

CHECK — French *checque*, or *draft*. Related to *checker* pieces, which in Europe are (also) called *draughts*. Further relates to a cross-checking or verification process, especially in French. A bank *draft* is a kind of cross-comparison against what is in one's account at a bank. Draft also means a *drawing out*, where a stove draws air from (out of) a room.

CO-CONSPIRATOR — Irrational term; vulgarism. The term *co-conspirator* is as rational as: a law-firm co-partner; a fraternal organization's co-brother or co-sister; a team's co-member; and a business executive's co-associate. "Co-" is redundant.

COIN — French *quoin*, meaning *wedge*, where a wedge is a tool used in making dies (which in turn are stamping tools). Another name for *wedge* is the Latin *cuneum*, where *cune* (kyew + knee) is used in the modern *pecuniary*, meaning *related to money*. The earliest coins were made from lumps of electrum, a naturally occurring amalgam of gold and silver. These rude lumps of metal were marked, usually on only one side, to indicate their weight. The tool used to mark them was a wedge-shaped implement whose markings are called *cuneiform* marks, meaning *formed by a cune*. Our word *cow*, a bovine animal, may be indirectly related to the *cu* (*kew*) in pecuniary.

COLLATERAL — Literally, *with side* or *parallel*. A thing promised as a guarantee of payment of a sum owed. If the sum owed is not paid, the collateral is taken in lieu of whatever sum was owed.

COMMERCE — Traffic. From the Latin *cum*, meaning *with*, and *merx*, meaning *merchandise*. Related to *mercenarius*, meaning *hireling*. Possibly parallel development of *hireling*, to *helper*, to *aide* or *aid*, which would ultimately compare with *mutually aiding* or *mutually beneficial*. Possibly related to co-mercy.

COMMERCIAL — See COMMERCE.

COMMODITY MONEY — Redundant terms. Used today to distinguish *money* from money-substitutes (paper currency, *fiat* or otherwise). See also Fiduciary Money.

COMPEL — *Compel* includes a requirement that officially issued coins and paper currencies of the United States be accepted in tenders for the payment of debts. The requirement has a conditional *OR* associated with it. If someone owes you *ten Dollars*, and if he tenders a Ten-Dollar gold certificate to you, if you do not accept it **AS** payment of the debt, the court will hold that you thereby waived your right to collect interest on the unpaid debt. However, if someone owes you *ten Dollars*, and tenders twenty-five German Marks to you (even though twenty-five Marks today has approximately the same purchasing power as ten Dollars in FRTs), you would not waive your claim to interest payment in the eyes of the courts if you rejected the twenty-five Marks. This position of the courts gave rise to widespread, although incorrect, informal usage of the two-word phrase *legal-tender*. Moreover, in the late 1800s, the silver content of the fifty-cent, twenty-five-cent and ten-cent coins was increased slightly so that the amount of silver in ten dimes, for example, would be a few percent more than the silver content of a silver Dollar coin. This modification helped reduce mischief, such as paying a bill of $150 in dimes. Alternately, the nation's courts compelled acceptance of silver dimes, quarter-Dollar and half-Dollar coins in tenders of up to and including $10. Compelled acceptance of U.S. coin is controlled by statute, and varies from time to time, depending on monetary circumstances and the mood of the nation's legislators. See also Chapter 7, Tender.

COMPENSATION — From Latin *compensare*, meaning *to weigh against* or *compare*. The word *pens* means *weigh* or *weight*. The sense of compensation is expressed in *balance the slate*, *even things up*, *settle accounts* and other American idioms.

CONSPIRATOR — A conspirator is one who, in secret, plans with another to commit a crime. *Con* is Latin for "with," *spire* is Latin for "breathe," and the two words together imply two or more people breathing the same air in the same place at the same time, in secret to plan a crime. See also CO-CONSPIRATOR.

CONSPIRE — Secretly, with at least one other person, plan to commit a crime.

CONTINENTAL — Colonial American paper currency (a token, *circa* 1775). Value declined to almost nothing. *Not worth a Continental*, derisive Colonial idiom. See photos, Figure 9-3.

CONTRACT — From Latin *contrahere*, where *con* means *together* or *with*, and *trahere* means *to draw*. See also Chapter 6, Note.

COPPER — Nickname for coin manufactured by element of same name, the penny or one-cent piece in the United States. Also, an element of matter.

COST — From Latin *costare*, to *stand* or *last* (endure). In Europe, *costly* means expensive, and thus expected to last a long time, endure weathering, or remain standing (for ages).

COUNTERFEIT — Literally, *against* and *make*. From the Latin *contra*, meaning *against*, and *facere*, meaning *to make* or *to do*. Compare with facsimile, facility, and surfeit.

COUNTRY — A geographically-defined area on the Earth. See also NATION.

CREDIT — From the Latin *credo*, meaning *to trust* or *to believe*.

CURRENCY, HARD — 1) A circulating medium, usually paper, which is redeemable in precious metal coinage on demand; or 2), a paper currency which is relatively stable in its purchasing power. While no nation's paper currency today meets the criteria in definition 1), above, the Swiss Franc is considered a relatively stable currency because its purchasing power remains steady from year to year. A soft currency is the opposite of a hard currency. The United States' currency (FRTs) is considered *hard* because it is less volatile in its purchasing power than the paper currency of many other countries.

CURRENCY, SOFT — (See CURRENCY, HARD).

D

DEBASE — Literally, *remove the basis*. If a coin is labeled as weighing *One Dollar*, removal of any of the precious metal of that coin, without deleting the label ("*One Dollar*"), is *debasing* that particular coin. A theoretical example of debasement of the nation's metallic currency would be government issuance of coins which bore the label *One Dollar* but did not contain 371.25 grains, plus or minus one-half percent, of pure silver. Counterfeiting is a felony punishable by fifteen years at hard labor in a federal penitentiary. Debasement is a form of counterfeiting.[2]

DEBIT — Latin *debitum*, from *debere*, meaning *to owe*.

DEBT — See DEBIT.

DEPRESSION — Variously defined, most often as an economic condition in which a lack of purchasing media causes a slowdown in the flow of goods and services from producer to consumer, which in turn causes a decline in the standard of living of the average citizen every quarter year for four or more consecutive quarters. See also RECESSION.

DIME — A ten-cent piece; a silver coin officially issued by the United States Mint; one tenth part of one Dollar of silver. The word *dime* is related to the Latin *decima*, meaning *tithe* and *one tenth part*. Dime, anciently spelled *disme*, is directly related to our words *decimal* and *decade*. Because the United States' principal monetary unit, the Dollar, is divided into a hundred parts, ours is the world's first metric monetary system.

---

[2] Debasement is also a form of adulteration, condemned by the Seventh Commandment. Debasement of coin and other currencies is also a violation of the Holy admonition in Proverbs 20:10: *Divers weights, and divers measures, both of them <u>are</u> alike abomination to the LORD*. (Emphasis in original.)

DOUBLOON — Spanish gold coin. *Doubloon* means *double pistole*, where *pistole* is a smaller Spanish coin.

DRAFT — See CHECK.

DUE — Derived from Old French *de voir*, meaning *to owe*.

E

EAGLE (COIN) — United States, ten Dollars of gold, containing 247.5 grains of pure gold.

ECONOMICS — From Greek *oiko*, or Latin *eco*, meaning *household* or *environment*, and *nomic*, meaning *to name* or *to number,* or *to manage*. Economics is the action of naming and numbering things in an environment; that is, quantifying and qualifying identifiable components of a society, culture, industry, etc. In Greek, "oikonomia" is said to (figuratively) mean "household manager." Literally, however, "oiko" is "the environment" and "nomia" is "naming and numbering things in an environment," which tells us that whether we discuss the Greek or Latin origin of *economics*, we arrive at the same current meaning, deriving it from the same ancient meaning.

ELECTRUM — A naturally-occurring amalgam of gold and silver. Also, the name of the first (and very crude) coins. See Kingdom of Lydia (or the Lydian Empire) at the western end of Turkey.

ELEMENT — An essential part of a legal document. For example, the four elements of a Note are *Maker, Payee, Dollar amount*, and *Due Date*. See Chapter 6, Note. Also a naturally occurring form of matter: Silver is an element, gold is an element, but salt is a compound of two elements, sodium and chlorine.

EPISTEMOLOGY — A philosophic theory (and study) of the method or basis of human knowledge. Term seen frequently in "Austrian" (school) economics texts. Relates to predictability of economic activity.

EXTRINSIC — From the outside, not belonging to the nature of a thing. The extrinsic value or worth of a clad coin may be *one dime*, while the intrinsic value or worth of the same coin may be less than one cent. A $10 Silver Certificate has an extrinsic worth of $10 in terms of lawful money of the United States, but it has an intrinsic worth of less than one cent.

F

FASCISM — A dictatorship, from *fasces*, a bundle of sticks. Benito Mussolini, in Italy in the early 1930s, was the *fascisti* party leader. The party's symbol was a bundle of sticks (to represent unity of purpose) and an ax (representing military might). Mussolini reportedly boasted that, "The *fascisti* party was the first [political party] to recognize that as society grows more complex, the more government is required."

FASCIST — A member of the *fascisti* party of Italy. See FASCISM.

FEE — Anglo Saxon *feoh*, meaning *cattle* or *money*; German *vieh*, meaning *cattle*. Also Latin *pecu*, meaning *cattle*, and possibly distantly related to our *cow*, which in German is *kuh* (pronounced *coo*). Also related to *fief*, as in *fiefdom*, and *feud*, as in *feudal*. A *fiefdom* is the land area in which a person *held in fee* (or in a bonded relationship, not free or sovereign) lives. See also (not in this work) *tenant in fee* and *tenant in fee simple*, in re Law. *Feud* also means *perpetual*.

FIAT — French for *decree*. Latin: *Let it be done*. Fiat *money* is a currency which is NOT money but is used **as** money (a currency, a medium of exchange) under order or decree and under threat or coercion, not voluntarily.

FIDUCIARY MONEY — Irrational term used today by some writers to indicate money substitutes, bogus and legitimate. Ex: Silver Certificate, redeemable Federal Reserve Note, Federal Reserve Token, etc. Term is irrational because *money* involves no fiduciary or other promissory relationship between its creator and any other owner. A better term might be *fiduciary media* (of exchange).

FINANCE — From Old French, *finer*, meaning *to end, to finish*, or *to settle*. Note *fin* in *finish*. See also Latin *finis*. Related to *fine*, meaning a payment to end a criminal or civil process, etc., from the Latin *fine* (pronounced fee + nay´) which means *ended*.

FINE — Anciently, a verb which describes the process of purifying precious metals, that is, removing impurities. Consider also *refine*. *Fine* is referred to in the Bible at Job 28:1 ("Surely there is a vein for the silver, and a place for gold *where* they fine *it*." Italics in original.) Also, in the Bible at Proverbs 25:4 ("Take away the dross from the silver, and there shall come forth a vessel for the finer.") *Fine* may also indicate small particles, and it may also indicate superior quality in goods and services, or a fabric with a tight mesh or weave.

FINE GOLD — In this context, *fine* means *pure*, or as fine a quality or purity as is possible. *Fine* means 100% pure, and *fine* also means *end*, wherein the purification process has come to an end — *fine gold* cannot be refined to a higher degree or level of purity. You may wish to remember that *fine* has two pronunciations: one, as in a *fine* of $25 for violating a traffic ordinance, and two, as the French would say *fee-nay*, meaning *end*. See also the Latin *finis*. The word *fine*, as it is used in the two-word phrase *fine gold* seen in U.S. law, is pronounced as we would use it in *a parking fine*.

FIX — From Latin *figere*, meaning *to figure* or *establish*. As related to the London gold *fixing* each day, the price established and then made public by a committee of banking and financial authorities without benefit of free-market influences, that is, solely by political or other arbitrary considerations.

FRANCHISE — From French *franc*, meaning *free* or *frank* (uninhibited). A license to commit an act or refrain from acting, wherein such act or forbearance to act could constitute a civil or criminal offense. Related to *franking privilege*, free postage for Members of Congress, etc. *Franked* mail is delivered without postage.

FUND — From the Latin *fundus*, meaning *bottom*. If you receive a check, then *cash* the check and receive redeemable currency (silver certificates, for example), and then redeem the currency for silver coin, you now possess *funds*, which means you've gone through all the transactions necessary to reach the *bottom* or most *fundamental* item(s). *Funds* is synonymous with *coins of gold or silver*. Also related to our modern word *foundation*.

G

GLOSSARY — From the German *glossa*, with a long *o*, meaning *language*. Specifically, a list of words and their definitions which relate to a narrow field of interest, such as a glossary of terms related to fishing, cheese, or money, etc.

GOLD — An elemental form of matter. Atomic symbol: Au. Atomic weight: 196.967; atomic number: 79. Related to the German *geld*, meaning *money*. Also possibly related to the German *gelb*, meaning the color *yellow*. Gold is said to be named for its color. The word *gold* is NOT synonymous with the word *money*. The former is an element of matter; the latter, a manufactured device. *Au* comes from the Latin word for gold, *aurum*.

GRAIN — A unit of measure of weight common to both avoirdupois and troy measure. See also WEIGHT.

GRAM — Unit of measure of weight in the metric system. 1 gram = 15.432 grains.

GRESHAM'S LAW — "Bad money drives out good." Sir Thomas Gresham (1519 - 1579), English financier. An informal economic law. If gold coins circulate in a society, and if a corrupt government then compels the citizenry to use *fiat* currency, the gold coins will soon disappear and everyone will "spend" just the *fiat* currency and save the gold coins. Once the government stops forcing the public to accept the bogus currency, the *fiat* currency will no longer be accepted in trade and the gold coins will return to circulation.

H

HOARD — As a noun, a *hoard* is a relatively large collection of things. As a verb, *hoard* means to accumulate as much as possible of something. People who store a year's supply of food in case of unforeseen emergency are said to be paranoid but harmless. People who seek to store food in anticipation of an emergency seen and accepted as a real emergency by the community at large are said to be bad because they are hoarding, and they are called hoarders. Hoarding is okay as long as everybody else thinks it's a stupid thing to do. Hoarding is not okay when everybody thinks it's the right thing to do. Look up *hypocrite* in any dictionary and you'll find a good description of a lot of today's voters.

I

ILLEGAL TENDER — A tender for an act which is prohibited by law. See Chapter 7, Tender.

INGOT — A bar or brick of cast metal. A typical ingot of 999 fine gold weighs about 400 troy ounces or 27.4 pounds (*avoir.*).

INSTRUMENT — A document, at law. Examples: Agreement, contract, bill, certificate, Note, will, testament, etc. See also NEGOTIABLE.

INTEREST — See Chapter 10, Usury.

INTRINSIC — Antonym of extrinsic. Cattle have intrinsic worth; bills of lading for cattle have only extrinsic worth. See EXTRINSIC.

INVEST — Literally, to *place in the garments of*, meaning to place in the possession of another. When you invest money in the capital shares of an incorporated entity, you place that money in the *clothing* (under the corporate control) of that corporation and its officers.

IOU — Idiomatic term in English-speaking countries. Refers to a written acknowledgment of a debt or obligation, which is (humorously) an "*I owe you.*"

K

KARAT — Unit of measure of purity of precious-metal plating. *24 karat gold plate* means 100% gold. *12 karat silver plate* means 50% silver and 50% base metal. Caution: In some books you may see *karat* spelled incorrectly, as *carat*. See also CARAT.

KESEF — Hebrew word for *money*, literally, *silver.*

L

LAWFUL MONEY — Precious metal coinage manufactured pursuant to law, particularly public law in the United States. The phrases *lawful money* and *lawful money of the United States* are synonymous, at law, in the United States. See Title 31, United States Code.

LEGAL TENDERS — See Chapter 7, Tender.

LEND — Effectively synonymous with loan (v). Derived in part from the Gothic *leihwan*, which is akin to the Latin *linquere*, the present-tense of *liqui*, from which we currently see *liquid assets* and *liquidity*, etc.

LEVERAGE — Literally, *use of a lever*. The term given to an investment in which a relatively small amount of capital is used to obtain control of a relatively large amount of capital. If $1,000 of stock is controlled with an investment of only $200, this investment is said to be *leveraged at five to one*. Successful, leveraged investments grow more quickly than straight or unleveraged investments. In the sample investment given above, a 10% gain in the value of the stock (to $1100) would produce a 50% ($100) gain to the investor; conversely, a 10% decline in the value of the stock would produce a 50% loss to the investor.

LUCRE — From the Latin *lucrum*, meaning *gain*. Also related to an Irish term *lauch*, meaning *price* or *wages*. Greek and Russian variants equate to *booty*. Today, *lucre* is a principle motivation of greedy people. In Scripture, *lucre* is used in lieu of *money* when discussing the gain of people who vigorously and enthusiastically seek wealth in unethical or unprincipled ways. Today we might use *lucre* (or *filthy lucre* or *dirty money*) to describe the earnings of one who sells illicit drugs to children, or one who perpetrates fraud.

M

M1 – Quoted as "em one," where "M" supposedly means "money." In general terms, M1 is the main "money supply" indicator in today's economic reporting. A statistic issued weekly by the Federal Reserve, M1 is described as the total of cash (coin and paper currency) in circulation plus the sum of all demand (commercial and private checking) accounts and travelers checks, etc. M2 is M1 plus savings account balances and small-denomination time deposits. M3 is M2 plus large-denomination time deposits. M4 is M3 plus certain other liquid assets. The statistic should be referred to as "C1," etc., where the "C" stands for "Credit," because in the U.S. today, none of our exchange media are *money*. Today's exchange media in the U.S. are *fiat* currency in the form of FRTs and metallic tokens.

MAKE — Synonymous with *create*, *originate* or *manufacture*. *Make* is only informally related to compel or force. Article 1, Section 10 of the United States Constitution uses *make* in the sense of the verb *use*, not *compel*. The federal Constitution has no authority to compel the states to compel a citizen of a state to do anything or forebear doing anything. Some may argue that Article 1, Section 10 authorizes the states to compel citizens to tender only certain things (objects) in payment of their (the citizens') debts, and that those things are only coins of gold and silver. This argument might have merit if the Founders had not been Christians, and if they had believed the states could morally, ethically and legally compel you to pay your debts with only the materials your state government gave you permission to use. In reality, Article 1, Section 10 commands the state governments (not the citizens of the state) to use only coins of gold and silver to pay their (the state's) debts. Citizens are free to use coins of gold or silver, or cattle, or almost anything else to pay their debts. If a creditor is unhappy with what has been tendered to him, he may seek recovery and remedies in a court of law. But since most debts are incurred through operation of a contract or agreement, and since the terms of payment in most contracts and agreements in the United States are described using the *Dollar sign* or symbol, or the word *Dollar*, or both, the designated medium of payment is therefore lawful money, that is, coins of gold or silver which were manufactured in a United States Mint, and which are weighed in Dollar units. Summing up, your state cannot compel you to use gold or silver coin in payment of your debts; whatever you and your creditors agree upon will be upheld in your state's courts. But *all state governments are compelled by Article 1, Section 10 to use only coins of gold or silver in their tenders for their payment of their debts.*

MAKER — The originator of a Note. See Chapter 6, Note.

MERCANTILE — Indirectly related to *negotiate*. See also COMMERCIAL.

MERCHANT — *Trader*, *negotiator*, from the Latin *mercator*. A map drawn so that the true bearings of courses may be measured directly is called a *Mercator Projection Map*, invented in the 1600s.

MINT — Stems from Latin *monere*, and later from *moneta*. The name of a building or other structure designed and erected primarily for manufacturing *money*, that is, coins of gold, silver, and other precious metals, and also non-precious metals (the latter called *minor coins*).

MONETA — Epithet of Roman Goddess *Juno*. See Chapter 2, Money.

MONETARY — Related to *money*. See Chapter 2, Money.

MONETIZE — Action of converting precious-metal bullion, dust, nuggets or plate into *coins*. See Chapter 2, Money.

MONEY — 1. Coins of gold, silver or other precious metal manufactured in a mint to be media of exchange. 2. A system by which we measure the relative value of goods and services. See also DOLLAR.

MORTGAGE — Literally, a *death pledge*. From the Old French *mort*, meaning *dead*, and the Teutonic *gage*, or *pledge*. See also mortal, mortician and mortuary, and amortize, etc. A form of a Note in which payments of principal and interest extend for many years, possibly until after, at, or just before the death of the borrower. Sometimes literally taken to mean a pledge of payment which is expected to continue beyond the *mortal* life of a borrower.

N

NATION — A group of people who share one or more common bonds, beliefs, principles or racial characteristics, and whose form of government has been patterned after those things. Consider Navaho (Navajo) *nation*. Compare versus COUNTRY.

NATIONAL SOCIALISM ("*Nazi*") — A socialist political party from Germany in the 1930s, whose leader, Adolf Hitler, plunged the world into World War II. The party is cited as the *Nazional Sozialistiche Arbeiter Partie* (National Socialist Worker Party).

Nazi — See NATIONAL SOCIALISM.

NEGOTIABLE — In financial matters, a *negotiable* instrument is one which can make its way from one person to another in the economy without losing its power. A ten-Dollar bill, because it is payable to the bearer, is a negotiable instrument; it can negotiate its way through the economy. Conversely, a power of attorney you give to your brother-in-law, empowering only him to sell only your car only while you are on a lengthy vacation in Siberia, is not a negotiable instrument because it so restricted in its powers.

NICKEL — An elemental form of matter. A *white* metal. A nickname for a United States coin made largely from this metal, that is, a five-cent piece. One of the United States' two minor coins (penny, or cent, and nickel).

NUGGET — A naturally-occuring lump of gold, silver or other precious or semiprecious metal. An Americanism which came to us from the provincial English word *nug*, meaning *a block of wood*. Possibly also derived, at least in part, from another English word, *nigg*, which meant *a small piece*. Also related to our word *noggin*, meaning *head*.

O

OBLIGATION — From *oblige*, which is derived from the Latin *obligere*, where *ob* means *near* and *ligere* means *to bind* (as in our word *ligament*). If I mow your lawn for you while you are ill, you may feel you have an obligation to reciprocate my act of kindness. Some obilgations may be monetary but others may not be monetary. *Obligation*, therefore, may or may not relate to payment (a tender and acceptance of money). See Chapter 8, Bill.

OFFER — A *bid* or *proposal*. See Chapter 7, Tender.

OUNCE — Unit of weight in either troy or avoirdupois measure. Also, unit of fluid measure. See also GRAIN.

OWE — Derived from Anglo Saxon *agen*, meaning to possess, have, or own, but specifically *to possess the property of another* (person), and therefore have an obligation to return it to that person.

OWN — See OWE.

P

PAY — Give money to another, or the money given to (or received by) another. Inherent in the meaning of *pay* is the use of money. Transfers of things other than money should be called *compensation*.

PAYEE — One of the four mandatory elements of a Note. Recipient of a payment, particularly of a Note or a Bill. See Chapter 6, Note; Chapter 7, Tender; and Chapter 8, Bill. The *payee* on a check is the person to whom money is to be paid; the person issuing the check is the *payor*. The *payor* pays the *payee*.

PEACE — Absence of war. See Chapter 5, Pay. *Peace*, in Latin, is *pax*.

PECUNIARY — From the Latin *pecuniarius*, meaning *money* or other *property*. Also from Old Latin *pecu*, meaning *cattle*; cattle have intrinsic worth or value. See German *kuh*, pronounced *coo*, meaning *cow*. Also related to Anglo Saxon *feoh* and German *vieh*, both of which mean *cattle*.

PENCE — Middle English contraction of *pennies*.

PENNY — Thought to be derived from *pan*, a bowl-shaped cooking utensil shaped like some early, small-denomination coins. Obscure origin but some etymologists (Thorpe, and later, Skeat) see a tie to *pending*, which is based upon *pand*, which means a *token* (small payment) or a *pawn* or *pledge*. "Penny" is a nickname for the *cent* coin.

PENURY — Being *in want of* something, or *needy*. From the Latin *penuria*, meaning *want*. A cognate of the Latin *paene*, meaning *hardly* (that is, *hardly enough* or *hardly sufficient*). Greek for *hunger*.

PIECE OF EIGHT — Spanish silver coin, divided into eight parts called *reales*. *Piece of Eight, dolaro* and *Pillar Dollar* were colonial nicknames for the coin, whose official name was *Colonata*.

POOR — From the Latin *pauper*, which means *poor*. Came to us via the French *povre*, then to the Middle English *poure*, both of which meant *poor*. Allied with the Latin *paucus* which means *few*. Possibly also related to Latin *parare*, meaning *to provide*, or literally *provided with little*.

POUND — Unit of weight in troy or avoirdupois measure. See GRAIN. 12 troy ounces = 1 troy pound; 16 avoirdupois ounces = 1 avoirdupois pound. Also, British monetary unit.

POVERTY — Originally from the Latin *paupertas*, (poverty), then to the French *pauvreté*, and the Middle English *pourertee*. Poverty is the great lack of money and other resources.

PRAXEOLOGY – The study (or theory) of the practical application or exercise of a branch of learning, such as economics. Includes study of economic customs, practices and habits of societies, tribes, countries, etc.

PRICE — Today related to *prize*, as in how (much) do you prize your goods (or time or services). Also related to *precious*, which is derived from the Latin *pretiosus*, which means *valuable*, and from the Latin *pretium*, meaning *price* or *cost*. *Price* is not related to *prestige*, and also not *etymologically* tied to *prize* (which relates to the Latin *prise*, meaning *a lever*, and which also means *a seizure* or *a thing captured from an enemy or won in a lottery or other contest*). Indirectly related to the French *priser*, meaning *to esteem*.

PRIVATE — Taken from the Latin *priuatus*, meaning *apart*, and from the Latin *priuus*, which means *single*, the latter interpreted literally as *put forward* or *sundered from the rest*. Sundered means broken (away from) or cut off. Compare with *person*.

PRIVILEGE — The modern extension of the Latin *privilegium*, in which *privi* means *for one's own* and *legi* means *law* and the suffix *ium* informally means *relating to*. *Leg* is directly tied to the Latin *lex*, meaning *law*. A privilege is a special law for one person or for a select class or group of persons. See also FRANCHISE.

PRIZE — See PRICE.

PROFFER — In a classical sense, synonymous with *tender*. See Chapter 7, Tender. In current usage, however, a *proffer* is simply a *formal* offer, one made in writing and with great attention to legal and other detail. The word *proffer* is derived from the Latin *profere*, where *pro* means *forward* (*in front of*, or *to the front*) and *fere* means *to bring* (and from which we get our *ferry boat*). *Fere* is a cognate of *bear*, meaning to carry or lift. Indeed, in a classical sense, *proffer* and *offer* differ only slightly in meaning. Offer stems from the Latin *offere*, where *of* means *near*, and *fere* means *to bring* or *to bear* (that is, to carry). Today, an *offer* or *proffer* is a written or spoken presentation of an acceptable price to the attention of a seller; a *tender* is the action of placing the sum agreed upon (or at least acceptable to the buyer) *in motion toward (and in plain view of)* the seller.

PROFIT — From the Latin *profectum*, and *proficere*, both of which mean *to make progress* or *to bring forward*. See also *proficient*, which also stems from *proficere*.

PUBLIC — Current spelling of the Latin *publicus*, meaning *belonging to the people*. Related to the Latin *populus*, which means *the people*.

PUBLICAN — The Latin *publicanus* means *a tax gatherer*. See Luke 3:12. Originally an adjective which meant *belonging to the public revenue*, where *revenue* means to *come back* or to *return*.

R

REALES — Division(s) of *Piece of Eight* (or *Colonata* or *Pillar Dollar* or *dolaro*), a Spanish silver coin which circulated widely in the American Colonies prior to and shortly after the American Revolutionary War. In purchasing power, one *dolaro* equaled eight *Reales*.

REBATE — Interestingly, this word actually means *to blunt a sword's edge*. Our current usage stems from the Old French term *rebatre*, where *re* means *back* and *batre* means *to beat* (hit with a stick). The French usage literally meant *to beat back again*, as one might do with the ball in a game of tennis. If you have an etymological dictionary, look up *batter* (*one who bats*, not a mixture of flour, water, and other ingredients).

RECESSION — An informal term, widely taken to mean a period during which the standard of living of a society declines for two or more consecutive quarter-year periods.

REGULATE — As it applies to Article 1, Section 8 of the United States Constitution, Congress is to *regulate the value thereof*, meaning assign and then abide by constraints on weights of coins manufactured in the United States Mint. Weight-deviation tolerances established by Congress are plus and minus one half of one percent, meaning coins which deviate more than 0.5% from their assigned weight are to be scrapped, with the resulting melt used to make new coins. Article 1, Section 10, empowers Congress to establish the *legal* ratio of worth between equal weights of silver and gold coin, that is, 15 to 1, 16 to 1, etc. Silver is the standard; the *legal* worth of gold coins is set by Congress in *regulating the Dollar value* of gold *in terms of silver*.

REMUNERATE — From the Latin *munus*, which means *gift* or *office*, from which also comes *municipal* and *munificent*. A tip given to a waitress is a form of *remuneration*.

RENT — Past tense of *rend*, meaning *to tear*. Allied to *render*, which comes from the Latin *reddare*, which means *to give back*. Rent, as a payment made or received, is a form of *usury* because it is a payment for the using up of a thing.

REVENUE — From the Latin *reuenire*, where *re* means *back* and *uenire* means *to come*. Tied to *venture*, an opportunity or chance. In its journey from Latin to modern English, the Latin *reuenire* lived in the French language for a time as *revenu* and *revenue*, which meant *rent* (as in the rent of one's property to another). See also RENT.

RICH — Derived from the Latin *rex* or *regis*, meaning king, which implies *kingly* or *having the wealth of a king*.

S

SALARY — From the Latin *salarium*, a payment given to soldiers for their purchases of salt. Roman troops would be given part of their compensation in salt, and those who did receive such payments were termed *saltiers*, the forerunner of our word *soldiers*. This custom of partial compensation with salt is the basis of modern exclamations like *he's not worth his salt*.

SALE — Derived from the Old High German *sala*, meaning *to hand over* or *delivery*. Allied to *sell* and to the German word *handsel*.

SALT — Natural crystalline formation of sodium and chlorine (NaCl). See also SALARY.

SCRIP — Two meanings: 1) particularly in Scandinavian lands, a small cloth bag made from a scrap of fabric; and 2) a piece of writing, stemming from the Latin *scriptum*, which is a form of *scribere*, which means *to write*. *Scrip* is a paper currency which is not redeemable in money, and which circulates in an economy due to governmental edict or decree, that is, *fiat* currency. See also *ASSIGNAT*.

SEIGNIORAGE — From the Old French *seignor* or *seigneur*, meaning *lord*, a political title. Stems from the Latin word *seniorem*, meaning *older* or *greater in authority*. The United States Mint, when it manufactured gold or silver coins for a private party, would retain some of the precious metal as its fee for making the coins. This fee, the *seigniorage,* paid for the work done by the Mint's employees. The United States government made a small profit on the manufacture of official coins for private persons. When a miner delivered his refined metal to the Mint, the Mint would pay him right away with coins, and would place his metal in inventory to be ready for use when still more coins were to be made. If someone gave the United States Mint 100 ounces of gold bullion, he would be given perhaps ninety-nine ounces of coins and the Mint would keep the remaining one ounce of gold as *seigniorage*. Since the one ounce was taken out of the 100 ounces *first*, that is (supposedly), *before* any coins were made of the bullion, the term *seigniorage* came into use.

SELL — Allied to SALE. Derived from the Old High German (and Gothic) *saljan*, meaning *to hand over* or *deliver*.

SHEKEL — Unit of *weight* of money in Biblical times. Later was the name of the *coin* weighed in the same units, much like Dollar became the name of the coin which was weighed in Dollar units. One Dollar (pure silver) = 371.25 grains; one Dollar (pure gold, in 1792) = 24.7 grains; one shekel (silver, in Maccabean times) = 218 grains. A gold shekel was also produced but was not used as widely as the silver shekel, hence most references to the shekel refer to its silver form, and unless *gold* is expressly stated, the usage always refers to the silver coin.

SHIN-PLASTER — Sarcastic nickname for any "doubtful" paper currency. Alludes to the worthless nature of the currency, that is, its non-redeemability. Means that the paper is usable for few things, among which might be to hold an ointment applied to a bruise on one's shin.

SILVER — An elemental form of matter and considered a precious metal. Atomic symbol: Ag. Atomic number: 47. Atomic weight: 107.868 (±0.001). Nickname of coins manufactured from this metal. Called a *white* metal, highly valuable in industry because of its ability to conduct electricity and heat, reflect light and heat, resist oxidation, and for its innate toxicity to bacteria — which is why eating utensils plated with silver, called *silverplate*, are so highly esteemed. Aerosols which dispense silver compounds are used to treat burns and open wounds. *Ag* is taken from the Latin word for silver: *Argentum. Ar* was thought the best atomic symbol for *argon,* leaving *Ag* to be the atomic symbol for *silver*.

SOVEREIGN — A British gold coin. Our modern word *sovereign* comes from the Late Latin *superanus*, which means *chief* or *above*. We, the people of the United States, are the sovereigns of this country. As a sovereign — more accurately, as a sovereign American freeman at law — your legal status is that of a *creator and controller* of governments. You supervise all civil-service workers at all levels of government; all civil service workers are your employees. The sovereign American freemen in colonial times penned the laws which created, control, and constrain all levels of government, especially the federal government.[3]

SPECIE — From *species*, meaning *in actual form*. As applied to financial affairs, payment in *specie* means payment in *actual* form, meaning Dollars of silver or Dollars of gold, not in or by tokens, scrip, redeemable currency, bonds, stocks, certificates, or other written or printed instruments. In brief, *specie* means *the real thing*, coins of gold or coins of silver. Pronounced spee´ + she, emphasizing the first syllable.

STAGFLATION — An American idiom, an informal combination of stagnant and inflation, that is, *stag* plus *flation*. The term suggests an economic condi-

---

[3] In the United States, we, the people, are the sovereigns. Most of us take orders only from God; everyone else takes orders from us. Sovereignty, in the United States, is the legal *status* of a child of God, meaning a person who is superior to temporal laws. In England, the only sovereign individuals are the members of the royal family and those to whom they grant sovereignty.

tion in which some inflationary effects are detected but they don't revive the economy, which inflation often does temporarily.

STIPEND — From the Latin *stip-pendium*, a *payment in money*, because a *stips* was a small coin, and *pendium* refers to *pendere*, literally meaning *to weigh out*, *to pay out*, or just *to pay*.

SUBSIDIARY COINAGE — Officially minted half-, quarter-, and tenth-dollar silver coins were limited in making payments not more than $10. Because they are not made of precious metals, at various times, American courts compelled acceptance of our minor coins, pennies or nickels, in tenders of only twenty-five cents or less, and for a while, of nickels up to $1.25. See also COMPEL.

T

TAKE — To *seize* or *grasp*, often implying the *involuntary* seizure of a thing from its rightful owner. Allied to *tax*. Vernacular term of the underworld wherein *the take* refers to the sum *taken* in a robbery or other crime.

TALENT — Unit of *weight*, equivalent to 3,000 shekels. Much like our Dollar is equivalent to 100 cents or, in pure silver, equal to 371.25 grains. 3,000 shekels equal about 93.5 pounds (*avoirdupois*).

TALLY — A *stick* notched to exactly match another stick, used to keep accounts. Allied distantly to *toll*, as in a *toll* road, and *tell*, to relate a story in the order events occurred. Also, *to count*.

TAX — Anciently (Biblically) related to *yoke*. Doublet of *task*. Also theoretically related to the French word *tagsere*, which means to touch or handle, the root *tag* giving us the name of the children's game of *tag*. Our word *tax* comes to us from the Bible's reference to kings who laid a heavy *yoke* (burden, task, tax) upon the people. A *yoke* is a device for joining a draft animal to a wagon or other device. Use of the word yoke to describe an involuntary tax or tribute implied that the wearer of the *yoke* was being treated as a domesticated animal, not a sovereign child of God. *Yoke* is the ancient root of *jugular* vein, so named because it is the chief vein in the neck. When one is *yoked*, one is not free. Therefore *yoke*, in a sense, is synonymous with *tax* or *tribute*, especially when they are involuntary exactions. Hence, persons who pay taxes involuntarily are *yokels*.[4]

TELLER — One who *tallies* or *counts*. A bank employee.

THE — A definite article. Indicates a unique entity.

THEFT — The *involuntary* transfer of property from its rightful owner to another person, or the forceful or deceitful seizure of property rightfully belonging to another. *All theft is a form of warfare. War is theft at its ultimate or maximum level. War is maximized theft, and petty theft is a small act of war.* See WAR.

TOKEN — A thing having little intrinsic worth which is used as a substitute for a thing having considerable intrinsic worth. See Chapter 6, Note.

TOLL — A *tax*, *exaction*, or *excise*. Something *taken* or *charged*, such as the fee for use of a *toll* road. See TALLY.

TRANSACTION — An *exchange*. If one person grows wheat and another grows apples, each grower produces a crop which is a result of his own *actions*. When the growers trade part of their crops to one another, the exchange is a trans-*action*, or figuratively, *a transfer of one's actions* or *a transfer of the results (or fruits) of one's actions*. Involuntary transactions are *crimes*. *Theft* is an *involuntary transaction*.

TREASON — From the Latin *tradere*, meaning *to deliver over*. Doublet of *tradition*, from the Latin *traditionem*.

TREASURE — Derived from the Latin *thesaurum*, which is the accusative form of the Latin *thesaurus*, a treasure (albeit only of words, at least today). Our

---

[4] The nation's Founders knew about the Bible's Eighth Commandment (*Thou shalt not steal*) and the admonition that Christians should not permit themselves to be *unequally yoked*. Hence, all taxes in the United States were to be *voluntary* and either *uniform* or *apportioned*. Taxes on corporations, since they are *not* sovereign entities, need not conform to this standard.

current usage of *treasure* is probably derived more directly from the Greek version of it, which means *a storehouse of* or *a hoard of*.

TREASURY —A place where treasure is kept. See TREASURE.

TROY — A *system of measure*. One ounce troy = 480 grains. See also *AVOIRDUPOIS*.

U

UNIT — One. A single thing or entity. The *unit* of measure of the weight of officially-minted precious-metal coins in the United States is Dollar. The *unit* of measure of the weight of precious stones is carat. A *unit* of measure of the weight of precious-metal coins in Biblical times was shekel.

V

VALUE — A Middle French term *valu*, which stems from *valoir*. These words, in turn, stem from the Latin *uallere*, which means *to be worth*. Also related to our modern *valor*, which means *to be strong* or *to be worth(y)*. Distantly related to *true* and *troth* (as in betroth, or marry). Compare with *true to the cause* vice *strong in adherence to the cause*. *Uallere* may also be distantly related to *weal*, as in *commonweal* and *wealth*.

VENUE — Strangely, this word comes to us from the world of fencing (sword fighting), where *venue* means *a thrust* or *a turn*. Sometimes spelled *venew*, as in Middle English period writing, where it meant *a locality*, which was a variation of the fencing usage wherein a vernacular version of *thrust* was expressed as *thrusting home*. It appears as if, over time, the term took on a special meaning related to *coming home*, from which a *location* was inferred. Tied to the Latin *venire*, which means *to come*, and which is used today in *veniremen*, meaning members of the jury, persons who have *come* to court to hear evidence in a trial. Also related to the Latin *uicinus*, which means *near*, and from which we derive our word *vicinity*. Further, related to our word *avenue*, meaning *a route by which to come*.

W

WAR — From the Low Latin *werre*, and later *guerre*. The Old High German word *werre* meant *(em)broil* or *confusion*. Allied to *worse*. Also note the Spanish pronunciation of words which begin with the letter *g*, spoken much in the same way we say *wh*, as in *which*. In practice, war is *theft* at its maximum level. Every theft or other crime is an act of war by the perpetrator against the victim. See THEFT. (See also John Locke's second *Treatise on Government*.)

WEALTH — Related to *weal*, as in the *Commonweal* or *Commonwealth*. The etymological history of this word is somewhat complex, as *wealth* has ties to words like *well*, meaning *healthy* and *a source of water*; and to words like *wall*, a protective barrier. If you can, explore the etymology of *wealth* in the etymological dictionaries at any good library. You should find it a fascinating experience.

WEIGHT — From the Middle English *weghen* and the Anglo Saxon *wegan*, which meant *to carry* or *to bear*. Related to the Dutch *wegen* and the Icelandic *vega*, which mean *to move* or *to lift*. See also the Danish *vagt*, and the Swedish *vigt*, and the German *gewicht*. Anciently, all coins were named for their intended or initial weight: Shekel, hin, daric, yehud, mina, talent, denarius, quadrans, peruta, and lepton, although archeologists have found a relatively wide range of weights of ancient coins of the same denomination, indicating that manufacturing tolerances were loose, at least by today's standards. *Talenton*, the Greek variant of the coin, talent, means *weight*. *Shekel*, the basic current coin of the Old Testament, comes from the Hebrew word *skl*, which means *to weigh* or *to pay*. See also the tables below.

WORTH — From the Latin *uereri*, which means *respect*. Tied to *wary* and *ware* (as in house*ware*). Possibly also related to our modern *rare*.

Y

YOKE — See TAX.

YOKEL — See TAX.

Tables

Note: In the tables below, *avoirdupois* is abbreviated *avoir*. Also, some equivalent weights are approximate, not exact. For exact values, see the Measures section of any good dictionary, encyclopedia, or physics or chemistry reference book. Also, recall there are two systems of weight measure: Apothecary and Customary, and each weight has a metric equivalent. To simplify this presentation, we do not distinguish between weight systems except in Table 17-2, for *dram*. Blank areas within each table indicate fields for which equivalents or other data is not necessary or not applicable.

This weight	Equals this weight	Or a gold "price" per troy ounce
480 grains	1 ounce troy	
437.5 grains	1 ounce *avoir*.	
5,760 grains	1 pound or 12 ounces troy	
7,000 grains	1 pound or 16 ounces *avoir*.	
1 Dollar (pure silver)	371.25 grains or 0.77 ounces troy	
1 Dollar (pure gold, 1792, 15 to 1 ratio, Ag to Au)	24.75 grains or 0.048 ounces troy	$15.00
1 Dollar (pure gold, 1900, 16 to 1 ratio, Ag to Au)	23.22 grains or 0.045 ounces troy	$18.75
1 Dollar (pure gold, 1933)		$31.36
1 Dollar (pure gold, 1934)		$35.00
1 Dollar (pure gold, 1969 thru 1979) for the Insiders.		$35.00
1 Dollar (pure gold, 1969 thru 1979) for you and your family.		Unavailable to regular citizens.
1 Dollar (pure gold, early 1998, for the Federal Reserve Bank owners and their families)	11.37 grains	$42.22 (FRT)
1 Dollar (pure gold, early 1998, for you and your family)	1.5 grains	$320.00 (FRT)

Table 17-1. Gold "price" versus weights, 1792 until 1998.

Primary unit	First alternative unit	Second alternative unit
Ton, short	2,000 pounds	32,000 ounces *avoir.*
Ton, long	2,240 pounds	35,840 ounces *avoir.*
Pound	464.29 grams	16 ounces *avoir.* or 12 ounces troy
Stone	14 pounds	6.5 kilograms
Ounce (troy)	1/12 pound	38.69 grams
Ounce (*avoir.*)	1/16 pound	1/32,000 ton, short
Gram	0.0265 ounce troy	0.0344 ounce *avoir.*
Grain	0.002285 ounce *avoir.*	0.065 gram
Carat	200 milligrams	
Dollar, U.S.	371.25 grains pure silver	24.75 grains pure gold
Dram	U.S. Customary System: 1/16 of an ounce or 27.34 grains or 1.77 grams	Apothecary weight: 1/8 of an ounce or 60 grains or 3.89 grams
Cent, U.S.	1 hundredth of a Dollar	10 mills
Talent	60 minas	3,600 shekels
Shekel	1/60 mina	8.25 grams
Daric (gold)	8.4 grams	

Table 17-2. Cross-references of a few units of weight.

Note: *Talent, shekel, daric,* and *mina* are the names for coins of the Biblical era, and virtually all the names of coins of that and subsequent eras were (also or originally) units of weight. The Mark of Germany was a unit of weight long before it became the name of a coin of that weight of silver. Most coins were named after the units of their weight, an ethical practice which ended in the United States in 1963 when the country's federal civil-service workers decided to stop redeeming our paper currency. Our civil-service workers kept the precious metal and forced us to keep the pieces of paper currency. Since then, the civil-service workers have continued to create more "credit" and pieces of paper currency, and they "spend" that "money" first, thereby getting a bigger bang for their buck than the rest of us get when we "spend" that "money" later.

•

19

Postscript

IT is a truism of authorship that, no matter how much care one takes — and we have taken much — errors will leap off the page, as soon as a book is published. This is one of God's ways of keeping authors humble, and we're sure this book is no exception. In spite of considerable research and fact-checking by the author and editors, it is likely that errors will still be found after the book is printed. Thus, we stress the reader's understanding of the importance of our Notice and Disclaimer on page xvi.

Unless otherwise indicated, Biblical quotations are from the King James Version.

This book is not intended to be a complete exposition on money or fractional-reserve banking. We presented only the most important fundamentals today's concerned citizen should know.

Next, the Banking Deregulation and Monetary Control Act (1980) effectively reduced banks' so-called reserve requirements to zero; it effectively ended Congress' control over how much artificial purchasing power banks may create. Our examples of "six times demand deposits" and "sixteen times time-deposits" are only approximations, used to simplify our explanation of the mechanics of fractional-reserve banking. At times, that practice may be even more egregious than we said it is.

The Federal Reserve banks are permitted to keep only about fifteen percent of the interest they are paid for their "loans" to the federal government. The remaining eighty-five percent of the interest is forwarded to the United States Treasury. This *curious* arrangement is often cited by the "Fed" as their answer to complaints that they are making a killing from their "loans" to government. It is also part of the reason some political personalities, when speaking of the national debt, say "we owe it to ourselves." We didn't discuss this point earlier because we wanted to keep our illustration of government bond sales as simple as possible. But now you're ready for a little deeper understanding.

Yes, it's true; the "Fed" retains fifteen percent of the interest they get because that's all they're allowed to keep, and that amount is allowed only to cover their overhead. They return eighty-five percent. But there's a subtle trick here. Yes, they give back eighty-five percent of the interest they receive but the real power of the "Fed" is not in the interest they receive, but in their ability to control the rest of the economy. The Federal Reserve's Open Market Committee, with its direct control over the supply of "money and credit," that is, the purchasing power of FRTs and other forms of credit, controls the ups and downs of every market. By knowing for sure when markets are going to move, and by knowing for sure which way, the folks who run the Open Market Committee, *and their close friends*, can make their killings in those markets, often through leveraged investments. When it comes to market timing, the rest of us are at a distinct disadvantage.

Confusion abounds regarding the mechanics of how banks use the real paybacks of fake loans, so we offer this simplified explanation.

You are a banker, and after Adam deposits $1,000, you loan Bill $6,000. As Bill writes checks against the $6,000, you cover those checks by simply stamping them PAID and deducting their face amount(s) from Bill's checking account (where you "deposited" the "loan" you made to him). When Bill pays you back, giving you $6,000 in FRTs, you reserve $1,000 (plus a little interest) for Adam, and you use the rest for "loans" of your bank's capital.

As a bank's net capital grows, its stockholders (often through leveraged purchases) make out like, well, "bandits" is probably as good a word to use as any.

If you are amazed that bankers do this sort of thing and get away with it, consider that President James E. ("Jimmy") Carter hired his pal, Bert Lance, top officer of several southern banks, to be Director of the Office of Management and Budget. Lance left office shortly after accepting the appointment when certain "irregularities" were discovered about the way he ran his banking operation. One item that raised eyebrows was that Mr. Lance was "overdrawn" — that's the word the dominant media used — about $450,000 in his checking accounts at just one of his banks. If you hadn't read this book you might wonder how a small-town bank could continue to operate when just one of its customers was almost a half a million dollars overdrawn on his several checking accounts. Some researchers say the bankers' slogan must be something like, "Ya know, it doesn't get any better'n this!"

We admonish every reader to please stop calling Federal Reserve Tokens something which they are not: Federal Reserve Notes. Calling them Notes gives them undeserved credibility and delays public understanding. Call them FRTs or Tokens, terms which may stimulate intelligent inquiry.

Some suggest that we reduce our use of banks. Use of money orders in lieu of checks, and cash in lieu of credit cards, might hasten the demise of fractional-reserve banking, they say. Borrowing from non-bank sources (personal friends, relatives, businesses, etc.) might also serve the nation's best interests, these voices urge. While we don't question their motives, and while we recognize that these suggestions may seem sensible, we disagree with them and we do not think they are appropriate for most readers.

We think you should continue to conduct your financial affairs as you have in the past. Our purpose is not to cause you to change abruptly or end any financial relationships you may have. If you wish to discuss your financial questions, a certified financial planner or other competent specialist may be your best source of counsel.

If you can afford to do so, buy extra copies of this book and give them to others as gifts; give them to special friends, business or professional associates, or to persons of means and professional accomplishment. Those recipients might be most likely to read the book and then act responsibly on its message. This book might also perform a valuable service as a home-school textbook.

We strongly urge readers not to use this book or any part of it as the basis of an action at law or as the basis for a refusal to obey any particular law or group of laws. In particular, no reader should even consider opposing the IRS or any state tax authority, based on what is in this book. To start solving those problems, send us your name and address using the Reader Registration form in Appendix B.

Fort Knox, Kentucky

One last thing. We have recently received disturbing details about the inventory of gold in Fort Knox. The federal depository at Fort Knox was built in 1934 to store all the gold coins and bullion the federal government rounded up from U.S. citizens in 1933. Fort Knox is under the control of the U.S. Mint, which is part of the Treasury Department, and we've recently learned that several investigators have been unsuccessful at getting the Treasury to release information about inventories of the gold stored there.

The Fort Knox operation is so sensitive that the only available official photo of the facility was taken in 1934. The last known inventory of the gold was done in 1944, although a perfunctory audit was reportedly performed early in 1953. The results of that audit have raised more questions than they answered, and the main question still unanswered relates to the amount and fineness of the gold stored at Fort Knox and elsewhere under control of the U.S. government.

Here's what we know. From the 1930s until about 1949, you and I and all the other U.S. citizens owned about 702 million troy ounces of pure gold, but it was stored for us in the U.S. Treasury's depository in Fort Knox, Kentucky and at other government facilities. In 1950, Fort Knox held about 650 million troy ounces of gold, the most gold ever stored in one place. From 1958 until 1968, fully half of our gold was shipped to buyers in foreign countries. By 1971, the amount of pure gold stored at Fort Knox had dropped to about 291 million troy ounces. Treasury reports tell us that during the ten-year period prior to 1979, that is, from 1969 until 1979, 500 million troy ounces of pure gold were shipped to foreigners who made claims on our gold, at $35 per troy ounce, through their banks (in Germany, Switzerland, France, and other foreign countries).

What interests us most about this hemorrhage of our gold is that it occurred in the period just prior to the repeal of the 1933 laws which barred U.S. citizens from owning gold. We, the People, could again own gold personally.

But in the decade just before that, the U.S. government sold our gold to foreign claimants, and the price was $35 per troy ounce. Then, after two-thirds of the gold was gone, it became legal for you and me to own gold, and the price we'd have to pay for it ranged as high as $800 per troy ounce; the price is now about $300 per troy ounce. Would you rather pay $300 per troy ounce, or $35 per troy ounce?

Guess what? An investigation into this puzzling series of events hints that the "foreigners" who made claims on 500 million troy ounces of our gold, in the period between 1969 and 1979, weren't really foreigners at all. No, it looks like they were *agents* of U.S. citizens, nominees if you will, who made the claims on behalf of U.S. citizens but did so in foreign countries.

Want to know one little item that tipped the investigators off? Here it is. Get a world map. Find Africa. Now look at North Africa and find Libya; it's on the North African coast of the Mediterranean Sea, and west of Egypt. Okay, after you find Libya, look just below it, to the south. Notice the country named Chad? Good.

Now peek at your current *World Almanac*. Look in the section which gives details of all the countries in the world. Find Chad in that material and notice the following details: Its per-capita gross domestic product in 1993 was about $550 — the U.S. per-capita GDP is about $27,607 (in 1995) — which suggests that Chad is not a particularly heavy player in the world financial scene.

Well, what would you say if we told you that someone in Chad, in the early 1970s, made a claim against our gold in the amount of about $50 million dollars (at $35 per troy ounce), and thus received about 1.2 million troy ounces of pure gold? How many people in Chad would have $50 million lying around to invest in gold? So, we are curious as to who was the buyer and for whom did he buy.

Other suspicious transactions dot the official record, which was withheld until a Freedom of Information Act request by the George Edward Durell Foundation was honored in about 1980. Once the investigators had the official record of the transactions, they discovered that the information they were given was incomplete. Conspicuous by its absence was any clue as to the name of the ultimate recipient of the gold. In not one instance have the investigators been able to identify a recipient, either as to the name of an individual or as to the name of the business or other organization he or she may have represented. If we aren't provided information on who received the gold, how can we establish the citizenship of that recipient?

Also, since the law banning ownership of gold applied to U.S. citizens, what would have prevented a U.S. citizen from buying shares in a foreign corporation, and then having that corporation make claims against the U.S. gold reserve? Apparently nothing.

So if you had been around in 1970, for example, you could have formed a small corporation in, say, Chad, and then bought a lot of stock in that corporation, maybe all of it. The corporation then could have used its capital to make a claim on our gold, the gold stored in Fort Knox.

In fact, if your president were a lawyer, and if he were instructed to ship or hand-deliver the gold to a private, numbered account in a Swiss bank, you could then fire him and make your corporation inactive. Since you are the sole (or at least major) stockholder of that corporation, you could elect yourself president at any time and withdraw the gold from the corporation's Swiss bank account. We wonder if one or more U.S. citizens, Insiders, bought more than 300 million troy ounces of our gold from Fort Knox, at $35 per troy ounce, effecting those purchases through foreign nominees.

We will continue to dig into this matter and we would like to keep you up to date on our efforts. Please be sure to send us the Reader Registration form in Appendix B.

Spread the Word?
It will help the nation if you spread the word about the topics covered in this book. Obviously, we would love it if you bought a zillion copies to give to your friends, relatives and acquaintances. On the other hand, we would also love it if you mentioned the book to others, to prompt them to investigate our concerns. But there is one thing we'd like to leave you with, a bit of advice on *how* to spread the word.

We think it not so good if you talk to others about this book and the topics it discusses. Too often, some people respond to new information in ways which seem irrational. If their response is extremely irrational, they may attack you physically. For this reason, we respectfully suggest you avoid direct confrontation with anyone who challenges you in the slightest over anything you might try to tell him. Back off, be agreeable, ask a series of neutral questions ("When are we going to break for lunch?"), or simply change the subject.

The unwillingness of some of their neighbors even to discuss the subject will likely come as no surprise to many readers. Perhaps you've already experienced a problem or two in this area with a co-worker or close relative. Discussion of some subjects becomes taboo, mostly because some people are terribly sensitive about them.

Here are a few hypothetical examples.

- You tell a co-worker that you think there are some flaws in the government's official view of Vince Foster's death, that suicide does not seem reasonable to you. You are surprised to hear this worker say, "Well, if you can't trust the government to investigate the death of one of their own workers, who can you trust?" This response implies that you don't support the government, and that your mind is therefore unbalanced or there is something else wrong with you mentally.

- You tell a relative that you are think the United States should not bail out South Korea financially, that its recent (mid-1990s) financial problems stem from bad decisions which should not be made a burden on U.S. taxpayers. Your relative says that if there was any kind of problem like that, it would be the talk of the town, that all the newspapers, magazines and electronic media would be full of complaints about it. In this example, your audience believes that the failure of the dominant media to support your view or concern is proof that your view is without merit.

- You discuss the recent crash of TWA Flight 800 and mention that you are as suspicious of that crash as you were and still are about some aspects of the shoot-down of Korean Air Lines flight 007 in 1983, and you mention that you've seen plenty of evidence in the newspapers to support your suspicions. Your audience responds by saying, "Just because something is in the papers doesn't mean it is true; a lot of what's in the news is exaggerated, or imbalanced, or preliminary."

- You mention that you have just read a book on the war in Vietnam and were surprised to learn that B-52 pilots were ordered to bomb Hanoi by flying, one after another, on the same approach to the target, and that this predictable flight path made it easy for North Vietnamese missile batteries to knock down our planes. Your audience challenges your information, saying that just because someone writes a book doesn't mean what the author says or quotes is the truth.

In each of the preceding examples, your audience responded in a way which, whether logical or not, erodes the value of what you said. Those responses also attempt to justify your audience's ignorance of the information you bring into the conversation. There may be a more appropriate term for this behavior but you may wish to consider it a defense mechanism. Please hold that thought for a moment.

Many years ago I read a *Scientific American* magazine article on a study conducted by a major eastern university, possibly Columbia. The article described the behavior of rats which, when selectively given electrical shocks in the company of other rats, the shocked rat would turn abruptly and bite the nearest rat. The study showed that when the shocked rat felt pain, he turned and attacked the nearest, and therefore most likely, cause of his pain.

People may react the same way. We sometimes lash out at the nearest possible source of pain when we feel pain. A teenage boy, for example, under stress because of poor grades in school, may be very difficult to deal with because he may lash out and attack others for the slightest or possibly even imaginary slights.

An adult under stress of marital problems may exhibit "road rage" when another driver follows too closely.

These examples of illogical behavior may remind you that just because you offer a reasoned argument, and just because you are sincere in your attempt to inform your audience, there is no guarantee that your audience will respond rationally to what you say.

So in the interest of achieving the most effective communications, and to maximize the chance you'll not become a victim of road rage or other irrational behavior, avoid personal discussion of these topics with others. But, you may ask, if you avoid discussion, how can you spread the word?

We offer this suggestion for you: Don't *discuss* these subjects, that is, don't *talk* about them. Restrict your communications to making sure, as much as you are able, that whomever you want to understand these things is first exposed to appropriate *printed* materials. Have you ever heard of anyone getting into an argument or fight with a book? Books are safe sources of information because they are non-threatening. If someone reads a book which offends him, he can tear the book up and burn the pieces, relieving stress and bringing the matter to a psychological and physical end. Closure, if you will.

Your *preferred* method of educating your friends might be to send them extra copies of this book. Better yet, call ZNS and have us ship several copies as gifts in your name, or we can send them as anonymous gifts — after which some of those recipients may excitedly tell you what they learned in their new copy of *MONEY*!

You should also make sure you mail us your Reader Registration form (Appendix B) so we'll be able to let you know when we have inexpensive items available.

Finally, please keep in mind the wisdom of the ages, as written by Edward Bulwer-Lytton (1803 - 1873):

> Beneath the rule of men entirely great
> The pen is mightier than the sword.[1]

---

[1] *Richelieu* (1839) act ii. sc. 2, l. 307.
The Concise Oxford Dictionary of Quotations, 3 ed.
(Oxford: Oxford University Press, 1994)

Yes, we've all heard that last line since we were children: The pen *is* mightier than the sword. You may see the power of that line when you pass out copies of *MONEY* and other printed matter because you'll be repeating the work of a great American of yesteryear: the nearly forgotten New York newspaper editor and publisher of 1735, **John Peter Zenger**.

•

"The only thing necessary for the triumph of evil is for good men to do nothing."

[Attributed to Edmund Burke (1729 -1797); also seen as, "It is necessary only for the good man to do nothing for evil to triumph," but neither quotation — nor variations thereof — is found in Burke's writings. je.]

"When bad men combine, the good must associate; else they will fall, one by one, an unpitied sacrifice in a contemptible struggle."

Edmund Burke, 1770 (1729 - 1797)

20

Appendices

Appendix A
Bibliography, resources and references

DICTIONARIES AND THESAURI

Anderson, William C. *A Dictionary of Law*. Chicago: T. H. Flood and Company, Law Publishers, 1891.

Ballentine, James A. *Ballentine's Law Dictionary*. Third edition, edited by William S. Anderson. Rochester, New York: The Lawyers Co-operative Publishing Company; and San Francisco: Bancroft-Whitney Company, 1969.

——— *Law Dictionary with Pronunciations*. Rochester, New York: The Lawyers Co-operative Publishing Company; and San Francisco: Bancroft-Whitney Company, 1948.

Black, Henry Campbell. *Black's Law Dictionary*, First Edition. Saint Paul, Minnesota: West Publishing Company, 1891.

——— *Black's Law Dictionary*, Revised Fourth Edition. Saint Paul, Minnesota: West Publishing Company, 1951.

——— *Black's Law Dictionary*, Fifth Edition. Saint Paul, Minnesota: West Publishing Company, 1979.

——— *Black's Law Dictionary*, Revised Sixth Edition. Saint Paul, Minnesota: West Publishing Company, 1991.

Bouvier, John. *Bouvier's Law Dictionary*. Boston: The Boston Book Company, 1897.

——— *Bouvier's Law Dictionary*, Baldwin's Century Edition. Cleveland: Banks-Baldwin Law Publishing Company, 1934.

——— *Bouvier's Law Dictionary and Concise Encyclopedia*, Third Revision (Using the Eighth Edition). Kansas City, Missouri: Vernon Law Book Company; and Saint Paul, Minnesota: West Publishing Company, 1914.

Brewer, E. Cobham. *The Dictionary of Phrase & Fable*, Classic Edition. New York: Avenel Books, 1991.

Byrne, Josefa Heifitz. *Mrs. Byrne's Dictionary*. Secaucas, New Jersey: Lyle Stuart, 1974.

Gifis, Steven H. *Law Dictionary*. Hauppauge, New York: Barron's Educational Series, Inc., 1984.

Hoad, T. F., ed. *Concise Oxford Dictionary of English Etymology*. New York: Oxford University Press, 1986.

Kinney, J. Kendrick. *A Law Dictionary and Glossary*. Chicago: Callaghan and Company, 1893.

Klatt, E., and Golze, G. *Langensheidt's German-English English-German Dictionary*. New York: Washington Square Press, 1952.

The Lawyers Co-operative Publishing Company and Bancroft-Whitney Company. *American Jurisprudence*, Second Edition, Volume 54. Rochester, New York: The Lawyers Co-operative Publishing Company and San Francisco: Bancroft-Whitney, 1971.

Ludes, Francis J., ed. *Corpus Juris Secundum*, Volume LVIII. Brooklyn, New York: The American Law Book Company, 1948.

March, Francis Andrew and March, Francis Andrew Jr. *A Thesaurus Dictionary of the English Language*. Philadelphia: Historical Publishing Company, 1913.

McMillan Publishing Company. *Cassell's Latin Dictionary*, Fifth Edition. New York: McMillan Publishing Company, 1968.

Morris, William and Morris, Mary. *Morris Dictionary of Word and Phrase Origins*. New York: Harper & Row, 1977.

Merriam-Webster, Inc. *Merriam-Webster New Book of Word Histories*. Springfield, Massachusetts: Merriam-Webster, 1991.

——— *Webster's Seventh New Collegiate Dictionary*. Springfield, Massachusetts: Merriam-Webster, 1967.

National Reporter System. *Judicial and Statutory Definitions of Words and Phrases*. Saint Paul, Minnesota: West Publishing Company, 1904.

Onions, C. T., ed. *Oxford Dictionary of English Etymology*, 1992 reprint. New York: Oxford University Press, 1966.

Oxford University Press. *Oxford American Dictionary*. Oxford: Oxford University Press, 1972.

——— *Oxford English Dictionary*. Oxford: Oxford University Press, 1989.

Partington, Angela, ed. *Oxford Dictionary of Quotations*. Oxford: Oxford University Press, 1994.

Partridge, Eric. *A Dictionary of Slang and Unconventional English*, Eighth Edition. New York: MacMillan Publishing Company, 1985.

Pope, Benjamin W. *Legal Definitions*. Chicago: Callaghan and Company, 1920.

Skeat, Rev. Walter W. *A Concise Etymological Dictionary of the English Language*. New York: Perigee Books, G. P. Putnam's Sons, 1980.

Thorndike, E. L., and Barnhart, Clarence L. *Scott, Foresman Advanced Dictionary*, Doubleday Edition. Garden City, New York: Doubleday & Company, 1983.

Tripp, Rhoda Thomas. *International Thesaurius of Quotations*. New York: Harper & Row, Publishers, 1987.

Webster, Noah. *Noah Webster's First Edition of an American Dictionary of the English Language*, 1828, eighth facsimile edition. Washington, D.C.: Foundation For American Christian Education, 1995.

Weekley, Ernest. *A Concise Etymological Dictionary of Modern English*. New York: E. P. Dutton, 1952.

——— *An Etymological Dictionary of Modern English*. New York: Dover Publications, 1967.

West Publishing Company. *Words And Phrases*. Saint Paul, Minnesota: West Publishing Company, 1961.

OTHER REFERENCES

Achtemeier, Paul J., General Editor. *Harper's Bible Dictionary*. New York: Harper & Row, 1985.

Balsiger, David, and Sellier, Charles E. Jr. *The Lincoln Conspiracy*. Los Angeles: Schick Sunn Classics Books, 1977.

Bancroft, George. *A Plea For the Constitution*. New York: Harpers, 1886; reprint Sewanee, Tennessee: Spencer Judd, Publishers, 1982.

Bates, Larry. *The New Economic Disorder*. Lake Mary, Florida: Creation House, 1994.

Blanchard, James U. III. *Golden Insights*. Jefferson, Louisiana: Jefferson Research, Inc., 1997.

Bolander, Donald O. *Instant Quotation Dictionary*. Mundelein, Illinois: Career Publishing, 1987.

Burris, W. Alan. *A Liberty Primer*, second edition. Rochester, New York: Society for Individual Liberty, Genesee Valley Chapter, 1983.

Cook, John. *The Rubicon Dictionary of Positive, Motivational, Life-Affirming & Inspirational Quotations*. Newington, Connecticut: Rubicon Press, 1994.

Cruden, Alexander. *Cruden's Complete Concordance*. Grand Rapids, Michigan: Zondervan Publishing House, 1968.

Del Mar, Alexander. *A History of Monetary Crimes*. New York: Gordon Press, 1899.

——— *History of Monetary Systems*. New York: Gordon Press, 1983.

——— *History of Money in America*. New York: Gordon Press, 1969.

——— *History of Money in Ancient Countries From Earliest Times to the Present*. New York: Ben Franklin Books,?

——— *Money & Civilization*. New York: Ben Franklin Books, 1886?

——— *Roman & Moslem Moneys*. New York: Gordon Press, ?

Donlon, William P. *United States Large Size Paper Money, 1861 to 1923.* Utica, New York: William P. Donlon, Publisher, 1973.

Ewart, Neil. *Cassell Everyday Phrases.* London: Blandford Press Limited, 1991.

Federer, William J. *America's God and Country (Encyclopedia of Quotations).* Coppell, Texas: FAME Publishing, 1994.

Fick, Paul. *The Dysfunctional President.* New York: Citadel Press, 1995.

Golitsyn, Anatoliy. *New Lies For Old.* New York: Dodd, Mead & Company, 1983.

Hein, Paul. *All Work and No Pay.* Sewanee, Tennessee: Spencer Judd, Publishers, 1986.

Henry, Lewis C. *Best Quotations for All Occasions.* New York: Fawcett, 1945.

Hewitt Brothers. *Hewitt-Donlon Catalog of United States Small Size Paper Money.* Chicago: Hewitt Brothers, 1974.

Katz, Howard S. *The Paper Aristocracy.* New York: Books In Focus, 1976.

Larson, Martin A. *The Federal Reserve and our Manipulated Dollar.* Old Greenwich, Connecticut: Devin-Adair Company, 1975.

Leitch, Gordon Jr. *The Monetary Errors and Deceptions of the Supreme Court.* Portland, Oregon: Bicentennial Era Enterprises, 1978.

───── *From Dollar to Counterfeit.* Portland, Oregon: Bicentennial Era Enterprises, 1981.

Lynch, Daniel C., and Lundquist, Leslie. *Digital Money.* New York: John Wiley & Sons, 1996.

McGuigan, Patrick B. and Rader, Randall R. *A Blueprint for Judicial Reform.* Washington, D.C.: Free Congress Research & Education Foundation, 1981.

Michie Company. *Michie on Banks and Banking.* Charlottesville, Virginia: The Michie Company, Law Publishers, 1952.

Mullins, Eustace. *The Secrets of the Federal Reserve.* Second printing. Staunton, Virginia: Bankers Research Institute, 1984.

Pick, Franz, and Sédillot, René. *All The Monies of the World.* New York: Pick Publishing Corporation, 1971.

Quigley, Carroll. *Tragedy and Hope: A History of the World in Our Time.* New York: The McMillan Company, 1966.

Sennholz, Hans F. *Age of Inflation.* Belmont, Massachusetts: Western Islands, 1979

Shafer, Neil. *Guide Book of Modern United States Currency.* Racine, Wisconsin: Western Publishing Company, 1973.

Spencer Judd. *Documents Illustrative of the Formation of the Union of the American States.* Sewanee, Tennessee: Spencer Judd, Publishers, 1982.

Sutton, Antony C., and Paiva, Chanti A. *Gold Versus Paper.* Phoenix, Arizona: Phoenix International Publishers, 1981.

U. S. Government Printing Office. *Federal Reserve Act of 1913, With Amendments and Laws Relating to Banking*, Gerard P. Walsh, Jr., Compiler, Superintendent, Document Room, House of Representatives. Washington, D.C.: U.S. Government Printing Office, 1982.

───── *Laws of the United States Concerning Money, Banking, And Loans, 1778 - 1909*, compiled by Huntington and Mawhinney, originally published in 1910 by the U.S. Government Printing Office, Washington, D.C. Westport, Connecticut: Greenwood Press, 1978.

Veitia, Diego J. *50 Great Investments for the 21st Century.* Chicago, Illinois: Dearborn Financial Publishing, 1997.

Werlich, Robert. *United States, Canadian, and Confederate Paper Money.* Washington, D.C.: Quaker Press, 1974.

Whitlock, Charles R. *Easy Money.* New York: Kensington Books, 1994.

Zondervan. *The Student Bible.* Grand Rapids, Michigan: Zondervan, 1984.

───── *The Zondervan Expanded Concordance.* Grand Rapids, Michigan: Zondervan Publishing House, 1968.

RECOMMENDED BOOKS

The reader should bear in mind that although I heartily recommend all of the following works, *none* focus on etymologies of monetary terms, so none regularly distinguish between precise and colloquial monetary terminology. Also, I don't agree with everything some author's advocate, although I do agree that their interest is commendable and I don't question their sincerity. My disagreements stem most often from an author's imprecise use of monetary or legal terms, or with logic based on false or incomplete premises (usually because the author misunderstands one or two monetary, political, philosophical, legal, economic, financial, or other terms).

For example, what an author or editor calls "money" may be redeemable paper currency, or *fiat* (irredeemable) paper currency, or silver or gold coins, or tokens, or exchange media generally, or wealth.

Terms like "honest money," "sound money," "commodity money," and "Consitutional money" are likely synonyms for *money,* coins of gold and silver.

The term "fiduciary money" may refer to redeemable as well as *fiat* (irredeemable) paper currency, chits, scrip, paper tokens, or other money substitutes, but *fiduciary* usually implies that a promise or obligation is involved, as in *bona fide* redeemable paper currency.

Terms like "Frauds," "funny money," "*fiat* money," "greenies," "Federal Reserve Nots," and "FRNs" probably refer to irredeemable U.S. paper currency.

However, in spite of semantic problems, I believe you will likely benefit by exposure to the concepts, arguments, and history offered in these excellent works.

Allen, Gary. *None Dare Call It Conspiracy.* Seal Beach, California: Concord Press, 1971.

Bancroft, George. *A Plea For the Constitution.* New York: Harpers, 1886; reprinted: Sewanee, Tennessee: Spencer Judd, Publishers, 1982.

Bastiat, Frederic. *The Law.* Irvington, New York: The Foundation for Economic Education, 1972.

Blanchard, James U. III. *Golden Insights.* Jefferson, Louisiana: Jefferson Research, 1997.

—— *Silver Bonanza.* New York: Simon & Schuster, 1993.

Cribb, Joe. *Money.* New York: Alfred A. Knopf, 1990.

Griffin, G. Edward. *The Capitalist Conspiracy*. Westlake Village, California: American Media, 1982.

—— *The Creature From Jekyll Island.* Westlake Village, California: American Media, 1994.

McManus, John. *Financial Terrorism.* Appleton, Wisconsin: The John Birch Society, 1993.

Mullins, Eustace. *The Secrets of the Federal Reserve.* Staunton, Virginia: Bankers Research Institute, 1984.

Sarnoff, Paul. *Silver Bulls.* Westport, Connecticut: Arlington House, 1980.

Smith, Jerome. *Silver Profits in the Seventies.* Vancouver, B.C., Canada: ERC Publishing, 1971.

—— *The Coming Currency Collapse.* New York: Books in Focus, 1980.

Stormer, John. *None Dare Call It Treason.* Florissant, Missouri: Liberty Bell Press, 1963.

Sutton, Antony and Paiva, Chanti A. *Gold Versus Paper.* Phoenix, Arizona: Phoenix International Publishers, 1981.

Sutton, Antony. *National Suicide.* New Rochelle, New York: Arlington House, 1974.

—— *Wall Street and the Rise of Hitler.* Seal Beach, California: '76 Press, 1976.

—— *War on Gold.* Seal Beach, California: '76 Press, 1977.

—— *The Best Enemy Money Can Buy.* Billings, Montana: Liberty House Press, 1986.

—— *America's Secret Establishment.* Billings, Montana: Liberty House Press, 1986.

—— *Wall Street and the Bolshevik Revolution.* Morley, Western Australia: Veritas Publishing Company, 1981.

Weber, Christopher. *". . . Good As Gold."* Berryville, Virginia: George Edward Durell Foundation, 1988.

Vieira, Edwin Jr. *Pieces of Eight: The Monetary Powers and Disabilities of the United States Constitution.* Old Greenwich, Connecticut: The Devin-Adair Company, 1983.

RECOMMENDED PERIODICALS

Bank Note Reporter*.* Tabloid, about 80 pages, dynamite monthly newspaper for persons interested in collecting or trading banknotes. International scope, lots of display ads and classifieds, and articles of interest to almost everyone. 700 E. State St., Iola, WI 54990; (subscription orders only: 800-258-0929), 715-445-2214, fax 715-445-4087; http://www.krause.com.

Barron's, 200 Burnett Road, Chicopee, MA 01020. Weekly financial tabloid newspaper, includes extensive lists of stock and commodity prices, etc. Invaluable resource for equities investors. Available at most magazine stores, etc.

The Economist*,* 111 West 57th Street, New York, NY 10019; 212-554-0500 or at 25 St. James's Street, London SW1A 1HG, United Kingdom, phone 0171-830-7000. Carefully reasoned and thorough reports on international economic issues, often the first to report on potential upheavals in the international political arena.

The Financial Privacy Report, monthly, international scope, remarkably informative, sometimes shocking. If you value individual liberty, of which privacy is a major part, check out this *gem* of a newsletter. Published by Daniel Rosenthal, edited by Michael Ketcher. P.O. Box 1277, Burnsville, MN 55337; 612-875-8757, fax 6122-882-4962.

Fleet Street Letter. International perspective on politics and investments, excellent source of information for individual investors. Contact Agora Publishing, 1217 Saint Paul Street, Baltimore, MD 21202. 800-433-1528, 410-223-2500, fax 410-223-2553.

Forecasts & Strategies. Mark Skousen's steady but highly interesting analysis of contemporary political and economic (financial) matters recognizes the long-term value of precious metal investments but is also aware of the profit potential of equities investments, etc. Balanced coverage for the mature, professional investor. Contact Phillips Publishing, 7811 Montrose Road, Potomac, MD 20854; 800-211-7662 (subscriptions only), 301-340-2100, fax 301-424-5059.

Gold Newsletter. From Jim Blanchard's Jefferson Financial, Inc., this monthly is an excellent source of insight on U.S. and international investments, monetary policy, and ethics (or the lack of same) in government. This newsletter has been around for about thirty years and has a global following — for good reason. 800-877-8847, 504-837-3033, fax 504-837-4885; email: gnlmail@jeffinc.com; http://www.jeffinc.com.

International Speculator. Doug Casey writes a penetrating analysis of today's markets and socio-political affairs. His is one of the best newsletters I've ever read. He's been calling the shots correctly for around twenty years. Contact Agora Publishing, 1217 Saint Paul Street, Baltimore, MD 21202. 800-433-1528, 410-223-2500, fax 410-223-2553.

Investor's Business Daily, P.O. Box 661750, Los Angeles, California 90066-8950. 310-448-6600 or 800-831-2525. Better than the *Wall Street Journal* and *Barron's* re editorial content. These folks show the courage that made U.S. journalism famous throughout the world. More gutsy, more up front, more courageous than any other business newspaper. Not extreme, just straightforward, to the point. At most magazine stores, etc.

McAlvany Intelligence Advisory, 166 Turner Drive, Durango, CO 81301. Phone 800-525-9556 (subscription orders only), 970-259-4100, fax 970-259-0306. This *excellent* newsletter, edited and published by Donald S. McAlvany, has been around for close to twenty years, maybe longer. It is consistently insightful, packed with pertinent information, and always worth much more than its subscription price, $125 per year. I've recommended it to my friends for probably fifteen years, possibly longer. It's about twenty-four pages monthly. An ideal reference letter for serious adults.

The New American, P.O. Box 8040, Appleton, WI 54913. Phone 800-342-6491, 920-749-3783, http://www.jbs.org. Excellent, glossy, news magazine, packed with in-depth reports on all the major events of the day. Far better than *Time, Newsweek* and the other "news" magazines. I like *NA* as much for what it *doesn't* have as for what it has. It covers the big stories with excellent research, writing, and organization (pictures, graphs, layout, etc.), but it doesn't include the usual "news" magazine garbage about movies, sports, food and cooking, or what's the latest with daytime-teevee "star" what's-his-face. [I think *The New American* is the world's best news magazine today. je.]

Remnant Review, P.O. Box 8204, Fort Worth, Texas 76112. Gary North, Ph.D., Editor. I've recommended *Remnant Review* to my friends since the early 1970s. An absolutely excellent newsletter, always informative (and occasionally mind-boggling). Twelve pages, monthly, and easily worth ten times the price. Christian, free-market, pro-American perspective, well written (sometimes extremely funny), *never* dull. Contact Agora Publishing, 1217 Saint Paul Street, Baltimore, MD 21202. 800-433-1528, 410-223-2500, fax 410-223-2553.

Strategic Investment. James Dale Davidson, founder and president of the National Taxpayers Union and The Sovereign Society, is senior editor of *SI*. He keeps the newsletter sharply focused on the most important, serious topics of the day. Excellent but brief coverage of international affairs. Contact Agora Publishing, 1217 Saint Paul Street, Baltimore, MD 21202. 800-433-1528, 410-223-2500, fax 410-223-2553; http://www.strategicinvestment.com.

Wall Street Journal, 200 Liberty Street, New York, NY. Well known and respected internationally, "the *Journal*" is *the* preferred source of daily stock market and other business and financial information. However, the editorial policy of the paper is thought by some to be too cautious, too willing to ignore reports damaging to political heavyweights or companies with political and financial clout. In a word, the *Wall Street Journal* may not be a good source of information on the Insiders because it is "too establishment" (or whatever phrase you prefer).

Washington Times, 3600 New York Ave. N.E., Washington, D.C. 20002. 202-636-3000. This daily paper covers the "politically incorrect" stories the *Washington Post* and other local papers don't touch. A weekly edition, available nationally by mail, covers virtually all of the political intrigues in the D.C. area, although some criticize it for its "establishment" position on the death of Vince Foster, etc. Also at many newsstands and magazine stores. 800-363-9118, fax 202-269-3419. email: letter@twtmail.com http://www.washtimes.com

RECOMMENDED ORGANIZATIONS, SOURCES

Acton Institute for the Study of Religion and Liberty. Father Robert A. Sirico, founder and president of the Acton Institute, conducts highly professional seminars and produces and sells equally high quality educational materials supporting Lord Acton's famous dictum: "Power tends to corrupt, and absolute power corrupts absolutely." Solidly pro-freedom and pro-American, not just for Catholics but for Americans generally. 161 Ottawa N.W., Suite 301, Grand Rapids, MI 49503, 616-454-3080, fax 616-454-9454; email: info@acton.org; http:www.action.org.

America's Legal & Professional Bookstores. Full inventory of law-related items, most used, some new, excellent prices and service. They carry *American Jurisprudence* and *Corpus Juris Secundum, Bouvier's, Black's*, and other valuable reference works. 725 J Street, Sacramento, CA 95814. 800-359-8010; 916-441-0410; fax 916-441-4641.

 **American Media** is the publisher of not just *The Creature From Jekyll Island* but also a wide assortment of equally thought-provoking books, video tapes, audio tapes, and other products for voters, parents, students, veterans, or retirees. G. Edward Griffin's *Creature* is available in hardback and paper. Contact American Media, P.O. Box 4646, Westlake Village, CA 91359, 800-595-6596 (orders only), 805-496-1649, fax 805-381-0191. Email: info@realityzone.com; http://www.realityzone.com.

Atlas Economic Research Foundation. Atlas creates privately-supported independent public policy institutes internationally for freedom-oriented educational and research activity. Visit their outstanding web site to access a free, on-line database of links to entities and individuals supporting economic freedom. 4084 University Drive, Suite 103, Fairfax, VA 22030-6812; http://www.atlas-fdn.org; 703-934-6969, fax 703-352-7530; email: atlas@atlas-fdn.org.

Better Business Bureau. Visit them at http://www.bbb.org.

Brooks Enterprises, Inc. (BEI). Dave Upham, former banker, founded and runs this investment advisory service. Top quality financial planning, investment guidance, excellent prices. Sponsors investment-seminar cruises to the Caribbean; ZNS and BEI may co-sponsor one to Europe soon. Free monthly newsletter. P.O. Box 1093, Redmond, OR 97756; 800-460-7238; phone and fax 541-923-3794; http://www.come.to/bei; email: beidbu@bendnet.com.

Bureau of Engraving and Printing, U.S. Treasury Department. Check out their web site to read dozens of the most-requested U.S. Treasury documents, and to buy products offered by the BEP. Also, for fun, peek at the page which shows the new $20 bill; see if you spot *both* errors in that display. http://www.bep.treas.gov.

Catacombs Press. ZNS Editor Alan Stang has written two *great* books likely to interest *MONEY* readers: *The Offshore Asset Protection Workbook*, $49.00 (plus $3 s/h in U.S.), and *Taxscam*, $9.95 (plus $2 s/h in U.S.). Both books are available now. Order from Catacombs Press, P.O. Box 261642, Encino, CA 91426; 818-996-2585; fax 626-966-7226. Cash, check, money order. *Highly recommended* by ZNS.

Cato Institute. A "think tank" of scholars and other professionals who seek to advance individual liberty and responsibility and a prosperous society. Great list of very high quality and carefully researched educational products. Free catalog. 1000 Massachusetts Avenue N.W., Washington, D.C. 20001; 202-842-0200; fax 202-842-3490, email cato@cato.org; http://www.cato.org.

Claitor's Law Books. 3165 S. Acadian @ I-10 (Interstate Hiway Ten), Baton Rouge, LA 70821. 800-274-1403; 504-344-0476; fax 504-344-0480. Full inventory of law books, new and used, including full sets of U.S.C., *Words and Phrases*, etc. Also carry reprint of *Black's* First Edition (1891) at about $100 per copy.

Federal Reserve Bank of Chicago. Readers of *MONEY* may be interested in obtaining a free copy of the Fed's interesting booklet, "Modern Money Mechanics," which is printed by the Chicago bank. This official Fed publication uses *interesting terminology* to explain what the Fed does and why it does it. The bank's Visitor Center and marvelous coin and currency display is open weekdays and entry is free. 230 South La Salle Street, Chicago, IL 60604; 312-322-5322, fax 312-322-5515; http://www.frbchi.org.

Federal Reserve Bank of New York. Visit the bank and view its superb exhibit of coins and paper currency (and tokens, etc.) from around the world. Outstanding collection, warm and friendly atmosphere, free tours of the bank, great for young and old. For groups of ten or more, please call for reservations at least one month in advance. 33 Liberty Street, New York, NY 10045; Public Information office phone 212-720-6130; email: FRBNYTOURS@ny.frb.org; http://www.ny.frb.org.

Federal Reserve Bank of San Francisco. See the spectacular American Currency Exhibit, open to the public daily, and it's free. Fascinating, educational, for everyone; boasts more than 400 specimens, some rare and irreplaceable. For groups of ten or more, please make reservations by calling 415-974-3252. 101 Market Street, San Francisco, CA 94105; 415-974-2561 (public relations office, mail stop 1110), fax 415-974-3341.

Foundation for Economic Education (FEE). Publishes a host of educational products supporting free enterprise, individual liberty and responsibility. Excellent quality and reasonably priced. Free catalog. 30 S. Broadway, Irvington, NY; 10533; 914-591-7230; fax 914-591-8910, email: freeman@fee.org; http://www.fee.org.

Foundation for the Advancement of Monetary Education, Inc., New York, New York; Lawrence Parks, Executive Director. Focuses on Internet distribution of materials in support of individual liberty and economic sanity. Visit their web site at http://www.fame.org. Great people offering excellent information.

Gold & Silver Reserve, Inc. Outstanding concept, now across the U.S. and in many foreign countries. Internet based, secure, e-gold® (e-metal®) transactions, or in a currency of your choice, in an instant. Leading edge technology guided by top-quality management. Easily establish *your* e-gold account at http://www.e-gold.com. G&SR, Inc. 1013 Centre Road, Suite 350, Wilmington, DE 19805; 800-909-6590, fax 302-994-4750, email: admin@e-gold.com; http://www.e-gold.com. *Highly recommended* by ZNS.

International Society for Individual Liberty. Educational effort across the U.S. and many foreign countries, includes great seminars, newsletter, pamphlets, books, and other materials. ISIL has recently offered several-day seminars, the most recent in British Columbia. Another will be held in Germany soon (late summer 1998). 836-B S. Hampton Road, Suite 229, Benicia, CA 94510-1960; 707-746-8796, fax 707-746-8797, email: isil@isil.org; http://www.isil.org.

Jefferson Coin & Bullion, Inc. Precious metals expert James U. Blanchard III, founder and CEO, has been in the precious metals business for at least thirty years. Excellent, reliable source for gold and silver coins, etc. 2400 Jefferson Hiway, Suite 600, Jefferson, LA 70121; 800-593-2585, 504-837-3033, fax 504-837-1165; email: jcbmail@jeffinc.com; http://www.jeffinc.com.

Jeremiah Films. Excellent documentary videos on the Clinton administration, Vince Foster death, etc., but one of their newest tapes, "THE CRA$H," discusses several of the most important points made in *MONEY*. $19.95 plus $3.50 s/h. P.O. Box 1710, Hemet, CA 92546; 800-828-2290, 909-925-6460, fax 909-652-5848; email: jeremiah@pe.net; http://www.jeremiahfilms.com. Free catalog.

John Birch Society. National field staff coordinates civic action and educational program in all fifty states. Possibly the largest inventory of high quality books on current history, political chicanery, and traditional American values. The world's best source of high-quality information on the Insiders. Information package $5.00. P.O. Box 8040, Appleton, WI 54913; 800-342-6469 (orders only), 920-749-3780, fax 920-749-3785; email: jbs@jbs.org; http://www.jbs.org.

Laissez Faire Books. Mail-order book dealer, catering to liberty-lovers everywhere for twenty-five (plus) years. Customers in the U.S. and ninety foreign lands. Outstanding selection of high-quality pro-freedom materials. Get on their mailing list and get their free catalog quarterly. Laissez Faire Books, 938 Howard Street, Suite 202, San Francisco, CA 94103; 800-326-0996 (orders only), 415-541-9780, fax 415-541-0597; email: orders@laissezfaire.org; http://laissezfaire.org (Note: This *is* the correct URL; no "www" is used. je.).

Libertarian Party. The Libertarian Party favors dramatically shrinking the size and cost of government, and eliminating laws that stifle the economy and control people's personal choices. The party's platform calls for vigorous defense of the Bill of Rights, free enterprise, civil liberties, free trade, no meddling overseas, and private charity. 2600 Virginia Avenue NW, Suite 100, Washington, D.C. 20037; 202-333-0008, fax 202-333-0072; email: lphq@digex.com and hq@lp.org; http://www.lp.org.

LibertyTree. David J. Theroux's mail-order catalog, a splendid array of freedom-oriented books, games, audio and video tapes, and even collectibles, *all* classy products for thinking people, young and not so young. New address as of Oct. 1997: 100 Swan Way, Suite 200, Oakland, CA 94621. 800-927-8733, 510-568-6047, fax 510-568-6040; email: order@independent.org; http://www.independent.org.

Minaret of Freedom Institute. Pro-freedom educational effort for Muslims in the United States and internationally. Dean Ahmad, Ph.D., president and founder. Reliable and comprehensive source for Islamic view on contemporary and foundational issues. Dr. Ahmad graduated *cum laude* from Harvard and obtained a Ph.D. in astronomy and astro-physics from the University of Arizona. He did postdoctoral work in astronomy at Harvard, the University of Maryland, Goddard Space Flight Center and for private firms. He founded the Institute in 1993 to help other Muslims better understand the concepts of freedom. 4323 Rosedale Avenue, Bethesda, MD 20814; 301-907-0947, fax 301-656-4714; email: deanahmad@yahoo.com; http://www.minaret.org.

National Alliance for Constitutional Money, Inc. Edwin Vieira, Jr., Ph.D., J.D., founder and president, publishes monograph series on Constitutional money and writes books on monetary topics. P.O. Box 3634, Manassas, VA 20108-0976.

National Fraud Information Center. Internet site for reporting Inernet or telephone fraud in the U.S., includes an e-zine (Internet "electronic" magazine): *Internet Fraud Watch.* Visit NFIC at http://www.fraud.org.

Toward Tradition. Educational effort for Jews and Christians, stressing traditional American Judeo-Christian values, wholesome living, and honesty in government. Rabbi Daniel Lapin, founder and president, is a local business executive and popular talk-show host. Call or write for a list of educational tapes and printed items. Excellent quality. P.O. Box 58, Mercer Island, WA 98040; 800-591-7579, 206-236-3046, fax 206-236-3288.

The Welch Foundation. In respectful remembrance of Robert H. W. Welch, founder of the John Birch Society, this entity focuses on production and distribution of educational materials in support of "constitutionally sound free market solutions to the multitude of problems facing our nation today." This organization, founded by J. R. Smeed in mid-1997, now issues "The Welch Report," both a monthly newsletter and weekly radio show. 2650 Mission St., #207, San Marino, CA 91108; 626-441-5471, fax 626-441-5474;
email: liberty@welchfoundation.org
http://www.welchfoundation.org.

World Marketing Alliance. More than $2.5 billion in sales in 1997, WMA, Inc. and its subsidiaries offer insurance, equities investments, and other services to help clients become financially independent. This company has an amazing debt-elimination plan for those in financial trouble: pay the same amount each month as now but for fewer months, or pay for as many months as now but less each month. Estimated 10,000 agents nationally. WMA, 11315 Johns Creek Pkwy, Duluth, GA 30097-1517; 770-453-9300, fax 770-447-7433; http://www.wmas.com.

Other Recommended Sources or Products

American Dictionary of the English Language, facsimile edition of Noah Webster's 1828 dictionary, about $60 per copy plus shipping from the Foundation for American Christian Education (FACE), P.O. Box 9588, Chesapeake, VA 23321. 800-352-3223, 757-488-6601; fax 757-488-5593.

Bouvier's Law Dictionary (two volumes). Contact the bookstores listed above.

CAS (Clinton Administration Scandals). A free but very interesting and professionally moderated Internet email list. Read a constant steam of topical and worthwhile items, recently averaging about seventy-five messages per day, on the Clinton administration and related issues. Make "subscribe cas" the body of an email message to majordomo@majordomo.pobox.com. It's automatic, it's free, and you can unsubscribe just as easily as you subscribe; brief, simple instructions are at the end of every message. [I've subscribed for about three years and found it very valuable. je.]

Encyclopædia Britannica. Printed version of the 15th Edition, 32 volumes, about $1,200 plus shipping. A children's edition add-on costs about $150. A CD is available for about $75. An Internet on-line service for residential access costs about $85 per year. In Chicago, call 800-621-3900 or 312-347-7900.

Oxford English Dictionary. This world-famous reference work is available several ways. The full set of twenty volumes is $3,000. A compact edition of just two volumes but containing all the information in the twenty-volume set costs $350 (and includes a special magnifying glass). A shorter, abridged edition is also available. CDs, in Mac or PC versions, are available for $395 (full version) and $95 (abridged version). Call for details. In North Carolina, 800-451-7556, or 919-677-0977; fax 919-677-1303.

•

Appendix B
Reader Registration Form

READER REGISTRATION FORM

(We recommend you use a photocopy* of this page, and ask you to please print clearly.)

☐ Please put a $ (Dollar sign) in this space if you would consider supporting a ZNS project with a donation.

☐ Please put a $ (Dollar sign) in this space if you are interested in investing in ZNS.

Your Name: _____

Company name, if needed: _____

Mailing address: _____

City: _____ State: _____ ZIP: _____ Country: _____

Your weekday phone: _____

Eves and weekend phone: _____

Your fax number: _____

Your email address: _____

Now, if you don't mind, please give us an idea of any abilities or assets you might offer to ZNS for a special project. You might mention your education, employment, and military service, etc., or just comment on the book. All replies are confidential. Data supplied will be used for official ZNS business only. Please print clearly. You may also send or attach a supplementary sheet. We thank you for your support.

_____
_____
_____
_____

Please mail a copy of the completed form to ZNS, P.O. Box 98950, Seattle, WA 98198, or fax to 253-815-0265. If you have questions, call ZNS at 253-874-2704. Attention Kinko's and other copy-center workers: * Copyright is waived for persons wishing to copy this page for its intended purpose. Form and copyright waiver expire December 31, 2002.

Appendix C
Quotations on Money

OUR quotations are organized into two sections. Quotations in the first section relate to money; those in the second section relate to a wide range of subjects but all of these quotations are wise, or humorous, and sometimes both wise and humorous.

In each section, quotations are ordered somewhat chronologically, with older quotations given first.

To aid children who read these pages, we show the titles of U.S. Presidents, Members of Congress, and a few others, but not academic degrees or professional titles, etc.

"If a common man slaps the face of another common man, he must pay ten shekels of silver as compensation." Hammurabi, king of Babylonia (1792 - 1750 B.C.), Law 204.

"Thou shalt not steal." Exodus 20:15, *ca.* 700 B.C., and the Eighth Commandment.

"Money's the wise man's religion." Euripides, *The Cyclops* (c. 425 B.C.).

"Money alone sets all the world in motion." Publilius Syrus, *Moral Sayings* (1st c. B.C.).

"When gold argues the cause, eloquence is impotent." Publilius Syrus, *Moral Sayings* (1st c. B.C.).

"When reason rules, money is a blessing." Publilius Syrus, *Moral Sayings* (1st c. B.C.).

Old Testament

Leviticus 19:
"36 Just balances, just weights, a just ephah, and a just hin, shall ye have: I am the LORD your God, which brought you out of the land of E'gypt.
37 "Therefore shall ye observe all my statutes, and all my judgments, and do them: I *am* the LORD."

Deuteronomy 25:
13 "Thou shalt not have in thy bag divers weights, a great and a small."
14 "Thou shalt not have in thine house divers measures, a great and a small."
15 "*But* thou shalt have a perfect and just weight, a perfect and just measure shalt thou have; that thy days may be lengthened in the land which the LORD thy God giveth thee."
16 "For all that do such things, and all that do unrighteously, *are* an abomination unto the LORD thy God."

Proverbs 11:1:
"A FALSE balance is abomination to the LORD: but a just weight *is* his delight."

Proverbs 16:11.
"A just weight and balance *are* the LORD'S: all the weights of the bag *are* his work."

Proverbs 20:10.
"Divers weights and divers measures, both of them are alike an abomination to the Lord."

Ecclestiastes 10:19.
"A feast is made for laughter, and wine maketh merry: but money answereth all *things*."

Isaiah 1:22.
"Thy silver has become dross, thy wine mixed with water."

Micah 6:10 and 11.
"Are there yet the treasures of wickedness in the house of the wicked, and the scant measure that is abominable? Shall I count them pure with the wicked balances, and with the bag of deceitful weights?"

New Testament

Matthew 25: 14 - 30.
14 For *the kingdom of heaven is* as a man traveling into a far country, *who* called his own servants, and delivered unto them his goods.
15 And unto one he gave five talents, to another two, and to another one; to every man according to his several ability; and straightway took his journey.
16 Then he that had received the five talents went and traded with the same, and made *them* other five talents.
17 And likewise he that *had received* two, he also gained other two.
18 But he that one, went and digged in the earth, and hid his lord's money.
19 After a long time, the lord of those servants cometh, and reckoneth with them.
20 And so he that had received five talents came and brought other five talents, saying, Lord, thou deliveredst unto me five talents; behold, I have gained beside them five talents more.
21 His lord said unto him, Well done, *thou* good and faithful servant: thou hast been faithful over a few things, I will make thee ruler over many things; enter thou into the joy of thy lord.
22 He also that had received two talents came and said, Lord, thou deliveredst unto me two talents: behold, I have gained two other talents beside them.
23 His lord said unto him, Well done, good and faithful servant: thou hast been faithful over a few things, I will make thee ruler over many things: enter thou into the joy of thy lord.
24 Then he which had received the one talent came and said, Lord, I knew thee that thou art an hard man, reaping where thou hast not sown, and gathering where thou hast not strawed:
25 And I was afraid, and went and hid thy talent in the earth: lo, *there* thou hast *that is* thine.
26 His lord answered and said unto him, *Thou* wicked and slothful servant, thou knewest that I reap where I sowed not, and gather where I have not strawed:
27 Thou oughtest therefore to have put my money to the exchangers and *then* at my coming I should have received mine own with usury.
28 Take therefore the talent from him, and give *it* unto him which hath ten talents.
29 For unto every one that hath shall be given, and he shall have abundance: but from him that hath not shall be taken away even that which he hath.
30 And cast ye the unprofitable servant into outer darkness: there shall be weeping and gnashing of teeth.

1 Timothy 6:

9 But they that will be rich, fall into temptation, and a snare, and *into* many foolish and hurtful lusts, which drown men in destruction and perdition.

10 For the love of money is the root of all evil; which while some coveted after, they have erred from the faith, and pierced themselves through with many sorrows.

Miscellaneous Related to Money

"Yahya related to me from Malik that Yahya ibn Said heard Said ibn al-Musayyab say, 'Keeping gold and silver out of circulation is part of working corruption in the land.'

"Malik said, 'There is no harm in buying gold with silver or silver with gold without measuring if it is unminted or a piece of jewellery which has been made. Counted dirhams and counted dinars should not be bought without reckoning until they are known and counted. To abandon number and buy them at random would only be to speculate. That is not part of the business transactions of Muslims. As for what is weighed of unminted objects and jewellery, there is no harm in buying such things without measuring. To buy them without measuring is like buying wheat, dried dates, and such food-stuffs, which are sold without measuring, even though things like them are measured.'"
—Hadith 31.16 (37b) from *Al-Muwatta* of Imam Malik (8th century A.D.), trans. by A. A. at-Tarjumana and Y. Johnson, Cambridge: Diwan Press, 1982.

"Bad money drives out good." Sir Thomas Gresham (1519 - 1579), English Financier. *See* Blanchard.

"Take care of the pence and the pounds will take care of themselves." William Lowndes (1652 - 1724).

"Go into the street, and give one man a lecture on morality, and another a shilling, and see which will respect you most." Samuel Johnson, quoted in Boswell's *Life of Samuel Johnson*, July 20, 1763.

"Paper money eventually returns to its intrinsic value — zero." Voltaire (1694 - 1778).

"Permit me to issue and control the money of a nation and I care not who makes its laws." Mayer Amschel Rothschild, founder of the Rothschild banking dynasty in the early 1700s. [This statement may also be seen quoted as: "Permit me to issue and control the money of a nation and I care not how its citizens vote." je.] *See* Frederic Morton, *The Rothschilds, A Family Portrait* (New York: Antheneum, 1962).

"Paper money polluted the equity of our laws, turned them into engines of oppression, corrupted the justice of our public administration, destroyed the fortunes of thousands who had confidence in it, enervated the trade, husbandry, and manufactures of our country, and went far to destroy the morality of our people." Peletiah Webster, 1789, as quoted in *Massachusetts Liberty*, Jan. - Mar. 1988, Vol. XIV, Number 1.

"When national debts have once been accumulated to a certain degree, there is scarce, I believe, a single instance of their having been fairly and completely paid. The liberation of the public revenue, if it has ever been brought about at all, has always been brought about by a bankruptcy; sometimes by an avowed one, but always by a real one, though frequently by a pretended overpayment." Adam Smith (1723 - 1790), *The Wealth of Nations*, 1776. *See* Blanchard.

"To emit an unfunded paper as the sign of value ought not to continue . . . being, in its nature, pregnant with abuses." Alexander Hamilton (1757 - 1804), Thomas Jefferson's Secretary of the Treasury.

"Money, when considered as the fruit of many years' industry, as the reward of labor, sweat and toil, is not to be sported with, or trusted to the airy bubble of paper currency." Thomas Paine (1737 - 1809).

"Religion is what keeps the poor from murdering the rich." Napoleon Boneparte (1769 - 1821)

"What has the law done? It has given the privilege of coining money in the form of paper, to a particular company. . . . In a word . . . the bank is coining false money." Napoleon Bonaparte. *See* Kiser.

"Though it [paper money] has no intrinsic value, yet, by limiting its quantity, its value in exchange is as great as an equal denomination of coins, or of bullion in that coin. . . . Experience, however, shows that neither a State nor a Bank ever have had the unrestricted power of issuing paper money without abusing that power; in all States, therefore, the issue of paper money ought to be under some check and control; and none seems so proper for that purpose as that of subjecting the issuers of paper money to the obligation of paying their notes in either gold coins or bullion." David Ricardo (1772 - 1823), *Principles of Political Economy and Taxation*, 1817. Ricardo was a Member of Parliament from 1819 to 1823, and is considered by many to be England's greatest economist of the nineteenth century. *See* Blanchard.

"Ready money is Aladdin's lamp." Byron, *Don Juan*, 1824.

"Banking establishments are more dangerous than standing armies." President Thomas Jefferson, 1826. *See* Blanchard.

"I place economy among the first and most important virtues and public debt as the great danger to be feared. To preserve our independence, we must not let our leaders load us with perpetual debt. We must make our choice between economy and liberty, or profusion and servitude." President Thomas Jefferson. *See* Blanchard.

"If the American people ever allow private banks to control the issuance of their currency, first by inflation and then by deflation, the banks and corporations that will grow up around them will deprive the people of all their prosperity until their children will wake up homeless on the continent their fathers conquered. . . .

"I believe that this banking institution is more dangerous to our liberties than a standing army. Already they have raised up a money aristocracy that has set the government at defiance. The issuing power of money should be taken from the banks and restored to the Government and the people to whom it properly belongs." President Thomas Jefferson. *See* Kiser.

"All the perplexities, confusion and distress in America arise, not from defects in their Constitution or Confederation, not from want of honor or virtue, so much as from the downright ignorance of the nature of coin, credit and circulation." President John Adams.

"We are in danger of being overwhelmed with irredeemable paper, mere paper, representing not gold nor silver; no sir, representing nothing but broken promises, bad faith, bankrupt corporations, cheated creditors and a ruined people." Daniel Webster, speech in the U.S. Senate, 1833.

"Gentlemen, I have had men watching you for a long time and I am convinced that you have used the funds of the bank to speculate in the foodstuffs of the country. When you won, you divided the profits amongst you, and when you lost, you charged it to the bank. You tell me that if I take the deposits from the bank and annul its charter I shall ruin ten thousand families. That may be true, gentlemen, but that is your sin; should I let you go on, you will ruin fifty thousand families, and that would be my sin. You are a den of vipers and thieves. I have determined to rout you out, and by the Eternal God, I will rout you out." President Andrew Jackson, opposing the Bank of the United States' attempt to renew its corporate powers under a federal charter. *See* Kiser.

"Whenever the paper has not been convertible into specie, and its quantity has depended on the policy of the government, a depreciation has been produced by an undue increase, or an apprehension of it." President James Madison (1751 - 1836).

"A disordered currency is one of the greatest political evils. It undermines the virtues necessary for the support of the social system and encourages propensities destructive to its happiness. It wars against industry, frugality and economy, and it fosters the evil spirits of extravagance and speculation. Of all the contrivances for cheating the laboring classes of mankind, none has been more effectual than that which deludes them with paper money." Daniel Webster (1782 - 1852). *See* Blanchard.

"Behind every great fortune there is a crime." Honoré de Balzac (1799 - 1855).

"Moral principle is a looser bond than pecuniary interest." President Abraham Lincoln, speech, October 1856.

"Government possessing the power to create and issue currency and credit as money and enjoying the right to withdraw both currency and credit from circulation by taxation and otherwise, need not and should not borrow capital at interest as the means of financing Government work and public enterprise. The Government should create, issue and circulate all the currency and credit needed to satisfy the spending power of the Government and the buying power of the consumers. The privilege of creating and issuing money is not only the supreme prerogative of Government, but it is the Government's greatest creative opportunity....

"As a result of war, corporations have been enthroned and an era of corruption in high places will follow; the money power of the country will endeavor to prolong its reign until all wealth is concentrated in a few hands and the Republic is destroyed." —President Abraham Lincoln. *See* Kiser. [Lincoln's confusion, evident here, became the basis of much of today's confusion about monetary terms and monetary policy. je.]

"The money power preys upon the nation in times of peace and conspires against it in times of adversity. It is more despotic than monarchy, more insolent than autocracy, more selfish than bureaucracy. It denounces, as public enemies, all who question its methods or throw light upon its crimes." President Abraham Lincoln.

"My agency in procuring the passage of the national Bank Act was the greatest financial mistake of my life.
"It has built up a monopoly that affects every interest in the country... It should be repealed. But before this can be accomplished the people will be arrayed on one side and the banks on the other, in a contest such as we have never seen before in the country." Salmon P. Chase, Secretary of the Treasury under Abraham Lincoln, on his (Chase's) death bed. *See* Kiser.

"Whoever controls the volume of money in any country is absolute master of industry and commerce." President James A. Garfield, as quoted by Paul Hein, M.D., *All Work & No Pay* (Sewanee, Tennessee: Spencer Judd, 1986).

"The coin is a delicate meter of civil, social and moral changes.... It is the finest barometer of social storms, and announces revolution." Ralph Waldo Emerson (1803 - 1882), essay on "Wealth," 1860. *See* Blanchard.

"Money is coined liberty, and so it is ten times dearer to a man who is deprived of freedom. If money is jingling in his pocket, he is half consoled, even though he cannot spend it." Dostoevsky, *The House of the Dead* (1862).

"Dear Sirs: A Mr. John Sherman has written us from a town in Ohio, U.S.A. as to the profits that may be made in the National Banking business under a recent act of your Congress, a copy of which act accompanied his letter. Apparently this act has been drawn upon the plan formulated here last summer by the British Bankers Association and by that Association recommended to our American friends as one that if enacted into law, would prove highly profitable to the banking fraternity throughout the world....
"Mr. Sherman declares that there has never before been such an opportunity for capitalists to accumulate money, as that presented by this act and that the old plan of State Banks is so unpopular that the new scheme will, by contrast, be most favorably regarded, notwithstanding the fact that it gives the National Banks an almost absolute control of the National finance. 'The few who can understand the system,' he says, 'will either be so interested in its profits, or so dependent on its favors, that there will be no opposition from that class, while on the other hand, the great body of people, mentally incapable of comprehending the tremendous advantages that derives from the system, will bear its burdens without complaint and perhaps without even suspecting that the system is inimical to their interests.'
"Please advise us fully as to this matter and also state whether or not you will be of assistance to us, if we conclude to establish a National Bank in the City of New York.... Awaiting your reply, we are Your respectful servants, Rothschild Brothers." Brothers Rothschild, in a letter dated June 25, 1863, referring to the National Banking Act of 1863, and addressed to Messers. Ikheimer, Morton and Vandergould, No. 3, Wall Street, New York, U.S.A.

"Lawful money of the United States" includes only gold and silver coin, or that which by law is made its equivalent, so as to be exchangeable therefor at par and on demand, and does not include a currency note which though nominally exchangeable for coin at its face value, is not redeemable on demand. *Bronson v. Rodes*, 74 U.S. 229, 247 (1869), 7 Wall. 229, 247. 19 L.Ed. 141.

"This business of lending blood money is one of the most thoroughly sordid, cold blooded, and criminal that was ever carried on, to any considerable extent, amongst human beings. It is like lending money to slave traders, or to common robbers and pirates, to be repaid out of their plunder. And the man who loans money to governments, so called, for the purpose of enabling the latter to rob, enslave and murder their people, are among the greatest villains that the world has ever seen." Lysander Spooner, *No Treason* (Boston, 1870), as quoted in *The Best Enemy Money Can Buy*, by Antony C. Sutton.

"We boast of having liberated 4,000,000 slaves ... but we are careful to conceal the ugly fact that by our iniquitous monetary system we have nationalized a system of oppression more refined, but none the less cruel, than the old system of chattel slavery." Horace Greeley. *See* Kiser.

"Money is the counter that enables life to be lived socially: it is life as truly as sovereigns [British coins. je.] and banknotes [*sic*] are money." George Bernard Shaw, preface, *Major Barbara* (1905). [George Bernard Shaw got a lot of things right but his terminology here is not among them. je.]

"The few who can understand the system (check money and credits[)] will either be so interested in its profits, or so dependent on its favors, that there will be no opposition from that class, while on the other hand, the great body of the people mentally incapable of comprehending the tremendous advantage that capital derives from the system, will bear its burdens without complaint, and perhaps without even suspecting that the system is inimical to their interests." Rothschild Brothers of London. (*See* Emery, below.) [*Nota bene*: I suspect the parenthetical inclusion, "check money and credits," was supplied by Emery, and is not part of the original material. I supplied the closing parenthesis, in brackets. je.]

"It is extraordinary how many emotional storms one may weather in safety if one is ballasted with ever so little gold." William McFee, *Casuals of the Sea* (1916).

"Picture a party of the nation's greatest bankers stealing out of New York on a private railroad car under cover of darkness, stealthily hieing hundreds of miles South, embarking on a mysterious launch, sneaking on to an island deserted by all but a few servants, living there a full week under such rigid secrecy that the names of not one of them was once mentioned lest the servants learn the identity and disclose to the world this strangest, most secret expedition in the history of American finance.
"I am not romancing. I am giving to the world, for the first time, the real story of how the famous Aldrich currency report, the foundation of our new currency system, was written." "Men Who Are Making America," by B. C. Forbes, *Leslie's Weekly*, October 19, 1916. *See* Griffin, p. 423. [The Aldrich report was the basis of the Aldrich bill which became the basis of the Federal Reserve Act of December 23, 1913. je.]

"A sentiment of trust in the legal money of the State is so deeply implanted in the citizens of all countries that they cannot but believe that someday this money must recover at least a part of its former value. To their minds it appears that value is inherent in money as such, and they do not comprehend that the real wealth, which this money might have stood for, has been dissipated once and for all.

"This sentiment is supported by the various legal regulations with which the governments endeavor to control prices, and so to preserve some purchasing power for their legal tender. Thus, the force of law preserves a measure of immediate purchasing power over some commodities and the force of sentiment maintains a willingness to hoard paper — which is really worthless.

"If, however, a government refrains from regulation and allows matters to take their own course, essential commodities soon attain a level of price out of the reach of all but the rich, the worthlessness of the money becomes apparent, and the fraud upon the public can be concealed no longer." John Maynard Keynes (1883 - 1946), *The Consequences of the Peace*, 1920. *See* Blanchard.

"Banking was conceived in iniquity and born in sin. . . . Bankers own the world. Take it away from them, but leave them the power to create money . . . and with the flick of a pen, they will create enough money to buy it back again. . . . Take this great power away from bankers and all great fortunes like mine will disappear, and they ought to disappear because this would then be a better and a happier world to live in. . . . But if you want to continue to be the slaves of bankers, and pay the cost of your own slavery, let them continue to create money." Sir Josiah Stamp, President of the Bank of England, in an informal talk to students of the University of Texas, in 1920. [*Caveat*: Pastor Sheldon Emery, cited below, quotes the second sentence as, "Bankers own the earth." Emery also quotes the last sentence as ending, ". . . England, then let bankers continue to create money and control credit." Finally, Emery's quotation contains this parenthetical insertion after the word *disappear*: "(he was said to be the second richest man in Great Britain)." je.]

"The real menace of our republic is the invisible government, which, like a giant octopus, sprawls its slimy length over our city, state and nation. At the head is a small group of banking houses generally referred to as 'international bankers.' This little coterie of powerful international bankers virtually runs our government for their own selfish ends." Mayor John F. Hylan, New York City, March 26, 1922.

"Under the Federal Reserve Act, panics are scientifically created; the present panic is the first scientifically created one, worked out as we figure a mathematical solution." U.S. Representative Charles A. Lindberg, Sr., commenting on the financial turmoil of the 1920s.

"The destruction of a currency does not follow a straight, predictable course . . . like a cancer, the disease breaks out anew because inflation cannot be cured through monetary and fiscal measures alone; it requires a fundamental change in social and political attitudes and this change usually does not occur until complete monetary chaos forces a change." G. Carl Wiegand, "The Great Inflation: Germany," 1923. *See* Blanchard.

"The individualistic capitalism of today . . . presumes a stable measuring rod of value and cannot be efficient — perhaps cannot survive — without one." John Maynard Keynes, "Tract on Monetary Reform," 1923. *See* Blanchard.

"The greatest monopoly in this country is the money monopoly, and a great industrial nation is controlled by its system of credit. Our system of credit is concentrated. The growth of the nation therefore, and all our activities are in the hands of a few men, who, even if their actions be honest and intended for the public interest, are necessarily concentrated upon the great undertakings in which their own money is involved and who, necessarily by every reason of their own limitations, chill and check and destroy genuine economic freedom. This is the greatest question of all, and to this statesmen must address themselves with an earnest determination to serve the long future and the liberties of men." President Woodrow Wilson. *See* Kiser.

"If you want to destroy capitalism and the society that goes with it, you must begin by debauching the currency." Lenin (1870 - 1924). Quoted by John Maynard Keynes, Ph.D. [This statement, which Keynes attributes to Lenin, has not been found in Lenin's writings and speeches by scholars at the Ludwig von Mises Institute, Auburn University, Auburn, Alabama. je.] *See* Blanchard.

"No one can earn a million dollars honestly." William Jennings Bryan (1860 - 1925)

"For the last five years, we have been in a new era in this country. We are making progress industrially and economically, not by leaps and bounds, but on a heroic scale." – *Forbes* magazine, in its issue for June, 1929. [Sent to me by Hal Lindsey's office. Mr. Lindsey is the author of *The Late Great Planet Earth* and is co-host of the international intelligence digest program on Trinity Broadcasting Network. je.]

"In the autumn of 1910, six men went out to shoot ducks. That is to say, they told the world that was their purpose. Mr. Warburg, who was of the number, gives an amusing account of his feelings when he boarded a private [railroad - je] car in Jersey City, bringing with him all the accoutrements of a duck shooter. The joke was in the fact that he had never shot a duck in his life and had no intention of shooting any. . . . The duck shoot was a blind." Nathaniel Wright Stephenson, *Nelson W. Aldrich in American Politics* (New York: Scribners, 1930; rprt. New York: Kennikat Press, 1971). *See* Griffin, p. 373.

"The modern banking system manufactures money out of nothing. The process is perhaps the most astounding piece of sleight of hand that was ever invented." Investment advisor Major L. B. Angus, in an article entitled "Slump Ahead in Bonds." (*See* Emery, below.)

"Bankers fought the Federal Reserve legislation — and every provision of the Federal Reserve Act — with the tireless energy of men fighting a forest fire. They said it was populistic, socialistic, half-baked, destructive, infantile, badly conceived, and unworkable. . . .

"These interviews with bankers led me to an interesting conclusion. I perceived gradually, through all the haze and smoke of controversy, that the banking world was not really as opposed to the bill as it pretended to be." McAdoo, William G., U.S. Treasury Secretary, *Crowded Years*. New York: Houghton Mifflin, 1931. Rept. New York: Kennikat Press, 1971. *See* Griffin, p. 464.

"I could never understand the popular belief that because a man makes a lot of money, he has a lot of brains. Some very wealthy men who have made huge fortunes have been among the most stupid people I have ever known." Julius Rosenwald, philanthropist and chairman of Sears from 1924 to 1932. Quoted in Ann Landers' column, *The Seattle Post-Intelligencer*, Seattle, Washington, Sunday, March 1, 1998.

"Despite my views about the value to society of greater publicity for the affairs of corporations, there was an occasion, near the close of 1910, when I was as secretive — indeed, as furtive — as any conspirator. . . . I do not feel it is any exaggeration to speak of our secret expedition to Jekyll Island as the occasion of the actual conception of what eventually became the Federal Reserve System. . . .

"We were told to leave our last names behind us. We were told, further, that we should avoid dining together on the night of our departure. We were instructed to come one at a time and as unobtrusively as possible to the railroad terminal on the New Jersey littoral of the Hudson, where Senator Aldrich's private car would be in readiness, attached to the rear end of a train for the South. . . .

"Once aboard the private car we began to observe the taboo that had been fixed on last names. We addressed one another as "Ben," "Paul," "Nelson," "Abe" — it is Abraham Piatt Andrew. Davidson and I adopted even deeper disguises, abandoning our first names. On the theory that we were always right, he became Wilbur and I became Orville, after those two aviation pioneers, the Wright brothers. . . .

"The servants and train crew may have known the identities of one or two of us, but they did not know all, and it was the names of all printed together that would have made our mysterious journey significant in Washington, in Wall Street, even in London. Discovery, we knew, simply must not happen, or else all our time and effort would be wasted. If it were to be exposed publicly that our particular group had got together and written a banking bill, that bill would have no chance whatever of passage by Congress." "From Farm Boy to Financier," by Frank A. Vanderlip, *The Saturday Evening Post,* Feb. 9, 1933, pp. 25, 70. The identical story was told two years later in Vanderlip's book bearing the same title as the article (New York: D. Appleton-Century Company, 1935). *See* Griffin, pp. 210-219.

"Since the cost of living rose faster than money wages during the war, real wages declined and laborers suffered. This has been the experience in all countries and at all times with inconvertible paper money currencies; and it is such experiences in France of many generations ago that gave rise to the French saying: The guillotine follows the paper money press, the two machines complementary one to the other." Edwin Walter Kemmerer, 1933. *See* Blanchard.

"The Federal Reserve (privately owned banks) are one of the most corrupt institutions the world has ever seen." U.S. Senator (*sic*) Louis T. McFadden (for twenty-two years Chairman of the U.S. Banking and Currency Commission [*sic*]). (*See* Emery, below.) [*Nota bene*: McFadden was a U.S. *Representative* and he chaired the *House* Banking and Currency *Committee.* je.]

"Some men worship rank, some worship heroes, some worship power, some worship God, and over these ideals they dispute — but they all worship money." Mark Twain, *Notebook* (1935).

"In the first place, then, it is patent that in our days not alone is wealth accumulated, but immense power and despotic economic domination are concentrated in the hands of a few, and that those few are frequently not the owners, but the trustees and directors of invested funds, who administer them at their good pleasure. . . . This power becomes particularly irresistible when exercised by those who, because they hold and control money, are able to govern credit and determine its allotment, for that reason supplying so to speak, the life-blood to the entire economic body, and grasping, as it were, in their hands the very soul of production, so that no one dare breathe against their will." Pope Pius XI.

"I had never thought the Federal Bank System would prove such a failure. The country is in a state of irretrievable bankruptcy." U.S. Senator Carter Glass, June 7, 1938. (*See* Emery, below.)

"We can smile today at an age when economists were seriously of the opinion that the value of currency was determined by the reserves in gold and foreign exchange lying in the vaults of the national banks, and above all was guaranteed by them. Instead of that we have learned to realize that the value of currency lies in a nation's power of production." Adolf Hitler, January 30, 1939. *See* Blanchard. [Compare with: "The productivity of the people backs the currency." William E. Simon, Secretary of the Treasury, July 12, 1978. *See* Blanchard.]

"If a nation values anything more than freedom, it will lose its freedom; and the irony of it is that if it is comfort or money that it values more, it will lose that too." Somerset Maugham, 1941.

"From the testimony of Marriner Eccles, Chairman of the Federal Reserve Board, before the House Banking and Currency Committee, September 30, 1941;
 'Congressman Patman: "Mr. Eccles, how did you get the money to buy those two billions of government securities?
 'Eccles: "We created it.
 'Patman: "Out of what?
 'Eccles: "Out of the right to issue credit-money.'"

"By a continuing process of inflation, governments can confiscate, secretly and unobserved, an important part of the wealth of their citizens. By this method, they not only confiscate, but they confiscate arbitrarily; and while the process impoverishes many, it actually enriches some. . . . The process engages all of the hidden forces of economic law on the side of destruction and does it in a manner which not one man in a million is able to diagnose." John Maynard Keynes, British socialist economist whose theories and philosophies are the backbone of most economic texts used today in the world's high schools, colleges and universities. Keynes' foremost disciple in the United States is considered to be Harvard Professor John Kenneth Galbraith, Ph.D., regular advisor to numerous U.S. presidents and Federal Reserve entities. Galbraith's writings on the U.S. economy and related topics are usually given wide distribution and credibility in serials such as *Time, Newsweek,* and *The New York Times*. Quotation taken from *The McAlvany Intelligence Advisor,* June 1988.

"Lenin is said to have declared that the best way to destroy the Capitalistic system was to debauch the currency. Lenin was right. There is no subtler, no surer means of overturning the existing basis of society. The process engages all the hidden forces of economic law on the side of destruction, and does it in a manner which not one man in a million can diagnose." John Maynard Keynes, British socialist and economist. [*N.B.* According to a scholar at the Ludwig von Mises Institute, Auburn University, in a telephone contact with me in January 1998, searches of Lenin's writings and speeches have failed to find any phrase or passage even similar to what Keynes attributes to Lenin. je.]

"Money is indeed the most important thing in the world; and all sound and successful personal and national morality should have this fact for its basis." George Bernard Shaw, preface, *The Irrational Knot,* 1950.

"Whenever destroyers appear among men, they start by destroying money, for money is men's protection and the base of a moral existence. Destroyers seize gold and leave to its owners a counterfeit pile of paper. This kills all objective standards and delivers men into the arbitrary power of an arbitrary setter of values. Gold was an objective value, an equivalent of wealth produced. Paper is a mortgage on wealth that does not exist, backed by a gun aimed at those who are expected to produce it. Paper is a check drawn by legal looters upon an account which is not theirs; upon the virtue of the victims. Watch for the day when it bounces, marked: Account overdrawn." Ayn Rand, *Atlas Shrugged. See* Blanchard.

"You will recall that the first act of the Marxists, who were surreptitiously infiltrated into key positions in our government in 1933, was to depreciate the dollar and deny to the American people the right of redemption because these conspirators had learned from Karl Marx that the surest way to overturn the social order was to debauch the currency. To accomplish this they installed the Laski-Keynes-Marxist monetary system of a so-called 'managed currency.'" Honorable John T. Wood, *American Mercury,* May 1957, p. 145. (*See* Emery, below.)

"Thoughtful men can hardly have failed to notice that the spoilation of peoples in our day by inflationary thievery, disguised with Machiavellian slyness as necessity or welfare, has doubtless exceeded by far the looting by the world's greatest conquerors." Malcolm Bryan, President, Federal Reserve Bank of Atlanta, March 19, 1959. *See* Blanchard.

"I'm living so far beyond my income that we may almost be said to be living apart." e e cummings (1894 - 1962).

"The Federal Reserve System is the only instrumentality endowed by law with discretionary power to create (or extinguish) the money that serves as bank reserves or as the public's pocket cash. Thus the ultimate capability for expanding or reducing the economy's supply of money rests with the Federal Reserve." Board of Governors, *The Federal Reserve System, Purposes and Functions, Fiftieth Anniversary Edition,* Federal Reserve System, Washington, 1963. *See* McManus.

"The fact is an independent Federal Reserve means something that is not in the framework of our constitutional system, which says that Congress will make the laws and the President will execute them. Those who desire a dictatorship on money matters by a 'banker's club' — away from the Congress and the President — are in effect advocating a form of government alien to our own." U.S. Representative Wright Patman, in a speech to the U.S. House of Representatives, April 3, 1964. See *Congressional Record,* August 3, 1964, p. 17840. *See* McManus.

"Although a creature of Congress, the Federal Reserve is, in practice, independent of that body in its policy making.... The Federal Reserve neither requires nor seeks the approval of any branch of government for its policies. The system itself decides at what ends its policies are aimed and then takes whatever actions it sees fit to reach those ends." U.S. House Banking Committee's *Primer on Money*, issued in 1964. *See* McManus.

"From birth to age 18, a girl needs good parents, from 18 to 35 she needs good looks, from 35 to 55 she needs a good personality, and from 55 on she needs cash." Sophie Tucker (1884 - 1966)

"In the U.S. today we have in effect two governments.... We have the duly constituted government.... Then we have an independent uncontrolled and uncoordinated government in the Federal Reserve System, operating the money powers that are reserved to Congress by the Constitution." U.S. Representative Wright Patman, chairman of the House Banking Committee, in his newsletter to his constituents, June 6, 1968.

"Many Germans, who at great risk defied Hitler's orders in the 1930s that all holdings of gold were to be declared, found at the end of the war that their gold saved their lives. They bribed Russian soldiers with it or saved their families from near starvation by using it to buy food on the black market. Remembering this, the Germans still buy between $5 and $12 million worth of gold each year." Timothy Green, *The World of Gold*, 1971. *See* Blanchard.

"The value of money is always the anticipated use value of what it will buy. Permitting politicians to manipulate the quantity of money permits them to affect indirectly the values involved in every market transaction. In fact, it permits them to disrupt, prevent and otherwise hamper transactions that would increase the satisfaction of every member of the society. Increasing the quantity of money does not increase the quantity of goods people want to buy. It only helps some at the expense of others. If men are to remain free and if Western civilization is to continue, people must regain the right to limit the political expansion of the quantity of money and/or credit. We must never again permit politicians to print money or get their hands on the money we put in banks and think is always there. A free market economy cannot permanently operate on a politically manipulated paper money standard. Free men need a market-selected money. Under present conditions, this means a gold standard." Percy L. Greaves, Jr., *Understanding the Dollar Crisis*, 1973. *See* Blanchard.

"Warburg's revolutionary plan to get American Society to go to work for Wall Street was astonishingly simple. Even today, . . . academic theoreticians cover their blackboards with meaningless equations, and the general public struggles in bewildered confusion with inflation and the coming credit collapse, while the quite simple explanation of the problem goes undiscussed and almost entirely uncomprehended. The Federal Reserve System is a legal private monopoly of the money supply operated for the benefit of the few under the guise of protecting and promoting the public interest." Anthony Sutton, *Wall Street and FDR* (New Rochelle, New York: Arlington House, 1975), p. 94. *See* Griffin, pp. 18-19.

"Misconceptions about the 'ownership' [of the Federal Reserve] have resulted from the fact that member banks own 'stock' in the System. The word 'stock' is a misnomer — in reality it is not stock in any generally accepted definition of the word.

"Four points about this so-called 'stock' clearly differentiate it from the ordinary meaning of the term:

"First. It carries no proprietary interest. In this respect, the stock is unlike the stock of any private corporation;

"Second. It cannot be sold or pledged for loans. It thus does not represent an ownership claim;

"Third. In the event of the dissolution of the Federal Reserve Act, the net assets after payment of the liabilities and repayment of the stock go to the U.S. Treasury rather than to the private banks; and

"Fourth. The stock does not carry the ordinary voting rights of stock. The method of electing officers of the Federal Reserve banks is in no way connected to the amount of stock ownership. Instead, each bank in a district has one vote within its class, regardless of its stock ownership." Gary Allen, "Federal Reserve: The Trillion Dollar Conspiracy," *American Opinion*, February 1976. *See* McManus.

"This so-called stock ownership, however, is more in the nature of an enforced subscription to the capital of the Federal Reserve banks than an ownership in the usual sense. The stock cannot be sold, transferred, or hypothecated, nor can it be voted in accordance with the par value of the shares held. Thus, the smallest member bank has an equal vote with the largest. Member banks have no right to participate in earnings above the six percent statutory dividend, and upon liquidation, any funds remaining after retirement of the stock revert to the government." Marriner S. Eccles, chairman of the Federal Reserve's Board of Governors, in a letter dated April 18, 1941 to U.S. Representative Wright Patman, as cited by Gary Allen, "Federal Reserve: The Trillion Dollar Conspiracy," *American Opinion*, February 1976. *See* McManus.

"The first function of money is to pay a debt. To do this one must give back to the creditor something of intrinsic worth equal to the goods or services the parting with which by the creditor incurred the debt. If the creditor gets less than this, he is being defrauded." John E. Holloway, *Gold Newsletter*, October 1976. *See* Blanchard.

"Rafe Mair, British Columbia's consumer and corporate affairs minister, has complained repeatedly that the federally chartered banks are breaking various provincial statutes . . . (Inspector General of Banks William) Kennett said his office refers any complaints to senior officers of the bank involved 'to ensure it received a fair hearing in the bank.'" From the *Vancouver Sun*, April 13, 1978. *See* Stewart, p. 152.

"The productivity of the people backs the currency." William E. Simon, Secretary of the Treasury, July 12, 1978. *See* Blanchard. [Compare Treasury Secretary Simon's view with a similar one: "We can smile today at an age when economists were seriously of the opinion that the value of currency was determined by the reserves in gold and foreign exchange lying in the vaults of the national banks, and above all was guaranteed by them. Instead of that we have learned to realize that the value of currency lies in a nation's power of production." Adolf Hitler, January 30, 1939. *See* Blanchard.]

"I am not anti-gold. I like gold — I would like to get as much of it as possible. But that has nothing to do with its role in the international monetary system." William E. Simon, Secretary of U.S. Treasury, when pressed about his anti-gold reputation, July 1978. *See* Blanchard.

"Inflation is like a country where nobody speaks the truth. Our failure to deal effectively with inflation results largely from our failure to regard it as a moral issue. We do not know whether the most valuable part of the contract may not turn out to be the paper it is written on. This condition is hard to reconcile with simple honesty." Henry C. Wallich, Governor of the Federal Reserve System, December 1978.

"I do not believe the world can meet the needs of billions of people when it bases its monetary system on a commodity whose availability and supply is unpredictable and comes from limited sources." William G. Miller, U.S. Secretary of the Treasury under President Carter (1977 - 1979). *See* Blanchard.

"The official inflation statistics do not include the decline in quality of goods and services. Poorly built homes and new cars, poor education and other public services — and more — are not figured in official figures. If you include declining quality as an inflationary factor, a good rule of thumb is that the actual inflation rate is twice the official rate." George Steve, associate of Franz Pick, June 27, 1980. *See* Blanchard.

"Money is the greatest invention of all time for economic betterment. It began as private property for purposes of exchange. But with passing time and the rise of states, the state control of money developed as a means of gaining and holding authoritarian power. . . . 'Coin clipping' by the state, in whatever form and by whatever name, has been a traditional method by which the state exerts and extends power over its subjects." F. A. Harper, "Introduction," *Inflation and Price Control*, 1980. *See* Blanchard.

"The Reagan economic program is a tightly knit, multi-faceted program, intelligently conceived and coherent in all of its parts. Unfortunately, it is also a fraud and a hoax and it is not going to work." Murray N. Rothbard, June 1981. *See* Blanchard.

"You're not dealing with the Salvation Army." Alix Granger, *Don't Bank on It, 1981*. *See* Stewart, p. 43. [Presumably this quotation is a banker's response to an inquiry about the bank's questionable dealings. je.]

"I don't know why Canadians are upset about bank profits. We've stopped screwing Canadians. Now we're screwing foreigners." Bank of Nova Scotia executive, November 1981. *See* Stewart, p. 185.

"I am not sure if the Fed is supplying too much money or not. . . . The problem is, nobody understands precisely just what is money and how much is being supplied." Donald T. Regan, Reagan Administration Secretary of the Treasury, March 21, 1983.

"I will give you no pleasure of any kind. You are all victims of past, present and future expropriation and I have not the slightest pity for you, because you give in and you are not intelligent. I do not understand how you can accept to be ruled by corruption, by crooked politicians, by absolutely idiotic bankers and by the criminal people of the New York Stock Exchange. I cannot understand how you bow to the dictates of one of the most horrible races of people called security analysts and how you can accept being cheated from morning to night with your currency. You are not aware, when you go to the supermarket, that your currency is a minidollar worth only five pennies (of its 1940 value)." Franz Pick, in a seminar speech entitled "The Beginning of the End," 1985. *See* Blanchard.

"It is important to question how well the Federal Reserve, which was established 73 years ago, is structured and whether it is adequately empowered to make a contribution to future economic and financial stability. . . . Total debt in the United States has soared to $7.7 trillion from only $62 billion when the Fed was founded." Henry Kaufmann, speaking before the Federal Reserve in Atlanta, April 1986.

"The market place is a crime and punishment world, and this Federal Reserve credit expansion is the greatest monetary crime of all time. Accordingly, the punishment will be far and away the greatest market punishment of all time." John Exter, *Gold Newsletter*, June 1987. *See* Blanchard.

"Who thought the day would arrive when a letter saying you could be the winner of a million dollars would be classified as junk mail?" *Salt Lake Tribune*, July 29, 1987.

"Throughout history, periods of high moral attainment have been periods of sound money, while periods of moral disintegration have followed the debasement of the monetary unit. Fiat money, printing press money, or money without intrinsic value is dishonest money, and the moral laws having been violated, moral degradation is inevitable." Howard E. Kershner, *Gold, God and Government*, as quoted in *Gold Newsletter*, March 1988. *See* Blanchard.

"Federal Reserve notes are I.O.U.'s from the Fed to the bearer and are also liabilities, but unlike most, they promise to pay back the bearer solely with Federal Reserve notes; that is, they pay off I.O.U.'s with other I.O.U.'s. Accordingly, if you bring a $100 bill to the Federal reserve and demand payment, they will give you two $50s, five $20s, ten $10s, or one hundred $1 bills." Mishkin, F. S. *The Economics of Money, Banking, and Financial Markets*, 2nd Ed. Glenview, Illinois: Scott, Foresman and Company, 1989. [As shown on the web site of Gold & Silver Reserve, Inc., http://www.e-gold.com.]

"Inflation is the result of the government's creating extra currency and credit unmatched by extra goods or services. Government produces this essentially worthless, but temporarily acceptable money to use as payment for what the majority instructs or permits government to do for some or all citizens at which is naïvely supposed to be government expense. Such 'government expense' turns into a consumer tax and the consumer cannot escape it. Where an unwise attempt is made to refund the tax as a 'cost-of-living' adjustment, it goes right back into a compounded, higher tax of inflation hidden deceitfully in higher prices which have so far been wrongly but successfully blamed on business, whose silence is taken to be a confession of guilt as charged." Lemuel R. Boulware, "The Menace of Inflation," 1990. *See* Blanchard.

"As a former banker, I have literally created millions of dollars out of thin air with the stroke of my pen. . . . under the Monetary Control Act of 1980 the Federal Reserve lobbied for a change in banking law and was granted the authority under this act to lower the reserve requirement to zero. . . . Deposit insurance and its sole surviving agency, the Federal Deposit Insurance Corporation (FDIC), is not designed to protect you. It is designed to protect bankers from runs on the bank by depositors. . . . The FDIC is a fraud foisted on the American public. Even using their own values in their balance sheet, they can cover, at most, only 0.5 percent of all the deposit fund liabilities they insure. * * * A single failure of one of the major money center banks in New York would more than break the FDIC. When you challenge the FDIC with this fact, they are quick to respond, 'Oh, but we are backed by the full faith and credit of the United States Government.' What does that mean in plain English? It means that if the FDIC does not have the money and they must bail out a banking system that has gone under, they will go and borrow the money from the United States Treasury. . . . Where does the United States Treasury get the money? Here we go again – it either has to tax us for it, borrow it, or print it. Either way, you pay for the bailout. . . . It's a system you cannot leave. It is the heart of power of the economic and political elite who have created a monster that entices you to be a slave to it and the monster system, while making your slavery appear so convenient." Larry Bates, former banker, author, *The New Economic Disorder* (Lake Mary, Florida: Creation House, Strang Communications Company, 1994).

"Suppose you saw me pick up a two-pound bag of coffee at the local supermarket. You were behind me in the checkout line as I said to the clerk, 'Just pour out the coffee and give me the two pounds.' What would you think? I know what you would think. You would think, 'Wow, he's really lost it!' But that's exactly what you've done with your dollar.

"We've all said together, 'Just forget the gold; give me the dollar.' This is precisely how the economic and political elite of this world have been able to accomplish the biggest Robin Hood theft of all times. They have simply taken from the ignorant and given it to themselves, the well informed." Larry Bates, former banker, author of *The New Economic Disorder,* page 109 (Lake Mary, Florida: Creation House, Strang Communications Company, 1994).

"It [the Great Depression] was not accidental. It was a carefully contrived occurrence. The international bankers sought to bring about a condition of despair so that they might emerge as the rulers of us all." U.S. Representative Louis T. McFadden on the Federal Reserve Corporation; remarks in Congress, as quoted in *The Federal Reserve Hoax*, by Wickliffe B. Vennard (Boston: Forum Publication Company, 1934), as quoted on page 63 of *The New Economic Disorder*, by Larry Bates, former banker. Lake Mary, Florida: Creation House, Strang Communications Company, 1994.

"A world central bank is essential for the twenty-first century for sound macro-economic management for global financial stability and for assisting the economic expansion of the poor nations. * * * It will take some time and probably some international financial crisis before a full-scale world central bank can be created." *Human Development Report of the Economic and Social Council of the United Nations,* June 1994, page 84, as quoted on page 64 of *The New Economic Disorder,* by former banker Larry Bates (Lake Mary, Florida: Creation House, Strang Communications Company, 1994).

"The transition from gold to fiat money will be greatly smoothed if the State has previously abandoned ounces, grams, grains, and other units of weight in naming its monetary units and substituted unique names, such as dollar, mark, franc, etc. It will then be far easier to eliminate the public's association of monetary units with weight and to teach the public to value the names themselves. Furthermore, if each national government sponsors its own unique name, it will be far easier for each State to control its own fiat issue absolutely." Murray N. Rothbard, *Man, Economy and [the] State,* Volume II, 1995. *See* Blanchard.

"The book *How to Beat Inflation* has just gone from $9.95 to $14.95." As quoted on page 159, 9th ed., *The Self-Publishing Manual,* Santa Barbara, California: Para Publishing, 1996.

"Federal reserve notes, to be issued at the discretion of the Board of Governors of the Federal Reserve System for the purpose of making advances to Federal reserve banks through the Federal reserve agents as hereinafter set forth and for no other purpose, are authorized. The said notes shall be obligations of the United States and shall be receivable by all national and member banks and Federal reserve banks and for all taxes, customs, and other public dues. They shall be redeemed in lawful money on demand at the Treasury Department of the United States, in the city of Washington, District of Columbia, or at any Federal Reserve bank." 12 U.S.C. § 411 (01/16/96).

"Logically, we need a sound currency, but if the world were always logical, men would ride side-saddle.
"The reason governments hate gold is that it limits their spending and prevents them from stealing their citizen's money via inflation. By running deficits, some politicians can satisfy more voters, and selfishly tend to their re-elections, thus sticking it to the next generation. Running the printing presses, more paper chases the same goods, the inexorable result of which is higher prices, which governments then blame on unions, or anybody else, and the public just doesn't get it." James Dines, *Gold Newsletter,* May 1997. *See* Blanchard.

"Q: What was a typical week's wages in the United States at the start of World War II?
"A: About $20. Specifically, the 1941 annual median income was $1,070." Syndicated "Mike Mailway" column, *Seattle Post-Intelligencer,* September 24, 1997.

"The first civilized money was the gold coinage struck by King Croesus of Lydia after 560 B.C. It was one of history's great inventions, which led almost instantly to the deepening of markets and the rapid accumulation of wealth. Before long, as Herodotus reports in amazement, Lydian women held enough wealth in gold that they became free to choose their own husbands. That was merely one among many instances in history when gold has helped individuals attain and preserve freedom.
"Unhappily, gold, freedom and civilization were eclipsed in the modern age by paper money. The good news is that the modern age is ending. Microprocessing is making possible new forms of economic and social organization and post-modern money. In the Information Age, a new form of money will emerge, encrypted digital receipts that will be transferable across the globe at the speed of light.
"The question is: receipts for what? The civilized answer is gold. Unlike the paper money receipts issued by governments during the gold standard eras, the new digital gold standard will be all but immune from counterfeiting. Each receipt will be verifiably unique. The new digital money of the Information Age will return control over the medium of exchange to the owners of wealth, who wish to preserve it, rather than to nation-states that wish to spirit it away." James Dale Davidson, *Gold Newsletter,* May 1997. *See* Blanchard.

"The only sound monetary system is a voluntary one. The free market always chooses the best possible form, or forms, of money. To date, the market's choice throughout the centuries, wherever a free market for money has existed, has been and remains precious metal and currency redeemable in precious metal. This preference will undoubtedly remain until a better form of money is discovered and chosen.
"Until then, prices for goods and services should be denominated not in state fictions such as dollars or yen or francs, but in specific weights of today's preferred monetary metal, i.e., in grams of gold. Anyone might issue promissory notes as currency, but the acceptance of such paper certificates would then be an individual decision, and risks of loss through imprudence or dishonesty would be borne by only a few individuals by their own conscious choice after considering the risks. Critical to the understanding of the wisdom of such a system is the knowledge that private issuers of paper against gold have every long-run incentive to provide a sound product, just as do producers of any product. As a result, risks would be minimal, as the market would provide its own policing." Robert Prechter, "At the Crest of the Tidal Wave," 1997. *See* Blanchard.

"For 5,000 years, mankind has viewed gold as money. In every part of the world, in every civilization, this has been true. For the last 25 years, the world's central bankers have thought themselves too sophisticated for gold. For me, I'll go with the 5,000 years." Adrian Day, *Gold Newsletter,* May 1997. *See* Blanchard.

"The record is a grim one and it was predicted by everyone who knew the inevitable results of giving politicians and central banks a printing press and letting them go hog-wild." U.S. Representative Ron Paul, M.D. *See* Blanchard.

"Trillions of dollars have been borrowed by Americans — as individuals, as homeowners, as businessmen and as taxpayers whose government has sold bonds — all on the assumption that they would be able to borrow dear and pay off cheap. Everyone has become accustomed to inflation over the last fifteen years. Everyone has learned the wonders of leverage in an age of price inflation: Buy now, pay later. Pyramid. Borrow to refinance. And pray for inflation." Gary North. *See* Blanchard.

"This country is a one-party country. Half of it is called Republican and half is called Democrat. It doesn't make any difference. All the really good ideas belong to the Libertarians." Hugh Downs, co-host, ABC-TV's 20/20, March 31, 1997.

"Federal Reserve Tokens are like the 'green stamp' premiums of the 1950s, except that when you turn *these* green stamps in, all you get are more green stamps." Mobley Milam, former assistant U.S. Attorney in San Diego, in a telephone conversation with the author in March 1998.

"The value of our dollar and the level of our interest rates are not supposed to be manipulated by a few members of the power elite meeting secretly in a marble palace. The Federal Reserve is unconstitutional, pure and simple. The only Constitutional money is gold and silver, and notes redeemable in them. Not Fed funny money. Without the Federal Reserve, our money could not be inflated at the behest of big government or big banks. Your income and savings would not lose their value. Just as important, we wouldn't have this endless string of booms and busts, recessions and depressions, with each bust getting worse. They aren't natural to the free market; they're caused by the schemers at the Fed. President Andrew Jackson called the 19th-century Fed 'The Monster' because it was a vehicle for inflation and all sorts of special-interest corruption. Let me tell you, things haven't changed a bit." U.S. Representative Ron Paul, M.D., April 1998.

"The rich have a passion for bargains as lively as it is pointless." Françoise Sagan.

"On January 28, 1965 President Johnson asked Congress to repeal the gold reserve requirement against Federal Reserve deposit liabilities. The bill passed and became law on March 3, 1965. Ended at last, and perhaps forever, was that vision of a currency system serving the needs of the people rather than the necessities of the government, a credit system that does not promote speculation and credit crises, but rather prevents them, a money system that is built upon substance rather than on illusory faith in government promises, and an economic system that rests upon private, individual responsibility rather than government edict and paternalism." Elgin Groseclose, "Fifty Years of Managed Money." *See* Blanchard.

"Rampant inflation destroys the capital markets which are the very wellspring of productive enterprise. A great deal of 'unproductive' labor is needed to cope with the complexities of calculation and dealing with rapidly changing prices. Finally, the greatest danger to economic production and well-being looms in sudden government intervention. Having recklessly depreciated the currency at two-digit rates, the same government may want to legislate and regulate the economic actions of the people. It may suddenly impose price, wage and rent controls, restrict imports or exports, levy new taxes, or commit some other new folly; all in order to treat some symptoms of its own policies." Hans E. Sennholz. *See* Blanchard.

"Whoever said money can't buy happiness didn't know where to shop." Unknown source.

"Save a little money each month and at the end of the year you'll be surprised at how little you have." Ernest Haskins.

"Better to be *nouveau* than never to have been *riche* at all." Unknown.

"Economists are people who work with numbers but who don't have the personality to be accountants." Unknown.

"A man can't get rich if he takes proper care of his family." Navajo saying.

"When I had money[,] everyone called me brother." Polish proverb.

"When money speaks, the truth keeps silent." Russian proverb. [Also quoted as: "When money speaks, the truth is silent." je.]

"With money in your pocket, you are wise and you are handsome and you sing well too." Yiddish proverb.

"Gold is too valuable to be used as money." Tom Wolfe, one-time U.S. Treasury Department staffer. *See* Blanchard.

"Money is the most liquid form of capital." *See* Smith.

"Let every man divide his money into three parts, and invest a third in land, a third in business, and a third let him keep by him in reserve." Hebrew Proverb. *See* Smith (pg. 97).

"I object to the claim that banks are a rip-off. They're part of the monetary system. Sure, there is hocus-pocus in the money game, but people know that. It's an acceptable fraud." A middle rank Canadian banker. *See* Stewart, pg. 1.

"No branch of the U.S. government owns any part of the Fed." *See* McManus.

"Do the member banks own the Fed? No. Their stock is 'an enforced subscription to the capital' of the regional bank, not ownership. For providing some of the capital of the regional Fed bank, they receive a proportionate dividend from it.
"Who does own the Fed? This pivotal question hasn't been directly answered by anyone who can do so. If it were an agency of the federal government, however, it would not have been able to withstand inquiries directed its way by members of Congress. All of the secrecy surrounding the Fed is one of many reasons why there is a demand, by Congressman Crane and others, that the organization be audited." *See* McManus.

"Legal Tender and the Promise to Pay – Legal Tender – The concept of legal tender is often misunderstood. Contrary to popular opinion, legal tender is **not** a means of payment that **must** be accepted by the parties to a transaction, but rather a legally defined means of payment that **should not be refused by a creditor** in satisfaction of a debt.
"The current series of Bank of England notes are legal tender in England and Wales, although not in Scotland or Northern Ireland, where the **only** currency carrying legal tender status for unlimited amounts is the pound coin." From the Internet site of the Bank of England, *circa* May 1998. Emphasis in original.

"Promise to pay – the '...promise to pay the bearer the sum of ...' on Bank of England notes has nothing to do with legal tender status. The promise to pay stands good for all time and means that the Bank will pay out the face value of any genuine Bank of England note no matter how old.
"The promise to pay also holds good for damaged notes, as long as enough of the note survives to prove that it was genuine and no previous claim for it has been received. The Bank's mutilated notes department receives some 23,000 claims a year for anything from fire damage to notes eaten by all manner of household pets." From the Internet site of the Bank of England, *circa* May 1998.

"The Great Seal of the U.S. (paper money) (currency)" – "Both the obverse and the reverse of the Great Seal of the United States, adopted in 1782, are reproduced on the back of the $1 bill. The obverse depicts an American eagle breasted by our national shield. The eagle holds in it [*sic*] right talon an olive branch of 13 leaves and 13 berries, symbolic of peace. In the left talon are 13 arrows signifying the original colonies' fight for freedom. A ribbon flying from the beak of the eagle is inscribed with the Latin motto, 'E Pluribus Unum', translated 'One out of many', in reference to the unity of the 13 colonies as one government. Over the eagle's head is a constellation of 13 five-pointed stars surrounded by a wreath of clouds. The reverse depicts a pyramid, with 1776, the year of the Declaration of Independence in the Roman Numerals 'MDCCLXXVI' on its base. The pyramid represents permanance [*sic*] & strength. Its unfinished condition symbolizes that there was still work to be done to form a more perfect government and signifies the expectation that new states would be admitted to the Union. The eye represents an all-seeing Deity. The words 'Anniut [*sic*] coeptis' translated as 'He (God) has favored our undertakings,' refer to the many interpositions of Divine Providence in the forming of our Government. 'Novus Ordo Seclorum' means 'A new order of the ages', signifying a new American era. Dubinsky, Thelma. (ed.) 'Facts about United States Money'. Department of the Treasury. (no date)" Taken from the web site of the United States Treasury, http://www.ustreas.gov, *circa* 1995. The current version of the Treasury's web site is considerably different from the way it appeared in 1995. [Punctuation, spelling, and other oddities or errors shown above were in the material on the web site but perhaps not in the Dubinsky work. je.]

"After the 1893 and 1907 financial panics, the Federal Reserve Act of 1913 was passed. It created the Federal Reserve System as the nation's central bank to regulate the flow of money and credit for economic stability and growth. The System was authorized to issue Federal Reserve Notes, now the only U.S. currency produced and representing 99 percent of all currency in circulation." From the Internet web site of the United States Bureau of Engraving and Printing: http://www.bep.treas.gov/currency/facts6.cfm, as of about July 1998.

OTHER QUOTES

"The great thieves lead away the little thief." Diogenes The Cynic (4th c. B.C.)

"Those who are too smart to engage in politics are punished by being governed by those who are dumber." Plato (427 - 347 B.C.).

"I call a fig a fig, a spade a spade." Menander, 342 - 292 B.C.

"Cessation of work is not accompanied by cessation of expenses." Cato the Elder (234 - 149 B.C.). *See* Blanchard.

"A nation can survive its fools, and even the ambitious. But it cannot survive treason from within. An enemy at the gates is less formidable, for he is known and carries his banner openly. But the traitor moves amongst those within the gate freely, his sly whispers rustling through all the alleys, heard in the very halls of government itself. For the traitor appears not a traitor; he speaks in accents familiar to his victims, and he wears their face and their garments, he appeals to the baseness that lies deep in the heart's of all men. He rots the soul of a nation, he works secretly and unknown in the night to undermine the pillars of the city, he infects the body politic, so that it can no longer resist. A murderer is less to fear." Marcus Tullius Cicero, 42 B.C.

"No sane man will dance." Cicero (106 - 43 B.C.).

"I knew a very wise man that believed that, if a man were permitted to make all the ballads, he need not care who should make the laws of a nation." Andrew Fletcher of Saltoun (1653 - 1716).

"The number of malefactors authorizes not the crime." Thomas Fuller, M.D., *Gnomologia* (1732).

"The right of self-defense is the first law of nature; in most governments it has been the study of rulers to confine this right within the narrowest limits possible. Wherever standing armies are kept up, and when the right of the people to keep and bear arms is, under any color or pretext whatsoever, prohibited, liberty, if not already annihilated, is on the brink of destruction." Henry St. George Tucker, in Blackstone's 1768 *Commentaries on the Laws of England.*. [Special thanks to Mr. Vin Suprynowicz, editor, *Las Vegas Review Journal*, who sent this quotation to me in April 1998. je.]

"Anything that is too stupid to be spoken is sung." Voltaire (1694 - 1778).

"It is dangerous to be right when the government is wrong." Voltaire (1694 - 1778).

"If it were not for the government, we would have nothing to laugh at in France." Sébastian Chamfort (1740 - 1794).

"Against stupidity the very gods Themselves contend in vain." Friedrich von Schiller (1759 - 1805) — *Maid of Orleans*. [Also seen as: "With stupidity the gods themselves struggle in vain." je.]

"To take from one, because it is thought his own industry and that of his fathers had acquired too much, in order to spare to others who, or whose fathers have not exercised equal industry and skill, is to violate arbitrarily the principle of association, the guarantee to everyone a free exercise of his industry and the fruits acquired by it." President Thomas Jefferson.

"It should be our endeavor to cultivate the peace and friendship of every nation. . . . Our interest will be to throw open the doors of commerce and to knock off all its shackles." President Thomas Jefferson (1743 - 1826).

"Liberty is impossible without secure private property." President Thomas Jefferson (1743 - 1826).

"I tremble for my country when I reflect that God is just." President Thomas Jefferson (1743 - 1826).

"The man who reads nothing at all is better educated than the man who reads nothing but newspapers." President Thomas Jefferson (1743 - 1826).

"I do not take a single newspaper, nor read one a month, and I feel myself infinitely the happier for it." President Thomas Jefferson (1743 - 1826).

"Advertisements contain the only truths to be relied on in a newspaper." President Thomas Jefferson (1743 - 1826).

"When ideas fail, words come in very handy." Goethe (1749 - 1832).

"Man can live and satisfy his wants only by ceaseless labor; by the ceaseless application of his faculties to natural resources. This process is the origin of property. . . . But it is also true that a man may live and satisfy his wants by seizing and consuming the products of the labor of others. This process is the origin of plunder. . . ." [Thus,] " . . . when plunder is organized by law for the profit of those who make the law, all the plundered classes try somehow to enter . . . into the making of laws . . . . It is impossible to introduce into society a greater change and a greater evil than this: the conversion of the law into an instrument of plunder." Frederic Bastiat, *The Law*, 1848.

"One should forgive one's enemies, but not before they are hanged." Heinrich Heine (1797 - 1856).

"Laws are like sausages. It's better not to see them being made." Otto von Bismarck (1815 - 1898).

"The difference between an almost correct phrase and a correct phrase is the difference between the lightning bug and lightning." Mark Twain.

"In the first place, God made idiots. That was for practice. Then he made school boards." Mark Twain (1835 - 1910).

"There is no such thing as an independent press in America, if we except that of little country towns. You know this and I know it. Not a man among you dares to utter his honest opinion. Were you to utter it, you know beforehand that it would never appear in print. . . . It is the duty of a New York journalist to lie, distort, to revile, to toady at the feet of Mammon, and to sell his country and his race for his daily bread, or what amounts to the same thing, his salary. We are the tools and the vassals of the rich behind the scenes. We are the marionettes. These men pull the strings and we dance. Our time, our talents, our lives, our capacities are all the property of these men — we are intellectual prostitutes." John Swinton, Editor of the *New York Times*, from remarks he gave at the annual dinner of the American Press Association in 1914.

"I don't make jokes. I just watch the government and report the facts." Will Rogers (1879 - 1935).

"Journalism largely consists in saying 'Lord Jones is dead' to people who never knew Lord Jones was alive." George K. Chesterton (1874 - 1936).

"If a nation values anything more than freedom, it will lose its freedom; and the irony of it is that if it is comfort or money that it values more, it will lose that too." Somerset Maugham, 1941.

"What luck for rulers that men do not think." Adolf Hitler (1889 - 1945).

"Those who cannot remember the past are condemned to repeat it." George Santayana (1863 - 1952). [Also quoted as: "Those who fail to learn from the mistakes of history are condemned to repeat them." je.]

"He who passively accepts evil is as much involved in it as he who helps to perpetrate it. He who accepts evil without protesting against it is really cooperating with it." Martin Luther King, Jr., *Stride Toward Freedom*, 1958.

"Listen, there is no courage or any extra courage that I know of to find out the right thing to do. Now, it is not only necessary to do the right thing, but to do it in the right way and the only problem you have is what is the right thing to do and what is the right way to do it. That is the problem. But this economy of ours is not so simple that it obeys to the opinion of bias or the pronouncements of any particular individual, even to the President. This is an economy that is made up of 173 million people and it reflects their desires, they're ready to buy, they're to spend, it is a thing that is too complex and too big to be affected adversely or advantageously just by a few words or any particular — say, a little this and that, or even a panacea so alleged." President Dwight David Eisenhower (1890 - 1969) in response to the question: "Has government bee lacking in courage and boldness in facing up to the recession?"

"To get profit without risk, experience without danger, and reward without work is [as] impossible as it is to live without being born." President Harry Truman (1884 - 1972).

"Tyranny results from the operation of the Iron Triangle. That's a coalition between the beneficiaries of any governmental program, the legislators seeking votes from them and the bureaucrats who administer the program. You've got a tyranny of the beneficiaries, politicians and bureaucrats. Nobody else is welcome." Milton Friedman, *Gold Newsletter*, October 8, 1984. *See* Blanchard

"The government consists of a gang of men exactly like you and me. They have, taking one with another, no special talent for the business of government, they have only a talent for getting and holding office. Their principal device to that end is to search out groups who pant and pine for something they can't get and promise to give it to them. Nine times out of ten, that promise is worth nothing. The tenth time it is made good by looting A to satisfy B. In other words, government is a broker in pillage, and every election is a sort of an advance auction of the sale of stolen goods." H. L. Mencken.

"Who asked for revisions of the neutrality law? Was it American labor? Did the call come from the farmers? From the pulpit? From the homes of Americans? From American youth?

"No, it came from the war hounds of Europe. It is supported by manufacturers of munitions who are seeking the profit which they cannot make under the present law.

"If the law is revised and adopted according to the New Deal's program, the European war will become *our war*. Then, the old cry of 'save the world for democracy' will arise again, as it did before when the United States entered the world conflict.

"If the belligerents become financially pinched after two or three years of war, an effort will be made to collect for the munitions which they will have purchased in America and the burden again will fall on the American taxpayer.

"If I believed in going into this thing at all, I myself could not sap from the lives of helpless children a few dollars to get cash. You cannot be a national benefactor and a Shylock at the same time." William E. Borah, U.S. Senator from Idaho. *See* Kiser.

"I do solemnly swear that I will support and defend the Constitution of the United States against all enemies, foreign and domestic; that I will bear true faith and allegiance to the same; that I will take this obligation freely, without any mental reservation or purpose of evasion, and that I will well and faithfully discharge the duties of the office on which I am about to enter. So help me God." 5 U.S.C. 3331, Congressional oath of office.

Whoever, knowing that an offense against the United States has been committed, receives, relieves, comforts or assists the offender in order to hinder or prevent his apprehension, trial or punishment, is an accessory after the fact.

"Except as otherwise expressly provided by any Act of Congress, an accessory after the fact shall be imprisoned not more than one-half the maximum term of imprisonment or (notwithstanding section 3571) fined not more than one-half the maximum fine prescribed for the punishment of the principal, or both; or if the principal is punishable by life imprisonment or death, the accessory shall be imprisoned not more than 15 years." 18 U.S.C. 3, "Accessory after the fact."

"Whoever, having knowledge of the actual commission of a felony cognizable by a court of the United States, conceals and does not as soon as possible make known the same to some judge or other person in civil or military authority under the United States, shall be fined under this title or imprisoned not more than three years, or both." 18 U.S.C. 4, "Misprision of felony."

"Every government is run by liars and nothing they say should be believed." I. F. Stone.

"Necessity is the plea for every infringement of human freedom. It is the argument of tyrants; it is the creed of slaves." William Pitt.

"Treason doth never prosper: what's the reason? For if it prosper, none dare call it treason." John Harrington, *Epigrams*.

"Trust in Allah, but tie your camel." Arab proverb.

GUIDE TO INTERMEDIATE SOURCES

Blanchard: Items attributed to "Blanchard" are from *Golden Insights: A Collection of My Favorite Quotes on Sound Money and Free Markets* (Jefferson, Louisiana: Jefferson Research, 1997), compiled by James U. Blanchard III, from the pages of *Gold Newsletter*.

Emery: Copied from an undated flyer from the late Pastor Sheldon Emery, America's Promise Ministries, Phoenix, AZ, received by the author *circa* 1986.

Griffin: Quoted by G. Edward Griffin, *The Creature From Jekyll Island* (Westlake Village, California: American Media, 1994).

Kiser: As quoted by Kiser, Fred H., *The Hidden Power of Money* (Los Angeles: Wetzel Publishing Company, 1941).

McManus: From *Financial Terrorism,* McManus, John F. (Appleton, Wisconsin: The John Birch Society, 1993.)

Smith: As quoted by Jerome Smith, *The Coming Currency Collapse* (New York: Books in Focus, 1980).

Stewart: As quoted in *Towers of Gold, Feet of Clay,* by Walter Stewart (Don Mills, Ontario, Canada: Collins Publishers, 1982).

Appendix D

Act of April 2, 1792

ACT OF APRIL 2, 1792
The following pages include the full text of the Act of April 2, 1792, the federal legislation which brought about the construction of the United States Mint in Philadelphia, Pennsylvania, and the manufacture of official United States silver coins and gold coins.

BY AUTHORITY OF CONGRESS.

THE

Public Statutes at Large

OF THE

UNITED STATES OF AMERICA,

FROM THE

ORGANIZATION OF THE GOVERNMENT IN 1789, TO MARCH 3, 1845.

ARRANGED IN CHRONOLOGICAL ORDER.

WITH

REFERENCES TO THE MATTER OF EACH ACT AND TO THE SUBSEQUENT ACTS ON THE SAME SUBJECT,

AND

COPIOUS NOTES OF THE DECISIONS

OF THE

Courts of the United States

CONSTRUING THOSE ACTS, AND UPON THE SUBJECTS OF THE LAWS.

WITH AN

INDEX TO THE CONTENTS OF EACH VOLUME,

AND A

FULL GENERAL INDEX TO THE WHOLE WORK, IN THE CONCLUDING VOLUME.

TOGETHER WITH

The Declaration of Independence, the Articles of Confederation, and the Constitution of the United States;

AND ALSO,

TABLES, IN THE LAST VOLUME, CONTAINING LISTS OF THE ACTS RELATING TO THE JUDICIARY, IMPOSTS AND TONNAGE, THE PUBLIC LANDS, ETC.

EDITED BY

RICHARD PETERS, ESQ.,

COUNSELLOR AT LAW.

The rights and interest of the United States in the stereotype plates from which this work is printed, are hereby recognised, acknowledged, and declared by the publishers, according to the provisions of the joint resolution of Congress, passed March 3, 1845.

VOL. I.

BOSTON:
LITTLE, BROWN, AND COMPANY.
1853.

SECOND CONGRESS. Sess. 1. Ch. 14, 15, 16. 1792.

STATUTE I.

March 28, 1792.

[Obsolete.]
1795, ch. 44, sec. 18.

President of the U. S. may appoint not more than four B. Generals.

CHAP. XIV.—*An Act supplemental to the act for making farther and more effectual provision for the protection of the frontiers of the United States.*

Be it enacted by the Senate and House of Representatives of the United States of America in Congress assembled, That it shall be lawful for the President of the United States, by and with the advice and consent of the Senate, to appoint such number of brigadier generals as may be conducive to the good of the public service. Provided the whole number appointed or to be appointed, shall not exceed four.

APPROVED, March 28, 1792.

STATUTE I.

April 2, 1792.

[Obsolete.]

Secretary of Treasury to finish the lighthouse on Baldhead in North Carolina.

CHAP. XV.—*An Act for finishing the Lighthouse on Baldhead at the mouth of Cape Fear river in the State of North Carolina.*

Be it enacted by the Senate and House of Representatives of the United States of America in Congress assembled, That the Secretary of the Treasury, under the direction of the President of the United States, be authorized, as soon as may be, to cause to be finished in such manner as shall appear advisable, the lighthouse heretofore begun under the authority of the state of North Carolina, on Baldhead at the mouth of Cape Fear river in the said state: And that a sum, not exceeding four thousand dollars, be appropriated for the same, out of any monies heretofore appropriated, which may remain unexpended, after satisfying the purposes for which they were appropriated, or out of any other monies, which may be in the treasury, not subject to any prior appropriation.

APPROVED, April 2, 1792.

STATUTE I.

April 2, 1792.

Mint established at the seat of government.

Director to employ workmen, &c.

CHAP. XVI.—*An Act establishing a Mint, and regulating the Coins of the United States.*(a)

SECTION 1. Be it enacted by the Senate and House of Representatives of the United States of America in Congress assembled, and it is hereby enacted and declared, That a mint for the purpose of a national coinage be, and the same is established; to be situate and carried on at the seat of the government of the United States, for the time being: And that for the well conducting of the business of the said mint, there shall be the following officers and persons, namely,—a Director, an Assayer, a Chief Coiner, an Engraver, a Treasurer.

SEC. 2. And be it further enacted, That the Director of the mint shall employ as many clerks, workmen and servants, as he shall from time to time find necessary, subject to the approbation of the President of the United States.

SEC. 3. And be it further enacted, That the respective functions and

---

(a) The acts establishing and regulating the mint of the United States, and for regulating coins, have been: An act establishing a mint and regulating the coins of the United States passed April 2, 1792, chap. 16; an act regulating foreign coins, and for other purposes, February 9, 1793, chap. 5; an act in alteration of the act establishing a mint and regulating the coins of the United States, March 3, 1794, chap. 4; an act supplementary to the act entitled, "An act to establish a mint and regulating the coins of the United States," passed March 3, 1795, chap. 47; an act respecting the mint, May 27, 1796, chap. 33; an act respecting the mint, April 24, 1800, chap. 34; an act concerning the mint, March 3, 1801, chap. 21; an act to prolong the continuance of the mint at Philadelphia, January 14, 1818, chap. 4; an act further to prolong the continuance of the mint at Philadelphia, March 3, 1823, chap. 43; an act to continue the mint at the city of Philadelphia, and for other purposes, May 19, 1828, chap. 67; an act concerning the gold coins of the United States, and for other purposes, June 28, 1834, chap. 95; an act to establish branches of the mint of the United States, March 3, 1835, chap. 39; an act supplementary to an act entitled, "An act establishing a mint, and regulating the coins of the United States," January 18, 1837, chap. 3; an act to amend an act entitled, "An act to establish branches of the mint of the United States," February 13, 1837, chap. 14; an act amendatory of an act establishing the branch mint at Dahlonega, Georgia, and defining the duties of the assayer and coiner, 1843, ch. 46. General Index.

SECOND CONGRESS SESS. I. CH. 16. 1792.

duties of the officers above mentioned shall be as follow: The Director of the mint shall have the chief management of the business thereof, and shall superintend all other officers and persons who shall be employed therein. The Assayer shall receive and give receipts for all metals which may lawfully be brought to the mint to be coined; shall assay all such of them as may require it, and shall deliver them to the Chief Coiner to be coined. The Chief Coiner shall cause to be coined all metals which shall be received by him for that purpose, according to such regulations as shall be prescribed by this or any future law. The Engraver shall sink and prepare the necessary dies for such coinage, with the proper devices and inscriptions, but it shall be lawful for the functions and duties of Chief Coiner and Engraver to be performed by one person. The Treasurer shall receive from the Chief Coiner all the coins which shall have been struck, and shall pay or deliver them to the persons respectively to whom the same ought to be paid or delivered: he shall moreover receive and safely keep all monies which shall be for the use, maintenance and support of the mint, and shall disburse the same upon warrants signed by the Director.

Duty of the officers.
Assayer.
Act of March 3, 1794, ch. 4, sec. 2.
Chief Coiner.
Engraver.
Treasurer.

SEC. 4. *And be it further enacted,* That every officer and clerk of the said mint shall, before he enters upon the execution of his office, take an oath or affirmation before some judge of the United States faithfully and diligently to perform the duties thereof.

To take oath.

SEC. 5. *And be it further enacted,* That the said assayer, chief coiner and treasurer, previously to entering upon the execution of their respective offices, shall each become bound to the United States of America, with one or more sureties to the satisfaction of the Secretary of the Treasury, in the sum of ten thousand dollars, with condition for the faithful and diligent performance of the duties of his office.

And give bond.
Act of March 3, 1794, ch. 4, sec. 2.

SEC. 6. *And be it further enacted,* That there shall be allowed and paid as compensations for their respective services—To the said director, a yearly salary of two thousand dollars, to the said assayer, a yearly salary of one thousand five hundred dollars, to the said chief coiner, a yearly salary of one thousand five hundred dollars, to the said engraver, a yearly salary of one thousand two hundred dollars, to the said treasurer, a yearly salary of one thousand two hundred dollars, to each clerk who may be employed, a yearly salary not exceeding five hundred dollars, and to the several subordinate workmen and servants, such wages and allowances as are customary and reasonable, according to their respective stations and occupations.(*a*)

Salaries.

SEC. 7. *And be it further enacted,* That the accounts of the officers and persons employed in and about the said mint and for services performed in relation thereto, and all other accounts concerning the business and administration thereof, shall be adjusted and settled in the treasury department of the United States, and a quarter yearly account of the receipts and disbursements of the said mint shall be rendered at the said treasury for settlement according to such forms and regulations as shall have been prescribed by that department; and that once in each year a report of the transactions of the said mint, accompanied by an abstract of the settlements which shall have been from time to time made, duly certified by the comptroller of the treasury, shall be laid before Congress for their information.

Accounts how and where to be settled.

SEC. 8. *And be it further enacted,* That in addition to the authority vested in the President of the United States by a resolution of the last session, touching the engaging of artists and the procuring of apparatus

President of U. S. to cause buildings to be provided.

(*a*) The acts relating to the salaries of the officers of the mint now in force, are: An act to continue the mint in the city of Philadelphia, May 19, 1828, chap. 67, sec. 6; an act supplementary to the act entitled, "An act establishing a mint, and regulating the coins of the United States," January 18, 1837, chap. 3, sec. 7; an act to establish branches of the mint of the United States, Feb. 13, 1837, chap. 14, sec. 2.

248   SECOND CONGRESS. Sess. I. Ch. 16. 1792.

for the said mint, the President be authorized, and he is hereby authorized to cause to be provided and put in proper condition such buildings, and in such manner as shall appear to him requisite for the purpose of carrying on the business of the said mint; and that as well the expenses which shall have been incurred pursuant to the said resolution as those which may be incurred in providing and preparing the said buildings, and all other expenses which may hereafter accrue for the maintenance and support of the said mint, and in carrying on the business thereof, over and above the sums which may be received by reason of the rate per centum for coinage herein after mentioned, shall be defrayed from the treasury of the United States, out of any monies which from time to time shall be therein, not otherwise appropriated.

Expense how to be defrayed.

Species of the coins to be struck.
Eagles.

Sec. 9. *And be it further enacted,* That there shall be from time to time struck and coined at the said mint, coins of gold, silver, and copper, of the following denominations, values and descriptions, viz. Eagles—each to be of the value of ten dollars or units, and to contain two hundred and forty-seven grains and four eighths of a grain of pure, or two hundred and seventy grains of standard gold. Half Eagles—each to be of the value of five dollars, and to contain one hundred and twenty-three grains and six eighths of a grain of pure, or one hundred and thirty-five grains of standard gold. Quarter Eagles—each to be of the value of two dollars and a half dollar, and to contain sixty-one grains and seven eighths of a grain of pure, or sixty-seven grains and four eighths of a grain of standard gold. Dollars or Units—each to be of the value of a Spanish milled dollar as the same is now current, and to contain three hundred and seventy-one grains and four sixteenth parts of a grain of pure, or four hundred and sixteen grains of standard silver. Half Dollars—each to be of half the value of the dollar or unit, and to contain one hundred and eighty-five grains and ten sixteenth parts of a grain of pure, or two hundred and eight grains of standard silver. Quarter Dollars—each to be of one fourth the value of the dollar or unit, and to contain ninety-two grains and thirteen sixteenth parts of a grain of pure, or one hundred and four grains of standard silver. Dismes—each to be of the value of one tenth of a dollar or unit, and to contain thirty-seven grains and two sixteenth parts of a grain of pure, or forty-one grains and three fifth parts of a grain of standard silver. Half Dismes—each to be of the value of one twentieth of a dollar, and to contain eighteen grains and nine sixteenth parts of a grain of pure, or twenty grains and four fifth parts of a grain of standard silver. Cents—each to be of the value of the one hundredth part of a dollar, and to contain eleven penny-weights of copper. Half Cents—each to be of the value of half a cent, and to contain five penny-weights and half a penny-weight of copper.(a)

Half Eagles.

Quarter Eagles.

Dollars or Units.

Half Dollars.

Quarter Dollars.

Dismes.

Half Dismes.

Cents.

Half Cents.
Act of May 8, 1792.

Of what devices.

Sec. 10. *And be it further enacted,* That, upon the said coins respectively, there shall be the following devices and legends, namely: Upon one side of each of the said coins there shall be an impression emblematic of liberty, with an inscription of the word Liberty, and the year of the coinage; and upon the reverse of each of the gold and silver coins there shall be the figure or representation of an eagle, with this inscription, "United States of America" and upon the reverse of each of the copper coins, there shall be an inscription which shall express the denomination of the piece, namely, cent or half cent, as the case may require.

Sec. 11. *And be it further enacted,* That the proportional value of gold to silver in all coins which shall by law be current as money within

---

(a) The acts regulating the gold and silver coins of the United States, are: An act establishing a mint and regulating the coins of the United States, April 2, 1792, chap. 16, sec. 9; an act concerning the gold coins of the United States, and for other purposes, June 28, 1834, chap. 9; an act supplementary to the act entitled, "An act to establish a mint, and regulating the coins of the United States, January 18, 1837, chap. 3, sec. 8, 9, 10.

SECOND CONGRESS. Sess. I. Ch. 16. 1792.

the United States, shall be as fifteen to one, according to quantity in weight, of pure gold or pure silver; that is to say, every fifteen pounds weight of pure silver shall be of equal value in all payments, with one pound weight of pure gold, and so in proportion as to any greater or less quantities of the respective metals.(*a*)

Proportional value of gold to silver.

SEC. 12. *And be it further enacted*, That the standard for all gold coins of the United States shall be eleven parts fine to one part alloy; and accordingly that eleven parts in twelve of the entire weight of each of the said coins shall consist of pure gold, and the remaining one twelfth part of alloy; and the said alloy shall be composed of silver and copper, in such proportions not exceeding one half silver as shall be found convenient; to be regulated by the director of the mint, for the time being, with the approbation of the President of the United States, until further provision shall be made by law. And to the end that the necessary information may be had in order to the making of such further provision, it shall be the duty of the director of the mint, at the expiration of a year after commencing the operations of the said mint, to report to Congress the practice thereof during the said year, touching the composition of the alloy of the said gold coins, the reasons for such practice, and the experiments and observations which shall have been made concerning the effects of different proportions of silver and copper in the said alloy.(*b*)

Standard for gold coins, and alloy how to be regulated.

Director to report the practice of the mint touching the alloy of gold coins.

SEC. 13. *And be it further enacted*, That the standard for all silver coins of the United States, shall be one thousand four hundred and eighty-five parts fine to one hundred and seventy-nine parts alloy; and accordingly that one thousand four hundred and eighty-five parts in one thousand six hundred and sixty-four parts of the entire weight of each of the said coins shall consist of pure silver, and the remaining one hundred and seventy-nine parts of alloy; which alloy shall be wholly of copper.(*c*)

Standard for silver coins—alloy how to be regulated.

Alloy.

SEC. 14. *And be it further enacted*, That it shall be lawful for any person or persons to bring to the said mint gold and silver bullion, in order to their being coined; and that the bullion so brought shall be there assayed and coined as speedily as may be after the receipt thereof, and that free of expense to the person or persons by whom the same shall have been brought. And as soon as the said bullion shall have been coined, the person or persons by whom the same shall have been delivered, shall upon demand receive in lieu thereof coins of the same species of bullion which shall have been so delivered, weight for weight, of the pure gold or pure silver therein contained: *Provided nevertheless*, That it shall be at the mutual option of the party or parties bringing such bullion, and of the director of the said mint, to make an immediate exchange of coins for standard bullion, with a deduction of one half per cent. from the weight of the pure gold, or pure silver contained in the said bullion, as an indemnification to the mint for the time which will necessarily be required for coining the said bullion, and for the advance which shall have been so made in coins. And it shall be the duty of the Secretary of the Treasury to furnish the said mint from time to time whenever the state of the treasury will admit thereof, with such sums as may be necessary for effecting the said exchanges, to be replaced as speedily as may be out of the coins which shall have been made of the bullion for which the monies so furnished shall have been exchanged; and the said deduction of one half per cent. shall constitute a fund towards defraying the expenses of the said mint.

Persons may bring gold and silver bullion, to be coined free of expense;

Act of April 24, 1800, ch. 34. how the director may exchange coins therefor, deducting half per cent.

Duty of Secretary of Treasury herein.

The half per cent. to constitute a fund, &c.

SEC. 15. *And be it further enacted*, That the bullion which shall be brought as aforesaid to the mint to be coined, shall be coined, and the equivalent thereof in coins rendered, if demanded, in the order in which

Order of delivering coins to persons bringing bullion, and

(*a*) See note to section 9. (*b*) See note to section 9. (*c*) See note to section 9.

SECOND CONGRESS. Sess. I. Ch. 16. 1792.

penalty on giving undue preference, &c.
Act of March 3, 1795, ch. 86.

the said bullion shall have been brought or delivered, giving priority according to priority of delivery only, and without preference to any person or persons; and if any preference shall be given contrary to the direction aforesaid, the officer by whom such undue preference shall be given, shall in each case forfeit and pay one thousand dollars; to be recovered with costs of suit. And to the end that it may be known if such preference shall at any time be given, the assayer or officer to whom the said bullion shall be delivered to be coined, shall give to the person or persons bringing the same, a memorandum in writing under his hand, denoting the weight, fineness and value thereof, together with the day and order of its delivery into the mint.

Coins made a lawful tender,

SEC. 16. *And be it further enacted*, That all the gold and silver coins which shall have been struck at, and issued from the said mint, shall be a lawful tender in all payments whatsoever, those of full weight according to the respective values herein before declared, and those of less than full weight at values proportional to their respective weights.

and to be made conformable to the standard weights, &c.

SEC. 17. *And be it further enacted*, That it shall be the duty of the respective officers of the said mint, carefully and faithfully to use their best endeavours that all the gold and silver coins which shall be struck at the said mint shall be, as nearly as may be, conformable to the several standards and weights aforesaid, and that the copper whereof the cents and half cents aforesaid may be composed, shall be of good quality.

The Treasurer to reserve not less than three pieces or each coin to be assayed;

when and by whom, &c.

1801, ch. 21.

SEC. 18. And the better to secure a due conformity of the said gold and silver coins to their respective standards, *Be it further enacted*, That from every separate mass of standard gold or silver, which shall be made into coins at the said mint, there shall be taken, set apart by the treasurer and reserved in his custody a certain number of pieces, not less than three, and that once in every year the pieces so set apart and reserved, shall be assayed under the inspection of the Chief Justice of the United States, the Secretary and Comptroller of the Treasury, the Secretary for the department of State, and the Attorney General of the United States, (who are hereby required to attend for that purpose at the said mint, on the last Monday in July in each year,) or under the inspection of any three of them, in such manner as they or a majority of them shall direct, and in the presence of the director, assayer and chief coiner of the said mint; and if it shall be found that the gold and silver so assayed, shall not be inferior to their respective standards herein before declared more than one part in one hundred and forty-four parts, the officer or officers of the said mint whom it may concern shall be held excusable; but if any greater inferiority shall appear, it shall be certified to the President of the United States, and the said officer or officers shall be deemed disqualified to hold their respective offices.

Penalty on debasing the coins.

SEC. 19. *And be it further enacted*, That if any of the gold or silver coins which shall be struck or coined at the said mint shall be debased or made worse as to the proportion of fine gold or fine silver therein contained, or shall be of less weight or value than the same ought to be pursuant to the directions of this act, through the default or with the connivance of any of the officers or persons who shall be employed at the said mint, for the purpose of profit or gain, or otherwise with a fraudulent intent, and if any of the said officers or persons shall embezzle any of the metals which shall at any time be committed to their charge for the purpose of being coined, or any of the coins which shall be struck or coined at the said mint, every such officer or person who shall commit any or either of the said offences, shall be deemed guilty of felony, and shall suffer death.

Money of account to be expressed in dollars, &c.

SEC. 20. *And be it further enacted*, That the money of account of the United States shall be expressed in dollars or units, dismes or tenths, cents or hundredths, and milles or thousandths, a disme being the tenth part of a dollar, a cent the hundredth part of a dollar, a mille the thou-

SECOND CONGRESS. Sess. 1. Ch. 17, 18. 1792.

sandth part of a dollar, and that all accounts in the public offices and all proceedings in the courts of the United States shall be kept and had in conformity to this regulation.

Approved, April 2, 1792.

STATUTE I.

CHAP. XVII.—*An Act supplementary to the act for the establishment and support of lighthouses, beacons, buoys, and public piers.*

April 12, 1792.

1789, ch. 9.

SECTION 1. *Be it enacted by the Senate and House of Representatives of the United States of America in Congress assembled,* That all expenses which shall accrue from the first day of July next, inclusively, for the necessary support, maintenance, and repairs of all lighthouses, beacons, buoys, the stakeage of channels, on the sea-coast, and public piers, shall continue to be defrayed by the United States, until the first day of July, in the year one thousand seven hundred and ninety-three, notwithstanding such lighthouses, beacons, or public piers, with the lands and tenements thereunto belonging, and the jurisdiction of the same, shall not in the mean time be ceded to, or vested in the United States, by the state or states respectively, in which the same may be, and that the said time be further allowed, to the states respectively to make such cession.

Expenses of beacons, &c. to be borne till July 1793.

1793, ch. 27.

SEC. 2. *And be it further enacted,* That the secretary of the treasury be authorized to cause to be provided, erected, and placed, a floating beacon, and as many buoys, as may be necessary for the security of navigation, at and near the entrance of the harbor of Charleston, in the state of South Carolina. And also to have affixed three floating beacons in the bay of Chesapeak; one at the north end of Willoughby's Spit, another at the tail of the Horse Shoe; and the third on the shoalest place of the middle ground.

Floating beacons to be placed at Charleston harbor and Chesapeak bay.

APPROVED, April 12, 1792.

STATUTE I.

CHAP. XVIII.—*An Act to erect a Lighthouse on Montok Point in the state of New York.*

April 12, 1792.

Be it enacted by the Senate and House of Representatives of the United States of America in Congress assembled, That as soon as the jurisdiction of such land on Montok Point in the state of New York as the President of the United States shall deem sufficient and most proper for the convenience and accommodation of a lighthouse shall have been ceded to the United States it shall be the duty of the secretary of the treasury, to provide by contract which shall be approved by the President of the United States, for building a lighthouse thereon, and for furnishing the same with all necessary supplies, and also to agree for the salaries or wages of the person or persons who may be appointed by the President for the superintendence and care of the same; and the President is hereby authorized to make the said appointments. That the number and disposition of the lights in the said lighthouse shall be such as may tend to distinguish it from others, and as far as is practicable, prevent mistakes.

Lighthouse on certain conditions to be built on Montok Point in State of N. Y.

APPROVED, April 12, 1792.

The following act of Congress, although strictly a private act, has application to so large a body of lands in the state of Ohio, as to justify its insertion in the form of a note.

An act for ascertaining the Bounds of a Tract of Land purchased by John Cleves Symmes.

Be it enacted by the Senate and House of Representatives of the United States of America, in Congress assembled, That the President of the United States be and he hereby is authorized at the request of John Cleves Symmes, or his agent or agents, to alter the contract made between the late board of treasury and the said John Cleves Symmes, for the sale of a tract of land of one million of acres, in such manner that the said tract may extend from the mouth of the Great Miami, to the mouth of the Little Miami, and

Appendix E
Balance Sheets

83rd Annual Report 1996

Board of Governors of the Federal Reserve System

1. Detailed Statement of Condition of All Federal Reserve Banks Combined, December 31, 1996 and 1995

Thousands of dollars

Item	1996		1995	
ASSETS				
Gold certificate account		11,048,036		11,050,060
Special drawing rights certificate account		9,718,000		10,168,000
Coin		591,170		424,452
Loans and securities				
Loans to depository institutions		85,337		135,440
Federal agency obligations				
Bought outright		2,224,700		2,633,995
Held under repurchase agreement		1,612,000		1,100,000
U.S. Treasury securities				
Bought outright				
Bills	190,646,505		183,115,712	
Notes	150,921,721		151,013,150	
Bonds	49,338,894		44,068,604	
Total bought outright	390,907,120		378,197,466	
Held under repurchase agreement	19,971,000		12,762,000	
Total U.S. Treasury securities	410,878,120		390,959,466	
Total loans and securities		414,800,157		394,828,901
Items in process of collection				
Transit items	11,740,684		4,179,015	
Other items in process of collection	1,387,061		1,101,279	
Total items in process of collection		13,127,745		5,280,294
Bank premises				
Land	191,902		166,903	
Buildings (including vaults)	934,260		882,954	
Building machinery and equipment	241,454		230,523	
Construction account	194,470		128,934	
Total bank premises	1,562,087		1,409,314	
Less depreciation allowance	329,185		283,562	
Bank premises, net		1,232,901		1,125,753
Other assets				
Furniture and equipment	1,230,372		1,192,205	
Less depreciation	706,846		671,613	
Total furniture and equipment, net	523,526		520,592	
Denominated in foreign currencies[1]	19,263,604		21,099,289	
Interest accrued	3,891,457		4,101,149	
Premium on securities	6,004,465		5,410,827	
Overdrafts	5,666		22,920	
Prepaid expenses	991,247		865,525	
Suspense account	3,029		13,398	
Real estate acquired for banking-house purposes	10,103		11,507	
Other	299,326		312,533	
Total other assets		30,992,423		32,357,740
Total assets		**481,510,432**		**455,235,200**

Figure E-1. The top entry, "Gold certificate account," should have a footnote to indicate that its $11 billion value is calculated at $42.2222 (FRT) per troy ounce, not the roughly $300 (FRT) per troy ounce you would have to pay. The value of this entry, if it were calculated at $300 (FRT) per troy ounce, would be about $77 billion, or about $66 billion more than shown. This puzzling omission is just one of several puzzling omissions in the Report.

REC'D OCT 2 0 1997

UNITED STATES GOVERNMENT ANNUAL REPORT

FISCAL YEAR 1996

Compiled and Published by
Department of the Treasury
Financial Management Service *fms*

BALANCE SHEET

IN MILLIONS OF DOLLARS

	September 30, 1996	September 30, 1995
Assets		
Cash and monetary assets:		
U.S. Treasury operating cash:		
Federal reserve account	7,700	8,620
Tax and loan note accounts	36,525	29,329
Special drawing rights:		
Total holdings	10,177	11,035
Special drawing rights certificates issued to Federal Reserve banks	-9,718	-10,168
Monetary assets with International Monetary Fund (IMF)	15,428	14,682
Other cash and monetary assets:		
U.S. Treasury monetary assets	87	356
Cash and other assets held outside the Treasury Account	21,133	29,697 r
U.S. Treasury time deposits	4,724	528
Total cash and monetary assets	86,056	84,080 r
Loan financing accounts:		
Guaranteed loans	-14,022	-12,714
Direct loans	32,780	19,732
Miscellaneous asset accounts	-1,655	-1,748 r
Total assets	103,159	89,349 r
Excess of liabilities over assets		
Excess of liabilities over assets at beginning of fiscal year	3,584,917	3,421,723 r
Add: Total deficit for fiscal year	107,277	163,916 r
Subtotal	3,692,194	3,585,639 r
Deduct: Other transactions not applied to surplus or deficit	615	722
Excess of liabilities over assets at close of fiscal year	3,691,579	3,584,917 r
Total assets and excess of liabilities over assets	3,794,738	3,674,266 r
Liabilities		
Borrowing from the public:		
Public debt securities outstanding	5,224,812	4,973,985
Premium and discount on public debt securities	-77,932	-79,996
Total public debt securities	5,146,880	4,893,989
Agency Securities Outstanding	35,043	26,955 r
Total Federal securities	5,181,923	4,920,944 r
Deduct: Net federal securities held as investments by Government accounts	1,448,967	1,317,645 r
Total borrowing from the public	3,732,957	3,603,299 r
Accrued interest payable	45,605	50,611
Special drawing rights allocated by IMF	7,052	7,380
Deposit fund liabilities	7,218	8,186
Miscellaneous liability accounts (checks outstanding, etc.)	1,906	4,790 r
Total liabilities	3,794,738	3,674,266 r

Details may not add to totals due to rounding.
r = revised

Figure E-2. Balance sheet, United States Government.

NOTES TO THE FINANCIAL STATEMENTS

1. *Description of Accounts Related to Cash Operations*

The classes of accounts maintained in connection with the cash operations of the Government include:

- The accounts of fiscal officers or agents who receive money for deposit in the U.S. Treasury or for other authorized disposition or who make expenditures by drawing checks on the Treasury;

- The accounts of administrative agencies that classify receipt and outlay transactions according to the individual receipt, appropriation, or fund account, and

- The accounts of the Treasury of the United States, which is responsible for the receipt and custody of money deposited by fiscal officers or agents.

A set of central accounts is maintained by the Financial Management Service for the purpose of consolidating financial data reported periodically from these three sources, in order to permit the results of cash operations in central financial reports, for the Government as a whole and as a means of internal control.

The central accounts relating to cash operations disclose monthly and fiscal year information on:

- The Government's receipts by principal sources, and its outlays according to the different appropriations and other funds involved, and

- The cash transactions, classified by type, together with certain directly related assets and liabilities that underlie such receipts and outlays.

Accounting for receipts is on the basis of collections; refunds of receipts are treated as deductions from gross receipts. Accounting for outlays is on the basis of checks issued and cash payments made (cash basis). Revolving and management fund receipts and reimbursements of moneys previously expended are treated as deductions from gross outlays. The interest on the public debt, public issues, is recognized on the accrual basis; however, the interest on special issues is on the cash basis. The structure of the accounts provides for a reconciliation, on a firm accounting basis, between the published reports of receipts and outlays for the Government as a whole and changes in the Treasury cash balance by means of such factors as checks outstanding, deposits in transit, and cash held outside the Treasury. Within the central accounts, receipt and outlay accounts are classified as:

- General fund receipt accounts;
- Special fund receipt accounts;
- General fund expenditure accounts;
- Revolving fund accounts;
- Consolidated working fund accounts;
- Management fund accounts;
- Trust fund accounts, and
- Transfer appropriation accounts.

These accounts are described in detail in the Annual Report Appendix.

2. *U.S. Treasury Operating Cash*

Major sources of information used by the Financial Management Service to determine Treasury's operating cash include the Daily Balance Wires from the Federal Reserve banks, reporting from the Bureau of the Public Debt, and electronic funds transfers and reconciling wires from the Internal Revenue Service Centers. Operating cash is presented on a modified cash basis: deposits are reflected as received and withdrawals are reflected as processed.

3. *Special Drawing Rights (SDR's)*

The special drawing rights act of 1968 and the Bretton Woods Agreements Act of 1945 authorize the United States to participate in the Special Drawing Rights Department of the International Monetary Fund and accept the resulting financial obligations of the Fund. The Special Drawing Rights Act provides the permanent authority for the United States to meet its financing requirements in connection with the acquisition and use of SDR's (the unit of account for fund transactions) by the issuance of SDR certificates to Federal Reserve banks.

4. *Miscellaneous Asset Accounts*

Included in miscellaneous assets are gold assets and their related certificates in the following amounts:

	Fiscal 1996	Fiscal 1995
Gold assets	$11,050	$11,051
Liabilities	$11,050	$11,051

5. *Other Transactions Not Applied to Surplus or Deficit*

Seigniorage is the difference between the value of coins as money and their cost of production. Seigniorage on coins arises from the exercise of the Government's monetary powers and differs from receipts coming from the public, since there is no corresponding payment by another party. Therefore, seigniorage is excluded from receipts and treated as a means of financing a deficit or as a supplementary amount to be applied to reduce debt or to increase the cash in the Treasury in a year with a surplus.

Profit resulting from the sale of gold as a monetary asset is treated like seigniorage, since the value of gold is determined by its value as a monetary asset rather than as a commodity.

6. *Federal Securities Outstanding*

These consist of public debt and include all public and agency issues outstanding.

- Public debt is that portion of the Federal debt incurred when the Treasury or the Federal Financing Bank (FFB) borrows funds directly from the public or another fund or account. To avoid double counting, FFB borrowing from the Treasury is not included in the public debt. (The Treasury borrowing required to obtain the money to lend to the FFB is already part of the public debt.)

- Agency debt is that portion of the Federal debt incurred when a Federal agency, other than the Treasury or the FFB, is authorized by law to borrow funds directly from the public or another fund or account. To avoid double counting, agency borrowing from Treasury or the FFB and Federal fund advances to trust funds are not included in the Federal debt. (The Treasury or FFB borrowing required to obtain the money to lend to the agency is already part of the public debt.)

7. *Deposit Fund Liabilities*

These include certain accounts established to record amounts either (a) held in suspense temporarily and later refunded or paid upon administrative or legal determination as to proper disposition thereof, or (b) held by the Government as agent for others (for example, State and local income taxes withheld from Federal employees' salaries and payroll deductions for the purchase of savings bonds by civilian employees of the Government).

8. *Undistributed Offsetting Receipts*

These receipts are composed of the following types of payments:

- Payments to trust funds by Government agencies for their employees' retirement;

- Interest paid to trust funds on their investments in Government securities; and

- Proprietary receipts from rent royalties on the Outer Continental Shelf lands.

Undistributed offsetting receipts are not deducted from outlays at the function, subfunction, or agency levels. They are deducted from the budget totals.

9. *Where applicable, prior year amounts have been revised to reflect realignment to the current Budget of the U.S. Government.*

Comments on the U.S. Treasury Report

Please observe that on the "Miscellaneous assets accounts" line there is no indication that a footnote might apply. However, on page 30 of the Report, the second of two pages of "NOTES TO THE FINANCIAL STATEMENTS," we see the following:

4. *Miscellaneous Asset Accounts*

Included in miscellaneous assets are gold assets and their related certificates in the following amounts:

	Fiscal 1996	Fiscal 1995
Gold assets	$11,050	$11,051
Liabilities	$11,050	$11,051

Now please permit me to direct your attention to a few points.

A. Notice that this note gives no clue that the term "gold assets" relates to the Federal Reserve in any way, or that between the "Fed" and the U.S. Treasury, this $11,050 million (FRT) is based on a gold value of $42.2222 (FRT) per troy ounce. Maybe the officials at the "Fed" and the U.S. Treasury assume that "everyone knows" that a footnote would apply, and that "everyone knows" that "we" owe the "Fed" all this gold, and that "everyone knows" that the "Fed" and the U.S. Treasury value the gold at $42.2222 (FRT) per troy ounce. Who benefits by a misunderstanding of these points?

B. The U.S. Treasury Report balance sheet does not list the actual FRT value of this asset. Instead, it lists the *net* value of the asset, in this case a negative value, which suggests that in addition to the $11 billion (FRT) claim the "Fed" has on the U.S. Treasury for gold, the "Fed" has an additional claim on gold or other "miscellaneous asset" of the U.S., and that the additional claim is valued at $1.655 billion (FRT), although one can't be sure whether this claim is for gold and valued at $42.2222 (FRT) per troy ounce, or for something other than gold, and at what valuation. In any event, this statement indicates that "we" owe the "Fed" more gold than "we" own, that is, more than our civil service workers have stored for us at Fort Knox, and at West Point, and at every other gold depository. Normally, a balance sheet for the U.S. Treasury would show Fort Knox's gold under Assets, and show the Federal Reserve's claim on that gold under Liabilities. Who benefits from such a strange organization of this balance sheet?

C. Note 4 does not indicate that the amounts shown are *millions* of dollars. If a novice (average U.S. voter) were to quickly glance at this note, there is at least a chance he or she would think the Fiscal 1996 Gold assets amount was $11,050 (FRT), or a millionth the actual amount. Who benefits by such a misunderstanding?

D. Notice also the bizarre language in note 5, *Other Transactions....* The two sentences in this note make sense only if we accept the bogus definitions of terms *implied* by their use here. Changing definitions by malicious use of the term, or "verbicide," is a common practice today of many civil service workers and their Insider bosses. These people don't care what the words actually mean. You and I are supposed to use the words in the way the civil service workers use the words, and if you don't use those words *their* way, you are just a "nobody" or a "know nothing," an ignoramus and a fool, and for your "stupidity" you may be fined or go to jail, or both. The Insiders and our civil service workers want you to obey them. You must obey them or you lose your freedom. Some of our nation's civil service workers are out of control. They are drunk with power. They think that your purpose in life is to serve them. Who benefits by such a misunderstanding?

•

Appendix F
Miscellaneous

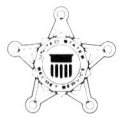

DEPARTMENT OF THE TREASURY
UNITED STATES SECRET SERVICE

REC'D JUN - 1997

915 Second Avenue, Suite 890
Seattle, Washington 98174

May 30, 1997

File: 800.000

Zenger News Service
Attn: Mr. James E. Ewart, ZNS President
P.O. Box 98950
Seattle, Washington 98198

Dear Mr. Ewart,

Reference is made to your letter of May 30, 1997.

Recognizing the restrictions imposed upon you by Title 18 United States Code (USC) secton 474, 18 USC 475, 18 USC 481, and 18 USC 504, I hereby grant a limited and temporary permission as outlined below:

You have permission, on this occasion, to reproduce U.S. currency, in full color and a size of less than three-quarters or greater than one and one-half the size of the original specimen for publication in your educational book entitled *Money*. You are aware that you must destroy any negatives, plates, films, videotape, etc. utilized in the preparation of this book for publication. It is not necessary for a U.S. Secret Service Special Agent to observe this destruction.

Should you have any questions concerning this, please contact Assistant Special Agent in Charge Thomas R. Moyle at (206) 220 6800.

Sincerely,

Charles A. Brewster
Special Agent in Charge

Appendix G
Biography of John Peter Zenger

John Peter Zenger earned a place in history by his dedication to virtue. He published *THE New York Weekly Journal* in the difficult period between 1733 and his death in 1746. Opposing the government-controlled *New York Gazette*, Zenger's newspaper featured daring columns about individual freedoms. The essence of those columns would reappear several generations later – in the Declaration of Independence and the Constitution of the United States of America.

On November 17, 1734, for printing articles critical of the despotic colonial government, Zenger was imprisoned on charges of seditious libel. Held for nine months under excessive bail, he continued to issue his newspaper by communicating his thoughts to his wife through a hole in his jail cell door.

At his trial, which began in April 1735, Zenger openly admitted publishing opposition to government actions. He also admitted that he knew it was against the law to publish articles critical of the colonial government. But, he argued that the law itself was just one more manifestation of despotism by government, that suppression of truth was tyrannical and contrary to justice, decency, and his religious beliefs.

Defense attorney Andrew Hamilton[1] first pointed out to the jury that only if there were falsehood in Zenger's newspapers could he be guilty of libel.

Second, Hamilton courageously informed the jury that despite explicit instructions to the contrary from the judge, they, the jurors, had the right to determine both the law and the facts in the case. Addressing the alleged sedition, and stressing the importance of the jury ruling upon the law in the case, Hamilton drove home the concept that they, the jurors, were the final authority as to what constituted the law.

Hamilton's argument was clear. It was not enough that the legislature might enact a statute. For any statute to become living law, jurors must decide whether that statute truly reflects their moral and ethical beliefs. If a statute conflicts with those beliefs, and if juries refuse to convict persons charged with violating it, that statute is as dead as if it had never been enacted. When juries refuse to convict under a particular statute, they are said to be exercising their right, duty, and power to nullify bad law.

Hamilton then warned the jurors that the liberties of their country were at stake, since a bad precedent in one government – meaning *colony* – is soon set up for an authority in another. He asked the jury to "secure that to which nature and the laws of our country have given us a right – the liberty of both exposing and opposing arbitrary power, in these parts of the world at least" by speaking and writing truth.

History records that the honorable members of Zenger's jury reached a unanimous verdict of not guilty, thereby setting legal precedent in two important ways.

First, for there to be libel there must be falsehood, and Zenger's jury unanimously agreed that he had simply told the truth about tyrannical British rule. This precedent, codified in the First Amendment to the United States Constitution, helps protect our freedom of speech and, thereby, the freedom of the press.

Second, the jury has the right, the power, and the duty to rule on the facts of a case and upon the law. When this right is exercised, it often results in nullification of bad law by We, the People, as jurors.

However, judges, in at least one important way, also have legitimate power to rule on the law. If someone were charged with *felony* theft but the facts of the case established that *petty* theft should be the charge, a judge would likely refuse to allow the matter to come to trial until the accused was charged under the appropriate statute. The judge would be described as having ruled on the law of the case. But the absolute power of juries to also rule on the law of a case becomes clear when we realize that jurors reach

---
[1] Not related to Alexander Hamilton.

their individual verdicts in the privacy of their own minds and consciences. Because each juror's mind is beyond the control of others, there is no possible bar to a panel of jurors, with a verdict of not guilty, ruling on and nullifying the law of a case.

Concerned Americans today sense a return of the injustices in the nation prior to Zenger's trial. Many citizens today might echo the prophetic wisdom of Andrew Hamilton, observing that our liberties are at risk. In the United States today, we see symptoms of anarchy in the courts, in the offices and bureaus of every stratum of government, and even in the halls of Congress. Thus, jurors in some criminal trials today apply the lessons of the Zenger case.

Zenger News Service is dedicated to the memory and ideals of John Peter Zenger, and to the virtuous character he boldly evidenced in his dedication to publishing the truth.

ZNS began operations on June 14, 1983, the 206th anniversary of the Continental Congress' act which established the Stars and Stripes as the flag of the Union. We commemorate this important date by supporting the principles which guided John Peter Zenger, so we'll build a reputation – a kind of flag or banner by which we are known – as a news service of virtue.

Figure G-1. The trial of John Peter Zenger. Photo courtesy of Brown Brothers. All rights reserved. Reproduced with permission.

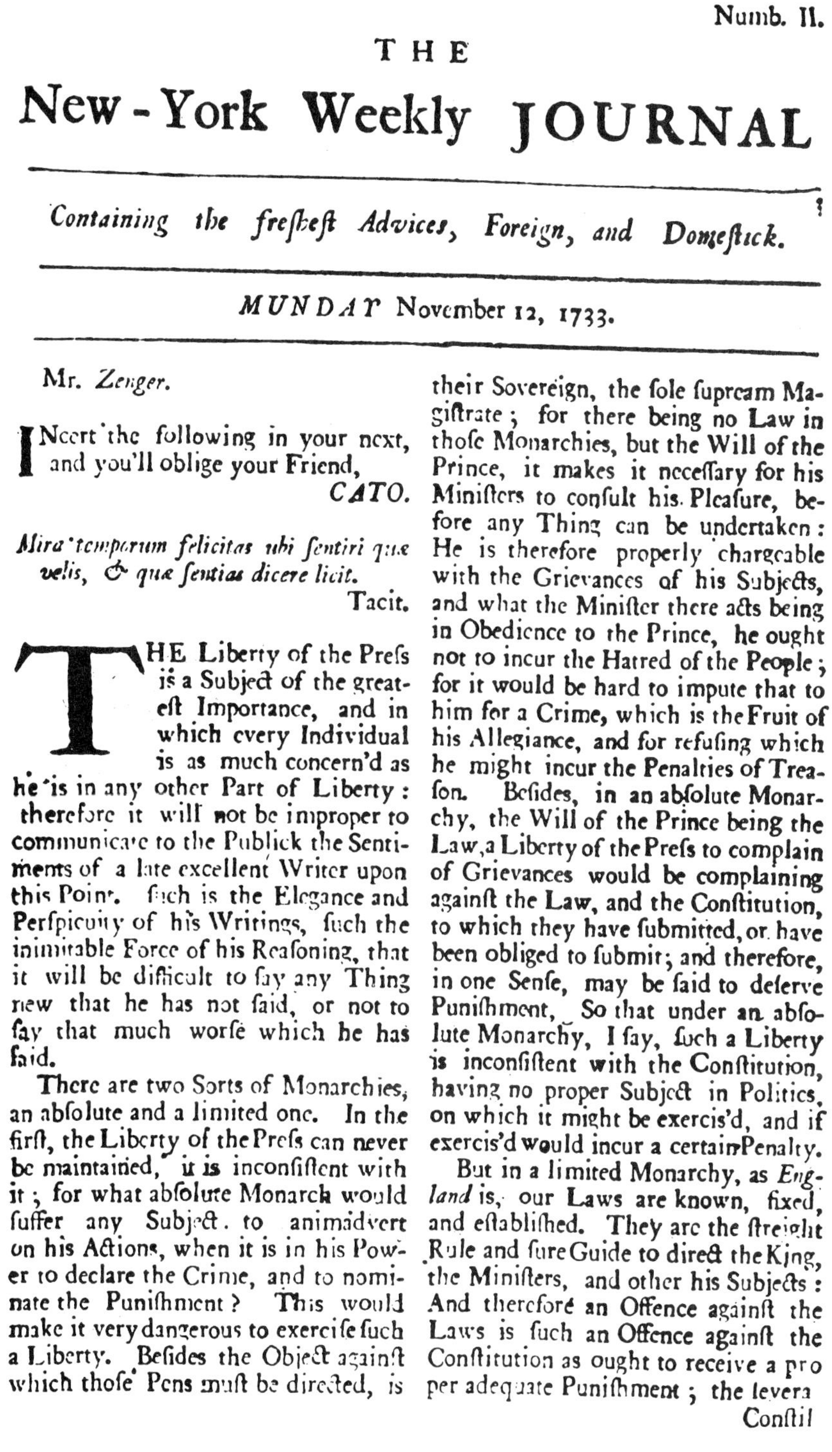

THE
New-York Weekly JOURNAL

Numb. II.

Containing the freſheſt Advices, Foreign, and Domeſtick.

MUNDAY November 12, 1733.

Mr. Zenger.

INcert the following in your next, and you'll oblige your Friend,
CATO.

Mira temporum felicitas ubi ſentiri quæ velis, & quæ ſentias dicere licit.
Tacit.

THE Liberty of the Preſs is a Subject of the greateſt Importance, and in which every Individual is as much concern'd as he is in any other Part of Liberty: therefore it will not be improper to communicate to the Publick the Sentiments of a late excellent Writer upon this Point. Such is the Elegance and Perſpicuity of his Writings, ſuch the inimitable Force of his Reaſoning, that it will be difficult to ſay any Thing new that he has not ſaid, or not to ſay that much worſe which he has ſaid.

There are two Sorts of Monarchies, an abſolute and a limited one. In the firſt, the Liberty of the Preſs can never be maintained, it is inconſiſtent with it; for what abſolute Monarch would ſuffer any Subject to animadvert on his Actions, when it is in his Power to declare the Crime, and to nominate the Puniſhment? This would make it very dangerous to exerciſe ſuch a Liberty. Beſides the Object againſt which thoſe Pens muſt be directed, is their Sovereign, the ſole ſupream Magiſtrate; for there being no Law in thoſe Monarchies, but the Will of the Prince, it makes it neceſſary for his Miniſters to conſult his Pleaſure, before any Thing can be undertaken: He is therefore properly chargeable with the Grievances of his Subjects, and what the Miniſter there acts being in Obedience to the Prince, he ought not to incur the Hatred of the People; for it would be hard to impute that to him for a Crime, which is the Fruit of his Allegiance, and for refuſing which he might incur the Penalties of Treaſon. Beſides, in an abſolute Monarchy, the Will of the Prince being the Law, a Liberty of the Preſs to complain of Grievances would be complaining againſt the Law, and the Conſtitution, to which they have ſubmitted, or have been obliged to ſubmit; and therefore, in one Senſe, may be ſaid to deſerve Puniſhment. So that under an abſolute Monarchy, I ſay, ſuch a Liberty is inconſiſtent with the Conſtitution, having no proper Subject in Politics, on which it might be exercis'd, and if exercis'd would incur a certain Penalty.

But in a limited Monarchy, as *England* is, our Laws are known, fixed, and eſtabliſhed. They are the ſtreight Rule and ſure Guide to direct the King, the Miniſters, and other his Subjects: And therefore an Offence againſt the Laws is ſuch an Offence againſt the Conſtitution as ought to receive a proper adequate Puniſhment; the ſevera
Conſtil

Figure G-2. *Zenger's newspaper,* THE New-York Weekly JOURNAL, *Monday, November 12, 1733. Photo courtesy of Brown Brothers. All rights reserved. Reproduced with permission.*

Appendix H
Oxford English Dictionary: money

THE OXFORD ENGLISH DICTIONARY

SECOND EDITION

Prepared by

J. A. SIMPSON *and* E. S. C. WEINER

VOLUME IX

Look–Mouke

CLARENDON PRESS · OXFORD

1989

Oxford University Press, Walton Street, Oxford OX2 6DP
Oxford New York Toronto
Delhi Bombay Calcutta Madras Karachi
Petaling Jaya Singapore Hong Kong Tokyo
Nairobi Dar es Salaam Cape Town
Melbourne Auckland
and associated companies in
Berlin Ibadan

Oxford is a trade mark of Oxford University Press

© Oxford University Press 1989

All rights reserved. No part of this publication may be reproduced,
stored in a retrieval system, or transmitted, in any form or by any means,
electronic, mechanical, photocopying, recording, or otherwise, without
the prior permission of Oxford University Press

British Library Cataloguing in Publication Data
Oxford English dictionary.—2nd ed.
1. English language-Dictionaries
I. Simpson, J. A. (John Andrew), 1953-
II. Weiner, Edmund S. C., 1950-
423
ISBN 0-19-861221-4 (vol. IX)
ISBN 0-19-861186-2 (set)

Library of Congress Cataloging-in-Publication Data
The Oxford English dictionary.—2nd ed.
prepared by J. A. Simpson and E. S. C. Weiner
Bibliography: p.
ISBN 0-19-861221-4 (vol. IX)
ISBN 0-19-861186-2 (set)
1. English language—Dictionaries. I. Simpson, J. A.
II. Weiner, E. S. C. III. Oxford University Press.
PE1625.O87 1989
423—dc19   88-5330

Data capture by ICC, Fort Washington, Pa.
Text-processing by Oxford University Press
Typesetting by Filmtype Services Ltd., Scarborough, N. Yorks.
Manufactured in the United States of America by
Rand McNally & Company, Taunton, Mass.

monepiscopacy (mɒnɪˈpɪskəpəsɪ). [f. MON(O)- + EPISCOPACY.] Government of the Church by bishops endowed with monarchical authority.

1889 GORE *Ministry Chr. Ch.* ii. 73 No one . . can maintain that the existence of what may be called, for lack of a distinctive term, monepiscopacy is essential to the continuity of the Church. **1903** *Dublin Rev.* Jan. 84 St. Peter is commonly said by the Fathers to be the type of monepiscopacy.

So **moneˈpiscopal** *a.*, pertaining to or of the nature of a monepiscopacy; ‖**moneˈpiscopus** (quasi-Latin), a monepiscopal bishop.

1891 G. G. FINDLAY tr. *Sabatier's Apostle Paul* App. 396 The mon-episcopal *régime* of Ignatius. *Ibid.* 399 The failure of Baur's attempt to identify the bishop of the Pastorals with the mon-episcopus (or monarchical bishop) of the second century.

moner (ˈməʊnə(r)). *Biol.* Also **monere**. Anglicized form of *moneron*, sing. MONERA.

1868 HUXLEY in *Q. Jrnl. Microsc. Sci.* VIII. 210, I propose to confer upon this new 'Moner' the generic name of *Bathybius*. **1869** tr. *Haeckel* ibid. IX. 219 Detaching themselves . . from the periphery of the Moner-colony. *Ibid.*, This Moner-form would be intimately allied to Protogenes. **1873** MAX MÜLLER in *Fraser's Mag.* July 5 The physiologist . . sees in the lowest Moneres the living proof of an independent beginning of life. **1882** COUES *Biogen.* (1884) 33 The chain of life is unbroken from moner to man.

moner, obs. form of MANNER.

‖**monera** (mɒˈnɪərə), *sb. pl.* [mod.L., badly f. Gr. μονήρης single.] Haeckel's name for a group of protozoa composed of organisms of the simplest form. Also sing. moˈneron, one of the monera.

1869 tr. *Haeckel* in *Q. Jrnl. Microsc. Sci.* IX. 28, I have called those forms of life standing at the lowest grade of organization Monera. *Ibid.* 35 A Protozoan organism of the Monera group. **1876** tr. *Haeckel's Hist. Creat.* I. 184 The first complete observations on the natural history of a Moneron . . were made by me . . in 1864. **1894** E. CLODD in *Academy* 7 July 14/1 The theory of the continuity of life from moneron to man.

Hence **moˈneral**, **moˈneric** *adjs.* = MONERAN *a.* **moˈneran** *a.*, of or belonging to the monera; *sb.* a moneron.

1877 HUXLEY *Anat. Inv. Anim.* ii. 95 An endoplastic repetition of the moneran Protomonas. **1881** CARPENTER *Microsc. & Rev.* (ed. 6) §394 Another very interesting 'moneric' type is the *Vampyrella*. **1891** *Q. Jrnl. Microsc. Sci.* XXXII. 611 Haeckel was mistaken in assuming their disappearance in a 'moneran stage'.

monergism (ˈmɒnədʒɪz(ə)m). *Theol.* [ad. mod.L. (and Ger.) *monergismus*, f. Gr. μόνος (see MONO-) + ἔργον work: see -ISM.] **a.** The doctrine of some Lutherans that regeneration is entirely the work of the Holy Spirit; opposed to SYNERGISM. **b.** Applied by some mod. writers to the doctrine (closely akin to Monothelitism) that the two natures in Christ have only 'one operation' (μία ἐνέργεια). (In this sense some Ger. writers have, more correctly, *monenergismus*.) Hence ˈ**monergist** *sb.*, one who professes monergism; also *adj.* = next. **monerˈgistic** *a.*, of or pertaining to monergism. See also MONENERGIST(IC *adjs.*

1867–80 M'CLINTOCK & STRONG *Cycl. Bibl. Lit.* VII. 481 (Cassell *Suppl.*) It is held by monergists that the will of sinful man has not the least inclination towards holiness . . until it has been acted upon by divine grace. **1893** E. K. MITCHELL tr. *Harnack's Outl. Hist. Dogma* 300 The Monergistic and Monotheletic Controversies. **1898** SPEIRS & MILLAR tr. *Harnack's Hist. Dogma* IV. 252 The Monergist and Monothelite Controversies.

‖**monerozoa** (mɒnɪərəʊˈzəʊə), *sb. pl.* *Zool.* [mod.L., f. Gr. μονήρης single + ζῷον animal.] An alternative name for MONERA.

1881 CARPENTER *Microsc. & Rev.* (ed. 6) §392 Monerozoa (as they have been designated by Prof. Haeckel, who first drew attention to them).

Hence **moneroˈzoan** *a.*, of, belonging to, or characteristic of the monerozoa; *sb.* one of the monerozoa; **moneroˈzoic** *a.* = prec. adj.

1879 CARPENTER in *Encycl. Brit.* IX. 375/1 Living organisms of the simplest possible 'monerozoic' type.

mones, monesche, obs. forms of MONISH *v.*

monesia (məʊˈniːʃ(ɪ)ə). [Origin unknown.] An astringent substance obtained from the bark of a Brazilian tree, *Chrysophyllum Buranhem* (*C. glycyphlœum*). Hence **monesin** (mɒˈniːsɪn) *Chem.*, an acrid principle obtained from monesia.

1843 *Pharm. Jrnl.* III. 292 Dr. G. Martin St. Ange . . says: 'A vegetable substance, called *monesia*, has lately been imported from South America, in the form of hard thick cakes. . . M. Bernard Derosne, the druggist, who introduced it, informs me that some travellers call the monesia bark, *goharem*; and others, *buranhem*'. **1858** HOGG *Veg. Kingd.* 500 An acid [*read* acrid] principle, analogous to saponin, called *monesin*.

monest, obs. form of MONISH *v.*

monestar, -er, -re, obs. forms of MONASTERY.

monestycall, obs. Sc. form of MONASTICAL.

monetain, obs. form of MOUNTAIN.

† **moneˈtarian**, *a.* *Obs.* *rare*⁻¹. [f. L. *monētāri-us* (see MONETARY *a.*) + -AN.] Of or pertaining to money or coins; numismatic.

1716 M. DAVIES *Athen. Brit.* III. 80 The last of all the Medal-kind Authors and Monetarian Writings.

monetarism (ˈmɒn-, ˈmʌnɪtərɪz(ə)m). [f. MONETARY *a.* + -ISM.] The economic doctrine or theory of a monetarist or of monetarists.

1969 *Newsweek* 6 Jan. 48 The combination of Stansian horse-and-buggy finance with Friedmanian go-go monetarism. **1970** *Times* 13 Mar. 10 The lecture was a full-blooded onslaught on 'the new monetarism', the doctrines of the Chicago school of economists led by the celebrated Professor Milton Friedman. **1971** *Times* 2 Aug. 13/4 Professor Paul Samuelson . . describes monetarism as a disease and defines it as a 'pathological belief . . that only the rate of growth of the money supply can affect significantly the rate of inflation or the level of unemployment'. **1971** *Sunday Times* 8 Aug. 4 Monetarism, the belief that the state of the economy can be decisively manipulated through regulating the flow of money, became an accepted cult in the White House after Dr Burns had left it to assume the chairmanship of the Federal Reserve Board. **1975** *Times* 28 Aug. 24/5 The Treasury['s] . . distrust of 'monetarism' arises from a belief that it has only one equation, that which links the money supply and the money national income.

monetarist (ˈmɒn-, ˈmʌnɪtərɪst), *a.* and *sb.* [f. MONETARY *a.* + -IST.] **A.** *adj.* Of a monetary character or having a monetary basis.

1914 GEDDES & THOMSON *Sex* x. 239 This order of things—avowedly mechanical, militarist, and monetarist at best, . . seems to many of us . . the only possible form of industrial civilisation. **1971** *Times* 2 Aug. 13/4 The father of the current monetarist school of economic thought. **1972** *Times* 6 Dec. 22/8 The distinctive monetarist assertion is that inflation is attributable solely to increase in the money supply. **1973** *Times* 16 Aug. 15/2 It is not . . true—even in terms of the monetarist theories on which Mr Powell relies—that the Government deficit uniquely determines the money supply. **1974** *Financial Times* 21 Oct. 16/8 The basic argument of the sadly mislabelled 'monetarist' school is that attempts by monetary and fiscal stimulation to lower the level of unemployment below a sustainable minimum, determined by underlying forces, will not bring about a lasting drop in the level of unemployment.

B. *sb.* One who places emphasis on monetary matters, *spec.* one who advocates tighter control of the money supply as an important remedy for inflation.

1963 *Economist* 27 Apr. 299/2 To control inflation by curtailment, as prescribed by the 'monetarists'. **1965** *Ibid.* 25 Sept. p. xxiv/1 The main battle was between the 'monetarists' (who . . believe that screwing down the money supply is always the answer to inflations of any sort) and the 'structuralists'. **1971** *Daily Tel.* 25 Jan. 12/2 It is argued by monetarists that lower rates of interest would contribute to inflation. **1971** *Times* 2 Aug. 13/4 In a highly controversial article in today's *Washington Post* influential monetarists in the United States are compared to water diviners.

Hence **monetaˈristic** *a.*

1972 *Publisher's Weekly* 6 Mar. 60/1 Nixon's two-and-a-half-year dalliance with laissez-faire and the monetaristic theories of Milton Friedman.

monetary (ˈmɒn-, ˈmʌnɪtərɪ), *a.* [ad. L. *monētāri-us* of or belonging to the mint, f. *monēta* mint: see MONEY.]

1. Of or pertaining to the coinage or currency. ***monetary unit***, the standard unit of value of a country's coinage.

1802–12 BENTHAM *Ration. Judic. Evid.* (1827) I. 148 Monetary forgery—forgery in relation to the current coin. **1830** GEN. P. THOMPSON *Exerc.* (1842) I. 208 The principles of what he terms monetary value. **1832** tr. *Sismondi's Ital. Rep.* iv. 85 The whole monetary system of Europe was . . abandoned to the depredations of sovereigns, who continually varied the title and weight of coins. **1853** HUMPHREYS *Coin Coll. Man.* vi. 56 The effigy of Pan was adopted as a monetary type by the Panticapeans. **1874** GREEN *Short Hist.* i. §6. 53 Laws which regulated the monetary standard.

2. Pertaining to or concerned with money, pecuniary.

1860 RUSKIN *Mod. Paint.* V. IX. xi. 330 Monetary asceticism, consisting in the refusal of pleasure and knowledge for the sake of money. **1865** BRIGHT *Sp. Canada* 13 Mar. (1876) 67/1 Men who are deep in great monetary transactions. **1866** CRUMP *Banking* iii. 74 The person who introduces a customer to a bank is expected to have some knowledge . . of his friend's monetary affairs. **1872** J. H. GLADSTONE *Faraday* ii. 76 But it was not in monetary gifts alone that his kindness to the distressed was shown. **1936** J. M. KEYNES *Gen. Theory Employment* xv. 203 A monetary policy which strikes public opinion as being experimental in character or easily liable to change may fail in its objective. **1944**, etc. [see *International Monetary Fund* s.v. INTERNATIONAL *a.* 2]. **1951** R. FIRTH *Elements of Social Organization* iv. 142 Even where monetary rewards for labour are largely current, he has noted that work may be undertaken for other than money symbols. **1961** *Ann. Reg. 1960* 475 The measures ranged from the traditional restraints to a new and previously untried monetary instrument. **1973** *Times* 6 July 17/1 The 'Smithsonian' agreement, which President Nixon characterized . . as 'the most significant monetary agreement in the history of the world'.

moneth(e, obs. forms of MONTH.

monethyl (mɒˈnɛθɪl). *Chem.* Also **mono-**. [f. MON(O)- + ETHYL.] An organic compound in which one atom of hydrogen is replaced by one molecule of ethyl. Hence **moˈnethylic** *a.*

1868 *Fownes' Chem.* (ed. 10) 615 Monethylic borate $C_2H_5BO_2$. **1869** ROSCOE *Elem. Chem.* 339 Monœthyl [*sic*] phosphine. **1881** *Academy* 14 May 360/2 An ethylether malic acid isomeric with the monethyl malate of Desmondisir.

ˈ**monetism**. *nonce-wd.* [f. L. *monēta* (see MONEY) + -ISM.] The worship of money. So also ˈ**monetist**, one who practises monetism.

1707 J. STEVENS tr. *Quevedo's Com. Wks.* (1709) 488 For founding the new Sect of Monetism, changing the Name of Atheists into that of Money-mongers, or Monetists [translating Sp. *dinerismos* and *dineristas*].

monetite (ˈməʊnɪtaɪt). *Min.* [f. *Moneta*, name of a small island near Puerto Rico: see -ITE¹.] A hydrogen phosphate of calcium, $CaH(PO_4)$, occurring as translucent, pale yellowish white crystals.

1882 C. U. SHEPARD in *Amer. Jrnl. Sci.* CXXIII. 400 The Moneta mineral, which we call monetite from its locality, is accompanied by two other species. **1968** I. KOSTOV *Mineral.* 458 Monetite and stercorite are triclinic.

monetization (ˌmɒn-, ˌmʌnɪtaɪˈzeɪʃən). [f. next + -ATION. Cf. mod.F. *monétisation*.] The action of monetizing.

1864 in WEBSTER. **1890** G. B. SHAW *Fabian Ess. Socialism* 191 Monetization of silver, import duties.

monetize (ˈmɒn-, ˈmʌnɪtaɪz), *v.* [f. L. *monēt-a* MONEY + -IZE. Cf. F. *monétiser*.] *trans.* To give a standard value to (a metal) in the coinage of a country; to put into circulation as money.

1880 in WEBSTER, Suppl. **1903** *Speaker* 10 Oct. 52/1 He demonetised silver in Germany and monetised gold.

Moneto, obs. variant of MANITOU.

1773 *Hist. Brit. Domin. N. Amer.* XIII. xi. 241 They assert, there are two monetoes or spirits; that the one sends all the good things they have, and the other all the bad.

moneur, obs. form of MONEYER.

money (ˈmʌnɪ), *sb.* Pl. **moneys**. Forms: 3–6 **moneye**, 4–5 **monoie, -oye, moone**, 4–6 **monay(e, monei(e, mone(e, monye**, 4–8 **mony**, 5–7 **monny**, 6–7 **monie**, 4– **money**. [a. OF. *moneie*, *mon(n)oie* (mod.F. *monnaie*) = Pr., Sp. *moneda*, Pg. *moeda*, It. *moneta*:—L. *monēta* (?f. *monēre* to warn, remind): orig. the name of a goddess (in classical times regarded as identical with Juno), in whose temple at Rome money was coined, hence, a mint, money. Cf. MINT *sb.*¹

For the plural the irregular spelling *monies* is still not uncommonly met with, esp. in sense 4.]

1. a. Current coin; metal stamped in pieces of portable form as a medium of exchange and measure of value. ***piece of money***: see PIECE *sb.* 3 c.

c **1330** R. BRUNNE *Chron.* (1725) 238 Edward . . wille wite certeyn, who schent has his mone. Of clippers, of roungers, of suilk takes he questis. **1340** *Ayenb.* 26 Of guod metal hy makeþ ualse moneye. **1377** LANGL. *P. Pl.* B. xv. 343 Þe merke of þat mone is good, ac þe metal is fieble. **1611** BIBLE *1 Kings* xxi. 2, I will giue thee the worth of it in money. **1680** MORDEN *Geog. Rect., Asiat. Tartaria* (1685) 396 The Mony of this kingdom is of a good Alloy. **1711** ADDISON *Spect.* No. 3 ¶5 Behind the Throne was a prodigious Heap of Bags of Mony. **1859** GEO. ELIOT *A. Bede* ix, It's no use filling your pocket full of money if you've got a hole in the corner.

fig. **1651** HOBBES *Leviath.* I. iv. 15 Words are wise mens counters, they do but reckon by them: but they are the mony of fooles.

b. Applied occas. by extension to any objects, or any material, serving the same purposes as coin.

c **1400** MAUNDEV. (1839) xxii. 239 He [the great Khan] . . makethe no Money, but of Lether emprented, or of Papyre. **1553** EDEN *Treat. Newe Ind.* (Arb.) 24 The monie which they vse, is made of a certayne paper . . with ye kinges ymage printed theron. **1600** J. PORY tr. *Leo's Africa* Introd. 22 Salt is the principall thing which runneth currant for money throughout all the emperours dominions. **1807** ROBINSON *Archæol. Græca* II. xix. 177 In cases of emergency . . the Spartans were allowed the use of money made from the skins of beasts.

c. In mod. use commonly applied indifferently to coin and to such promissory documents representing coin (esp. government and bank notes) as are currently accepted as a medium of exchange. See PAPER MONEY.

1819 *Noble's Instr. Emigr. U.S.* 107 The best money to take to the United States, is either guineas or Spanish milled dollars; . . Bank of England notes will not do. **1864** *Chamb. Encycl.* VI. 529/2 No one hesitates in counting a £5 Bank of England note as money. **1880** BON. PRICE in *Fraser's Mag.* May 675 Only 3*l.* in each 100*l.* were cash—that is, coin and bank notes, true money. **1903** *Westm. Gaz.* 18 June 2/1 In international commerce the form of money most used is a bill of exchange, and a good bill is good money.

† **d.** ***black money*** (= med.L. *moneta nigra*), copper coinage; ? also, debased silver coin. ***white money***, standard silver coin. *Obs.*

[**1335** *Act 9 Edw. III*, stat 2, c. 1 §4 Que totes maneres de noire monoie, que courent ja communalment en notre roialme . . soient tote oultrement ostez.] **1423** *Rolls of Parlt.* IV. 256/2 For as muche as gret scarcite of Whit money is wyth inne this land, because that silver is bought. **1469** *Sc. Acts Jas. III* (1597) §40 That there be na Deniers of France,

..nor nane vther counterfaictes of black money, be tane in payment in the Realme, bot our soveraine Lords awin black money. **1567** HARMAN *Caveat* 42 He plucked oute viii. shyllinges in whyte money. **1607** MIDDLETON *Phœnix* I. vi, He had so much grace before he died to turn his white money into gold, a great ease to his executor. **1642** FULLER *Holy & Prof. St.* IV. v. 264 Receiving black money from cheatours, he payes them in good silver.

2. (With *pl.*) A particular coin or coinage. Also, a denomination of value representing a fraction or a multiple of the value of some coin; in full, ***money of account*** (see ACCOUNT *sb.* 1).

1426 LYDG. *De Guil. Pilgr.* 17614 Thys hand in frenshe.. Ys callyd 'Poitevyneresse', For yt forgeth.. A monye callyd Poytevyn. **1481** CAXTON *Myrr.* III. xiv. 165 The monoyes were establisshed first; for as moche as they had not of alle thinges necessarye to gydre. **1588** J. READ tr. *Arcæus' Compend. Meth.* 69, I made an orifice with the Trepan, to the greatnes of a siluer mony called a Roiall. **1617** MORYSON *Itin.* I. 285 Now I will set downe the divers moneys of Germany with the severall values of them. *c* **1630** MUN *Eng. Treas.* (1664) 4 He ought to know the Measures, Weights, and Monies of all forraign Countries. *a* **1637** B. JONSON *Discov. Consuetudo* etc. (1640), Custome is the most certaine Mistresse of Language, as the publicke stampe makes the current money. **1648** C. WALKER *Hist. Independ.* I. 169 Francis Allen a poor Goldsmith... In honour of whom Clipped moneys are now called (Allens). **1756** NUGENT *Gr. Tour, Germany* II. 62 At Cologne, the most remarkable money is the rixdollar. **1837** *Penny Cycl.* VIII. 328/1 Constantine I. introduced the milliarensis, worth somewhere about a shilling of our money. **1839** *Ibid.* XV. 322/1 The denominations.. of the different moneys current among the chief nations of antiquity. **1885** *Athenæum* 30 May 690/1 The reasons for these changes in coinage, the intentions of those who issued moneys.. are often almost unknown.

3. a. Coin considered in reference to its value or purchasing power; hence, property or possessions of any kind viewed as convertible into money or having value expressible in terms of money.

c **1290** *S. Eng. Leg.* I. 262/41 Non oþur Moneye, heo seide, ich ne habbe bote mi-self her. **1377** LANGL. *P. Pl.* B. XIII. 394 To marchaunden with monoye [*v.r.* moneie] and maken her eschaunges. *c* **1386** CHAUCER *Prol.* 705 Up-on a day he gat him more moneye Than that the person gat in monthes tweye. *c* **1430** LYDG. *London Lyckpeny* i, But for lack of mony I cold not spede. **1529** MORE *Suppl. Soulys* Wks. 325/2 Then were he very cruell in that he deliuereth them not without monei. **1539** BIBLE *1 Tim.* vi. 10 For couetousnes of money is the rote of all euyll. **1651** HOBBES *Leviath.* II. xxii. 122 Sometimes Iustice cannot be had without mony. **1718** LADY M. W. MONTAGU *Lett.* (1887) II. 237 'Tis his business to get money, and hers to spend it. **1753** HANWAY *Trav.* II. I. iii. 15 They have introduced the custom of giving money to servants. **1776** ADAM SMITH *W. N.* IV. i. ¶1 Wealth and money.. are, in common language, considered as in every respect synonymous. **1879** FROUDE *Cæsar* xviii. 301 He already owed half a million of money. **1890** *Murray's Mag.* June 764 He'll come into a lot of money some fine day.

b. with demonstrative or possessive adj., designating a sum applied to a particular purpose or in the possession of a particular person.

a **1300** *Cursor M.* 16475 Here i yeld yow yur mone, ges me a-gain mi war. *c* **1330** R. BRUNNE *Chron.* (1725) 308 Þat tyme no þing he wrouht, bot spendid his mone. **1463** *Bury Wills* (Camden) 27 This mony not to be delyuerid to noon of hem. **1590** SHAKS. *Com. Err.* IV. i. 63 The monie that you owe me for the Chaine. *c* **1645** [see FOOL *sb.*[1] 1 d]. **1684** BUNYAN *Pilgr.* II. (1862) 351 Then said one of them, I will pay you when I take my Mony. **1818** CRUISE *Digest* (ed. 2) I. 477 Notwithstanding the father paid the whole money. **1838** D. JERROLD *Men of Character* (1851) 320 The highway laconism of 'your money or your life!' **1891** KIPLING *Light that Failed* iii, Come back when your money's spent.

c. considered as a commodity in the market (for loan, etc.).

a **1687** PETTY *Pol. Arith.* vi. (1691) 100 It is certain that mony which payeth those Rents, and driveth on Trade, must have increased also. **1691** SIR D. NORTH *Disc. Trade* Pref. B 2, Money is a Merchandize, whereof there may be a glut, as well as a scarcity. **1776** ADAM SMITH *W. N.* IV. i, It is not any scarcity of gold and silver, but the difficulty which such people find in borrowing, and which their creditors find in getting payment, that occasions the general complaint of the scarcity of money. **1797** BURKE *Regic. Peace* iii. Sel. Wks. III. 208 The value of money must be judged, like every thing else, from it's rate at market. **1878** *Encycl. Brit.* XVI. 721/1 In mercantile phraseology the value of money means the interest charged for the use of loanable capital. Thus, when the market rate of interest is high money is said to be dear, when it is low money is regarded as cheap.

¶ **d.** ***a certain money*** (see CERTAIN *sb.* 5 b).

c **1380** *Antecrist* in Todd 3 *Treat. Wyclif* 149 To sett þereon her syngnet for a certeyne moneye. **1556** *Chron. Gr. Friars* (Camden) 70 [She] gave hare husbande a sartyne mony a yere dureynge hys lyffe.

e. Wages, salary; one's pay.

1887 PARISH & SHAW *Dict. Kentish Dial.* 103 He's getting good money, I reckon. **1916** G. B. SHAW *Pygmalion* II. 143 His proper trade's a navvy; and he works at it sometimes.. and earns good money at it. **1920** E. O'NEILL *Beyond the Horizon* II. i. 85 If that's the case, you can go to the devil... You'll get your money tomorrow when I get back from town. **1963** H. GARNER in R. Weaver *Canad. Short Stories* (1968) 2nd Ser. 45 Nobody really liked working for Malloy-Harrison, but the money was better than most places.

4. *pl.* Properly = 'sums of money', but often indistinguishable from the sing. (sense 3). Now chiefly in legal and quasi-legal parlance, or as an archaism.

1382 WYCLIF *2 Macc.* iii. 6 And tolde to hym the tresorie in Jerusalem for to be ful with moneys [Vulg. *pecuniis*] vnnoumbreable. **1625** BACON *Ess., Usury* (end), No Man will Lend his Moneyes farre off, nor put them into Vnknown Hands. **1632** LITHGOW *Trav.* IV. 140 [He] furnished him with great moneys, and other necessaries. **1734** tr. *Rollin's Anc. Hist.* XIX. v. (1827) VIII. 163 To make him a present of the monies arising from that sale. **1822** BYRON *Werner* II. ii, But to steal The moneys of a slumbering man! **1865** *Morn. Star* 3 Feb., A young woman, was charged.. with stealing from the person of Robert Tharston,.. 7*s.* 6*d.*, his moneys. **1866** CRUMP *Banking* v. 118 An agreement to pay the bill when certain monies were realised. **1871** R. ELLIS tr. *Catullus* xxix. 22 Is not all his act To swallow monies, empty purses heap on heap?

¶ From Shakspere onwards, the use of the pl. for the sing. has been commonly attributed to Jews, whose supposed pronunciation is sometimes ridiculed by the spelling 'monish'.

1596 SHAKS. *Merch. V.* I. iii. 117 You come to me, and you say, Shylocke, we would haue moneyes. **1794** CUMBERLAND *Jew* II. ii, *Sheva.* Why truly, monies is a goot thing. **1819** SCOTT *Ivanhoe* xi, 'O', said the Jew, 'you are come to pay moneys... And from whom dost thou bring it?'

5. With defining word, forming specific phrases, as **big money**: see BIG *a.* B. 2; † **chief money** = capital; **dirty money**: see DIRTY *a.* 6 b; **even money**, equal betting, also *attrib.*; † **present**, † **real money** = READY MONEY; † **single, small money**, small change; † **Spanish money** *slang* (see quot. 1700).

For *hard*, *soft money* see HARD *a.* 2, SOFT *a.* Freq. with prefixed sb., denoting the reason or purpose for which money is expended, as *beer-money* (BEER *sb.*[1] 4), BLOOD-MONEY, *card-money* (CARD *sb.*[2] 14), *conscience-money* (CONSCIENCE 16 c), †COPY-MONEY, *gate-money* (GATE *sb.*[1] 13), HUSH-MONEY, POCKET-MONEY, SMART-MONEY, etc.

a **1380** *St. Bernard* 738 in Horstm. *Altengl. Leg.* (1878) 53 3if i take þe þe chef moneye [L. *capitale*] Wiþ to pleye. **1553** *Stanford Churchw. Acc.* in *Antiquary* XVII. 117 It. of ye parisheoners for crowche monay or paschull monay iiijs. vijd. **1590** SHAKS. *Com. Err.* IV. i. 34, I am not furnish'd with the present monie. **1591** GREENE *2nd Pt. Conny-c.* (1592) D 2, [There] came another and bought a knife and should haue single money again. **1611** DONNE *Anat. World, 1st Anniv.* 234 And that rich Indie which doth gold interre, Is but as single money coyn'd from her. **1685** PETTY *Last Will* p. v, Which.. raised me an estate of about 13000*l.* in ready and real money. *a* **1700** B. E. *Dict. Cant. Crew*, *Spanish-money*, fair Words and Compliments. **1722** DE FOE *Plague* (1884) 106 Small Money to make up any odd Sum. **1903** *Daily News* 8 Aug. 4/5 If number five wins the bank collects all the even-money bets.

6. Phrases, etc.

a. Proverbs. ***money makes the mare*** (or †*horse*) ***to go***; ***money is the sinews*** (or †*nerves*) ***of war*** (cf. Cicero *Phil.* v. ii. 5 'nervos belli, pecuniam infinitam'); ***time is money***; etc.

c **1450** *Cov. Myst.* (Shaks. Soc.) 268 In old termys I have herde seyde That mony makyth Schapman. **1573** J. SANDFORD *Hours Recreat.* (1576) 213 Money makes the horsse to goe. **1605** BACON *Adv. Learn.* II. xxiii. §38 But that opinion I may condemne with like reason as Macchiauell doth that other: that monies were the sinews of the warres. **1611** BIBLE *I Tim.* vi. 10 The loue of money is the root of all euill. **1638** [see NERVE *sb.* 2]. *c* **1645** [see FOOL *sb.*[1] 1 d]. **1660** T. M. *C. Walker's Hist. Independ.* IV. 65 The Army could not subsist without money (which is the Nerve of War). **1659, 1698** [see MARE[1] 1 b]. **1681** A. BEHN *Rover* II. III. i. 43 Money speaks sense in a Language all Nations understand. **1748** B. FRANKLIN *Advice to Young Tradesman* in *Writings* (1905) II. 371 Remember that *time* is money. **1792** WOLCOT (P. Pindar) *More Money, Odes to Mr. Pitt* iv, 'Tis money makes the old mare trot. **1845** C. LEVER *Let.* in L. Stevenson *Dr. Quicksilver* (1939) ix. 149 You have paid your money, and you may take your choice. **1846** *Punch* 3 Jan. 17 (*caption*) You pays your money, and you takes your choice. **1853** T. T. LYNCH *Lect. Self Improvement* v. 113 Money is power—power for bread and power for tinsel. **1861** TRAFFORD *City & Suburb* xiv, Money makes money, it is said. **1886** BARING-GOULD *Court Royal* xliii, Time was money to Mr. Cheek. He did not allow the grass to grow under his feet. **1898** G. B. SHAW *Arms & Man* II. 57 A twenty leva bill! Sergius gave me that, out of pure swagger. A fool and his money are soon parted. **1903** *Sat. Even. Post* 5 Sept. 12/1 When money talks it often merely remarks 'Good-by'. **1905** 'O. HENRY' in *N.Y. World Mag.* 12 Nov. 8/1 Money talks. But you may think that the conversation of a little old ten-dollar bill in New York would be nothing more than a whisper. **1927** E. O'NEILL *Marco Millions* I. ii. 36 He'll have time enough for that, but with us time is money. *Ibid.* iii. 44 Money isn't everything, not always. **1930** G. B. MEANS *Strange Death of President Harding* IV. 72 One can do nothing—be nothing, without money, not even in the White House. Money is power. **1952** W. G. HARDY *Unfulfilled* 199 Money isn't everything. **1956** A. WILSON *Anglo-Saxon Attitudes* II. ii. 277 Yeah, he's on the Market... You know the sort of stuff. Money talks and so on. **1965** *Times* 14 July 8/4 In the Government today were known supporters of C.N.D. Why? Because the Prime Minister put them there. Why? Because he shared their views? Because it was expedient to do so? Because he was practising some duplicity? Why? 'You pays your money and you takes your choice.'

b. ***for money***: in return or exchange for money. ***for*** or ***at the money***: at the price paid. ***for love or money***: see LOVE *sb.*[1] 7 c. (***so and so***) ***for my money***, a colloq. expression of approbation = '..is what I desire or like', '..is my choice', 'give me..'; ***for my money***: also = in my opinion. † ***to take eggs for*** (***one's***) ***money***: see EGG *sb.* 4. ***to have a run for one's money***: see RUN *sb.*[1] 1 d.

c **1330** R. BRUNNE *Chron.* (1725) 246 Þei wer out of þe tour delyuerd for mone. *c* **1380** WYCLIF *Wks.* (1880) 241 Whanne prelatis.. fauouren hem in synne for moneye. **1513** BRADSHAW *St. Werburge* I. 1677 There was habundaunce Of all-maner pleasures to be had for monye. **1549** [see GO *v.* 24 b]. **1566** E. H. tr. *Erasmus's Diuersoria* sig. B2[v] This behauiour doth well beseme Frenchmen peraduenture, how be it the fashions of Duche lande shall go for my monye when all is done. **1589** [see GO *v.* 24 b]. **1599** SHAKS. *Much Ado* II. iii. 63 Well, a horne for my money when all's done. **1616** W. HAUGHTON (*title*) English-Men for my Money. **1667** DRYDEN & DK. NEWCASTLE *Sir M. Mar-All* v. i, They may talk what they will of Oxford for an university, but Cambridge for my money. **1700** [see GIVE *v.* 3 c]. *a* **1734** NORTH *Life Dudley North* (1744) 181 It is certain the Pamphlet is.. utterly sunk, and a Copy not to be had for Money. **1802-12** BENTHAM *Ration. Judic. Evid.* (1827) IV. 93 The higher you pay for your dispatch, the more delay you have for your money. **1840** *Spirit of Times* 21 Nov. 447/3 Give me the gall, I say, that *has an eye for dirt*, for she is the gall for my money. **1842** S. LOVER *Handy Andy* x, 'You're right', said Dick, 'Murphy is the very man for our money'. **1882** *Daily Tel.* 30 Jan., Khamseen, who cost 570 guineas at Mr. Vyner's sale, is reckoned a bargain.. at the money. **1932** D. L. SAYERS *Have his Carcase* xi. 138 Peter's the man for my money. He won't see a hardworking man lose a job for want of a good news story. **1943** *N.Y. Times* 9 May II. 5/5 Glenn was, and for my money is still tops. **1954** J. SYMONS *Narrowing Circle* xiv. 59 For my money, Marian was responsible.. for the trouble we'd had. **1969** D. CLARK *Death after Evensong* IV. 97, I wouldn't mind not finding who did Parseloe in. For my money he deserved it.

c. ***to make money***: to acquire or earn money; also, to get money by the sale *of*, make a profit *out of*. ***to coin money***: to acquire wealth rapidly (see COIN *v.*[1] 1 c). ***to cost money***: see COST *v.* 1 d.

1457 *Paston Lett.* I. 416 He.. resseyvyth but chaffr and waare for hys cornys and wollys, &c. and then most abyde along day to make money. **1472-1632** [see MAKE *v.* 29]. **1828** W. McDOWALL *Poems Galloway Dial.* 25 When Buonaparte in splendour shone, 'Twas then I made the money. **1901** *Spectator* 20 July 82/1 The War Office ought not to make money out of, any more than they should subsidise, the rifle clubs.

d. (***it is***) ***everybody's*** or ***every man's money***: in early use, what everybody prefers to buy; also, what everybody can afford to buy; now (mainly in negative context) what everybody would find worth its price. (Also in analogous phrases: see quots. 1625, 1712, 1851.) ***to be*** (***good, bad***, etc.) ***money***: to be a (good or bad) investment, to 'pay'. ***there is money in*** (***something***): money can be made out of it.

1601 HOLLAND *Pliny* I. 381 The ointment of Saffron confected at Soli in Cilicia, imported for a good while and caried the praise alone: but soone after that of Rhodes was every mans money. **1625** BACON *Ess., Riches*, When a Mans Stocke is come to that, that he can expect the Prime of Markets, and ouercome those Bargaines, which for their greatnesse are few Mens Money. **1653** GATAKER *Vind. Annot. Jer.* 29 The whole work.. consists of two great volumes, and the price consequently correspondent, not every mans money, and in fewer hands therefore. **1712** ADDISON *Spect.* No. 482 ¶1 Such a Discourse is of general Use, and every married Man's Money. **1851** MAYHEW *Lond. Lab.* I. 91/1, I sell dry fruit, sir, in February and March, because I must be doing something, and green fruit's not my money then. *Ibid.* 139/1 Mignonette's everybody's money. Dahlias didn't go off so well. *Ibid.* (1861) III. 103, I reckon Astley's is the worst money for any man. *Ibid.* 130 Richardson's used.. to be more money, but now it's as bad as the rest of 'em. **1887** *Pall Mall G.* 1 Mar. 14/1 There is undoubtedly money in guns.

e. ***money burns*** (***a hole***) (***in***) ***one's pocket*** (or †***purse***) (and similar phrases): one is impatient to spend one's money. Cf. BURN *v.*[1] 16.

1529 MORE *Dyaloge of Ymagys* II. x. f.lxi, Hauyng a lytell wanton money whyche hym thought brennyd out the botom of hys purs. **1702** FARQUHAR *Inconstant* v. iii. 77 My time lyes heavy on my hands, and my Money burns in my Pocket. **1875** S. SMILES *Thrift* viii. 125 A man who has more money about him than he requires.. is tempted to spend it... It is apt to 'burn a hole in his pocket'. **1943** M. LASSWELL *Suds in your Eye* xiv. 103 Her money was burning a hole in her pocket. **1958** L. DURRELL *Balthazar* xiii. 227 I've scraped a dowry together over the years... The money burns my pocket. **1972** A. S. NEILL *Neill! Neill! Orange Peel!* II. 238 Today, I don't see the young.. saving money. It burns a hole in their pockets.

f. ***your money or your life***: a formula used by highwaymen, etc., in threatening to kill a person if he does not hand over money.

1841 F. A. BURNEY *Jrnl.* 23 Feb. (1926) 321 Mr. Dixon attempted expostulation, upon which the Highwayman drew out a Pistol,.. exclaiming, with an oath, 'Your money or your life!' **1848** J. A. FROUDE *Let.* 16 May in W. H. Dunn *Froude* (1961) I. 118 Nothing will open rich John Bull's understanding but a hand at his throat and 'Your money or your life'. **1864** J. PAYN *Lost Sir Massingberd* II. xiii. 212 A pistol, was protruded into the carriage. 'Your money or your life!..', said a rough voice.

g. ***in the money***: among the prize-winners in a competition, show, or the like; amply or sufficiently supplied with money; rich.

1902 'D. DIX' *Fables of Elite* 48 It is True that when the Spurt is over I am generally in the Money. **1928** *Morning Post* 20 Oct. 6/1 One of them is to-day a full champion, the other three all winners, and 'in the money', as the fanciers say, whenever shown. **1945** G. CASEY in *Coast to Coast 1944* 3 Shift her round like you was doin' yesterday and you'll be in the money. **1946** L. BROMFIELD *World we live In* 325 Being in the money at the moment, I said that of course I'd lend her any reasonable amount. **1969** T. PARKER *Twisting Lane* 200 She said we could stay there rent free until I was in the money again.

h. ***money for jam***, ***money for old rope*** (and similar phrases): a profitable return for little or no trouble; a very easy job; someone or something easy to profit from, beat, etc.

1919 *Athenæum* 8 Aug. 727/2 The great use of jam in the Army..originated a number of phrases, such as 'money for jam' (money for nothing). **1927** T. E. Lawrence *Let.* 22 Sept. (1938) 540 Recently I made nearly ten pounds out of reviewing eleven books. Money for jam, as the airman says. **1936** J. Curtis *Gilt Kid* xiii. 134 He would spin her a fanny about the marriage laws, tie the poor kid up. It ought to be money for old rope. **1942** E. Waugh *Put out More Flags* 150 At the moment there were no mortars and he was given instead a light and easily manageable counterfeit of wood which was slung on the back of his haversack, relieving him of a rifle. At present it was money for old rope. **1958** 'A. Gilbert' *Death against Clock* iv. 47 If he saw the wallet it must have seemed money for jam. **1966** 'L. Lane' *ABZ of Scouse* 70 *Money fer owd rope*, something for nothing. Other similar phrases are *money fer dirt*; *money fer raggety kecks*; *money fer jam*, etc., etc. **1973** A. Hunter *Gently French* iii. 24 Wasn't no risk, it was money for jam. **1974** N. Bentley *Inside Information* v. 52 I'll advance you another two hundred. Christ, that's money for old rope.

i. ***not everybody's money***: not to everybody's liking.

1923 J. Manchon *Le Slang* 196 *You ain't everybody's money*, vous ne pouvez pas plaire à tout le monde. **1933** 'G. Orwell' *Let.* c 10 Dec. in *Coll. Ess.* (1968) I. 128 As to the actual writing in *Ulysses*, it isn't everybody's money, but personally I think it is superb in places.

j. ***to put one's money on***: to bet on (a horse, etc.); also *fig.*, to favour or depend on; to expect the success of.

1931 T. R. G. Lyell *Slang, Phrase & Idiom* 528 If you've got any sense, you'll put your money on that horse I told you of. **1963** *Listener* 21 Feb. 341/3 She does not put all her money on love. **1969** *Ibid.* 8 May 636/1 A century hence, prophesied one critic, it would be only 'the careless glance of curiosity, or the student's all-ranging eye' that would turn upon the Little Nells and Paul Dombeys; he put his money instead on Dickens's humour.

k. ***to put*** (or ***get***) ***one's money where one's mouth is***: to produce, bet, or pay out money to support one's statements or opinions. orig. *N. Amer.*

1942 Z. N. Hurston in A. Dundes *Mother Wit* (1973) 224/1 'Put your money where your mouth is!' he challenged. **1951** *Amer. Speech* XXVI. 99/1 *Get your money where your mouth is*, a phrase [in poker] which means, 'put up or shut up'. **1970** *Globe & Mail* (Toronto) 26 Sept. 7/3 Eventually it got to the point when he suggested that maybe I was the guy who should take it on. Sort of put your money where your mouth is. **1975** A. Price *Our Man in Camelot* v. 95 The squadron betting book the barman keeps..for guys who are ready to put their money where their mouth is.

l. ***to have money to burn***: see burn *v.*[1] 8 d.

7. *attrib.* and *Comb.* **a.** simple attrib., as ***money-affair***, ***-bond***, ***-chest***, †***-codger*** (= miser), ***-coffer***, ***-controversy***, ***-debt***, ***-draught***, ***-drawer***, ***-economy***, ***-fear***, ***-fine***, ***-flow***, ***-god***, ***-hunger***, ***-lust***, ***-market***, †***-means***, †***-miser***, ***-mulct***, ***-payment***, ***-price***, ***-purse***, ***-rent***, †***-sack***, ***-safe***, ***-sense***, ***-slave***, ***-standard***, ***-supply***, ***-system***, ***-till***, ***-token***, ***-transaction***, ***-valuation***, ***-value***, ***-wages***.

1702 Steele *Funeral* ii. i, Your Lordship will send for Him, when you are at Leisure to look upon *Money-affairs. **1837** Carlyle *Fr. Rev.* I. iii. viii, Rich if Court-titles and *Money-bonds can enrich him. **1836** Pusey in Liddon *Life* (1893) I. xvii. 393 To put a canker into the *money-chests of the Protestant landlords. **1818** *Blackw. Mag.* III. 402 Musty, frousy, stingy, *money-codger. **1525–6** *Rec. St. Mary at Hill* 331 For..mendyng of the lock of the *money cofur within the plate chest. **1597** Beard *Theatre God's Judgem.* (1612) 490 If there were anie *money-controuersies to be decided. **1711** M. Henry *Forgiv. Sin* Wks. 1853 II. 319/2 Our Saviour in his parables alludes to *money-debts. **1890** Sir G. F. Duckett *Visit. Eng. Cluniac Found.* 31 He found the house with a money-debt of 935. marks. **1758** *M. P.'s Let. on Navy* 19 These assigned Tickets would be equal to *Money-draughts upon any responsible Banker. **1880** W. Newton *Serm. for Boys & Girls* (1881) 372 She had lost the key of her *money-drawer. **1942** L. B. Namier *Conflicts* 50 It is not easy to translate into exact figures this barter business, which is..contrasted with the *money-economy and transactions of the Western Powers. **1962** H. R. Loyn *Anglo-Saxon Eng.* iv. 159 The earliest law-codes give evidence..of the importance of a money-economy. **1927** *Money-fear [see *money-lust* below]. **1875** Stubbs *Const. Hist.* I. iii. 47 Such are the proportions of the wer-gild and the *money-fines. **1953** C. F. Hockett in Saporta & Bastian *Psycholinguistics* (1961) 64/1 *Money-flow (at least in one direction) is *income*. **1590** Spenser *F. Q.* ii. vii. 39 'Suffise it then, thou *Money God,' (quoth hee) 'That all thine ydle offers I refuse'. **1891** Stevenson & Osbourne *Wrecker* (1892) vii. 120 Far from the *money-hunger of the West. **1965** *Times Lit. Suppl.* 25 Nov. 1047 (Advt.), A young manhood of scheming and money-hunger in Chicago. **1927** D. H. Lawrence *Let.* 18 Dec. (1962) II. 1027 They must first overthrow in themselves the money-fear and *money-lust. **1930** E. Pound *XXX Cantos* xiv. 61 The perverts, who have set money-lust Before the pleasures of the senses. **1600–12** Rowlands *Four Knaves* (Percy Soc.) 63 A knight.. Intreates his father..Some *mony-means to help him he would make. **1586** A. Day *Eng. Secretary* i. (1625) 45 A wretched ending of such *money-misers. **1650** Trapp *Comm. Exod.* xx. 17 Violence offered to a woman..if shee were not quick, it was onely a *monie-mulct. **1799** *Hull Advertiser* 15 June 1/2 The house is..subject to a *money payment in lieu of tithes. **1776** Adam Smith *W. N.* i. v. (1869) I. 49 Six shillings and eight pence..in the time of Edward I, I consider as the same *money-price with a pound sterling in the present time. **1861** Maine *Anc. Law* v. 157 The husband..pays a money-price to her relations for the tutelage which they surrender to him. c **1821** J. W. Masters in *Eng. Dial. Dict.* (1903) IV. 149 2 He brought our Jack a leather cap An' Sal a *money-puss. **1878** B. F. Taylor *Between Gates* 273 We stood under fig-trees hung with money-purses filled with seeds. **1966** A. R. Scammell *My Newfoundland* 33, I kept mine [sc. a dollar bill] for weeks in my little money-purse (we never called them purses). **1792** A. Young *Trav. France* I. iv. 340 Much the greater part of the lands of France are not let at a *money-rent, but at one-half or one-third produce. **1848** Mill *Pol. Econ.* I. ii. viii. 366 An attempt to introduce..a system of money rents and capitalist farmers. **1603** Davies *Microcosm.* 153 The *Money-Sacke best kept the Land from sack. **1799** *Hull Advertiser* 6 Oct. 3/3 Charged..with having broken open..the *money-safe within the said dwelling-house. **1865** D. G. Rossetti *Let.* 14 Sept. (1965) II. 571 This might have been..executed..more profitably in a *money-sense than what I did do. **1963** *Times Lit. Suppl.* 25 Jan. 62/3 Their hair-dressing or their money-sense. **1929** D. H. Lawrence *Pansies* 116 He can't help being a slave, a wage-slave, A *money-slave. **1771** Raper in *Phil. Trans.* LXI. 468, I discovered the Eginean Talent to have been the *money-standard of Macedon. **1878** F. A. Walker *Money* iv. 76 (*heading*) The importance of the *money supply. **1975** *Times* 18 June 29/7 For this year a 15 per cent rise in the money supply and a 12½ per cent rise in gnp..would be the right interim targets. **1929** D. H. Lawrence *Pansies* 109 Why don't we do something about the *money system? **1857** *Quinland* I. ii. ii. 289 If the stars were extinguished, it would not disturb him, unless his *money-till were upset. **1937** C. M. Arensberg *Irish Countryman* 175 His or her remittances would eventually reach his money-till. **1875** Jowett *Plato* (ed. 2) III. 242 They will need a market-place, and a *money-token for purposes of exchange. **1858** Ld. St. Leonards *Handy-Bk. Prop. Law* xviii. 133 Looking at this as a simple *money transaction. **1848** Mill *Pol. Econ.*, Prel. Remarks, I. 5 He accepted these [goods] at a *money valuation. **1870** Emerson *Soc. & Solit.*, *Eloquence* Wks. (Bohn) III. 32 In old countries, a high *money-value is set on the service of men who have achieved a personal distinction. **1817** Malthus *Popul.* (ed. 5) I. 31 An increased number of labourers receiving the same *money-wages will necessarily, by their competition, increase the money price of corn.

b. objective and objective genitive, as ***money-borrower***, ***-catcher***, ***-clipper***, ***-coiner***, ***-getter***, ***-grabber***, ***-hoarder***, ***-loser***, ***-lover***, ***-raiser***, ***-spender***, ***-teller***, †***-thirster***; ***money-breeding***, ***-catching***, ***-changing***, ***-clipping***, ***-earning***, ***-getting***, ***-grabbing***, ***-grasping***, ***-losing***, ***-loving***, ***-meditating***, ***-raising***, ***-saving***, ***-spending***, ***-sucking*** vbl. sbs. and ppl. adjs.; ***money-conscious***, ***-directed*** adjs.; **c.** advb. and instrumental, as ***money-bloated***, ***-distressed***, ***-mad***, ***-minded***, ***-mouthed***, †***spelled*** (= spellbound) adjs.

a **1845** Syd. Smith *Ballot* Wks. 1859 II. 306/1 The *money-bloated blockhead. **1766** Goldsm. *Vic. W.* iii, Though he was a *money-borrower. **1796** Mrs. M. Robinson *Angelina* I. 71 The blustering,..*money-breeding savage, her father. **1702** C. Mather *Magn. Chr.* vii. 33 The Disciples of this *Money-catcher became so Exceeding Fierce. **1841** Emerson *Lect., Man the Reformer* Wks. (Bohn) II. 236 The most bronzed and sharpened money-catcher. **1737** (*title*) The Pleasant Art of *Money-Catching. **1938** G. Greene *Nineteen Stories* (1947) 76 Mr. Calloway sat on his usual seat staring out over the *money-changing booths at the United States. **1759** B. Martin *Nat. Hist. Eng.* I. *Somerset* 68 A notorious shelter for Robbers and *Money-clippers. **1563–87** Foxe *A. & M.* (1596) 311/1 About which time also,..Iewes for *monie clipping were put to execution. **1715** Leoni *Palladio's Archit.* (1742) II. 78 The *Mensarii* had the inspection over *Money-Coiners, and Bankers. **1933** *Money-conscious [see conscious *a.* 12]. **1963** *Times* 1 May 15/4 The parties being money-conscious to the highest degree. **1970** T. Hilton *Pre-Raphaelites* vi. 171 The destructiveness of capitalist society, its callous and *money-directed disregard of culture. **1852** Thackeray *Esmond* i. xiv, Few fond women feel *money-distressed. **1912** J. London *Let.* 7 Sept. (1966) 364 My long stuff is pretty good at *money-earning. **1813** L. Hunt in *Examiner* 26 Apr. 257/2 An assembly of jobbers and *money-getters. **1653** Walton *Angler* i. 5 *Money-getting men. **1836** J. H. Newman *Par. Serm.* (ed. 2) II. xxviii. 395 A life of money-getting is a life of care. **1875** Jowett *Plato* (ed. 2) I. 190 Socrates makes a playful allusion to his money-getting habits. **1903** *Eng. Dial. Dict.* s.v., He's a regular *money grabber. **1933** *Times Lit. Suppl.* 27 Apr. 283/3 A money-grabber, notorious in a money-grabbing age. **1920** D. H. Lawrence *Touch & Go* 9 We say it is a mere material struggle, a *money-grabbing affair. **1789** Wolcot (P. Pindar) *Expost. Odes* iii, Perdition catch the *money-grasping wretch. **1643** Trapp *Comm. Gen.* xxiii. 16 It may well be said of *money-hoarders, they have no quick-silver, no currant money. **1795** Ld. Auckland *Corr.* (1862) III. 301 The *money-holders know..that the whole continental system is involved in calamity. **1928** *Weekly Dispatch* 6 May 15 About 30 [musical comedies] prove to be *money-losers. **1963** E. Humphreys *Gift* ii. iv. 239 If a reputation for being a money-loser had reached as far as Barrot's ears, there was very little hope of him ever making a film again. **1870** J. K. Medbery *Men & Myst. Wall St.* 200 It is the greatest money-making and *money-losing spot on the globe. **1960** *Farmer & Stockbreeder* 16 Feb. 87/2 All your life you have heard that farming is a money-losing proposition. **1832** Mrs. Grant *Mem.* (1844) III. 214 He is no *money-lover, and is kind-hearted. **1703** Rowe *Fair Penit.* i. i. 54 Sour, unrelenting, *Mony-loving Villains. **1768** *Woman of Honor* III. 219 That *money-mad avarice. **1929** D. H. Lawrence *Pansies* 79 Fear of my money-mad fellow-men. **1965** G. Jackson *Let.* 16 Mar. in *Soledad Brother* (1971) 69 The shocks and strains of this money-mad society are enough to ruin the purest of minds. **1974** A. Ross *Bradford Business* 169 Money-mad property developers. **1749** Fielding *Tom Jones* xi. ix, Not so travels the *money-meditating tradesman. **1588** W. Kempe *Educ. Children* sig. C3 One of these *money minded parents. **1957** *Times Lit. Suppl.* 20 Dec. 769/4 The insistence of the more money-minded directors on its premature exploration. **1604** Pricket *Honors Fame* (1881) 4 Some golden *mony mouthed eloquence, that vseth a detractors Oratory. **1909** *Westm. Gaz.* 11 Aug. 1/3 This remarkable man began his career as a *money-raiser fifteen years ago with an £8,000 collection. **1955** W. Dean in H. Van Thal *Fanfare for E. Newman* v. 61 *Don Giovanni* in Trianon's version and Nicolai's *Merry Wives of Windsor* had to be put on as money-raisers. **1960** *Farmer & Stockbreeder* 29 Mar. 105/3 The huge success of *money-raising efforts. **1826** E. Irving *Babylon* I. iv. 311 Legislation upon any principle but that of money-making, or *money-saving, hath gone to sleep. **1615** T. Adams *White Devil* 42 A mercenary tongue and a *money-spel'd conscience. **1920** *Edin. Rev.* July 163 Meleager was always a *money spender rather than a money maker. **1900** J. London *Let.* 1 Mar. (1966) 97 The habit of *money spending. **1911** H. Granville Barker *Madras House* iii. 91 The Middle Class Women of England form one of the greatest Money Spending Machines the world has ever seen. **1921** Galsworthy *To Let* ii. v. 162 A lot of slow-fly *money-sucking officials. **1594** R. Ashley tr. *Loys le Roy* 29 b, *Money-tellers, and changers. **1651** French *Distill.* Pref. *3 b, Did you never heare of a vapouring fellow..that ..was..caught aside by *money-thirsters?

8. Special combinations: **money-back** *a.*, designating a system, agreement, etc., whereby a customer will be refunded the money he pays, if he is not satisfied with the goods or service provided; †**money-bank** = bank *sb.*[3] 2 or 7; so †**money-banker**; †**money-batterer**, a clipper or sweater of coin; †**money-bawd**, derisive name for a userer; **money-belt** orig. *U.S.*, a belt designed for carrying money; **money-bill**, a bill in Parliament for granting supplies; **money-broker**, a money-dealer; **money bug** *U.S. slang*, a person having great wealth or financial power; **money centre** *U.S.*, a place of pre-eminent importance in the financial affairs of a region or country; *spec.* New York; **money-clause**, a clause (in a Parliamentary bill) for granting supplies; **money-column**, (*a*) a portion of an account-book page or the like, marked off by vertically ruled lines for the reception of figures denoting sums of money; (*b*) the column of a newspaper devoted to the money-market; **money-cowrie** = cowrie 1 a; **money crop** *U.S.*, a crop that is grown mainly for selling and not for the grower's consumption; = *cash-crop*; **money-dealer**, one who deals in money in the way of exchange, banking, lending, etc.; so **money-dealing** *vbl. sb.*; †**money-dropper**, a sharper who drops a piece of money and then pretends to have found it, in order to obtain the confidence of his intended dupe; **money-flower**, the plant Honesty, *Lunaria biennis*; †**money-gentleman**, a 'money-man' (see below) of good position; **money-gold** *rare*, gold coin; **money illusion** (orig. *U.S.*), the illusion that money has a fixed value in terms of its purchasing power; **money-jobber**, a dealer in money or coin; so **money-jobbing** *vbl. sb.*; **money king** *U.S.*, a magnate in finance; a person of great wealth; **money-letter**, a letter containing money; **money-man**, a financier; also (*nonce-use*) one who desires money; **money market**, (*a*) the sphere of operation of the dealers in loans, stocks and shares, etc.; (*b*) a place in which the financial activity of a region is centred; †**money-master**, one who possesses large funds with which he does business, a capitalist; †**money-merchant**, a trader in money, money-dealer; **money-order**, an order for payment of a specified sum, issued at one post-office and payable at another (in British official use restricted to what is popularly called a *post-office order*, in which the name of the payee does not appear on the order, but is transmitted from the issuing to the paying office in a 'letter of advice'; thus distinguished from the *postal order*); **money-player**, (*a*) *U.S.*, a type of gambler (see quot. 1935); (*b*) a professional, as opposed to an amateur; **money-pot**, an earthenware money-box from which coins can be taken only by breaking the vessel; **money-power**, (*a*) the power to coin money, regulate its use, etc.; (*b*) the power exercised by money or by wealthy people, firms, etc.; **money-quake**, a financial smash of seismic magnitude; †**money-scrivener**, one whose business it is to raise loans, put money out at interest, etc., on behalf of his clients (see scrivener); **money-shark** orig. *U.S.*, an avaricious money-dealer; **money shop**, a shop where money can be obtained; *spec.* an establishment which performs more conveniently many of the functions of a bank, and specializes in arranging loans; **money-spider** = next (*a*); also, a spider of the genus *Salticus*; **money-spinner**, (*a*) a small spider, *Aranea scenica*, supposed to bring good luck in money or other matters to the person over whom it crawls; (*b*) one who makes great profits by speculation or usury; also, a person who, or thing which, makes a lot of money;

something that is very profitable; hence **money-spinning** *vbl. sb.* and *ppl. a.*; **money-taker**, † (*a*) one who takes bribes; (*b*) one who is appointed to receive payments of money, *esp.* one who is set at the entrance of a place of entertainment to receive the money for admission.

1922 *Weekly Dispatch* 12 Nov. 4 (Advt.), All our business is conducted on the '*Moneyback' principle; that is to say, if you are not perfectly satisfied with your purchase return it to us within seven days and we will refund your money in full by return of post. 1955 *Radio Times* 22 Apr. 2/3 Sisco paints are sold on a 'money back' guarantee. 1972 *Farm & Country* 19 Dec. 13/3 We are certain that you will be satisfied and offer a money back guarantee. *a*1628 F. GREVIL *Sidney* (1652) 230 That provident Lady..made his credit swell through all the *money-banks of Europe. 1677 YARRANTON *Eng. Improv.* 18 All persons that have designs to get considerable Sums of Moneys into their hands for intended designs, or hazardous adventures, apply themselves to the *Money-Bankers. *c*1515 *Cocke Lorell's B.* (Percy Soc.) 11 Players, purse cutters, *money baterers, Golde washers. 1626 B. JONSON *Staple of N.* 2nd Intermeane, Old Couetousnesse,..the *Money-bawd, who is a flesh-bawd too, they say. 1846 *St. Louis* (Missouri) *Reveille* 9 Sept. 3/2 The stock consists, in part, of Shirts, Collars,..*Money Belts. 1923 *Outward Bound* Mar. 408/2 Among cowboys..one might..leave one's money-belt full of gold and notes beside the fire. 1958 P. KEMP *No Colours or Crest* viii. 174, I had a hundred gold sovereigns in my money belt. *a*1715 BURNET *Own Time* III. (1724) I. 439 The House of Commons gave a *money bill for this. 1827 HALLAM *Const. Hist.* (1876) III. xiii. 27 The long agitated question of the right of the lords to make alterations in money-bills. 1616 B. JONSON in *Browne's Past.* II. To Author, Or, like our *Money-Brokers, take vp names On credit, and are cossen'd. 1833 J. HOLLAND *Manuf. Metal* II. v. 113 Mr. Rothschild, the eminent capitalist and money-broker. 1898 *People* 20 Mar. 4/4 The happiness or the misery of 3 millions of people wholly dependent on the whims and caprices of, say, half a dozen '*money bugs', as they are called in the States. 1922 *Public Opinion* 11 Aug. 132/2 The profiteering class, money bugs as the Americans call them. 1838 D. D. BARNARD *Speeches & Rep.* 36 Composed of twenty-six local sovereignties, of all which New-York is the *money centre, as London is the money centre of half the world. 1900 *Congress. Rec.* 17 Feb. 1897/2 Gilt-edged paper can be placed in the money-centers at a small per cent. 1844 LD. BROUGHAM *Brit. Const.* xvii. (1862) 266 The assent of the Lords to a *money-clause is just as necessary as to any other part of a Bill. 1727-51 CHAMBERS *Cycl.* s.v. *Book-keeping*, They may keep the debt and credit both on one side, by double *money-columns. 1861 *Chamb. Encycl.* II. 227/2 The first money-column on each page is for the discount, and the second for the cash. 1906 *Daily Chron.* 23 May 6/4 A keen eye intent on the money-column [of a newspaper]. 1839 SOWERBY *Conch. Man.* 65 *Money Cowry, *Cypræa Moneta*. 1881 *Harper's Mag.* Oct. 723/1 Cotton is the *money crop. 1904 T. WATSON *Bethany* 5 They never failed to make it their object to produce on the farm the necessary supplies, tobacco or cotton being merely the surplus crop, the money crop. 1974 S. MARCUS *Minding the Store* (1975) xii. 243 Until about 1932, Texas had essentially an agriculturally based economy. By 1905 cotton was the money crop. 1787 HAWKINS *Life Johnson* 423 A company of *money-dealers, who, in their time, held the balance of the Antwerp exchange. 1866 CRUMP *Banking* i. 1 Some authorities assert that the Lombard merchants commenced the business of *money-dealing. 1748 SMOLLETT *Rod. Rand.* xv, A rascally *money-dropper, who made it his business to decoy strangers in that manner to one of his own haunts. 1578 *Mony floure, 1597 money flower [see *penny-flower*, PENNY 12]. 1665 PEPYS *Diary* 7 Apr., Unless the King can get some nobleman or rich *money-gentleman to lend him money. 1841 *N.Z. Jrnl.* No. 32. 92 Natives talk about *money-gold. 1842 *Lett. Settlers in Wellington, Nelson & New Plymouth* (1843) 137 We can get them [*sc.* pigs] from the natives for blankets, or for 'money gold' as they call it, which we call sovereigns. 1925 J. GREGORY *Bab of Backwoods* xxiii. 283 Gold that had..been dull bits of ore dug from rocky hillsides; that men had taken and made into money-gold. 1928 I. FISHER *Money Illusion* (1929) i. 4 The '*Money Illusion'..., the failure to perceive that the dollar, or any other unit of money, expands or shrinks in value. 1975 *Times* 30 June 12/8 Money illusion is, as in Germany, dying..as people spend indexed wages rather than save. 1696 J. CARY *Ess. Coyn* 9 The People were again furnish'd by the *Money-Jobbers, with new Arguments against the Government. 1798 BP. WATSON *Address People Gt. Brit.* 5 Money-jobbers, who deal in large speculations on credit. 1790 BURKE *Fr. Rev.* 277 By this means the spirit of *money-jobbing and speculation goes into the mass of land itself. 1838 D. D. BARNARD *Speeches & Rep.* 106 To see him [*sc.* the President] sit as a great *money king over the nation. 1900 *Congress. Rec.* 7 Feb. 1610/1 Where ought control of the currency to rest?.. At present the banks and the money kings wield this power. 1886 W. J. TUCKER *E. Europe* 85 As to those with the parcels, or *money-letters, ask them to wait. 1575-85 ABP. SANDYS *Serm.* i. 5 As before he exhorted vs to come and buie freely, without monie; because God is no *monie man. 1662 PEPYS *Diary* 18 Sept., To dinner to Sheriff Maynell's, the great money-man. 1928 Money man [see DATE *v.* 2 d]. 1958 Money-man [see CACKLE *sb.* 3 a]. 1973 *Times* 2 Feb. 14/7 New York money men have been known to quake in the knowledge that they have on deposit $1,000m of overnight money. 1791 A. HAMILTON *Establishment of Mint* in *Wks.* (1810) I. 291 In Holland, the greatest **money* market of Europe, gold was to silver..as 1 to 14·88. 1816 SCOTT *Antiquary* II. vii. 190 In the present state of the money-market. 1861 GOSCHEN *For. Exch.* 10 The power which foreign capitalists, holders of bills of exchange upon England, may exert over our money-market. 1883 *Century Mag.* Sept. 691/2 Wall Street..is the money market of the whole country. 1964 *Financial Times* 12 Mar. 10/2 South Africa has developed a money market which, in relation to national income, handles a larger volume of funds than the traditional London discount market. 1604 T. M. *Black Bk.* in *Middleton's Wks.* (Bullen) VIII. 28 An hoary *money-master..his only recreation was but to hop about the Burse. 1630 *R. Johnson's Kingd. & Commw.* 339 They are great Bankers and mony Masters. 1647 TRAPP *Comm. Matt.* xxi. 12 Christ is everyday casting out of his Church all these *money merchants. *a*1656 HALES *Gold. Rem.* III. *Serm.*, etc. (1673) 26 Augustinus Chiessius, a Banker, a Money-merchant at Rome. 1802 in H. Joyce *Hist. Post Office* (1893) 438 At Sight pay..one Pound..and place the same to the Account of the *Money Order Office. *a*1861 A. H. CLOUGH *Mari Magno* in *Poems* (1871) 320 The money-order had been cashed. 1893 in H. Joyce *Hist. Post Office* (1893) 420 The Money Order Office had been established in 1792. 1972 *Post Office Guide* 590 Inland money orders are issued by and payable at all money order offices. 1935 A. J. POLLOCK *Underworld Speaks* 77/1 **Money player*, the tougher the game, this particular gambler excels on account of having lots of nerve. 1944 *Gen* 11 Mar. 30 It is one of the die-hard notions that no money-player is fit to lead an England team. 1681 GREW *Musæum* IV. §iv. 381 A Roman *Money-Pot..fashion'd almost like a Pint Jug without a Neck. Closed at the top, and having a Notch on one side, as in a Christmas-Box. 1829 *H. R. Doc. 21st U.S. Congress 1 Sess.* No. 6. 12 The application of the *money power of the Government to regulate the unequal action. 1831 T. H. BENTON in *Reg. Deb. Congress U.S.* 2 Feb. 50/2 The money power of the bank is both direct and indirect. 1840 J. S. MILL in *Edin. Rev.* LXXII. 11 The additions to the 'money-power' of the higher ranks, consist of the riches of the *novi homines* who are continually aggregated to that class from among the merchants and manufacturers. 1926 R. H. TAWNEY *Religion & Rise of Capitalism* ii. 89 When he [*sc.* Luther] looks at German social life, he finds it ridden by a conscienceless money-power, which incidentally ministers ..to the avarice and corruption of Rome. 1959 *Ann. Reg. 1958* 90 The United Party was pictured as being.. dominated by jingoes and in the hands of the money-power. 1841 HOR. SMITH *Moneyed Man* III. iii. 67 A **money-quake*, whose explosion should hurl all their fortunes into the air. 1852 MUNDY *Our Antipodes* (1857) 20 At the time of the general money-quake he fell like the rest—failing for an immense sum. 1704 LUTTRELL *Brief Rel.* (1857) V. 414 Mr. Adams, an eminent *money scrivener of this citty,..is gone aside (as tis said) for 50,000*l.* *a*1784 JOHNSON in Boswell *Life* (1816) III. 20 Jack Ellis, a money scrivener behind the Royal Exchange. 1844 *Congress. Globe* 28th Congress 2 Sess. App. 37/2 Banks..managed..by a set of irresponsible *money sharks. 1972 G. F. NEWMAN *You Nice Bastard* 347 *Moneyshark*, unlicenced money-lender (operating at especially high rates of interest). 1816 SCOTT *Let.* 23 July (1932) I. 502 You had better be looking out & inquiring after some *money-shop, as we shall have enough of bills. 1972 *Guardian* 9 June 11 The new 'money shop' branches which are sprouting up in the High Streets... Money shops are not really banks at all... 'Loan shop'..is still the best shorthand description. 1875 MELLISS *St. Helena* 217 *Salticus nigrolimbatus*, Cambr.—The large black and white 'Fly-catcher' or '*Money-spider', as it is commonly called. 1879 *N. & Q.* Ser. v. XII. 229 The superstition in connexion with so-called 'money-spiders'. 1756 MRS. F. BROOKE *Old Maid* No. 36. 289 Last night you were more pleased than a wise woman ought to have been, at seeing a *money-spinner upon your handkerchief. 1859 G. A. SALA *Twice round Clock* 69 The clown, the dunderheaded moneyspinner who votes that books are 'rubbish'. 1862 SALA *Seven Sons* I. x. 253 The son of a city money-spinner of mushroom extraction. *c*1880 A. W. PINERO *Money Spinner* (1890) 22 Have you forgotten my father's [gaming] house... Have you forgotten what they called me then, because of my never-failing good fortune—because of my *luck*. They called me the *Money Spinner*! 1952 W. GRANVILLE *Dict. Theatr. Terms* 119 *Money-spinner*, a successful play or artiste. 1954 G. SMITH *Flaw in Crystal* 87 He found he had a pretty knack of writing so that ordinary men and women could understand and feel something of the beauty he saw around him. And he turned that touch into a money-spinner. 1958 A. WILSON *Middle Age of Mrs Eliot* II. 237 If he publishes anything it'll have every chance of being a money spinner. 1970 *Times* 23 Jan. 25/5 (Advt.), Their products range from fertilizers and basic heavy chemicals to..complex petro-chemicals..big money-spinners for Britain's export. 1855 CHAMIER *My Travels* III. iv. 95 *Money-spinning defies even a sirocco or a pestilence. 1936 J. BUCHAN *Island of Sheep* vi. 105 He's a stockbroker—a one-man firm which he founded himself. His interests? Not financial exclusively —indeed, he professes to despise the whole money-spinning business. 1973 *Courier & Advertiser* (Dundee) 1 Mar. 2/2 The money spinning lager boom already accounts for some 12 per cent. of the beer drunk in Britain. 1616 R. C. *Times' Whistle* IV. 1442 Sayth master *mony-taker, greasd i' th' fist, 'And if thou comst in danger, for a noble I'le stand thy friend'. 1825 HONE *Every-day Bk.* 5 Nov. I. 1185, I paid my penny to the money-taker.

money ('mʌnɪ), *v.* [In sense 1, ad. F. *monnayer*; in the other senses, f. MONEY *sb.*]

1. *trans.* To coin or mint (money). *rare.*

*c*1430 *Pilgr. Lyf Manhode* I. cxii. (1869) 59 And therfore on him was forged and moneyed thi ransoum; the wikkede smithes forgeden him on his bak and moneyden [orig. Fr. *monnoyerent*] him. 1691 LOCKE *Lower. Interest* Wks. 1727 II. 44 If your Exportation will not balance your Importation ..away must your Silver go again, whether Monied or not Monied. 1865 SALA *Amer. in War* I. 136 The American.. double-eagle..is perhaps the most beautiful and splendid coin ever moneyed in any mint.

†**2.** To supply with money, bestow money upon. In bad sense, to bribe. *Obs.*

1528 TINDALE *Obed. Chr. Man.* D ij b, How many yeres they will prolonge the sentence with cavillacions & suttelte, if they be well monyed on both parties. 1530 —— *Pract. Prel.* G j, Then come in the embassadours of Fraunce and monye a fewe prelates..to betraye both the kynge and the royalme to. 1611 SPEED *Hist. Gt. Brit.* IX. xi. (1623) 674 Some perfidious English, whom King Robert had monyed. 1624 HEYWOOD *Captives* I. i. in Bullen *O. Pl.* IV, Thou hast monied me in this, Nay landed me. *a*1625 FLETCHER & MASS. *Laws of Candy* I. i, He out of his own store Hath monied Cassilanes the General.

†**b.** To furnish money for (an undertaking).

*a*1697 AUBREY *Lives, Ingelbert* (1898) II. 1 He was a poore-man, but Sir Hugh Middleton..moneyed the businesse.

3. To dispose of for money. *rare.*

*c*1611 CHAPMAN *Iliad* XI. 590 Our prey was rich and great; Twice fiue and twentie flockes of sheepe [etc.];..And these soone-monied wares We draue into Neileus towne. 1895 *Funk's Stand. Dict.*, *Money v.*...2. (Rare.) To dispose of for money; as, to money a cargo.

4. *to money out*: to state in detail the prices of; to 'price out' or 'figure out' (a tender or estimate). *Sc.*

1833 LOUDON *Encycl. Archit.* §1059 (Scottish Specification) A detailed bill of every article contained in the estimate, together with the price at which each article was monied out, must accompany such tender. 1893 *Westm. Gaz.* 1 Nov. 7/3 The high prices at which they moneyed out their tenders.

'**moneyage.** *Hist.* [a. OF. *monneage* (mod.F. *monnayage*), mint, tax upon money, f. *monnayer* MONEY *v.* Cf. med.L. *monētāgium* and *monētāticum*.] 'A payment by the moneyers for the privilege of coining; otherwise explained as a payment by the subjects to prevent loss by the depreciation or change of coinage' (Stubbs *Sel. Charters* Gloss. s.v. *Monetagium*).

1747 CARTE *Hist. Eng.* I. 482 Moneyage was a duty of twelve pence paid every third year in Normandie to the Duke for not altering the coin. 1762 HUME *Hist. Eng. to Hen. VII*, I. App. II. 414 Moneyage was also a general land-tax.. levied by the two first Norman kings, and abolished by the charter of Henry I.

'**money-bag.**

1. A bag for holding money. Often used jocularly in pl. to denote 'wealth'.

1565 COOPER *Thesaurus* s.v. *Numarius*, *Theca numaria*, a money bagge. 1596 SHAKS. *Merch. V.* II. v. 18, I did dreame of money bags to night. 1713 ADDISON *Guard.* No. 106 ¶4, I found my place taken up by an ill-bred, aukward puppy, with a money-bag under each arm. 1825 LAMB *Elia* II. *Stage Illusion*, The insecure tenure by which he [*sc.* the miser] holds his money bags and parchments? 1884 *St. James's Gaz.* 9 July 6/1 The elder had possession of the money-bags; and so Prince Victor was forced to eat the leek.

2. *transf.* (*pl.*) A person who is chiefly remarkable as a possessor or lover of money.

1818 KEATS *Isabella* xviii, How could these money-bags see east and west? 1898 J. ARCH *Story of Life* 378 Though squarsons and squires, landlords and money-bags leagued together against me, I was returned by a majority of 34.

money-bound, *a. jocular.* [after *weather-bound*.] Detained by want of money.

1825 MOORE *Mem. Sheridan* II. 488 His letters to the treasurer of the theatre on these occasions were generally headed with the words 'Money-bound'. 1863 JEAFFRESON *Sir Everard's Dau.* 85 When you were often money-bound for a month at a time at a manor-house, because you hadn't the requisite amount of cash wherewith to tip the servants on leaving. 1867 SMYTH *Sailor's Word-bk.*, *Money-bound*, a phrase expressive of such passengers as are detained on board till a remittance arrives for paying the passage made.

'**money-box.** A box in which money is kept; *esp.* a closed box into which savings or contributions are dropped through a slit.

1585 HIGINS tr. *Junius' Nomencl.* 249 *Capsella fictilis*..a mony box made of potters clay, wherein boyes put their mony to keepe, such as they hang in shops, &c. towards Christmas. 1611 COTGR., *Cachemaille*, a money box. 1755 JOHNSON, *Moneybox*, a till. 1848 DICKENS *Dombey* xviii, The juggler's wife is active with the money-box in another quarter of the town. 1858 O. W. HOLMES *Aut. Breakf.-t.* vii. (1895) 169 The brains also are shaken up [by riding] like coppers in a money-box.

'**money-changer.** One whose business it is to change money at a fixed or authorized rate.

1382 WYCLIF *John* ii. 14 And he fond in the temple men sellinge scheep, and oxen, and culueris, and chaungeris [*v.r.* money chaungeris] sittinge. *c*1440 *York Myst.* xxvi. 73 In oure temple..Where tabillis full of tresoure lay..Of oure cheffe mony-changers. 1526 TINDALE *Matt.* xxi. 12 And overthrew the tables of the mony chaungers. 1727 ARBUTHNOT *Coins*, etc. 212 The Usurers or Money-changers being a sort of a scandalous employment at Rome. 1827 MACAULAY *Ess.*, *Machiavelli* ¶13 The tables of Italian money-changers were set in every city.

moneyche, obs. form of MONISH.

moneyed ('mʌnɪd), *a.* Forms: 5-7 **monyed**, 6 **monide**, 6-9 **monied**, 6- **moneyed**. [f. MONEY *sb.* + -ED[2].]

1. Having or possessing money, rich in money. ***moneyed man*** often *spec.* = CAPITALIST.

1457 *Paston Lett.* I. 416 Of such chaffr takyng he shall nevere be monyed. 1573 L. LLOYD *Pilgr. Princes* 104 Hee should bee the most monyed Prince that euer shoulde raigne in India. *c*1592 MARLOWE *Jew of Malta* I. (1633) C, Thou art a Merchant and a monied man. 1597 BACON *Ess.*, *Colours* v. (Arb.) 143 When a great moneyed man hath deuided his chests and coines and bags. 1625 *Ibid.*, *Usury* ¶4 To inuite Moneyed Men, to lend to the Merchants, for the Continuing and Quickning of Trade. 1647 CLARENDON *Hist. Reb.* VI. §288 The Marquis of Worcester was generally reputed the greatest monied man of the kingdom. 1712 SWIFT *Cond. Allies* Wks. 1751 VIII. 119 That Set of People, who are called the Monied Men; such as had raised vast Sums by trading with Stocks and Funds and lending Money upon great Interest. 1727 A. HAMILTON *New Acc. E. Ind.* I. xii. 139 The Insolence of the Portugueze makes it unsafe for money'd strangers to dwell among them. 1803 WORDSW. *Poems Nat. Indep.* I. xx. *Sonnet*, These times strike monied worldlings with dismay. 1822 J. FLINT *Lett. Amer.* 108 To appropriate to themselves the labour of less moneyed citizens. 1844 STANLEY *Arnold* (1858) I. vi. 237 The landed aristocracy and moneyed aristocracy. 1868 RUSKIN *Time & Tide* (1872) 154 The monied men and leaders of commerce.

Appendix I

Encyclopædia Britannica:1768 (First) Edition

Encyclopædia Britannica;

OR, A

DICTIONARY

OF

ARTS and SCIENCES,

COMPILED UPON A NEW PLAN.

IN WHICH

The different SCIENCES and ARTS are digested into distinct Treatises or Systems;

AND

The various TECHNICAL TERMS, &c. are explained as they occur in the order of the Alphabet.

ILLUSTRATED WITH ONE HUNDRED AND SIXTY COPPERPLATES.

By a SOCIETY of GENTLEMEN in SCOTLAND.

IN THREE VOLUMES.

VOL. III.

EDINBURGH:

Printed for A. BELL and C. MACFARQUHAR;
And sold by COLIN MACFARQUHAR, at his Printing-office, Nicolson-street.

M.DCC.LXXI.

MOHILA, one of the Comora islands in the Indian ocean, situated between Madagascar and the continent of Africa: E. long. 43° 30', S. lat. 12°.

MOIDORE, a Portuguese gold coin, value 1l. 7s. Sterling.

MOIETY, the half of any thing.

MOLA, in geography, a town of Italy, seven miles east of the city of Barri, in the kingdom of Naples.

MOLA, in ichthyology. See TETRODON.

MOLARES, or DENTES MOLARES, in anatomy, the large teeth called in English grinders. See ANATOMY, p. 165.

MOLDAVIA, a province of European Turky, separated from Poland by the river Neilter.

MOLE, in zoology. See TALPA.

MOLE CRICKET. See GRYLLUS.

MOLE, in midwifery, a mass of fleshy matter, of a spherical figure, generated in the uterus, or womb, and sometimes mistaken for a child. See MIDWIFERY.

MOLE, in geography, a river in Surry, so called from its running, for part of its course, under ground.

MOLE, is also a massive work of large stones laid in the sea by means of cofferdams; extending before a port, either to defend the harbour from the impetuosity of the waves, or to prevent the passage of ships without leave.

ACTION OF MOLESTATION, in Scots law. See LAW, Tit. xxx. 19.

MOLLUGO, in botany, a genus of the triandria trigynia class. The calix consists of five leaves; the corolla is wanting; and the capsule has three cells and three valves. There are five species, none of them natives of Britain.

MOLLOSSES, in commerce, the thick fluid matter remaining after the sugar is made, resembling syrup.

In Holland molosses are much used in the manufacture of tobacco, and by the poor people for sugar. A brandy is also distilled from them, but it is said to be unwholesome.

MOLOSSUS, in Greek and Latin poetry, a foot composed of three long syllables, as *delectant*.

MOLUCCA ISLANDS, five islands in the Indian ocean, the largest of which is scarce thirty miles round; they are called Bachian, Machian, Motyr, Ternate, and Tydor; they produce sago, oranges, lemons, and some other fruits; but what is peculiar to these islands, is their producing cloves. They are subject to the Dutch, and are situated in 125° of east longitude, and between 50' south, and 2° north latitude.

MOLUCCELLA, in botany, a genus of the didynamia gymnospermia class. The calix is bell-shaped, and larger than the corolla. There are three species, none of them natives of Britain.

MOLWITZ, a town of Silesia, in the kingdom of Bohemia: E. long. 16° 45', N. lat. 50° 26'.

MOLYBDIA, in natural history, the name of a genus of crystals, of a cubic form, or composed of six sides, at right angles, like a dye.

MOMBAZA, or MONBASA, an island and city on the east coast of Africa, opposite to the country of Mombaza, in Zanguebar: E. long. 48°, N. lat. 4°.

MOMENT, in the doctrine of time, an instant, or the most minute and indivisible part of duration.

MOMENTUM, in mechanics, signifies the same with impetus, or the quantity of motion in a moving body; which is always equal to the quantity of matter multiplied into the velocity; or, which is the same thing, it may be considered as a rectangle under the quantity of matter and velocity.

MOMORDICA, in botany, a genus of the monœcia syngenesia class. The calix of the male and female consists of five segments; the corolla of the male has six segments; and the filaments are three. The corolla of the female consists of five segments; and it has three styli. There are eight species, none of them natives of Britain.

MONA, an island in the Baltic, south west of the island of Zealand, subject to Denmark: E. long. 12° 30', N. lat. 55° 20'.

MONADELPHIA, in botany. See BOTANY, p. 635.

MONAGHAN, a county of Ireland, in the province of Ulster, bounded by Tyrone, on the north; by Armagh, on the east; by Cavan and Louth, on the south; and by the county of Farmanagh, on the west.

MONANDRIA, in botany. See BOTANY, p. 635.

MONARCHY, a government in which the supreme power is vested in a single person. See GOVERNMENT.

MONARDA, in botany, a genus of the diandria monogynia class. The corolla is unequal, the superior lip involving a linear filament. It has four seeds. There are five species, none of them natives of Britain.

MONASTERY, a convent, or house built for the reception and entertainment of monks, mendicant friars, or nuns, whether it be an abbey, priory, &c.

Monasteries are governed by different rules, according to the different regulations prescribed by their founders. The first regular and perfect monasteries were founded by St. Pachomius, in Egypt: but St. Basil is generally considered as the great father and patriarch of the Eastern monks; since in the fourth century he prescribed rules for the government of the monasteries, to which the Anachorets and Coenobites, and the other ancient fathers of the deserts, submitted. In like manner St. Benedict was styled the patriarch of the Western monks. He appeared in Italy towards the latter end of the fifth century, and published his rule, which was universally received throughout the west. St. Augustin being sent into England by St. Gregory the pope, in the year 596, to convert the English, he, at the same time introduced the monastic state into this kingdom; which made such progress here, that within the space of two hundred years, there were thirty kings and queens who preferred the religious habit to their crowns, and founded stately monasteries, where they ended their days in solitude and retirement.

MONASTIC, something belonging to monks. See MONK.

MONCON, a town of Spain, in the province of Arragon, fifty miles north-east of Saragossa.

MONDAY, the second day of the week, so called as being anciently sacred to the moon, *q. d.* moon-day.

MONEMUGI, a country in the south of Africa, situated between Angola and Zanguebar.

MONEY, a piece of matter, commonly metal, to which public authority has affixed a certain value and weight to serve as a medium in commerce.

Of artificial or material money.

I. From the infancy of the world, at least as far back as our accounts of the transactions of mankind reach, we find they had adopted the precious metals, that is, silver and gold, as the common measure of value, and as the adequate equivalent for every thing alienable.

The metals are admirably adapted for this purpose: They are perfectly homogeneous: When pure, their masses, or bulks, are exactly in proportion to their weights: No physical difference can be found between two pounds of gold, or silver, let them be the production of the mines of Europe, Asia, Africa, or America: They are perfectly malleable, fusible, and suffer the most exact division which human art is capable to give them: They are capable of being mixed with one another, as well as with metals of a baser, that is, of a less homogeneous nature, such as copper: By this mixture they spread themselves uniformly through the whole mass of the composed lump, so that every atom of it becomes proportionally possessed of a share of this noble mixture; by which means the subdivision of the precious metals is rendered very extensive.

Their physical qualities are invariable; they lose nothing by keeping; they are solid and durable; and though their parts are separated by friction, like every other thing, yet still they are of the number of those which suffer least by it.

If money, therefore, can be made of any thing, that is, if the proportional value of things vendible can be measured by any thing material, it may be measured by the metals.

II. The two metals being pitched upon as the most proper substances for realizing the ideal scale of money, those who undertake the operation of adjusting a standard must constantly keep in their eye the nature and qualities of a scale, as well as the principles upon which it is formed.

The unit of the scale must constantly be the same, although realized in the metals, or the whole operation fails in the most essential part. This realizing the unit is like adjusting a pair of compasses to a geometrical scale, where the smallest deviation from the exact opening once given must occasion an incorrect measure. The metals, therefore, are to money what a pair of compasses is to a geometrical scale.

This operation of adjusting the metals to the money of account implies an exact and determinate proportion of both metals to the money unit, realized in all the species and denominations of coin, adjusted to that standard.

The smallest particle of either metal added to, or taken away from any coin, which represent certain determinate parts of the scale, overturns the whole system of material money. And if, notwithstanding such variation, these coins continue to bear the same denominations as before, this will as effectually destroy their usefulness in measuring the value of things, as it would overturn the usefulness of a pair of compasses, to suffer the opening to vary, after it is adjusted to the scale representing feet, toises, miles, or leagues, by which the distances up the plan are to be measured.

III. Debasing the standard is a good term; because it conveys a clear and distinct idea. It is diminishing the weight of the pure metal contained in that denomination by which a nation reckons, and which we have called the money unit. Raising the standard requires no farther definition, being the direct contrary.

IV. Altering the standard (that is, raising or debasing the value of the money unit) is like altering the national measures or weights. This is best discovered by comparing the thing altered with things of the same nature which have suffered no alteration. Thus if the foot of measure was altered at once over all England, by adding to it, or taking from it, any proportional part of its standard length, the alteration would be best discovered, by comparing the new foot with that of Paris, or of any other country, which had suffered no alteration. Just so, if the pound sterling, which is the English unit, shall be found any how changed, and if the variation it has met with be difficult to ascertain, because of a complication of circumstances, the best way to discover it, will be to compare the former and the present value of it with the money of other nations which has suffered no variation. This the course of exchange will perform with the greatest exactness.

V. Artists pretend, that the precious metals, when absolutely pure from any mixture, are not of sufficient hardness to constitute a solid and lasting coin. They are found also in the mines mixed with other metals of a baser nature, and the bringing them to a state of perfect purity occasions an unnecessary expence. To avoid, therefore, the inconvenience of employing them in all their purity, people have adopted the expedient of mixing them with a determinate proportion of other metals, which hurts neither their fusibility, malleability, beauty, or lustre. This metal is called *alloy*; and, being considered only as a support to the principal metal, is accounted of no value in itself. So that eleven ounces of gold, when mixed with one ounce of silver, acquires, by that addition, no augmentation of value whatever.

This being the case, we shall, as much as possible, overlook the existence of alloy, in speaking of money, in order to render language less subject to ambiguity.

Incapacities of the metals to perform the office of an invariable measure of value.

I. Were there but one species of such a substance as we have represented gold and silver to be; were there but one metal possessing the qualities of purity, divisibility, and durability; the inconveniences in the use of it for money would be fewer by far than they are found to be as matters stand.

Such a metal might then, by an unlimited division into parts exactly equal, be made to serve as a tolerably steady and universal measure. But the rivalship between the metals, and the perfect equality which is found between all their physical qualities, so far as regards purity and divisibility, render them so equally well adapted to serve as the common measure of value, that they are universally admitted to pass current as money.

What is the consequence of this? That the one measures the value of the other, as well as that of every other thing. Now the moment any measure begins to be measured

Appendix J
Encyclopædia Britannica: 1911 Edition

THE
ENCYCLOPÆDIA BRITANNICA

A

DICTIONARY

OF

ARTS, SCIENCES, LITERATURE AND GENERAL INFORMATION

ELEVENTH EDITION

VOLUME XVIII
MEDAL to MUMPS

Cambridge, England:
at the University Press
New York, 35 West 32nd Street
1911

above sea-level, the upper 1834 ft. There is a school of the industrial arts and handicrafts, and majolica, paper, and silk cocoons are produced. The upper town contains the hexagonal piazza, a citadel, erected in 1573 by Emanuel Philibert, the cathedral of S. Donatus, a spacious episcopal palace, and higher up is a tower, the Belvedere, with a fine view. At the foot of the hill along the banks of the Ellero (a tributary of the Po) lie the industrial and commercial suburbs of Breo, Borgatto, Pian della Valle and Carassone, with their potteries, tanneries, paper-mills, marble-works, &c. The mansion of Count San Quintino in Pian della Valle was the seat of the printing-press which from 1472 issued books with the imprint Mons Regalis.

Mondovì—Mons Vici, Mons Regalis, Monteregale—did not take its rise till about A.D. 1000. The bishopric dates from 1388. About 2 m. to the east is the sanctuary of Vico, a church designed by Ascanio Vittozzi in 1596 and crowned by a famous dome (1730–1748), which has been declared a national monument. In the square before it is a monument (1891) to Charles Emmanuel I. of Savoy.

See L. Melano Rossi, *The Sanctuario of the Madonna di Vico* (London, 1907).

MONET, CLAUDE (1840–   ), French painter, was born in Paris on the 14th of November 1840. His youth was passed at Hâvre, where his father had settled in 1845. Until he was fifteen years old he led a somewhat irregular life, learning little at school, and spending all his time in decorating his books with drawings and caricatures which gave him notoriety in Hâvre. At the same time he became acquainted with Boudin, a clever sea-painter, under whose guidance he learned to love and to understand nature. At the age of twenty he became a soldier, and spent two years of his military time with the regiment of the Chasseurs d'Afrique in the desert. Falling ill with fever, he was sent home, and entered the studio of Gleyre. This classical painter tried in vain to keep him to conventional art and away from truth and nature, and Monet left his studio, where he had become acquainted with two other "impressionistic" painters—Sisley and Renoir. At that time he also knew Manet (*q.v.*), and in 1869 he joined the group of Cézanne, Degas, Duranty, Sisley, and became a *plein air* painter. During the war of 1870 he withdrew to England, and on his return was introduced by Daubigny to a dealer, M. Durand-Ruel, in whose galleries almost all his works have been exhibited. In 1872 he exhibited views of Argenteuil, near Paris; in 1874 a series entitled "Cathedrals," showing the cathedral of Rouen under different lights. He afterwards painted views of Vétheuil (1875, see Plate), Pourville and cliffs of Etretat (1881), of Bordighera (1886), of the Creuse (1889), Le Meules (1891), and some further views of cathedrals (1894). In December 1900 he exhibited some pictures called "Le Bassin des Nymphéas," and was engaged at the beginning of 1901 in painting views of London. Several of Monet's paintings, bequeathed by M. Caillebotte, are in the Luxembourg Museum, Paris. (See IMPRESSIONISM.)

MONETARY CONFERENCES (INTERNATIONAL). These assemblies were one of the features of the latter half of the 19th century, due to the decided tendency towards securing reforms by concerted international action. The disorganized state of the European currencies, which became more serious in consequence of the great expansion in trade and industry, came into notice through the great gold discoveries and their effect on the relations between the two precious metals. Both by its situation and its currency system, France was the country that was first led to aim at the establishment of a currency union, in which French ideas and influences would be predominant. A preliminary step was the formation of the Latin union, whereby the currencies of France, Italy, Belgium and Switzerland were—in respect to their gold and silver coins—assimilated. In 1867 the Paris Exhibition furnished the occasion for summoning a monetary conference, to which the principal countries of the world sent representatives. The guiding spirit of this assembly was the eminent economist, De Parieu, who had originated the Latin Union. By his advice a scheme was approved recommending the adoption of the single gold standard, the use of the decimal system, and the co-ordination of the various currencies with the French system. Difficulties as to the mode of bringing these principles into practical operation were discussed, and full liberty had to be given to the several nations to carry out the proposals in the way that seemed best. The result proved that the obstacles were insurmountable, *e.g.* the British government could not obtain the assent of a Royal Commission to the assimilation of the sovereign to the 25-franc piece; and the course of political events soon completely altered the relative position of the leading countries, even in their monetary relations. Germany and the United States reformed their currencies, without reference to any international considerations.

The meeting of the next international conference took place under very different conditions. A great fall in the value of silver as measured in gold, in progress from 1873, had affected the relations of silver-using countries, and disturbed the level of prices. Indian interests as well as those of American producers of silver suffered, while the management of all double-standard currencies became a task of increasing difficulty. The government of the United States invited the representatives of the leading powers to meet in Paris for the purpose of considering (1) the desirability of retaining the unrestricted use of silver for coinage, (2) the adoption of international bimetallism (*q.v.*), by the acceptance of a ratio to be fixed by agreement. Eleven nations sent delegates, Germany being the only great power unrepresented. After somewhat protracted discussion and the presentation of a large number of documents the European states accepted the American proposition "that it is necessary to maintain in the world the monetary functions of silver"; but declined to bind the discretion of particular states as to the methods to be employed. They further declared it impossible to enter into an agreement for a common ratio. The conference, therefore, separated without any result being obtained.

In consequence of the continuing fall in the value of silver, which stimulated the bimetallic agitation, a third conference was convened by the joint action of France and the United States; it also met in Paris, and was more influential than its predecessor, since Germany sent representatives, as did Spain, Portugal, Denmark and India. The characteristic of this conference was the greater strength of the support given to the bimetallic proposal by France and the United States, together with the opposition of the delegates of the smaller European countries, and the refusal of Germany to promise any co-operation. The inevitable consequence of this situation was the adjournment of the conference to obtain fresh instructions, which, however, were never furnished.

After several abortive attempts the fourth (and last) of the conferences of this class was brought together at Brussels in November 1892 on the initiative of the United States. A full representation of the powers attended, but delay arose from the absence of definite proposals by the American government. These, when they were presented, proved to be only a reaffirmation of the bimetallic policy, and showed no advance. The conference, therefore, proceeded to consider the plans of Levy, Baron de Rothschild and Sotbeer for the more extended use of silver. Such devices, being merely alleviations, failed to gain any effective support. Appeals to England and Germany to grant some concessions likewise failed. Thus, like its Paris forerunners, the Brussels conference adjourned, but never resumed its sittings.

After 1892 the currency problem passed into a new stage, in which action was national rather than international. The method of procedure by conference was for the time abandoned.

The proceedings of the several conferences have been issued by the governments taking part in them. Those of the United States are the most convenient for English and American readers. See also H. B. Russell, *International Monetary Conferences* (New York, 1898). (C. F. B.)

MONEY. 1. *Definition and Functions.*—The difficult question as to the best definition of money has been complicated by the efforts of writers so to define the term as to give support to their particular theories. It is hard to frame a precise account which will hold good of the many objects that have served for monetary use. From denoting coined metal, money has come to include anything that performs the money work: though there has been considerable hesitation in extending the term to those forms of credit that are in modern societies the chief instrument of exchange. It is therefore best to avoid a formal definition; and, instead, to bring out the character of money by describing the functions that it performs in the social system. The most important is, clearly, that of facilitating exchange. It is not necessary to dwell on the great importance of this office. The slightest consideration of industrial organization shows that it is based on the division of employments; but the earliest economic writers saw plainly that division of employments was only possible through the agency of a medium of exchange. They recognized that the result of increasing specialization of labour was to establish a state of things in which each individual produced little or nothing for the direct satisfaction of his own wants, and had therefore to live by exchanging his product for the products of others. They saw, further, that this only became feasible by the existence of an article that all would be willing to accept for their special products; as otherwise the difficulty of bringing together persons with reciprocal wants would prove an insurmountable obstacle to that development of exchange, which alone made division of labour possible. A *second* function hardly inferior in importance to the one just mentioned is that of affording a ready means for estimating the comparative values of different commodities. Without some common object as a standard of comparison this would be practically impossible. " If a tailor had only coats and wanted to buy bread or a horse, it would be very troublesome to ascertain how much bread he ought to obtain for a coat or how many coats he should give for a horse "; and as the number of commodities concerned increased the problem would become harder, " for each commodity would have to be quoted in terms of every other commodity." There is, indeed, a good deal to be said for the view that the conception of general exchange value could never have been formed without the previous existence of money; it has certainly support from the evidence of competent observers respecting the methods of exchange followed by savage communities. The selection of some particular article as the criterion makes the comparison of values easy. " The chosen commodity becomes a *common denominator*, or *common measure of value* in terms of which we estimate the value of all other goods," and in this way money, which in its primary function renders exchange possible by acting as an intermediate term in each transfer, also makes exchanges easier by making them definite. Still another function of money comes into being with the progress of society. One of the most distinctive features of advancing civilization is the increasing tendency of people to trust each other. There is thus a continuous increase in relations arising from contract, as can be seen by examining the development of any legal system. Now, a contract implies something to be done in the future, and for estimating the value of that future act a standard is required; and here money which has already acted as a *medium of exchange* and as a *measure of value* at a given time, performs a *third* function, by affording an approximate means of estimating the present value of the future act; in this respect it may be regarded as a *standard of value*, or as some prefer to say, of *deferred payments*. Nor does this exhaust the list of services that money renders. In the earlier stages of economic life it acts as a *store of value*; for in no other way could a large body of wealth be concentrated. Though this is no longer needed by individuals, even at the present day the great banks find that their reserves must take the form of a monetary store. Again, money in its various forms has been the great agency for transmitting values from place to place. Its international function in this respect still continues. The balance of debt between countries is ultimately settled by the passage of bullion from the debtor to the creditor nation. But, though money has these powers, it is nevertheless correct to say that its essential functions are three in number, *i.e.* it supplies: (1) the common medium by which exchanges are made possible; (2) the common measure by which the comparative values of those exchanges are estimated; (3) the standard by which future obligations are determined.

2. *The Value of Money, its Determining Causes. The Quantity of Money required by a Country.*—The value of money is in principle only a special case of the general problem of value; but owing to its peculiar position the medium of exchange has in this respect become surrounded by difficulties that need to be removed. The very phrase " value of money " is employed in two senses, which on the surface seem to have no connexion with each other, and are the cause of much confusion to those who have not looked into the matter. In mercantile phraseology the value of money means the interest charged for the use of loanable capital. When the market rate of interest is high, money is said to be dear; when it is low, money is regarded as cheap. Without entering into the reasons for this use of the term, it is sufficient to state the other and for our present purpose more correct meaning of the phrase. As the value of a thing is what it will exchange for; so " the value of money is what money will exchange for, or its purchasing power. If prices are low, money will buy much of other things, and is of high value; if prices are high, it will buy little of other things, and is of low value. The value of money is inversely as general prices, falling as they rise and rising as they fall." Now the *proximate* condition under which value is determined is admittedly the establishment of an equation between demand and supply. In the case of money, however, some explanation as to the nature of both these elements in the problem becomes necessary. In what forms is the supply of, and the demand for, money exhibited? The supply of a commodity is the quantity of it which is offered for sale. But in what shape does the sale of money take place? Plainly, by being offered for goods. The supply of money is the quantity of it which people are wanting to lay out, *i.e.* all the money in circulation at the time. Demand, in like manner, means the quantity of a commodity desired, or, according to another mode of expression, the amount of purchasing power offered for it. Taking the latter as the more convenient for the case of money, we can say that the demand for it consists in all goods offered for sale. The position of money as the medium of exchange introduces a further novel feature; for the market in its case is world-wide and the demand is unceasing; money is consequently in a constant state of supply and demand. It thus appears that the factors determining the value of money at a given time are: (1) the amount of money in circulation, and (2) the amount of goods on sale. Closer examination reveals other influencing conditions. The mere quantity of money is not the only element on the supply side. The varying circulation of the monetary units must be taken into account. Some coins do not make a single purchase in a year, while others change hands in transactions hundreds of times. By averaging, we may estimate the effect of the rapidity with which money does its work, or, to employ a technical term, the " efficiency of money." Similarly, the amount of sales rather than the quantity of commodities is the determining element on the demand side. Thus, if the influence of credit be omitted, it is true to say that the value of money varies inversely as its quantity multiplied by its efficiency, the amount of transactions being assumed to be constant. Some additional explanation is required before this formula can be accepted as an expression of the whole truth on the subject. It must be noticed that it is not commodities only that are exchanged for money. Services of all kinds constitute a large portion of the demand for the circulating medium, while the payment of interest on the many kinds of obligations makes a further call on it. The potent influence of credit must also be recognized. The latter force is indeed the chief agency to be considered in dealing with the variations of prices; though so far as it is based on deposits of metallic money it may be regarded as a form of increased monetary efficiency, and therefore as coming within the formula given above. In its wider aspect, credit acts as a substitute for ordinary money, and may be interpreted as equivalent to a system of perfected barter, or, better, as a new currency development. An interesting but paradoxical conclusion should be noticed: it is that increased

Appendix K

Encyclopædia Britannica: Fifteenth Edition, 1997 Printing

The New Encyclopædia Britannica

Volume 24

MACROPÆDIA

Knowledge in Depth

FOUNDED 1768
15 TH EDITION

Encyclopædia Britannica, Inc.
Jacob E. Safra, Chairman of the Board
James E. Goulka, Chief Operating Officer

Chicago
Auckland/London/Madrid/Manila/Paris
Rome/Seoul/Sydney/Tokyo/Toronto

Money

The subject of money has fascinated wise men from the time of Aristotle to the present day because it is so full of mystery and paradox. The piece of paper labelled one dollar or 100 francs or 10 kroner or 1,000 yen is little different, as paper, from a piece of the same size torn from a newspaper or magazine, yet it will enable its bearer to command some measure of food, drink, clothing, and the remaining goods of life while the other is fit only to light the fire. Whence the difference?

The easy answer, and the right one, is that people accept money as such because they know that others will. The pieces of paper are valuable because everyone thinks they are, and everyone thinks they are because in his experience they always have been. At bottom money is, then, a social convention, but a convention of uncommon strength that people will abide by even under extreme provocation. The strength of the convention is, of course, what enables governments to profit by inflating the currency. But it is not indestructible. When great variations occur in the quantity of these pieces of paper—as they have during and after wars—they may be seen to be, after all, no more than pieces of paper. People will then seek substitutes—like the cigarettes and cognac that for a time became the medium of exchange in Germany after World War II. As John Stuart Mill wrote:

> There cannot, in short, be intrinsically a more insignificant thing, in the economy of society, than money; except in the character of a contrivance for sparing time and labour. It is a machinery for doing quickly and commodiously, what would be done, though less quickly and commodiously, without it; and like many other kinds of machinery, it only exerts a distinct and independent influence of its own when it gets out of order. (*Principles of Political Economy*, W.J. Ashley [ed.], 1909, p. 488.)

Mill was perfectly correct, although one must add that there is hardly a contrivance man possesses that can do more damage to a society when it goes wrong.

This article is divided into the following sections:

Functions of money 323
Varieties of money 323
  Metallic money
  Paper money
Standards of value 324
  The gold standard
  The decline of gold
  The dollar standard
Modern monetary systems 325
  Public money holdings
  Central banking
Monetary theories 326
  The quantity theory of money
  The Keynesian critique
  The monetarist view
Bibliography 329

FUNCTIONS OF MONEY

The basic function of money is to enable buying to be separated from selling, thus permitting trade to take place without the so-called double coincidence of barter. If a person has something to sell and wants something else in return, it is not necessary to search for someone able and willing to make the desired exchange of items. The person can sell the surplus item for general purchasing power—that is, "money"—to anyone who wants to buy it and then use the proceeds to buy the desired item from anyone who wants to sell it.

The importance of this function of money is dramatically illustrated by the experience of Germany just after World War II, when paper money was rendered largely useless because, despite inflationary conditions, price controls were effectively enforced by the American, French, and British armies of occupation. People had to resort to barter or to inefficient money substitutes. The result was to cut total output of the economy in half. The German "economic miracle" just after 1948 reflected partly a currency reform by the occupation authorities, but some economists hold that it stemmed primarily from the German government's elimination of all price controls, thereby permitting a money economy to replace a barter economy.

Separation of the act of sale from the act of purchase requires the existence of something that will be generally accepted in payment—this is the "medium of exchange" function of money. But there must also be something that can serve as a temporary abode of purchasing power, in which the seller holds the proceeds in the interim between the first sale and the subsequent purchase, or from which the buyer can extract the general purchasing power with which to pay for what is bought. This is the "asset" function of money.

VARIETIES OF MONEY

Anything can serve as money that habit or social convention and successful experience endow with the quality of general acceptability, and a variety of items have so served—from the wampum (beads made from shells) of American Indians to cowries (brightly coloured shells) in India, to whales' teeth among the Fijians, to tobacco among early colonists in North America, to large stone disks on the Pacific island of Yap, to cigarettes and liquor in post-World War II Germany. The wide use of cattle as money in primitive times survives in the word pecuniary, which comes from the Latin *pecus*, meaning cattle.

Metallic money. The use of metals as money has occurred throughout history. As Aristotle observed,

> The various necessities of life are not easily carried about, and hence man agreed to employ in their dealings with each other something which was intrinsically useful and easily applicable to the purposes of life, for example, iron, silver, and the like. Of this the value was at first measured by size and weight, but in process of time they put a stamp upon it, to save the trouble of weighing and to mark the value.

The use of metal for money can be traced back to more than 2,000 years before the birth of Christ. But standardization and certification in the form of coinage, as referred to by Aristotle, did not occur except perhaps in isolated instances until the 7th century BC. Historians generally assign to Lydia, a state in Anatolia, priority in using coined money. The first coins were made of electrum, a natural mixture of gold and silver, and were crude, bean-shaped ingots bearing a primitive punchmark certifying to either weight or fineness, or both.

The use of coins enabled payment to be by "tale," or count, rather than weight, greatly facilitating commerce. But this in turn encouraged clipping (shaving off tiny slivers from the sides or edges of coins) and sweating (shaking a bunch of coins together in a leather bag and collecting the dust that was thereby knocked off) in the hope of passing on the lighter coin at its face value. Gresham's law (that "bad money drives out good" when there is a fixed rate of exchange between them) came into operation, and heavy, good coins were held for their metallic value, while light coins were passed on. The coins became lighter and lighter, and prices higher and higher. Then payment by weight would be resumed for large transactions, and there would be pressure for recoinage. These particular defects were largely ended by the "milling" of coins (making serrations around the circumference of a coin), which began in the late 17th century.

A more serious matter was the attempt by the sovereign to benefit from the monopoly of coinage. In this respect,

Debasing the currency

Greek and Roman experience offers an interesting contrast. Though Solon, on taking office in Athens in 594 BC, did institute a partial debasement of the currency, for the next four centuries, until the absorption of Greece into the Roman Empire, the Athenian *drachma* had an almost constant silver content (67 grains of fine silver until Alexander, 65 grains thereafter) and became the standard coin of trade in Greece and in much of Asia and Europe as well. Even after the Roman conquest, the *drachma* continued to be minted and widely used.

The Roman experience was very different. Not long after the silver *denarius*, patterned after the Greek *drachma*, was introduced in about 212 BC, the prior copper coinage (*aes*, or *libra*) began to be debased until, by the time the empire began, its weight had been reduced from one pound to half an ounce. The silver *denarius* and the gold *aureus* (introduced about 87 BC) suffered only minor debasement until the time of Nero (AD 54), when almost continuous tampering with the coinage began. The metal content of the gold and silver coins was reduced, and the proportion of alloy was increased to three-fourths or more of its weight. Debasement in Rome (as ever since) was a reflection of the state's inability or unwillingness to finance its expenditures through explicit taxes. But the debasement in turn worsened Rome's economic situation and undoubtedly contributed to the collapse of the empire.

Paper money. In the late 18th and early 19th centuries, paper money and bank notes spread widely. The bulk of the money in use came to consist not of actual gold or silver but of fiduciary money—promises to pay specified amounts of gold and silver. These promises were initially issued by individuals or companies as bank notes or as the transferrable book entries that came to be called deposits. But gradually the state assumed a role.

From fiduciary paper money promising to pay gold or silver, it is a short step to fiat paper money—that is, notes that are issued on the "fiat" of the sovereign, are specified to be so many dollars or francs or yen, and are legal tender but are not promises to pay something else. The first large-scale issue in a Western country occurred in France in the early 18th century (though there are reports of paper money in China many centuries earlier). Later, the French revolutionary government issued paper money in the form of assignats from 1789 to 1796. The American colonies and later the Continental Congress issued bills of credit that could be used in making payments. These early experiments gave fiat money a deservedly bad name. The money was overissued, and prices rose drastically until the money became worthless or was redeemed in metallic money (or promises to pay metallic money) at a small fraction of its initial value.

Subsequent issues of fiat money in the major countries during the 19th century were temporary departures from a metallic standard. In Great Britain, for example, payment of gold for the outstanding bank notes was "suspended" during the Napoleonic Wars (1797–1815). As a result, gold coin and bullion became more expensive in terms of paper. Similarly, in the United States during the Civil War, convertibility of Union currency (greenbacks) into specie was suspended, and resumption did not occur until 1879. At its peak, in 1864, the greenback price of gold, nominally equivalent to $100, reached more than $250.

STANDARDS OF VALUE

In the Middle Ages, when money consisted primarily of coins, silver and gold coins circulated simultaneously. As governments came increasingly to take over the coinage, and especially as fiduciary money was introduced, they tended to specify their nominal monetary units in terms of fixed weights of both silver and gold—to adopt a national bimetallic standard. Gresham's law, however, usually assured that the bimetallic standard degenerated into a monometallic standard: if the quantity of silver designated as the monetary equivalent of one ounce of gold was less than the quantity that could be purchased in the market for one ounce of gold (*i.e.*, if the mint overvalued silver), no one would bring gold to be coined. If one had gold, it was better to buy silver and bring it to be coined. Silver, the cheaper metal, "drove out" gold and became the standard. This happened in most of the countries of Europe, so that by the early 19th century all were effectively on a silver standard. In Britain, on the other hand, the ratio established in the 18th century at the advice of Sir Isaac Newton, then serving as master of the mint, overvalued gold and therefore led to an effective gold standard. In the United States a ratio of 15 ounces of silver to one ounce of gold was set in 1792. This ratio overvalued silver, so silver became the standard. In 1834 the ratio was altered to 16 to one, which overvalued gold, so gold became the standard.

The gold standard. The great gold discoveries in California and Australia in the 1840s and '50s produced a temporary decline in the value of gold in terms of silver. This price change, plus the dominance of Britain in international finance, led to a widespread shift from a silver standard to a gold standard. Germany adopted gold in 1871–73, the Latin Monetary Union (France, Italy, Belgium, Switzerland) in 1873–74, the Scandinavian Union (Denmark, Norway, and Sweden) and The Netherlands in 1875–76. By the final decades of the century, silver remained dominant only in the Far East (China, in particular). Elsewhere the gold standard reigned.

The early 20th century was the great era of the international gold standard. Gold coins circulated in most of the world; paper money, whether issued by private banks or by government, was convertible on demand into gold coins or gold bullion at an official price (with perhaps the addition of a small fee); and bank deposits were convertible into either gold coin or paper currency that was itself convertible into gold. In a few countries, a minor variant prevailed—the so-called gold-exchange standard, under which the currency was converted at a fixed price into the currency of another country (usually the British pound sterling) that was itself convertible into gold.

There was, in effect, a single world money called by different names in different countries. A U.S. dollar, for example, was defined as 23.22 grains of pure gold (25.8 grains of gold 0.9000 fineness). A British pound sterling was defined as 113.00 grains of pure gold (123.274 grains of gold 11/12th fine). Accordingly, one British pound equalled 4.8665 U.S. dollars (113.00/23.22) at the official parity. The actual exchange rate could deviate from this only by an amount that corresponded to the cost of shipping gold. If the price of the pound sterling in terms of dollars rose to a considerably higher value than this in the foreign exchange market, someone in New York City who had a debt to pay in London might find that, rather than buy the needed pounds on the market, it was cheaper to get gold for dollars at a bank or at the U.S. subtreasury, ship the gold to London, and get pounds for the gold from the Bank of England. This set an upper limit to the exchange rate. Similarly, the cost of shipping gold from Britain to the United States set a lower limit. These limits were known as the gold points.

Under such an international gold standard, the quantity of money in each country was determined by the specie-flow adjustment mechanism analyzed by 19th-century economists. If, for whatever reason, the quantity of money in a country rose unduly, this would tend to raise prices in that country relative to prices in other countries; the rise in prices would have the effect of discouraging exports and encouraging imports. The decreased supply of foreign currency from the sale of exports plus the increased demand for foreign currency to pay for imports would tend to raise the price of foreign currency in terms of domestic currency. As soon as this price hit the upper gold point, gold would be shipped out of the country to other countries. The decline in the amount of gold would produce in turn a reduction in the total amount of money—because banks and government institutions, seeing their gold reserves decline, would want to protect themselves against further demands by reducing the claims against gold that were outstanding. This would tend to lower prices at home. The influx of gold abroad would have the opposite effect, increasing the quantity of money there and raising prices. These adjustments would continue until the gold flow ceased or was reversed.

This is precisely the mechanism that operates within

Appendix L

Stock Ownership, Federal Reserve Bank of New York

THE NEW YORK TIMES, WEDNESDAY, SEPTEMBER 23, 1914.

BANKS' STOCK LIST FULL OF SURPRISES

Many Names Associated by Public with Big Stockholdings Not Found.

HETTY GREEN'S 30 SHARES

Frank Vanderlip Missing from Among Large Interests in National City.

Publication yesterday of lists of stockholders in some of New York City's largest banks aroused considerable interest in the financial district, as much because of the absences of expected names as of the amounts of the principal holdings. The date at which the lists were compiled was not made known, and important changes may have taken place since, although as a rule there is little activity in bank shares and the controlling interests in most institutions have been in the same hands for many years.

Among the surprises in the lists, as published by Dow, Jones & Co., was the discovery that Hetty Green, often spoken of as a very important factor in the conduct of the Chemical National, owns only 31 of the 30,000 shares of that institution. Frank Vanderlip, President of the National City Bank, is not down among the principal shareholders, while James Stillman, Chairman of the Board of Directors, holds 47,498 shares of the total of 250,000. Mr. Stillman is also a large holder in the Hanover and the Citizens' Central. J. P. Morgan & Co. have the biggest holdings of any firm.

The shareholders, capitalization, number of shares, dividends, and book value, follow:

National City Bank—Capital, $25,000; total stockholders, 1,013; book value, $230; par value, $100; annual dividend, 10 per cent. Stock also includes $10,000,000 capital of National City Company, which pays annual dividend of 6 per cent.

James Stillman	47,498	W. A. Rockefeller	10
J. P. Morgan & Co.	14,000	A. T. Russell	8,267
W. Rockefeller	10,000	A. C. Taylor	7,899
M. T. Pyne	8,267	J. W. Sterling	6,067
Percy Pyne	8,267	U. S. Trust Co.	
J. D. Rockefeller	1,750	New York	4,500
J. S. Rockefeller	100	J. P. Morgan, Jr.	1,000
*Trustee.			

National Bank of Commerce—Capital, $25,000,000; total stockholders, 3,013; book value, $180; par value, $100; annual dividend, 8 per cent.

Equitable Life	24,700	A. D. Juilliard	2,000
Mutual Life	17,294	J. J. Gerdan	1,696
G. F. Baker	10,000	J. P. Goodhart & Co.	
North. Finance Corporation	9,300	J. N. Jarvine	1,287
J. P. Morgan & Co.	7,800	F. A. V. Twombly	1,285
Mary W. Harriman	5,650	Kidder, Peabody & Co.	1,250
E. J. Berwind	5,650	J. P. Morgan, Jr.	1,125
T. F. Ryan	5,100	L. P. Morton	1,100
R. W. Winthrop Co. agents	4,900	H. B. Davison	1,500
S. J. Saltus	4,757	W. W. Astor	1,100
T. A. Reynolds	3,175	J. H. Schiff	1,000
*P. M. Warburg	3,000	V. P. Snyder	1,000
A. J. Hemphill	2,000	G. Whittell	1,000
		E. T. Nichols	1,000
*Since sold his holdings.			

First National—Capital, $10,000,000; total stockholders, 626; book value, $329; par value, $100; annual dividend, 40 per cent. Of this 28 per cent is paid on bank's stock and 12 per cent on stock of First Security Company.

G. F. Baker	20,000	G. F. Baker, Jr.	5,000
J. P. Morgan & Co.	13,900	J. J. Hill	4,000
H. C. Fahnestock	10,000	North'n Fin Co.	1,700
		F. L. Hine	1,400
Garland, Dodson & Eimmer Tr of est of J A Garland	6,000	H. B. Davison	1,010
		Mary C. Thompson	9,000

Chase National—Capital, $5,000,000; total shareholders, 309; book value, $299; par value, $100; annual dividend, 20 per cent.

G. F. Baker	13,408	H. W. Cannon	1,400
A. H. Wiggin	6,482	G. B. Schley	500
C. A. Edwards	4,500	S. Miller	500
A. B. Hepburn	2,873	J. J. Mitchell	500
J. J. Hill	1,500	Faith Moore	500
L. G. Thompson	1,500	W. H. Porter	500
E. Tuck	1,500	F. S. Thompson	
Trustees Princeton Univ.	1,000	U. S. T Co., Tr.	1,000

Hanover National—Capital, $3,000,000; total stockholders, 404; book value, $579; par value, $100; annual dividend, 16 per cent.

Wm. Woodward	6,909	Bessemer Invest. Co.	
James Stillman	4,000		525
Wm. Rockefeller	1,340	Wm. J. Clark	423
Wm. Barbour	1,200	Wm. J. Halls	410
Jas. M. Donald	1,025	C. Wodsworth	750
		Robt. M. Goelet	400

Facsimile of an article which appeared in The New York Times dated September 23, 1914. Listed are major stockholders of the five New York City banks which purchased 40% of the 203,053 shares of the Federal Reserve Bank of New York when the System was organized in 1914. They thus obtained control of that Federal Reserve Bank and have held it ever since. As of Tuesday, July 26, 1983, the top five surviving New York City banks have increased their ownership of the Federal Reserve Bank of New York to 53% of the shares.

91

Figure L-1. This New York Times *article and caption are taken from page 91 of the 1984 edition of Eustace Mullins' book,* The Secrets of the Federal Reserve, *and is reproduced with permission. Copyright © 1998 by The New York Times. Reprinted with permission.*

ADDENDUM

As of 11:05 Tuesday, July 26, 1983, the list of member banks holding Federal Reserve Bank of New York stock includes twenty-seven New York City banks. Listed below are the number of shares held by ten of these banks, amounting to 66% of the total outstanding number of shares, namely 7,005,700:

	Shares	Percent
Bankers Trust Company	438,831	(6%)
Bank of New York	141,482	(2%)
Chase Manhattan Bank	1,011,862	(14%)
Chemical Bank	544,962	(8%)
Citibank	1,090,813	(15%)
European American Bank & Trust	127,800	(2%)
J. Henry Schroder Bank & Trust	37,493	(.5%)
Manufacturers Hanover	509,852	(7%)
Morgan Guaranty Trust	655,443	(9%)
National Bank of North America	105,600	(2%)

The tremendous number of shares held today as against the original purchases in 1914 is brought about by Section 5 of the original Federal Reserve Act which called for a member bank to buy and hold stock in the district Federal Reserve Bank equal to 6% of its capital and surplus.

Currently, shares held by five of the above named banks comprise 53% of the total Federal Reserve Bank of New York stock. An examination of the major stockholders of the New York City banks shows clearly that a few families, related by blood, marriage, or business interests, still control the New York City banks which, in turn, hold the controlling stock of the Federal Reserve Bank of New York.

It is notable that three of the banks holding Federal Reserve Bank of New York stock, in the amount of 270,893 shares, are subsidiaries of foreign banks. J. Henry Schroder Bank and Trust is listed by *Standard and Poors* as a subsidiary of Schroders Ltd. of London. The National Bank of North America is a subsidiary of the National Westminster Bank, one of London's "Big Five". European American Bank is a subsidiary of the European American Bank, Bahamas, LTD. It is interesting to note that the directors of the European American Bank & Trust include Milton F. Rosenthal president and Chief Operating Officer of the international gold company,

Engelhard Minerals and Chemical; Hamilton F. Potter, a partner in Sullivan and Cromwell (J. Henry Schroder Bank & Trust attorneys); Edward H. Tuck, partner of Shearman and Sterling (Citibank's attorneys); F.H. Ulrich and Hans Liebkutsch, managing directors of the Deutsche Bank (Germany); E.J.W. Helmuth and Jack Lendley, directors of the giant Midland Bank of London, one of the "Big Five"; and Roger Alloo, Paul-Emmanuel Janssen, and Maurice Laure of the Societe Generale de Banque (Brussels, Belgium). [See Chart III]

This information, derived from the latest issue of the tabulation available from the Board of Governors, Federal Reserve System, is cited as current evidence which indicates that the controlling stock in the Federal Reserve Bank of New York, which sets the rate and scale of operations for the entire Federal Reserve System is heavily influenced by banks directly controlled by "The London Connection", that is, the Rothschild-controlled Bank of England. [See Chart I]

Figure L-2. Mr. Mullins reports that in 1983, in response to his request, the New York Federal Reserve Bank sent him a stockholder computer printout from which he was able to update his records. The paragraphs above reflect the information in that printout, and are photocopies of pages 179 and 180 of his book, The Secrets of the Federal Reserve, *reproduced with permission. All rights reserved.*

Appendix M

Graphs: The Dow-Jones Industrial Average

Figure M-1. The DJIA (or just the "DOW") in terms of troy ounces of gold (top) and in terms of "dollars" (bottom). The vertical axis in these two graphs is logarithmic. Linear vertical axes are used in the graphs on the next page. Graphing the DJIA in terms of troy ounces of gold may reduce the confusion of dealing with "dollars," a unit of measure whose value may vary relatively widely due to political and criminal manipulation. See also Appendix A, Topline Investment Graphics.

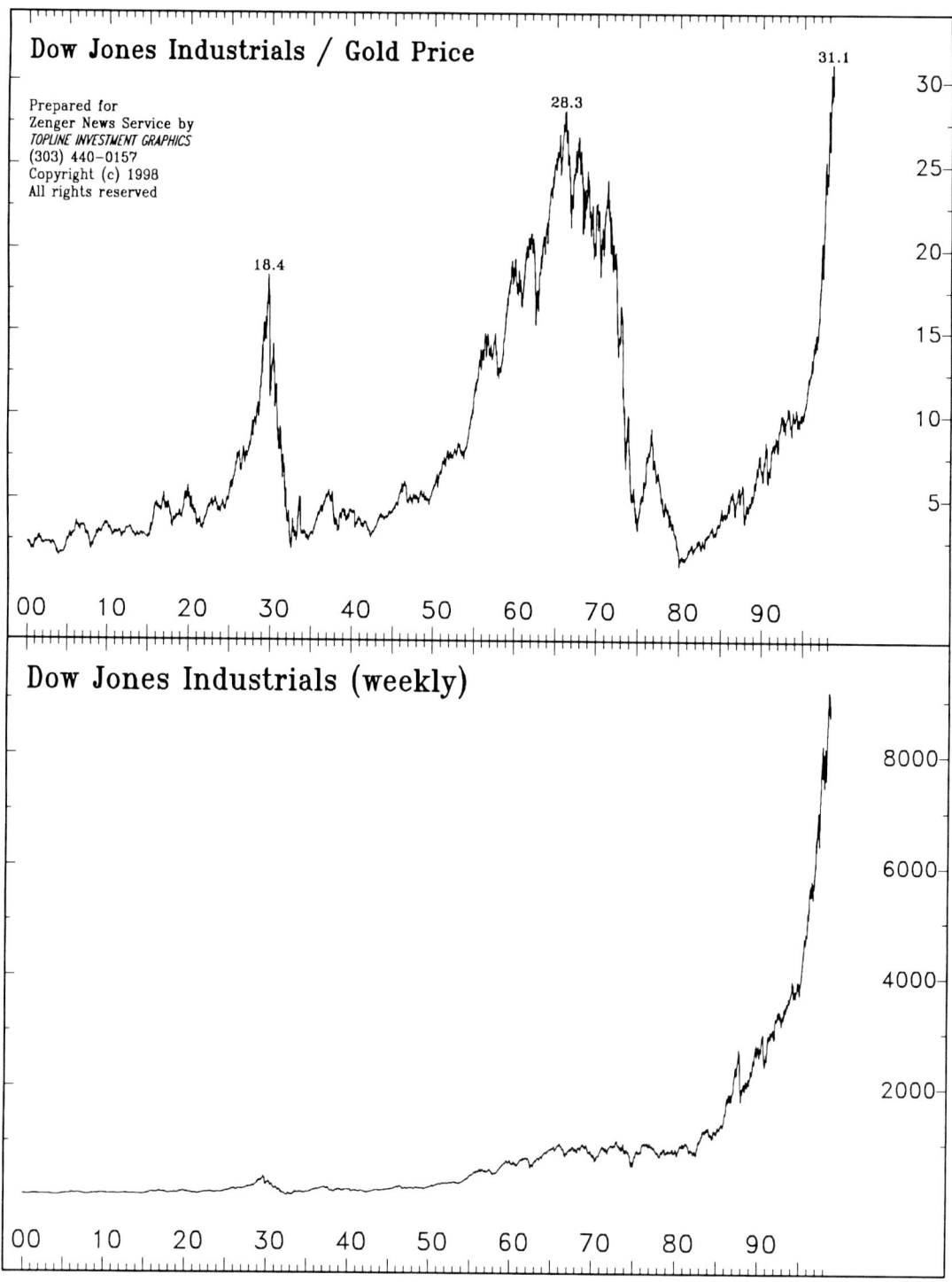

Figure M-2. The DJIA (or just the "DOW") in terms of troy ounces of gold (top) and in terms of "dollars" (bottom). The vertical axis in these two graphs is linear. Logarithmic vertical axes are used in the graphs on the previous page. Graphing the DJIA in terms of troy ounces of gold may be reduce the confusion of dealing with "dollars," a unit of measure whose value may vary relatively widely due to political and criminal manipulation. See also Appendix A, Topline Investment Graphics.

Appendix N
Cases and Dictionary Definitions

Most of the material in this appendix is taken from the following copyrighted sources[1] and is used with the kind permission of the publishers. All rights reserved.
1. *American Dictionary of the English Language*, Noah Webster, 1828.
2. *Bouvier's Law Dictionary*, 1870.
3. *Black's Law Dictionary*, First edition, 1891.
4. *Words & Phrases*, 1904.
5. *Black's Law Dictionary*, Fourth edition, 1951.
6. *Words & Phrases*, 1957.
7. *Black's Law Dictionary*, Sixth edition, 1991.

Words & Phrases is an encyclopedic work, a set of about fifty volumes of some 500 pages each. *W&P* contains brief descriptions of court positions on the meanings of words or phrases which played a significant role in the outcome of a trial.

You will soon see that a definition used by one court may appear to contradict a definition used in another court. Thus, we caution you to not rely on this material without first fully investigating other possible definitions, or how a definition may vary, depending upon the context in which the word may be used.

Finally, you should also not rely upon these or other definitions without first discussing your interests or purposes with competent legal counsel.

Nevertheless, in spite of the caution you must exercise while reading this information, we believe it will be a highly rewarding experience for everyone, especially law professionals.

Material is arranged alphabetically on the word or phrase of interest. We highlight the word of interest, then give the source and its year of publication. Many cases in the 1904 and 1957 editions of *Words & Phrases* were decided prior to 1900; a few were decided prior to 1850.

Unless otherwise indicated, emphasis is in the original. In the older sources, a space may precede a semi-colon or colon. Such odd punctuation has been preserved here, except where other factors suggested that no space preceded the punctuation. Also, where the source included material in a smaller font than other text, we approximated that feature in our reproductions.

In several places you will see phrases like "a chose in action" or "a thing in action." These phrases refer to redeemable currency, bills or promissory notes or bank notes which, presumably, are or will be turned in for redemption, that is, presented to a bank or the U.S. Treasury in a demand for payment. The phrase "in action" signifies that the action of redemption or payment is incomplete, and that it may never be complete.

One more possibly misunderstood phrase is that which, in a court opinion, a silver certificate is not considered a promissory note. The courts occasionally took this position because the need for a silver certificate to be paid was statutory, that is, the need was established by a specific law related to the issue of that certificate, not part of the body of law which governs routine commercial transactions. For the purposes of this book, however, every redeemable paper currency in the United States is, etymologically, a promissory note because the language on its face includes a promise to pay, and identifies the maker, the payee, the dollar amount, and the due date (usually "on demand").

Finally, when the source material continues but we reach the end of appropriate or topical material, our decision to quote no more of the source is signified with triple asterisks, ***. We also use triple asterisks to indicate where we may have skipped multiple sentences to avoid quoting inapplicable text, etc.

Apparent contradictions in the following material may have two causes. First, courts and editors of law books may not have always considered the etymology of important terms, possibly because etymological dictionaries were not readily available. Second, courts and legal professionals may have drifted away from formal, technical definitions in attempts to interpret colloquialisms, to assure that justice was served.

However, don't forget that criminals often use words inappropriately, to defraud or otherwise manipulate victims and others. Most notorious in this regard may be candidates for elective office; they take advantage of (and often exacerbate) public confusion about the meanings of monetary and economic words and phrases. I suspect that "verbicide" may be habitual for more than a few candidates for national office.

BILL: (Webster, 1828) 2. In *law* and in *commerce*, in England, an obligation or security given for money under the hand, and sometimes the seal of the debtor, without a condition or forfeiture for non-payment. In the latter circumstance, it differs from a bond. In the United States, this species of security is usually called a note, a note of hand, or a promissory note. ***
7. A *bill of exchange* is an order drawn on a person, in a distant place, requesting or directing him to pay money to some person assigned by the drawer, or to his order, in consideration of the same sum received by the drawer. Bills of exchange are either *foreign* or *inland*; *foreign*, when drawn by a person in one country upon one residing in another; *inland*, when both the drawer and drawee reside in the same country. The person who draws the bill is called the *drawer*; the person on whom the request or demand is made, is called the *drawee*; and the person to whom the money is directed to be paid, is called the payee.

BILL: (Bouvier, 1870) 5. **As a Contract.** An obligation; a deed, whereby the obligor acknowledges himself to owe unto the obligee a certain sum of money or some other thing, in which, besides the names of the parties, are to be considered the sum or thing due, the time, place, and manner of payment or delivery thereof. It may be indented or poll, and with or without a penalty. West, Symb. §§ 100, 101.

BILL OF CREDIT: (Bouvier, 1870) Paper issued by the authority of a state on the faith of the state, and designed to circulate as money. 11 Pet. 257.

Promissory notes or bills issued by a state government, exclusively, on the credit of the state, and intended to circulate through the community for its ordinary purposes as money, re-

---
[1] Except for Webster, all are from West Publishing Company, Saint Paul, Minnesota

deemable at a future day, and for the payment of which the faith of the state is pledged. 4 Kent, Comm. 408.

BILL: (Black, 1891) A formal declaration, complaint, or statement of particular things in writing. As a legal term, this word has many meanings and applications, the more important of which are enumerated below. ***

    7. **As a contract**. An obligation; a deed, whereby the obligor acknowledges himself to owe unto the obligee a certain sum of money or some other thing, in which, besides the names of the parties, are to be considered the sum or thing due, the time, place, and manner of payment or delivery thereof. It may be indented or poll, and with or without a penalty. West, Symb. §§ 100, 101.

BILL: (Black, 1951) 7. [**Bill single**. A written promise to pay to a person or persons named a stated sum at a stated time, without any condition. When under seal, as is usually the case, it is sometimes called a "bill obligatory," *(q.v.)* It differs from a "bill penal," *(q.v.)* in that it expresses no penalty.]

    8. **In commercial law**[.] A written statement of the terms of a contract, or specification of the items of a transaction or of a demand; also a general name for any item of indebtedness, whether receivable or payable.

    Accounts for goods sold, services rendered, or work done. Newman v. San Antonio Traction Co., Tex.Civ.App., 155 S.W. 688, 690.

    As a verb, as generally and customarily used in commercial transactions, "bill" is synonymous with "charge" or "invoice." George M. Jones Co. v. Canadian Nat. R. Co., D.C.Mich., 14 F.2d 852, 855.

    9. **In the law of negotiable instruments**

    A promissory obligation for the payment of money.

    Standing alone or without qualifying words, the term is understood to mean a bank note, United States treasury note, or other piece of paper circulating as money. Green v. State, 28 Tex.App. 493, 13 S.W. 785.

    —**Bill of credit.** In constitutional law. A bill or promissory note issued by the government of a state or nation, upon its faith and credit, designed to circulate in the community as money, and redeemable at a future day. Hale v. Huston, 44 Ala. 138, 4 Am.Rep. 124. In mercantile law. A license or authority given in writing from one person to another, very common among merchants, bankers, and those who travel, empowering a person to receive or take up money of their correspondents abroad.

    —**Bill of exchange.** A written order from A. to B., directing B. to pay to C. a certain sum of money therein named. Byles, Bills, 1. An open (that is, unsealed) letter addressed by one person to another directing him, in effect, to pay, absolutely and at all events, a certain sum of money therein named, to a third person, or to any other to whom that third person may order it to be paid, or it may be payable to bearer or to the drawer himself. 1 Daniel, Neg.Inst. 27.

    An unconditional order in writing addressed by one person to another, signed by the person giving it, requiring the person to whom it is addressed to pay on demand or at a fixed or determinable future time a sum certain in money to order or to bearer. Clayton Town-Site Co. v. Clayton Drug Co., 147 P. 460, 20 N.M. 185; Smythe v. Sanders, 101 S. 435, 436, 136 Misc. 382; Sometimes called a "trade acceptance." Jones v. Revere Preserving Co., 247 Mass. 225, 142 N.E. 70, 71.

    A "check" differs from a "bill of exchange" in that it is always drawn on a deposit whereas a bill is not. Wilson v. Buchenau, D.C.Cal., 43 F.Supp. 272, 275.

BILL: (Black, 1991) *Commercial transactions*. A written statement of the terms of a contract, or specification of the items of a transaction or of a demand. Also, a general name for any item of indebtedness, whether receivable or payable; an account for goods sold, services rendered, or work done. As a verb, as generally and customarily used in commercial transactions, "bill" is synonymous with "charge" or "invoice." ***

    Commercial paper. A promissory obligation for the payment of money.

    Bill of credit. A bill or promissory note issued by the government, upon its faith and credit, designed to circulate in the community as money. *See* Federal reserve notes; Treasury bill.

    Bill of exchange. An unconditional order in writing addressed by one person to another, signed by the person giving it, requiring the person to whom it is addressed to pay on demand or at a fixed or determinable future time a sum certain in money. A three party instrument in which the first party draws an order for the payment of a sum certain on a second party for payment to a third party at a definite future time. Same as "draft" under U.C.C. A check is a demand bill of exchange.

CASH: (Webster, 1828) *n.* [Fr. *caisse*; Sp. Port. *caxa*, a chest, box, coffer. See *Case*.] Money ; primarily, ready money, money in chest or on hand, in bank or at command. It is properly silver and gold ; but since the institution of banks, it denotes also bank notes equivalent to money. *To pay in cash* is opposed to payment in goods, commodities, or labor, as in barter.

    CASH, *v.t.* To turn into money, or to exchange for money ; as, to *cash* a note or an order.

    2. To pay money for ; as, the clerks of a bank *cash* notes when presented.

CASH: (Bouvier, 1870) That which circulates as money, including bank bills, but not mere bills receivable.

    Cash price is the price of articles paid for in cash at the time of purchase, in distinction from the barter and credit prices.

CASH: (Black, 1891) Ready money ; whatever can be used as money without being converted into another form; that which circulates as money, including bank-bills.

    Cash payment means the opposite of credit. 6 Md. 37; 24 N. J. Law. 96.

CASH: (Black, 1951) Money or its equivalent; usually ready money. Kerlin v. Young, 159 Ga. 95, 125 S.E. 204, 207; Britain v. Rice, Tex.Civ.App., 204 S.W. 254, 256.

CASH: (Black, 1991) Money or the equivalent; usually ready money. Currency and coins, negotiable checks, and balances in bank accounts. That which circulates as money. *See* Legal tender; Petty cash.

COUNTERFEIT: (Bouvier, 1870) In Criminal Law. To make something false in the semblance of that which is true. It always implies a fraudulent intent. Vide Viner, Abr. *Counterfeit* ; Forgery.

CREDIT: (Bouvier, 1870) The ability to borrow, on the opinion conceived by the lender that he will be repaid.

    A debt due in consequence of a contract of hire or borrowing of money.

    The time allowed by the creditor for the payment of goods sold by him to the debtor.

    That which is due to a merchant, as distinguished from debit, that which is due by him.

That influence connected with certain social positions. 20 Toullier, n. 19.

See, generally, 5 Taunt. 338 ; 3 N. Y. 344.

COIN: (Webster, 1828) 1. Money stamped ; a piece of metal, as gold, silver, copper, or other metal, converted into money, by impressing on it marks, figures or characters. To make good money, these impressions must be under the authority of government. That which is stamped without authority is called false or counterfeit coin. Formerly, all coin was made by hammering; but it is now impressed by a machine or mill.

Current coin is coin legally stamped and circulating in trade.

Ancient coins are chiefly those of the Jews, Greeks and Romans, which are kept in cabinets as curiosities.

COIN: (Black, 1891) *n.* Pieces of gold, silver, or other metal, fashioned into a prescribed shape, weight, and degree of fineness, and stamped, by authority of government, with certain marks and devices, and put into circulation as money at a fixed value.

Strictly speaking, coin differs from money, as the species differs from the genus. Money is any matter, whether metal, paper, beads, shells, etc., which has currency as a medium in commerce. Coin is a particular species, always made of metal, and struck according to a certain process called "coinage." Wharton.

COIN: (Black, 1951) *n.* Pieces of gold, silver, or other metal, fashioned into a prescribed shape, weight, and degree of fineness, and stamped, by authority of government, with certain marks and devices, and put into circulation as money at a fixed value, Com. v. Gallagher, 16 Gray, Mass., 240; Latham v. U. S., 1 Ct.Cl. 150; Borie v. Trott, 5 Phila., Pa., 403, or any metal disc, State v. Kelleher, 127 A. 503, 504, 2 W.W.Harr., Del., 559.

COINAGE: (Black, 1891) The process or the function of coining metallic money; also the great mass of metallic money in circulation.

COINAGE CLAUSE. Provision in U.S. Constitution granting to Congress the power to coin money, Art. I, § 8, par. 5.
[Absent from the 1991 *Black's* is any reference to "coin." je.]

CURRENCY: (Webster, 1828) *n.* [See *Current.*] Literally, a flowing, running or passing ; a continued or uninterrupted course, like that of a stream ; as the *currency* of time. Ayliffe.

3. A continual passing from hand to hand, as the *currency* of cents, or of English crowns; the *currency* of bank bills or treasury notes.

6. That which is current or in circulation, as a medium of trade. This word may be applied to coins, or to bills issued by authority. It is often applied to bank notes, and to notes issued by government. *Crawford.*

CURRENCY: (Black, 1891, 1951, and 1991) Coined money and such bank-notes or other paper money as are authorized by law and do in fact circulate from hand to hand as the medium of exchange.

CURRENT ASSETS. (Black, 1991) Any property that will be or could be converted into cash in the normal operation of a business or at an earlier date, usually within one year. Short-term assets; *e.g.* cash, accounts receivable, inventory.

CURRENT FUNDS: (Black, 1891) This phrase means gold or silver, or something equivalent thereto, and convertible at pleasure into coined money. 4 Ala. 90.

CURRENT FUNDS: (Black, 1991) Cash and other assets readily convertible into cash. Money which circulates as legal tender. Formerly, this phrase meant gold or silver, or something equivalent thereto, and convertible at pleasure into coin money. *See* Current money.

CURRENT LIABILITIES: (Black, 1991) An obligation that will be paid in the ordinary course of a business or within one year. A current liability is paid by expending a current asset. The phrase "current liability" carries with it the idea of a liability that is presently enforceable.

CURRENT MONEY: (Black, 1891, 1991) The currency of the country; whatever is intended to and does actually circulate as currency; every species of coin or currency. 5 Lea, 96. In this phrase the adjective "current" is not synonymous with "convertible." It is employed to describe money which passes from hand to hand, from person to person, and circulates through the community, and is generally received. Money is current which is received as money in the common business transactions, and is the common medium in barter and trade. 41 Ala. 321.

DEBT: (Bouvier, 1870) (Lat. *debere,* to owe; *debitum,* something owed). **In Contracts**. A sum of money due by certain and express agreement. 3 Blackstone, Comm. 154.

All that is due a man under any form of obligation or promise. 3 Metc. Mass. 522.

Any claim for money. Penn. Stat. March 21, 1806, § 5.

*** Debts are discharged in various ways, but principally by payment.

DECEIT: (Bouvier, 1870) A fraudulent misrepresentation or contrivance, by which one man deceives another, who has no means of detecting the fraud, to the injury and damage of the latter.

2. Fraud, or the intention to deceive, is the very essence of this injury ; for if the party misrepresenting was himself mistaken, no blame can attach to him. The representation must be made *malo animo;* but whether or not the party is himself to gain by it is wholly immaterial.

It may be by the deliberate assertion of a falsehood to the injury of another, by failure to disclose a latent defect, or by concealing an apparent defect. See CAVEAT EMPTOR.

The party deceived must have been in a situation such as to have no means of detecting the deceit.

3. The remedy for a deceit, unless the right of action has been suspended or discharged, is by an action of trespass on the case. The old writ of deceit was brought for acknowledging a fine, or the like, in another name, and, this being a perversion of law to an evil purpose and a high contempt, the act was laid *contra pacem,* and a fine imposed upon the offender. See Brooke, Abr. *Disceit;* Viner, Abr. *Disceit.*

When two or more persons unite in a deceit upon another, they may be indicted for a conspiracy.

DOLLAR: (Webster, 1828) *n.* [G. *Thaler;* D. *Daalder ;* Dan. and Sw. *daler ;* Sp. *dalera ;* Russ. *taler;* said to be from *Dale,* the town where it was first coined.

A silver coin of Spain and of the United States, of the value of one hundred cents, or four shillings and sixpence sterling. The dollar seems to have been originally a German coin, and in different parts of Germany, the name is given to coins of different values.

DOLLAR: (Bouvier, 1870) (Germ. *Thaler*). The money unit of the United States.

2. It was established under the confederation by resolution of congress, July 6, 1785. This was originally represented by a silver piece only ; the coinage of which was authorized by the act of congress of Aug. 8, 1786. The same act also established a decimal system of coinage and accounts. 1. Brown 4 D. U. S. Laws, 646. But the coinage was not effected until after the passage of the act of April 2, 1792, establishing a mint, 1 U.S. Stat. at Large, 246; and the first coinage of dollars commenced in 1794. The law last cited provided for the coinage of "dollars or units, each to be the value of a Spanish milled dollar, as the same was then current, and to contain three hundred and seventy-one grains and four-sixteenths parts of a grain of pure silver, or four hundred and sixteen grains of standard silver." ***

DOLLAR: (Black, 1891) The unit employed in the United States in calculating money values. It is coined both in gold and silver, and is of the value of one hundred cents.

DOLLAR: (Black, 1951) The unit employed in the United States in calculating money values. It is coined both in gold and silver, and is of the value of one hundred cents. People v. Alba. 46 Cal.App.2d 859, 117 P.2d 63. Money or currency issued by lawful authority and intended to pass and circulate as such. Neufield v. United States, 118 F.2d 375, 387, 73 App.D.C. 175. The dollar of nine-tenths fine consisting of the weight determined under the 31 U.S.C.A. § 321, shall be the standard unit of value, and all forms of money issued or coined shall be maintained at a parity of value with this standard. 31 U.S.C.A. § 314.

DOLLAR: (Black, 1991) [Not found in *Black's Law Dictionary*, Sixth edition, © 1991. je.]

DOLLAR: (*Words & Phrases*, 1957)
Miscellaneous cases
"Dollars," as used in a decree requiring an executor to account for a certain sum in dollars, means the constitutional currency of the country, and will not be held to apply to depreciated issue of worthless banks. Bailey v. Dilworth, 18 Miss. (10 Smedes & M.) 404, 410, 48 Am.Dec. 760.

In Act Dec. 22, 1840, providing that the salary of the president of a certain bank should be given seven hundred dollars, and the cashier's one thousand eight hundred dollars, "dollars" legally means gold or silver, and for services rendered as such officers of the bank the officers acquired the right to demand and receive in payment gold or silver, and could not lawfully be compelled to accept the depreciated paper of the banks of the state. State Bank v. Crease, 6 Ark. (1 Eng.) 292, 295.

Coined dollar
When from the judgment record it appears that the complaint was upon a contract which by law was payable in coin, the term "dollars," without the prefix of "coined," "gold," or "silver," in the subsequent parts of the record, means coined dollars. Ransford v. Marvin, N.Y., 8 Abb.Prac.N.S. 432, 436.

"The dollar note is an engagement to pay a dollar, and the dollar intended is the coin dollar of the United States ; a certain quantity in weight and fineness of gold or silver, authenticated as such by the stamp of the government. No other dollar had before been recognized by the legislation of the national government as lawful money." New York ex rel. Bank of New York v. Board of Sup'rs of New York County, 74 U.S. 26, 30, 7 Wall. 26, 30, 19 L.Ed. 60.

Coin of certain weight
Taking the definition from the statute book, "dollar" is a silver coin weighting 412 grains, or a gold coin weighting 25 4/5 grains, of nine-tenths pure to one-tenth alloy of each metal. Borie v. Trott, Pa., 5 Phila. 366, 404.

The government note payable in "dollars" intends coined dollars of the United States; a certain quantity in weight and fineness of gold or silver, authenticated as such by the stamp of the government. Bank of New York v. New York County Sup'rs, 74 U.S. 26, 30, 7 Wall. 26, 30, 19 L.Ed. 60.

A contract to pay a certain number of "dollars" in gold or silver coin is an agreement to deliver a certain weight of standard gold, to be ascertained by a count of coins, each of which is certified to contain a definite proportion of that weight. Bronson v. Rodes, 74 U.S. 229, 250, 7 Wall. 229, 250, 19 L.Ed. 141.

The term "dollar" has a known legal meaning, as much so as any other word or form of expression designating or having reference to a standard of measurement prescribed and established by law. It is a silver coin of a fixed weight and fineness, issued and made current by the authority of Congress, in the exercise of its constitutional power to that end. By the same authority other gold and silver coins are issued and made current, each as a legal equivalent of an ascertained number of dollars or fractions of a dollar. Undoubtedly the word "dollar" may be used in a contract in a sense other than this, its statute definition, and effect will be given to it accordingly if the intention to use it in such modified sense is so evidenced that the law can take cognizance of it. Austin v. Kinsman, S.C., 13 Rich.Eq. 259, 262.

Descriptive of value
An indictment charging that the defendant stole "sixty dollars of the current gold coin" of the United States is equivalent to saying "sixty pieces of gold coin called sixty dollars," there being in our money a piece of gold coin called a "dollar." McKane v. State, 11 Ind. 195.

The term "dollar" is both the name of a coin and an expression of value. It may be that the phrase used is intelligible in common parlance, but, in an indictment charging the conversion of "nineteen thousand dollars" in money and in bank notes, without some description of their number or denomination, is insufficient. State v. Stimson, 24 N.J.L.(4 Zab.) 9, 27. [This court's concern for the number of bank notes was likely founded on its awareness that at least some of the bank notes may have been worthless. je.]

Legal tender
"Dollars," in a check, meant dollars in lawful money of the United States, and could not be explained by verbal agreement, custom, or any mercantile or other usage, to mean otherwise. Howes v. Austin, 35 Ill. 396, 398.

Medium of exchange
In view of Kirby's Dig. § 1826, making the difference between grand and petit larceny to depend upon whether the value of the property stolen exceeds $10 or not, in a prosecution for larceny of gold, silver, and paper money, proof that the owner had "cashed" his pay check and had in his pockets $31.05 and in

answer to the question, "How much money did you have in your pocket?" he had replied, "One dollar and a nickel," and in answer to the question, "How much greenback or curency," [*sic*] he replied "Two tens, a five, two twos, and a one, and one dollar in silver and a nickel," was a sufficient proof of the value of the property taken, since the words "money," "cash," "silver," "greenback," "currency," and "dollar" were used in each instance in referring to the medium of exchange in use in this country; and, as money itself is the standard of value, it is not only unnecessary, but impossible, to prove its value, and while "money" in its technical sense is coined metal, in its popular sense it is any currency, token, bank notes, or other circulating medium in general use as the representative of value and a generic term. Cook v. State, 196 S.W. 922, 924, 130 Ark. 90.

Specie currency

A promise to pay a specific sum in "dollars," or to pay so many dollars, is a contract to pay a particular kind of currency. It is a contract to pay a specie currency. Hilb. v. Peyton, Va., 22 Grat. 550, 561.

DOLLAR NOTE

A legal tender currency redeemable in gold or silver coin of the United States; an engagement by the United States to pay a dollar. Cincinnati v. Anderson, 10 Ohio Cir.Ct. 265, 6 Ohio Cir.Dec. 594, 595; Bank of New York v. Board of Supervisors of County of New York, 74 U.S. 26, 30, 7 Wall. 26, 30, 19 L.Ed. 60.

DOLLARS AND CENTS

When a debt is agreed to be paid in "dollars and cents," in the absence of an agreement, express or implied, for its payment in some other way, a payment in money is meant, and not a payment by the delivery of property, the transfer of notes, the delivery of checks, or through the medium of an accord and satisfaction. Simons v. Douglas' Ex'r, 225 S.W. 721, 722, 189 Ky. 644.

FRAUD: (Bouvier, 1870) The unlawful appropriation of another's property, with knowledge, by design, and without criminal intent.

Fraud is sometimes used as a term synonymous with *covin, collusion,* and *deceit,* but improperly so. *Covin* is a secret contrivance between two or more persons to defraud and prejudice another of his rights. *Collusion* is an agreement between two or more persons to defraud another under the forms of law, or to accomplish an illegal purpose. *Deceit* is a fraudulent contrivance by words or acts to deceive a third person, who, relying thereupon, without carelessness or neglect of his own, sustains damage thereby. Coke, Litt. 357 *b;* Bacon, Abr. *Fraud.*

I.O.U.: (Bouvier, 1870) **In Common Law**. A memorandum of debt in use among merchants. It is not a promissory note, as it contains no direct promise to pay. See 4 Carr. & P. 324; 1 Mann. & G. 46; 1 C. B. 543; 1 Esp. 426; Parson, Bills & Notes.

LAUNDERING: [No "illegal" usage included in any of my dictionaries prior to *Black's Law Dictionary*, Sixth edition, ©1991. je.]

LAUNDERING: (Black, 1991) Term used to describe investment or other transfer of money flowing from racketeering, drug transactions, and other illegal sources into legitimate channels so that its original source cannot be traced. Money laundering is a federal crime. 18 U.S.C.A. § 1956.

LAWFUL MONEY: (Webster, 1828) [No definition in Webster's 1828 dictionary. je.]

LAWFUL MONEY: (Bouvier, 1870) Money which is a legal tender in payment of debts; *e.g.* gold and silver coined at the mint. 2 Salk. 446; 5 Mod. 7; 3 Ind. 358; 2 How. 244; 3 *id.* 717; 16 Ark. 83. See 1 Hempst. C. C. 236.

LAWFUL MONEY: (Black, 1891) Money which is a legal tender in payment of debts; *e.g.,* gold and silver coined at the mint. [Citations follow in original. On a page before this definition we see "LAWFUL: Legal; warranted or authorized by the law; having the qualifications prescribed by law; not contrary to nor forbidden by the law." *MONEY* readers may wish to reflect on the phrase "authorized by the law" when considering the material in Chapter 2, Money, *et seq.* je.]

LAWFUL MONEY: (*Words & Phrases*, 1904) "Lawful money of the United States" includes only gold and silver coin, or that which by law is made its equivalent, so as to be exchangeable therefor at par and on demand, and does not include a currency note which, though nominally exchangeable for coin at its face value, is not redeemable on demand. Bronson v. Rodes, 74 U. S. (7 Wall.) 229, 247, 19 L. Ed. 141.

LAWFUL MONEY: (Black, 1951) Money which is a legal tender in payment of debts. [Citations follow in original. The phrase from the 1891 edition, "*e.g.,* gold and silver coined at the mint" is no longer shown, although in 1951 the nation's circulating media included silver coins, silver certificates, United States Notes, and Federal Reserve Notes. Those paper media were regularly redeemed on demand in silver coin. je.]

LAWFUL MONEY: (*Words & Phrases*, 1957)

"Lawful money of the United States," as used in an indictment charging the larceny of $75 of the "lawful money of the United States," cannot be construed to include the notes of national banks. Lawful money of the United States might consist of gold or silver coin or United States treasury notes and fractional currency. Hamilton v. State, 60 Ind. 193, 194, 28 Am. Rep. 653.

LAWFUL MONEY: (Black, 1991) Money which is a legal tender in payment of debts. *See* Legal tender. [No citations or other material follows this definition. je.]

LEGAL TENDER: (Webster, 1828) ["LEGAL TENDER" is not found in Webster's 1828 dictionary. je.]

LEGAL TENDER: (Bouvier, 1870) That currency which has been made suitable by law for the purposes of a tender in the payment of debts.

The following descriptions of currency are legal tender in the United States:—

All the gold coins of the United States, according to their nominal value, for all sums whatever. *The silver dollar* of the United States is a legal tender for all sums whatever. *The silver coins* below the denomination of the dollar, coined prior to 1854, are a legal tender in payment of any sum whatever. *The silver coins below the dollar,* of the date 1854 and of subsequent years, are a legal tender in sums not exceeding five dollars. *The three-cent silver coins* of the date of 1851, 1852, and 1853 are a tender in sums not exceeding thirty cents. Those of subsequent dates are a tender in sums not exceeding five dollars.

The cent is not a legal tender.

The laws at one time in force making certain foreign coins a legal tender was repealed by the act of Feb. 21, 1857, § 3 (Stat. at Large, vol. 11, p. 163). No foreign coins are now a legal tender.

By recent legislation, treasury notes have been issued, which are a legal tender for all debts, public and private, except duties on imports and interest on the public debt. (Act of Congress of May 23, 1862.)

LEGAL TENDER: (Black, 1891) That kind of coin, money, or circulating medium which the law compels a creditor to accept in payment of his debt, when tendered by the debtor in the right amount.

LEGAL TENDER: (Black, 1951) [*Black's* 1951 edition does not include "LEGAL TENDER." je.]

LEGAL TENDER: (Black, 1991) All coins and currencies of the United States (including Federal Reserve notes and circulating notes of Federal Reserve banks and national banking associations), regardless of when coined or issued, are legal tender for all debts, public and private, public charges, taxes, duties, and dues. 31 U.S.C.A. § 392. *See also* United States currency.

LEGAL TENDER: (*Words & Phrases*, 1957)
— Cross References
Money

To constitute a "legal tender" it is essential to prove an actual offer of the sum due, unless the actual production and offer of the money be dispensed with by the express declaration of the creditor that he will not accept it, or by some equivalent act. Greenwood v. Watson, 171 F. 619, 621, 96 C.C.A. 421, citing Buchanau v. Horney, 12 Ill. 336.

The terms "lawful sum in money" and "legal tender" are not synonymous, but have different meanings. A tender, to be good in law, must be made in legal tender notes or coin of the United States. National bank notes and gold and silver certificates are lawful money, and so recognized in the commercial exchanges of the United States; but they are not legal tender. Martin v. Bott, 46 N.E. 151, 153, 17 Ind.App. 444.

LEGAL TENDER NOTE: (*Words & Phrases*, 1957)

A legal tender note is a contract on the part of the government to pay its nominal value in coin. O'Neil v. McKewn, 1 S.C. (1 Rich.) 147, 148.

MINT: (Webster, 1828) *n.* [Sax. *mynet*, money or stamped coin; D. *munt, mint,* coin; G. *münze* ; SW. *mynt* ; Dan. *myndt*, coin. this word is doubtless a derivative from *mine*, or *moneta*, from the same root.]

1. The place where money is coined by public authority. In Great Britain, formerly, there was a *mint* in almost every county; but the privilege of coining is now considered as a royal prerogative in that country, and as the prerogative of the sovereign power in other countries. The only *mint* now in Great Britain is in the Tower of London. The *mint* of the United States is in Philadelphia. [In the United States, "the sovereign power" resides in you and your neighbors, as "sovereign freemen," and you have delegated some of your power to the workers at the United States mint and instructed them to manufacture this country's coins. *You* are the sovereign power in this country. je.]

MONETARY: (Black, 1951) The usual meaning is "pertaining to coinage or currency or having to do with money", but it has been held to include personal property. In re Kipp's Will, Sur., 37 N.Y.S.2d 541, 543.

MONEY: (Webster, 1828) *n.* plu. *moneys.* [Sax. *mynet* ; D. *munt,* mint ; G. *münze* ; Sw. *mynt* ; Dan. *myndt,* money or mint ; Fr. *monnoie* ; Ir. *monadh* ; W. *mwnai* ; Sp. *moneda* ; Port. *moeda,* contracted ; L. It. *moneta. Money* and *mint* are the same word varied.]

1. Coin ; stamped metal ; any piece of metal, usually gold, silver or copper, stamped by public authority, and used as the medium of commerce. We sometimes give the name of money to other coined metals, and to any other material which rude nations use as a medium of trade. But among modern commercial nations, gold, silver and copper are the only metals used for this purpose. Gold and silver, containing great value in a small compass, and being therefore of easy conveyance, and being also durable and little liable to diminution by use, are the most convenient metals for coin or money, which is the representative of commodities of all kinds, of lands, and of every thing that is capable of being transferred in commerce.

2. Bank notes or bills of credit issued by authority, and exchangeable for coin or redeemable, are also called *money* ; as such notes in modern times represent coin, and are used as a substitute for it. If a man pays in hand for goods in bank notes which are current, he is said to pay in ready *money.*

3. Wealth ; affluence.

Money can neither open new avenues to pleasure, nor block up the passages of anguish. *Rambler.*

MONEY: (Bouvier, 1870) Gold and silver coins. The common medium of exchange in a civilized nation.

There is some difference of opinion as to the etymology of the word money ; and writers do not agree as to its precise meaning. Some writers define it to be the common medium of exchange among civilized nations; but in the United States constitution there is a provision which has been supposed to make it synonymous with coins: "The congress shall have power to coin money." Art. 1, sect. 8. Again : "No state shall coin money, or make any thing but gold and silver a legal tender in payment of debt." Art. 1, sect. 10. [sic] Hence the money of the United States consists of gold and silver coins. And so well has the congress of the United States maintained this point, that the copper coins heretofore struck, and the nickel cent of recent issues, although authorized to "pass current," are not money in an exact sense, because they are not made a legal tender in the payment of debts. The question has been made whether a paper currency can be constitutionally authorized by congress and constituted a legal tender in the payment of private debts. Such a power has been exercised and adjudged valid by the highest tribunal of several of the states, but has not been passed upon by the supreme court of the United States.

For many purposes, bank-notes, 1 Younge & J. Exch. 380; 3 Mass. 405 ; 14 *id.* 122; 17 *id.* 560; 4 Pick. Mass. 74; 2 N. H. 333; 7 Cow. N.Y. 662; Brayt. Vt. 24; a check, 4 Bingh. 179, and negotiable notes, 3 Mass. 405, will be considered as money. To support a count for money had and received, the receipt by the defendant of bank-notes, promissory notes, 3 Mass. 405; 9 Pick. Mass. 93; 14 Me. 285; 7 Johns. 132, credit in account in the books of a third person, 3 Campb. 199, or any chattel, is sufficient, 4 Pick. Mass. 71; 17 Mass. 560, and will be treated as money. See 7 Wend. N.Y. 311; 8 *id.* 641; 7 Serg. & R. Penn. 246; 8 Term,

687; 3 Bos. & P. 559; 1 Younge & J. Exch. 380. [In the foregoing material, just before my "*sic*," the U.S. Constitution, Art. 1, Sect. 10 should be quoted as: "No State shall . . . make any Thing but gold and silver Coin a Tender in Payment of Debts; . . . ." je.]

MONEY: (Black, 1891) A general, indefinite term for the measure and representative of value; currency; the circulating medium; cash.

"Money" is a generic term, and embraces every description of coin or bank-notes recognized by common consent as a representative of value in effecting exchanges of property or payment of debts. 5 Humph. 140.

Money is used in a specific and also in a general and more comprehensive sense. In its specific sense, it means what is coined or stamped by public authority, and has its determinate value fixed by governments. In its more comprehensive and general sense, it means wealth,—the representative of commodities of all kinds, of lands, and of everything that can be transferred in commerce. 31 Tex. 10.

In its strict technical sense, "money" means coined metal, usually gold or silver, upon which the government stamp has been impressed to indicate its value. In its more popular sense, "money" means any currency, tokens, bank-notes, or other circulating medium in general use as the representative of value. 45 Tex. 305.

The term "moneys" is not of more extensive signification than "money," and means only cash, and not things in action. 14 Johns. 1; 1 Johns. Ch. 231.

MONEY: (*Words & Phrases*, 1904)
Money.

Webster defines money: "(1) Coin; stamped metal; pieces of metal, usually gold, silver, or copper, stamped by public authority, and used as the medium of commerce. (2) Hence any currency usually and lawfully employed in buying and selling as the equivalent of money, as bank notes and the like" Carter v. Cox, 44 Miss. 155.

"Money," in its strict technical sense, is coined metal, usually gold or silver, upon which the government stamp has been impressed to indicate its value. In its more popular sense, "money" means any currency token, [*sic*] bank-notes, or other circulating medium in general use as the representative of value; a generic term, covering everything which by consent is made to represent property, and passes as such currently from hand to had. The word designates the whole volume of the medium of exchange, regardless of its character or denomination. State v. Downs, 47 N.E. 670, 671, 148 Ind. 324; Hopson v. Fountain, 24 Tenn. (5 Humph.) 140; Miller v. McKinney, 73 Tenn. (5 Lea) 93, 96; Graham v. State, 24 Tenn. (5 Humph.) 40, 41; State v. Hill, 66 N. W. 541, 559, 47 Neb. 456; United States v. Lucius Beebe & Sons (U. S.) 122 Fed. 762, 767, 58 C. C. A. 562. [The "*sic*" above indicates a suspected typographic error. Other, earlier sources quote this passage as, ". . . any currency, tokens, bank-notes, . . ." je.]

Money is not only a medium of exchange, but it is a standard of value. Nothing can be such a standard which has no intrinsic value, or which is subjected to frequent changes in values. From the earliest period in the history of civilized nations, we find pieces of gold and silver used as money. Those metals are scattered over the world in small quantities. They are susceptible of division, capable of easy impression, and have more value in proportion to weight than size, and are less subject to loss by wear and abrasion, than any other material possessing these qualities. Legal Tender Cases, 4 Sup. Ct. 122, 137, 110 U. X. 421, 28 L. Ed. 204.

The term "money" or "moneys," wherever used in the chapter relating to the revenue, shall be held to mean gold, silver, or other coin, and paper or other currency, used in barter and trade as money. Rev. S. Mo. 1899, § 9123.

Bank bills or notes. See also, "Bank Note."

The word "money" may be extended to bank notes, when they are known and approved of, and used in the market as cash. Judah v. Harris (N. Y.) 19 Johns. 144, 145.

The term "money" does not include a bank note. Such a note does not differ in its nature from any other promissory note payable to bearer. Filgo v. Penny, 6 N. C. 182, 183.

Same—Criminal law.

It is not accurate to call currency in the shape of bills or notes money, for in the true sense they are not money. State v. Hoke, 84 Ind. 137, 139 (citing Boyd v. Olvey, 82 Ind. 294; Hamilton v. State, 60 Ind. 193, 28 Am Rep. 653). [This is an 1849 case. je.]

"The term 'money,' though it may have a popular import which in ordinary parlance means, or at least includes, bank notes, in its true technical import means lawful money of the United States, or, in other words, gold or silver coin, and, when used in judicial proceedings, is always to be taken in its technical sense; and thus an indictment for keeping a gaming table, at which a game of chance was charged to have been played for money, is not supported by proof that bank notes were played for. [*sic*] Pryor v. Commonwealth, 32 Ky. (2 Dana) 298. [The "*sic*" indicates where I believe the closing quotation mark should be. je.]

"Money," as used in Crimes Act, § 18, providing that any person stealing any money, the property of another, shall be guilty of larceny, cannot be construed to include bank bills, for strictly bank bills are not money, though for many purposes they are treated as such. Johnson v. State, 11 Ohio St. 324, 325.

The term "money," in the statute defining robbery as taking from the person of another any money or personal property of any value whatsoever, with force and by violence, and with intent to steal or rob, does not include bank notes. Turner v. State, 1 Ohio St. 422, 426.

In Rev. St. § 152, declaring that the State Treasurer shall have charge of all moneys paid into the state, the term does not include promissory notes. State v. McFetridge, 54 N. W. 1, 16, 84 Wis. 473, 20 L. R. A. 223.

Promissory notes are not the kind of notes which pass as money, for they are not public tokens. Bank notes are public tokens—as much so as weights and measures or the alnager's seal. In practice, they represent the coin of our country, and pass currently as money. State v. Patillo, 11 N. C. 348, 349. [An alnager is a specialized inspector and tax collector for the King. je.]

Treasury notes or greenbacks

"Money" does not include treasury notes. Foquet v. Hoadley, 3 Conn. 534, 536.

In legal acceptance, "money" means current metallic coins; therefore an indictment for embezzling "money" is not sustained by proof of embezzling greenbacks or national currency notes. Block v. State, 44 Tex. 620, 622.

"The generic term 'money,' since the introduction and free use of bank notes and treasury notes as a circulating medium and standard of value, is understood to include such notes, as well as the authorized coin of the country." Noble v. State, 59 Ala. 73, 80.

"Money" as used in an indictment charging the betting of money, does not include United States treasury notes, such notes not being money in the legal acceptation. Williams v. State, 20 Miss. (12 Smedes & M.) 58, 63.

MONEY: (Black, 1951) In usual and ordinary acceptation it means gold, silver, or paper money used as circulating medium of exchange, and does not embrace notes, bonds, evidences of debt, or other personal or real estate. Lane v. Railey, 280 Ky. 319, 133 S.W.2d 74, 79, 81. Currency; the circulating medium; cash.
The term "moneys" is not of more extensive signification than "money," and means only cash, and not things in action. Mann v. Mann, 14 Johns., N.Y., 1; 7 Am.Dec. 416.
In its strict technical sense, "money" means coined metal, usually gold or silver, upon which the government stamp has been impressed to indicate its value. In its more popular sense, "money" means any currency, tokens, bank-notes, or other circulating medium in general use as the representative of value. Kennedy v. Briere, 45 Tex. 305; Cook v. State, 130 Ark. 90, 196 S.W. 922, 924; Vick v. Howard, 136 Va. 101, 116 S.E. 465, 467, 31 A.L.R. 240.
The simple meaning of "money" is current coin, but it may mean possessions expressible in money values. "Money" has no technical meaning, but is of ambiguous import, and may be interpreted having regard to all surrounding circumstances under which it is used. "Money" is often and popularly used as equivalent to "property." "Money" means wealth reckoned in terms of money; capital considered as a cash asset; specifically such wealth or capital dealt in as a commodity to be loaned, invested, or the like; wealth considered as a cash asset. Salt Lake County v. Utah Copper Co., C.C.A. Utah, 23 F.2d 127, 132.
In its more comprehensive and general sense, it means wealth,—the representative of commodities of all kinds, of lands, and of everything that can be transferred in commerce. Paul v. Ball, 31 Tex. 10. A general, indefinite term for the measure and representative of value.

MONEY: (Black, 1991) In usual and ordinary acceptation it means coins and paper currency used as circulating medium of exchange, and does not embrace notes, bonds, evidences of debt, or other personal or real estate.
A medium of exchange authorized or adopted by a domestic or foreign government as a part of its currency. U.C.C. § 1—201(24).
See also Currency; Current money; Flat money; Legal tender; Near money; Scrip. ["Flat" is F-L-A-T, not F-I-A-T. je.]
Public money. Revenue received from federal, state, and local governments from taxes, fees, fines, etc. *See* Revenue.

NOTE: (Webster, 1828) *n.* [L. *nota* ; Fr. *note* ; W. *nod* ; from L. *notus, nosco,* to know.]
***

13. A written or printed paper acknowledging a debt and promising payment ; as a promissory *note;* a bank-*note;* a *note* of hand; a negotiable *note.*

NOTE: (Bouvier, 1870) [There is no definition for "Note" in *Bouvier*. je.]

NOTE: (Black, 1951) *n.* A unilateral instrument containing an express and absolute promise of signer to pay to a specified person or order, or bearer, a definite sum of money at a specified time. Shawno Finance Corporation v. Julius, 214 Wis. 637, 254 N.W. 355. *** See Bought Note; Notes; Judgment Note; Promissory Note; Sold Note.

NOTE: (*Words & Phrases*, 1957)
In general
A "note" is not "payment" but only a "promise to pay". Fidelity Savings State Bank v. Grimes, 131 P.2d 894, 896, 156 Kan. 55.

The characteristics of a "note" are a definite obligor, a definite obligee (either by name or designation), a definitely ascertainable obligation, and a time of maturity, either definite or that will become definite. Commissioner of Internal Revenue v. Meridian & Thirteenth Realty Co., C.C.A.7, 132 F.2d 182, 188.

Debt
A "note" is a written acknowledgment of a debt and a promise to pay, and a "debt" is that which is due from one person to another. Almond v. Gilmer, 49 S.E.2d 431, 442, 188 Va. 1.

Draft
The term "bills or notes," in a statute providing that no banking association shall issue or put in circulation any bills or notes, etc., means any circulating bill or note deposited and likely to be used as a substitute for money. The term does not include a draft not payable by its terms to order or bearer, although expressed in dollars and not in foreign coin, and drawn on a domestic and not a foreign place. Curtis v. Levitt, N.Y., 17 Barb. 309, 341.

Evidence of debt
A "note", is merely the evidence of existence of the obligation. Magnolia Petroleum Co. v. Police Jury of Vermillion Parish, La. App., 11 So.2d 36, 38.

Money
A note is a written promise made by a certain person to pay a certain sum of money to a certain person at a certain time. Brown v. First Nat. Bank, 18 N.E. 56, 59, 115 Ind. 572, 577; Grissom v. Commercial Nat. Bank, 10 S.W. 774, 779, 87 Tenn. (3 Pickle) 350, 3 L.R.A. 273, 10 Am.St.Rep. 669.

Promissory note
Promissory "notes" are forms of intangible property and are evidence of debts owing their holders. Department of Taxation v. Weber, 113 N.E.2d 141, 142, 94 Ohio App. 511.

NOTE: (Black, 1991) *n.* An instrument containing an express and absolute promise of signer (*i.e.* maker) to pay to a specified person or order, or bearer, a definite sum of money at a specified time. The borrower's legally binding written promise to repay a debt to a lender on a specified date. An instrument that is a promise to pay other than a certificate of deposit. U.C.C. § 3—104(2)(d). Two party instrument made by the maker and payable to payee which is negotiable if signed by the maker and contains an unconditional promise to pay sum certain in money, on demand or at a definite time, to order or bearer. U.C.C. § 3—104(1). A note not meeting these requirements may be assignable but not negotiable. ***

NOTE OF HAND: (Bouvier, 1870) A popular name for a promissory note.

PAY: (Webster, 1828) *v.t.* pret. and pp. *paid.* ***
  1. To discharge a debt; to deliver to a creditor the value of the debt, either in money or goods, to his acceptance or satisfaction, by which the obligation of the debtor is discharged. ***

PAY: (Black, 1891) To pay is to deliver to a creditor the value of a debt, either in money or in goods, for his acceptance, by which the debt is discharged. 36 N. Y. 522.

PAY: (Black, 1951) *v.* To discharge a debt; to deliver to a creditor the value of a debt, either in money or in goods, for his acceptance. Beals v. Home Ins. Co., 36 N.Y. 522. Carpenter v. Dummit, 221 Ky. 67, 297 S.W. 695, 700; Vollmer v. Automobile Fire Ins. Co. of Hartford, Conn., 207 App.Div. 67, 202 N.Y.S. 374, 375.

The term, however, is sometimes limited to discharging an indebtedness by the use of money. Krahn v. Goodrich, 164 Wis. 600, 160 N.W. 1072, 1075. In re Bailey's Estate, 276 Pa. 147, 119 A. 907, 909.

PAY: (Black, 1991) *v.* To discharge a debt by tender of payment due; to deliver to a creditor the value of a debt, either in money or in goods, for his acceptance. U.C.C. §§ 2—511, 3—604. To compensate for goods, services or labor. *See also* Discharge; Payment.

PAYABLE: (Black, 1891) A sum of money is said to be payable when a person is under an obligation to pay it. "Payable" may therefore signify an obligation to pay at a future time, but, when used without qualification, "payable" means that the debt is payable at once, as opposed to "owing." Sweet.

PAYABLE: (Black, 1951) Capable of being paid; suitable to be paid; admitting or demanding payment; justly due; legally enforceable. In re Advisory Opinion to the Governor, 74 Fla. 250, 77 So. 102, 103.

A sum of money is said to be payable when a person is under an obligation to pay it. "Payable" may therefore signify an obligation to pay at a future time, but, when used without qualification, "payable" means that the debt is payable at once, as opposed to "owing." Sweet. And see First Nat. Bank v. Greenville Nat. Bank, 84 Tex. 40, 19 S.W. 334; Easton v. Hyde, 13 Minn. 91, Gil. 83.

PAYABLE ON DEMAND: (Black, 1951) A bill payable on demand is payable on its date or within a reasonable time without grace. Waggoner Banking Co. v. Gray County State Bank, Tex.Civ.App., 165 S.W. 922, 925.

At common law an instrument is payable on demand where no time for payment is expressed, unless the circumstances show a different intention. Coleman v. Page's Estate, 202 S.C. 486, 25 S.E.2d 559.

PAYEE: (Black, 1891) In mercantile law. The person in whose favor a bill of exchange, promissory note, or check is made or drawn; the person to whom or to whose order a bill, note, or check is made payable. 3 Kent, Comm. 75.

PAYER, or **PAYOR**: (Black, 1891) One who pays, or who is to make a payment; particularly the person who is to make payment of a bill or note. Correlative to "payee."

PAYER, *or* **PAYOR**: (Black, 1991) One who pays, or who is to make a payment; particularly the person who is to make payment of a check, bill or note. Correlative to "payee."

PAYMENT: (Bouvier, 1870) The fulfillment of a promise, or the performance of an agreement.

The discharge in money of a sum due. ***

4. According to Comyns, payment by merchants must be made in money or by bill. Comyns, Dig. *Merchant* (F).

It is now the law for all classes of citizens that payment must be made by money, unless the obligation is, by the terms of the instrument creating it, to be discharged by other means. In the United States, congress has, by the constitution, power to decide what shall be a legal tender; that is, in what form the creditor may demand his payment or must receive it if offered; and congress has determined this by statutes. The same power is exercised by the governments of all civilized countries. Payment in the United States must be made in coined money (or treasury notes made legal tender), if the creditor insists upon having it, 3 Halst. N. J. 172; 4 N. H. 296; 4 Dev. & B. No. C. 435; and copper cents are not legal tender under the United States constitution. 2 Nott & M'C. So. C. 519. ***

5. Upon a plea of payment, the defendant may prove a discharge in bank-notes, negotiable notes of individuals, or a debt already due from the payee, delivered and accepted or discounted as payment. Phillipps, Ev. Cowen & H. ed. n. 387. Bank-notes, in conformity to usage and common understanding, are regarded as cash. 1 Burr. 452; 3 *id.* 1516; 9 Johns. N. Y. 120; 6 Md. 37; unless objected to. 1 Metc. Mass. 356; 8 Ohio, 169; 10 Me. 475; 2 Crompt. & J. Exch. 16, n.; 5 Yerg. Tenn. 199; 4 Esp. 267; 3 Humphr. Tenn. 162; 6 Ala. N. S. 226. Treasury notes are not cash. 3 Conn. 534. Giving a check is not considered as payment; but the holder may treat it as a nullity if he derives no benefit from it, provided he has not been guilty of negligence so as to cause injury to the drawer. 2 Parsons, Contr. 136; 2 Campb. 515; 8 Term., 451; 2 Bos. & P. 518, 4 Ad. & E. 952; ***

7. If a bill of exchange or promissory note be given to a creditor and accepted as payment, it shall be a good payment. Comyns, Dig. *Merchant* (F); 30 N. H. 540; *** But regularly a bill of exchange or note given to a creditor shall not be a discharge of the debt till payment of the bill, unless so accepted. Skinn. 410; 1 Salk. 124. *** [*Bouvier's Law Dictionary*, 1870 edition, provides five pages of discussion of various aspects of *payment.* je.]

PAYMENT: (Black, 1991) The fulfillment of a promise, or the performance of an agreement. A discharge of an obligation or debt, and part payment, if accepted, is a discharge pro tanto.

In a more restricted legal sense payment is the performance of a duty, promise, or obligation, or discharge of a debt or liability, by the delivery of money or other value by a debtor to a creditor, where the money or other valuable thing is tendered and accepted as extinguishing debt or obligation in whole or in part. Also the money or other thing so delivered. U.C.C. §§ 2—511, 3—604. ***

PROMISSORY: (Webster, 1828) *a.* Containing a promise or binding declaration of something to be done or forborne. *Arbuthnot.*

2. In *law,* a promissory note is a writing which contains a

promise of the payment of money or the delivery of property to another, at or before a time specified, in consideration of value received by the promiser. In England, *promissory* notes and bills of exchange, being negotiable for the payment of a less sum than twenty shillings, are declared to be void by Stat 15. Geo. III. *Blackstone.*

PROMISSORY NOTE: (Bouvier, 1870) A written promise to pay a certain sum of money, at a future time, unconditionally. 7 Watts & S. Penn. 264; 2 Humphr. Tenn. 143; 10 Wend. N. Y. 675; 1 Ala. 263; 7 Mo. 42; 2 Cow. N. Y. 536; 6 N. H. 364; 7 Vern. Ch. 22.

2. A promissory note differs from a mere acknowledgment of debt without any promise to pay, as when the debtor gives his creditor an I O U. See 2 Yerg. Tenn. 50; 15 Mees. & W. Exch. 23. But see 2 Humphr. Tenn. 143; 6 Ala. n. s. 373. In its form it usually contains a promise to pay, at a time therein expressed, a sum of money to a certain person therein named, or to his order, for value received. It is dated and signed by the maker. It is never under seal.

He who makes this promise is called the *maker,* and he to whom it is made is the payee. Bayley, Bills, 1: 3 Kent, Comm. 46.

3. Although a promissory note, in its original shape, bears no resemblance to a bill of exchange, yet when indorsed it is exactly similar to one; for then it is an order by the indorser of the note upon the maker to pay the indorsee. The indorser is as it were the drawer; the maker, the acceptor; and the indorsee, the payee. 4 Burr. 669; 4 Term, 148; 3 Burr. 1224.

Most of the rules applicable to bills of exchange equally affect promissory notes. No particular form is requisite to these instruments: a promise to deliver the money, or to be accountable for it, or that the payee shall have it, is sufficient. Chitty, Bills, 53, 54.

4. There are two principal qualities essential to the validity of a note: *first*, that it be payable at all events, not dependent on any contingency, 20 Pick. Mass. 132; 22 *id.* 132, nor payable out of any particular fund. 3 J. J. Marsh. Ky. 170, 542; 5 Ark. 441; 2 Blackf. Ind. 48; 1 Bibb, Ky. 503; 9 Miss. 393; 3 Pick. Mass. 541; 4 Hawks, No. C. 102; 5 How. 382. *Second,* it is required that it be for the payment of money only, 10 Serg. & R. Penn. 94; 4 Watts, Penn. 400; 11 Vt. 268, and not in bank-notes; though it has been held differently in the state of New York. 9 Johns. N. Y. 120; 19 *id.* 144.

5. A promissory note payable to order or bearer passes by indorsement, and, although a chose in action, the holder may bring suit on it in his own name. Although a simple contract, a sufficient consideration is implied from the nature of the instrument. See 5 Comyns, Dig. 133, n., 151, 472; Smith, Merc. Law, b. 3, c. 1; 4 Barnew. & C. 236; 1 Carr. & M. 16. See Bill of Exchange; Indorsement; Notice.

PROMISSORY NOTE: (Black, 1891) A promise or engagement, in writing, to pay a specified sum at a time therein limited, or on demand, or at sight, to a person therein named, or to his order, or bearer. Byles, Bills, 1, 4; 5 Denio, 484.

A promissory note is a written promise made by one or more to pay another, or order, or bearer, at a specified time, a specific amount of money, or other articles of value. Code Ga. 1882, § 2774.

A promissory note is an instrument negotiable in form, whereby the signer promises to pay a specified sum of money. Civil Code Cal. § 8244.

An unconditional written promise, signed by the maker, to pay absolutely and at all events a sum certain in money, either to the bearer or to a person therein designated or his order. Benj. Chalm. Bills & N. art. 271.

PROMISSORY NOTE: (Black, 1951) A promise or engagement, in writing, to pay a specified sum at a time therein limited, or on demand, or at sight, to a person therein named, or to his order, or bearer. Byles, Bills, 1, 4; Hall v Farmer, 5 Denio, N.Y. 484. A written promise made by one or more to pay another, or order, or bearer, at a specified time, a specified amount of money, or other articles of value. Pryor v. American Trust & Banking Co., 15 Ga.App. 822, 84 S.E. 312, 314. An unconditional written promise, signed by the maker, to pay absolutely and at all events a sum certain in money, either to the bearer or to a person therein designated or his order. Benj. Chalm. Bills & N. art. 271; Harrison v. Beals, 111 Or. 563, 222 P. 728, 730; at a time specified therein, or at a time which must certainly arrive. Iowa Sate Savings Bank v. Wignall, 53 Okl. 641, 157 P. 725; Lanum v. Harrington, 267 Ill. 57, 107 N.E. 826, 828.

A written promise to pay a certain sum of money, at a future time, unconditionally. Brooks v. Owen, 112 Mo. 251, 19 S.W. 723, 20 S.W. 492. By the Uniform Negotiable Instruments Act, a *negotiable promissory note* is defined as an unconditional promise in writing made by one person to another signed by the maker engaging to pay on demand, or at a fixed or determinable future time, a sum certain in money to order or to bearer. Where a note is drawn to the maker's own order, it is not complete until indorsed by him. Section 184.

NOTE: (*Words & Phrases*, 1957)
PROMISSORY NOTE
In general

A "promissory note" is merely evidence of an indebtedness which exists independently of the note, and the instrument itself is merely a facility to creditor in proving the fact of the obligation. LSA-C.C. art. 1762. Oak Appliance Co. v. Clayton, La. App., 1 So.2d 157, 159.

A "promissory note" is an evidence of indebtedness from the maker to the payee, by which the maker agrees to pay the payee a definite sum at a certain time. Gregory v. Williams, 189 P. 932, 933, 106 Kan. 819.

A promissory note is merely a promise to pay money in the future, and when without consideration is but a promise to make a gift in the future, and the gift is not completed until the note is paid. Brooks v. Owen, 19 S.W. 723, 725, 112 Mo. 251; Conrad v. Manning's Estate, 83 N.W. 1038, 125 Mich. 77.

Absolute and unconditional payment

It is essential to the validity of a promissory note that it contain no contingency or uncertainty as to the person by whom it is payable or to whom it is payable. Frazier v. Moore's Adm'r, 11 Tex. 755, 759.

A "promissory note" is a written promise by one person to pay another person therein named or order a fixed sum of money at all events and at a time specified therein or at a time which must certainly arise. Clarke v. Hunter, 83 Ill.App. 100.

A "promissory note" may be defined to be a written engagement by one person to pay absolutely and unconditionally to another person therein named, or to his order or to the bearer, a certain sum of money at a specified time, or on demand, or at sight. Hall v. Farmer, N.Y., 5 Denio, 484, 487; Bank of Peru v. Farnsworth, 18 Ill. (8 Peck) 563, 565.

Instrument in writing

A "promissory note" is a promise in writing to pay to a person therein named a certain sum of money at a specified time. Digan v. Mandel, 79 N.E. 899, 902, 167 Ind. 586, 119 Am.St.Rep. 515.

Payment of money only

To constitute a good promissory note, it must be for the payment of money in specie—that is, not that the words "in specie" must be included in the note, but it must be for the payment of money generally without limitation or restriction, which will then in legal acceptation mean gold and silver; so where a note is made payable in current bank notes of Tennessee it is not a promissory note within the meaning of the law merchant. Whiteman v. Childress, 25 Tenn. (6 Humph.) 303, 306.

Silver certificates or treasury notes

Treasury notes issued by authority of Act Oct. 12, 1837, 5 Stat. 201, were promissory notes within the meaning of Act March 3, 1825, 4 Stat. 114, prohibiting or providing a penalty for concealing such notes, or receiving them knowing them to be stolen. They contain a promise to pay money by the United States, and are substantially a demand imposed by the law. United States v. Hardyman, 38 U.S. 176, 178, 13 Pet. 176, 178, 10 L.Ed. 113.

The term "promissory note," as used in Code, art. 30, § 101, providing for the punishment of any one who shall steal any promissory note, does not include a silver certificate. "A silver certificate is not, in common parlance, a promissory note; and to charge one with stealing a promissory note would not, under such an instruction, inform the accused as to the nature of the offense for which he is called upon to answer, nor would the jury before whom the case was tried know it was the offense which the grand jury intended to present." Stewart v. State, 62 Md. 412, 416.

PROMISSORY NOTE: (Black, 1991) A promise or engagement, in writing, to pay a specified sum at a time therein stated, or on demand, or at sight, to a person therein named, or to his order, or bearer. An unconditional written promise, signed by the maker, to pay absolutely and at all events a sum certain in money, either to the bearer or to a person therein designated or his order, at a time specified therein, or at a time which must certainly arrive.

A signed paper promising to pay another a certain sum of money. An unconditional written promise to pay a specified sum of money on demand or at a specified date. Such a note is negotiable if signed by the maker and containing an unconditional promise to pay a sum certain in money either on demand or at a definite time and payable to order or bearer. U.C.C. § 3—104.

SPECIE: (Webster, 1828) *n. spe'shy.* Coin; copper, silver or gold coined and used as a circulating medium of commerce. [See *Special.*]

SPECIE: (Bouvier, 1870) Metallic money issued by public authority.

This term is used in contradistinction to paper money, which in some countries is emitted by the government, and is a mere engagement which represents specie. Bank-paper in the United States is also called paper money. Specie is the only constitutional money in this country. See 4 T. B. Monr. 483.

SPECIE: (Black, 1891) 1. Coin of the precious metals, of a certain weight and fineness, and bearing the stamp of the government, denoting its value as currency. 5 Hill, 523, 536.

2. When spoken of a contract, the expression "performance *in specie*" means strictly, or according to the exact terms. As applied to things, it signifies individuality or identity. Thus, on a bequest of a specific picture, the legatee would be said to be entitled to the delivery of the picture *in specie; i.e.,* of the very thing. Whether a thing is due *in genere* or *in specie* depends, in each case, on the will of the transacting parties. Brown. [In the United States of America, in contracts in which the dollar sign ($) is used to define terms or conditions and payments, etc., *specie* refers to coins of gold and silver, meaning lawful money of the United States. je.]

SPECIE: (Black, 1951) Coin of the precious metals, of a certain weight and fineness, and bearing the stamp of the government, denoting its value as currency. Trebilcock v. Wilson, 12 Wall. 695, 20 L.Ed. 460; Walkup v. Houston, 65 N.C. 501; Henry v. Bank of Salina, 5 Hill, N.Y., 536.

When spoken of a contract, the expression "performance *in specie*" means strictly, or according to the exact terms. As applied to things, it signifies individuality or identity. Thus, on a bequest of a specific picture, the legatee would be said to be entitled to the delivery of the picture *in specie; i.e.,* of the very thing. Whether a thing is due *in genere* or *in specie* depends, in each case, on the will of the transacting parties. Brown.

SPECIE: (*Words & Phrases*, 1957)

"Specie" is a coin of the precious metals of a certain weight and fineness, with government's stamp thereon denoting its value as a medium of exchange or currency. Henry v. Bank of Salina, N.Y., 5 Hill, 523, 536.

"Specie," as used in an instrument payable in specie, means that the designated number of dollars should be paid in so many gold or silver dollars of the coinage of the United States. Trebilcock v. Wilson, Iowa, 79 U.S. (12 Wall.) 687, 695; Belford v. Woodward, 41, N.E. 1097, 1099, 158 Ill. 122, 29 L.R.A. 593.

SPECIE: (Black, 1991) **Specie** /spiyshiy(iy)/. Coin of the precious metals, of a certain weight and fineness, and bearing the stamp of the government, denoting its value as currency. Metallic money; *e.g.* gold or silver coins.

When spoken of a contract, the expression "performance *in specie*" means strictly, or according to the exact terms. As applied to things, it signifies individuality or identity. Thus, on a bequest of a specific picture, the legatee would be said to be entitled to the delivery of the picture *in specie; i.e.,* of the very thing. Whether a thing is due *in genere* or *in specie* depends, in each case, on the will of the transacting parties. [Compare *Black's* Sixth's strange pronunciation guide, "/spiyshiy(iy)/," with the short and notably adequate one given by Webster in his 1828 dictionary, above. je.]

SPECIES: (Webster, 1828) ***

8. Coin, or coined silver and gold, used as a circulating medium; as the current *species* of Europe. *Arbuthnot.*

In modern practice, this word is contracted into *specie*. What quantity of *specie* has the bank in its vault? What is the amount of all the current *specie* in the country? What is the value in *specie*, of a bill of exchange? We receive payment for goods in *specie*, not in bank notes. ***

TENDER: (Webster, 1828) *n.* [from *tend.*] One that attends or takes care of ; a nurse.

3. [Fr. *tendre*, to reach.] In *law*, an offer, either of money to pay a debt, or of service to be performed, in order to save a penalty or forfeiture which would be incurred by non-payment or non-performance; as the *tender* of rent due, or of the amount of a note or bond with interest. To constitute a legal tender, such money must be offered as the law prescribes; the offer of bank notes is not a legal tender. So also the tender must be at the time and place where the rent or debt ought to be paid, and it must be to the full amount due. ***

4. Any offer for acceptance. The gentleman made me a *tender* of his services.

5. The thing offered. This money is not a legal *tender.*

TENDER: (Bouvier, 1870) (Lat. *tendere*, to extend, to offer). An offer to deliver something, made in pursuance of some contract or obligation, under such circumstances as to require no further act from the party making it to complete the transfer.

Legal tender, money of a character whch by law a debtor may require his creditor to receive in payment, in the absence of any agreement in the contract or obligation itself. See LEGAL TENDER.

In Contracts. It may be either of money or of specific articles. ***

6. The effect of a tender is to put a stop to accruing damages and interest. 5 C. B. 365; 3 Bingh. 290; 9 Cow. N. Y. 641; *** [If you and I enter a contract and my part is to "pay" you 300 horses, but instead of horses I deliver 300 cows to you, which you reject, I would not have made a legal tender to you and the courts would probably award damages and interest to you. In this case, a (the) *legal* tender would have been my delivery of 300 *horses* to you. je.]

TENDER: (Black, 1891) An offer of money; the act by which one produces and offers to a person holding a claim or demand against him the amount of money which he considers and admits to be due, in satisfaction of such claim or demand, without any stipulation or condition.

Tender, in pleading, is a plea by defendant that he has been always ready to pay the debt demanded, and before the commencement of the action tendered it to the plaintiff, and now brings it into court ready to be paid to him, etc. Brown.

Legal tender. Money is said to be legal tender when a creditor cannot refuse to accept it in payment of a debt.

TENDER: (Black, 1951) An offer of money; the act by which one produces and offers to a person holding a claim or demand against him the amount of money which he considers and admits to be due, in satisfaction of such claim or demand, without any stipulation or condition. Kastens v. Ruland, 94 N.J.Eq. 451, 1220 A. 21, 22; ***

The offer of performance, not performance itself, and, when unjustifiably refused, places other party in default and permits party making tender to exercise remedies for breach of contract. Walker v. Houston, 215 Cal. 742, 12 P.2d 952, 953, 87 A.L.R. 937.

The actual proffer of money, as distinguished from mere proposal or proposition to proffer it. Caplan v. Shaw, W.Va., 30 S.E.2d 132, 140. Hence mere written proposal to pay money, without offer of cash, is not "tender." Wardlaw v. Woodruff, 175 Ga. 515, 165 S.E. 557, 560.

"Tender," though usually used in connection with an offer to pay money, is properly used in connection with offer of property other than money. Maxwell Implement Co. v. Fitzgerald, 86 Ind.App. 206, 146 N.E. 883, 885; ***

Tender, in pleading, is a plea by defendant that he has been always ready to pay the debt demanded, and before the commencement of the action tendered it to the plaintiff, and now brings it into court ready to be paid to him, etc. Brown.

Legal tender is that kind of coin, money, or circulating medium which the law compels a creditor to accept in payment of his debt, when tendered by the debtor in the right amount. ***

TENDER: (Black, 1991) An offer of money. The act by which one produces and offers to a person holding a claim or demand against him the amount of money which he considers and admits to be due, in satisfaction of such claim or demand, without any stipulation or condition. *** [The remainder of the definition of Tender in *Black's* Sixth edition is essentially the same as that in *Black's* Fourth edition. je.]

TOKEN: (Bouvier, 1870) A document or sign of the existence of a fact.

Tokens are either public or general, or privy tokens. They are either true or false. When a token is false and indicates a general intent to defraud, and is used for that purpose, it will render the offender guilty of the crime of cheating. 12 Johns. N. Y. 292; but if it is a mere privy token, as, counterfeiting a letter in another man's name, in order to cheat but one individual, it would not be indictable. 9 Wend. N. Y. 182; 1 Dall. Penn. 47; 2 Const. S. C. 139; 2 Va. Cas. 65; 4 Hawks No. C. 348; 6 Mass. 72; 12 Johns. N. Y. 293; 2 Dev. No. C. 199; 1 Rich. So. C. 244.

In Common Law. In England, this name is given to pieces of metal, made in the shape of money, passing among private persons by consent at a certain value. 2 Chitty, Comm. Law, 182.

TREASON: (Bouvier, 1870) **In Criminal Law**. This word imports a betraying, treachery, or breach of allegiance. 4 Sharewood, Blackst. Comm. 75.

2. The constitution of the United States, art. 3, s. 3, defines treason against the Unites States to consist only in levying war against them, or in adhering to their enemies, giving them aid or comfort. This offense is punished with death. Act of April 30, 1790, 1 Story, U. S. Laws, 83. By the same article of the constitution, no person shall be convicted of treason unless on the testimony of two witnesses to the same overt act, or on confession in open court. See, generally, 3 Story, Const. 39, p. 667; Sergeant, Const. c. 30; United States *vs.* Fries, Pamph.; 1 Tucker, Blackst. Comm. App. 275, 276; ***

•

Appendix O

United States Code, Constitution

Title 5 . Government Organization and Employees
Part III - Employees
Subpart B - Employment and Retention

Chapter 33 - Examination, Selection and Placement
Subchapter II - Oath of Office

§ 3331. Oath of office

An individual, except the President, elected or appointed to an office of honor or profit in the civil service or uniformed services, shall take the following oath: "I, AB, do solemnly swear (or affirm) that I will support and defend the Constitution of the United States against all enemies, foreign and domestic; that I will bear true faith and allegiance to the same; that I take this obligation freely, without any mental reservation or purpose of evasion; and that I will well and faithfully discharge the duties of the office on which I am about to enter. So help me God." This section does not affect other oaths required by law.

Title 10. Armed Forces
Subtitle A - General Military Law
Part II - Personnel

Chapter 31 - Enlistments

§ 502. Enlistment oath: who may administer

Each person enlisting in an armed force shall take the following oath: "I, _ _ _ _ _ _ _ _ _ _, do solemnly swear (or affirm) that I will support and defend the Constitution of the United States against all enemies, foreign and domestic; that I will bear true faith and allegiance to the same; and that I will obey the orders of the President of the United States and the orders of the officers appointed over me, according to regulations and the Uniform Code of Military Justice. So help me God." This oath may be taken before any commissioned officer of any armed force.

U.S. Constitution, Article II, Section 1: Oath of office for the President:

"I do solemnly swear (or affirm) that I will faithfully execute the Office of President of the United States, and will to the best of my Ability, preserve, protect and defend the Consitution of the United States."

U.S. Constitution, Article I, Section 8:

"The Congress shall have Power . . . To coin Money, regulate the Value thereof, and of foreign Coin, and fix the Standard of Weights and Measures; . . . ."

U.S. Constitution, Article I, Section 10:

"No State shall . . . make any Thing but gold and silver Coin a Tender in Payment of Debts; . . . ."

Title 18. Crimes and Criminal Procedure
Part I - Crimes

Chapter 1 - General Provisions

§ 3. Accessory after the fact

Whoever, knowing that an offense against the United States has been committed, receives, relieves, comforts or assists the offender in order to hinder or prevent his apprehension, trial or punishment, is an accessory after the fact.

Except as otherwise expressly provided by any Act of Congress, an accessory after the fact shall be imprisoned not more than one-half the maximum term of imprisonment or (notwithstanding section 3571) fined not more than one-half the maximum fine prescribed for the punishment of the principal, or both; or if the principal is punishable by life imprisonment or death, the accessory shall be imprisoned not more than 15 years.

§ 4. Misprision of felony

Whoever, having knowledge of the actual commission of a felony cognizable by a court of the United States, conceals and does not as soon as possible make known the same to some judge or other person in civil or military authority under the United States, shall be fined under this title or imprisoned not more than three years, or both.

Title 18 § 241. Conspiracy against rights

If two or more persons conspire to injure, oppress, threaten, or intimidate any person in any State, Territory, or District in the free exercise or enjoyment of any right or privilege secured to him by the Constitution or laws of the United States, or because of his having so exercised the same; or

If two or more persons go in disguise on the highway, or on the premises of another, with intent to prevent or hinder his free exercise or enjoyment of any right or privilege so secured -

They shall be fined under this title or imprisoned not more than ten years, or both; and if death results from the acts committed in violation of this section or if such acts include kidnapping or an attempt to kidnap, aggravated sexual abuse or an attempt to commit aggravated sexual abuse, or an attempt to kill, they shall be fined under this title or imprisoned for any term of years or for life, or both, or may be sentenced to death.

Title 18 § 242. Deprivation of rights under color of law

Whoever, under color of any law, statute, ordinance, regulation, or custom, willfully subjects any person in any State, Territory, or District to the deprivation of any rights, privileges, or immunities secured or protected by the Constitution or laws of the United States, or to different punishments, pains, or penalties, on account of such person being an alien, or by reason of his color, or race, than are prescribed for the punishment of citizens, shall be fined under this title or imprisoned not more than one year, or both; and if bodily injury results from the acts committed in violation of this section or if such acts include the use, attempted use, or threatened use of a dangerous weapon, explosives, or fire, shall be fined under this title or imprisoned not more than ten years, or both; and if death results from the acts committed in violation of this section or if such acts include kidnapping or an attempt to kidnap, aggravated sexual abuse, or an attempt to commit aggravated sexual abuse, or an attempt to kill, shall be fined under this title, or imprisoned for any term of years or for life, or both, or may be sentenced to death.

Title 18 § 474. Plates or stones for counterfeiting obligations or securities

(a) Whoever, having control, custody, or possession of any plate, stone, or other thing, or any part thereof, from which has been printed, or which may be prepared by direction of the Secretary of the Treasury for the purpose of printing, any obligation or other security of the United States, uses such plate, stone, or other thing, or any part thereof, or knowingly suffers the same to be used for the purpose of printing any such or similar obligation or other security, or any part thereof, except as may be printed for the use of the United States by order of the proper officer thereof; or

Whoever makes or executes any plate, stone, or other thing in the likeness of any plate designated for the printing of such obligation or other security; or

Whoever sells any such plate, stone, or other thing, or brings into the United States any such plate, stone, or other thing, except under the direction of the Secretary of the Treasury or te, stone, or other thing be used for the printing of the obligations or other securities of the United States; or

Whoever has in his control, custody, or possession any plate, stone, or other thing in any manner made after or in the similitude of any plate, stone, or other thing, from which any such obligation or other security has been printed, with intent to use such plate, stone, or other thing, or to suffer the same to be used in forging or counterfeiting any such obligation or other security, or any part thereof; or

Whoever has in his possession or custody, except under authority from the Secretary of the Treasury or other proper officer, any obligation or other security made or executed, in whole or in part, after the similitude of any obligation or other security issued under the authority of the United States, with intent to sell or otherwise use the same; or

Whoever prints, photographs, or in any other manner makes or executes any engraving, photograph, print, or impression in the likeness of any such obligation or other security, or any part thereof, or sells any such engraving, photograph, print, or impression, except to the United States, or brings into the United States, any such engraving, photograph, print, or impression, except by direction of some proper officer of the United States -

Is guilty of a class C felony.

(b) For purposes of this section, the terms "plate", "stone", "thing", or "other thing" includes any electronic method used for the acquisition, recording, retrieval, transmission, or reproduction of any obligation or other security, unless such use is authorized by the Secretary of the Treasury. The Secretary shall establish a system (pursuant to section 504) to ensure that the legitimate use of such electronic methods and retention of such reproductions by businesses, hobbyists, press and others shall not be unduly restricted.

Title 18 § 474A. Deterrents to counterfeiting of obligations and securities

(a) Whoever has in his control or possession, after a distinctive paper has been adopted by the Secretary of the Treasury for the obligations and other securities of the United States, any similar paper adapted to the making of any such obligation or other security, except under the authority of the Secretary of the Treasury, is guilty of a class C felony.

(b) Whoever has in his control or possession, after a distinctive counterfeit deterrent has been adopted by the Secretary of the Treasury for the obligations and other securities of the United States by publication in the Federal Register, any essentially identical feature or device adapted to the making of any such obligation or security, except under the authority of the Secretary of the Treasury, is guilty of a class C felony.

(c) As used in this section -

> (1) the term "distinctive paper" includes any distinctive medium of which currency is made, whether of wood pulp, rag, plastic substrate, or other natural or artificial fibers or materials; and

(2) the term "distinctive counterfeit deterrent" includes any ink, watermark, seal, security thread, optically variable device, or other feature or device;

(A) in which the United States has an exclusive property interest; or

(B) which is not otherwise in commercial use or in the public domain and which the Secretary designates as being necessary in preventing the counterfeiting of obligations or other securities of the United States.

Title 18 § 475. Imitating obligations or securities; advertisements

Whoever designs, engraves, prints, makes, or executes, or utters, issues, distributes, circulates, or uses any business or professional card, notice, placard, circular, handbill, or advertisement in the likeness or similitude of any obligation or security of the United States issued under or authorized by any Act of Congress or writes, prints, or otherwise impresses upon or attaches to any such instrument, obligation, or security, or any coin of the United States, any business or professional card, notice, or advertisement, or any notice or advertisement whatever, shall be fined under this title.

Title 18 § 479. Uttering counterfeit foreign obligations or securities

Whoever, within the United States, knowingly and with intent to defraud, utters, passes, or puts off, in payment or negotiation, any false, forged, or counterfeited bond, certificate, obligation, security, treasury note, bill, or promise to pay, mentioned in section 478 of this title, whether or not the same was made, altered, forged, or counterfeited within the United States, shall be fined under this title or imprisoned not more than three years, or both.

Title 18 § 481. Plates or stones for counterfeiting foreign obligations or securities

Whoever, within the United States except by lawful authority, controls, holds, or possesses any plate, stone, or other thing, or any part thereof, from which has been printed or may be printed any counterfeit note, bond, obligation, or other security, in whole or in part, of any foreign government, bank, or corporation, or uses such plate, stone, or other thing, or knowingly permits or suffers the same to be used in counterfeiting such foreign obligations, or any part thereof; or

Whoever, except by lawful authority, makes or engraves any plate, stone, or other thing in the likeness or similitude of any plate, stone, or other thing designated for the printing of the genuine issues of the obligations of any foreign government, bank, or corporation; or

Whoever, except by lawful authority, prints, photographs, or makes, executes, or sells any engraving, photograph, print, or impression in the likeness of any genuine note, bond, obligation, or other security, or any part thereof, of any foreign government, bank, or corporation; or

Whoever brings into the United States any counterfeit plate, stone, or other thing, engraving, photograph, print, or other impressions of the notes, bonds, obligations, or other securities of any foreign government, bank, or corporation -

Shall be fined under this title or imprisoned not more than five years, or both.

Title 18 § 504. Printing and filming of United States and foreign obligations and securities

Notwithstanding any other provision of this chapter, the following are permitted:

(1) the printing, publishing, or importation, or the making or importation of the necessary plates for such printing or publishing, of illustrations of -

(A) postage stamps of the United States,

(B) revenue stamps of the United States,

(C) any other obligation or other security of the United States, and

(D) postage stamps, revenue stamps, notes, bonds, and any other obligation or other security of any foreign government, bank, or corporation. Illustrations permitted by the foregoing provisions of this section shall be made in accordance with the following conditions:

(i) all illustrations shall be in black and white, except that illustrations of postage stamps issued by the United States or by any foreign government and stamps issued under the Migratory Bird Hunting Stamp Act of 1934 may be in color;

(ii) all illustrations (including illustrations of uncanceled postage stamps in color and illustrations of stamps issued under the Migratory Bird Hunting Stamp Act of 1934 in color) shall be of a size less than three-fourths or more than one and one-half, in linear dimension, of each part of any matter so illustrated which is covered by subparagraph (A), (B), (C), or (D) of this paragraph, except that black and white illustrations of postage and revenue stamps issued by the United States or by any foreign government and colored illustrations of canceled postage stamps issued by the United States may be in the exact linear dimension in which the stamps were issued; and

(iii) the negatives and plates used in making the illustrations shall be destroyed after their final use in accordance with this section. The Secretary of the Treasury shall prescribe regulations to permit color illustrations of such currency of the United States as the Secretary determines may be appropriate for such purposes.

(2) The (FOOTNOTE 1) provisions of this section shall not permit the reproduction of illustrations of obligations or other securities, by or through electronic methods used for the acquisition, recording, retrieval, transmission, or reproduction of any obligation or other security, unless such use is authorized by the Secretary of the Treasury. The Secretary shall establish a system to ensure that the legitimate use of such electronic methods and retention of such reproductions by businesses, hobbyists, press or others shall not be unduly restricted.

(FOOTNOTE 1) So in original. Probably should not be capitalized.

(3) the making or importation, (FOOTNOTE 2) of motion-picture films, microfilms, or slides, for projection upon a screen or for use in telecasting, of postage and revenue stamps and other obligations and securities of the United States, and postage and revenue stamps, notes, bonds, and other obligations or securities of any foreign government, bank, or corporation.

No prints or other reproductions shall be made from such films or slides, except for the purposes of paragraph (1), without the permission of the Secretary of the Treasury.

(FOOTNOTE 2) So in original. The comma probably should not appear.

For the purposes of this section the term "postage stamp" includes postage meter stamps.

Title 42 § 1981. Equal rights under the law

(a) Statement of equal rights

All persons within the jurisdiction of the United States shall have the same right in every State and Territory to make and enforce contracts, to sue, be parties, give evidence, and to the full and equal benefit of all laws and proceedings for the security of persons and property as is enjoyed by white citizens, and shall be subject to like punishment, pains, penalties, taxes, licenses, and exactions of every kind, and to no other.

(b) "Make and enforce contracts" defined

For purposes of this section, the term "make and enforce contracts" includes the making, performance, modification, and termination of contracts, and the enjoyment of all benefits, privileges, terms, and conditions of the contractual relationship.

(c) Protection against impairment

The rights protected by this section are protected against impairment by nongovernmental discrimination and impairment under color of State law.

Appendix P

Libertarian Party press release

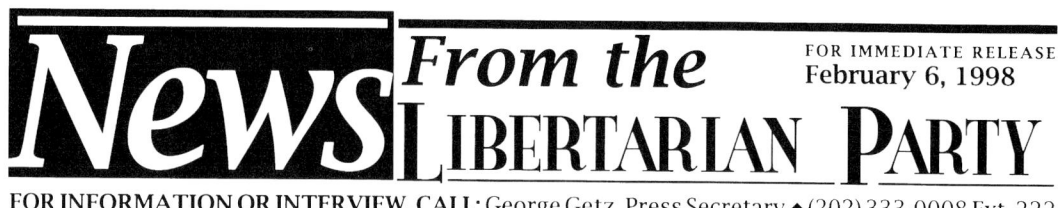

FOR IMMEDIATE RELEASE
February 6, 1998

FOR INFORMATION OR INTERVIEW, CALL: George Getz, Press Secretary ♦ (202) 333-0008 Ext. 222

The GOP's "vast conspiracy" to beat Clinton at tax-and-spending increases

If the GOP wants smaller government, why did they out-spend Clinton?

WASHINGTON, DC — Think President Clinton's $1.73 trillion budget is obscenely expensive? Wait until the Republicans get hold of it, Libertarians say.

"Last year, the Republicans criticized Bill Clinton's massive budget publicly. Then, when no one was looking, they loaded it up with $5 billion more of their own pork-barrel programs," said Libertarian Party Chairman Steve Dasbach.

> "If they do the same thing this year, they'll prove there *really is* a right-wing conspiracy in Washington: A Republican conspiracy to give Bill Clinton an even larger government than he asked for — again."

This week, Clinton sent to Congress a budget that he claims will result in a $9.5 billion surplus by 1999. The president wants to increase spending on education, child care, health care, and the environment while raising taxes by nearly $100 billion over five years. House Speaker Newt Gingrich immediately assailed it as "a budget only a liberal could love," and Senate Budget Committee Chairman Pete Domenici called it a "magnificent contradiction."

"The *real* contradiction is the difference between what Republicans say and what they do," Dasbach said. "Last year, Republicans gave Bill Clinton *more* money than he wanted for 35 separate programs, **adding a staggering $5 billion to America's total tax bill.**"

Specifically, the GOP handed Clinton $200 million more than he demanded for the Agency for International Development; $1 billion more for education programs; $54 million more for agriculture programs; and tens of millions more for AIDS programs, the Energy Department, and public housing, according to an analysis by the Cato Institute of last year's 13 appropriations bills.

"Incredibly, the GOP even authorized $5 million for a football field for the NFL's Carolina Panthers, by quietly inserting the money into a bill funding the Appalachian Regional Commission — proving that sports welfare is alive and well in the Republican-controlled Congress," said Dasbach.

> **This year, Republicans may be tempted to increase spending even more because of predictions of a budget surplus, Dasbach warned.**

"Fantasies of a budget surplus have already seduced Republicans into going on another tax-and-spend orgy," he said. GOP plans include $219 billion for highway construction, a multi-billion-dollar tobacco tax, and $2 billion to restore food stamp benefits to legal aliens.

"These GOP spending plans prove that the only *real* difference between Republicans and Democrats is which government programs they want to spend your money on," Dasbach said. "Democrats want to spend it on child care, health care, and the environment, and Republicans prefer highways, food stamps, and football fields.

"Republican politicians claim they want smaller government, but year after year, their budget speaks louder than their words. **And this year, taxpayers may learn another expensive lesson about what GOP really stands for: Groveling Over Pork.**"

# # #

6. Article I, § 8, cl. 6

The final monetary provision in the Constitution requires little exegesis. Self-evidently, Article I, § 8, cl. 6 relates in a derivative fashion: (i) to the power "To borrow Money" in Article I, § 8, cl. 2, out of which arise "the Securities * * * of the United States";[366] and (ii) to the power "To coin Money, regulate the Value thereof, and of foreign Coin" in Article I, § 8, cl. 5, out of which arises the "current Coin of the United States". [367]

Once again, the Framers chose painstakingly precise language -- referring specifically to "the Securities and current Coin of the United States" only, while avoiding such terms as "bills of credit", "paper currency", or even "money" generally. This careful distinction between "Securities" and "current Coin" strongly emphasizes once again that all "Money" of the United States is and must be coin: Article I, § 8, cl. 5 authorizes Congress "To coin Money" -- and Article I, § 8, cl. 6 empowers Congress to punish counterfeiting the evidence of this "borrow[ing]" alone. But Article I, § 8, cl. 6 does not empower Congress to punish counterfeiting anything else, unequivocally implying that the Constitution recognizes only two, mutually exclusive financial instruments: "Money" itself, composed of properly "regulate[d]" domestic and foreign "Coin"; and "Securities", composed of appropriate promises to pay "borrow[ed] Money".[368] Or, conversely, a "Securit[y]" can never be "Money"; and the power "To borrow Money" can never function to create "Money".[369]

[366] E.g., 2 J. Story, Commentaries, ante note 9, (§) 1123, at 61-62.

[367] At the time of the Federal Convention, the term "current Coin" was synonymous with the term "lawful Coin". See, e.g., Wharton v. Morris, 1 U.S. (1 Dall.) 125, 126 (Pa. 1785). The Framers added the adjective "current" apparently to bring within Article I, § 8, cl. 6 the counterfeiting of any foreign "Coin" that might be given "currency" (or made "lawful") by its "regulat[ion]" in the United States. 1 W. Crosskey, Politics and the Constitution, ante note 215, at 476-77.

[368] Whether a mere promise to pay can qualify as a constitutional "securit[y]" is doubtful. As late as the middle of the nineteenth century the term "security" had a restricted meaning that excluded such promises. In re Astor's Estate, 62 N.Y.S.2d 117, 118 (N.Y. City Surrogate's Ct. 1946). See Black's Law Dictionary, ante note 15, at 1522, which defines "security" as "an obligation * * * given by a debtor to make sure the payment or performance of his debt, by furnishing the creditor with a resource to be used in case of failure in the principal obligation". Blackstone, for example, drew a distinction between "bills of exchange" (which he classified as "securities") and "promissory notes". 2 W. Blackstone, Commentaries, ante note 10, at 466-70. But c.f. Bank v. Supervisors, 74 U.S. (7 Wall.) 26, 31 (1868): "[United States] notes are obligations. They bind the national faith. They are, therefore, strictly securities. They secure the payment stipulated to the holders, by the pledge of the national faith, the only ultimate security of all national obligations, whatever form they may assume."

[369] On the other hand, as is obvious, "Money" can never be a "Securit[y]", and the power "To coin Money" can never function to borrow "Money".

•

Edwin Vieira, Jr., A.B., Harvard College; A.M., Ph.D., Harvard Graduate School of Arts and Sciences; J.D., Harvard Law School. Member of the Maryland and District of Columbia Bars.

Figure P-1. From page 87, Pieces of Eight: The Monetary Powers and Disabilities of the United States Constitution, *by Edwin Vieira, Jr., founder and president of the National Alliance for Constitutional Money. This is part six of a multipart analysis of the Constitutional aspects of United States monetary law. Here Dr. Vieira discusses the United States Constitution, Article I (one), Section 8, clause 6. Copyright © 1983 by Edwin Vieira, Jr. All rights reserved. Reproduced with permission. Fort Lee, New Jersey: Sound Dollar Committee, 1983. ISBN 0-8159-6226-6; LCCN 83-18898.*

INDEX

900 number 151, 152

A

A Blueprint for Judicial Reform xiv, xvii, 233
abrasion 303
accountant 128, 129
Act of April 2, 1792 vii, 9, 19, 34, 41, 45, 47, 253, 300
act of God 105
activist xiv, xv, 186
Acton Institute 190, 236
Actuary 209
adulteration 212
Advanced Research Projects Agency (ARPA) 173
aerosols 220
affidavit 151
Africa 154, 155, 165, 227
Ag 220, 223
Air Force 2
Alaska 153
Aldrich, Nelson W. 243
Aldrich report 243
Allen, Gary 193
alloy 9, 17, 18, 19, 300
Amazon.com 174
Amendment, 16th 186
Amendment, Balanced Budget 206
Amendment, Fifth 186
Amendment, Flat Tax 206
American Dictionary of the English Language xvii, 232, 238, 297
American Embassy 5
American Numismatic Association (ANA) xvii, 201
American Numismatic Society (ANS) xvii, 201
amortize 209, 217
Andrew, Abraham Piatt 244
Angell, Wayne 5
anonymity 130, 163, 170
anti-social 155, 161, 162, 163, 166
anti-virus software 178, 179
Apothecary 223, 224
Ar 220

Arab 182, 251
Arapaho 69
Argentum 220
Arkansas 172
ARPAnet 173
arson 144, 195, 233, 305
Article 1, Section 10, U.S. Constitution 41, 141, 216, 219, 303
Article 1, Section 8, U.S. Constitution 19, 41, 219
artificial persons 137
ASCII 178
assault 123, 162
assets 14, 47, 120, 123, 132, 133, 160, 176, 186, 187, 198, 202, 215, 216, 239, 246, 267, 299
assignat 209, 219
AT&T 203
attorney 50, 129, 137, 139, 154, 176, 187, 188, 189, 198, 217, 248, 271
Au 214, 223
audit 209, 227, 249
Aurum 214, 221
Australia xix, 234
Austrian xix, 213
avoirdupois 132, 214, 217, 218, 221, 223

B

bait and switch 154
balance sheet, U.S. Treasury 267
Balanced Budget 206
Bancroft, George v
Bank of England xix, 244, 249
Bank of Nova Scotia 247
Banking Deregulation and Monetary Control Act 225
bankrupt 108, 210, 242, 245
barratry 210
Barron's 231, 234, 235
barter 8, 210, 298, 299, 303
Bastiat, Frederic iii, 250
beak 45, 249
Berlin vii, ix, xvi, xxii, 1, 2, 3, 4, 5, 6
Berlin Wall xxii, 3
Best Enemy Money Can Buy 234, 243

Better Business Bureau   154, 156, 236
Bible, King James Version   225
bill of credit   297, 298
bill of exchange   297, 298, 305, 306, 307
bill of lading   45
bill of materials   45
Bill of Rights   45, 206, 237
Black Tuesday   111
Black's Law Dictionary   xvii, 29, 44, 182, 231, 297, 300, 301
Blanchard, James U., III   xvii, 108, 164, 208, 232, 234, 237, 242, 243, 244, 245, 246, 247, 248, 249, 250, 251
Bohemia   17, 99
bond   5, 51, 115, 225, 243, 297, 308, 311
Borah, William E.   242, 251
border   xxii, 2, 3, 155
Boulware, Lemuel R.   247
Bouvier's Law Dictionary   xix, 231, 238, 297, 305
Bowers and Merena Galleries, Inc.   xvii
brass   9
Brazil   139
breach   32, 106, 139, 308
Bretton Woods   181, 182
British Royal Mint   xix, 9
broker   120, 121, 122, 128, 198, 251
Brooklyn   129, 159, 232
Bryan, Malcolm   245
Bryan, William Jennings   244
budget   143, 163, 168, 187, 199, 206
bull   102, 197
bullion   9, 20, 21, 111, 133, 139, 216, 220, 226, 242
Bulwer-Lytton, Edward   1, 229
Bureau of Engraving and Printing   xix, 14, 85, 115, 141, 236, 249
Business Week   133

C

California gold   x, 98
capital, preservation of   127
carat   46, 215, 222
Carnegie Mellon University   178
Carter, James E. ("Jimmy")   226
Casuals of the Sea   243
Cato Institute   190, 236
cattle   103, 213, 215, 216, 217
caveat   147, 170, 244, 299
caveat emptor   147
certificate of deposit   116, 117, 304
Certified mail   43, 152
Chad   227, 228
Chase Manhattan Bank   xix
Chase, Salmon P.   243
chattel   210, 211, 243, 302
cheat   159, 308

checking account   114, 116, 117, 118, 119, 120, 121, 122, 169, 170, 190, 226
Cherokee   ix, 60
child of God   220, 221
Choctaw   ix, 60
CIA   3, 4
Cicero, Marcus Tullius   250
citizen   5, 39, 43, 58, 163, 200, 203, 212, 216, 225, 228
civics   iii
Civil War, American   xviii, 15, 35, 38
class-action suit   139
clergy   156
clipping   9, 18
code   vii, xiii, xvii, 29, 52, 138, 139, 145, 151, 152, 157, 160, 165, 167, 175, 178, 186, 188, 189, 215, 306, 307, 309, 330
collateral   103, 104, 115, 123, 124, 211
Colonata   18, 218, 219
colonial   x, xvii, xviii, 97, 212, 218, 220, 271
colony   ix, 34, 51, 53, 271
color of law   137, 310
Colorado Springs   xvii, 201
commodity   xviii, 19, 211, 234, 246, 304
communist   3, 4, 130, 135, 143, 193
Computer Professionals for Social Responsibility   179
con artist   5, 6, 150, 153, 156
Confederate States of America   ix, 62
confederation   41, 49, 241, 300
Consequences of the Peace   244
conspiracy   29, 137, 138, 144, 163, 199, 232, 234, 246, 299, 309
conspirator   137, 211, 212, 244
Constitution   vii, xii, xiv, xv, xvii, xix, 8, 18, 19, 26, 40, 41, 49, 107, 112, 137, 141, 143, 162, 193, 200, 206, 216, 219, 232, 234, 242, 246, 251, 271, 299, 302, 303, 305, 308, 309, 310
Constitutional Convention   141, 206
Consulate   xvii, xix, 99
Consumer Price Index   196, 202
Continental   ix, 38, 54, 141, 196, 212, 272
cookie   179
copper   18, 97, 141, 212, 299, 302, 303, 304, 305, 307
Costa Rica   166, 181
counter check   171, 172
counterfeit   29, 39, 52, 113, 173, 212, 233, 245, 298, 299, 310, 311
coupon   21, 47, 205
courier   129, 152, 153, 154
cow   34, 102, 211, 213, 217, 302, 306, 308
Creature From Jekyll Island   xvi, 207, 234, 236, 251
crisis   136, 158, 163, 201, 246, 247
Croesus, King (of Lydia)   248

crook   5, 150, 153, 155, 157, 160, 161, 165, 167, 171, 172, 180
Cruden, Alexander   232
Cuba   5
culture   iii, 107, 112, 199, 213
cuneiform   211
CyberCash   178
Czech Republic   x, xvii, 17, 99
Czechoslovakia   17, 99

D

daalder   297
Daily Worker   135
daler   299
Danish Mint   xix
Danish Trade Office   xix
daric   222, 224
Davidson, James Dale   248
Day, Adrian   248
de Balzac, Honoré   243
De La Rue Currency and Security Print   xviii
debit   140, 160, 161, 167, 168, 171, 183, 212, 298, 330
default   123, 127, 308
defense   2, 15, 113, 128, 136, 142, 143, 173, 198, 204, 205, 229, 237, 250, 271
deficit   202
deflation   242
Del Mar, Alexander   iii
demand deposit   116
democracy   204
demonetize   8
denarii   7
denarius   222
Denmark   xix
deposit   ix, 12, 13, 14, 47, 48, 116, 117, 118, 121, 122, 158, 169, 170, 171, 172, 173, 181, 183, 188, 247, 248, 298, 304
depression   xi, 111, 208, 212, 247
Depression, Great   111
Deuteronomy   v, 104, 241
Dies, Martin   iii
DigiCash   176
digital money   176, 233, 248
dime   9, 17, 141, 157, 210, 212, 213
Dines, James   248
diplomacy   191
disclaimer   vii, xxi, 225
disinformation   5, 6
disme   212
disordered currency   242
dolaro   218, 219
dominant media   131, 134, 138, 163, 185, 226, 228
dominion   104, 131
Don't Bank on It, 1981   247

Dostoevsky, Fedor   134, 243
doubloon   213
Dow Jones   vii, xviii, 130, 133, 203
Downey, Barry   176
draft   24, 187, 188, 211, 213, 221, 298, 304
dram   223, 224
dross   210, 214, 241
drought   104, 112
Drug   298
drug   123, 143, 162, 165, 166, 180, 182, 193, 197, 298, 301
due date   25, 213, 297
Durell, George Edward Foundation   227
dust   ii, xvii, 2, 8, 20, 21, 67, 82, 99, 216, 329
Dysfunctional President, The   198

E

e-cash   176, 183
e-gold   176, 177, 183, 237, 247, 330
e-metal   176, 183, 237
eagle   19, 213, 249
East Berlin   3
economic warfare   113, 137, 142
economics   101, 179, 206, 213, 218, 247
eel   155
Electronic Privacy Information Center (EPIC)   179
electrum   8, 211, 213
Emerson, Ralph Waldo   243
employment   26, 143, 151, 169, 192, 239, 309
encrypt   175
England   xvii, xviii, xix, 9, 220, 244, 249, 250, 297, 306, 308
environmentalists   204
epigrams   251
epistimology   213
epithet   7, 216
equity   111, 124, 127, 128, 129, 242
Ervin, Sam J., Jr.   xiv
escrow   149
Estonia   xix
etymology   7, 11, 109, 222, 231, 232, 297, 302
Euripides   241
Euro   181
exchange media   7, 216, 234
excise   221
Exodus   104, 105, 241
Export-Import Bank   180
Exter, John   247
extrinsic   14, 213, 215

F

face value   x, 38, 39, 79, 97, 113, 132, 205, 243, 249, 301
Farewell Address   xiv
fascism   106, 213

fascist 213
FBI 128, 146, 153, 172
Federal Reserve Act xi, xviii, 233, 243, 244, 246, 249
Federal Reserve Bank v, vii, ix, xix, 14, 46, 48, 53, 54, 61, 64, 65, 66, 69, 73, 74, 75, 77, 115, 132, 141, 198, 203, 236, 245, 248, 293, 294
Federal Reserve Bank of Chicago 236
Federal Reserve Bank of New York vii, 53, 54, 61, 64, 66, 77, 115, 132, 236, 293
Federal Reserve Bank of San Francisco 65, 69, 236
Federal Reserve Note ii, ix, x, 14, 20, 23, 28, 29, 30, 41, 46, 51, 73, 82, 83, 86, 88, 92, 93, 198, 213
Federal Reserve System vii, xix, 25, 131, 132, 207, 244, 244, 246, 248, 249
Federal Reserve Token (FRT) ix, 20, 22, 213
Federalist Papers 141
fee 26, 101, 102, 105, 129, 135, 148, 149, 158, 161, 166, 170, 189, 210, 213, 220, 221, 237
felony 39, 137, 212, 251, 271, 309, 310
fiat 131, 164, 208, 209, 211, 213, 214, 216, 219, 234, 247, 248
Fick, Paul 198
fiduciary 139, 211, 213, 234
finance xxi, 31, 46, 51, 129, 209, 213, 243, 304
fine gold 214, 215
finis 213, 214
Finland xix, 9
First Virtual Holdings, Inc. 178
fix 41, 150, 165, 180, 214, 309
flat tax 199, 206
food-reserve coupons 205
forbearance 214
Forbes, B. C. 243
Ford, Harrison 129
foreknowledge 43
forgiveness 51, 105
Fort Knox xviii, xix, 226, 227, 228, 267
Fortune 133
Foster, Vince 235
foundation xiv, 112, 129, 201, 214, 243
Foundation for American Christian Education (FACE) xvii, 238
Foundation for Economic Education (FEE) 190, 234, 237
Foundation for the Advancement of Monetary Education (FAME) xviii, 237
Fractional Currency ix, 61, 301
Franc 164, 212, 214, 248
France iii, 9, 209, 227, 245, 250
Free Congress Foundation xiv, xvii
free market 26, 103, 246, 248
Freemen 199
freemen 220, 302

Friedman, Milton 251
From Dollar to Counterfeit 233
fruits of crime 101, 138
full faith and credit 204, 205, 247
Fuller, Thomas 250
Fund for Constitutional Government 179

G

Galbraith, John Kenneth 245
gelb 214
geld 214
Germany ix, x, xix, xxii, 2, 4, 17, 133, 142, 168, 200, 217, 224, 227, 237, 244, 299
Gestapo 3
glasnost 143
Gold & Silver Reserve, Inc. 176, 177, 237, 247
gold certificate ii, ix, x, 28, 72, 81, 84, 211, 262
Gold Coin Certificate ix, 64, 66, 77
Gold, God and Government 208, 247
Gold Newsletter 108, 164, 208, 235, 246, 247, 248, 251
gold standard 131, 132, 246, 248
Gold Versus Paper 233, 234
Golden Insights xvii, 232, 234, 251
Gordon, George 189
grain 214, 217, 218, 224, 300
gram ii, 214, 224
grand jury 123, 124, 127, 185, 307
Granger, Alix 247
Great Depression 111, 208, 247
Greaves, Percy L. 246
Greek 210, 213, 215, 218, 222
Greeley, Horace 243
Green, Timothy 246
greenback ix, 20, 37, 39, 59, 301
Greenspan, Alan 132
Gresham, Sir Thomas 214, 242
Griffin, G. Edward xvi, 207, 251
grind 8, 18
Groseclose, Elgin 249
groshen 17, 99
guard xiv, 2, 3, 10, 146, 170, 173, 195
guillotine 245
gulag 3
gulden groshen 17, 99
Gulf War 193
guns 172, 197

H

hacker 171
hammer 11
Hamilton, Alexander 242, 271
Hamilton, Andrew 272
Hand, Learned xv
hard labor 39, 212

Harper, F. A.   247
Harrington, Sir John   251, 306
Herodotus   248
Hidden Power of Money   251
hin   222, 241
Hitler   106, 133, 136, 169, 193, 200, 202, 217, 234, 245, 246, 250
Hobza, Gordon   3
Hoge, Robert   xvii
Holloway, John E.   246
Holmes, Oliver Wendell   xiii
holocaust   131, 202
Holy Bible   101, 104
Homo sapiens   110
House of the Dead   134, 243
How to Beat Inflation   248
Hyde, John   305

I

IBM   203
ID   2, 169
illegal tender   32, 33, 38, 40, 215
income   25, 120, 146, 167, 186, 191, 192, 198, 199, 207, 245, 248
income tax   25, 146, 186, 191, 192, 199, 207
ingot   10, 210, 215
instrument   10, 20, 24, 25, 27, 28, 29, 35, 38, 42, 45, 46, 140, 183, 187, 215, 217, 250, 298, 304, 305, 306, 307, 311
insurance   105, 123, 130, 155, 156, 157, 158, 167, 172, 174, 190, 238, 247
intent   28, 39, 40, 41, 42, 43, 46, 52, 144, 145, 187, 206, 298, 301, 303, 308, 309, 310, 311
International Monetary Fund (IMF)   143
intrinsic   10, 14, 21, 114, 134, 141, 208, 213, 215, 217, 221, 242, 246, 247, 303
invest   128, 133, 146, 202, 215, 227, 249
IOU   42, 47, 188, 215
Iraq   103, 193
iris   169
Iron Triangle   251
IRS   11, 25, 45, 146, 186, 187, 188, 189, 199, 202, 226
Israel   103

J

Jackson, Douglas L. (M.D.)   176
Jefferson Financial   xvii, 235
Jefferson, Thomas   xi, 114, 134, 242, 250
Jesus   99, 200
Jews   199, 202, 238, 299
Joachim's Thal   17
Job   214
Jochymov   x, 99
John Birch Society   138, 234, 237, 251
Johnson, Samuel   242
Jordan   103
Jubilee   104, 105
Judeo-Christian   104, 108, 202, 238
judge   xiv, 11, 32, 33, 185, 187, 188, 198, 251, 271, 309
judicial activist   xiv
judicial verbicide   xiv, xv
jugular   221
Juno   7, 8, 216
Juno Moneta   8
Jupiter   7
jury   24, 123, 124, 127, 138, 162, 185, 187, 188, 198, 222, 271, 304, 307

K

karat   215
Kellems, Vivian   iii
Kemmerer, Edwin Walter   245
Kennett, William   246
Kershner, Howard E.   208, 247
Keynes, John Maynard   244, 245
KGB   3, 4, 5, 6, 128
King James Version   225
King, Martin Luther, Jr.   250
Kiser, Fred H.   242, 243, 244, 251
Knox v. Lee   40
Kope, Spencer   xviii
Korea   5, 228
Korean Air Lines flight 007   5, 228
Korean War   4, 5, 193
Kourdakov, Sergei   iii
Kurland, Philip B.   xv

L

La Guardia   147
laissez faire   110, 237
lamprey   155, 196
Lance, Bert   226
Lapin, Daniel (Rabbi)   238
Latvia   9
laundering   182, 301
Lebanon   103
legalized theft   105
legislature   271
Lehrman Bell Mueller Cannon, Inc.   xviii
Leitch, Gordon (M.D.)   xviii, 233
Lemon Motor Company   204, 205
Lenin, Vladimir L.   143, 155, 244, 245
lepton   222
leverage   205, 215, 248
liabilities   14, 24, 120, 132, 246, 247, 248, 267, 299
liability   xxi, 25, 299, 305
Libertarian Party   vii, 200, 237, 313

Libya 227
Limbaugh, Rush xi
Lincoln, Abraham 15, 20, 35, 36, 111, 202, 243
liquidating our inventory 152
Lira 48, 180
loan committee 124
Locke, John iii
Lord Acton 15, 130
Lowndes, William 242
lucre 215
Luke 104, 219
Lundquist, Leslie 176, 233
Lydia 8, 213, 248
Lynch, Daniel C. 176, 233

M

Madison, James 207, 242
Mair, Rafe 246
maker 25, 28, 41, 46, 51, 213
Malaysia 174
mania 136
manipulate 6, 43, 130, 131, 133, 159, 204, 246, 297
Marbury v. Madison xiv
Mark Twain Bank 176
Massachusetts Bay Colony Note ix, 34, 51, 53
MasterCard 153, 178
maxim 138
maximized theft 26, 221
Mayflower 8
McAdoo, William G. 244
McAlvany, Donald S. 235, 245
McAlvany Intelligence Advisor 245
McFadden, Louis T. iii, 245, 247
McFee, William 243
media of exchange 8, 9, 13, 14, 21, 26, 48, 110, 200, 216
Medicare 150
Mediterranean 8, 227
megalomania 163
Megalopolis Enterprises 129
memoranda 28, 189
memorandum 42, 301
Mencken, H. L. 251
mens rea 43, 187
mercantile 200, 216, 298, 300, 305
Mercator Projection Map 216
Mercedes 205
merchant 298, 307
Metcalf, Jack xix
metric 212, 214, 223
Mexico 139, 183
Miami 156, 172
Micah 241
Milam, Mobley 50, 198, 248
military personnel 192

militia 131
mill 9, 18, 35, 98, 112, 299
millennium 163, 165, 199
Miller, William G. 246
mina 222, 224
misdemeanor 32, 137
misfeasance 139
misprision 251, 309
missile batteries 229
missing dollar 106, 146, 203
mission statement 191
Mondex 178
monere 7, 216
Moneta 7, 8
monetize 8, 216
money laundering 182, 301
money order 152, 183, 187, 236
monie 8
monopoly 207, 243, 244, 246
Montana 234
moral v, 102, 105, 106, 143, 187, 208, 241, 243, 245, 246, 247, 271
Moral Sayings 241
morality 102, 242, 245
Mormon x, 98
mortgage xi, 42, 125, 157, 188, 216, 245
Moses 103
Mueller, John xviii
Mullins, Eustace xviii, 233, 234, 294
music iii, 163, 194, 197
Mussolini, Benito 106, 213
mynt 8, 302
Myth 41, 43, 106
mythology 7

N

National Banking Act 141, 243
national currency ix, 70, 74, 75, 76, 141, 304
National Gold Bank ix, 64
national socialist 106, 142, 217
Nazi 4, 106, 217
Nazional Sozialistiche Arbeiter Partei 217
NetBill 178
New York Stock Exchange 247
New York Times 245, 250, 293
New Zealand xix, 8
nickel 97, 135, 141, 217, 301, 302
Nightly Business Report 133
No Treason 243
nominee 128
North, Gary 235, 248
notary 27, 128
Notice vii, xxi, 16, 33, 41, 88, 89, 102, 107, 115, 123, 127, 163, 170, 174, 225, 227, 267, 306
Numismatic Guaranty Corporation xvii

O

oath   139, 251, 309
obligee   23, 297, 298, 304
obligor   23, 297, 298, 304
oligarchy   xv
Open Market, Inc. (OMI)   178
Orwell, George   107, 136
Oxford English Dictionary   vii, xvii, 29, 232, 238, 275
Oxford University Press   xvii, 229, 231, 232

P

paper emission   38
Para Publishing   xviii, 248
Parks, Lawrence   xviii, 237
Paine, Thomas   108, 242
Patman, Wright   iii, 245, 246
Patton, George S., Jr. (U.S. General)   186
Paul, Ron   xix, 248
pax   23, 217
pay to the order of   24
payroll   169, 170
peace   v, 23, 26, 136, 178, 217, 243, 244, 249, 250
pecuniary   211, 217, 243
pen is mightier   229, 230
pence   218, 242
penny   138, 139, 212, 217, 218, 303
penury   218
perestroika   143
perjury   139
perpetrator   144, 145, 146, 149, 153, 156, 222
Peter the Great   7
pfennig   17
PGP   175, 176, 180
Pick, Franz   iii, 108, 246, 247
Pieces of Eight   xvii, 18, 40, 234, 314
pigeon drop   148, 156
PIN   160
pistole   213
Pitt, William   175, 251
plate   20, 21, 39, 82, 189, 215, 216, 310, 311
platinum   9, 177
Plymouth Rock   8, 51, 53
points   xiii, 29, 49, 122, 148, 189, 237, 246, 267
Ponzi, Charles A.   146, 147, 148
portfolio   127, 198
Pound   48, 113, 181, 182, 224
Prechter, Robert   248
pretend   25, 115, 116, 117, 119, 120, 121, 122
Pretty Good Privacy (PGP)   175
price level   109, 110, 112, 113, 119, 130, 133, 134, 136, 143, 144, 197, 202, 203, 206
principal   xiii, 102, 103, 117, 120, 121, 122, 123, 124, 125, 127, 144, 167, 168, 212, 217, 251, 306, 309

privacy   125, 128, 142, 175, 177, 178, 179, 180, 183, 187, 234, 272
pro per   188, 211
pro se   188
productivity   94, 110, 113, 131, 135, 140, 245, 246
proffer   218, 308
promissory note   28, 297, 298, 301, 303, 304, 305, 306, 307
prosecute   136, 151, 155, 199
Proverbs   104, 212, 214, 241
proxy   129
psychopath   136
public debt   10, 39, 70, 75, 242, 302
public key   175
publican   219
puzzle   146, 203

Q

quill   45

R

Rand, Ayn   245
ratio   19, 139, 140, 219, 223
reales   18, 218, 219
reasonable man   105
rebate   219
recession   xi, 111, 112, 212, 219, 251
redeem   25, 38, 39, 49, 182, 214
Regan, Donald T.   247
regulate the value   41, 140, 219, 309
Reichsbanknote   x, 94
republic   ix, x, xvii, xix, 17, 19, 33, 56, 99, 106, 108, 111, 112, 140, 141, 155, 243, 244
Republic of Texas   ix, 56
Republican   200, 201, 248
reputation   51, 103, 246, 272
reserve requirement   118, 247, 248
retina   169
retire   135, 146, 173, 201
revenue   116, 191, 219, 242, 303, 304, 311, 312
Ricardo, David   242
Richelieu   229
risk   xxi, 103, 104, 117, 118, 123, 169, 185, 192, 246, 251, 272
road rage   229
Rogers, Will   250
Roman   7, 8, 216, 219, 232, 249
Roosevelt, Franklin   111
Roosevelt, Theodore ("Teddy")   xiii
Russia   3, 5
Russian   1, 2, 3, 4, 143, 148, 171, 215, 246, 249

S

safe-deposit   170, 173
salary   202, 219, 250, 300

salt 98, 213, 219, 247, 304
Salvation Army 247
Samuel 104, 242
San Jose xviii, 181
sanctity 199
Santayana, George 250
Sardis 8
Saturday Evening Post 245
Saudi Arabia 181
savings account 116, 117, 121, 169, 171, 216
scanner 161, 169, 173
scholar 245
Scientific American 229
scientific socialist 110
Scotland iii, 166, 249
Scottish 8, 39
scrip 219, 220, 234, 304
SDR 181, 182
Seattle i, ii, v, xvi, xviii, xix, 154, 239, 244, 248, 329, 330
Seattle Post-Intelligencer 244, 248
Secrets of the Federal Reserve xviii, 233, 234, 293, 294
seigniorage 220
Senate Banking Subcommittee 161
Sennholz, Hans 233, 249
Serengeti Plains 154
Service of Process 43
Shafer, Neil 132, 233
share 143, 146, 155, 192, 217
Shaw, George Bernard 114, 243, 245
shekel 48, 220, 222, 224
Sherman, Roger iii
shilling 242
shin-plaster 220
short-term 14, 104, 128, 299
Siberia 4, 217
silver certificate ii, ix, x, 28, 65, 67, 69, 78, 80, 87, 90, 100, 198, 213, 297, 307
silverplate 220
Simon, William E. 245, 246
Singapore xix
Sirico, Robert (Fr.) 236
Skeat iii, 218, 232
skl 222
slave 4, 143, 243, 247
slave labor camp 4
smart card 168, 169, 178
Smith, Adam 242
Smith, Jerome 251
Smithsonian Institution xvii, 53, 54, 55, 57, 58, 60, 63, 67, 68, 83, 84, 98
socialism 107, 188, 217
socialist 1, 106, 107, 110, 136, 142, 217, 245
sodium 213, 219

soldier iii, 1, 2, 3, 5
sovereign 213, 220, 221, 235, 302
Soviet xxii, 1, 2, 3, 4, 110, 136, 143
Spangdahlem Air Base 2, 3, 4
Spanish Milled Dollar 18, 300
Special Drawing Rights (SDR) 181
specie 40, 131, 207, 220, 242, 301, 307
spiritual iii, 26, 143, 144, 193
Spooner, Lysander iii, 243
Spree 2
spy 136, 189
St. Louis 176
stagflation 220
standard xvi, 17, 18, 41, 110, 111, 113, 121, 124, 127, 131, 132, 133, 137, 141, 143, 169, 170, 201, 212, 219, 221, 246, 248, 300, 301, 303, 304, 309
standing armies 114, 242, 250
Stang, Alan vii, xi, 236
status 131, 220, 249
statute of limitations 199
steal xi, 26, 137, 156, 161, 221, 241, 303, 307
steel 9, 97, 170
Sterling xviii, 299
Steve, George 108, 246
Stewart, Walter 164, 251
stick 45, 103, 151, 219, 221
stipend 221
stips 221
stock vii, 32, 103, 111, 120, 121, 122, 127, 128, 129, 130, 131, 138, 142, 154, 181, 196, 198, 203, 204, 208, 210, 215, 228, 234, 235, 246, 247, 249, 293
stockholder 103, 129, 203, 228, 294
Stone, I. F. 224, 251
stone 19, 131, 310, 311
subsidiary 34, 221
Supreme Court xiii, xiv, xv, 5, 40, 186, 187, 188, 233, 302
survival training 131
Sutton, Antony C. 193, 207, 233, 234, 243, 246
Swiss 48, 176, 181, 201, 202, 212, 228
Switzerland xviii, 129, 176, 201, 202, 227
sword 222, 229, 230
syphilis 112
Syria 103
Syrus, Publius 241

T

tag 221
talent 26, 48, 130, 221, 222, 224, 241, 251
talenton 222
tallies, tally 221
Tanana 153
teacher 192, 197

telephone bill   46, 49
television   3, 151, 163, 176, 185, 187, 193
teller   24, 46, 47, 160, 165, 172, 183, 221
teller checks   183
Texas   iii, ix, xix, 56, 157, 158, 199, 233, 235, 244
theft   11, 18, 21, 26, 104, 105, 113, 114, 119, 124, 130, 137, 138, 144, 145, 149, 155, 187, 221, 222, 247, 271
theft by fraud   11, 18, 21, 104, 113, 114, 119, 124, 130, 137, 144, 149
Thomas De La Rue Limited   xviii
three-card Monte   159, 160
time deposit   117
Timothy   242, 247
tithe   212
toast   186, 188, 189
token   ix, 14, 20, 22, 212, 218, 221, 301, 303, 308
Tokyo   169
toll   221
ton   46, 106, 188, 224
tool   10, 175, 211
Topline Investment Graphics   xviii, 295, 296
totalitarian   106
Toward Tradition   190, 238
Towers of Gold   164, 251
traditional American values   26, 104, 110, 162, 194, 237
transaction   14, 19, 31, 102, 122, 128, 129, 150, 160, 161, 165, 167, 168, 169, 175, 176, 178, 180, 182, 183, 221, 246, 249, 298
travelers check   183
treason   29, 137, 144, 221, 234, 243, 250, 251, 308
treasure   200, 221, 222
Treasury, U.S., balance sheet   267
trend   110, 133, 204
trial   x, xviii, 43, 137, 149, 157, 158, 187, 188, 198, 222, 251, 271, 272, 297, 309
tribal   162
trick   15, 21, 107, 117, 121, 123, 156, 158, 159, 170, 225
Trier (German city)   4
trillion   116, 167, 168, 184, 246, 247
Truman, Harry   251
Trust   251, 306
trust   48, 104, 139, 146, 150, 196, 212, 228, 243, 251, 306
TWA Flight 800   228
Twain, Mark   176, 245, 250
tyranny   xv, 251
Tyson, Mike   162

U

U.S. Army   186
U.S. Bureau of Engraving and Printing   xix, 85
U.S. Mint   xix, 226
U.S. Navy   5
U.S. Secret Service   vii
U.S. Treasury   xix, 63, 95, 96, 132, 182, 196, 236, 244, 246, 249, 267, 297
Ukraine   5
ultima   xiii
Understanding the Dollar Crisis   246
unfunded   116, 168, 242
union   1, 110, 127, 143, 233, 235, 249, 272
United Nations   180, 248
United States Note   ix, x, xviii, 36, 71, 76, 79, 85, 89, 91
university   xiv, xvii, xvii, 21, 178, 179, 192, 201, 229, 231, 232, 236, 244, 245
Upham, David   236
usufruct   101
usurious interest rates   101, 122
usury   vii, 101–109, 121, 197, 215, 219, 241
Utah   137, 302
utility   101, 102, 178
utter   10, 51, 52, 250

V

Vancouver Sun   246
Vanderlip, Frank   245
vault   128, 170, 171, 307
vending machine   140
venue   222
verbicide   vii, xiii, xiv, xv, 107, 267, 297
VeriFone   178
Vieira, Edwin, Jr.   xvii, 40, 234, 237
Vietnam   4, 5, 193, 229
VISA   153, 178, 330
visa   2
Voltaire   10, 134, 164, 242, 250
voluntary   105, 155, 166, 186, 196, 200, 221, 248
von Mises, Ludwig   244, 245
von Schiller, Friedrich   250
von Schlick, Count Steven   17, 18, 99
vulgar   107, 162

W

Wall Street and FDR   207, 246
Wall Street and the Bolshevik Revolution   234
Wall Street and the Rise of Hitler   234
Wall Street Journal   133, 235
Wall Street Week   133
Wallich, Henry C.   246
wampum   10, 13
War Department   113
Warburg, Paul and Felix   244
ware   222
warning   7, 37, 108, 189, 204
Washington, Booker T.   iii
Washington, George   xiv

Washington, Martha ii, ix
Watergate xiv
Wealth of Nations 242
Weber, Christopher 234, 304
Webster, Noah 297
Webster, Peletiah 242
Welch Foundation 238
Welch, Robert H. W. iii
West Point 267
West Publishing Company xvii, 11, 44, 231, 232, 297
White House 115, 116, 202
white metal 217, 220
Wiegand, G. Carl 244
Will Pay vii, ix, 51, 71
will pay ix, 25, 29, 46, 48, 51, 91, 92, 102, 116, 147, 148, 167, 249
Willow Creek Press of Washington xviii
Wilson, Woodrow 244
wire transfer 166
Wirtschaftswunder 142
withdrawn 18, 20, 111
Wolfe, Tom 249
World Almanac 133, 227
World Bank 117, 143
World Dollar Base xviii
World Gold Council xviii
World of Gold 246
World Trade Center 129
World War I iii, 4, 5
World War II xviii, 4, 5, 97, 106, 107, 113, 142, 186, 193, 202, 217, 248
World War III 109
worth 14, 18, 19, 21, 32, 34, 38, 41, 54, 103, 106, 124, 127, 132, 141, 149, 152, 158, 160, 167, 170, 179, 181, 182, 190, 201, 212, 213, 215, 217, 219, 221, 222, 235, 246, 247, 251
wrench 10
Wright brothers 244

X

XYZ Bank 172

Y

Yankee 18
yehud 222
yoke 221, 222
yokel 222
yuppies 6

Z

Zenger, John Peter vii, x, xviii, 230, 271, 272
Zenger News Service (ZNS) ii, xvi, 125, 272
Zimmerman, Phil 175
ZIP code 189
ZNS ii, xvii, xix, 190, 191, 192, 193, 229, 236, 237, 239, 272, 330
Zondervan Publishing House 232, 233
ZYNDEX ii